Real World
Adobe Photoshop CS2

Real World
Adobe Photoshop CS2
Industrial-Strength Production Techniques

Bruce Fraser
David Blatner

Peachpit Press

Adobe

David
For Fay, Harry, Ann, Abe, Katie, and Rita,
who laid the foundation in my family.

Bruce
For the photographers, everywhere.
Without them, we would have no images.

Real World Adobe Photoshop CS2

Bruce Fraser and David Blatner

Copyright ©2006 by David Blatner and Bruce Fraser

Peachpit Press

1249 Eighth Street, Berkeley, CA 94710

510/524-2178 Fax: 510/524-2221

Find us on the Web at www.peachpit.com.

Peachpit Press is a division of Pearson Education.

Real World Adobe Photoshop CS2 is published in association with Adobe Press.

Interior design by Stephen F. Roth/Open House

Project Editor: Rebecca Gulick   Production Editor: Lisa Brazieal

Proofreader: Liz Welch   Indexer: Karin Arrigoni

Cover Designer: Charlene Charles-Will   Illustration: Ben Fishman, Artifish, Inc.

Image credits and permissions, page 915

ISBN 0-321-33411-6

9 8 7 6 5 4 3 2 1

Printed and bound in the United States of America

Overview

The Big Picture

Contents

What's Inside

Preface

Photoshop in the Real World

If you're reading this book because you want to produce embossed type, fractalized tree branches, or spherized images in Photoshop, you're in the wrong place. If you're after tips and tricks on how to get the coolest special effects in your images, look elsewhere. There are (at least) half a dozen good books on those subjects.

But if you're looking to move images through Photoshop—getting good scans or digital captures in, working your will on them, and putting out world-class final output—this is the book for you. Its *raison d'être* is to answer the many questions that people in production environments ask every single day (and not without some frustration).

► What settings should I use in the Color Settings dialog box?

► How do I bring out shadow details in my images without blowing away the highlights?

► What methods are available to neutralize color casts?

► How do I calibrate my monitor? (And should I?)

► How do I put a drop shadow on top of a process-color tint in Quark-XPress or Adobe InDesign?

► What's the best way to silhouette an image for catalog work?

These questions, and dozens of others, face Photoshop users all the time. And unfortunately, the books we've seen on Photoshop—much less Photoshop's own online help, which is itself a poor substitute for the sorely missed manuals of yore—simply don't address these crucial, run-of-the-mill, day-in-and-day-out production issues. This book does.

Ask Your Printer

We wrote this book for a lot of reasons, but the biggest one was probably our frustration with the knee-jerk advice we kept hearing about desktop prepress: "Ask your printer."

Go ahead. Ask your printer what values you should enter in the Color Settings and Proof Setup dialog boxes. In our experience, with nine out of ten printers you'll be lucky if you get more than wild guesses. In this new age of desktop prepress, there's simply no one you can ask (whether you're a designer, a prepress shop… or a printer). *You're* in the pilot's seat, with your hand on the stick (and the trigger). Where do you turn when the bogies are incoming?

We're hoping that you'll turn to this book.

Developing Your "Spidey Sense"

Flipping through nine hundred pages isn't exactly practical, though, when you've got a missile on your tail. So we try to do more with this book than tell you which key to press, or what value to enter where. We're trying to help you develop what our friend and colleague Greg Vander Houwen calls your "spidey sense" (those who didn't grow up on Spider-Man comics may not relate completely, but you get the idea).

When you're in the crunch, you've gotta have an intuitive, almost instinctive feel for what's going on in Photoshop, so you can finesse it to your needs. Canned techniques just don't cut it. So you'll find a fair amount of conceptual discussion here, describing how Photoshop "thinks" about images, and suggesting how you might think about them as well.

The Step-by-Step Stuff

Along with those concepts, we've included just about every step-by-step production technique we know of. From scanning to silhouettes and drop shadows, to tonal correction, sharpening, and color separation, we've tried to explain how to get images into Photoshop—and back out again—with the least pain and the best quality. And yes, in the course of explaining those techniques, we *will* tell you which key to press, and what values to enter in what dialog boxes.

History Is Important

We hear some of you mumbling under your breath, "We've been doing prepress for 30 years, and we don't need to learn a new way of doing it." We beg to differ. Print manufacturing, of which prepress is the handmaiden, is in the throes of change. For example, direct-to-plate printing has largely replaced the practice of making plates from film. This cuts out the quality loss inherent in a generation of optical duplication, but takes away our old film-based proofs. Digital photography (which in a few years will almost certainly be called simply "photography") makes the drum scanner obsolescent, and in today's ultra competitive marketplace, the old industry-standard 3.2 rounds of proofing and correction just don't cut it any more.

Our goal is not to detract from the way you've been doing things. It's to show you how those approaches can be incorporated with the new tools, improved, and pushed to new limits.

Whither Photography?

This book isn't just about prepress. It's also about photography and about images. We believe that photographers understand tone and color as well as any other skilled group of professionals, and one of our aims has been to help photographers translate their own understanding of images into Photoshop's digital world.

Digital imaging has undoubtedly changed the practice of photography, but images still come from an intentional act on the part of the image maker, and that isn't going to change, whether the photons are captured by goo smeared on celluloid or by photoelectric sensors. We believe that digital imaging offers the photographer as many opportunities as it creates pitfalls. To all the photographers out there who are nervous about the digital revolution, we say, "Come on in, the water's fine." And more to the point, we can't *do* this stuff without you.

The Depth of Understanding

We were crazy to take on this book when we started in 1993, and we're no less crazy today. If we weren't, we wouldn't have tried to unravel such an insanely complex subject. We don't claim to have the ultimate answers, but the answers we do have are tried, tested, and effective. The methods presented in this book may not be the only way to get good results from Photoshop, but they're the product of endless days and nights of research and testing, of badgering anyone we thought might have an answer with endless questions, then trying to present these insights in some coherent form. (Bruce vaguely remembers wondering, while making coffee at 4 AM, why one of his kitchen faucets was labeled "cyan"….)

While our grasp on reality may have occasionally been tenuous during the production of this book, the techniques we present are firmly grounded in the real world—hence the title.

How the Book Is Organized

The biggest problem we face in writing about Photoshop is not just that it's the "deepest" program we've ever used, but that almost every technique and feature relies on every other technique and feature. It's impossible to talk about Photoshop without circular reasoning.

However, we have tried to impose some structure to the book. In the first five chapters, we attempt to lay the groundwork for the rest of the book, covering *Building a Photoshop System, Essential Photoshop Tips and Tricks, Image Essentials, Color Essentials*, and *Color Settings* (all the color management stuff). We put all this information first because it's patently impossible to be effective in Photoshop without it.

Once we've laid the groundwork, we jump into really working with images. In the next four chapters, we explore techniques you'll want to employ with almost every image you work with in Photoshop: *Image Adjustment Fundamentals; The Digital Darkroom; Making Selections;* and *Sharpness, Detail, and Noise Reduction.*

The origin and type of the images you work with determine what you can or need to do with them, so the next two chapters discuss these issues: *Spot Colors and Duotones;* and *Building a Digital Workflow.*

In the course of any book project, the authors find that they have a boatload of information that simply doesn't fit any single category. Fortunately, we're lucky enough to have a chapter called *Essential Image Techniques.*

The tips in this chapter are like the tools in your toolbox—you never know when you'll need one, so it's good to have the whole box nearby.

Sometimes it's hard to remember that there is life outside of Photoshop. In the last two chapters of the book, we show how to get those images out of Photoshop into the real world: *Image Storage and Output*, and *Multimedia and the Web*.

This Edition

Real World Photoshop has grown in size with each subsequent edition. This one is no exception, but in this revision we've taken the opportunity to go through the entire book with a fine-tooth comb and remove all the stuff that may have made sense in the twentieth century but has now either been superseded, rendered moot by new tools and techniques, or simply drifted into that category our friend and colleague Fred Bunting succinctly terms "more interesting than relevant."

Photoshop has changed over the years, and, for better or worse, so have we. Many techniques we thought brilliant in our salad days now seem like cleverness for the sake of cleverness. Given the choice between dazzling you with our skill and knowledge, and telling what you need to know to get the job done quickly and effectively without compromising quality, we've gone for the latter.

A Word to Windows Users

This book covers tips and techniques for both the Macintosh and Windows versions of Photoshop. However, we have chosen to illustrate dialog boxes, menus, and palettes using screen shots from the Macintosh version. Similarly, when discussing the many keyboard shortcuts in the program, we include the Macintosh versions. In almost every case the Command key translates to the Ctrl key and the Option key translates to the Alt key. In the case of the very few exceptions to this rule, we have included both the Macintosh and the Windows versions. We apologize to all you Windows users, but because the interface between the two programs is so transparent we picked the platform we know best and ran with it.

Thank You!

We'd like to give special thanks to a few of the many people who helped evolve a shadow of an idea into what you hold in your hands. Rebecca Gulick, our editor of this seventh edition, was helpful, patient, and unflappable as usual; production heroine extraordinaire Lisa Brazieal and our other friends at Peachpit took our work and made it fly.

A huge vote of thanks must go to Thomas Knoll, without whom there would be no Photoshop. For answering all our ridiculous questions while performing extraordinary feats of engineering, we thank Chris Cox, Marc Pawliger, Russell Williams, John Nack, Jeff Chien, Todor Georgiev, David Howe, Scott Byer, and the rest of the Photoshop team.

Several vendors were generous in providing equipment, support, and encouragement. Special thanks go to Dano Steinhardt and Eddie Murphy at Epson America, Brian Levey at Colorvisions, Thomas Kunz and Liz Quinlisk at GretagMacbeth, Marc Levine at Monaco Systems, Mark Duhaime at Imacon USA, Kaz Kajikawa at EIZO, Will Hollingworth at NEC/Mitsubishi, John Panozzo at Colorbyte Software, and Jamie L. Martin for Xerox. We owe thanks to Karl Lang for developing the Sony Artisan display, and hope for even better things to come.

Special thanks go to Stephen Johnson and Michael Kieran for their generosity of spirit, their constant encouragement, and the many hours they spent with us in deep discussions that ranged from the technical to the philosophical; and to Greg Gorman for proving, gracefully but indubitably, that it's possible to immerse oneself in digital imaging yet still have a life. If we see further than others, it's because we stand on the shoulders of Photoshop giants, including Julianne Kost, Katrin Eismann, Jeff Schewe, Martin Evening, Andrew Rodney, and Deke McClelland, pixel-meisters all.

Bruce. "To photographers everywhere; various musicians who helped keep me semisane while I worked on this book, to my friends, colleagues and peers in the Photoshop community, to the Pixel Mafia—you know who you are—and to my lovely wife Angela, for more than I can say here."

David. "My deepest appreciation to Debbie Carlson, my friend and partner, and to my family and friends who have had to put up with 'the book is almost done' for way too long. My sincere appreciation to my two sons, Gabriel and Daniel, who helped immeasurably by sleeping at all the right times."

Building a Photoshop System

Putting It All Together

Photoshop is about as rich a program as you'll ever encounter, and much of this book focuses on ways to make you more efficient in your use of it. But no quantity of tips, tricks, and workarounds can compensate for hardware that's inadequate to the task, or a poorly configured system. So in this chapter we look at building an environment in which Photoshop can excel.

Hardware

Photoshop takes full advantage of fast Macs and PCs—the faster the better—but the speed of the computer is only one part of the equation. Even the fastest computer available will seem sluggish if you don't have enough RAM, and Photoshop refuses to work at all if you don't have enough hard disk space. How much is enough? It depends entirely on the size of the files you're working with, and the kinds of operations you're carrying out on them.

Choosing a Platform

Discussions of Macs versus PCs usually tend to degenerate into "my Dad can beat your Dad"—they produce a lot of heat, but little light. We're firmly convinced that price and performance are at parity on the two platforms. The Mac has richer support in terms of dual monitors, plug-ins, and color measurement equipment. The PC has a greater range of general business software.

The bottom line: if you're happy with your current hardware platform, there's probably no reason to switch. You may, however, want to think about upgrading machines that are more than three or four years old. If you're still running Mac OS 10.2 or earlier, or Windows 98, you'll need to upgrade your OS to run Photoshop CS, and the new operating systems make their own heavy demands on hardware.

If you're planning to upgrade to the latest-and-greatest Windows 2000, Windows XP, or Mac OS 10.4, do yourself a favor—get a machine that was designed with the new OS in mind. You'll save yourself a ton of time and frustration. It's possible to run Photoshop CS on fairly old machines—the minimum Mac OS requirement is Mac OS 10.2.8, and the minimum Windows requirement is Windows 2000 with Service Pack 4—but we can tell you from bitter experience that it will be an uphill struggle. If your time is worth anything, trying to run a third-millennium application like Photoshop CS2 on a second-millennium machine is a false economy.

Macintosh. Many Photoshop operations involve really large quantities of number crunching, so the speed of your Mac's processor makes a big difference. Photoshop CS unequivocally demands at least a G3—it won't run at all on anything less—and in practice it makes little sense to use anything less than a G4, since Photoshop makes very effective use of the G4's AltiVec acceleration. If you want to take advantage of more than 2 GB of RAM, which Photoshop CS2 can do, you want a G5!

Photoshop really benefits from dual processors, as do the operating systems under which it runs. If you're planning to upgrade, a dual-processor Mac with a slightly lower clock speed will generally outperform a somewhat faster single-processor model.

Windows. Photoshop CS demands a Pentium III-class machine, but it's distinctly happier on a Pentium 4, as are Windows 2000 and Windows XP, the required operating systems. If you have a 64-bit machine and want to take advantage of more than 2 GB of RAM, Windows XP 64 is highly recommended.

RAM

The old adage that you can never be too thin, too rich, or have too much RAM holds true for Photoshp CS2 just as it did for previous versions. Just how much RAM you need depends on your file size and work habits—remember that additional layers and channels increase the size of the file—but we don't recommend even trying to run Photoshop on a system with less than 512 MB of RAM, and more, *much* more is better. The absolute minimum configuration, according to Adobe, is 320 MB. It may be doable—barely—but you won't enjoy it. If you typically work on Web-resolution images, use layers sparingly, and use few or no History states, you may be able to run Photoshop quite happily in our minimum suggested RAM complement. But if *any* of the above don't apply, you'll want more—much more. Fortunately, RAM is cheap these days.

We used to have various rules about how much RAM is enough, but as Photoshop has added more features that use scratch space, they've largely gone out the window. Photoshop uses RAM as a cache for its scratch file—if what it needs at any given moment is in the cache, it can fetch it quicker. But unless you only work on small flat files, it's a near certainty that at some point the scratch disk will come into play.

32-bit hardware. On 32-bit systems, Photoshop can use all the RAM installed in your system, up to the 2 GB limit. You *don't* want to allocate all this RAM to Photoshop, because if you do, you'll starve the OS, and force it to page memory out to its swapfile constantly.

According to Adobe, the default ram allocation settings—70 percent for Mac and 55 percent for Windows— will be optimal under normal use for most users. But we don't know anyone who uses Photoshop normally!

You can fine tune your settings based upon your own system, installed RAM and the way in which you use Photoshop. Depending upon the number of system processes running, and the number of other applications you typically run, you can try increasing the RAM allocation incrementally while checking the available unused RAM with a system utility. You should always leave a few hundred megabytes free to avoid starving the system. For Mac, you can use Activity Monitor (built in OS X) to watch RAM usage. For Windows you can watch Performance Monitor, which is also built in.

64-bit hardware. With 64-bit hardware, Photoshop CS2 can in theory address up to about 3.5 GB of RAM (in practice it uses 3072 MB directly), but if you're working on huge images, you may see benefits from even more RAM, because when Photoshop sees that more than 4 GB of RAM is installed, Photoshop lets the OS buffer scratch data into RAM instead of writing it directly to disk.

Photoshop doesn't normally use those buffers because it "costs" extra to copy the data to and from the buffers instead of using the disk. If the data can use the RAM buffer instead of using the disk, this is more than worth it. Photoshop's access patterns to its scratch file mostly don't match what the OS is expecting. The OS assumes that if you just read or wrote it, you're likely to need it again soon, which is generally not the case with Photoshop's scratch disk. However, when you've got more RAM than the program can use directly, there's little to lose by letting the OS cache it.

During the Photoshop CS2 beta period, Bruce added RAM incrementally to his G5, and saw performance improvements at each increment all the way up to 8 GB (but he typically works on fairly enormous files).

A reliable way to figure if you'd benefit from more RAM is to keep an eye on the Efficiency indicator while you work (click in the lower-left corner of the document window; see Figure 1-1). If the reading drops below 100 percent, more RAM would help. (If you've already maxed out your machine with as much RAM as Photoshop can address, and your efficiency is still below 100 percent, see "Scratch disk space," later in this chapter.)

Figure 1-1
The Efficiency indicator

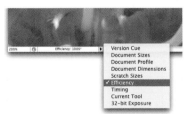

RAM allocation. Memory allocation is dynamic under both Macintosh OS X and Windows XP, but you can (and should) still tell Photoshop how much of the available RAM to gobble. A good starting point is to allocate 50 percent of the available RAM to Photoshop, which you do in the Memory & Image Cache panel of Preferences (see Figure 1-2). If you have a large amount of RAM—3 GB or more—you can try increasing that percentage, but if you go too far you'll hear the hard disk start to thrash whenever the OS or another application needs to grab some RAM.

Figure 1-2
Allocating RAM
to Photoshop

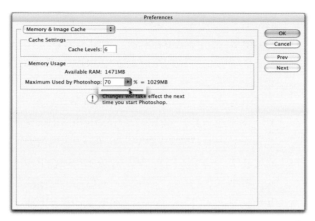

Mac OS X actually gives you an extra clue: When an application is waiting for the computer, you see the all-too-familiar spinning wristwatch cursor, but when the OS is the one causing the delay, you see a spinning multicolored wheel—Bruce calls it "The Spinning Pizza of Death." If you see the SPOD on Mac OS X, or you hear the hard disk thrashing on Windows when you're working on an image that should fit into RAM, it's a sign that you've set the memory allocation too high and need to back it off a little.

Note that a few Photoshop filters (Lens Flare, for instance) require that you have enough physical RAM to load the entire image into memory. Even though Photoshop has a virtual-memory scheme, if you don't have the RAM, these effects just won't work.

The Power Mac G5s and the new 64-bit Windows machines let you add up to 8 GB of RAM. If your work typically lets you stay at 100 percent efficiency, you won't get any benefit from adding more RAM, but if you want to allocate 100 percent of the available RAM to Photoshop, you need to install at least 4 GB—4.5 is better. Don't allocate 100 percent on a 32-bit system—you'll starve the operating system of RAM.

Image cache. The Cache Levels setting in the Memory and Image Cache panel of the Preferences dialog box also has an impact on RAM usage. Increasing the Image Cache value speeds screen redraw when you're working with larger files that contain a lot of layers. However, the Image Cache doesn't do too much for small files. The default setting is 6 levels. If you routinely work with larger multilayered files, try increasing the cache level to 8. If you work with smaller files, try reducing it.

Virtual Memory

Virtual memory is a programming trick that fools the computer into thinking it has more RAM than it really does. It works by reserving a specially marked amount of space on your hard drive that gets treated as RAM. The real, physical RAM is then used as a cache for the "virtual memory" stored on the disk. If the data that the computer is looking for is cached in RAM, you don't see any slowdown, but if the computer has to go searching on the hard disk instead, things can slow down a lot.

Operating systems create a swap file on your hard disk that serves as virtual memory to let multiple applications grab RAM as needed. Photoshop also has its own private virtual memory scheme called Scratch Disk, which it uses to let you do things that wouldn't fit in physical RAM, such as storing 1,000 history states on a 300 MB image (which we don't actually recommend doing). To get optimum performance, you need to configure both the operating system's virtual memory scheme and Photoshop's scratch disk space so that they play nicely together.

Photoshop scratch disk and the OS swap file. Both Windows and Macintosh OS X use the startup drive for the swap file unless you have told them to do otherwise. On Windows systems, you can change the swap file setting by bringing up Properties for My Computer, selecting the Performance tab, clicking the Virtual Memory button, and selecting the Change option. This lets you specify maximum and minimum swap file sizes as well as which drive gets used.

On Mac OS X, the procedure for pointing the swap file at a drive other than the startup is way more complex, so much so that it's crazy to try to move it when it's so much easier to move Photoshop's scratch instead (see "Scratch disk space," on the next page). Ultimately, the only reason we can see to move the swap file is if your startup drive is also the fastest one, and you want to let Photoshop use it as a scratch disk.

Photoshop performs much better if you put the swap file and Photoshop's scratch file on different physical mechanisms, so a second hard drive is always desirable. This way, the same set of read-write heads don't have to scurry around like gerbils on espresso while trying to serve the dual demands of the operating system swap file and Photoshop's scratch space. It's fine to keep images, applications, or just about anything else *except* the OS swap file on the same drive as Photoshop's scratch space, but it's a good idea to dedicate a partition on that drive to Photoshop's scratch space, because otherwise the scratch space may become fragmented and slow Photoshop down. A dedicated partition shouldn't need defragmenting, but you can do so very easily by simply erasing it—you don't need to run a fancy disk optimizer.

If all you have is one single hard disk, you'll have to let Photoshop and the OS fight it out—fortunately, if you're careful with the percentage of memory you allocate to Photoshop, the conflicts shouldn't be too bad or frequent.

Scratch disk space. Photoshop requires scratch disk space at least equal to the amount of RAM you've allocated to Photoshop—it uses RAM only as a cache for the scratch disk space. That means if you've given Photoshop 120 MB of RAM, you must also have 120 MB of free disk space. If you have less, Photoshop will only use an amount of RAM equivalent to the free space on the scratch disk. In practice, you're likely to need more, and if you work with layered high-bit files or many history states, *much* more.

Photoshop constantly optimizes the scratch space. Those of you who learned in the stone age to view disk access as a warning that things are about to get very slow should learn to accept it as normal Photoshop behavior. People are often especially concerned when they see disk access immediately after opening a file. This, too, is normal: Photoshop is simply setting itself up to be more efficient down the line. Photoshop has a couple of ways to tell you when you're relying on the scratch disk.

In the lower-left corner of the document window, there's a popup menu that shows, among other things, document size, scratch size, or "efficiency" (see Figure 1-3). If you set this to Scratch Sizes, the first number shows the amount of RAM being used by all open documents, and the second number shows the amount of RAM currently allocated to Photoshop. If the first number is bigger than the second, Photoshop is using your hard drive as virtual memory. When the indicator is set to Efficiency, a reading of less than 100 percent indicates that virtual memory is coming into play.

RAID arrays. A striped RAID hard disk array can be a very worthwhile investment, particularly if you're dealing with images too large for your available RAM on a regular basis. Photoshop can write to a RAID disk much faster than to a single fixed disk, so your performance will improve. The current speed champ is a dual-channel Ultra320 SCSI array with one, two, or three 15,000-RPM drives on each channel, but fast SCSI drives are small

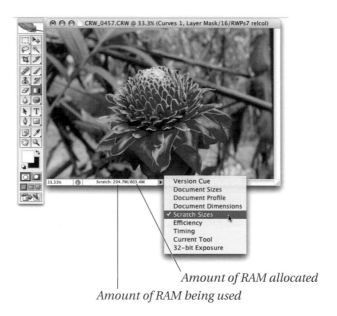

Figure 1-3
Scratch size

Amount of RAM allocated
Amount of RAM being used

and expensive. A software RAID combining two Serial ATA drives is almost
as fast, with a much lower cost per megabyte. FireWire 800 arrays also
show great potential, but only if you add multiple FireWire 800 channels
by adding extra controllers—a single-channel FireWire 800 array is only
about 10–15 percent faster than a single FireWire 800 drive. Three channels will get you almost the same speed as Ultra320 SCSI, and four channels (if you have enough PCI slots to burn) will exceed Ultra320 SCSI on a
good many operations. Given the high cost and relatively low capacity of
SCSI drives, we recommend exploring the alternatives unless you already
have a SCSI array—SATA and FireWire 800 drives in the 250 GB range are
relatively inexpensive by comparison.

Opening and saving large files is also faster with a RAID array. But if you
have a choice between buying RAM and buying a fast hard drive, max out
the RAM first unless opening and saving large files already constitutes a
significant bottleneck in your workflow.

Tip: Use the Purge Commands. You know that Photoshop gets sluggish
when you run out of RAM. And you know that whenever you take a new
snapshot, or copy a large chunk of your document to the clipboard, Photoshop guzzles RAM. When you don't have any more RAM for Photoshop
to guzzle, life slows down significantly. You can clear up the amount of
RAM that Photoshop is using by "emptying" the Histories, Clipboard, and

Undo buffers. We used to need all sorts of clever tricks to do this. Nowadays, we just select one of the following from from the Purge submenu (at the bottom of the Edit menu): Clipboard, Histories, Pattern, Undo, or All. If a Purge command is dimmed, it means the buffer is already empty, so there's nothing there to purge.

Monitors

The CRT versus LCD debate continues to rage, but it has in many ways been rendered moot since manufacture of high-end CRTs has essentially ceased. All we can really say is that it's a personal decision. LCDs have improved enormously over the past few years, but the viewing angle is still an issue—the color changes when you move your head from side to side—and it's still difficult to manufacture a large LCD with uniform brightness since all the light is produced by a backlight and a diffuser.

CRT monitors also improved a lot over the past few years, with higher brightness and better uniformity than the previous generations. Some CRT monitors, notably the Sony Artisan and LaCie Electron series with BlueEye, offer a USB connection between the monitor and the host CPU that allows the bundled calibration system to automatically adjust the individual R, G, and B gains to achieve the correct white point. Third-party calibrators such as the ones we discuss later in this chapter allow you to do the same thing manually with only slightly more effort, as long as your monitor offers separate R, G, and B gain controls. If you have one of these displays, we suggest you baby it as much as possible, because you won't be able to replace it.

Bruce has punted on the question—his main Photoshop system features both a Sony Artisan CRT and an EIZO ColorEdge CG21 LCD. He trusts shadow rendition and overall color a little more on the CRT, but finds the LCD much sharper, and almost as accurate. He's also been working with a prototype of the NEC/Mitsubishi 2180 WG (the WG stands for wide gamut)—an LCD display that uses red, green, and blue LEDs for the backlight instead of a fluorescent tube. It's a very bright display with a huge color gamut, and if you can afford it you'll probably be able to buy one by the time you read this. However, displays like this one won't likely become mainstream, with mainstream pricing, until 2007 or 2008.

Video acceleration. There's a widespread but ill-founded belief that accelerated video boards speed up Photoshop screen redraw. The bottleneck in redrawing Photoshop images on the screen is almost never the video system—it's getting the image data out of RAM (or even worse, from disk) to the video system. A super-fast video card may make your system feel faster and more responsive, but if you analyze what's going on, you'll usually find that the difference is a screen redraw of two-tenths of a second rather than five-tenths of a second. (Of course, those tenths of a second can add up—in a month you may even save enough time to grab a cup of coffee.)

Most video acceleration these days is aimed at 3D graphics performance—useful if you do a lot of 3D work or play a lot of games—but the 2D performance of just about any current video card is good enough that it won't constitute a significant bottleneck in your Photoshop work.

Dual-monitor support. Just about any Mac video card installed in a desktop machine other than the iMac can support two calibrated displays. That's not always the case with Windows video cards, many of which report themselves to the operating system as a single device with which only one display profile can be associated.

Neither of us has any significant experience with dual-monitor Windows setups, though we know they can be made to work because we've seen them. Our best advice is to assume nothing, and do plenty of research before making any purchase decisions.

Monitor calibration. If you want to trust what you see on screen (which we certainly do), some kind of monitor calibration is essential. The free, eyeball-based, software-only monitor calibrators (such as Adobe Gamma and ColorSync Default Calibrator) are better than nothing, but unless you work in a cave, you'll find it's extremely difficult to get consistent results because your eyes—and hence your "monitor calibration"—adapt to changing lighting conditions.

We believe that every serious Photoshop user would be better served using a hardware puck to measure the behavior of the monitor, and accompanying software to set it to a known condition and to write a monitor profile. There are several good, relatively inexpensive hardware-based monitor calibration packages available—we like the i1 (or Eye-One) Display from GretagMacbeth, the OPTIX from Monaco Systems, BasIC-

Color Display with the "squid" (or even better, with the Monaco OPTIX), or OptiCal and its less-expensive sibling, PhotoCal, from ColorVisions. All of these can calibrate both CRT and LCD monitors, and any of them will do a better job of keeping your displays accurately profiled than any of the eyeball-based tools.

The Power of Photoshop

Photoshop is not a island, complete unto itself. Rather, it's surrounded by hardware and software that supports or hinders it. If you focus on any piece of the whole and ignore the rest, you'll run into trouble (or at the very least, you'll be less efficient than you might have been).

We're going to focus on Photoshop for the rest of the book, but while you read, keep in mind these other factors: memory considerations, hardware, and third-party software. That way, you'll really be prepared to harness the power of Photoshop.

Essential Photoshop Tips and Tricks

Making Photoshop Fly

In the previous chapter, we talked about tweaking the hardware to speed up your work. Hardware is important, and few applications make heavier demands on it than does Photoshop, but the biggest speed bump you can make to Photoshop is to accelerate the wetware: the component that exists between keyboard and chair—in short, gentle reader, the most important part of any digital imaging system: your good self.

If you get paid by the hour, rather than by the amount of work accomplished, you may want to skip this chapter. If you want to realize the full potential of Photoshop as a lean, mean, pixel-processing machine, read on! We'll break you of the habit of choosing tools by clicking on their icons, and help you avoid those lengthy mouse voyages up to the menu bar.

Upgrading to a New Version

Like death and taxes, upgrading your software is inevitable but not necessarily fun. Some people upgrade as soon as the box hits the proverbial shelf; others take years, buying a new version only after their service bureau or printer refuses to take their old files anymore. Sooner or later, though, you'll be faced with new features, new challenges, and a new bottle of aspirin.

What's New in "CS2"

The most sweeping change in Photoshop CS2 is the replacement of the File Browser with Bridge, an entirely new standalone application. Depending on how you use Photoshop, it may affect you hardly at all, or it may present an opportunity to rethink your entire workflow. Some color management features have been moved or renamed, but there's no new functionality there. Ultimately, most of the new features provide either improvements, or entirely new functionality; a few may provoke some head-scratching.

Here are a few important changes in Photoshop CS2 (we're not listing every new feature here, just the ones you'd better know about before jumping into the rest of the book).

Bridge. Bridge is a new standalone application that's more than a browser but a little less than an asset manager (though it seems irrevocably headed in that direction). While almost everyone will find it useful for managing collections of images, digital Raw shooters will especially find that its ability to host the Camera Raw plugin without tying up Photoshop opens up some interesting new workflow possibilities. We cover Bridge in depth in Chapter 11, *Building a Digital Workflow*.

Multiple layer selection. Seemingly, the most common reason for linking layers, according to Adobe's usability testing, is to move them simultaneously. In Photoshop CS2, you can simply select multiple layers and move them—Shift-click to select contiguous layers, Command-click to select discontiguous ones.

However, it's now also possible to have *no* layers selected in the Layers palette—we're hard-pressed to find a use for that! Layer linking is still possible via the link icon in the Layers palette, but the links are only visible when one of the linked layers is selected. This makes some people crazy, but we found we got used to it pretty quickly. We discuss the new behavior later in this chapter.

Reduce Noise. Noise reduction has traditionally not been one of Photoshop's strengths, and in the past we've used some fairly demented workarounds. The new Reduce Noise filter is a step in the right direction, but but doesn't quite eliminate the need for these workarounds—we discuss it in detail in Chapter 9, *Sharpness, Detail, and Noise Reduction*.

Smart Sharpen. Sharpening is an area that's been largely ignored since the Unsharp Mask filter first made its appearance. Photoshop CS2 introduces an all-new sharpening filter, Smart Sharpen. It's interesting, and possibly useful, though it shows signs of being a 1.0 implementation—we cover it in depth in Chapter 9, *Sharpness, Detail, and Noise Reduction*.

Lens Correction. Rounding out the new offerings that address detail is the new Lens Correction filter, which allows you to fix barrel and pincushion distortion, chromatic aberration, and perspective errors. It doesn't turn an SLR into a view camera, but it's a fair substitute for tilt/shift lenses. We discuss it in detail in Chapter 9, *Sharpness, Detail, and Noise Reduction*.

Menu and workspace customization. Now you can personalize your copy of Photoshop to the nth degree, hiding stuff you never use, and making the things you use all the time more accessible. The downside is that you can also render your copy of Photoshop incomprehensible to everyone (including yourself) if you aren't careful. We'll look at the new customization features later in this chapter.

Spot healing. Spotting for dust or scratches usually involves mind-numbing drudgery. The healing brush tool, which debuted in Photoshop 7, helps a great deal, but the new spot healing brush in Photoshop CS2 saves lots of time by eliminating the requirement that you set a source point for healing. We'll look at it in Chapter 12, *Essential Image Techniques*.

Camera Raw. The Camera Raw plugin, now at version 3, has become something very close to an application within an application. The tonal fine-tuning allowed by the Curve tab, along with the crop and straighten tools, and the ability to batch save directly from Camera Raw, add up to less time spent post-conversion in Photoshop. With digital Raw capture, Photoshop becomes a tool for making localized corrections and layering images rather than a mandatory step in the workflow. We cover Camera Raw in much more detail in Chapter 11, *Building a Digital Workflow*.

Merge to HDR. If you want to capture the entire dynamic range of real-world scenes, from brightest specular highlight all the way into deep shadows, it's unlikely that you can do so with a single exposure. Merge to HDR lets you combine multiple bracketed exposures of the same scene (ideally in Camera Raw format) in an HDR (High Dynamic Range) file, which uses 32 bits of floating point data per pixel, per channel to record an essentially unlimited dynamic range. We'll look at Merge to HDR in Chapter 12, *Essential Image Techniques*.

Smart Objects. The new Smart Objects feature lets you place vector or pixel-based files—including Camera Raw images—as editable, rotatable, and scalable objects without turning them into pixels. It's an evolutionary rather than revolutionary feature—you can't see the Smart Object in context in the Photoshop document when you edit it, so it's really just a shortcut for going back to the source object, editing it, and bringing the edited version back into Photoshop—but it's a big time-saver nonetheless. We look at it in Chapter 12, *Essential Image Techniques*.

Perspective cloning. The new Vanishing Point filter makes cloning objects to match the perspective of existing ones much easier. Add an extra ten stories to the Empire State Building or a second deck to the Golden Gate Bridge with just a few mouse clicks. We'll look at Vanishing Point in Chapter 12, *Essential Image Techniques*.

Animation features. Photoshop's huge gravitational force continues to attract features from its little brother ImageReady. The newest casualty is the Animation palette, which lets you create animated GIFs based on the visual appearance of layers. For those who need this sort of thing, we cover it in Chapter 14, *Multimedia and the Web*.

Other stuff. Photoshop CS2 offers a number of other smaller changes, such as image warping (hiding in the Transform submenu, under the Edit menu), a Red Eye tool for removing those hideous red camera flash reflections, the ability to change the size of some of the user-interface elements, and a WYSIWYG font menu. We were going to say these were all improvements until we got to the font menu "feature"—fortunately, this is one you can easily turn off in the new Type panel of the Preferences dialog box.

Windows

Screen space is at almost as great a premium as memory these days—every little bit helps. We like to work in Full Screen mode with Photoshop (see

Figure 2-1) instead of wasting space on title bars, scroll bars, and the like. You can switch to either of two full-screen modes in the Tool palette or by pressing F. The first time you press F (or click on the middle icon on the palette), the image window takes over the screen (up to the menu bar) and the background becomes 50-percent gray. The second time, the menu bar disappears, too, and the background becomes black. (See "Make the Palettes Go Away," later in this chapter, for an important related tip.)

Figure 2-1
Full Screen mode

Click here or press F to switch to Full Screen mode.

If you have extra time on your hands, you can also pick Full Screen mode from the Screen Mode submenu (under the View menu).

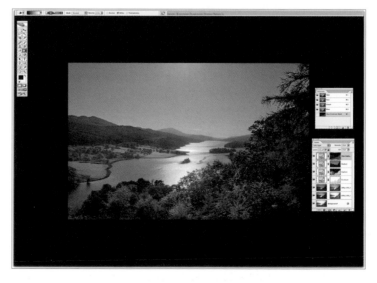

Tip: Full Screen Scroll. Just because your image is in Full Screen mode doesn't mean you can't scroll around using the Grabber Hand tool: Just hold down the spacebar and click-and-drag. If the image doesn't fill the screen, the Grabber Hand tool moves the whole image around.

Tip: Showing the Menu Bar. When you're in either of the full-screen modes, you can hide or show the menu bar by pressing Shift-F.

Tip: Changing the Matte Color. You can change the neutral gray background color that surrounds your image when you're in Full Screen mode or when you expand the document window larger than the image itself. Just pick a foreground color and then Shift-click on the background with the Paint Bucket tool (it's in the Gradient tool's flyout menu). At first glance, this is nothing more than a good trick to play on your colleagues. However, it's also a good way to preview how an image will look if you're going to place it on a colored background.

Tip: Spread Out Those Windows. When you have two or more document windows open at the same time, Photoshop will neatly arrange them on your screen if you choose Tile Horizontally, Tile Vertically, or Cascade from the Arrange submenu (under the Window menu). The difference? The Tile options resize and reposition the windows so that you can see all the windows at once. Cascade repositions the windows so that they're stacked on top of each other, with only their title bars showing.

Tip: Rotating Through Your Windows. We often find ourselves in Photoshop with five or more windows open at a time—a frustrating situation when we need to move through them all quickly. You can press Control-Tab to switch from one open document to the next. (In this case, it's the Control key on both Macintosh and Windows.) This way, you can rotate through the windows without taking your hands off the keyboard, even if you're in Full Screen mode with no menus.

Tip: Use New Window. You often want to see your image at Actual Pixels view (where screen pixels equal image pixels) but work at some other magnification. Instead of jumping back and forth between different magnification views, try opening a second window by selecting New Window from the Arrange submenu (under the Window menu). You can leave one window set to Actual Pixels and change the other window to whatever view you want to work at. Whenever you change something in one window, Photoshop updates the other window almost immediately. You can also use this technique to display an image in RGB and CMYK Preview modes simultaneously.

Tip: From Window to Folder. If you want to open an image that you know is in the same folder as one that is currently open in Photoshop, Command-click on the title in the document window's title bar (this is a Macintosh-only feature, as far as we know) and select the folder from the popup menu that appears. This tells Photoshop to switch to the desktop and open that folder.

Navigation

In this section, we first explore some of the fastest ways to move around your image, including zooming in and out. Then we discuss moving pixels around both within your document, and from one document to another. It's funny, but we find that even expert users forget or never learn this basic stuff, so we urge you to read this section even if you think you already know all there is to know about navigating in Photoshop. And as usual, Photoshop CS2 snuck in some new zoom and scroll tricks.

Magnification

Images got pixels. Computer screens got pixels. But how does one type of pixel relate to the other type of pixel? When you display an image on your screen, Photoshop has to match the image pixels to screen pixels (see Figure 2-2). The percentage in the title bar of the document window tells you how Photoshop is matching up those pixels.

The key to understanding this percentage stuff is to remember two things. First, at 100-percent view (otherwise known as Actual Pixels), each image pixel is represented by a single screen pixel. This view has nothing to do with how big the image will appear in print (or even on the Web, because different monitors have different resolutions). Second, at any percentage other than 100, you're probably not seeing a fully accurate view of your image.

Figure 2-2
Matching pixels

Sixteen image pixels are represented by a single screen pixel.

Sixteen screen pixels represent a single image pixel.

At 400 percent, the image is magnified four times. At 50 percent, it's reduced by half, so you're only seeing half the pixels in the image because you're zoomed farther out and Photoshop has to downsample the image on the fly. When you're viewing at an integral multiple of 100 (25, 50, 200, 400 percent, and so on), Photoshop displays image pixels evenly. At 200 percent, four screen pixels (two horizontal, two vertical) equal one image pixel; at 50 percent, four image pixels equal one screen pixel, and so on.

However, when you're at any "odd" percentage, the program has to jimmy the display in order to make things work. Photoshop can't cut a screen pixel or an image pixel in half, so instead it fakes the effect using anti-aliasing. The moral of the story is, always return to Actual Size (100 percent) view to peruse your image.

By the way, while it's tempting to select Print Size from the View menu (in order to see how large the image will be on paper), this setting is *only* accurate on 72 pixels-per-inch monitors—in other words, on those old 13-inch Apple monitors and hardly anything else. We just ignore it.

Tip: Don't Select the Zoom Tool. We never select the Zoom tool from the Tool palette. You can always get the Zoom tool temporarily by holding down Command-spacebar (to zoom in) or Command-Option-spacebar (to zoom out). Each click reduces from actual size to two-thirds (66.7 percent), to one-half (50 percent), to one-third (33.3 percent), and so on when zooming out, and magnifies in 100-percent increments when zooming in.

(Actually, it jumps from 800 to 1200 percent, and from 1200 to 1600 percent, which is the maximum magnification available.)

You can also drag around an area with the Zoom tool. The pixels within the marquee are magnified to whatever percentage best fills the screen.

Tip: Zoom with Keystrokes. If you just want to change the overall magnification of an image, press Command-plus (+) or Command-minus (-) to zoom in or out. We find this especially handy because it resizes the window at the same time if necessary. But if any palettes are open, this keystroke won't increase the document window beyond the edges of the palettes unless you click the Ignore Palettes checkbox in the Options bar while the Zoom tool is selected. Note that adding the Option key to this mix tells Photoshop to zoom in or out without changing the size of the window. For some reason, it's just the opposite in Windows: The Ctrl key zooms without resizing, and holding down Ctrl and Alt zooms *and* resizes.

Tip: Zoom with the Scroll Wheel. If your mouse has a scroll wheel, you can use it to scroll or zoom. By default, it's set to scroll, and pressing Option while turning the wheel makes it zoom instead. To reverse this behavior, check Zoom with Scroll Wheel in General Preferences.

Tip: Get to 100-Percent View Quickly. You can jump to 100-percent view quickly by double-clicking on the Zoom tool in the Tool palette. This is just the same as clicking the Actual Pixels button in the Options bar or choosing Actual Pixels from the View menu. Faster still, press Command-Option-0 (zero).

Tip: Fit Window in Screen. Double-clicking on the Hand tool, on the other hand (no pun left unturned), is the same as clicking Fit on Screen in the Options bar when the Zoom tool or Hand tool is selected, or pressing Command-0 (zero)—it makes the image and the document window as large as it can, without going out of the screen's boundaries.

Tip: Zoom Factor. At the bottom-left corner of the window, Photoshop displays the current magnification percentage. This isn't only a display: You can change it to whatever percentage you'd like (double-click to select the whole field). Type the zoom percentage you want, then press Return or Enter when you're done. If you're not sure exactly what percentage you want, note that you can press Shift-Return instead of Return and the field remains selected after Photoshop zooms in or out, letting you enter a different value (see Figure 2-3).

Figure 2-3
Zoom factor

Type the zoom percentage you want here, then press Return or Enter.

Moving

If you're like most Photoshop users, you find yourself moving around the image a lot. Do a little here . . . do a little there . . . and so on. But when you're doing this kind of navigation, you should rarely use the scroll bars. There are much better ways.

Tip: Use the Grabber Hand. The best way to make a small move around your image is with the Grabber Hand. Don't choose it from the Tool palette. Instead, hold down the spacebar to get the Grabber Hand. Then just click-and-drag to where you want to go.

Grab Every Image. Wouldn't it be cool if you could use the Grabber Hand on more than one open image window at the same time? No problem: Just hold down the Shift key with the Grabber Hand tool (or press Shift-spacebar with any other tool). This works when zooming in and out, too: Just add the Shift key and your magnification change gets applied to all open images.

Tip: End Up Down Home. We like the extended keyboard—the kind with function keys and the built-in keypad. Most people ignore the very helpful Page Up, Page Down, Home, and End keys when working in Photoshop, but we find them invaluable for perusing an image for dust or scratches.

When you press Page Up or Page Down, Photoshop scrolls the image by almost an entire page's worth of pixels up or down. It leaves a small band of overlap, just in case. While there's no Page Left or Page Right button, you can jump a screen to the left or right by pressing Command-Page Up or

Command-Page Down. You can scroll in 10-pixel increments by pressing Shift-Page Up or Shift-Page Down (or, again, add the Command key to go left or right).

Also note that pressing the Home button jumps you to the upper-left corner, and the End button jumps you to the lower-right corner of the document. David often uses this technique when using the Cropping tool. He lazily sets the cropping rectangle approximately where he wants it, then zooms in to the upper-left corner to precisely adjust that corner point. Then, with one hit of the End key, he's transported to the lower right, where he can adjust that corner.

Tip: Match Up Your Images. When you're working on two or more images at the same time, it's often helpful to see the same part of each image at the same magnification. Several commands on the Arrange submenu (under the Window menu) automate this process. The Match Zoom feature sets the magnification percentage for every open image to the zoom level of the current document. Match Location leaves the magnification alone but scrolls each document window to the same part of the image as the current file—for instance, if the current file displays the lower-right corner, then all the images will scroll to the lower-right corner. (Unfortunately, Match Location is only approximate; it won't match to the exact pixel.) The one we use most often is Match Zoom and Location. You can guess what it does.

Tip: Moving Among the Layers. The Grabber Hand and scroll bars only let you move around your image on a two-dimensional plane. What about moving into the third dimension—the layer dimension?

You can move among layers (without ever touching the Layers palette) by using keystrokes: Option-[or Option-] (the square brackets) move to the previous or next visible layer (even if that layer is in a different layer set). Add Shift to extend the selection to multiple layers. Option-. (period) and Option-, (comma) select the top and bottom layers, respectively.

One cool feature here is that if only one layer is visible when you press these keystrokes, Photoshop hides that layer and shows the next layer. This is great for cycling through a number of layers, though it doesn't always work when you have layer groups.

By the way, if you want to *move* the layers rather than just select them, you can press Command-Shift-[or Command-Shift-] to move the selected layer to the bottom and top of the layers stack, respectively.

Tip: Faster Layer Selection. Perhaps the fastest way to select a layer is to select the Move tool and then turn on the Auto Select Layer checkbox in the Options bar. Now you can switch to a layer simply by clicking with the Move tool on a pixel on that layer. If you don't have the Move tool selected when you want to switch layers, simply Command-click (which gives you the Move tool temporarily). On the other hand, we personally find Auto Layer Select somewhat infuriating because it's too easy to select the wrong layer. Instead, we like using the Move tool's context-sensitive menu.

Tip: Context-Sensitive Menus. When you Control-click (Macintosh) or click with the right mouse button (Windows), Photoshop displays a context-sensitive menu that changes depending on what tool you have selected in the Tool palette. We find the menu for the various painting tools pretty useless (though if you had to do a lot of painting, it might be helpful). But the menus you get when you Control-click (or right-mouse-button-click) with the Move tool and the selection tools are great.

The context-sensitive menu for the Move tool lets you choose a layer to work on. If you have four layers in an image, and three of them overlap in one particular area, you can Control-click (or right-mouse-button- click) on that area and Photoshop asks you which of the three layers you want to jump to. (Note that you can almost always get the Move tool's context-sensitive menu by Command-Control-clicking or, in Windows, clicking the right mouse button with the Ctrl key held down.)

The context-sensitive menu for the Marquee tool contains a mish-mosh of features, including Delete Layer, Duplicate Layer, Load Selection, Reselect, Color Range, and Group into New Smart Object (we have no idea why Adobe picked these and left others out). Many of these features don't have keyboard shortcuts, so this menu is the fastest way to perform them.

Tip: Click on Your Layer. Here's another way to select a different layer without clicking on it in the Layers palette: Command-Option-Control-click (with any tool; in Windows, you Ctrl-Alt-click with the right mouse button). If you click on pixels that "belong" to a different layer than the one you're on, Photoshop jumps to that layer. For instance, if you've got a picture of your mom on Layer 3, and you're currently on the Background layer, you can Command-Option-Control-click (or Ctrl-Alt-right-mouse-button-click) on your mom to jump to Layer 3.

This typically works only when you click on a pixel that has an opacity greater than 50 percent. (We say "typically" because it sometimes *does* work if the total visible opacity is less than 50 percent. See "Info Palette," later in this chapter.) If your mom has a feathered halo around her, you may not be able to get this to work if you click on the feathered part.

Navigator Palette

The Navigator palette acts as command central for all scrolling and zooming (see Figure 2-4). We rarely use this palette because we find that it's usually either too precise or not precise enough, and it takes too much mousing around. Of course, this is largely a personal bias on our part; if you find it useful, more power to you.

Figure 2-4
Navigator palette

Most of the palette is occupied by a thumbnail of the image, with a red frame indicating the contents of the active window. (If your image has a lot of red in it, you might want to change the frame color by choosing Palette Options from the palette's flyout menu). Dragging the outline pans the contents of the active window. Command-dragging lets you define a new outline, thereby changing the zoom percentage.

The percentage field at the lower left of the palette works exactly like the one at the lower left of the image window. Clicking the zoom-in and zoom-out buttons has the same effect as pressing Command-plus and Command-minus. David's favorite feature in this palette is the magnification slider, which lets him change the zoom level dynamically. It's not a particularly useful feature, but it's mighty fun.

Moving Pixels

If you simply make a selection, then drag it with one of the selection tools, you move the selection boundary but not its contents. If you want the pixels to move as well, you have to use the Move tool. Fortunately, no matter what tool is selected, you can always temporarily get the Move tool by holding down the Command key. Note that you can hold down the Option key while you drag to copy the pixels as you move them (moving a duplicate of the pixels).

When you move or copy selected pixels with the Move tool, you get a floating selection (sort of like a temporary layer that disappears when you deselect). While the selection is still floating, you can use the Fade command (in the Edit menu) to change its opacity or blend mode.

With the Move tool, you can move an entire layer around without selecting anything. When you do have something selected, you don't have to worry about positioning the cursor before you drag. This is a great speedup, especially when you're working with heavily feathered selections.

Tip: Arrow Keys Move, Too. When moving pixels around, don't forget the arrow keys. With the Move tool selected, each press of an arrow key moves the contents of your selection by one pixel. If you add the Shift key, the selection moves 10 pixels. Modifier keys work, too: hold down the Option key when you first press an arrow key, and the selection is duplicated, floated, and moved one pixel (don't keep holding down the Option key after that, unless you want a *lot* of duplicates).

Remember that you can always get the Move tool temporarily by adding the Command key to any of these shortcuts. Pressing the arrow keys with any tool other than the Move tool moves the selection without moving the pixels it contains. This is an essential technique for precision placement of a selection.

If you've got the Move tool selected (press V), and nothing is selected when you press the arrow keys, the entire layer moves by one pixel. Add the Shift key to move 10 pixels instead.

Tip: Moving Multiple Layers. One of the problems with layers is that you often can't do the same thing to more than one layer at the same time. An obvious exception in Photoshop CS2 is moving layers.

If you wanted to move more than one layer at a time in previous versions of Photoshop, you had to link them. In Photoshop CS2, you can simply select all the layers you want to move: Shift-click in the Layers palette to select contiguous layers, Command-click to select noncontiguous ones.

Tip: Duplicating Layers. Duplicating a layer is a part of our everyday workflow, so it's a good thing that there are various ways to do it.

▶ You can drag the layer's tile on top of the New Layer button in the Layers palette.

▶ You can press Command-J (if some pixels are selected, then only those pixels will be duplicated).

▶ You can select Duplicate Layer from the Layer menu.

▶ You can select Duplicate Layer from the context-sensitive menu you get when Control-clicking (Macintosh) or right-mouse-button-clicking (Windows) with the Marquee, Lasso, or Cropping tool.

The method you use at any given time should be determined by where your hands are. (Keyboard? Mouse? Coffee mug?)

Tip: Duplicating and Merging Layers. You can merge a copy of all the currently visible layers in a document into a new layer (without deleting the other layers) by holding down the Option key when selecting Merge Visible from the Layer menu (or, better yet, just press Command-Shift-Option-E). In previous versions of Photoshop, Option-Merge Visible copied all the visible pixels into the currently selected layer—in CS2, it always creates a new layer unless the currently selected layer is empty.

Tip: Copying Pixels. Layers are a fact of life, and with Photoshop it's not uncommon to find yourself with more layers than you know what to do with. If you make a selection and select Copy, you only get the pixels on the currently active layer(s) (the one(s) selected on the Layers palette). If you want to copy all the visible layers, select Copy Merged instead (or press Command-Shift-C).

Some people use this technique to make a merged copy of the entire image (not just a selection). It works, but the previous tip provides a faster and less memory-intensive way of doing the same thing.

Tip: Pasting Pixels. Pasting pixels into a document automatically creates a new layer (unless your image is in Indexed Color mode). So what about the Paste Into (Command-Shift-V) and Paste Behind (Command-Shift-Option-V) features (which are available when you've made a selection)? When invoked, each of these adds a new layer, but it also adds a layer mask to that layer in the form of the selection. This is one of the fastest ways to build a layer and a layer mask in one step: Draw a selection the shape of the layer mask you want, then perform a Paste Into or a Paste Behind (depending on the effect you're trying to achieve).

Tip: Drag-and-Drop Selections and Layers. Most Photoshop users can't envision a world without Cut and Paste. However, there are times to use the Clipboard and times not to. In Photoshop, you often want to avoid the Clipboard because you're dealing with large amounts of data. Every time you move something to or from the clipboard, you eat up more RAM or hard drive space, which can slow you down.

If you want to move a selection of pixels (or a layer) from one document to another, you can do so by dragging it from one window into the other (if you've got a selection, remember to use the Move tool, or else you'll just move the selection boundary itself). Photoshop moves the pixels "behind the scenes," so as to avoid unneeded memory requirements. If you're trying to copy an entire layer, you can also just click on its tile in the Layers palette and drag it to the other document's window.

Tip: Placing your Drag-and-Drop Selection. In the last tips we talked about how you can drag and drop a selection or layer from one image into another. When you let go of the mouse button, the selection is placed into the image right where you dropped it. However, if you hold down the Shift key, Photoshop centers the layer or selection in the new image. If the two images have the same pixel dimensions, the Shift key "pin-registers" it—the layer or selection falls in exactly the same place it was in the original document.

Tip: Copying Layer Masks. In previous versions of Photoshop, copying layer masks from one layer to another was a fairly painful process. In Photoshop CS2, you can simply click the layer mask's tile in the Layers palette, and Option-drag it to the target layer.

Guides, Grids, and Alignment

Moving pixels is all very well and good, but where are you going to move them to? If you need to place pixels with precision, you should use the ruler, guides, grids, and alignment features. The ruler is the simplest: you can hide or show it by pressing Command-R. Wherever you move your cursor, faint tick marks appear in the rulers, showing you exactly where you are (you can also follow the coordinates on the Info palette).

Guides. You can add a guide to a page by dragging it out from either the horizontal or vertical ruler. Or, if you care about specific placement, you can either carefully watch the measurements on the Info palette as you drag, or select New Guide from the View menu. (If you don't think in inches, you can change the default measurement system; see "Tip: Switch Units," later in this chapter.)

You can always move a guide with the Move tool (don't forget you can always get the Move tool temporarily by holding down the Command key). Table 2-1 lists a number of grids and guides keystrokes that can help you use these features effortlessly.

	To do this...	Press this...
Table 2-1 **Grids and guides** **keystrokes**	Hide/Show All Extras (grids, guides, etc.)	Command-H
	Hide/Show Guides	Command-' (quote)
	Hide/Show Grid	Command-Option-'
	Snap To Guides	Command-; (semicolon)
	Lock/Unlock Guides	Command-Option-;

Tip: Snap to Ruler Marks. We almost always hold down the Shift key when dragging a guide out from a ruler; that way, the guide automatically snaps to the ruler tick marks. If you find that your guides are slightly sticky as you drag them out without the Shift key held down, check to see what layer you're on. When Snap To Guides is turned on, objects snap to the guides *and* guides snap to the edges and centers of objects on layers.

Tip: Switching Guide Direction. Dragged out a horizontal guide when you meant to get a vertical one? No problem: Just Option-click on the guide to switch its orientation (or hold down the Option key while dragging out the guide).

Tip: Mirroring Guides. If you rotate your image by 90 degrees, or flip it horizontally or vertically, your guides will rotate or flip with it. You can stop this errant behavior by locking down the guides first (press Command-Option-semicolon).

Tip: Guides on the Pasteboard. Just because your pixels stop at the edge of the image doesn't mean your guides have to. You can place guides out on the gray area outside the image canvas and they're still functional. This is just the ticket if you've got a photo that you need to place so that it bleeds off the edge of your image by 0.25 inch.

Tip: Changing Guides and Grids. Guides are, by default, cyan. Grid lines are, by default, set one inch apart. If you don't like these settings, change them in the Guides, Grid & Slices pane of the Preferences dialog box (you can select this from the Preferences submenu), or just double-click on any guide with the Move tool (or Command-double-click with any other tool).

Alignment and distribution. People often use the alignment features in page-layout applications, but Photoshop has alignment and distribution features, too, and they're a godsend for anyone who really cares about precision in their images (we find them particularly useful when building images for the Web). Here's how you can align objects on two layers.

1. Select two or more layers in the Layers palette. Remember that you can Command-Shift-click on each layer to select more than one discontiguous layer.

2. Make sure you have no selections by pressing Command-D (or choosing Deselect from the Select menu), and then choose among

the options on the Align submenu (under the Layer menu; see Figure 2-5). Or, even faster, click on one of the Align buttons in the Options bar when you have the Move tool selected. If you don't deselect first, Photoshop aligns to the selection instead of to the layers.

Tip: Locking Alignment. Normally, when you align along the left edges, Photoshop moves all the layers except for the one that has the leftmost data. (Or the rightmost data when aligning left, and so on.) You can force Photoshop to lock one layer and move the others by *linking* the layers instead of selecting them: Select them all, click the Link icon in the Layers palette, then click on the layer you want to remain in place. Now when you choose from the Align submenu, all the layers move except for the currently selected one.

Figure 2-5
Aligning layers

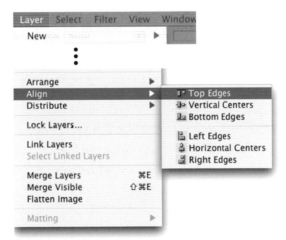

If you select three or more layers, you can also distribute the layers instead of aligning them. For example, if you have four small pictures that you want evenly spread across your Photoshop image, you can put each one on a separate layer, link them all together, and choose Horizontal Centers from the Distribute submenu (it, too, is under the Layer menu; see Figure 2-6).

When distributing layers vertically, Photoshop "locks" the layers that are closest to the top and the bottom of the image canvas; when distribut-

Figure 2-6
Distributing layers

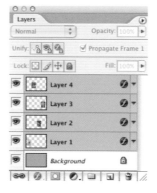

Align Linked:
Horizontal Centers,
Distribute Linked:
Horizontal Centers

ing horizontally, it locks the leftmost and rightmost layers. All the layers in between get moved. For example, if you choose Vertical Centers from the Distribute Linked submenu, Photoshop moves the layers so that there is an equal amount of space from the vertical center point of one layer to the next.

Tip: Aligning to the Canvas. Aligning two layers together is all well and good, but we often find we want to align something to the image canvas itself. For instance, you might want to center some text horizontally in the picture. Here's how you can do it.

1. Press Command-A to select the whole image.

2. Select the layer(s) you want to move.

3. Choose from among the Align buttons in the Options bar (when you have the Move tool selected) or the Align to Selection submenu (under the Layer menu). If you choose the Horizontal Centers button, then Photoshop centers your layer to the selection (which, in this case, is the size of the canvas).

Dialog Boxes

Dialog boxes seem like simple things, but since you probably spend a good chunk of your time in Photoshop looking at them, wouldn't it be great to be more efficient while you're there? Here are a bunch of tips that will let you fly through those pesky beasts.

Tip: Scroll 'n' Zoom. The most important lesson to learn about dialog boxes in Photoshop is that just because one is open doesn't mean you can't do anything else. For instance, in many dialog boxes—such as the Levels and Curves dialog boxes—you can still scroll around any open documents (not just the active one) by holding down the spacebar and dragging. You can even zoom in and out of the active window using the Command-spacebar and Command-Option-spacebar techniques.

Tip: Save your Settings. Many dialog boxes in Photoshop have Save and Load buttons that let you save to disk all the settings that you've made in a dialog box. They're particularly useful when you're going through the iterative process of editing an image.

For instance, let's say you're adjusting the tone of an image with Curves. You increase this and decrease that, and add some points here and there…. Finally, when you're finished, you click OK and find—much to your dismay—that you need to make one more change. If you jump right back into Curves, you degrade your image a second time—not good (see Chapter 6, *Image Adjustment Fundamentals*). If you undo, you lose the changes you made the first time. But if you've saved the curve to disk before leaving the dialog box, you can undo, go back to the dialog box, and load in the settings you had saved. Then you can add that one last move to the curve, without introducing a second round of image-degrading corrections.

Tip: Instant Replay. There's one other way to undo and still save any tonal-adjustment settings you've made. If you hold down the Option key while selecting *any* feature from the Adjust submenu (under the Image menu), Photoshop opens the dialog box with the last-used settings. Similarly, you can add the Option key to the adjustment's keyboard shortcut. For instance, Command-Option-L opens the Levels dialog box with the same settings you last used. This is a great way to specify the same Levels or Curves (or Hue/Saturation, or any other adjustment) for several different images. But as soon as you quit Photoshop, it loses its memory.

Tip: Opening Palettes from Dialog Boxes. We almost always work with the Info palette open. However, every now and again it gets closed or covered up with some other palette. Unfortunately, while you're in a dialog box (like the Curves or Levels dialog box), you cannot click on any palette without leaving the dialog box by clicking OK or Cancel. Fortunately for efficiency, you *can* select a palette from the Window menu. To display the Info palette, select Show Info from this menu. (Unfortunately, this *still* doesn't work for palettes that are docked in the palette well.)

Keystrokes in Dialog Boxes

We love keystrokes. They make everything go much faster, or at least they make it *feel* like we're working faster. Here are a few keystrokes that we use all the time while in dialog boxes.

Option. Holding down the Option (or Alt) key while in a dialog box almost always changes the Cancel button into a Reset button, letting you reset the dialog box to its original state (the way it was when you first opened it). If you want to go keystrokes the whole way, press Command-Option-period to do the same thing (this doesn't work on Windows).

Command-Z. You already know Command-Z because it's gotten you out of more jams than you care to think about. Well, Command-Z performs an undo within dialog boxes, too. It undoes the last change you made. We use this all the time when we mistype.

Arrow keys. Many dialog boxes in Photoshop have text fields where you enter or change numbers (see Figure 2-7). You can change those numbers by pressing the Up or Down arrow key. Press once, and the number increases or decreases by one. If you hold down the Shift key while pressing the arrow key, the number changes by 10. (Note that some dialog box values change by a tenth or even a hundredth; when you hold down Shift, they change by 10 times as much.)

A few dialog boxes use the arrow keys in a different way. In the Lens Flare filter, for instance, the arrow keys move the position of the effect.

Figure 2-7
Numerical fields
in dialog boxes

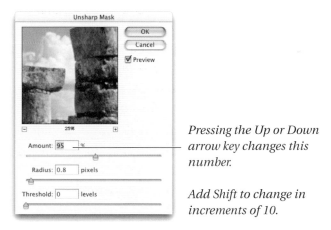

Pressing the Up or Down arrow key changes this number.

Add Shift to change in increments of 10.

Tab key. As in most Macintosh and Windows applications, the Tab key selects the next text field in dialog boxes with multiple text fields. You can use this in conjunction with the previous tip in dialog boxes such as the Unsharp Mask filter, or you can simply tab to the next field and type in a number if you already know the value you want. Shift-Tab to move to the previous field instead.

Previewing

Most of Photoshop's tonal- and color-correction features and many of its filters offer a Preview checkbox in their dialog boxes. Plus, all the filters that have a dialog box have a proxy window that shows the effect applied to a small section of the image (some dialog boxes have both). If you're working on a very large file on a relatively slow machine, and the filter you're using has a proxy window, you might want to turn off the Preview checkbox so that Photoshop doesn't slow down redrawing the screen while you're making adjustments. However, most of the time, unless we're working with a very slow filter like Smart Sharpen, we just leave the Preview feature on.

We use the Preview checkbox to view "before" and "after" versions of our images, toggling it on and off to see the effect of the changes without leaving the dialog box—sometimes the changes we make are subtle and gradual, but a before-and-after usually lets us see exactly what we've accomplished.

Proxies. The proxy in dialog boxes shows only a small part of the image, but it updates almost instantly. Previewing time-consuming filters such as Smart Sharpen or Reduce Noise on a large file can take a long time. Some very time-consuming filters such as the Distort filters offer a large proxy instead of a preview.

Tip: Before and After in Proxies. You can always see a before-and-after comparison by clicking in the proxy. Hold down the mouse button to see the image before the filter is applied, and release it to see the image after the filter is applied.

Tip: Changing the Proxy View. To see a different part of the image, click-and-drag in the proxy (no modifier keys are necessary). Alternatively, you can click in the document itself. The cursor changes to a small rectangle—wherever you click shows up in the Preview window.

Similarly, you can zoom the proxy in and out. The *slow* way is to click on the little (+) and (-) buttons. Much faster is to click the proxy with either the Command or Option key held down—the former zooms in, the latter zooms out. However, we rarely zoom in and out because you can't see the true effect of a filter unless you're at 100-percent view.

Note that proxies only show the layer you're working on at any one time. This makes sense, really; only that layer is going to be affected.

New Dialog Box

Before we move on to essential tips about tools, we need to take a quick look at the New dialog box, which has a few very helpful (and in some cases hidden) features. For instance, note that the New dialog box has an Advanced button; when you click this, you're offered two additional settings: Color Profile and Pixel Aspect Ratio. Color Profile lets you specify a profile other than the working space for your image. (You can choose the default working space too, but since that's what you'd get anyway, it's a bit pointless to choose it here.) Note that we cover working spaces in Chapter 5, *Color Settings*. Pixel Aspect Ratio lets you choose a nonsquare pixel, in case your image is destined for video. If video isn't in your game plan, then avoid this popup menu entirely. (Neither of us are video experts, so we're pretty darn happy with plain ol' square pixels.)

Tip: Preset Document Sizes. The Preset popup menu in the New dialog box lets you pick from among 24 common document sizes, such as A4, 640 × 480, and 4 × 6 inches.If you need a preset other than the ones on the list, jusr set the New dialog box the way you want it, then click the Save Preset button (see Figure 2-8). You can delete user-created presets using the Delete Preset button, but the built-in ones that ship with Photoshop are there to stay.

Figure 2-8
The New
dialog box

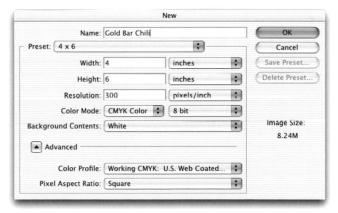

When you save a document preset, Photoshop gives you the choice of which settings to remember: Resolution, Mode, Bit Depth, Content, Profile, and Pixel Aspect Ratio. For example, let's say you turn off the Profile checkbox; when you later choose your preset from the Preset popup menu, Photoshop leaves the image's profile set to the current working space instead of overriding it.

Note that some built-in presets (those having to do with video), can also automatically add guides to the document. Unfortunately, there's currently no way to save presets with guides yourself.

Tip: Clairvoyant Image Size. The New dialog box tries to read your mind. If you have something copied to the Clipboard when you create a new document, Photoshop automatically selects Clipboard from the Preset popup menu and plugs the pixel dimensions, resolution, and color model of that copied piece into the proper places of the dialog box for you. If you'd rather use the values from the last new image you created, hold down the Option key while selecting New from the File menu (or press Command-Option-N).

Tip: Breaking Up Measurements. Photoshop is just trying to help make your life easier: When you select a measurement system (inches, picas, pixels, or whatever) in the New dialog box—or the Image Size or the Canvas Size dialog box—Photoshop changes both the horizontal and vertical settings. If you want vertical to be set to picas and horizontal to be millimeters, then hold down the Shift key while selecting a measurement system. That tells the program not to change the other setting, too.

Tip: Copying Sizes from Other Documents. Russell Brown, that king of Photoshop tips and tricks, reminded us to keep our eyes open. Why, for instance, is the Window menu not grayed out when you have the New dialog box open? Because you can select items from it!

If you want your new document to have the same pixel dimensions, resolution, and color mode as a document you already have open, you can select that document from the bottom of the Window menu or the bottom of the Preset popup menu. Voilà! The statistics are copied.

This trick also works in the Image Size and Canvas Size dialog boxes.

Keyboard Shortcuts

In the early days of desktop publishing software, programmers figured it was good enough to assign various keyboard shortcuts to menu items. Even if the keyboard shortcut (which engineers abbreviate KBSC) made no sense, we users were forced to memorize it if we were to become efficient. Today, the times they are a-changin', at least for some programs. While QuarkXPress is still living in the dark ages, Photoshop CS2 lets you edit *every* keyboard shortcut to your own liking, and even add shortcuts where there weren't any before.

Of course, the ability to change keyboard shortcuts is great for users, but wreaks havoc for those of us who write books about the software! Throughout this book we describe the keyboard shortcuts in the Photoshop Defaults set. (Someday you'll know you're really living in the future when you change your shortcuts and our book—printed on "digital paper"—automatically updates.)

Tip: Use Your Own Set. To change or add a keyboard shortcut, select Keyboard Shortcuts from the bottom of the Edit menu (or press Command-Option-Shift-K, unless you've changed it to something else). If you edit the default set, it gets saved as "Photoshop Default (modified)", so you can still get the original default back (just choose Photoshop Defaults from the Set menu). But we recommend saving sets with useful names instead. To save a new set, click the New Set button (see Figure 2-9); by default, Photoshop saves the set in the proper location on your hard drive (inside your Photoshop application folder, in Presets>Keyboard Shortcuts).

To customize keyboard shortcuts, follow these steps.

1. Pick Application Menus, Palette Menus, or Tools from the Shortcuts For popup menu. All of Photoshop's shortcuts fall into one of these three areas.

2. Choose from the feature list (you have to click on the little "expand" icon to the left of a menu or palette name to see its features).

Figure 2-9
Edit keyboard
shortcuts

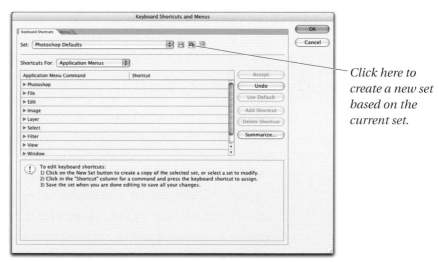

Click here to create a new set based on the current set.

3. Note that the field in the Shortcut column is highlighted; now you can type the keyboard shortcut you want to apply to this feature. If the shortcut is already in use, Photoshop alerts you—if you proceed, the shortcut is removed from the other feature and applied here.

4. If you want to create another shortcut for the same feature (there's no reason you can't have more than one shortcut that does the same thing), click the Add Shortcut button. If you're done with this feature and want to change another, click the Accept button. When you're done applying shortcuts, click OK.

Note that you can save keyboard shortcuts for palette menus and tools in addition to regular menu commands. In fact, you can even save shortcuts for third-party features like Import and Automate plug-ins, filters, or scripts!

Tip: What Was That Shortcut Again? With the advent of editable keyboard shortcuts, the number of different shortcuts for you to keep track of is not infinite, but it's a very large number indeed, and probably too much for any mortal brain. Fortunately, you can click the Summarize button in the Keyboard Shortcuts and Menus dialog box to export a list of every feature and its shortcuts. Photoshop saves this file in HTML format, so you can open it in any Web browser and print it out for future reference.

Menu Customization

Photoshop CS2 takes customization further than ever before by letting you customize menus by colorizing or hiding menu commands. While legend has it that a beta version of QuarkXPress once shipped without a Quit command, you can't hide Photoshop's Quit or Close commands, but you *can* hide the New, Open, and Save commands, if you're sufficiently deranged to try. (The keyboard shortcuts will still work, so if your goal is total sabotage, you'll have to delete those too.)

As you can probably tell from the preceding paragraph, we have mixed feelings about menu customization. But once you buy into the concept, Photoshop's implementation is pretty slick, and most users don't use anywhere near all of Photoshop's commands. To edit menu commands, choose Menus from the Edit menu (press Command-Option-Shift-M) to open the Keyboard Shortcuts and Menus dialog box—it's the same dialog box used for customizing keyboard shortcuts, but when opened with the Menus command, it opens showing the Menus panel (see Figure 2-10).

Figure 2-10
Edit menus

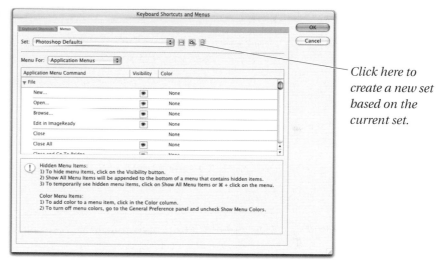

Click here to create a new set based on the current set.

For most (but not all) menu commands, you can control visibility—whether or not they show up on the menu bar—and assign one of seven colors, or None. (Bruce *hates* extraneous color appearing in Photoshop, but even he has to admit that the available colors are fairly tasteful.)

All the caveats about naming sets apply equally to menu customization as they do to keyboard shortcuts. If you get hopelessly confused and wind up with a copy of Photoshop that doesn't let you do anything, one of the menu commands you *can't* hide is Reset Menus, which lurks on the Workspace submenu (in the Window menu), so you always have an escape route!

Workspaces

Rounding out the customization features, we have workspaces. Workspaces let you save any combination of palette locations, keyboard shortcuts, and custom menu sets for quick and easy recall. To save a workspace, set the palettes the way you want them, and optionally load any custom keyboard shortcut and menu sets, then choose Save Workspace from the Workspace submenu on the View menu—see Figure 2-11.

Figure 2-11
Saving workspaces

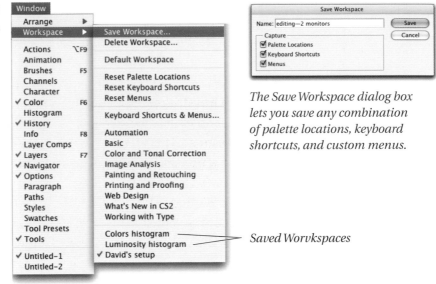

The Save Workspace dialog box lets you save any combination of palette locations, keyboard shortcuts, and custom menus.

Saved Workspaces appear at the foot of the Workspace submenu. For even easier recall, you can use Actions to assign function keys to different workspaces.

We used saved workspaces in many ways. When Bruce uses his laptop at home, it's always connected to a second monitor, and he uses the laptop screen for palettes, but when he's on the road, everything has to be shoehorned into the laptop's 1024 × 768 resolution, so he's created workspaces for each configuration. When he's writing Actions, Bruce likes to make the Actions palette as long as possible. The rest of the time he keeps it compact, or docks it in the palette well, so again, workspaces automate changing the palette.

Essentially, the use of the customization features is limited mostly by your ingenuity, but if you make too many customizations, it may become difficult to remember what each one does! So experiment, but use common sense—it's easy to go hog-wild with this stuff.

Tools

After you're finished moving around in your image, zooming in and out, and moving pixels hither and yon, it's time to get down to work with Photoshop's tools. The tools have all sorts of hidden properties that can make life easier and—more important—more efficient. Let's look at a number of tips and techniques for getting the most out of these instruments of creation.

Tip: Tool Keystrokes. The most important productivity tip we've found in Photoshop to date has been the ability to select each and every tool with a keystroke. Unlike most programs, the keystrokes for Photoshop's tools do not use any modifier keys. You press the key without Command, Control, or Option. Figure 2-12 shows the keystroke for each tool.

Some tools in the Tool palette have multiple modes. For instance, the Dodge tool also "contains" the Burn and the Sponge tools. The slow way to access the different modes is to press the tool icon to bring up the flyout palette containing the different modes. A faster method is to press the tool's keystroke once to select it, and then hold down the Shift key while pressing it again to toggle among the choices. Press M once, and you jump to the Marquee tool; then press Shift-M, and it switches to the elliptical Marquee tool; press Shift-M once more, and it switches back to the rectangular Marquee tool. Note that this keystroke doesn't cycle through the single-row marquee or the single-column marquee.

(Photoshop lets you change this behavior: If you turn off the "Use Shift Key for Tool Switch" checkbox in the General panel of the Preferences dialog box—see "Preferences," later in this chapter—then you don't have to hold down the Shift key to rotate through the tools; each time you press M, you'll get a different tool.)

Tip: Changing Blend Modes. You can also change blend modes (Normal, Screen, Multiply, and so on) by pressing Shift-minus and Shift-plus, or by holding down Shift and Option and pressing the first letter of the mode (such as Shift-Option-S for Screen). If you have a painting tool selected (like the Brush tool), this changes the mode of the selected tool; otherwise, it changes the mode of the layer itself.

Tip: Swap Tool Effect. While we rarely use the Blur, Sharpen, Dodge, or Burn tools (the first two are kind of clunky and we prefer to use adjustment layers rather than the last two), it is kind of fun to know that if you hold down the Option key, the Blur tool switches to the Sharpen tool (and vice versa), and the Dodge tool switches to the Burn tool (and vice versa).

Figure 2-12
Keystrokes for tools

Of course, these are just the defaults; you can edit the shortcuts by selecting Keyboard Shortcuts in the Edit menu.

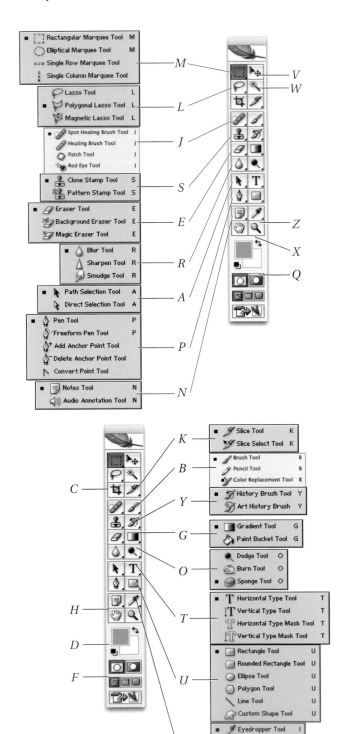

Tip: Options Bar Keystrokes. The tools on the Tool palette only go so far. You often need to modify the tool's default settings on the Options bar. Try this: select a tool, then press Return. The Options bar, even if hidden, appears at this command. Plus, if there is a number-input field on the Options bar, Photoshop selects it for you. When you press Return with the Lasso or Marquee tools selected, for example, the Feather field becomes highlighted on the Options bar.

If there is more than one number-input field on the Options bar, you can press Tab to jump from one to the next. Finally, when you're finished with your changes, press Return again to exit from the bar and resume work.

Tool Presets

Each tool in the Tool palette offers one or more options, such as how large a brush diameter, or whether a selection is feathered, or what mode a tool will paint in (Multiply, Screen, and so on). It's a hassle to remember to set all the tool options, but fortunately Photoshop can remember them for you if you use the Tool Presets feature.

The Tool Presets feature lives in two places: at the far left side of the Options bar, and in the Tool Presets palette (which you can select from the Window menu). We find that the palette is most useful for fine artists who need to switch among various tool presets often within the same image (see Figure 2-13). Production folks like us tend to keep the palette closed and select tools from the Tool Presets popup menu in the Options bar (see Figure 2-14).

Figure 2-13
Tool Presets palette

To create a new tool preset, select any tool in the Tool palette, change the Options bar to the way you want it, click on the Tool Presets popup menu in the Options bar, then click the New Tool Preset button (it looks like a little page with a dog-eared corner). Or, faster, after setting up the tool, you can Option-click on the Tool Presets icon in the Options bar.

Figure 2-14
Tool Preset
popup menu

When Photoshop asks you for a name, we suggest giving the tool preset a descriptive name, like "ShapeTool Circle 50c20m."

Photoshop also comes with several premade collections of tool presets, such as Art History and Brushes. The trick to finding these (and doing all sorts of other things with tool presets, like saving your own sets), is to click once on the Tool Presets flyout menu in the Options bar, and then click once on the popout menu icon (the little triangle on the side of the menu). Or, if the Tool Presets palette is open, you can find all these same options in the palette's flyout menu.

Unfortunately, there's no way to edit a tool preset once you make it—you can only create a new one and delete the old one by choosing Delete Tool Preset from the Tool Preset flyout menu.

Tip: Resetting the Tools. Photoshop power users are forever changing the settings for the tools on the Options bar. But every now and again, it's nice to level the playing field. You can reset the tool options for either a single tool or for all the tools by Control-clicking on the Tool Presets popup menu on the far left edge of the Options bar (or right-mouse-button in Windows).

Eyedropper

Matching colors by eye can be difficult. Instead, use the tool designed for the job: the Eyedropper.

Tip: Eyedropper Keystroke. You can always grab the Eyedropper from the Tool palette (or press I), but if you already have a painting tool selected, it's faster just to use the Option key to toggle between the Eyedropper tool and the painting tool.

Tip: How Many Pixels Are You Looking At? Almost every image has noise in it—pixels that are just plain wrong. If you're clicking around with the Eyedropper tool, there's a reasonable chance that you'll click right on one of those noise pixels, resulting in a color you don't expect (or want). The key is to change what the Eyedropper is looking at.

David usually changes the Sample Size popup menu in the Options bar to 3 by 3 Average. This way, the Eyedropper looks at nine pixels (the pixel you click on, plus the eight surrounding it) and averages them. If he's working on a very high-resolution image, however, he switches to 5 by 5 Average. Bruce, on the other hand, lives on the edge: he always leaves the Eyedropper set to Point Sample. If he thinks there's a danger of picking up a noise pixel, he just zooms in far enough to see exactly which pixel he's sampling.

Tip: Don't Limit Your Eyedropping. Don't forget that when you're working with the Eyedropper tool, you can click on *any* open Photoshop document, or even the Picker, Swatches, or Scratch palettes. This usually even works when a dialog box is open. If you want to select a color from someplace else on screen (outside of Photoshop), first click down inside a Photoshop document, and then drag the mouse (with the button held down) over the color you want. Note that this only captures the RGB color values of whatever is visible on screen (there's no way for Photoshop to find out what the underlying color value is if you sample, say, a CMYK color from a QuarkXPress document).

Tip: Lock Your Sample Points. The Color Sampler (which is hidden as an alternate to the Eyedropper tool) lets you place a sample point at any location in your image and expands the Info palette to show the readings at this coordinate (see Figure 2-15). This is most helpful when performing

Figure 2-15
Locking sample points

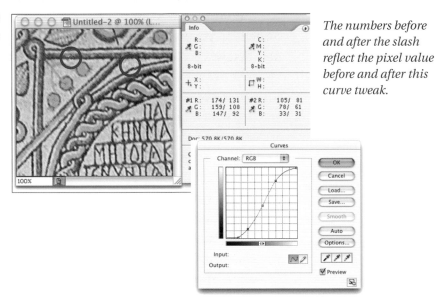

The numbers before and after the slash reflect the pixel value before and after this curve tweak.

color or tonal adjustments, because you can quickly see how your tweaks affect various areas of your image while you're making changes. (See Chapter 6, *Image Adjustment Fundamentals,* for more on this technique.)

We almost never choose the actual Color Sampler tool from the toolbox. Instead, we just Shift-click with the normal Eyedropper tool (or Option-Shift-click with any of the painting tools), which does the same thing. If you want to move a sample point someplace else, you can just click-and-drag it with the Color Sampler tool (or Shift-drag with the Eyedropper tool). To delete a sample point, just Option-click with the Color Sampler tool (or Option-Shift-click on it with either the Eyedropper tool or any painting tool).

Gradient Tool

One of the complaints Adobe heard most in times gone by was that blends in Photoshop resulted in banding. The answer they always gave was to "add noise" to the blend. It's true; adding noise reduces banding significantly. Fortunately, Photoshop adds noise for us. Of course, you can stop it by turning off the Dither checkbox in the Options bar, but there's almost no reason to do so. You *may* want to turn dithering off if you're doing scientific imaging or printing to a continuous-tone device that can actually reproduce the gradient without banding.

Tip: Adding More Noise. If you're still getting banding even with Dither turned on, you may want to add even more noise to a blend. However, note that you don't always need to apply the Add Noise filter to the entire gradient; use the filter selectively.

Instead, you might find it better to add noise to only one or two channels. View each channel separately (see Chapter 8, *Making Selections*) to see where the banding is more prevalent. Then add some noise just to the blend area in that channel.

Tip: Blends in CMYK. Eric Reinfeld pounded it into our heads one day: if you're going to make blends in Photoshop images that will end up in CMYK mode, create them in CMYK mode. Sometimes changing modes from RGB to CMYK can give you significant color shifts in blends.

Many custom CMYK profiles produce strange results when you make a blend—in particular, blues tend to have a saturation "hole" and become less saturated when you expect them to become more so. You can often get better results by creating the blend in one of the CMYK working spaces that ship with Photoshop, then assigning your custom profile to the result. Photoshop's CMYK profiles may not represent your printing conditions, but they tend to offer much smoother gradients than third-party profiles built with any of the common profiling tools. This is a mildly perverse use of color management, but it works—see Chapter 5, *Color Settings*, for more detail about assigning profiles.

Tip: Gradients on Layers. Some people make hard work of creating a blend that fades away into transparency. They go through endless convolutions of Layer Masks and Channel Options, or they spend hours building custom gradients, and so on. They're making it difficult for themselves by not opening their eyes. When you have the Gradient tool selected, the Options bar offers a popup menu with various gradients in it, and one of the defaults blends from Foreground to Transparent, or from Transparent to Foreground. If that option isn't available, someone may have edited your gradient presets. You can create or edit a gradient by clicking once on the gradient swatch in the Options bar. You can also select a different set of gradient presets from the popout menu to the right of the swatch (see Figure 2-16).

Figure 2-16
Gradient options

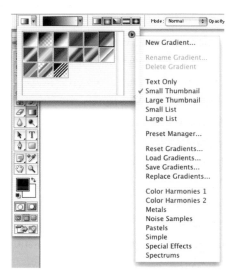

Paint Brushes

We can't tell you how to make great art using Photoshop's painting tools, but we can give you some hints about how to use them more efficiently.

Photoshop 7 dramatically increased the ability to customize your brushes (see Figure 2-17). It's important to remember that these brush styles aren't only for painting with the Brush tool—they also work with the Eraser tool, the Clone Stamp tool, the History Brush tool, and so on. While most of the new brush features are designed for fine art work (simulating charcoal, water colors, and so on), every now and again you may find them helpful in a production environment, too—especially for detailed retouching. Note that in Photoshop CS and later you can use the Brush tool in 16-bit images, too.

Figure 2-17
The Brushes palette

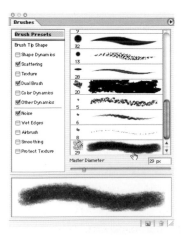

Tip: Brush Keystrokes. Did you know that the [and] keys (the square brackets) increase and decrease the diameter of a brush? Plus, Shift-[and Shift-] change the brush's hardness. We now keep one hand on the keyboard and one on our mouse (or tablet pen); when we want to change tools, we press the key for that tool. When we want to change brush size, we cycle through the brushes with the [and] keys until we find the size we like. Here's one more shortcut, too: the Command and period keys move up and down through the brush presets.

Tip: Fastest Brush Selection. Actually, one of the best ways to select a brush is probably via the context-sensitive menu. On the Macintosh, hold down the Control key when you click with any of the painting tools and Photoshop displays the Brushes menu wherever you click. In Windows, right-mouse-button-click to see the menu. After selecting a brush size, press Enter or Esc to make the palette disappear.

Tip: Hovering Pseudo-Selections. Instead of selecting a brush from the Brushes palette, then painting with it to see how it will really look, hover the cursor over the preset for a moment and Photoshop will display a sample of that brush at the bottom of the palette. If you don't like it, hover over another brush. When you find one you like, click on it to select it.

Tip: Opacity by the Numbers. In between changing brush sizes, we're forever changing brush opacity while painting or retouching. If you're still moving the sliders around on the Options bar, stop it. Instead, just type a number from 0 to 9. Zero gives you 100-percent opacity, 1 gives you 10 percent, 2 gives you 20 percent, and so on. For finer control, press two number keys in quick succession—for example, pressing 45 gets you 45-percent opacity. If you have a non-painting tool selected in the Tool palette, then typing a number changes the opacity of the layer you're working on (unless it's the Background layer, of course). Note that if the Airbrush feature in the Options bar is turned on, then typing numbers affects the Flow percentage rather than the Opacity setting.

Tip: Touching Up Line Art. We talk about scanning and converting to line art in Chapter 12, *Essential Image Techniques*, but since we're on the topic of painting tools, we should discuss the Pencil tool for just a moment. One of the best techniques for retouching line-art (black-and-white) images is the Auto Erase feature on the Options bar. When Auto Erase is turned on, the Pencil tool works like this: if you click on any color other than the foreground color, that pixel—along with all others you touch before lifting the mouse button—is changed to the foreground color (this is the way it works, even with Auto Erase turned off). If you click on the foreground color, however, that pixel—along with all others you encounter—is changed to the background color. This effectively means you don't have to keep switching the foreground and background colors while you work.

Tip: Use All Layers. If you're working on a multilayer image, you may find yourself frustrated with tools like the Smudge, Blur, Magic Wand, or the Clone Stamp tools. That's because sometimes you want these tools to "see" the layers below the one you're working on, and sometimes you do not. Fortunately, Photoshop gives you a choice for each of these tools with the Use All Layers checkbox on the Options bar. (Note that in older versions, this was called Sample Merged.)

When Use All Layers is turned off, each tool acts as though the other layers weren't even there. But if you turn it on, look out! Photoshop sees the other visible layers (both above and below it) and acts as though they were merged together (see Figure 2-18).

The benefit of this is great, but people often don't see the downside. Let's say your background contains a blue box, and Layer 1 has an overlapping yellow box. When you paint or smudge or blur or whatever with Use All Layers turned on, Photoshop "sucks up" the blue and paints it into Layer 1. If you think about it, that's what it should and has to do. But it can really throw you for a loop if you're not prepared.

Cropping Tool

We almost always scan a little bigger than we need, just in case. So we end up using the Cropping tool a lot. The nice thing about the Cropping tool (as opposed to the Crop feature on the Image menu) is that you can make fine adjustments before agreeing to go through with the paring. Just drag one of the corner or side handles. Here are a couple more ways you can fine-tune the crop.

Tip: See What Gets Cropped. By default, Photoshop darkens the area outside the cropping rectangle so that you can see what's going to get

Figure 2-18
Use All Layers

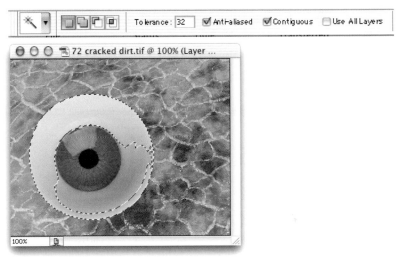

When Use All Layers is turned off and we click on the eyeball,
Photoshop only selects portions of the eye.

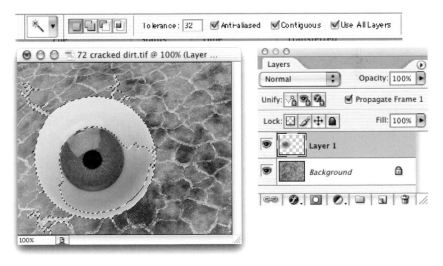

When Use All Layers is turned on, the selection extends past the eye
because there is some white in the background.

cropped out before you press Enter. However, David likes to change this behavior so that it ghosts the cropped out pixels instead (turns them near white). You can do this by clicking on the Color swatch in the Options bar (when the Cropping tool is selected) and picking white from the Color Picker instead of black. You may want to increase the opacity of the color in the Options bar, too (David usually uses 80 percent).

Tip: Rotating and Moving While Cropping. If cropping an image down is the most common postscan step, what is the second most common? Rotating, of course. You can crop and rotate at the same time with the Cropping tool: after dragging out the cropping rectangle with the Cropping tool, just place the cursor outside the cropping rectangle and drag. The rectangle rotates. When you press Return or Enter, Photoshop crops and rotates the image to straighten the rectangle. It can be tricky to get exactly the right angle by eye—keep an eye on the Info palette. Also, if the cropping rectangle isn't in the right place, you can always move it—just place the cursor inside the cropping rectangle and drag.

Tip: Adjusting for Keystone. What do you do about lines in your image that are supposed to be vertical or horizontal but aren't? For example, if you take a picture of a painting hanging on a wall, you often need to do so from one side to avoid flash reflections, so the subject ends up being skewed rarther than rectangular. Fortunately, our faithful Cropping tool offers a cool option: adjusting for perspective. The key is to turn on the Perspective checkbox in the Options bar after drawing the cropping rectangle; this lets you grab the corner points and move them willy-nilly where you will.

However, positioning the corner points of the cropping "rectangle" can be tricky. You must first find something in the image that is supposed to be a rectangle, and set the corner points on the corners of that shape. In the example of a building, you might choose the corners of a window. Then, hold down the Option and Shift keys while dragging one of the corner handles; this expands the crop but retains its shape. When you have the cropping shape the size you want it, drag the center point icon to where the camera was pointing (or where you imagine the center of the focus should be). Then press Enter or Return (see Figure 2-19).

By the way, we find that when using this tool Photoshop often alerts us that either the center point or the corner points are in the wrong position. This usually happens when you haven't selected the corner points of something that *should* be rectangular. In other words, Photoshop acts as a safety net, stopping you when you choose a distortion that isn't likely to happen in a real photograph. Sometimes simply moving the center point to a different location (by trial and error) does the trick.

Figure 2-19
Adjusting perspective
with the Cropping tool

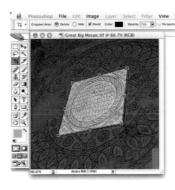

*It was impossible
to photograph this
floor mosaic without
keystone distortion.*

*The cropping
corners set to
a rectangle in
the image*

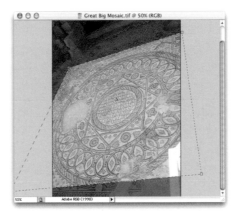

*The crop is extended by holding down
Option and Shift while dragging
the corner points.*

*Press Enter or Return to crop
and adjust for perspective.*

For serious perspective corrections, though, you're better off using the new Lens Correction filter, which we discuss in Chapter 9, *Sharpness, Detail, and Noise Reduction.*

Tip: Save That Layer Data. In early versions of Photoshop, the cropping tool would throw away pixels outside the cropping rectangle. If you changed your mind and wanted to crop the image differently, you would have to select Undo and then try again. But Photoshop now gives you the option (by selecting the Hide button in the Options bar after dragging the cropping rectangle) of saving the cropped-out pixels as *big data*—material that hangs outside the actual visible image rectangle. Then, if you didn't get the crop just right, you can either move the image around with the Move tool or re-crop using a different rectangle (see "Tip: Expand the Canvas by Cropping," later in this chapter). Note that this only works on layers other than the Background layer.

Tip: Resampling While Cropping. Warning: the Cropping tool may be changing your resolution or even resampling your image data without you knowing it! The Height, Width, and Resolution fields in the Options bar (when you have the Cropping tool selected) let you choose a size and resolution for your cropped picture. Basically, these fields let you save the step of visiting the Image Size dialog box after cropping. But remember that when you use them, they always change your image resolution or resample the image (see Chapter 3, *Image Essentials*, for more on the pros and cons of resampling).

In ancient versions of Photoshop, if you left the Resolution field blank and you specified a Height and Width without specifying any units (like pixels, inches, and so on), the program would constrain the cropping size to a particular aspect ratio (like four-by-six) but it wouldn't mess with your resolution. Alas, now the Height and Width fields always have units attached to them. If you leave the Resolution field blank, Photoshop adjusts the image resolution to accommodate the change in size. That means your image resolution can drop or increase without you realizing it. (In this case, Photoshop is *not* resampling the data—just adjusting the size of the pixels.) Instead, see the next tip for how to crop to an aspect ratio.

If you type a value into the Resolution field, Photoshop resamples the image to that value. This resampling behavior is handy when you want to resample down, but be careful that you don't ask for more resolution than you really have; resampling up is usually best avoided. (Note that you can only set the Height, Width, and Resolution values *before* you start cropping; once you draw a cropping rectangle, the Options bar changes.)

Tip: Cropping to an Aspect Ratio. Let's say you want to crop your image to a four-by-six aspect ratio (height-to-width, or vice versa), but you don't want to resample the image (which adds or removes pixels, causing blurring) or change the image resolution. The Cropping tool can't perform this task anymore, so you need a different technique. First, select the Marquee (rectangular selection) tool and choose Fixed Aspect Ratio from the Style popup menu in the Options bar. The Options bar then lets you type values in the Height and Width fields (here you'd type *4* and *6*). Next, marquee the area you want cropped, and then select Crop from the Image menu. See Chapter 8, *Making Selections*, for tips and tricks for the Marquee tool.

Tip: Expand the Canvas by Cropping. Once you've created a cropping rectangle with the Cropping tool, you can actually expand the crop past the boundaries of the image (assuming you zoom back until you see the gray area around the image in the document window). Then, after you press Enter, the canvas size actually expands to the edge of the cropping rectangle. This is David's favorite way to enlarge the canvas.

Tip: Cropping Near the Border. If you're trying to shave just a sliver of pixels off one side of an image, you'll find it incredibly annoying that Photoshop snaps the cropping rectangle to the edge of the image whenever you drag close to it. Fortunately, you can turn this behavior off by selecting Snap in the View menu (or pressing Command-Shift-;). Or, you can hold down the Control key to temporarily disable the snapping behavior.

Eraser Tool

The Eraser tool has gotten a bad rap because people assume you have to use a big, blocky eraser. No, you can erase using any brush—soft or hard, like an airbrush or even with the textured brushes in the Brushes palette. And what's more, you can control the opacity of the Eraser (don't forget you can just type a number on the keyboard to change the tool's opacity). This makes the eraser fully usable, in our opinion. However, just because a tool is usable doesn't mean you have to use it. Whenever possible, we much prefer masking to erasing. The difference? Masks (which we cover in Chapter 7, *The Digital Darkroom*) can "erase" pixels without actually deleting them. Masks just hide the data, and you can always recover it later. Nevertheless, the Eraser tool can on occasion get you out of a jam. Here are a few tips.

Tip: Erase to History. The Erase to History feature (it's a checkbox on the Options bar when you have the Eraser tool selected) lets you use the Eraser tool to replace pixels from an earlier state of the image (see "When Things Go Worng," later in this chapter, for more on the History feature). Erase to History more or less turns the Eraser into the History Brush tool. For instance, you can open a file, mess with it until it's a mess, then revert *parts of it* to the original using the Eraser tool with Erase to History turned on.

The important thing to remember is that you can temporarily turn on the Erase to History feature by holding down the Option key while using the Eraser tool.

Tip: Watch Preserve Transparency When Erasing. Note that the Eraser tool (or any other tool, for that matter) won't change a layer's transparency when you have the Preserve Transparency checkbox turned on in the Layers palette. That means it won't erase pixels away to transparency; rather it just paints in the background color. Don't forget you can turn Preserve Transparency on and off by pressing / (slash).

Tip: Erasing to Transparency. When you use a soft-edged brush to erase pixels from a layer (rather than the Background layer), the pixels that are partially erased—that is, they're still somewhat visible, but they have some transparency in them—cannot be brought back to full opacity. For example, if you set the Eraser to 50-percent opacity and erase a bunch of pixels from a layer, there's no way to get them back to 100-percent again. The reason: You're not changing the pixel's color, you're only changing the layer's transparency mask. This isn't really a tip: it's just a warning. What you erase sometimes doesn't really go away.

Measurement Tool

We still sometimes hear people complain that Photoshop doesn't have a Measurement tool. Actually Photoshop does have one, but for some reason people don't notice it. That's too bad, because the Measurement tool is extremely useful for measuring distances and angles. The keyboard shortcut for this tool is "I" (or Shift-I if it's hiding under the Eyedropper tool). Here's a rundown of how this tool works.

▶ To measure between two pixels, click-and-drag from one point to the other with the Measurement tool.

▶ Once you have a measuring line, you can hide it by selecting any other tool from the Tool palette. To show it again, select the Measurement tool.

▶ You can move the measuring line by dragging the line (not the endpoints). If you drag an endpoint, you just move that one end of the line.

▶ You can't really delete a measuring line, but you can move it outside the boundaries of the image window, which is pretty much the same thing.

▶ You can turn the measuring line into a V-shaped compass in order to measure an angle by Option-clicking on one end of the measuring line and dragging (see Figure 2-20).

Figure 2-20
Measuring up

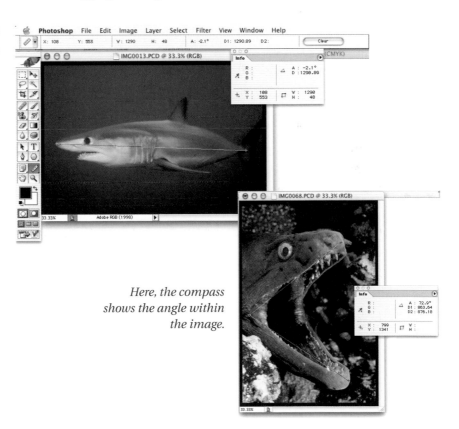

*Here, the compass
shows the angle within
the image.*

Where do you find the measurement? On the Info palette or the Options bar, of course. The palette displays the angle and the horizontal and vertical distances, along with the total distance in whatever measurement system you've set up in Units Preferences.

Tip: Measuring Before Rotating. We know you always make sure your images are placed squarely on the scanner before you scan them, but you may occasionally have to level someone else's crooked scan. Again, the Measurement tool can help immensely. If you select Arbitrary from the Rotate Canvas submenu (under the Image menu) immediately after using the Measurement tool, Photoshop automatically grabs the angle and places it in the dialog box for you.

There are two things to note here. First, the angle in the Rotate Canvas dialog box is usually slightly more accurate, so the number you see there may be slightly different from the one on the Info palette (usually within half a degree). Second, if the angle is above 45 degrees, Photoshop automatically subtracts it from 90 degrees, assuming that you want to rotate it counterclockwise to align with the vertical axis instead of the horizontal axis.

Notes Tools

While the majority of images touched by Photoshop are edited by a single person, people are increasingly working on pictures in teams. Perhaps the team is a retoucher and a client, or perhaps it's four Photoshop users, each with specific skills—whatever the case, it's important for these folks to communicate with each other. Enter Photoshop's Notes tools (press N). Photoshop has two Notes tools: one for text annotations and one for audio annotations. We suggest using audio annotations to your images only if you've never learned to type or if you're tired of having so much extra space on your hard drive—audio notes can make your files balloon in size (each 10 seconds of audio you add is about 140 K compared to about 1 K for 100 words of text notes).

To add a text annotation, click once on the image with the Notes tool and type what you will. If you type more than can fit in the little box, Photoshop automatically adds a scroll bar on the side. In addition, you can change the note's color, author, font, and size in the Options bar at any time.

Double-clicking on a note opens it (so you can read or listen to it) or closes it (minimizes it to just the Notes icon). Single-clicking on the Notes icon lets you move it or delete it (just press the Delete key). Or, if you want to delete all the notes in an image, press the Clear All button in the Options bar.

Tip: Move the Notes Away. By default, Photoshop places your notes windows at the same place in your image as the Notes icon. However, that means the little notes window usually covers up the image so you can't see what the note refers to. We usually drag the Notes icon off to the side slightly (just click-and-drag the note's title bar to move it), or—if there aren't many notes in a file—most of the way off the image, onto the gray area that surrounds the picture.

Tip: Show the Notes. If you can't see notes in your Photoshop file but you suspect they're there, make sure the Annotations item is turned on in the Show submenu (under the View menu). When this is off, no Notes icons appear.

Palettes

Bruce has a second monitor set up on his computer just so he can open all of Photoshop's palettes on it and free up his primary monitor's precious space. There's little doubt that palettes are both incredibly useful and incredibly annoying at times. Fortunately, Photoshop has some built-in but hidden features that make working with palettes a much happier experience. For instance, palettes are "sticky"—if you move them near the side of the monitor or near another palette, they'll "snap-to" align to that side or palette. (Even better, hold down the Shift key while you drag a palette to force it to the side of the screen.) This (if nothing else) helps you keep a neat and tidy screen on which to work.

Tip: Make the Palettes Go Away. If you only have one monitor on which to store both your image and Photoshop's plethora of palettes, you should remember two keyboard shortcuts. First, pressing Tab makes the palettes disappear (or reappear, if they're already hidden). We find this absolutely invaluable, and use it daily.

Second, pressing Shift-Tab makes all palettes except the Tool palette disappear (or reappear). We find this only slightly better than completely useless; we would prefer that the keystroke hid all the palettes except the Info palette.

Tip: Making Palettes Smaller. Another way to maximize your screen real estate is by collapsing one or more of your open palettes. If you double-click on the palette's name tab, the palette collapses to just the title bar and name (see Figure 2-21). Or if you click in the zoom box of a palette (the checkbox in the upper-right corner of the palette), the palette reduces in size to only a few key elements. For instance, if you click in the zoom box of the Layers palette, you can still use the Opacity sliders and Mode popup menu (but the Layer tiles and icons get hidden).

Figure 2-21
Collapsing palettes
(Macintosh on left,
Windows on right)

Full palette

*Double-click
to get minipalette.*

Tip: Mix and Match Palettes. There's one more way to save space on your computer screen: mix and match your palettes. Palettes in Photoshop have a curious attribute—you can drag one on top of another and they become one (see Figure 2-22). Then if you want, you can drag them apart again by clicking and dragging the palette's tab heading. (In fact, these kinds of palettes are called "tabbed palettes.")

For instance, David always keeps his Layers, Channels, and Paths palettes together on one palette. When he wants to work with one of these, he can click on that palette's tab heading. Or better yet, he uses a keystroke to make it active (see "Actions" in Chapter 12, *Essential Image Techniques*, for more on how to define your own keyboard shortcuts).

Bruce, on the other hand, always keeps his Layers and Channels palettes separate, even when he's working on a single-monitor system. Nei-

Figure 2-22
Mixing and matching
palettes

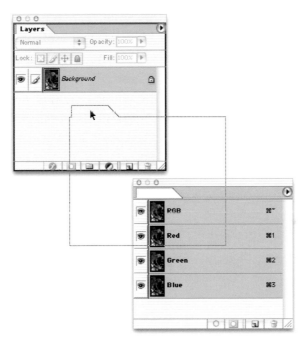

ther of us ever mixes the Info palette with another palette, because we want it open all the time.

Photoshop offers one more way to combine palettes: by docking them. Docking a palette means that one palette is attached to the bottom of another one. Docked palettes always move together, and when you hide one they both disappear. To dock one palette to another, drag it over the other palette's bottom edge; don't let go of the mouse button until you see the bottom edge of the palette become highlighted.

Tip: In-and-Out Palettes. You can store palettes in the Options bar as well: when your screen resolution is above 800 pixels wide, the Options bar contains a "palette well," onto which you can drag palettes. Then, to use one of these palettes, just click on its tab. When you press Enter or Return, or as soon as you start doing anything else (like use a tool or a menu), the palette minimizes into the well again. This behavior is perfect for the Swatches and Colors palettes, but is inappropriate for palettes you need open a lot, like the Info or Layers palette.

Tip: Scrubby Sliders. Some palettes—notably Layers, Character, and Paragraph—sport a hidden new feature called a "scrubby slider," which lets you change values by clicking and dragging to the left or the right. For example, you can change the Opacity field in the Layers palette by clicking *on the title* "Opacity" and dragging to the left (to reduce opacity) or the right (to increase it). Not all fields in all palettes have this feature yet, but you can always tell a scrubby slider by hovering the cursor over the title of a field—scrubby sliders change the cursor icon to a pointed finger with left and right arrows. For faster scrubbing, hold down the Shift key, which multiplies the normal adjustment by ten.

Tip: Reset Palette Positions. Every now and again, your palettes might get really messed up—placed partly or entirely off your screen, and so on. Don't panic; that's what Reset Palette Locations (in the Workspace submenu, in the Window menu) is for.

Layers Palette

In every version since 3.0 (the first time that the layers feature was introduced), the Layers palette has become increasingly important to how people use Photoshop. With such a crucial palette, there have to be at least a few good tips around here. No?

Tip: Displaying and Hiding Layers. Every click takes another moment or two, and many people click in the display column of the Layers palette (the one with the little eyeballs in it) once for each layer they want to show or hide. Cut out the clicker-chatter, and just click-and-drag through the column for all the layers you want to make visible. Or, Option-click in the display column of the Layers palette. When you Option-click on an eyeball, Photoshop hides all the layers except the one you clicked on. Then, if you Option-click again, it redisplays them all again. Even though this trick doesn't save you a lot of time, it sure feels like it does (which is often just as cool).

Tip: Creating a New Layer. Layers are the best thing since sliced bread, and we're creating new ones all the time. But if you're still making a new layer by clicking on the New Layer button in the Layers palette, you've got some learning to do: Just click Command-Shift-N (or Command-Option-

Shift-N, if you don't want to see the New Layer dialog box). If you're trying to duplicate the current layer, just press Command-J (if you have pixels selected when you press this, only those pixels will copy to a new layer).

Tip: Rename Your Layers. It's a very good idea to rename your layers from Layer 1 or Layer 2 to something a bit more descriptive. However, don't waste time looking for a "rename layer" feature. Instead, just double-click on the layer tile to rename it. Note that this works in the Channels, Paths, and File Browser palettes, too.

Tip: Creating Layer Groups. The more layers you have in your document, the more difficult it is to manage them. Fortunately, Photoshop now offers layer "sets" in which you can group contiguous layers (layers that are next to each other). Layer groups are so easy to use that they really don't require a great deal of explanation. Here are the basics, though.

▶ To create a layer group, click on the New Layer Group button in the Layers palette (see Figure 2-23).

Figure 2-23
Layer Group

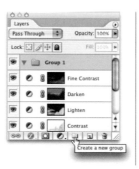

▶ To add a layer to a group, just drag it on top of the group. Or, to create a new layer inside the group automatically, select the group or any layer within the group (in the Layers palette) and click the New Layer button. You can remove a layer from a group simply by dragging it out.

▶ You can move layer groups in the same way you move layers: just drag them around in the palette. You can also copy a whole group of layers to a different document by dragging the layer group over.

▶ If you have more than one layer group, it's helpful to color-code them: just double-click on the layer group's name and pick a color in the

Group Properties dialog box. You should probably name the set, too, while you're there (the default "Group 1" doesn't help identify what's in it). Watch out, though: if you drag a color-coded layer out of the set, it still retains its color-coding!

▶ If you want to move all the layers within a layer group at the same time, select the layer group in the Layers palette. This is easier and faster than linking the layers together or selecting them all.

▶ You can add a layer mask to the layer group (see Chapter 7, *The Digital Darkroom*, for more on masks) and it'll apply to every layer in the group. Similarly, locking a set locks every layer within the group.

▶ Photoshop CS lets you nest one layer set inside another; just drag a set on top of another set, as though you were dragging a folder inside another folder. Or, if you select a layer inside a set first, when you create a new set, it will also be nested. You can nest your layer sets up to five deep.

▶ Layer sets act almost like a single layer, so when you show or hide the set, all the layers in that set appear or disappear.

▶ When you delete a layer set, Photoshop lets you choose to delete the set *and* the layers and sets inside it or just the set itself (leaving the layers and nested sets intact).

Unfortunately, you can't apply a layer effect (see Chapter 12, *Essential Image Techniques*) to a set or use a set as a clipping group (see Chapter 8, *Making Selections*).

Tip: Layer Sets and Blending Modes. If you had your coffee this morning, you'll notice that you can change the blending mode of a layer set. Normally, the blending mode is set to Pass Through, which means, "let each layer's blending mode speak for itself." In this mode, layers inside the set look the same as they do if they were outside the set. However, if you change the set's blending mode, a curious thing happens: Photoshop first composites the layers in the set together as though they were a single layer (following the blending modes you've specified for each layer), and then it composites that "single layer" together with the rest of your image using the layer set's blending mode. In this case, layers may appear very different whether they're inside or outside that set.

Similarly, when you change the opacity of the set, Photoshop first composites the layers in the set together (using their individual Opacity settings) and then applies this global Opacity setting to the result.

Layer Comps Palette

The Layer Comps palette was David's favorite new feature in Photoshop CS. David loves keeping his options open, and is forever trying to decide among various permutations of reality. For instance, he'll picture in his mind's eye five different ways to drive to the grocery store before committing to one. Photoshop's Layer Comps palette won't help him with his driving choices, but it's an awesome help when making decisions about how to edit an image in Photoshop.

The Layer Comps palette is like a clever combination of the Layers palette and the History palette: It lets you save the state of your document's layers so you can return to it later. It seems like the Layer Comps feature should be part of the Layers palette, but perhaps Adobe figured the Layers palette was already complex enough. While the snapshots feature of the History palette can perform most of the same tasks as the Layer Comps palette, the History palette is significantly more memory-intensive and—this is important—layer comps can be saved with the document while snapshots disappear when you close the file. Saving a layer comp makes almost no difference to your file size (each comp is only a few K on disk).

Tip: Layer Comps Don't Only Record Visibility. A "comp" details how each layer in the layer palette is composed. At first glance, it appears that each layer comp just records which layers are visible and which are hidden, but they can actually remember the position of items on each layer, layer effects, and the layer's blending mode, too. To create a layer comp, press the New Layer Comp button in the Layer Comps palette. Now Photoshop displays the New Layer Comp dialog box, which lets you name the layer comp, specify which settings Photoshop should remember, and insert a comment about the comp (see Figure 2-24).

It's a good idea to get into the habit of naming your layer comps and even writing a quick one-line comment about the comp. After you create three or four comps, you'll start to get confused as to what is what; and then if you save the file and come back to it later, you'll be totally lost if these aren't named or commented.

Figure 2-24
Layer Comps
palette

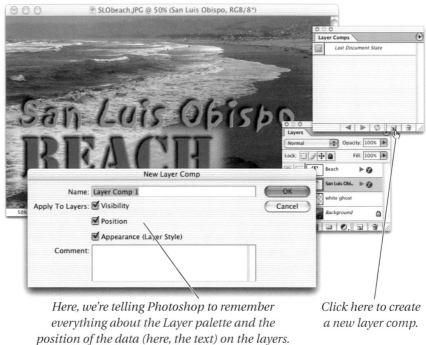

*Here, we're telling Photoshop to remember
everything about the Layer palette and the
position of the data (here, the text) on the layers.*

*Click here to create
a new layer comp.*

*Layer comp comments appear here
when you click on the triangle.*

*Clicking here applies this
layer comp to the file.*

*Cycles through
selected layer comps*

Photoshop can remember three kinds of information about your layer
comps: Visibility, Position, and Appearance.

▶ By default, layer comps just remember the *visibility* of each layer—that is, which layers and layer sets are visible and which are hidden in the Layers palette.

▶ When you turn on the Position checkbox, the layer comp remembers the geometry of all your layers—where on the layer the pixel data is sitting. For example, let's say you save a layer comp with Position turned on, and then use the Move tool to reposition the image or text on that layer. When you return to the saved layer comp, the image or text reverts back to where it was when you saved the comp.

▶ The Appearance option tells the program to remember any layer effects and blending modes that you've applied to your layers. For example, let's say you save a layer comp with Appearance turn *off*, then you change the blending modes of one or more layers in the Layers palette. When you return to the saved layer comp, the blending mode changes remain because you hadn't told the layer comp to retain the appearance of the layers.

For a quick and dirty layer comp with the default name, no comment, and the same attributes as the last comp you made (by default, just the Visibility option), hold down the Option (Alt) key while clicking the New Layer Comp button. Remember that, like layers and channels, you can always rename a layer comp by double-clicking on its name in the palette. If you double-click on the tile (anywhere other than its name), you open the Layer Comp Options dialog box.

Tip: Quick Display of Comps. Once you have saved one or more layer comps in the Layer Comps palette, you can return to a comp state by clicking the small square to the left of the comp name. You can also click the left and right arrow icons at the bottom of the Layer Comps palette. Better yet, if you have ten comps, but only want to cycle through three of them, select those three (Command- or Ctrl-click on the comps to select more than one) and then use the arrow buttons in the palette. If you use layer comps much, we strongly suggest that you use the Keyboard Shortcuts feature (in the Edit menu) to apply keyboard shortcuts to the Next Layer Comp and Previous Layer Comp features so you don't have to click those silly arrow buttons all the time.

You'll notice a layer comp called Last Document State in the Layer Comp palette. This is just the state of your document before you chose a layer comp. For example, let's say you display a layer comp, then hide some layers and move some text around. Now if you select any layer comp, your changes disappear—but if you click on the Last Document State comp, the changes return.

Tip: Updating Comps. Need to change the layer comp? You don't have to delete it and start over. Just set up the Photoshop document to reflect what you want the comp to look like, then select the comp in the palette, and click the Update Layer Comp button (that's the one that looks like two rotating arrows).

Tip: Sending Comps to Clients. The fact that Photoshop saves layer comps—comments and all—with your files is pretty cool. That means you can save a file as a PSD, TIFF, or PDF file and have someone else open the file in Photoshop and browse through the Layer Comp palette. Even cooler, however, are the three Export Layer Comp scripts in the Scripts submenu (under the File menu): Export Layer Comps to Files, Export Layer Comps to PDF, and Export Layer Comps to WPG. Each of these lets you save all (or the currently selected) layer comps to one or more flattened files on disk. The PDF can even be a slide-show presentation which progresses automatically every few seconds if you want. It took us some time before we figured out what WPG is: It's a Web Photo Gallery of your comps, ready to post on a Web site.

Note that when you run the last two of these scripts (each written in JavaScript, by the way), you'll see each of your comps appear twice. The first time, Photoshop is flattening and saving to disk; the second time, it's opening that flattened version and adding it to the presentation.

Tip: Clear Comp Warnings. If, after making one or more layer comps, you delete or merge a layer, you'll notice that small warning icons appear in the Layer Comps palette. These tell you that Photoshop can no longer return to the layer comp as saved (because the layer no longer exists like it did when you made the comp). You can still choose a layer comp that has a warning icon—it'll still apply to all the layers that still do exist. If you delete a layer and you don't want to see the warning icons anymore,

Control-click (or right-click on Windows) on one of the icons and choose Clear All Layer Comp Warnings from the context menu.

Info Palette

In a battle of the palettes, we don't know which Photoshop palette would win the "most important" prize, but we do know which would win in the "most telling" category: the Info palette. We almost never close this palette. It just provides us with too much critical information.

At its most basic task, as a densitometer, it tells us the gray values and RGB or CMYK values in our image. But there's much more. When you're working in RGB, the Info palette shows you how pixels will translate into CMYK or Grayscale. When working in Levels or Curves, it displays before-and-after values (see Chapter 6, *Image Adjustment Fundamentals*). Especially note the Proof Color option, which shows the numbers that would result from the conversion you've specified in Proof Setup, which may be different from the one you've specified in Color Settings (see Chapter 5, *Color Settings*). The Proof Color numbers appear in italics—a clue that you're looking at a different set of numbers than the ones you'd get from a mode change.

But wait, there's more! When you rotate a selection, the Info palette displays what angle you're at. And when you scale, it shows percentages. If you've selected a color that is out of the CMYK gamut (depending on your setup; see Chapter 5, *Color Settings*), a gamut alarm appears on the Info palette.

Tip: Finding Opacity. When you have transparency showing (e.g., on layers that have transparency when no background is showing), the Info palette can give you an opacity ("Op") reading. However, while Photoshop would display this automatically in earlier versions, now you have to do a little extra work: you must click on one of the little black eyedroppers in the Info palette and select Opacity (see Figure 2-25).

Tip: Switch Units. While we typically work in pixel measurements, we do on occasion need to see "real world" physical measurements such as inches or centimeters. Instead of traversing the menus to open the Units dialog box (on the Preferences submenu under the File menu), we find it's usually faster to select from the Info palette's flyout menu. Just click

Figure 2-25
The Info palette

on the XY cursor icon (see Figure 2-26). Another option: double-clicking in one of the rulers opens the Units Preferences dialog box. You can also do this by Control-clicking (Mac) or Right-button-clicking (Windows) on one of the rulers. (Press Command-R if the rulers aren't visible.)

Figure 2-26
Changing units

Color Palettes

The Color Picker and the Color palette both fit into one category, so we almost always group them together into one palette on our screen and switch between them as necessary. Or better yet, we just put them in the Options bar's palette well.

Most novice Photoshop users select a foreground or background color by clicking once on the icons in the Tool palette and choosing from the Color dialog box. Many pros, however, have abandoned this technique, and focus instead on these color palettes. Here are a few tips to make this technique more… ah… palettable.

Tip: Switching Color Bars. Instead of clicking on the foreground color swatch in the Tool palette, you might consider typing values into the Color palette. Are the fields labeled "RGB" when you want to type in "CMYK" or something else? Just choose a different mode from the flyout menu on the palette. If you like choosing colors visually rather than numerically, you can use the color bar at the bottom of the palette (no, the Color Bar is not just another place to meet people). While the spectrum of colors that appear here usually covers the RGB gamut, you can switch to a different spectrum by Shift-clicking on the area. Click once, and you switch to CMYK; again, and you get a gradient in grayscale; a third time, and you see a gradient from your foreground color to your background color. Shift-clicking again takes you back to RGB. You can also use the context menu to choose a color space.

Tip: Editing the Color Swatches. You've probably ignored all those swatches on the Swatches palette because they never seem to include colors that have anything to do with your images. Don't ignore… explore! You can add, delete, and edit those little color swatches on the Swatches palette. Table 2-2 shows you how. If you're looking for Web-safe colors, or other useful colors, check out the flyout menu at the top of the palette.

You can't actually edit a color that's already there. Instead, you can click on the swatch (to make it the current foreground color), edit the foreground color, then Shift-click back on the swatch (which replaces it with the current foreground color).

Table 2-2 Editing the Swatches palette	To do this…	Do this…
	Add foreground color	Click any empty area
	Delete a color	Command/Alt-click
	Replace a color with foreground color	Shift-click (Mac only)

Bridge

In Photoshop 7, a new palette called the File Browser was introduced. In Photoshop CS, the File Browser retained some palette-like attributes, but became more omnipresent, staying open even when images were opened. In Photoshop CS2, the tasks formerly handled by the File Browser have been handed over to a new standalone application called Bridge.

Bridge is a bit less than a full-blown asset manager, but much more than a simple file browser. Depending on the nature of your Photoshop usage, it may be anything from a mild convenience to a mission-critical workflow component. We'l cover Bridge in much more detail in Chapter 11, *Building a Digital Workflow*, but here are the basics.

The simplest way to launch Bridge is to do so the way you launch any other application on your platform of choice. However, you have the following additional options as shown in Figure 2-27:

▶ Choose Browse from Photoshop's File menu.

▶ Click the Go to Bridge button in the Options bar (it's the icon that looks like a magnifying glass over an open folder).

▶ Enable the Automatically Launch Bridge checkbox in the General panel of Photoshop's Preferences dialog box. That way, whenever you launch Photoshop, Bridge automatically launches too.

Figure 2-27
Launching Bridge

Choose Browse from the File menu.

Click the File Browser icon in the Options bar.

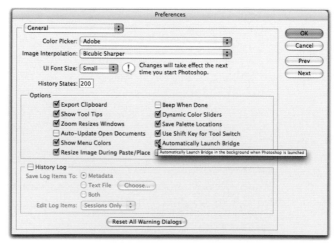

Launch Photoshop with the Automatically Launch Bridge Preference checked.

Once Bridge is open, you'll see that each window shows the contents of a single folder—if it contains subfolders, they show up as folder icons. Figure 2-28 shows the components of a Bridge window.

Bridge windows have six areas—the main thumbnail display, and five resizable palettes.

▶ **The Folders pallete** shows the folder hierarchy, and lets you navigate between folders and volumes. You can navigate up and down the folders list using the up and down arrow keys, and you can collapse and expand volumes or folders that contain subfolders using the left and right arrow keys. Command-up arrow moves you up to the next level in the folder hierarchy. The palette menu contains but one command, Refresh.

▶ **The Favorites palette** is a handy place for storing things that you often want to return to in a Bridge window. In addition to actual volumes and folders, the Favorites palette can hold Collections, which are saved

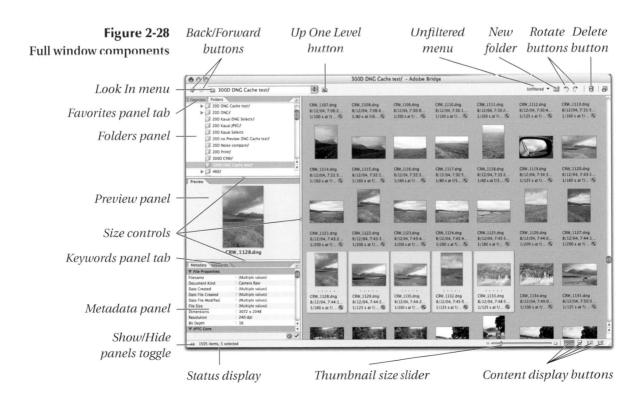

Figure 2-28
Full window components

Back/Forward buttons   Up One Level button   Unfiltered menu   New folder   Rotate buttons   Delete button

Look In menu
Favorites panel tab
Folders panel

Preview panel

Size controls

Keywords panel tab

Metadata panel

Show/Hide panels toggle

Status display   Thumbnail size slider   Content display buttons search criteria that act as "virtual" folders. It also contains an icon for Photoshop CS2. Clicking it transfers you to Photoshop CS2, launching it if it isn't already running. You can configure the preset items from Bridge's Preferences, and you can add items to it by dragging or by menu command.

▶ **The Preview palette** displays a preview for the selected image. Like the other palettes, you can collapse it by double-clicking on its tab and resize it by dragging, but it has no menu and no secrets.

▶ **The Metadata palette** displays the metadata associated with the currently selected image or images . When you have more than one image selected, many of the fields read "Multiple Values Exist."

  Metadata fields that are editable appear in the palette with a pencil icon next to the title. To edit these fields, select the images or images whose metadata you wish to edit, and then either click the pencil icon or click directly in the text area to enter the new metadata. To confirm entries, click the Apply checkbox at the palette's lower-right corner, or press Enter (Mac) or Alt-Enter (Windows). The only IPTC field that isn't editable here is the Keywords field—to edit keywords, you need to use the Keywords palette.

▶ **The Keywords palette** lets you create keywords (which you can group into categories called *keyword sets*), and apply them to a selected image or images. The keywords get written into the Keywords field of the IPTC metadata, so they're visible in the Metadata palette—you just can't edit or apply them there.

  Keyword sets appear as folders—the triangle to the left lets you expand and collapse them. When they're expanded, you can see the list of keywords in the set. To apply a keyword to selected images, click in the column at the left of the palette—a checkmark appears, indicating that the selected images contain this keyword. To apply all the keywords in a set, click beside the set name rather than the individual keyword. Icons at the bottom of the palette let you create a new keyword set or keyword, or delete an existing keyword set or keyword. Deleting keywords removes them only from the list, not from any files that contain them. You can also move keywords to a different set by dragging.

We'll cover Bridge in more detail in Chapter 11, *Building a Digital Work-flow*, but here are some handy tips.

Tip: Turn Each Way. Bridge lets you rotate images, but the image on disk isn't actually changed. Instead, Bridge instructs Photoshop to rotate the image as soon as you open it. To set one or more selected images to rotate, click on one of the two Rotate buttons at the top of the Bridge window. Each click rotates the image 90 degrees clockwise or counterclockwise. You can also rotate an image by Control-clicking (Mac) or right-button-click-ing (Windows) on it and selecting Rotate from the context-sensitive menu. Or, if you're trying to impress your supervisor, press Command-] (to turn selected images counterclockwise) or Command-[(clockwise).

Tip: Ratings. Usually, the first thing we do when looking at a folder full of images is to separate out the duds. In a "yes or no" first pass, we select one or more files and press Command 1 to apply a one-star rating—a single star appears below the image thumbnail. For more nuanced ratings, you can apply up to five stars (click on the stars or press Command-1 through Command-5 to apply the ratings). Once you've rated your images, you can use the Unfiltered/Filtered menu (it's the first item in the cluster of controls at the upper-right corner of the Bridge window) to control which files are displayed based on their ratings.

Tip: Drag Those Files. If you need to sequence images, as for a slide show, you can simply drag the thumbnails into the order you want. The Sort menu is automatically set to Manually when you do this; if you choose any other sort (such as sort by filename), you can restore your drag-order by choosing Manually from the Sort submenu on Bridge's View menu.

Tip: Batch Renaming. Most digital cameras assign names like P0001924. JPG to each image, which we find less than useful. To rename images in a batch, select their thumbnails, then choose Batch Rename from Bridge's Tools menu. This displays the Batch Rename dialog box, which gives you a number of options for naming files (see Figure 2-29). Careful with this one; you can't easily undo it after clicking OK, though you do get the option of preserving the current filename (the one it had before renaming) in metadata.

Figure 2-29
Bridge's Batch Rename

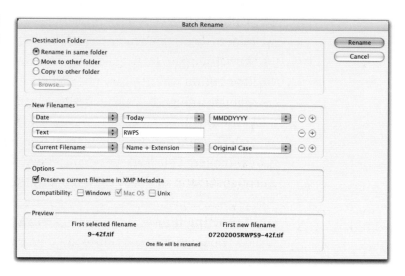

Tip: Moving and Copying Images. You can move files from one folder into another by dragging the file's thumbnail into any folder in the Folders palette. Add the Option key and the file is copied instead of moved.

Metadata. In the Metadata palette, Bridge displays whatever information it can glean from the file. At a minimum, it shows you the file's creation date, file format, and size. However, if the capture device or software application that created the image saved more information in the EXIF (exchangeable image file) format, then Photoshop can display it here, too. This is particularly useful for people who use digital cameras, which typically save a plethora of data, including the date and time the picture was snapped, the exposure setting, and focal length. Photoshop also lets you edit some of the metadata, such as keywords, description, and copyright information. You can later search for this information, or view it in the File Info window, or even view it from within InDesign's Links palette.

Tip: Opening the Composite. Do you have a large .TIF or .PSD file with a lot of layers, but you only want to open a flattened version? No problem: hold down Option and Shift while double-clicking on the image in Bridge or in the Open dialog box. Note that for .PSD files, this only works when the file was saved with a composite image. If you turn off the Always Maximize Compatibility for Photoshop (PSD) Files option in the Preferences dialog box, you won't be able to open the composite because there will be no composite to open (see "Preferences," later in this chapter).

Tip: Hide the Palettes. To maximize the views of the thumbnails (on the right side of the Bridge Window) and hide the palettes (on the left), click on the Show/Hide palettes toggle at the bottom of the Bridge window—that's the little button with the double-headed arrow. Note that you can also resize and rearrange the palettes by dragging them. Of course, you can also save various configurations of Bridge using Bridge's own Workspace feature, which works very like Photoshop's (see "Saving Workspaces," earlier in this chapter). One workspace might have a really large preview image and no metadata; another might have tiny thumbnails; and so on.

Tip: Exporting the Cache. The first time you use Bridge to view a folder of files, you'll notice that it takes some time to gather information and build a thumbnail for each image. It's usually worth waiting until it's done, as it's difficult to do anything in Bridge while it's busy making thumbnails. However, the next time you browse that folder, the images show up almost instantaneously. The trick? Bridge saves the thumbnails in a cache—along with file information, ranking, and rotation setting. The cache is saved in a compressed and proprietary format on your local hard drive.

Fortunately, Bridge lets you save a folder's cache file within the folder itself. To do this, select Export Cache from the Cache submenu (in Bridge's Tools menu). When the exported cache files are present in a folder, Bridge uses them instead of creating new cache files. If you later write the folder full of images to a CD, Bridge can even read the cache off the CD. However, any subsequent changes you make to the rankings or image rotation are only stored in your local cache (not on the CD, as it is read-only).

Preferences

There's a scene in Monty Python's *Life of Brian* where Brian is trying to persuade his followers to think for themselves. He shouts, "Every one of you is different! You're all individuals!" One person raises his hand and replies, "I'm not."

This is the situation we often find with Photoshop users. Even though each person uses the program differently, they think they need to use it just like everyone else. Not true. You can customize Photoshop in a number of ways through its Preferences submenu (in the Edit menu on Windows, and in the Photoshop menu in Mac OS X).

We're not going to discuss every preference here—we're just going to take a look at some of the key items. First we'll cover the General Preferences dialog box (press Command-K); then we'll look at some other preferences. (We also discuss preferences where relevant elsewhere in the book; for example, we explore Photoshop's color preferences more in Chapter 5, *Color Settings*.)

Tip: Return of Preferences. If you make a change in one of the many Preferences dialog boxes and then—after clicking OK—you decide to change to some other preference, you can return to the same Preferences panel by pressing Command-Option-K.

Tip: Navigating Through Preferences. The Preferences dialog box contains eight different "screens" (also called "panels" or "tabs"), each of which offers a different set of options (see Figure 2-30). Sure, you can select each screen from the popup menu at the top of the dialog box, or by clicking the Next and Prev buttons. But the fastest way to jump to a particular screen is by pressing Command-1 (for the first screen), Command-2 (for the second screen), and so on up to Command-9.

Tip: Propagating Your Preferences. Any time you make a change to one of the Preferences dialog boxes, Photoshop remembers your alteration, and when you quit, saves it in the "Adobe Photoshop CS2 Prefs" file. (In Mac OS X, it's in User>YourName>Library>Preferences>Adobe Photoshop CS2 Settings. On Windows systems, it's hidden.) If anything happens to that file, all your changes are gone. Because of this, on the Macintosh, we recommend keeping a backup of that file, or even the whole settings directory (people often back up their images without realizing they should back up this sort of data file, too).

Certain kinds of crashes can corrupt Photoshop's Preferences file. If Photoshop starts acting strange on us, our first step is always to replace the Preferences file with a clean copy (if no copy of the Preferences file is available, then Photoshop will build a new one for you). To reset the Preference files, hold down the Command, Option, and Shift keys (Ctrl, Alt, and Shift keys on Windows) immediately after launching the program—Photoshop will ask if you really want to reset all the preferences.

Note that if you administer a number of different computers that are running Photoshop, you may want to standardize the preferences on all

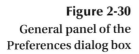
Figure 2-30
General panel of the
Preferences dialog box

machines. The answer: copy the Photoshop Prefs file to each computer. Finally, note that Photoshop doesn't save changes to the preferences until you Quit. If Photoshop crashes, the changes don't get saved.

Export Clipboard. When the Export Clipboard checkbox is on, Photoshop converts whatever is on the Clipboard into a PICT or WMF format when you leave Photoshop. This is helpful—indeed, necessary—if you want to paste a selection into some other program. But if you've got a megabyte or two or 10 MB on the Clipboard, that conversion is going to take some time. In situations when you're running low on RAM, it may even crash your machine, though this is now rare. Since the Clipboard is probably the least reliable mechanism for getting images from Photoshop into some other application, we recommend leaving Export Clipboard off until you really need it.

Save Palette Locations. This does what it says—it remembers which palettes were open, which were closed, and where they were located on the screen the last time you quit. But if you change your monitor resolution, the palettes return to their default locations. We leave this turned on, but we tend to rely on the Save Workspace feature to manage our palettes instead.

Tip: Use System Shortcut Keys. In Mac OS X, Apple appropriated two keyboard shortcuts that were crucial for Photoshop users: Command-H and Command-M. Photoshop users know these as "Hide Selection" and "Curves dialog box." The Mac OS X folks use these shortcuts for "Hide Application" and "Minimize Application." In Photoshop, the Photoshop keyboard shortcuts always win. However, you can hold down the Control key, too, to get the system shortcuts (press Command-Control-H to get Hide Application, and so on).

The File Handling panel contains several useful options—see Figure 2-31. Here are the ones we find most important.

Image Previews. When you save a document in Photoshop, the program can save little thumbnails of your image as file icons. These thumbnails can be helpful, or they can simply be a drag to your productivity. We always set Image Previews to Ask When Saving, so we get a choice for each file (see "Preview Options" in Chapter 13, *Image Storage and Output*).

Ask Before Saving Layered TIFF Files. Many benighted souls still don't realize that TIFF files are first-class citizens that can store anything a Photoshop (.psd) file can, including Photoshop layers. We discuss this in detail in Chapter 13, *Image Storage and Output*, but we should point out one thing here: When the Ask Before Saving Layered TIFF Files option is turned

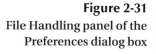

Figure 2-31
File Handling panel of the
Preferences dialog box

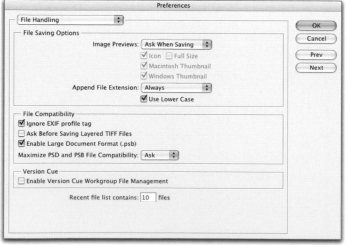

on in Preferences (it is by default), Photoshop will always alert you when you try to save a file that was a flat (nonlayered) TIFF but now has layers. For example, if you open a TIFF image and add some type, the text shows up on a type layer. Now if you press Command-S to save the file, Photoshop displays the TIFF Options dialog box, in which you can either flatten the layers or keep them.

If you find yourself staring at this dialog box too much, and you keep thinking to yourself, "If I wanted to flatten the image, I would have done it myself," then go ahead and turn this option off in the Preferences dialog box. Then Photoshop won't bother you anymore. David likes this option and leaves it turned on, Bruce finds it annoying and keeps it turned off.

Maximize PSD and PSB File Compatibility. We used to think that the Maximize Compatibility feature (previously known as "Maximize Backwards Compatibility in Photoshop Format," "Include Composited Image with Layered Files," or "2.5 Format Compatibility") was completely brain-dead. Now we think it's only "mostly useless." Basically, when you set the popup menu to Always, Photoshop saves a flattened version of your layered image along with the layered version. The main problem is that this feature makes your image sizes larger on disk (sometimes several times larger) than they would otherwise be.

We've always said: turn this off (by setting the popup menu to Never) and leave it off. However, there are now several very good exceptions which have tempered our opinion so that we now set this to Ask. (This tells Photoshop to add a checkbox in the Save As dialog box so you can choose whether or not you want it on a per-image basis.)

First, turn it on if you're using some other program that claims to open native Photoshop files, like Macromedia FreeHand, but which requires this flattened version to work. InDesign CS can import layered Photoshop files without this composite as long as they only have 8 bits per channel—16-bit per channel images require the composite. Another reason to leave it on is that future versions of Photoshop may interpret blending modes slightly differently than they do today. Adobe won't say what might change (or even if there will be changes), but if they do change something, and that change affects the look of your file, then you would at least be able to recover the flattened version if there is one. We discuss this in more detail in Chapter 13, *Image Storage and Output*.

Brush Size. By default, the Painting Cursors preference (in the Display & Cursors panel of the Preferences dialog box) is set to Brush Size (see Figure 2-32). However, if you'd prefer to see a little brush cursor icon instead of setting the cursor to the shape of the brush, you can change the preference to Standard. We can't figure out why anyone would want to do this, but ain't it great that Photoshop lets you?

Figure 2-32
Display & Cursors
panel of the
Preferences dialog box

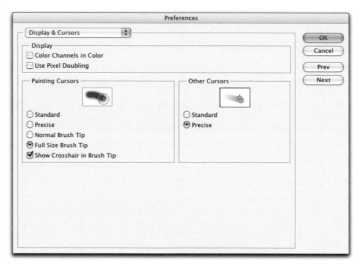

Tip: What Pixel? Because it's often difficult to tell which pixel a small painting tool will affect, Photoshop implemented the handy crosshairs feature: when Caps Lock is down, the cursor switches to a crosshair icon displaying precisely which pixel Photoshop is "looking at."

Gamut Warning. Bruce thinks the Gamut Warning is basically useless—he'd rather just see what's happening to the out-of-gamut colors when they're converted—but for the record, when you turn on Gamut Warning from the View menu (or press Command-Shift-Y), Photoshop displays all the out-of-gamut pixels in the color you choose here.

If you do want to use this feature (David likes it), we recommend you choose a really ugly color (in the Transparency & Gamut Preferences dialog box) that doesn't appear anywhere in your image, such as a bright lime green. This way, when you switch on Gamut Warning, the out-of-gamut areas are quite obvious.

Transparency. Transparency is not a color, it's a state of mind. Therefore, when you see it on a layer, what should it look like? Typically, Photoshop displays transparency as a grid of white and gray boxes in a checkerboard pattern. The Preferences dialog box lets you change the colors of the checkerboard and set the size of the squares, though we've never found a reason to do so (see Figure 2-33).

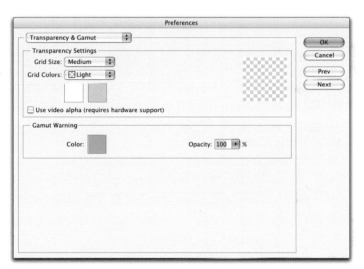

Figure 2-33
Transparency & Gamut
panel of the
Preferences dialog box

Image Cache. Adobe has been getting yelled at for years about Photoshop's handling of large images. Way back in version 4, Photoshop introduced a nominal concession toward large-image handling with the Image Cache feature. It wasn't a great step forward, but it was a step nonetheless. Unfortunately, Photoshop hasn't progressed any farther down the road since then. The Image Cache saves several downsampled, low-resolution versions of your image. That way, if you work on your image in a zoomed-out view, Photoshop can update your screen preview faster by displaying the cached image instead of downsampling the full-resolution one.

If you're low on RAM, you should probably turn off image caching (set the number of caches to 1 in the Image Cache Preferences dialog box; see Figure 2-34), because these downsampled versions of your image take up extra RAM (or space on your scratch disk, if you don't have enough RAM available).

If you've got plenty of RAM and you spend a lot of time working at zoom percentages less than 100 percent, an Image Cache setting of 4 or higher could help speed you up. Each cache level caches one increment of zoom,

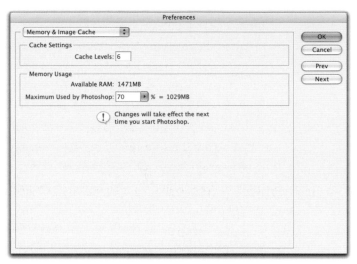

Figure 2-34
Memroy & Image Cache
panel of the
Preferences dialog box

so a setting of 4 caches the 66.7-, 50-, 33.3- and 25-percent views, while a setting of 6 adds the 16.7-percent and 12.5-percent views. The highest setting, 8 levels, caches all views down to 6.25 percent. This is really only useful on very large images, but the incremental difference in RAM footprint between 6 levels and 8 levels is so small that even if you'd benefit from a setting of 8 only occasionally, you'd probably be best off just setting the Image Cache to 8 and leaving it there.

When Things Go Worng

It's 11 PM on the night before your big presentation. You've been working on this image for thirteen hours, and you're beginning to experience a bad case of "pixel vision." After making a selection, you run a filter, look carefully, and decide that you don't like the effect. But before you can reach Undo, you accidentally click on the document window, deselecting the area.

That's not so bad, is it? Not until you realize that undoing will only undo the deselection, not the filter… and that you haven't saved for half an hour. The mistake remains, and there's no way to get rid of it without losing the last 30 minutes of brain-draining work. Or is there? In this section of the chapter, we take a look at the various ways you can save yourself when something goes terribly wrong.

Undo. The first defense against any offensive mistake is, of course, Undo. You can find this on the Edit menu, but we suggest keeping one hand conveniently on the Command and Z keys, ready and waiting for the blunder that is sure to come sooner or later. Note that Photoshop is smart enough not to consider some things "undoable." Taking a snapshot, for instance, doesn't count; so you can take a snapshot and then undo whatever you did just before the snapshot. Similarly, you can open the Histogram, hide edges, change foreground or background colors, zoom, scroll, or even duplicate the file, and Photoshop still lets you go back and undo the previous action.

Revert to Saved. You'd think this command is pretty easy to interpret. If you've really messed up something in your image, the best option is often simply to revert the entire file to the last saved version by selecting Revert from the File menu. In Photoshop CS, Revert occasionally caused us trouble because it ignored anything we'd done in the Missing Profile or Profile Mismatch dialog boxes—it reverted to the file that opened in Photoshop, not the one saved to disk. Photoshop CS2 punts on the whole issue by making Revert unavailable if you make changes in either of these dialog boxes.

The History Palette

There is a school of thought that dictates, "Don't give people what they want, give them what they need." The Photoshop engineering team appears to advocate this—they spend hours listening to and thinking about what people ask for, then they come back with a feature that goes far beyond what anyone had even thought to request. For example, people long asked Adobe for multiple Undos (the ability to sequentially undo steps that you've taken while editing a Photoshop image). The result is the History palette, which goes far beyond a simple Undo mechanism into a whole new paradigm of working in Photoshop.

The History palette, at its most basic, remembers what you've done to your file and lets you either retrace your steps or revert back to any earlier version of the image. Every time you do something to your image—paint a brush stroke, run a filter, make a selection, and so on—Photoshop saves this change as a *state* in the History palette (see Figure 2-35). At any time, you can revert the entire image to any previous state, or—using the History

Figure 2-35
The History palette

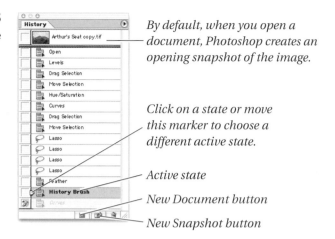

By default, when you open a document, Photoshop creates an opening snapshot of the image.

Click on a state or move this marker to choose a different active state.

Active state

New Document button

New Snapshot button

Brush tool or the Fill command, which we'll discuss in a moment—selectively paint back in time.

The only issue with using History is that it can consume a lot of scratch space. Sorry, did we say "a lot"? We meant "vast, awe-inspiring, mind-boggling quantities" of scratch space, particularly since Photoshop's old 100-state limit was increased to 1000 in Photoshop 7. It's unlikely that heavy History use will hurt performance significantly, though if Photoshop has to hunt for something in 50 GB of scratch disk space you may experience a momentary lapse in responsiveness—the bigger danger is that you run out of scratch disk space and find yourself unable to do anything, possibly including saving the file. If you plan on using 1000 history states, make sure you have plenty of scratch disk space!

Tip: Turning Off History. If you're doing straightlaced production work all day (the kind of work for which a single Undo is perfectly adequate), you may want to avoid the History feature's heavy scratch disk overhead by changing the History States value to 1 in the Preferences dialog box (press Command-K). Similarly, you can turn off Automatically Create First Snapshot in the History Options dialog box (which you can find on the History palette's flyout menu). You might also want to turn off these functions if you're going to batch-process a number of images using actions or the Automate "wizards" (because in these cases, History isn't necessary), but unless your scratch space is very limited, as on a laptop with a single internal drive, the default 20 history states are probably pretty safe.

The History palette has two sections: snapshots and states. Let's take a look at each of these and how you can use them.

Snapshots. The History palette lets you save any number of snapshots—representing a moment in time for your image—so that at any time you can go back to a specific state. There are two main differences between snapshots and states.

▶ Photoshop records almost everything you do to an image as a state. By default, snapshots are only recorded when you first open an image and when you click the New Snapshot button in the History palette.

▶ When the number of states recorded on the History palette exceeds the Maximum Remembered States value (set in the History Options dialog box), the oldest states start dropping off the list. Snapshots don't disappear until you close the document.

Tip: What's in the Snapshot. When you click the New Snapshot button on the History palette (or select New Snapshot from the palette's flyout menu), Photoshop saves the whole document (individual layers and all). Depending on how many layers you have and how large your document is, this might require a lot of scratch space. If you Option-click the button, Photoshop offers two other less-storage-intensive snapshot choices: a version of the image with merged layers, or just of the currently selected layer. (If you find yourself Option-clicking the button a lot in order to get these options, then turn on the Show New Snapshot Dialog By Default checkbox in History Options. That way, you don't have to press the Option key anymore.)

Stepping through states. As we mentioned earlier, Photoshop saves every brush stroke, every selection, every *any*thing you do to your image as a state on the History palette (though the state only remains on the palette until you reach the maximum number of states or you close the document). There are three ways to move among states of your image.

▶ To revert your image back to a state, you can click on any state's tile in the History palette.

▶ You can move the active state marker to a different state on the History palette.

▶ You can press Command-Z to step back to the last state (just as you've always been able to do). But you can also press Command-Option-Z to move backward one state at a time, and Command-Shift-Z to move forward one state at a time.

In general, when you move to an earlier state, Photoshop grays out every subsequent state on the History palette, indicating that if you do anything now these grayed-out states will be erased. This is like going back to a fork in the road and choosing the opposite path from what you took before. Photoshop offers another option: if you turn on the Allow Non-Linear History checkbox in the History Options dialog box, Photoshop doesn't gray out or remove subsequent states when you move back in time (though it still deletes old states when you hit the maximum number of states limit).

Non-Linear History is like returning to the fork in the road, taking the opposite path, but then having the option to return to any state from the first path. For example, you could run a Gaussian Blur on your image using three different amounts—returning the image to the pre-blurred state in the History palette each time—and then switch among these three states to decide which one you wanted to use.

The primary problem with Non-Linear History is that it may confuse you more than help you, especially when you're dealing with a number of different "forks in the road."

The History Brush. Returning to a previous state returns the entire image to that state. But Photoshop's History feature lets you selectively return portions of your image to a previous state, too, with the History Brush and the Fill command. Before painting with the History Brush, first select the source state in the History palette (click in the column to the left of the state from which you want to paint). For instance, let's say you sharpen a picture of a face with Unsharp Masking (see Chapter 9, *Sharpness, Detail, and Noise Reduction*) and find that the lips have become oversharp. You can select the History Brush, set the source state to the presharpened state, and brush around the lips (though you'd probably want to reduce the opacity of the History Brush to 20 or 30 percent by pressing 2 or 3 first).

The History Brush tool (press Y) is very similar to the Eraser tool when the Erase to History checkbox is turned on in the Options bar, but the History Brush lets you paint with modes, such as Multiply and Screen. We used to prefer the History Brush over Erase to History or Fill from History, because they didn't work on high-bit files, but that limitation has disappeared in Photoshop CS2, so now we use whichever gets the job done most easily.

Tip: Snap Before Action. If you run an action in the Actions palette that has more steps than your History States preference, you won't be able to "undo" the action. That's why before running the action you should either save a snapshot of your full document or set the source state for the History Brush to the current state. The latter works because Photoshop never "rolls off" the source state in the History palette, so you don't have to worry about its getting deleted after reaching the maximum number of states.

Fill with History. One last nifty technique that can rescue you from a catastrophic "oops" is the Fill command on the Edit menu (press Shift-F5). This lets you fill any selection (or the entire image, if nothing is selected) with the pixels from the current source state on the History palette. We usually use this in preference to the History Brush or Eraser tools when the area to be reverted is easily selectable. Sometimes when we paint with those tools, we overlook some pixels (it's hard to use a brush to paint every pixel in an area at 100 percent). This is never a problem when you use the Fill command.

You've always been able to press Option-Delete to fill a selection or layer with the foreground color. In version 4, Photoshop added the ability to automatically preserve transparency on the layer when you add the Shift key (slightly faster than having to turn on the Preserve Transparency checkbox in the Layers palette). Similarly, you can fill with the background color by pressing Command-Delete (add the Shift key to preserve transparency). To fill the layer or selection with the current history source state, press Command-Option-Delete. And, of course, you can add the Shift key to this to fill with Preserve Transparency turned on.

Tip: Persistent States. Remember that both snapshots and states are cleared out when you close a document. If you want to save a particular state or snapshot, drag its tile over the Create New Document button on the History palette. Now that state is its own document that you can save to disk. If you want to copy pixels from that document into another image, simply use the Clone Stamp tool (you can set the source point to one document and then paint with it in the other file).

Tip: Revert When Revert Doesn't Work. Deke McClelland taught us a trick at a recent Photoshop conference that has already saved David's buttocks several times. Because David has a tendency to type fast and loose, he'll often press Command-S (Save) when he really meant to press Command-A (Select All) or Command-D (Deselect). Of course, this saves over his file on disk, often ruining his original scan. The History palette to the rescue! Remember that the default preference for the History palette is to create a snapshot of the image when you first open it. If you save over your original image, you can drag the snapshot's tile over the Create New Document button in the History palette to re-create the original data in its own file.

Tip: Copying States. Although Photoshop lets you copy states from one document to another simply by dragging them from the History palette onto the other document's window, we can't think of many good reasons to do this. The copied state completely replaces the image that you've dragged it over.

Tip: When History Stops Working. Note that you cannot use the History Brush or the Fill from History feature when your image's pixel dimensions, bit depth, or color mode has changed. Pixel dimensions usually change when you rotate the whole image, use the Cropping tool, or use the Image Size or Canvas Size dialog boxes.

Tip: Purging States. As we said earlier, the History palette takes up a lot of scratch disk space. If you find yourself running out of room on your hard disk, you might try clearing out the History states by either selecting Clear History from the flyout menu on the History palette or choosing Histories from the Purge submenu (under the Edit menu). The former can be undone in a pinch; the latter cannot. Curiously, neither of these removes your snapshots, so you have to delete those manually if you want to save even more space. Remember that closing your document and reopening it will also remove all snapshots and history states.

Easter Eggs

It's a tradition in Macintosh software to include Easter Eggs—those wacky little undocumented, nonutilitarian features that serve only to amuse the programmer and (they hope) the user. Note that if your friends think you have no sense of humor, you might want to skip this section; it might just annoy you.

There are (at least) three Easter Eggs in Photoshop—two hidden screens and one quote list.

Dark Matter. A tradition even more venerable than Easter Eggs is code names. Almost all software has a code name that the developers use before the product is christened with a real shipping name. Photoshop 4 was code-named Big Electric Cat (it's an Adrian Belew reference, if you care). Photoshop 5 was code-named Strange Cargo. Photoshop 6 was called Venus in Furs. Photoshop 7 was called Liquid Sky. Photoshop CS was called Dark Matter. Photoshop CS2 was called Space Monkey. To see the original Space Monkey splash screen, hold down the Command key while selecting About Photoshop from the Photoshop menu. In Photoshop for Windows, press Control-Alt and select About Photoshop from the Help menu.

Quotes. If you watch either the standard About Photoshop screen or the Space Monkey splash screen, you'll notice that the credits at the bottom of the screen start to scroll by, thanking everyone and their dog for participating in the development process. Don't get impatient—the last person on the list is someone special. (Actually, if you *are* the impatient type, hold down the Option or Alt key once the credits start rolling; see Figure 2-36)

The now-legendary Adobe Transient Witticisms demonstrate just how twisted people get when building a new version of Photoshop, but they also get hidden deeper in each version. Here's how to find them in Photoshop CS2. Open the Space Monkey splash screen, and go all the way through the scrolling credits (the Option key helps), then, as soon as they've finished, Option-click in the white space between Version 9.0 and the credits.

Figure 2-36
Adobe Transient
Witticisms

Merlin lives! Finally (at least, this is the last one we know about), there's a little hidden dialog box nestled away. When you hold down the Option key while selecting Palette Options from the flyout menus in either the Paths, Layers, or Channels palettes, Merlin happily jumps out.

The World of Photoshop

If our publisher weren't screaming bloody murder to get this book to the printer, we'd still be writing tips. But instead of waiting until the next edition of the book, try finding them for yourself. The more you *play* with Photoshop, the more you'll be rewarded with treasures from the deep.

3 Image Essentials

It's All Zeros and Ones

Computers know nothing about images, or tone, color, truth, beauty, or art. They're just very complicated adding machines that crunch numbers. Every piece of data we store on a computer is comprised of numbers. All the commands we send to the computer are translated into numbers. Even this text that I'm typing is made up of numbers.

Fortunately, you don't have to learn hexadecimal or binary math to use Photoshop—we're living math-challenged proof of that—but if you want to put Photoshop under your control, rather than flailing around and occasionally getting good results by happy accident, you do need to understand the basic concepts that Photoshop and other image editors use to represent photographs using numbers.

We'll keep it simple and equation-free (the computer does the math for you), but unless you like heavily pixellated output and wildly unpredictable color shifts, you really want to understand the essential lessons about images that we lay out in this chapter.

Pixels and Paths

When you get down to the nitty-gritty, there are essentially two ways to make computers display pictures. In Photoshop terminology, the distinction is between pixels and paths. Other terms you may hear are "raster" (rasters are rows or lines, not reggae) and "vector." We call the stuff made up of pixels "images" and the stuff made of vectors "artwork."

Pixel-based images. Images are simply collections of dots (we call them *pixels* or *sample points*) laid out in a big grid. The pixels can be different colors, and the number of pixels can vary. No matter what the picture is—whether it's a modernist painting of a giraffe or a photograph of your mother—it's always described using lots of pixels. This is the only way to represent the fine detail and subtle gradations of photorealistic images.

Just about every image comes from one of three sources: capture devices (such as scanners, digital cameras, or video cameras), painting and image-editing programs (such as Photoshop), or screen-capture programs (like Snapz Pro, the operating system, and a host of others). If you create a document with any of these tools, it's an image.

Vector artwork. Vector artwork, also known as object-oriented graphics, is both more complex and more simple than a pixel-based image. On the one hand, instead of describing a rectangle with thousands (or millions) of dots, vector graphics just say, "Draw a rectangle this big and put it here." Clearly, this is a much more efficient and space-saving method for describing some kinds of art. Vector graphics can include many different types of objects, including lines, boxes, circles, curves, polygons, and text blocks. And all those items can have a variety of attributes—line weight, type formatting, fill color, graduated fills, and so on.

To use an analogy, vector graphics are like directions saying, "Go three blocks down the street, turn left at the 7-11, and go another five blocks," while pixel-based images are more like saying, "Take a step. Now take another step. And another …." At its core, Photoshop is a tool for working with pixels, but each iteration has offered more support for incorporating vector elements that retain their object-oriented characteristics, such as shapes or type, and you can also use vector elements as selections and masks on pixel-based images.

Outside Photoshop, vector graphics come from two primary sources: drawing programs (such as Adobe Illustrator), and computer-aided design (CAD) programs. You might also get vector artwork from other programs, such as a program that makes graphs.

Words, Words, Words

While terminology might not keep you up at night, we in the writin' business have to worry about such things. In fact, one of our first controversies in writing this book concerned the term *bitmap*.

Bruce maintains that, strictly speaking, bitmaps are only black-and-white images. This is how Photoshop uses the term. He prefers to describe images made up of colored dots as *raster* images (the word "raster" refers to a group of lines—in this case, lines of pixels—that collectively make up an image). David thinks that only people who wear pocket protectors (some of his best friends do) would use the word "raster." For years we compromised by using the term "bitmapped images"—which resulted in a lot of sentences with at least one wooden leg. So in this edition, we call documents comprised of pixels "images" and documents comprised of vectors "artwork."

Another problem we've encountered is what to call all those little dots in an image. As we mentioned earlier, when we talk about points in an image, we like to call them *pixels*, *samples*, or *sample points*.

The phrase "sample points" comes from what a scanner does: it samples an image—checking what color or gray value it finds—every 300th of an inch, every 100th of an inch, or whatever. But nowadays, many images are captured with a digital camera rather than being scanned, which makes the concept of sample points more questionable. Pixel is a more generic term because it specifies the smallest "picture element" in an image. Some people still call pixels *pels*. They may not wear pocket protec-

tors, but they've almost certainly had an unnaturally close relationship with an IBM mainframe somewhere in their past.

When we talk about scanning an image in, or printing an image out, we talk about samples or pixels per inch (while samples is closer to reality, everyone we know uses the latter, or *ppi*); and when we talk about the resolution of a bitmapped image saved on disk, we just talk about the total number of pixels. Note that many people use "dots per inch" (*dpi*) for any and all kinds of resolution. We reserve the term "dots per inch" for use when speaking of printers and imagesetters, which actually create dots on paper or film.

We use the term "pixels" for one other thing: screen resolution. But to be clear, we always try to specify "screen pixels" or "image pixels."

Crossing the line. The distinction between images and artwork occasionally gets fuzzy, because vector artwork can include pixel-based images as objects in their own right. For instance, you can put a digital camera capture into an Adobe Illustrator illustration. The image acts like an object on the page, much like a rectangle or oval. You can rotate it, warp it, and scale it, but you can't go into the image and change the pixels.

A vector artwork file may include a pixel-based image as its *only* object. In this situation, the file is an image that you can open for editing in a painting or pixel-editing application. Photoshop's PDF (Portable Document Format) files are good examples of this. While PDF is typically a vector file format, you can create a pixel-only PDF in Photoshop.

Just to round out the confusion, Photoshop lets you include vector elements in pixel-based images, either as stand-alone objects (like text) or as clipping paths. A clipping path in an image is invisible; it acts as a cookie cutter, allowing you to produce irregularly shaped images such as the silhouetted product shots you often see in ads (see "Clipping Paths" in Chapter 12, *Essential Image Techniques*).

Pixels and Images

Photoshop lets you do all kinds of nifty stuff, but at its heart, it pretty much all comes down to pixels. To use Photoshop effectively, you need to understand the basic attributes of pixel-based images.

Every pixel-based image has three basic characteristics: dimension, bit depth, and color model (which Photoshop refers to as *image mode*).

Dimension

Dimension is the attribute that is loosely related to size. Pixel-based images are always rectangular grids made up of little squares, like checkerboards or chessboards or parquet floors in your kitchen; those little squares are individual pixels (see Figure 3-1). The dimensions of the pixel grid refer to the number of pixels along its short and long dimensions. A chessboard is always eight squares by eight squares. The grid of pixels that makes up your computer screen might be 1200 by 1600. A 6-megapixel digital camera typically produces an image that's 3072 by 2048 pixels.

Image dimensions are limited by the capabilities of your capture device, the amount of available storage space, your patience—the more pixels in

Figure 3-1
Bitmaps as
grids of squares

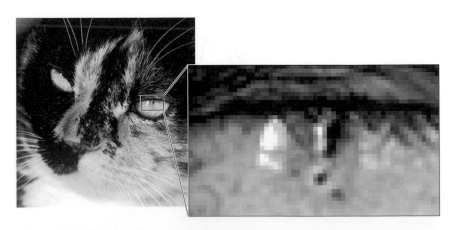

the image, the more space it needs, and the longer it takes to do things to it—and in Photoshop, by the 300,000-by-300,000-pixel image size limit.

Dimension is only indirectly related to physical size or resolution: Until you specify how large each pixel is (called "resolution") an image has no specific size. But resolution and size aren't innate to the digital image; they're fungible qualities. That is, the same 100-by-100 pixels can be made as small as a postage stamp or as large as a billboard. We'll discuss resolution and why it's important in more detail later in this chapter.

Bit Depth

Bit depth is the attribute that dictates how many shades or colors the image can contain. Because each pixel's tone or color is defined by one or more numbers, the range in which those numbers can fall dictates the range of possible values for each pixel, and hence the total number of colors (or shades of gray) that the image can contain.

For example, in a 1-bit image (one in which each pixel is represented by one bit of information—either a one or a zero) each pixel is either on or off, which usually means black and white. (Of course, if you printed with red ink on blue paper, the pixels would be either red or blue.)

With two bits per pixel, there are four possible combinations (00, 01, 10, and 11), hence four possible values, and four possible colors or gray levels (see Figure 3-2). Eight bits of information give you 256 possible values; in 8-bit/channel RGB images, each pixel actually has three 8-bit values—one each for red, green, and blue (see Figure 3-3), for a total of 24 bits per pixel. (In 8-bit/channel CMYK there are four channels rather than three, so a CMYK pixel takes 32 bits to describe.)

Figure 3-2
Bit depth

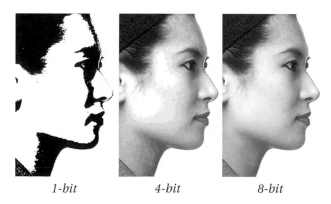

1-bit   *4-bit*   *8-bit*

Figure 3-3 When RGB and CMYK combine

Color images (like the one in the upper-left corner) can be described with RGB data (on the left) or CMYK data (on the right). This figure is somewhat complicated by the need to print the red, green, and blue versions using cyan, magenta, and yellow inks.

Photoshop lets you work with a variety of bit depths, up to the 32 floating-point bits per channel in the new HDR (High Dynamic Range) mode. But for most work, the common bit depths are 8-bit/channel (24-bit RGB and 32-bit CMYK) and 16-bit/channel (48-bit RGB).

How much is enough? 8-bits-per-channel provides 16.7 million possible RGB color definitions, which is a much larger number than the number of unique colors the human eye can distinguish, and certainly much larger than the number of unique colors we can print.

Why capture many more colors than we print, or even see? The simple answer is that the larger number of bits gives us much more editing flexibility. Whatever number of shades you start with, each edit you make has the inevitable result of reducing that number. As you'll see in Chapter 6, *Image Adjustment Fundamentals*, every edit opens up gaps between some adjacent pixel values and smooshes others together, reducing the total number of shades.

So bit depth has an important relationship to the quality of an image, which we'll cover more fully later in this chapter, and to its ability to withstand editing, which we'll cover in most of the rest of this book.

Image Mode

Bit depth and dimension each tell part of the story, but the third essential attribute of images, the image mode, is the one that dictates whether all those numbers represent shades of gray, or colors. As we mentioned earlier, computers know nothing about tone or color; they just crunch numbers. Image mode is the attribute that provides a human meaning for the numbers they crunch.

In general, the numbers that describe pixels relate to *tonal* values, with lower numbers representing darker tones and higher ones representing brighter tones. In an 8-bit/channel grayscale image, 0 represents solid black, 255 represents pure white, and the intermediate numbers represent intermediate shades of gray.

In the color image modes, the numbers represent shades of a primary color rather than shades of gray. So an RGB image is actually made up of three grayscale channels: one representing red values, one green, and one blue. A CMYK image contains four grayscale channels: one each for cyan, magenta, yellow and black.

The one exception we mentioned earlier is the Indexed Color mode, where each value represents an arbitrary color that gets loaded from a lookup table. Indexed Color images can contain only 256 colors, and since the color values are arbitrary (number 1 could be red, number 2 could be blue, and so on), most of Photoshop's editing tools don't work. In the other modes, we can change tone and color by adjusting the numbers to make a pixel, or one channel of a pixel, lighter or darker, but if we did that on an Indexed Color image, we'd end up with a completely different color! (So Photoshop sensibly prevents us from doing so.)

Resolution

Resolution is one of the most overused and least-understood words in desktop publishing. People use it when they talk about scanners and printers, images and screens, halftones, and just about anything else they can get their hands on. Then they wonder why they're confused. Fortunately, resolution is easy once you get the hang of it.

As we noted earlier, an image in its pure digital state has no physical size—it's just a bunch of pixels, and the pixels can be any size you want. So whenever you give an image tangible expression, whether on the screen or in printed form, you confer upon it the property of physical size, and hence resolution.

The resolution of an image is the number of pixels per unit of measurement—usually the number of pixels per inch (ppi) or pixels per centimeter (ppcm). If your image has 72 pixels wide and you tell it to be 72 pixels per inch, then it's an inch wide. If you print it at half the size, you'll still have the same number of pixels, but they'll be crammed into half the space, so each inch will contain 144 of them. Or, if you take the same image and change its resolution to 36 pixels per inch, suddenly the image is two inches wide (same number of pixels, but each one is twice as big as the original; see Figure 3-4).

You can also look at resolution in another way: If you know an image's size and resolution, you can figure out its dimensions. When you scan a picture that is three inches on each side at 100 pixels per inch, you know that the image has 300 pixels on each side (100 per inch). If you scan it at 300 pixels per inch, the dimensions shoot up to 900 pixels on each side.

The key to making resolution work for you is knowing how many pixels you need for the intended purpose to which you'll put the image.

Figure 3-4
Scaling and
resolution

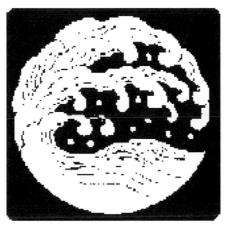

25 percent
(288 ppi)

50 percent
(144 ppi)

100 percent (72 ppi)

50 percent
(144 ppi)

100 percent (72 ppi)

300 percent (24 ppi)

How Much Is Enough?

If bigger were better, we'd be out of business (you'd be hard pressed to call us statuesque). And when it comes to image resolution, bigger isn't necessarily better. The higher the resolution of an image, the longer it takes to open, edit, save, or print. Back in Neolithic times, we used to point out the money you could save by working with smaller images. With storage costs dropping below $1 per gigabyte, that's a less compelling argument, but large images still take longer to transmit over even a gigabit Ethernet network, and even 500 GB hard drives fill up eventually.

But, smaller isn't necessarily better, either. If your image resolution is too low, your image will look pixelated (see Figure 3-5); you'll start seeing the

Terms of Resolution

Not everyone talks about resolution in terms of ppi. Depending on the circumstance, your personality, and the time of day, you might discuss a file's resolution in a number of ways, but they're all different ways of talking about the same essential concept: *how much information* the file contains. Here's a quick rundown of your options.

Dimensions. The least ambiguous way of talking about the resolution of images is by their pixel dimensions; that is, the number of pixels on each side of the grid. This doesn't tell you what physical size it is, but if you understand how much resolution you need for different output methods, it's useful shorthand for expressing how big the image *could be*, depending on what you wanted to do with it. It tells you how much information is in the file. Hard-core Photoshop users like to talk in dimensions because they don't necessarily know (or care) how large the final output will be.

For instance, you could say a capture from a 6-megapixel camera is a 2,048-by-3,076 image. What does that tell you? With experience, you'd know that your file size is in 8-bit/channel mode is 18 MB, and at 225 ppi you could print a full-bleed letter-size page. Later in this chapter, we discuss ways how you can figure all this out for yourself.

Image size. A wordier but equally unambiguous way to discuss resolution is to cite phyiscal dimensions and resolution. For example, you might say a file is 4 by 5 inches at 225 ppi. This makes the most sense to someone doing page layout, because they're typically concerned with how the image is going to look on the printed page. Note, however, that you have to specify both the size and the res-olution; otherwise you're telling only half the story.

File size. A third way to discuss resolution is by the file's size on disk. You can quickly get a sense of the difference in information content of two files when we tell you that the first is 900 K and the second is 12 MB. In fact, a lot of digital imaging gurus *only* think in file size. If you ask them, "What's the resolution of that file?" they look at you like you're an idiot.

Once you become accustomed to working with a number of different sizes, you'll recognize that the 900 K RGB file is about the size of a 640-by-480 RGB image. At 72 ppi (screen resolution) that's pretty big, but at 300 ppi (typical resolution for a high-quality print job), the image is only about two inches wide.

Megapixels. Digital cameras are often rated in megapixels, which is

pixels themselves, or adverse effects from excessively large pixels. Loss of detail and mottling are the two worst offenders in this category.

Maybe you thought you could save time by reducing your images to 150 ppi. But if the client rejects the job because the image is too pixelated, any savings are more than wiped out when you have to redo the job. So if bigger isn't better, and too small is even worse, how much is enough? How much image data do you need? The first consideration is image mode: The requirements are very different for line art than for grayscale and color.

simply the total number of pixels, obtained by multiplying the number of pixels on the short side by the number of pixels on the long side—see Table 3-1.

Single-side dimension. People who work with continuous-tone film recorders, such as the Solitaire or the Kodak LVT, frequently talk about a file's resolution in terms of the dimension of one side— typically the width—of the image. For instance, they might ask for "a 4 K file." That means the image should be exactly 4,096 pixels across.

K usually means file size (kilobytes). However, in this case it's 1,024 pixels.

The height of the image is relatively unimportant in this case, though if you're imaging to film, it's usually assumed that you know the other dimension of the image because it's dictated by the aspect ratio of the film you're using. High-quality film recorders usually write out to 4-by-5-inch

Table 3-1 Megapixels

MP	Dimensions*
1.6	1,536 by 1,024
2.8	2,048 by 1,365
3.1	2,048 by 1,536
4.1	2,464 by 1,648
6.3	3,072 by 2,048
8.2	3,504 by 2,336
11	4,604 by 2,704
17	5,120 by 3,413
22	6,144 by 4,096

actual pixel dimensions may vary with camera model

chromes (positive transparencies), so if you want to fill the image area, it's usually assumed that the short side of your 8 K image will contain somewhere around 6,550 pixels.

Res. One other method of discussing resolution uses the term *res*. Res is simply the number of pixels per millimeter, and it's a great deal more common in Europe than in the metrically challenged United States. People usually talk about res when they're

Table 3-2 Resolution in res

Res	Pixels per Inch
1	25.4
2	50.8
3	76.2
4	101.6
5	127
6	152.4
7	177.8
8	203.2
9	228.6
10	254
11	279.4
12	304.8
20	508
40	1,016
60	1,524
80	2,032

discussing capture resolution on drum scanners. For example, a file scanned at res 12 is scanned at 12 sample points (pixels) per millimeter—which is 120 sample points per centimeter, or—in common usage—304.8 sample points per inch (see Table 3-2).

Line Art

For bilevel (black-and-white, 1-bit, bitmap mode) images, the resolution never needs to be higher than that of the printer you're using. This is one situation where image pixels per inch equate to printer dots per inch. If you're printing to a 600-dpi desktop laser printer, there's no reason to have more than 600 pixels per inch in your image (the printer can only image 600 dots per inch, so any extras just get thrown away). However, when you print to a 2,400-dpi platesetter, that 600-ppi image appears jaggy.

If you're printing line art on press, plan on using an image resolution of *at least* 800 ppi—preferably 1,000 ppi or more (see Figure 3-6). Lower

Figure 3-5
Pixelation in images
when the resolution
is too low

100 percent
200 ppi

300 percent
66 ppi

resolutions often show jaggies and broken lines—on newsprint or very porous paper, you may get away with a lower resolution such as 400 or 600 ppi, because the jaggies will disappear with the spreading ink, but unless you have considerable experience with the print process at hand, you can't tell until the job has run, so err on the side of caution.

See Chapter 10, *Spot Colors, Duotones, and Line Art*, for more on the resolution and appearance of line art images.

Grayscale and Color Halftones

Here's a simple formula for the proper resolution for printing grayscale and color images to halftoning devices such as laser printers and platesetters: Image resolution should be no more than twice the screen frequency. For instance, if you're printing a halftone image at 133 lines per inch (*lpi*), the image resolution should be no larger than 266 ppi (see Figures 3-7 and 3-8). Any higher resolution is almost certainly wasted information.

Figure 3-6
Resolution of
line art

144 ppi   *300 ppi*

800 ppi   *1,200 ppi*

We've heard from people who claim to see a difference between 2 times the screen frequency and 2.5 times the screen frequency, but no one has ever shown us a print sample that supported this contention. It's an absolute certainty that anything higher than 2.5 times the screen frequency is wasted if you're printing to a PostScript output device.

If you go to print an image whose resolution exceeds that multiplier, Photoshop warns you, and PostScript just discards the extra information when it gets to the printer. You can print the image, but it takes longer to print, and you may even get worse results than you would with a lower-resolution version. In fact, we often use less than twice the line screen. With many images, you can use 1.5 times the screen frequency, and you can sometimes get away with less, sometimes even as low as 1.2 times the screen frequency. That means the resolution of the image you're printing at 133 lpi *could* be as low as 160 ppi (but if you want to play it safe, you might use 200 ppi).

Figure 3-7 Resolution and image reproduction

How much resolution do you need? All of these images are printed using the same 133-lpi halftone screen, but they contain different numbers of pixels. Look for details, such as readability of type.

2:1 sampling ratio, 266 ppi

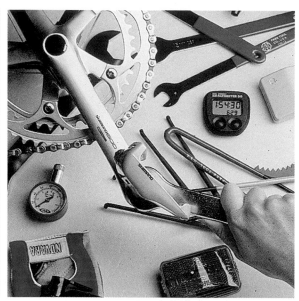

1.5:1 sampling ratio, 200 ppi

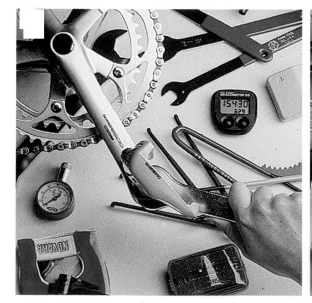

1.2:1 sampling ratio, 160 ppi

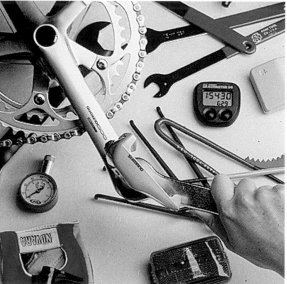

1:1 sampling ratio, 133 ppi

So which multiplier should you use? It depends on quality requirements, the quality of your reproduction method, the kind of images you're reproducing, and your output system.

Figure 3-8 Resolution of grayscale images

2:1 (266 ppi)   *1.5:1 (200 ppi)*

1.25:1 (166 ppi)   *1:1 (133 ppi)*

Quality requirements. The only reliable way we've found to answer the question of what's "good enough" is whether the person paying for the job smiles when they sign the check. There's no absolute index of quality, and clients have widely differing expectations. The best course of action is to prepare Kodak Approvals, Creo Spectrums, or other high-quality dot-based proofs of a few different images, using different multipliers to see where the trade-off works for you.

Reproduction method. Images destined for uncoated stock and newsprint can generally withstand a lower multiplier than those printed on coated stock at a high screen frequency, because the more porous stock causes greater dot gain: The halftone dots grow larger because the ink bleeds into the paper. If you're producing a rag or a newspaper and you're still using the two-times-frequency rule, you're wasting someone's time and money—we hope it's not yours.

Image detail. The need for higher resolution also depends on the content of the image itself. Reducing the multiplier reduces the clarity of small details, so higher resolution is most important with images that have small (and important) details.

Most pictures of people work fine at 1.25 times the screen frequency, but trees with fine branches and leaves might do best with 1.5 times screen frequency. And if the image has a lot of fine diagonal or curved lines (such as rigging on a sailboat, or small text), you may want to use a resolution of 2 times the frequency, particularly if you're paying through the teeth for a 200-lpi print job on high-quality coated stock. Of course, in those cases it's probably worth spending a little extra on high-quality proofs to test some of the more difficult images at different resolutions.

If a lot of this halftone talk is going over your head, we recommend a book that David coauthored with Steve Roth, Conrad Chavez, and Glenn Fleishman called *Real World Scanning and Halftones, 3rd Edition.*

Grayscale and Color Inkjet Output

Photo-inkjet printers don't use halftoning. Instead, they use a quite different technique of laying down dots, called *error diffusion.* (See Chapter 13, *Image Storage and Ouput,* for more on the differences between halftone and diffusion dithers.) A common mistake is to take the resolution of the printer in dots per inch, and then send the printer a file with that same resolution in pixels per inch. You do *not* want to send an inkjet printer with a resolution of 1440 × 2880 dpi a 2880 ppi file, or a 1440 ppi file, or even a 720 ppi file! If you do, you'll create an uneccessarily huge file, and you'll drown the printer with data, actually obscuring detail rather than revealing it.

There are all sorts of theories as to the "best" resolution for inkjet printing, some more grounded in reality than others. We'll spare you the more esoteric details and simply tell you that we've obtained good results using resolutions between 180 ppi for very large prints and 480 ppi for small prints. Most of the time we print at somewhere between 240 and 360 ppi, depending on the print size and the available resolution in the image. We've yet to find a reason to send more than 480 ppi to any inkjet printer.

Grayscale and Color Continuous-Tone Output

If you're printing to continuous-tone output devices such as film recorders or dye-sublimation printers, forget all that fancy math. You simply want the resolution of your file to match the resolution of the output device. If you're printing to a 300-dpi dye-sub printer, you want 300-ppi resolution—about 18 MB for a letter-size page. If you're printing to an 8 K film recorder, you really do want 8,096 pixels on the short side of the image, or an approximately 240 MB scan.

Sometimes, your image may have fewer pixels than you ideally need. Some film recorders and digital printers have excellent built-in upsampling capabilities that rival Photoshop's, in which case you can save time, effort, and disk space by letting the output device do the upsampling. But if you're a driven control freak, you may want to control the upsampling process yourself (see "Resampling," on the next page).

On-Screen Output (Multimedia and the Web)

Multimedia is another form of continuous-tone output, but where you often need very high resolution for film recorders, on-screen multimedia projects require very little. It's generally misleading to think in terms of resolution when you prepare images for use on screen. All that really matters is the pixel dimensions.

When people talk about monitor resolution, they almost invariably specify the number of pixels on the screen—800 by 600, 1,600 by 1,200, and so on. The polite fiction that screen resolution is 72 ppi is no more than that. You can run a 22-inch monitor at 800 by 600 (great for games) or a 17-inch monitor at 1,600 by 1,200 (great for images, bad for reading small type). These extreme cases produce actual resolutions much lower and higher than 72 ppi. Once your image escapes into the wilds of the Web, you have no control over the size at which it's viewed.

We almost never scan an image at screen resolution, however. We like to scan at a higher resolution so that we can crop and resize the image to get it just right; then we downsample it (see the next section).

Resampling

One of the most important issues in working with images—and, unfortunately, one which few people seem to understand—is how the resolution can change relative to (or independently of) the size of your image.

There are two ways that you can change resolution: scaling and resampling. Scaling doesn't change the number of pixels, just the resolution. Resampling changes the pixel dimensions. If you take a 2-by-2-inch, 300-ppi image and change the size to 1 inch square in QuarkXPress or InDesign, you're scaling: The pixels get smaller and the resolution gets higher (it increases to 600 ppi).

In Photoshop, you have a choice whether to scale or resample. If you scale that image down without changing the resolution, Photoshop has to throw away a bunch of pixels; that's called *downsampling*. If you double the size to four by four inches by *upsampling*, the program has to add more pixels by *interpolating* between the other pixels in the image.

Upsampling vs. Downsampling

We used to avoid upsampling when our images mostly came from scanned film, but in the digital age, it no longer makes sense to have a hard-and-fast rule. The lack of film grain in digital captures makes them much more amenable to upsampling than film scans ever were. We often upsample digital camera captures by 200 percent, sometimes even more. Upsampling still doesn't add details that weren't there in the capture, but sometimes it does an uncannily good impersonation! Nevertheless, a 4.1-megapixel capture rarely makes a good magazine cover!

Downsampling is much less problematic, because it's just throwing away data in a more or less intelligent manner. In fact, it's a common and necessary practice: We often scan at a higher resolution than is strictly necessary, to allow for cropping and for unanticipated changes in output size or method. We downsample to the required resolution before printing to save time and storage space.

Resampling methods. Photoshop offers five resampling methods: Nearest Neighbor, Bilinear, Bicubic, Bicubic Smoother, and Bicubic Sharper, the last two of which were introduced in Photoshop CS. You choose which you want in the General panel of the Preferences dialog box or in the

Image Size dialog box (see Figures 3-9 and 3-10). Each has its strengths and weaknesses, and we use them all in different situations.

▶ **Nearest Neighbor** is the most basic, and it's very fast: To create a new pixel, Photoshop simply looks at the pixel next to it and copies its value. Unfortunately, the results are usually lousy unless the image is made of colored lines or shapes (like an image from Illustrator or FreeHand), but it's often useful for preserving the readability of screen shots.

▶ **Bilinear** is slightly more complex and produces somewhat better quality: the program sets the color or gray value of each pixel according to the pixels surrounding it. Some pictures can be upsampled pretty well with bilinear interpolation. But we usually use one of the bicubic options instead.

▶ **Bicubic** interpolation creates better effects than Nearest Neighbor or Bilinear, but takes longer. Like Bilinear, it looks at surrounding pixels, but the equation it uses is much more complex and calculation intensive, producing smoother tonal gradations.

Figure 3-9
Photoshop's resampling
(interpolation) methods

General Preferences

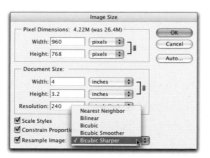

Image Size

Image Size Dialog Box

For those of us who have to teach Photoshop as well as use it, the Image Size dialog box is always one of the biggest sources of confusion, because the results you get depend not only on which buttons you click and which fields you type numbers into, but also on the order in which you do so.

The Image Size dialog box is split into the two most important ways of describing an image's resolution: its pixel dimensions and its print size.

▶ **Pixel Dimensions.** The best way to specify an image's size is by its pixel dimensions—these tell you exactly how much data you have to work with. The Pixel Dimensions section shows you both the dimensions and the file's size, in megabytes (or K, if it's under 1 MB).

▶ **Document Size.** A bitmapped image has no inherent size—it's just pixels on a grid. The Document Size section lets you tag the image with a size and resolution, so that when you import the file into some other program, it knows the image size.

Resample Image. The most important feature in the Image Size dialog box is the Resample Image checkbox. When this is turned on, Photoshop lets you change the image's pixel dimensions; when it's off, the dimensions

Figure 3-10 Image Size dialog box

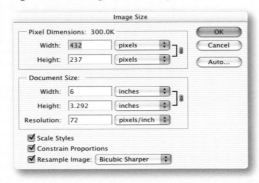

The Image Size dialog box is split into two editable areas: Pixel Dimensions and Document Size.

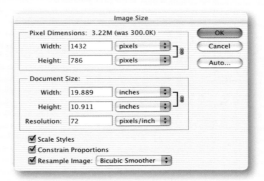

With Resample Image turned on, when you change the Pixel Dimensions, the Document Size changes, but the Resolution doesn't.

are locked. In other words, unless you turn on this checkbox, you cannot add pixels to or remove pixels from the image (upsample or downsample).

Although the dialog box is split into two areas, you really have three interdependent values you can adjust. With Resample Image turned on, you can change the pixel dimensions, the document size, or the resolution. You also

have the ability to choose which resampling method Photoshop should use (see "Upsampling vs. Downsampling," earlier in this chapter).

Note that when the pixel dimensions change, so does the size of the file. Photoshop displays both the old and new size in the Pixel Dimensions section of the dialog box.

Figure 3-10 Image Size dialog box, continued

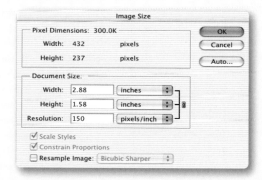

With Resample Image turned on, when you change the Resolution, the Pixel Dimensions change, but the Document Size doesn't.

With Resample Image turned off, the Pixel Dimensions never change. Changing Document Size affects Resolution and vice versa.

Changing sizes. Like we said, the Image Size dialog box takes some getting used to. One confusing element is that whenever you make a change to one field, some other fields change and others don't. Here's a quick summary of what to watch for.

When Resample Image is turned on and you change the Pixel Dimensions, the Document Size changes, but the Resolution does not. If you change the Document Size, the Pixel Dimensions change, too, and the Resolution remains unchanged. If you change the Resolution, the Pixel Dimensions change, and the Document Size stays the same. An often overlooked subtlety is that Image Size allows you to change the Document Size and the Resolution in a single operation (which then changes the pixel dimensions).

The key is that Document Size and Resolution are independent of one another when Resample Image is turned on. Just change one, then the other.

When Resample Image is turned off, the Pixel Dimensions never change, and changing either Document Size or Resolution always affects the other one (see Figure 3-10).

If the previous two paragraphs didn't make any sense, don't bother trying to memorize them; just go and play with the Image Size dialog box until you see what's going on.

Tip: Adjusting by Percent. The word "percent" appears in both the Pixel Dimensions and the Document Size popup menus. Percent isn't a size; it's based on the current size of the image you're working on. For example, if you have a 2-by-2-inch image and you type in 200 percent for Document Size Width and Height, the result will be a 4-by-4-inch image. The number of pixels in the image will depend on whether you have Resample Image turned on or off.

We find this especially helpful when we have to re-create an image that was scaled "for position only" in a layout program. First we write down the scaling values on a piece of paper, and then we open the image in Photoshop and type the percentages into the Image Size dialog box.

▶ **Bicubic Smoother** is a new interpolation method specifically designed for upsampling. As its name suggests, it gives a smoother result that handles subsequent sharpening better than Bicubic sampling.

▶ **Bicubic Sharper** is another new interpolation method, only this time designed for downsampling. It does a better job of preserving detail than does Bicubic.

The differences are often subtle, and since we always recommend sharpening after resampling, the resampling itself is only half of the story. The new simple rule: Use Bicubic Smoother for upsampling (but don't expect miracles, particularly with film scans) and Bicubic Sharper for downsampling.

Image Mode

As we said earlier, a pixel can have a value of 165, but that doesn't mean anything until you know what image mode the image lives in. That 165 could represent a level of gray, or a particular color, or it might be only one member of a set of three or four other 8-bit values. Fortunately, Photoshop makes it easy to see what image mode an image is in, as well as to convert it to a different mode, if you want.

Ultimately, an image mode is simply a method of organizing the bits to describe a color. In a perfect world, you could say to a printer, "I'd like this box to be navy blue," and they'd know exactly what you were talking about. However, even Bruce and David can't agree on what navy blue looks like, much less you and your printer. So color scientists created a whole mess of ways for us to describe colors with some precision—to each other and to a computer.

Photoshop reads and writes only a handful of the many different color modes they came up with. Fortunately, they're the most important of the bunch, at least for those in the world of graphic arts. Each of the following image modes appears on Photoshop's Mode menu. Note that the mode your image is in determines the file formats you can save in. For instance, you can't save as JPEG if the file is in Lab mode. We'll talk more about this in Chapter 13, *Image Storage and Output*.

Bitmap

David really wishes that Adobe had picked a different word for this image mode. He insists that all images in Photoshop are *bitmapped*, but only "flat" black-and-white images, in which each pixel is defined using one bit of data (a zero or a one), are *bitmaps*.

One-bit pictures have a particular difference from other images when it comes to PostScript printing: the white areas throughout the image can appear transparent, showing through to whatever the image is printing over. Ordinarily, images are opaque, except for the occasional white silhouetted background made with clipping paths (see "Silhouettes" in Chapter 12, *Essential Image Techniques*).

The other major difference between the other image modes and Bitmap mode is that you're much more limited in the sorts of image editing you can do. For instance, you can't use any filters, and because there's no such thing as anti-aliasing in 1-bit images, you just cannot use tools that require this, such as the Smudge tool, the Blur tool, or the Dodge/Burn tool.

Bilevel bitmaps are the most generic of images, so you can save them in almost any file format.

Grayscale

Grayscale files in Photoshop are always either 8- or 16-bit images: Anything less than 8-bit gets converted to 8-bit; anything more than 8-bit gets converted to 16-bit. Eight-bit is still more common, although most scanners now allow you to bring more than 8 bits into Photoshop.

With 8-bit grayscale, each pixel has a value from 0 (black) to 255 (white), so there are a maximum of 256 levels of gray possible. With 16-bit grayscale, each pixel has a value from 0 (black) to 32,768 (white), for a theoretical maximum of 32,769 possible gray shades.

Few capture devices can actually deliver all those gray shades, so 16-bit files usually have rather a lot of redundancy. But that redundancy translates into editing headroom, so if your camera or scanner can capture 12 or more bits per pixel, it's often worthwhile bringing the high-bit data into Photoshop.

Eight-bit grayscale images are pretty generic, so you can save them in almost any format this side of MacPaint. You can save 16-bit grayscale images in a number of formats, but if you add layers, your choices are limited to Photoshop, Large Document Format, PNG, PDF, and Photoshop Raw, and TIFF.

Duotone

When you print a grayscale image on a printing press, those 256 levels of gray often get reduced to 100 or so because of the limitations of the press. You can counter this flattening effect considerably—increasing the tonal range of the printed image—by printing the image with more than one color of ink. This is called printing a *duotone* (for two inks), a *tritone* (for three inks), or a *quadtone* (for four).

The key is that the extra colors aren't typically used to simulate colors in the image; rather, they're used to extend the dynamic range of the underlying grayscale image. Those expensive Ansel Adams books on your coffee table were very likely printed using three or four (or even five or six) *different* black and gray inks.

Photoshop has a special image mode for duotones, tritones, and quadtones, and even though the file may appear to be in color, each pixel is still saved using only eight bits of information. The trick is that Photoshop saves a set of contrast curves for each ink along with the 8-bit grayscale image. Creating a good duotone is as much art as science.

Note that if you want to place duotone images in a page-layout application for spot-color separation, the safest choice is still to save in EPS format, though InDesign supports Photoshop and PDF duotone-mode files. For more information, see Chapter 10, *Spot Colors and Duotones*.

Indexed Color

As we said, each pixel in a grayscale image is defined with eight bits of information, so the file can contain up to 256 different pixel values. But each of those values, from 1 to 256, doesn't have to be a level of gray. The Indexed Color image mode is a method for producing 8-bit, 256-color files. Indexed-color bitmaps use a table of 256 colors, chosen from the full 24-bit palette. A given pixel's color is defined by reference to the table: "This pixel is color number 123, this pixel is color number 81," and so on.

While indexed color can save disk space (it requires only 8 bits per sample point, rather than the full 24 in RGB mode—see below), it gives you only 256 different colors. That's not a lot of colors, when you compare it to the 16.7 million different colors you can get in RGB.

Another major limitation is that most editing tools won't work in Indexed Color, because they almost all rely on the numeric values having a relationship to how light or dark the pixel is. Therefore, you should always do your image editing in RGB mode and then convert to Indexed

Color mode as a last step—the relatively tiny size of Indexed Color images makes them useful for Web graphics, but not for many other uses.

You can save indexed-color images in Photoshop, GIF, PNG, PICT, Amiga IFF, or BMP format (see "Niche File Formats" in Chapter 13, *Image Storage and Output*).

RGB

Every color computer monitor and television in the world displays color using the RGB image mode, in which every color is produced with varying amounts of red, green, and blue light. (These colors are called *additive primaries* because the more red, green, or blue light you add, the closer to white you get.) In Photoshop, files saved in the RGB mode typically use a set of three 8-bit grayscale files, so we say that RGB files are *24-bit* files.

These files can include up to approximately 16 million colors—more than enough to qualify as photographic quality. This is the mode in which we prefer to work when editing color images. Also, most scanners save images in RGB format. High-end drum scanners include "color computers" that automatically convert files to CMYK mode (see below), but RGB scanning is becoming more common even in shops with these scanners.

If you're producing images for multimedia, or you're outputting files to a film recorder—to 35 mm or 4-by-5 film, for instance—you should always save your files in RGB mode.

Tip: To RGB or to CMYK. A great philosophical debate rages on whether it's better to work in RGB or in CMYK for prepress work. As with most burning philosophical questions, there's no easy answer to this one, but that doesn't deter us from supplying one anyway. If someone gives you a CMYK scan from a drum scanner, work in CMYK. In all other cases, we recommend staying in RGB for as long as possible. We discuss this question in much more detail in Chapter 6, *Image Adjustment Fundamentals*.

You can save 24-bit RGB files in Photoshop, EPS, TIFF, PICT, Amiga IFF, BMP, JPEG, PCX, PDF, Pixar, Raw, Scitex CT, or Targa format, but unless you have compelling reasons to do otherwise, we suggest you stick with Photoshop (PSD), TIFF, PDF, or EPS.

Photoshop also lets you work with 48-bit RGB files, which contain three 16-bit channels instead of three 8-bit ones. Layered 48-bit images offer great editing flexibility, so we're using them more often now.

CMYK

Traditional full-color printing presses can print only four colors in a run: cyan, magenta, yellow, and black. Every other color in the spectrum is simulated using various combinations of those colors. When you open a file saved in CMYK mode, Photoshop has to convert the CMYK values to RGB values on the fly, in order to display the image on your computer screen. It's important to remember that when you look at the screen, you're looking at an RGB version of the data.

If you buy high-end drum scans, they'll probably be CMYK files. Otherwise, to print your images on press or on some desktop color printers, you'll have to convert your RGB images to CMYK. We discuss Photoshop's tools for doing so in Chapter 5, *Color Settings*.

You can save CMYK files in Photoshop, TIFF, PDF, EPS, JPEG, DCS, Scitex CT, and Raw formats, but the first four are by far the most common.

Lab

The problem with RGB and CMYK modes is that a given RGB or CMYK specification doesn't really describe a *color*. Rather, it's a set of instructions that a specific output device uses to produce a color. The problem is that different devices produce different colors from the same RGB or CMYK specifications. If you've ever seen a wall full of television screens at a department store, you've seen what we're talking about: The same image—with the same RGB values—looks different on each screen.

And if you've ever sat through a printing press run, you know that the 50th impression probably isn't exactly the same color as the 5,000th or the 50,000th. So, while a pixel in a scanned image may have a particular RGB or CMYK value, you can't tell what that color really *looks like*. RGB and CMYK are both *device-specific* color modes.

However, a class of *device-independent* or *perceptually based* modes has been developed over the years. All of them are based, more or less, on a color space defined by the Commission Internationale de l'Éclairage (CIE) in 1931. The Lab mode in Photoshop is one such derivative.

Lab doesn't describe a color by the components that make it up (RGB or CMYK, for instance). Instead, it describes *what a color looks like*. Device-independent color spaces are at the heart of the various color management systems now available that improve color correspondence between your screen, color printouts, and final printed output.

A file saved in Lab mode describes what a color looks like under rigidly specified conditions; it's up to you (or Photoshop, or your color management software) to decide what RGB or CMYK values are needed to create that color on your chosen output device.

Photoshop uses Lab mode as a reference when switching between CMYK and RGB modes, taking the values in your RGB Setup and CMYK Setup dialog boxes into account (see Chapter 5, *Color Settings*, for more information on this conversion). You can save 24-bit Lab images in Photoshop, DCS, EPS, PDF, TIFF, or Raw format. (You can only save 48-bit Lab images as Photoshop, Large Document Format, PDF, TIFF, or Raw.)

Lab is considerably less intuitive than the other color modes. The Lightness channel is relatively easy to understand, but the a* and b* channels (pronounced "ay-star" and "bee-star") are less so. The a* channel represents how red or green a color is—negative values represent greens, positive ones reds—and the b* channel represents how blue or yellow the color is—negative values represent blue, positive ones yellow. Neutrals and near-neutrals always have values close to zero in both channels. Most hardcore Photoshop geeks have a few tricks that rely on Lab mode, but many of them can be accomplished more easily by using blend modes instead. Luminosity blending, for example, produces extremely similar results to working on the Lightness channel in Lab mode.

Multichannel

The last image mode that Photoshop offers is Multichannel mode. This mode is the generic mode: like RGB or CMYK, Multichannel mode has more than one 8-bit channel; however, you can set the color and name of each channel to anything you like.

This flexibility can be a blessing or a curse. Back in the days when color scanners cost a fortune, we used to scan color photographs on grayscale scanners by scanning the image three times through red, green, and blue acetate, combining the three images into a single multichannel document that we then turned into RGB. Ah, those were the days.

Today, many scientific and astronomical images are made in "false color"—the channels may be a combination of radar, infrared, and ultraviolet, in addition to various colors of visible light. Some of our gonzo digital photographer friends are using Multichannel mode to combine infrared and visible-spectrum photographs into composite images of surreal beauty.

We mostly use Multichannel mode as an intermediary step or for complex spot color images. For instance, you can use it to store extra channels for transparency masks or selections in other images. Your only options for saving multichannel images are the Photoshop, Raw, Large Document Format, and DCS formats.

Bitmaps and File Size

As we said at the beginning of this chapter, pixel-based images are rectangles with thousands (or even millions) of pixels. Each of those pixels has to be saved on disk. If each pixel is defined using 8 bits of color information, then the file is eight times bigger than a black-and-white bitmap. Similarly, a 24-bit file is a full three times bigger than the 8-bit image, and a 48-bit file is twice the size of a 24-bit one.

Big files take a long time to open, edit, print, or save. Many people who complain about how slow editing is in Photoshop are simply working with files much bigger than they need. Instead, you can save yourself the complaining and reduce your file size when you can. Here's a quick rundown of how each attribute of a pixel-based image affects file size.

Dimensions and resolution. When you increase the number of pixels, you increase the file's size by the square of the value. That means if you double the resolution, you quadruple the file size (2 × 2); triple the resolution, and your file is nine times as large (3 × 3). There can easily be a multimegabyte difference between a 300-ppi and a 225-ppi image. (And remember that a 225-ppi image is almost always plenty enough resolution for a 150-lpi halftone screen.)

Bit depth. Increasing bit depth increases file size by a simple multiplier. Therefore, a 24-bit image is three times as large as an 8-bit image, and 24 times as large as a 1-bit image.

Image mode. Image mode doesn't necessarily increase file size, but going from RGB (24-bit) to CMYK (32-bit) mode does. It adds an extra 8-bit channel, thereby increasing bit depth (because each pixel is 32 bits deep).

Figuring File Size

Now that you know the factors that affect the size of images, it's a simple matter to calculate file size using the following formula:

File size in kilobytes =
Resolution^2 × Width × Height × Bits per sample ÷ 8,192

For example, if you have a 4-by-5-inch, 1-bit image at 300 ppi, you know that the file size is 220 K (300^2 × 4 × 5 × 1 ÷ 8192). A 24-bit image of the same size would be 5,273 K (just about 5 MB). In case you were wondering, this formula works because 8,192 is the number of bits in a kilobyte.

Tip: Faster File Figuring. There's an even easier way to calculate file sizes than doing the math yourself—let the computer do it for you. Photoshop's New Document and Image Size dialog boxes are very handy calculators for figuring dimensions, resolution, and file size. Simply type in the values you want, and Photoshop shows you how big the file would be (see Figure 3-11).

Of course, all these calculations apply only to flat files. When you start adding layers, layer masks, and alpha channels, it becomes quite difficult to figure file size with any degree of reliability. Each channel or mask adds another 8 or 16 bits to the bit depth (depending on whether the document was in 8-bit/channel or 16-bit/channel mode), but layers are much harder to figure because Photoshop divides each layer into tiles. Empty tiles take up almost no space, but if a tile contains just one pixel, it takes up the same

Figure 3-11
The Image Size dialog box

As you change values in these fields…

…Photoshop shows you the file size that will result.

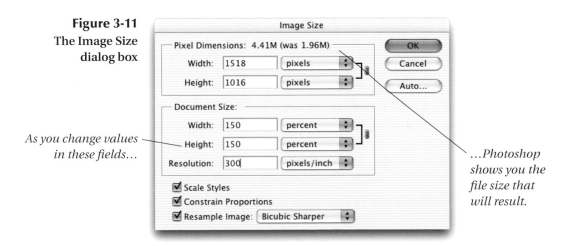

amount of space as a tile that's full of pixels. It's possible, and sometimes useful, to place layered TIFF or Photoshop files in a page-layout application, but we recommend flattening all files before final handoff to keep final files to a manageable size.

Some file formats also offer compression options. It's important to bear in mind that the file size that Photoshop reports is always the amount of RAM that the uncompressed, flattened image will occupy. We'll discuss compression options and file formats in much greater detail in Chapter 13, *Image Storage and Output*.

Billions and Billions of Bits

Would you hire a carpenter who didn't know anything about wood? Pixels are the wood of Photoshop; they're the material you use to construct your images. Without a firm understanding of the strengths as well as the weaknesses of your material, you won't get very far with this power tool of a program.

In this chapter, we've focused on the inherent attributes of pixel-based images, but one inherent attribute that we referred to only in passing is also one of the major sources of frustration to anyone who works with digital images. That attribute is color ambiguity: If you ask 100 people to visualize "red" you'll likely come up with 100 different colors. Likewise, if you display the same image on 100 monitors you may well end up with 100 different images unless you take steps to prevent that outcome. But before we examine the solution to the problem in Chapter 5, *Color Settings*, we need to tell you a bit about the nature of color itself, and go into a little more detail on the sometimes-mysterious relationship between color and numbers.

4 Color Essentials

What Makes a Color

You may have been taught back in kindergarten that the primary colors are red, yellow, and blue, and that all other colors can be made from them. Bruce still vividly recalls the day when his first-grade teacher, Mrs. Anderson, told him that he could make gray by using equal amounts of red, yellow, and blue. After looking at the lurid, weird, multicolored mess that was supposed to be a gray cat, he quite sensibly started over using a 2B pencil, and concluded that Mrs. Anderson was either color-blind or clueless. He traces his sometimes-inconvenient tendency to question authority to that day.

The details of Mrs. Anderson's lesson were certainly fallacious, but they contained an important kernel of truth—the notion that we can create all colors by combining three primary constituents. People have many different ways of thinking about, talking about, and working with color, but the notion of three ingredients that make up a color occurs again and again. Art directors may feel comfortable specifying color changes with the terms *hue*, *lightness*, and *saturation*. Those who came to color through the computer may be more at home with levels of RGB. Scientists think about color in all sorts of strange ways, including CIE Lab, HSB, and LCH. And dyed-in-the-wool prepress folks think in CMYK dot percentages.

Although Photoshop tries to accommodate all these ways of thinking about color—and it does a pretty good job—many Photoshop users find themselves locked into seeing color in only one way. This is natural and understandable—we all have one way of thinking about color that seems more sensible than the others—but it can make life with Photoshop more difficult than it needs to be. If you understand that all the different ways of looking at color are based on the same notion—combining three ingredients—you can learn to translate among the ways Photoshop lets you work with them, and choose the right one for the task at hand.

"Wait a minute," you say. "CMYK has four constituents, not three!" You question authority too, when that authority doesn't make sense. Well, in our role as temporary authority figures, we'll do what authority figures often do when asked hard questions: We ask you to trust us. Set this issue aside for the moment. We promise we'll deal with it later.

In this chapter, we take a hard look at some fundamental color relationships and how Photoshop presents them. This stuff might seem a little theoretical at times, but we urge you to slog through it; it's essential for our later discussions about tonal and color correction.

Primary Colors

The concept of *primary* colors is at the heart of much of the color work we do on computers. When we work with primary colors, we're talking about three colors that we can combine to make all the other colors. We can define colors by specifying varying proportions of primary colors, and we can color-correct images by adjusting the relationship of the primary colors. Ignoring for the moment which specific colors constitute the primaries, there are two fundamental principles of primary colors.

▶ They are the irreducible components of color.

▶ The primary colors, combined in varying proportions, can produce an entire spectrum of color.

The *secondary* colors, by the way, are made by combining two primary colors and excluding the third. But we don't much care about that. It is important to note, though, that what makes the primary colors special—indeed what makes them primary colors—is human physiology rather than any special property inherent in those wavelengths of light.

Additive and Subtractive Color

Before becoming preoccupied with the behavior of spherical objects like apples, billiard balls, and planets, Sir Isaac Newton performed some experiments with light and prisms. He found that he could break white light down into red, green, and blue components, a fairly trivial phenomenon that had been known for centuries. His breakthrough was the discovery that he could *reconstitute* white light by recombining those red, green, and blue components. Red, green, and blue—the primary colors of light—are known as the *additive primary* colors because as you add color, the result becomes more white (the absence of colored light is black; see Figure 4-1). This is how computer monitors and televisions produce color.

Figure 4-1
Additive and subtractive primaries

But color on the printed page works differently. Unlike a television, the page doesn't emit light; it just reflects whatever light hits it. To produce color images in print, you don't work with the light directly. Instead, you use pigments (like ink, dye, toner, or wax) that *absorb* some colors of light and reflect others.

The primary colors of pigments are cyan, yellow, and magenta. We call these the *subtractive primary* colors because as you add pigments to a white page, they subtract (absorb) more light, and the reflected color becomes darker. (We sometimes find it easier to remember: You *add* additive colors to get white, and you *subtract* subtractive colors to get white.) Cyan absorbs all the red light, magenta absorbs all the green light, and yellow absorbs all the blue light. If you add the maximum intensities of cyan, magenta, and yellow, you get black—in theory (see Figure 4-1).

Mrs. Anderson had the right idea about primary colors; she just picked the wrong ones. No matter how hard you try, you'll never be able to make cyan using red, yellow, and blue crayons.

An Imperfect World

A little while ago, we asked you to trust us on the subject of CMYK. Well, we just told you that combining cyan, magenta, and yellow would, *in theory*, produce black. In practice, however, it produces a muddy brown mess. Why? In the words of our friend and colleague Bob Schaffel, "God made RGB . . . man made CMYK." To that we add: "Who do you trust more?"

Imperfect pigments. If we had perfect CMY pigments, we wouldn't have to add black (K) as a fourth color. But despite our best efforts, our cyan pigments always contain a little red, our magentas always contain a little green, and our yellows always contain a trace of blue. Moreover, there's a limit to the amount of ink we can apply to the paper without dissolving it. So when we print in color, we add black to help with the reproduction of dark colors and to achieve acceptable density on press. See Chapter 5, *Color Settings*, for more on this.

Imperfect conversions. If we only had to deal with CMY, life would be a lot simpler. However, a large part of the problem of reproducing color images in print is that scanners—since they deal with light—see color in RGB, and we have to translate those values into CMYK to print them. Unfortunately, this conversion is a thorny one (see Chapter 5, *Color Settings*, for more on this subject).

The Color Wheel

Before moving on to weightier matters such as gravity, calculus, and his impending thirtieth birthday, Sir Isaac Newton provided the world of color with one more key concept: if you take the colors of the spectrum and arrange them around the circumference of a wheel, the relationships among primaries become much clearer (see Figure 4-2).

The important thing to notice about this color wheel is that the additive and subtractive primary colors are opposite each other, equidistant around the wheel. These relationships are key to understanding how color works. For instance, cyan sits opposite red on the color wheel because it is, in fact, the opposite of red: Cyan pigments appear cyan because they absorb red light and reflect blue and green. Cyan is, in short, the absence of red.

Figure 4-2
The color wheel

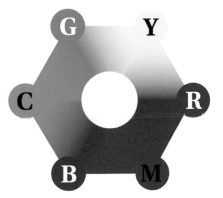

Emitted and reflected (additive and subtractive) colors are complementary to one another. Red is complementary to cyan, green to magenta, and blue to yellow.

Colors that lie directly opposite each other on the wheel are known as *complementary* colors.

Figuring Saturation and Brightness

So far, we've talked about color in terms of three primary colors. But there are other ways of specifying color in terms of three ingredients. The most familiar one use the terms of *hue* (the property we refer to when we talk about "red" or "orange"), *saturation* (the "purity" of the color), and *brightness*.

Newton's basic two-dimensional color wheel lets us see the relationships between different hues, but to describe colors more fully, we need a more complex, three-dimensional model. We can find one of these in the HSB (Hue, Saturation, Brightness) color cylinder (see Figure 4-3).

In the HSB cylinder, you can see the hues are arranged around the edge of the wheel, and colors become progressively more pastel as we move into the center—the farther in you go, the less saturated or pure the color is. The Apple Color Picker (which many programs use to specify color, but not Photoshop) is a graphical representation of the HSB color model—it displays a color wheel to pick hue and saturation, with a slider to control brightness.

Tristimulus Models and Color Spaces

Ignoring the inconvenience of CMYK, all the ways we've discussed of specifying and thinking about color involve three primary ingredients. Color scientists call these *tristimulus* models. (A *color* model is simply a way of thinking about color and representing it numerically: A tristimulus model represents colors by using three numbers.) If you go deep into the physiology of color, you'll find that our perceptual systems are

Figure 4-3
The HSB color cylinder

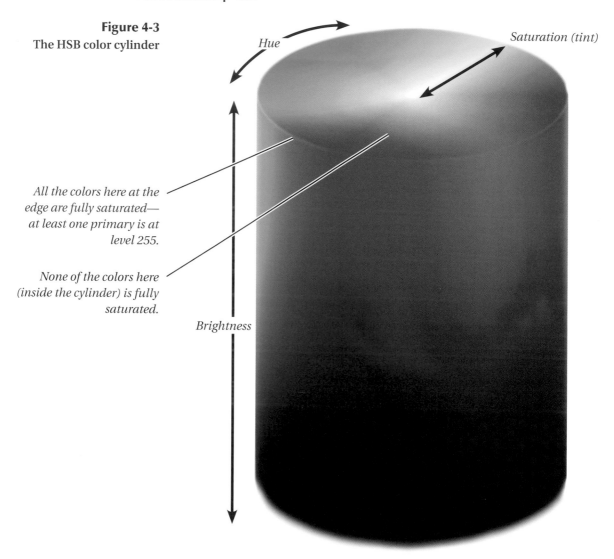

Hue

Saturation (tint)

All the colors here at the edge are fully saturated— at least one primary is at level 255.

None of the colors here (inside the cylinder) is fully saturated.

Brightness

actually wired in terms of three different responses to light that combine to produce the sensation of color. So the tristimulus approach isn't merely a mathematical convenience—it's inherent in the way our perceptual systems work.

But tristimulus models have another useful property. Because they specify everything in terms of three ingredients, you can (with very little effort) view them as three-dimensional objects with *x*, *y*, and *z* axes. Each color has a location in this three-dimensional object, specified by the three values. These three-dimensional models are called *color spaces*, a term that gets thrown around a great deal in the world of color.

We like to think of the HSB color space as a giant cylinder; the brightness slider in the Apple Color Picker determines which slice of the cylinder we're looking at. But, like any metaphor, there's a good side and a bad side to looking at color this way.

▶ **The good side.** The Apple Color Picker is a great way to start learning about color and how changing a single primary changes your colors.

▶ **The bad side.** The simple HSB model can't really describe how you *see* colors. For instance, you know that cyan appears much lighter than blue; but in the HSB cylinder, they both have the same brightness and saturation values.

Therefore, while the Color Picker is a step in the right direction, we have to go further to understand how to work with color.

How Colors Affect Each Other

There are a lot of times in Photoshop when we find ourselves working with one color space, but thinking about the changes in terms of another. As you'll see in Chapter 6, *Image Adjustment Fundamentals*, for instance, we often recommend that you use curves to adjust RGB values, but base your changes on the resulting CMYK percentages as displayed in the Info palette. So, it will speed up your work if you take some time to figure out how color spaces interact—what happens in one space when you work in another.

Here are some ways to think about RGB, CMY, and HSB colors, and how they relate to each other.

Tone. One of the least understood—yet most important—effects of adding colors together is that adding or removing primaries not only affects hue and saturation; it also affects tone. When you increase any RGB component to change the hue—adding light—the color gets lighter. The reverse is true with CMY because you're adding ink, making the color darker.

Hue. Every color, except the primaries, contains opposing primary colors. In RGB mode, red is "pure," but orange contains red alongside a good dose of green (and possibly some blue, too). In CMYK, magenta is pure, and red is not—it contains some amount of yellow in addition to magenta. So to change a color's hue, you add or subtract primary colors.

In the process, you will probably affect the color's tone—adding or removing light (or ink) so the color gets lighter or darker.

Saturation. A saturated RGB color is made up of only one or two primaries; the third primary is always zero. When you add a trace of the third color—in order to change the hue slightly, for instance—you desaturate the color.

Likewise, if you increase the saturation of a color using the Hue/Saturation dialog box (or any other), you're removing one of the primaries. If you get out to the edge, where one of the primaries is maxed out and the other two are still changing, you'll change the hue and the tone.

There's another important consideration pertaining to saturated colors. When you saturate a color in an RGB image, you wind up with detail in only one of the three channels. One of the others is always solid white, and the other is always solid black. It's this—not just the difficulty of reproducing them—that makes saturated colors in images difficult to handle, because all the detail is being carried by only one channel.

Neutrals. A color made up of equal values of red, green, and blue is always a neutral gray (though you may have to do quite a bit of work to make it come out that way on screen or—once you've converted it to CMYK—on press). The "darkness" of the gray depends on how much red, green, and blue there is—more light makes for a lighter gray. This is useful in a number of situations, including making monitor adjustments and correcting color casts.

For a quick summary of relationships among the color spaces, see the sidebar "Color Relationships at a Glance."

Device-Independent Color

Basically, the problem with HSB, RGB, and CMY (and even CMYK) is that they don't describe how a color looks; they only describe the color's ingredients. You've probably walked into a television store and seen about a hundred televisions on the wall, each of them receiving the same color information. But *none* of them displays the colors in the same way.

Color Relationships at a Glance

It's worth spending some time to understand the color relationships we're discussing in this chapter. We all have a favorite color space, but if you can learn to view color in more than one way—understanding how to achieve the same results by manipulating CMY, RGB, and HSB—you'll find the world of color correction much less alien, and you'll be much more able to select the right tool for the job.

We suggest memorizing these fundamentals.

▶ 100% cyan = 0 red

▶ 100% magenta = 0 green

▶ 100% yellow = 0 blue

▶ Increasing RGB values corresponds exactly to reducing CMY values, and vice versa.

▶ Reducing saturation (making something more gray) means introducing the complementary color; to desaturate red, for example, you add cyan.

▶ The complement of a primary color is produced by combining equal amounts of the other two primary colors.

▶ Lightening or darkening a saturated color desaturates that color.

▶ Changing the hue of a color often changes lightness as well.

▶ Saturation changes can cause hue changes.

Saturated Primaries—CMY versus RGB

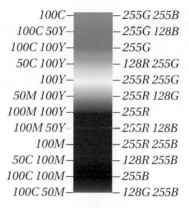

100C	255G 255B
100C 50Y	255G 128B
100C 100Y	255G
50C 100Y	128R 255G
100Y	255R 255G
50M 100Y	255R 128G
100M 100Y	255R
100M 50Y	255R 128B
100M	255R 255B
50C 100M	128R 255B
100C 100M	255B
100C 50M	128G 255B

The colors at left are fully saturated—each contains 100 percent of one or two primaries. The additive and subtractive primaries have an inverse relationship.

Desaturating Saturated Colors

| 255R 255G |
| 64R 128G 192B |
| 128R 128G 128B |
| 64R 192G 128B |
| 255R 255B |

Desaturating the reds removes red and adds other primaries to the red areas. Adding a third primary "pollutes" the saturated color, causing it to go gray. It may or may not affect lightness.

Lightness and Saturation

Lightening or darkening a saturated color (here, +50 and -50) desaturates it; either it pulls the primaries back from 100 percent, or it pollutes them with a third primary, or both. Also note the hue shift in the darkened version.

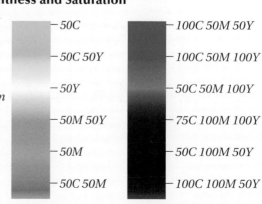

50C	100C 50M 50Y
50C 50Y	100C 50M 100Y
50Y	50C 50M 100Y
50M 50Y	75C 100M 100Y
50M	50C 100M 50Y
50C 50M	100C 100M 50Y

In fact, if you send the same RGB values to ten different monitors, or the same CMYK values to ten different presses, you'll end up with ten different colors (see Figure 4-4). We call RGB and CMYK *device dependent*, because the color you get varies from device to device.

So, Photoshop has a problem in trying to display colors properly on your monitor: It doesn't know what the colors should *look like* to you. It doesn't know what those RGB or CMYK values really mean.

Plus, the program has to take all the little quirks of human vision into account. For instance, our eyes are more sensitive to some colors and brightness levels than to others, and we're more sensitive to small changes in bright colors than we are to small changes in dark ones (if you've had trouble teasing all the subtle shadow details out of your scanned images, this is one reason why). RGB and CMYK don't give Photoshop the information it needs to know what color is actually being described.

Figure 4-4 **Device-dependent color and color gamuts**
Since this figure is printed with process inks on paper, it can only simulate the results of sending the same RGB or CMYK values to various devices. It depicts relative appearances, not actual results. Likewise, the color chart just represents the gamuts of different devices, rather than actually showing those gamuts.

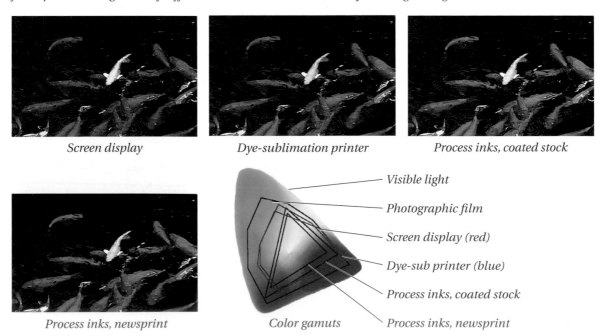

Screen display   *Dye-sublimation printer*   *Process inks, coated stock*

Process inks, newsprint   *Color gamuts*

— *Visible light*
— *Photographic film*
— *Screen display (red)*
— *Dye-sub printer (blue)*
— *Process inks, coated stock*
— *Process inks, newsprint*

Lab Color

Fortunately, there's CIE Lab, which appears on the Mode menu simply as Lab. Lab is designed to describe what colors *look like*, regardless of the device they're displayed on, so we call it *device independent*.

Whereas in HSB the hues are represented as lying around a wheel, Lab color uses a more accurate but significantly less intuitive arrangement. In Lab, the third axis (which lies perpendicular to the page and is roughly equivalent to brightness in HSB) is the luminance axis—it represents how bright the color appears to the human eye. But unlike brightness in HSB, it takes into account the fact that we see green as brighter than blue.

Whole books have been written on Lab color (we've even read some of them), and while they may be of great interest to color scientists, they're unlikely to help you get great-looking images on a deadline. For now, there are really only three things you need to know about Lab color.

▶ While HSB, HSL, and LCH are based on the way we think about color, and RGB and CMYK are based on the ways devices such as monitors and printers produce color, Lab is based on the way humans actually *see* color. A Lab specification describes the color that most people will see when they look at an object under specified lighting conditions.

▶ Photoshop uses Lab as a reference when it does mode changes. For instance, when you switch from RGB mode to CMYK mode, Photoshop uses Lab to decide what *color* is being specified by each device-dependent RGB value, and then comes up with the right device-dependent CMYK equivalent. You'll see why this is so important in the next chapter, *Color Settings*.

▶ Finally, you shouldn't feel dumb if you find it hard to get your head around Lab color. It *is* difficult to visualize, because it's an abstract mathematical construct—it isn't based on amounts of things we can understand readily, like RGB or HSB. It uses differing amounts of three primaries to specify colors, but those primaries don't really correspond to anything we can actually experience.

Working with Colors

When you work with Photoshop, it lets you view and adjust your colors in all sorts of different ways. It's difficult to adjust saturation in an image, for example, by manipulating RGB or CMYK values directly, so Photoshop provides tools that let you apply changes in hue, saturation, and brightness to the underlying RGB or CMYK data. Likewise, if you have an RGB image but you plan to print it in CMYK, you can use Photoshop's Info palette to keep track of what's happening to the CMYK values you'll eventually get when you do the mode change from RGB to CMYK.

You face two fairly large problems, however. The first is that every time you do a mode change, you lose some image information; if your images start with 256 shades of each color, some of these get lost due to rounding errors as you convert from one color space to another. Photoshop lets you work around this by providing information about what you'll get after you've done the color-space conversion, without your actually having to do so until we've perfected your images. We discuss this in much more detail in Chapter 6, *Image Adjustment Fundamentals*.

The second problem is that the color spaces in which most of your images are stored, RGB and CMYK, are device dependent—the color you'll get varies depending on the device you send it to. Worse, each device has a range of colors it can reproduce—called the *color gamut*—and some devices have a much wider gamut than others (see Figure 4-4, earlier in this chapter). For example, color film can record a wider range of colors than a color monitor can display, and the monitor displays a wider range of colors than you can reproduce with ink on paper; so no matter what you do, some of the colors captured on film simply can't be reproduced in print.

Fortunately, Photoshop has tools that let us remove some (if not all) of the ambiguity from your RGB and CMYK color definitions, and it lets you specify the gamut of your monitor and your CMYK output devices. The next chapter, *Color Settings*, is devoted to explaining what those tools are, how they work, and how to use them.

5 Color Settings

Understanding Photoshop's Color Management

Welcome to the heart of *Real World Photoshop CS2*. We consider every topic in this book to be important, but color management—and let's make no mistake here, this chapter is all about color management—is one of those topics that can quickly make anyone feel stupid. If you're under the delusion that you can use Photoshop *without* using color management, this chapter is a must-read. Without understanding how Photoshop handles color behind the scenes, there's no way to get great color (or black-and-white) images out of this program.

Fortunately, while behind the scenes Photoshop's color management system uses mathematics that approach rocket science, using these tools is much simpler: You need to understand a few key concepts, learn where the buttons are, and use common sense in deciding when to push them.

In the last chapter, we broke the sad news that RGB and CMYK are very ambiguous ways of specifying color, since the actual color you get will vary from device to device. In this chapter, we'll look at the features Photoshop offers to make what you see on the screen at least resemble, if not actually match, what you get in your printed output.

There aren't any major changes in functionality in the color management features of Photoshop CS2 since the last version. However, several key commands have been moved to different menu locations, and labels have changed.

Controlling Color

It may seem strange to devote a whole chapter to a handful of commands, but the settings that deal with defining, converting, and displaying color are so important that you really need to understand what they do, and when and how they do it. Use these features correctly, and you'll produce predictable, repeatable color more easily than ever; use them incorrectly, or ignore them, and you'll be doomed to "chase color" through cycle after cycle of corrections and proofs.

In this chapter, we'll focus on six features:

► Color Settings

► The Color Picker

► Assign Profile

► Convert to Profile

► Proof Setup

► Print with Preview

We'll explain what each does, how they interact, and how you can use them, both to communicate color clearly and to see what your output will look like ahead of time, whether it's print CMYK, print RGB, or the Web.

If you're new to the concepts behind color management, you'll likely find that just diving into Photoshop's dialog boxes is more than a tad overwhelming. Even experienced Photoshop users may find a 30,000-foot overview helpful. So before we look in detail at the color management features in Photoshop CS2, let's step back a little and discuss just what color management is and how it's supposed to work.

Color Management Systems Explained

A color management system (CMS) is a set of software tools that attempts to maintain the appearance of colors as they're reproduced by different devices. We stress the word "appearance" because it's simply impossible to reproduce many of the colors found in the world in print, or even on a color monitor.

Color management often gets dressed up in much fancier clothing, but it really does only two things.

▶ It lets you assign a specific color appearance to RGB or CMYK numbers that would otherwise be ambiguous.

▶ Within the physical limitations of the devices involved, it lets you keep that specific color appearance as you send your images to different displays and output devices.

The options may sometimes appear more complex, but if you break them down, you'll find that they always do some combination of the above two tasks.

CMS Components

All CMSs employ three basic components:

▶ The *reference color space* (also known as the *profile connection space*, or PCS) is a device-independent, perceptually based color space. Most current CMSs use a CIE-defined color space, such as CIE Lab or CIE XYZ. You never have to worry about the reference color space; it's the theory behind how the software works.

▶ The *color-matching engine* (sometimes known as the *color matching method*, or CMM) is the software that does the conversion between different device-specific color spaces. Photoshop CS supports other color matching engines besides the Adobe-branded one (ACE) that it shares with the other Adobe Creative Suite applications, but the only reason we can see for using a different engine is if you absolutely must obtain exactly the same conversions from non-Adobe products. In general, the differences between the various CMMs are slight.

▶ *Profiles* usually describe the behavior of a device like a scanner, monitor, or printer. For instance, a profile can tell the CMS "This is the reddest red that this device can output." A profile can also define a "virtual color space" that's unrelated to any particular device (the Adobe RGB space is an example of this; we'll see how it's useful later on). Profiles are the key to color management. Without a profile, 100-percent Red has no specific meaning; with a profile, the color management system can say "Oh, *that* color red!" Thanks to the ICC (International Color

Consortium), device profiles conform to a standard format that lets them work with all CMSs on all platforms. ColorSync profiles on the Mac and .icm or .icc profiles on Windows both follow the ICC spec and are interchangeable between platforms.

The key point is that profiles define the actual color appearance—the color that we see—that any given set of RGB or CMYK numbers produce on the device (a monitor, a desktop printer, a proofing system, a printing press) whose behavior the profile describes.

Conveying Color Meaning

The key concept in using a CMS is conveying color meaning—making those ambiguous RGB and CMYK values unambiguous. If the system is going to keep the color consistent among different devices, it needs to know what color appearance each device in the process represents using RGB or CMYK numbers. If a CMS knows what RGB values a scanner produces when it scans specific colors, and knows what colors a display produces when we send it specific RGB numbers, it can calculate the new RGB numbers it needs to send to the display to make it reproduce the colors represented by the scanner RGB numbers.

Profile embedding. When you embed a profile in an image, you aren't changing the image. You're simply providing a definition of what the numbers in the file mean in terms of actual colors you can see—you're assigning a specific color appearance to the RGB or CMYK numbers. If you don't embed profiles in your images, the numbers in the file are ambiguous and open to many different interpretations. Embedding a profile simply tells color-management-savvy applications which interpretation you want to place on the numbers. Profile embedding is the easiest way to convey the color meaning—the intended color appearance—of the numbers in the digital image.

Source and target profiles. When you ask the color management system to make a conversion—to change the numbers in the file—the CMS needs to know where the RGB or CMYK color values came from and where you want to send them. Whenever you open or create an image, you have to give the CMS this information by specifying a source profile and a target profile.

The source profile (which is sometimes already embedded in the file) says, "This RGB data is from such-and-such a scanner," or "This RGB data is from such-and-such a monitor." This tells the CMS what actual colors RGB or CMYK numbers represent. The target profile tells the CMS where the image is going, so that it can calculate the new RGB or CMYK numbers that will maintain the color in the image on the target device.

For example, imagine that color management systems work with words rather than colors. The purpose of the word-CMS is to translate words from one language to another. If you just feed it a bunch of words, it can't do anything. But if you give it the words and tell it that they were written by a French person (the source), it all of a sudden can understand what the words are saying. If you then tell it that you speak German (the target), it can translate the meaning faithfully for you.

The process. Back to pictures: When you scan some artwork, you end up with a lot of RGB data. But for Photoshop to know what specific colors those RGB values are meant to represent, you have to tell it that the RGB data came from this particular scanner. When you choose your scanner's device profile as the source profile, you're telling Photoshop that this isn't just any old RGB data; it's the RGB data carefully defined by the scanner's device profile.

To make the image on your printer match the original, you choose your printer profile as the target profile. The CMS takes the RGB values in the image and uses the scanner profile as the secret decoder ring that tells it what colors (in the reference color space) the RGB values represent. Then it calculates new RGB or CMYK values based on the printer profile, to produce the same colors when they're printed on your printer.

This is really the only thing CMSs do. They convert color data from one device's color space (one "language") to another. Pretty much everything you do with a CMS involves asking it to make the colors match between a source and a target profile, and this same two-step is integral to the way Photoshop CS handles color.

Rendering intents. There's one more wrinkle. Each device has a fixed range of color that it can reproduce, dictated by the laws of physics. Your monitor can't reproduce a more saturated red than the red produced by the monitor's red phosphor. Your printer can't reproduce a cyan more saturated than the printer's cyan ink, or a white brighter than the white of the paper. The range of color a device can reproduce is called the *color gamut*. Colors present in the source space that aren't reproducible in the destination space are called *out-of-gamut* colors. Since you can't reproduce those colors in the destination space, you have to replace them with some other colors.

The ICC profile specification includes four different methods of handling out-of-gamut colors, called *rendering intents*. (In Photoshop CS2, they're simply called intents.) The four rendering intents act as follows:

▶ **Perceptual.** The Perceptual intent attempts to fit the gamut of the source space into the gamut of the target space in such a way that the overall color relationships, and hence the overall image appearance, is preserved, even though all the colors in the image may change somewhat in lightness and saturation. It's a good choice for images that contain significant out-of-gamut colors.

▶ **Saturation.** The Saturation intent maps fully saturated colors in the source to fully saturated colors in the target without concerning itself with hue or lightness. It's mostly good for pie charts and such, where you just want vivid colors, but some profiling vendors use it as an alternate method of perceptual rendering, so it may be worth previewing the conversion using Saturation rendering to see if it does something useful—see "Soft-Proofing Controls," later in this chapter.

▶ **Relative Colorimetric.** The Relative Colorimetric intent maps white in the source to white in the target, so that white on your output is the white of the paper rather than the white of the source space, which may be different. It then reproduces all the in-gamut colors exactly, clipping out-of-gamut colors to the closest reproducible hue. For images that don't contain significant out-of-gamut colors, it's often a better choice than Perceptual because it preserves more of the original colors.

▶ **Absolute Colorimetric.** The Absolute Colorimetric intent is the same as Relative Colorimetric, except that it doesn't scale source white to target white. If your source space has a bluish white, and your output is on a yellowish-white paper, Absolute Colorimetric rendering makes the printer lay down some cyan ink in the white areas to simulate the white of the original. It's generally only used for proofing (see "Soft-Proofing Controls" later in this chapter).

When you use a CMS to convert data from one color space to another, you need to tell it three pieces of information: the source profile, the target profile, and the rendering intent. You can think of these three elements as where the color comes from, where the color is going, and how you want the color to get there. But before you go hog-wild, converting images willy-nilly from one space to another, a cautionary note is needed.

Space conversions and data loss. Bear in mind that even the best CMS degrades your image when you convert it from one color space to another. Even though the conversions may be very accurate, you still want to limit their number (any color space conversion involves some loss, due to rounding and quantization errors). That's why Photoshop has taken a somewhat different approach to color management than most other applications. Rather than make you transform images continually from one device's color space to another's, thus degrading the image, Photoshop offers a reasonable place for images to live: a device-independent RGB working space.

Color Management in Photoshop

A little history: In versions of Photoshop prior to 5, the program acted like almost all other applications at the time and simply sent RGB values straight to the screen. A little-understood feature called Monitor Setup let you tell Photoshop how your monitor behaved—what its white point, primaries, and tone reproduction characteristics were, in effect providing Photoshop with a monitor profile. If the information was correct, Photoshop knew what color you would see when a set of RGB numbers was displayed on the monitor, and it would attempt to preserve that color during color space conversions. You can think of this approach as a crude color management system, albeit a limited, closed, proprietary one.

But even when used correctly, this approach had no mechanism for telling other users how your monitor behaved, and hence no mechanism for conveying what colors the RGB numbers represented; so the image would appear different on each system, and would convert to other color spaces differently on each system. Most users just left Monitor Setup alone, so images converted the same but appeared different on different systems, giving rise to the myth that it's impossible to trust the monitor.

Working Spaces and Display Compensation

Photoshop 5 introduced the use of industry-standard ICC profiles to define the various color spaces, a practice continued in all subsequent versions. In Photoshop 5, your image's RGB space (called the *working space*) became uncoupled from the monitor's RGB space, or for that matter from any other physical device. Instead of keeping hundreds of images in different device-specific color spaces (each tied to whatever monitor last worked on it), Photoshop 5 more or less forced you to convert all your images into a single RGB working space.

Photoshop 5, like all subsequent versions, displayed everything through your monitor profile—it performed an on-the-fly transform from this one RGB space to your monitor's RGB space, but only to the data that it sent to the monitor; the actual image data wasn't changed. The huge advantage was that images displayed correctly on different systems, as long as they had accurate monitor profiles. But this also had some disadvantages.

One disadvantage of this approach was that it forced a one-time conversion of the image from whatever RGB space it was captured in to the RGB working space, which many users found scary. A bigger problem was that nobody could agree on *which* working space to use (though there was general agreement that the default, sRGB, was a Really Bad Idea). As a result, lots of people were confronted with strange dialog boxes warning them about profile mismatches and scary-looking progress bars that announced that Photoshop was "Converting colors"—which created confusion and discomfort, even when Photoshop was doing the right thing.

So Photoshop 6 replaced the strict (or, as some of the Photoshop team labeled it, "fascist") approach to working spaces with a more flexible approach (which we labeled "anarchist"), introducing the notion of *per-document* color. Documents could exist in any profiled space—a working space, a capture space, an output space. There are good reasons why you want to convert most of your images into a working space—we'll look at these in detail a little later—but the huge difference (and benefit) with per-document color is that you aren't forced to do so.

The consensus is that Photoshop 6 finally got color management right, and its approach has been carried over largely unchanged through Photoshop 7 to today's Creative Suite 2 applications, including Photoshop.

But if you jump blindly into the Color Settings dialog box (press Command-Shift-K, or select Color Settings from the Edit menu—this used to be in the Photoshop menu on the Macintosh) and start pressing buttons, they may hurt you. Color Settings is very deep indeed, and the interactions between the controls are often quite subtle (see Figure 5-1).

So rather than just waltzing through the various options in order, we need to step back a little and look at some of the concepts the controls embody. If you just want the CliffsNotes version, see the sidebar "Photoshop Color Management at a Glance."

Figure 5-1
The Color Settings
dialog box

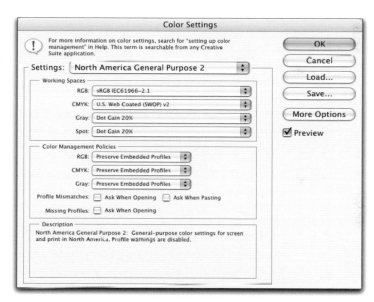

The Conceptual Framework

Photoshop's color management has some unique concepts, and places a different emphasis on some mainstream color management concepts than do other applications. So before we dive into dialog boxes, let's look at an overview of the controls and the kinds of things for which you'll use them.

Working Spaces and Device Spaces

In the Bad Old Days (and in many other applications today) you could use only one RGB space and only one CMYK space at a time. But Photoshop's "per-document color" means you can have multiple RGB and CMYK documents open at the same time, each one using a different color space. This is great for service bureaus and others who work with images from many

Photoshop Color Management at a Glance

The color architecture in Photoshop CS2 is deep but straightforward. Here, in a nutshell, are the controls you need to know about to make Photoshop CS produce the results you want.

▶ The Color Settings dialog box lets you set default working spaces for RGB, CMYK, and Grayscale, and set Color Management Policies, which dictate how Photoshop uses (or ignores) embedded profiles in images. It also lets you set warnings for missing or mismatched profiles.

▶ The default working spaces are the ones Photoshop always uses when it encounters untagged images (those with no embedded profiles), and are also the ones Photoshop always uses as the destination when you con-

vert between color modes by choosing RGB, CMYK, or Grayscale from the Mode submenu on the Image menu.

▶ Untagged images use whatever working space is currently set for that color mode. If you change the working space, Photoshop reinterprets the image as being in the new working space. Tagged images stay in the space represented by the embedded profile unless you explicitly ask for a conversion to another space.

▶ Color Management Policies let you control Photoshop's color management behavior. Preserve Embedded Profiles makes Photoshop open each image in the space represented by its embedded profile. Convert to Working RGB/CMYK/Gray-

scale forces a conversion from the embedded profile space to the working space. Off ignores embedded profiles and treats all images as being in the working space. Untagged images—those that don't contain an embedded profile—are always treated as being in the current working space.

▶ Photoshop *always* displays images through your monitor profile, which it picks up from the operating system. It performs an on-the-fly conversion on the data sent to the video card from the document's space (either the document's own embedded profile or the current working space) to your monitor space. This conversion is only for display—it doesn't affect the contents of the file.

different sources, but it also opens several cans o' worms. We now have to draw a distinction between the working space and the document space(s), and between working spaces and device spaces.

Most of us have become used to switching CMYK spaces as our output needs dictate (each output device or method requires a different CMYK space), but we've generally followed the practice of sticking with a single RGB space, mainly because Photoshop forced us to do so. Now that we're freed from the tyranny of the RGB working space, it's important to look at the pros and cons of leaving RGB images in the space in which they were opened or converting them to an RGB working space.

With per-document color, your chosen working space is just a fall-back position for untagged images (images that don't have embedded profiles). Photoshop offers several different RGB working spaces, and enterprising

- The Assign Profile command lets you assign a profile to any image. Assigning a profile doesn't change the numbers in the image, it just attaches a new meaning to those numbers, and hence it changes the appearance, sometimes dramatically.

- The Convert to Profile command lets you convert images to any profiled space, with a choice of rendering intents. Unlike Assign Profile, Convert to Profile changes the numbers in the image but preserves the appearance. Convert to Profile offers more control over color space conversions than changing modes from the Mode submenu, because it lets you preview different rendering intents, and it allows you to perform RGB-to-RGB or CMYK-to-CMYK conversions, which are impossible using the Mode commands.

- The Proof Colors command offers a live preview of conversions to any RGB, CMYK, or Grayscale output space. You can work in a working space while previewing the output space. Proof Colors offers separate control over the rendering from source space to proof space, and proof space to the monitor, providing very accurate previews.

- The Color Management Options panel of the Print with Preview dialog box lets you perform a conversion on the data that's sent to the printer. The conversion can be a simple one from document space to the output space, or a more complex one from the document space to the Proof Colors space to the output space. The former is handy for printing final art on a composite printer directly from Photoshop. The latter is useful for proofing final press output on a composite printer.

If you learn how to use all these controls effectively, you'll have achieved mastery of Photoshop's color management in its entirety. Maybe you should write a book!

On your way to mastering Photoshop's color management, just remember the basic principle that color management only does two things: assign a color appearance to the numbers, and change the numbers to preserve that appearance in a different scenario. Learn to figure out whether you're assigning an appearance or making a conversion.

third parties have created still more. It may seem sensible to edit in the space in which the image was captured—a scanner or digital camera space—or in the final output space, such as an RGB inkjet. But working spaces have important properties that make them better suited to image editing than the vast majority of device spaces.

- Most device color spaces are not *perceptually uniform*. That means that when you edit your file, the same editing increment in Levels, Curves, Hue/Saturation, or whatever, may have a much larger effect on some parts of the tonal range and color gamut than on others.

- Most device color spaces aren't gray-balanced. One of the key features of the abstract RGB working spaces built into Photoshop (as well as most third-party working spaces) is that when R=G=B, you know you have a neutral gray. This isn't true for most scanner RGB spaces, many digital camera RGB spaces, and pretty much all printer RGB spaces.

▶ Output device spaces typically clip some colors in the image because their gamut is almost always smaller than the original capture. For instance, if you simply apply a monitor or inkjet printer profile to an image you just scanned, you may not get all the colors you deserve.

Working spaces, in contrast, tend to be uniform, and are invariably gray-balanced. They do, however, differ widely in their gamuts, so gamut size is one of the key considerations when choosing an RGB working space for a particular job (see "Choosing an RGB Working Space," later in this chapter). So while you're no longer forced to use abstract RGB working spaces, you should do so for any serious image editing. Picking an RGB working space and sticking to it will also make your life easier.

Tagged and Untagged Images

Whenever you open or create an image, Photoshop treats it as a tagged or an untagged image from the moment of opening or creation, depending on how you set the Color Management Policies in Color Settings. Tagged and untagged images behave differently as follows:

Tagged images. Tagged images are those with an embedded profile, which may be different from the current working space profile. A tagged image keeps its original profile and stays in the "document space" rather than the working space, unless you explicitly assign a new profile, convert to a new profile, or untag the image, discarding the profile. The Color Management Policies let you automatically keep documents in their own space, convert them to the working space, or discard the profile.

Untagged images. Untagged images have no embedded profile. They exist as a bunch of numbers whose actual color meaning is open to interpretation. If you change the working space while an untagged image is open, the image gets reinterpreted to be in the new working space, and the appearance changes. If you move pixels (by either copy and paste or drag-and-drop) to another image in the same color mode, the numerical values are moved to the new document. For operations where Photoshop needs to make an assumption about the actual colors the numbers represent, such as mode changes or displaying on the monitor, Photoshop treats untagged images as being in the current working space for that mode. It also does so when you move pixels to a document in a different color mode, such as pasting from an RGB document to a CMYK one.

You can always convert a tagged image to an untagged one, or vice versa, by using the Assign Profile command (on the Mode submenu, under the Image menu), or the Embed Profile checkbox in the Save As dialog box, to embed a profile.

Tip: Document Profiles at a Glance. You can tell at a glance whether a document is tagged or untagged by choosing Document Profile from the popup menu at the lower left of the document window (see Figure 5-2). For tagged images, it shows the profile name. For untagged images, it displays "Untagged RGB" (or CMYK, or Grayscale, depending on the document's mode).

A subtler clue can be found in the document window's title bar (see Figure 5-3). The pound sign (#) at the end of the title bar display indicates an untagged document. An asterisk (*) at the end of the title bar display indicates a document that's tagged with a profile different from the current working space. If neither character appears, the document is tagged with the working space profile.

Figure 5-2
Watching the
document profile

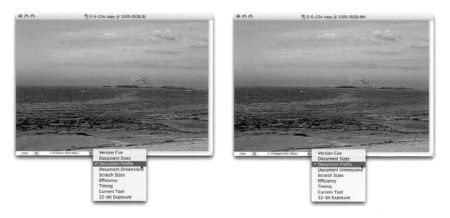

Figure 5-3
A subtle clue

untagged

tagged, not working space

tagged with working space

To tag or not to tag? In the vast majority of cases, untagged documents are a Bad Thing because they force us to guess the intended appearance portrayed by the numbers in the file, and hence create extra work for everyone. The only situations that justify untagged documents are those where the numbers are unambiguous because of the context, or the appearance generated by the numbers is irrelevant.

For example, we didn't embed profiles in any of the CMYK images we used in this book, because they're all going to the same printing condition, and we set InDesign's CMYK working space to the profile that describes that printing condition. Our CMYK profile is about 2.8 MB, so by not embedding it in each and every image, we saved a huge amount of disk space and FTP transmission time. The CMYK numbers are unambiguous, because they're governed by the working space profile for the InDesign document.

By the same token, we don't embed profiles in images destined for the Web. The very few Web browsers that pay any attention to embedded profiles assume that untagged RGB is sRGB, so we convert our web images to sRGB, then export the image without the profile.

When we work with profiling targets, the whole point of the exercise is to find out what colors the device in question produces when we feed it the numbers in the target, so there's no point in making any assumptions about the appearance represented by the numbers.

Last but not least, if you're working in a closed-loop CMYK workflow, where you just don't want the CMYK numbers to change when sent to your printing process, there's no point in embedding a profile.

In all other situations, we strongly recommend embedding profiles in your images. Doing so lets you convey your color intentions clearly to all the devices and all the people in your workflow. Failure to do so forces the people to guess your intentions, causing extra work and frustration for all concerned.

Proofing Simulations

One of the hardest—and most important—tasks in Photoshop is proofing what your final output will look like on your screen or on a color printer. Photoshop gives you very fine control over both, which we'll talk about in great depth later in this chapter and in Chapter 13, *Image Storage and Output*. Here's the quick version, though:

► The Proof Setup command (in the View menu) gives you full control over on-screen proofing simulations. Proof Setup's simulations are window-specific, so you can simultaneously view the same file in different simulations.

► You can view how different rendering intents will convert an image to a destination space before actually making the conversion.

► You can see how an image prepared for one output process will behave when sent to another without adjustment: This is particularly useful when you're faced with the prospect of repurposing CMYK files made for one printing condition to work with another.

► You can work inside an accurate output simulation to optimize your image for a particular output process.

But to make this magic work, you *must* calibrate and profile your monitor, and it's highly recommended that you take steps to control your viewing environment (see the sidebar "Creating a Consistent Environment").

Photoshop and the Monitor

In the days of film, when you could find out what the color should look like by looking at the film on a light table (assuming that the film was available), you could argue that monitor profiling and calibration was in the "nice but not essential" category. But with the advent of digital capture, the monitor is the first place where the image comes into existence in any meaningful way, so monitor calibration becomes an absolute mission-critical necessity!

When you work in any space except monitor RGB, Photoshop uses the monitor's profile to transform the data on the fly as it gets sent to the video card so that the monitor displays the color correctly. The great benefit of this approach is that it makes it possible for people using very different monitors on different platforms to view the same image virtually identically.

Remember: Photoshop displays *everything* through your monitor profile. If the profile doesn't describe the real behavior of your monitor accurately, everything you see, and hence everything you do to your images, will be off by a little or a lot, depending on how inaccurate the profile is.

Tip: If You Just Want to Go by the Numbers. It's possible to do good work with Photoshop using an uncalibrated, uncharacterized monitor—you just can't trust what you see on the screen. If you want to simply go by the numbers—reading the RGB levels and the CMYK dot percentages—you can use the Info palette to check your color and simply ignore what you see on the monitor. Even with a calibrated monitor, it's usually a good idea to check those numbers anyway.

If you aren't concerned with the monitor appearance, open Color Settings, pull down the RGB menu in the Working Spaces section, and choose Monitor RGB. We don't advocate this—we much prefer being able to work visually—but it is possible, particularly if you're working in a closed-loop environment where you always go to the same output conditions. Of course, if you do this, you may as well ignore the rest of this chapter....

But to make this magic happen for you, you need an accurate profile for each monitor, and you need to let Photoshop know which profile it should use for the monitor. To display color accurately, Photoshop needs to know how your monitor behaves—what color white it produces, what sort of tonal response it has, and what actual colors it produces when it's fed pure R, G, or B. Photoshop gets all its information about the monitor from the display profile. If you want the color on your monitor to be accurate, you *must* have a customized ICC profile that accurately describes the behavior of your monitor.

Evaluating Your Monitor

Monitors lose brightness over time, and eventually they simply wear out. Long before the menu bar is burned into the screen, the monitor has lost so much of its brightness range that it probably can't be accurately calibrated to ideal settings.

Calibration utilities work by selectively *reducing* the brightness of the red, green, and blue channels (making them dimmer). So when you calibrate your monitor, the first thing you'll notice is that it's not as bright as it was in its original uncalibrated state. If it wasn't very bright to begin with, it's a problem.

Here's our simple rule of thumb: turn the contrast control all the way up. If the monitor is brighter at that setting than you like, it's a worthwhile candidate for hardware calibration. If it isn't as bright as you'd like, it's a candidate for replacement—it's only going to get dimmer over time, and you'll find it very difficult to bring it to a specific white point. You can still get some life out of the monitor by running it in its raw state and simply profiling that state, but it won't last forever.

Creating a Consistent Environment

Three factors combine to produce the sensation we describe as color: the object, the light source that illuminates that object, and the observer. You are the observer, and your color vision is subject to subtle changes brought on by things as disparate as age, diet, mood, and how much sleep you've had. There isn't a lot you can do about those, and their effects are relatively minor, but it's good to bear them in mind because they make the phenomenon of color very subjective. The other factors that affect your color vision are, fortunately, easier to control.

Lighting. Consistent lighting is vital if you want to create a calibrated system. In the United States, color transparencies and print proofs are almost always evaluated using light with a controlled color temperature of 5000 Kelvins (K). In Europe and Asia, 6500 K is the standard—it's a little more blue. (Strictly speaking, the relevant standards—D50 and D65—are daylight curves that aren't absolutely identical to the black-body radiation described by the Kelvin scale, but for most practical purposes they're interchangeable.)

You need to provide a consistent lighting environment for viewing your printed output; otherwise the thing you're trying to match—the original image or the final output—will be constantly changing. You can go whole hog and install D50 lighting everywhere, bricking up any offending windows in the process, but for most of us that's impractical. But you can situate your monitor so that it's shielded from direct window light, turn off room lights for color-critical evaluations, and use a relatively inexpensive 4700 K Solux desk lamp for evaluating photographs and printed material. Be careful, though—many D50 lamps require a special fixture to avoid overheating, because the unwanted wavelengths are reflected through the back of the lamp into the fixture.

Theoretically, the ideal working situation is a low ambient light (almost dark) environment. This maximizes the apparent dynamic range of the monitor and ensures that no stray light is distorting your color perception. However, some shops that have tried this have noted a significant drop in the productivity of the employees forced to work in dark windowless rooms, so go as far toward approaching that ideal as you feel is reasonable.

Consistency is much more important than the absolute color temperature of the light source— the variations we've measured in the color temperature of viewing booths at various commercial printers are strong evidence of that. If you work in a studio with a skylight and floor-to-ceiling windows, the color of the light will change over the course of the day, and hence so will your perception of color. In a situation like that, you really need to create an area where you can view prints and transparencies under a light source that's shielded from the ambient light.

A hood to shield the monitor from stray reflections is also very worthwhile—a cardboard box spray-painted matte black may not be elegant, but it's every bit as effective as more expensive solutions, and doesn't distort the color the way most antiglare shields do.

Context. Your color perception is dramatically affected by surrounding colors. Again, you can go to extremes and paint all your walls neutral gray. (Bruce wound up doing this because his office was painted pale pink when he first moved in, and he found that it was introducing a color cast into almost everything— including his dreams.)

It's easier and more important, however, to make your desktop pattern a neutral, 50-percent gray. Pink-marble, green-plaid, or family-snapshot desktop patterns may seem fun and harmless, but they'll seriously interfere with your color judgment. We also recommend not wearing Hawaiian shirts when you're making critical color judgments. Designer black, you'll be happy to know, is just great.

You also have to maintain your monitor profile. Monitors drift over time, though LCDs tend to drift much more slowly than CRTs, so a profile that was accurate when it was created may not be accurate a week, a month, or a year later. In theory, there are two distinct ways to compensate for monitor drift.

▶ You can create a new profile regularly, a process technically known as *characterization*.

▶ You can adjust the behavior of the monitor regularly to bring its behavior into agreement with the behavior described by the profile, a process called *calibration*.

In practice, most monitor profiling tools do both, and make no clear distinction between the two. The practical distinction boils down to the aim points you choose, and the reasons for preferring one approach over the other stem entirely from the features offered by the monitor.

How White Are Your Whites?

For several years, we advocated calibrating monitors to a white point of D50 and a gamma of 1.8 to match the proofing illuminant and dot gain of the commercial printing industry. Hard lessons taught by bitter experience made us back away from that recommendation.

It's very difficult for a CRT monitor to achieve satisfactory brightness when calibrated to a D50 white point, because the blue phosphors are the most efficient of the three, and calibrating to D50 invariably involves turning down the blue channel. Often, the result is a monitor that looks dingy and yellow. Our eyes respond to brightness in a quite non-linear way, and when the brightness of the monitor is too low (below about 75 candelas/m^2) we see yellow instead of white.

But even with LCD displays that can produce a blindingly bright D50, a second problem seems to arise when you attempt to compare an image on the monitor side-by-side with hard copy in a D50 light box. We've been able to achieve close matches, but we've also noted that the highlights on the monitor tend to appear redder than those of the hard copy, even when both monitor and light box are calibrated to D50 and balanced to the same level of illumination.

We haven't yet heard a technical explanation of this phenomenon that completely satisfies us (and we're not sure we'd understand one anyway), but we've experienced it ourselves, and we've heard enough reports from others that we believe it's a real issue. Part of the explanation may be that, while a theoretically ideal D50 illuminant produces a continuous spectrum, both the lamps in light boxes and the phosphors in monitors produce spiky, discontinuous output that's con-

Calibration Parameters

Monitor profiling packages typically ask for the following parameters:

▶ White luminance: the brightness of pure white on the monitor, specified in candelas per square meter (cd/m^2), or foot-lamberts.

▶ White point: the color of monitor white, specified either in Kelvins or as a daylight temperature such as D50 or D65 (see the sidebar, "How White Are Your Whites?"). For practical monitor calibration purposes, you can treat 5000 K and D50, or 6500K and D65, as interchangeable.

▶ The tone response curve, usually specified as a gamma value.

Some packages also let you set a separate black luminance value, but only for CRT displays—LCD displays have a fixed contrast ratio, so the black luminance depends entirely on the white luminance.

Display Adjustments

The ability to calibrate a display depends on the controls that can affect its behavior. You can calibrate any display by changing the lookup tables

---

centrated in fairly narrow bands. There are many different combinations of wavelengths that produce the tristimulus values that add up to a D50 white point.

Bruce believes that there's also a perceptual effect in play. One of the well-documented tricks our eyes play on us is something called "discounting the illuminant"—if we look at a red apple under red light, we still see it as red rather than white, because we know it's red, and we discount the red light. But when we look at a monitor, we can't discount the illuminant because the image *is* the illuminant!

One solution is to separate the monitor and the light box—Bruce has taken to working with the monitor in front of him and the light box behind him, switching from one to the other—which seems to resolve the problem in large part. Interestingly enough, though, others have reported that calibrating the monitor to D65 rather than D50 creates a much better match with a D50 light box.

Another factor that nudges us towards D65 and away from D50 is that, whenever we measure the color temperature of daylight within a thousand meters of sea level, we invariably find that it's much closer to D65 than to D50. Our eyes seem to adapt easily to a D65 monitor white.

Obviously this subject needs a great deal more research, but we've come to the conclusion that it makes more sense to calibrate the monitor to D65 than to D50. Most LCD displays have a native D65 white point anyway, so for LCDs, just use the native white point. If you're happy with a D50 monitor white, don't fix what isn't broken; but if you're running into any of the aforementioned issues, we strongly recommend that you try D65 instead.

in the video card that drives the display, but the glaring weakness in this approach is that all current video card lookup tables (LUTs) are 8 bits per channel. As you'll learn in the next chapter, whenever you edit an 8-bit-per-channel image you end up with fewer levels than you had when you started, and the same holds true for tweaking the video card LUT.

Some displays allow you to make adjustments that change their behavior in the display itself, avoiding the losses inherent in tweaking the 8-bit video card lookup tables. With those displays, it makes sense to calibrate to a specific white point and/or gamma value.

Other displays, including most but not all LCD displays, have no physical adjustments other than the brightness of the backlight. With this type of display, it makes the most sense to profile their native unadjusted behavior, and let the color management system—which typically uses 20 bits per channel instead of the video card LUT's 8 bits—do the work of correcting the displayed colors.

CRT Monitors. CRT monitors are pretty much an orphaned technology now. Sadly, the high-end CRTs such as the Sony Artisan and the Barco Reference Calibrator have been discontinued. Manufacture of high-end CRT displays has largely ceased.

But there are still plenty of CRTs in good working order out in the field (Bruce hopes to get at least another year out of his Sony Artisan). Most CRT displays allow separate control over the RGB guns. (Some only let you control two of the three, in which case the master gain control, usually labeled "Contrast," controls the third.)

With CRT displays, we recommend adjusting the RGB gains to achieve the desired white point and target luminance. The gamma value, however, can only be achieved by adjusting the video card LUT. If the profiling package offers native gamma as an option, use it. Otherwise we recommend choosing gamma 2.2, because it's closer to the native gamma of CRT displays than any of the other likely choices, and hence involves the smallest tweaks to the video card LUT.

Basic LCD monitors. Most current LCD monitors, including the Apple Cinema Displays, allow only one adjustment, which is the brightness of the backlight. On these types of displays, it makes sense to set the brightness to a comfortable level (bearing in mind that, as with CRT monitors, the higher you set the white luminance, the faster you'll wear out the display), then just profile the monitor at its native white point and gamma. If the software forces you to choose an explicit gamma value, use gamma 2.2.

High-end LCD monitors. Some high-end LCD monitors—notably the EIZO FlexScan and ColorEdge series—contain their own lookup tables, independent of the video card, with 10, 12, or even 14 bits of precision. The extra bits don't let the monitor display more colors—the OS pipeline through which applications communicate with the display is only 8 bits per channel wide—but they do let you calibrate the display to a specific white point and gamma without incurring the losses inherent in doing so in the 8-bit video card LUT. For these displays, we recommend a white point of D65, native gamma if it's an option, and gamma 2.2 if it isn't.

LED-backlit monitors. Just to confuse matters, there's a new kid on the block. LED-backlit monitors use arrays of red, green, and blue LEDs for the backlight instead of a fluorescent tube. Since the colors are produced independently, you can adjust the white point by varying the strength of the red, green, and blue LEDs.

This type of display typically also has its own internal 12-bit (or higher) LUT. We prefer profiling the native tone response of the display when the profiling software lets us do so, but we typically use gamma 2.2 when it doesn't.

This type of display is just starting to appear on the market. (Bruce is typing these words on a hand-built pre-production model of the NEC/Mitsubishi 2180 WG. The WG stands for Wide Gamut, and they ain't kidding!) These displays will likely be expensive for the next couple of years, but we expect them eventually to replace fluorescent-backlit LCDs for serious imaging work—they're brighter and have much larger gamuts than fluorescent-backlit displays can produce.

Profiling Tools

If you're serious about working visually with Photoshop (rather than just going by the numbers), a profiling package that includes a hardware measurement device is highly recommended. (Bruce wanted to say "essential," but David persuaded him to take the softer line.) Various eyeball-based profiling utilities (such as Adobe Gamma) are available, but they have two major drawbacks:

▶ Most are designed for CRT displays, and don't do a good job of estimating the tonal response of LCD displays.

▶ They use the user's eyeballs as the measurement device. Our eyes are highly adaptable, which is great for a mammal living on planet Earth, but distinctly suboptimal when the goal is to return the monitor to a known state. Because human eyes involuntarily and uncontrollably adapt to the current ambient lighting conditions, they aren't accurate enough for consistent color.

Colorimeters and spectrophotometers have none of the eye's wonderful adaptability, so they always produce the same answer when fed the same stimulus. For monitor calibration and profiling, that's a big advantage!

However, if you must use eyeball-based tools, these guidelines may help improve the results:

▶ Don't try to use Adobe Gamma on LCD displays. It was designed for CRT monitors, and the mechanism it uses for estimating gamma doesn't work at all well on LCD monitors.

▶ Minimize your eyes' adaptability by profiling under the same lighting conditions each time you make a profile. Ideally, the monitor should be the brightest thing in your field of view. (This is always true, but it's particularly critical during profiling—see the sidebar "Creating a Consistent Environment," earlier in this chapter.)

▶ Give the display at least a half-hour warm-up time before profiling.

▶ Many eyeball-based profiling tools take an existing profile as their starting point. Often, if you take an existing display profile built with the eyeball-based tool as your starting point, the end result is very bad indeed. Start with a known good profile—see "Bad Monitor Profiles," later in this chapter.

A good many users are still reluctant to spend money on display profiling hardware and software. If you don't care how the image looks on the monitor and you're happy to just go by the numbers, you don't really need a custom monitor profile or the gear to build one. In all other cases, and especially if you're shooting digital cameras, trying to save money by doing eyeball calibration and profiling is a classic example of being penny wise and pound (or euro?) foolish. As with most things, you tend to get what you pay for with monitor profiling tools, but even the least expensive instrumented package will return more accurate and more consistent results than any of the visual tools.

Setting Aim Points

Use the capabilities of your monitor as a guide in setting aim points for calibration. The goal is to change the video card LUT as little as possible so that you get the full 256 shades per channel that the OS allows you to send to the monitor.

Aim points and the working space. We should make it abundantly clear that the white point and gamma of your display are entirely independent of the white point and gamma of your RGB working space. The color management system translates working space white point and gamma scamlessly to that of your display. The goal in setting white point and gamma for the display is simply to make the display behave as well as it can.

White luminance. The trade-off in setting the white luminance is that you want it high enough to be comfortable, but low enough to avoid wearing out the display prematurely. If a display can't reach 75 cd/m² after profiling, it's a candidate for replacement. LCD displays are typically much brighter than CRTs, but overdriving them will wear them out just like CRTs. A reasonable rule of thumb is to set the luminance at about 80 percent of full power (less if it appears too bright), until that setting becomes too dim. Then you can crank it up while starting to shop for a replacement.

Reasonable starting points are around 80-95 cd/m² for CRTs, and around 120 cd/m² for LCDs (though if the display can produce a much higher luminance, you may want to set it higher).

Target white point. On displays with genuinely adjustable white points—which means CRTs and a very few exotic LCDs at this point—we recommend adjusting the display to a D65/6500K white point. See the sidebar, "How White Are Your Whites?" for our detailed rationales for doing so. Some combinations of profiling package and display let the profiling package control the display's internal controls via a DDC (Display Data Channel) connection, either through a separate USB connection or through the monitor cable itself. Besides being easier than adjusting the display through the front panel, DDC connections often allow the profiling package to make finer adjustments than the front-panel interface allows.

If the white point isn't adjustable in the display itself, as is the case with most LCD displays, we recommend profiling with the native white point—it's usually very close to D65 anyway.

Target gamma. With those profiling packages that allow it, we generally prefer to use native gamma as the aim point. Sometimes this is a hidden feature—for example, the Sony Artisan software in Expert mode lets you enter "---" (three dashes) to use the display's native gamma.

If native gamma isn't an option, we use gamma 2.2 for CRT displays. LCD displays are a bit more complicated—the tonal response curve of an LCD display doesn't really match a gamma curve. With most LCD displays and most profiling packages, if forced to choose a gamma value, we'll use gamma 2.2.

Perhaps in recognition of the fact that LCDs don't really follow a gamma curve, some profiling packages now offer more exotic tone response curves. With "standard" LCD displays that don't have their own internal LUTs, we still prefer using native gamma if possible, but if that isn't an option, or if you're using a display with internal LUTs that the profiling software can address, we encourage you to investigate these options. We've obtained good results using the L* curve in Integrated Color Solutions' BasICColor Display and the DICOM curve in Mitsubishi/NEC's Spectraview II.

Bad Monitor Profiles

There's one further gotcha. A fairly large number of users wind up creating profiles with Adobe Gamma or Display Calibrator that turn all colors in Photoshop into a psychedelic mess. If accepting the situation and calling it art works for you, fine. Otherwise, start over. The problem is almost invariably caused by starting out with a bad profile. Pick a known good profile like sRGB or Apple RGB as the starting point, and repeat the whole exercise. This time it should work.

Also, if your monitor profile is invisible to Photoshop, it's probably bad—Photoshop rejects monitor profiles with white points that cannot reasonably be interpreted as white. We haven't seen this happen with any of the current versions of the popular profiling packages, but that doesn't mean it can't happen!

Color Settings

Once you've created a custom monitor profile, it's time to get to the meat of Photoshop's built-in color controls. The Color Settings dialog box (from the Edit menu, or press Command-Shift-K) is color central, letting you set up working spaces and color management policies for RGB, CMYK, and grayscale images. It also lets you tell Photoshop what you want to do about missing or mismatched profiles. You can choose each of these settings individually or just use one of the presets, which then makes all the choices for you (customizing the settings is more powerful, of course). If you click the More Options button, Photoshop expands the dialog box to let you change the color engine (CMM) and the default rendering intent for conversions, as well as a few more esoteric controls we'll discuss later in this section, and makes the full lists of installed profiles and presets available.

Color Settings Presets

The Settings menu at the top of the Color Settings dialog box lets you load presets to configure Color Settings with a single menu command that sets working spaces, policies, and warnings for you (see Figure 5-4). Presets are a reasonable place to start, but if you've gotten this far into this chapter, you're obviously the kind of person who believes presets are made to be overwritten.

Figure 5-4
Color Settings presets

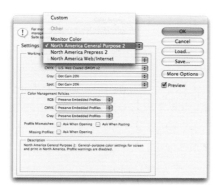

Color Settings Presets short list

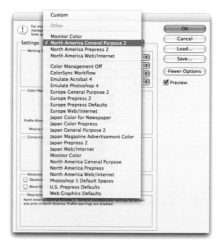

Color Settings Presets with More Options selected

The real power of the Settings popup menu isn't what ships with Photoshop, but rather the fact that you can save your own settings to disk and then recall them quickly later. Even better, while you can always load a Color Settings preset from anywhere on your hard drive (using the Load button), if you save your settings in the right place, they become available from the Presets popup menu. (On Mac OS X, the "right place" is inside the Library/Application Support/Adobe/Color/Settings folder; on Windows, it's inside Program Files/Common Files/Adobe/Color/Settings.)

Saving presets that appear on the Settings menu offers an easy way to configure Photoshop for an entire workgroup. And if you own the entire Creative Suite, you can even synchronize the color settings to the same preset across all the CS applications using the Creative Suite Color Settings command (press Command-Shift-K, just like in Photoshop) from Bridge's Edit menu.

The presets that Adobe offers fall into two broad categories: those that ignore color management, and those that use it. As you can probably guess, we fall squarely into the "use it" camp.

General Purpose 2. First introduced in Photoshop CS, the three General Purpose 2 presets (North American, Europe, and Japan) are Adobe's latest attempt to simplify color management (though Bruce was heard to mutter something about "rearranging deck chairs on the *Titanic*"). They set the RGB working space to sRGB; they set the CMYK working space to U.S. Web Coated (SWOP) v.2 (North American), Euroscale Coated v2 (Europe), or Japan Color 2001 Coated (Japan); they set the Gray working space to Dot Gain 20%; and they set all the policies to Preserve Embedded Profiles while disabling the missing profile and profile mismatch warnings.

In all fairness, these presets are an improvement over the General Purpose Default settings that first appeared in Photoshop CS, in that they now preserve embedded profiles for all color modes (which means you see the image displayed the same way it was when it was last saved), and they no longer use a different default rendering intent than all the other presets. The default rendering intent for all the Photoshop CS2 presets is relative colorimetric with Black Point Compensation.

Monitor Color. As its name suggests, Monitor Color loads your monitor profile as the RGB working space, and essentially tells Photoshop not to use color management, setting all the policies to Off (we discuss the meaning of policies later in this chapter). It treats all your documents as though they are in the working space for that color mode, ignoring any embedded profiles. For some inexplicable reason, though, it turns on the Profile Mismatch—Ask When Opening warning, which makes no sense since the profile will be ignored anyway.

Web/Internet. If you work *exclusively* for the Web, the new Web/Internet presets (one each for North America, Europe, and Japan) may be quite useful. The Web is, of course, the same in Japan as it is in North America or Europe—the only difference between the three presets is the CMYK working space, which is U.S. Web Coated (SWOP) v2 for North America, Japan Color 2001 Coated for Japan, and Europe ISO Coated FOGRA27 for Europe.

The dangerous aspect of the Web/Internet presets is that they set the policy for RGB to Convert to Working RGB. That's probably okay if all your work is destined for the Web, but since it automatically converts every RGB file to sRGB, you'll be unhappy when larger-gamut RGB images destined for print get squashed into sRGB with no intervention on your part!

Prepress 2. The three prepress settings—Europe, Japan, and U.S. Prepress 2—tell Photoshop to use color management wherever possible, and to give you as much feedback as possible about missing and mismatched profiles. They differ only in their choice of CMYK profiles and the dot gain for grayscale and spot colors (20 percent in the U.S., and 15 percent in Europe and Japan). If your work is destined for a printing press and you don't have a custom profile for your printing or proofing conditions, one of these choices may be a good starting point.

The North America and Japan Prepress 2 presets are identical to the prepress defaults that shipped with Photoshop CS. The Europe Prepress 2 preset uses the Europe ISO Coated FOGRA27 CMYK profile as the CMYK working space instead of the older Euroscale Coated v2, which unlike the new profile wasn't readily tracable to any standardized printing condition, so we have to consider it an improvement.

Extra Presets

When you click the More Options button in Color Settings, you gain access to all the presets that ship with Photoshop CS2—not just the ones designed for your region—and if you upgraded from a previous version of Photoshop, you'll see all the old presets from the previous version too. Most of the older presets had flaws, but some are downright dangerous.

Color Management Off. As its name suggests, Color Management Off tells Photoshop not to use color management, setting all the policies to Off (again, we discuss the individual policies later in this chapter). It treats all your documents as though they are in the working space for that color mode, ignoring any embedded profiles. It also loads your display profile as the RGB working space, so it could reasonably be called "Emulate Correctly Configured Photoshop 4," but since hardly anyone ever configured color correctly in Photoshop 4, we won't quibble.

Emulate Photoshop 4. Choosing Emulate Photoshop 4 is like reminiscing about the good old days, back when life was simpler. Somehow we always forget all the terrible aspects of the "good old days." This option ignores color management for the most part, setting different working spaces for RGB, CMYK, and grayscale (it uses Apple RGB as the working space on the Mac, and sRGB as the RGB working space on Windows). If you're in a strictly-by-the-numbers all-CMYK print, or all-RGB Web workflow, and you're firmly convinced that color management has nothing to offer, this option might make sense. (But then why are you reading this chapter?) Even then, however, with a decent monitor profile Color Management Off is a better alternative.

ColorSync Workflow. Macintosh users have one more option: ColorSync Workflow. This sets the ColorSync Default Profiles as the RGB, CMYK, and Gray working spaces. Since Tiger (Mac OS 10.4) has no mechanism for setting default ColorSync profiles, this option is rendered useless under Tiger, and we tended to avoid it under earlier OS versions because it set the Engine to the Apple CMM rather than Adobe's ACE, which we prefer.

Presets Are Only Starting Points

If you've read this far, the odds are that none of the Color Settings presets is ideal for you, so don't be afraid to customize them and create your own settings. The following sections deal with the individual settings in the Color Settings dialog box that are likely candidates for customization.

The RGB Working Space

So what are these strange things, the RGB working spaces, that you choose from the Color Settings RGB menu? They're arbitrary, device-independent RGB spaces. Some real techno-geeks will quibble with applying the term "device-independent" to an RGB space, preferring to reserve the term for purely synthetic perceptually based color spaces like CIE Lab. To those folks, we suggest that while a useful distinction can be made between perceptually based spaces and RGB spaces, that distinction does not revolve around device independence. Photoshop's RGB working spaces don't depend on the vagaries of any given piece of hardware, so we feel it's truthful to call them "device-independent RGB."

Why Use RGB Working Spaces?

The RGB working spaces built into Photoshop are designed to provide a good environment for editing images. As such, they have two important properties that aren't shared by the vast majority of device spaces.

▶ **Gray balance.** The working spaces are gray-balanced, meaning simply that equal amounts of R, G, and B always produce a neutral gray. This is hardly ever the case with device (scanner, camera, display, printer) spaces. Since one of the easiest ways to bring color into line is to find something that should be neutral, and make it so, gray balance is an extremely useful property.

▶ **Perceptual uniformity.** The working spaces are approximately perceptually uniform, meaning that changing the numeric values in the image by the same increment results in about the same degree of visual change, no matter whether it's in the highlights, the midtones, the shadows, the pastels, or the saturated colors. Again, device spaces generally don't work that way.

All color space conversions entail some data loss, but the conversion from capture (camera or scanner) to working space is, in our experience, invariably worthwhile, and when it's done in 16-bit/channel mode, the loss is so trivial it's just about undetectable. Even in 8-bit/channel mode, you're likely to produce much better results editing in a working space rather than a device space.

Why not just use Lab? After all, Lab is by design a device-independent, perceptually uniform color space. But Lab has at least two properties that make it less than ideal as a standard editing space.

First, Lab is pretty nonintuitive when it comes to making color corrections—small adjustments to a* and b* values often produce large changes in unexpected directions. A bigger problem, however, is that Lab, by definition, contains all the colors you can see, and as a corollary, it also contains many "colors" you can't see.

When we use eight bits per channel to represent this whole range of color, the distance from one value to the next becomes large—uncomfortably large, in fact. And since any real image from a scanner or digital camera contains a much smaller range of color than Lab represents, you wind up wasting bits on colors you can't capture, display, print, or even see. If you work with 16-bit-per-channel images, the gamut problem is much less of an issue, but editing in Lab is still not particularly friendly, and conversions from capture space to Lab generally involve more data loss due to quantization error than the conversion to RGB working spaces.

Choosing an RGB Working Space

The main difference between RGB working spaces is the gamut size—the range of color that they can represent. You may think you should just choose the largest gamut available so that you'll be sure of encompassing the gamuts of all your output processes, but (as is almost always the case in digital imaging) there's a trade-off involved—at least if you're using 8-bit-per-channel images.

As we explained in Chapter 3, *Image Essentials*, RGB images are made up of three grayscale channels, in which each pixel has a value from 0 to 255. This holds true for every 24-bit RGB image, irrespective of the working space it lives in. If you choose a very large-gamut space, the 256 possible data values in each channel are stretched to cover the entire gamut—the larger the gamut, the further apart each value is from its neighbors.

The practical implication is that you have less editing headroom in a large-gamut space than you do in a small one: When you edit images, you invariably open up gaps in the tonal range as levels that were formerly adjacent get stretched apart. In a small-gamut space, the jump from level 126 to level 129 may be visually insignificant, whereas in a larger space, you'll get obvious banding rather than a smooth transition.

The simplest option is to settle on a single RGB editing space for all your work, but you may wish to use a larger space for 48-bit images than you do for 24-bit ones, or a larger space for digital captures than for film scans. In a service bureau environment, you'll have to support all sorts of RGB spaces—which is easy in Photoshop CS2—in which case the default working space should simply be the one you use most.

That said, we've probably been guilty in the past of overstating the dangers of large-gamut working spaces. If you're working with legacy images that have already been edited in a small-gamut space, or JPEG digital captures, there's no good reason to convert them to a larger space, and if you do you may encounter some of the aforementioned issues. But if you work with scans from modern scanners, or raw captures from today's digital cameras, large-gamut spaces are not only safe, but may be needed to do full justice to the image. Bruce has been using ProPhoto RGB, which has a very large gamut indeed, for almost all his work for the past seven years, and has found that images are no more likely to fall apart in ProPhoto RGB than in smaller spaces.

Gamut Size Revisited

The naive presumption is that since RGB spaces are bigger than CMYK, they can hold all the CMYK colors we can print. That's not really the case. RGB color spaces all have a characteristic three-dimensional shape, where maximum saturation happens at fairly high luminance levels. Print spaces have a different characteristic gamut shape, where maximum saturation is reached at lower luminances. If you bear in mind that you increase RGB saturation by adding light, and you increase print saturation by adding ink, this makes perfect sense.

Two-dimensional gamut plots disguise this fact, which is why they can be seriously misleading. Three-dimensional gamut plots make the relationships between gamuts much clearer. Figure 5-5 shows three views of Adobe RGB and U.S. Sheetfed Coated v2 CMYK plotted in three dimensions. The differences in size are obvious, but note the difference in shape.

In fact, Adobe RGB (1998) just barely contains the gamut of U.S. Sheetfed Coated v2 except for the saturated CMYK yellow, which lies just outside the gamut of Adobe RGB (1998). So if your primary concern is with press output, Adobe RGB (1998) may be a safe choice of working space.

For inkjet printing printing, however, Adobe RGB (1998) may be on the small side. Figure 5-6 shows Epson Ultrachrome inks (the inks found in

Figure 5-5
3D gamut plots

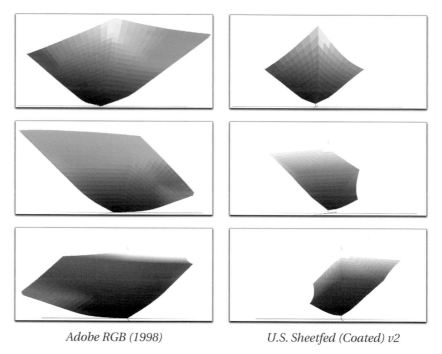

Adobe RGB (1998)   *U.S. Sheetfed (Coated) v2*

the Epson Stylus Photo 2200, 4000, 7600 and 9600 printers) on Premium Luster paper, plotted as a solid against Adobe RGB as a wireframe. Adobe RGB clips a huge chunk of the yellow-orange range, a significant chunk of saturated darker greens and blues, and a tiny bit of magenta-red. The pigmented Ultrachrome inks have a smaller gamut than the dye-based inks found in many inkjet printers, so this illustration is conservative.

Adobe RGB is the largest of the four "recommended" RGB working spaces that appear, along with Monitor RGB, in the RGB working space menu when Color Settings is opened with More Options turned off. Figure 5-7 shows Apple RGB, Colormatch RGB, and sRGB plotted against U.S. Sheetfed Coated v2.

Figure 5-6
Adobe RGB and
Epson Ultrachrome

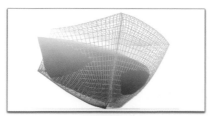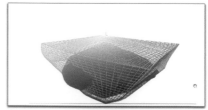

Epson Ultrachrome (solid) and Adobe RGB (wireframe). Note the significant degree to which Adobe RGB clips the yellow-oranges, greens, and blues.

Figure 5-7
Working RGBs and
U.S. Sheetfed Coated v2

Apple RGB

Colormatch RGB

sRGB

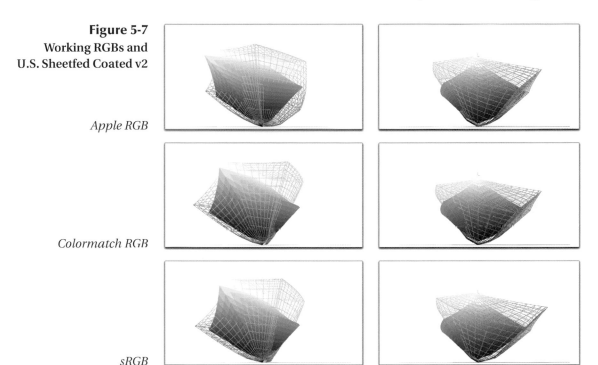

All three of the smaller spaces clip U.S. Sheetfed Coated v2 to a significant degree, though Colormatch clips the least. Needless to say (but we'll say it anyway), if the color can't be represented in the source space (in this case, working RGB), it won't be present in the output either. Since CMYK inks give us a fairly small box of crayons to play with anyway, we'd prefer to be able to make full use of them without having any of our printable colors clipped by our choice of working space, so we regard Adobe RGB (1998) as the minimum requirement for RGB destined for print. (David uses it even for preparing Web graphics, and then converts to sRGB before exporting the untagged GIF, JPEG, or PNG file.)

Apple RGB and Colormatch RGB are legacy monitor-based spaces whose time has passed. Apple RGB is based on the original Apple 13-inch color monitor—we doubt we could even find a working sample—and Colormatch RGB is based on the almost-as-long-gone Radius Pressview. Unless you have to deal with massive amounts of legacy imagery in one of these spaces, there's really no reason to use either as a working space. Essentially, the two rational choices from the four recommended spaces are sRGB for Web or multimedia images, and Adobe RGB for everything else. Then there's Monitor RGB....

Monitor RGB. When you choose Monitor RGB, Photoshop uses your monitor profile as the RGB working space: It's listed in the RGB Working Space menu as "Monitor RGB–YourMonitorProfileName."

Tip: Check Your Monitor Profile. Photoshop CS2 always displays images through your monitor profile. The only way to find out *which* monitor profile it's using is to look at the Monitor RGB listing in the RGB menu in the Color Settings dialog box; the name of the profile is listed there.

If you choose Monitor RGB, Photoshop displays RGB images by sending the numerical values in the RGB file directly to the video card. It uses the definition of those RGB values supplied by the monitor profile to convert RGB to other color spaces.

The only reason we can think of to choose Monitor RGB as your working space is if you're working exclusively on Web graphics, and you need the RGB color in Photoshop to match the RGB color in non-color-managed applications like Dreamweaver. Using your monitor profile as the working space will ensure that RGB in Photoshop looks exactly the same as RGB in all your non-color-managed applications—unfortunately, it will also ensure that RGB looks different on your machine than it does on everyone else's. (That's why Photoshop introduced the idea of an RGB working space in the first place.)

If you're a Windows user, you'll likely find that the differences between Monitor RGB and sRGB are quite small. Mac users, though, will typically see a bigger difference. Web designers who work on the Mac may want to do most of their work using Monitor RGB, and then convert the final result to sRGB. That way, Windows users will see something close to what was intended, while Mac users who use Safari, or Internet Explorer with ColorSync turned on, will also see something close to the intended color. Mac users who use Netscape will see dark images, but they should be used to that....

On the other hand, many images destined for the Web also end up in print as repurposing becomes increasingly important. That's why David uses the Adobe RGB working space even when he's creating Web graphics. Then he uses Photoshop's soft-proofing controls to see what the image will look like on the Web (see "Soft-Proofing Controls," later in this chapter).

Other RGB Working Spaces

If you turn on the Advanced Mode checkbox in Color Settings, the RGB menu expands to include every RGB profile installed on your machine. In Advanced mode, Photoshop allows you to use any RGB profile as an RGB working space, or even to create your own. Don't go hog-wild with this! Editing in your SuperHamsterScan 9000 Turbo Z profile's space is possible, but it probably won't be perceptually uniform, and, worse, it probably won't be gray-balanced. It's extremely hard to edit images well in a space that isn't gray-balanced, and almost impossible to do so in one that has color crossovers, which many capture profiles do.

However, you may want to consider some working spaces that aren't installed in Photoshop's Recommended folder. You can also define your own RGB working space, in which case you've definitely earned the title of Advanced User, but having already gone down that road, Bruce recommends that you do so only after identifying very specific problems and exhausting all other available solutions.

David likes to keep things simple, and uses Adobe RGB virtually all of the time. Bruce uses different RGB working spaces for different purposes. It isn't absolutely necessary to load these as working spaces in Color Settings—you can always use the Assign Profile command (see "Assign Profile" later in this chapter) to assign a profile other than the working space to an image—but if you're going to be working with a bunch of images in the same space, it makes life slightly easier to load that space as the working space. The following is by no means an exhaustive list, but we've found each of these spaces useful.

ProPhoto RGB. Formerly known as rgbMaster, and before that as ROMM (Reference Output Metric Method) RGB, Kodak's ProPhoto RGB is an extremely wide-gamut RGB space, so wide that its primaries are imaginary—there is no light source that could produce these colors, and we couldn't see them if there was. It needs these extreme primaries to be able to accommodate the dark saturated colors we can readily achieve in print and that get clipped by smaller spaces. It's wide enough that we recommend doing major edits only on high-bit files—small tweaks to 8-bit-per-channel files, however, are safe.

Bruce uses it for most of his work, especially for digital captures converted through Camera Raw. Before he switched from film to digital capture, Bruce was hesitant to make ProPhoto RGB his unequivocally recommended working space for two reasons:

▶ It's slightly less convenient than any of the four recommended spaces, in that you have to press the More Options button in Color Settings before you can choose it from the RGB working space menu.

▶ If you deliver ProPhoto RGB to someone who doesn't use color management correctly, the results will be much worse than if you deliver the color in a smaller space (though the results may still be pretty bad).

With the advent of digital capture, though, a relatively new problem crops up. Digital does a much better job of capturing dark saturated colors than film ever did, and converting digital raw to Adobe RGB or a smaller space often turns the gradations in things like dark green foliage or dark brown wood into solid blobs.

Figure 5-8 shows a relatively innocuous image converted into ProPhoto RGB via Camera Raw, with no saturation boost and only very mild tonal adjustments. Many of the foliage and flower colors lie well outside the gamut of Adobe RGB, and when the image is converted to Adobe RGB or a smaller space, all these out-of-gamut colors get clipped to the gamut boundary, wiping out subtle detail.

With the image converted to ProPhoto RGB, we can maintain the gradations when we optimize the image for print, whether by changing saturation, hue, lightness, or any combination thereof. It's the ability to hold *color difference* that represents detail, rather than the ability to represent ridiculously saturated colors, that drives Bruce to use ProPhoto RGB for all his digital, and much of his film work. The fact that it covers the entire gamut of all his output spaces is simply a nice bonus.

EktaSpace. Developed by photographer Joseph Holmes, EktaSpace is a large-gamut space that's a little more conservative, and hence a little more manageable, than ProPhoto RGB. There's been some debate over whether EktaSpace really covers the entire E6 gamut. Our experiments suggest that, while it may be possible to capture colors in-camera (without resorting to games like exposing the film with a monochromatic laser) that will be clipped by EktaSpace, it's not likely. EktaSpace will hold any colors you're likely to encounter on E6 film that's shot and processed under normal

Figure 5-8
Color spaces and
input clipping

The gamut plots below, produced using Chromix ColorThink, plot color in Lab space. You're looking at a side elevation of the color space, with the Lightness axis running vertically. The a* axis, from red to green, runs almost straight toward you out of the page; the b* axis, from blue to yellow, runs from left to right.

Even an innocuous image like the one at right can contain colors that lie well outside the range that either Adobe RGB (1998) or sRGB can represent.

The image above plotted (as squares) against the color gamut of Adobe RGB (shaded solid)

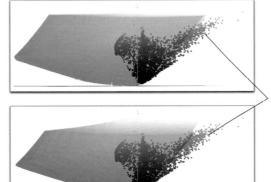

These dark yellows and oranges lie outside the gamut of Adobe RGB or sRGB.

The image above plotted (as squares) against the color gamut of sRGB (shaded solid)

conditions. It's possible to use 8-bit-per-channel images in EktaSpace, but you'll get much more editing headroom with 16-bit files.

Bruce uses EktaSpace for transparency scans when it's important to preserve the characteristics of the individual film stock. He finds it's easier to do this in EktaSpace than in any other space he's tried. You can download it from www.josephholmes.com.

BruceRGB. Unlike both ProPhoto RGB and EktaSpace, BruceRGB is a small-gamut space. Bruce designed it to offer the maximum editing headroom on 8-bit-per-channel images destined for CMYK printing. It's basically a compromise between Adobe RGB (1998), which is a little too big, and ColorMatch RGB, which is too small. It covers most of the gamut of CMYK offset printing and is a reasonable match to most RGB inkjet printers. It clips some cyans and oranges, but not much more so than Adobe RGB.

Nowadays, Bruce uses it only as an "emergency" space, mostly for legacy images that were scanned on flatbed scanners in the early 1990s and then edited to within an inch of their lives. He notes that today's scanners and cameras are so much better than those from 1998, when he developed the space, that he has much less need for BruceRGB. But it still comes in handy for those rare images that simply fall apart in larger spaces. You can define it yourself using the Custom RGB setting (see the next section).

Custom RGB Spaces

If you're a hard-core imaging geek who likes to live dangerously, you can define your own RGB working space. It's not that difficult, because an RGB working space is defined by just three primary xy values for red, green, and blue; a white point; and a gamma value. For example, if you use a high-quality scanning-back digital camera that lets you set the gray balance for each image, you may want to define a working space whose primaries are the same as the camera's, thereby (in theory) ensuring that your working space matches your input device.

To define a custom RGB working space, you first need to click the More Options button in Color Settings. This lets you choose Custom RGB from the RGB menu, which in turn opens the Custom RGB dialog box (see Figure 5-9). Custom RGB allows you to choose a name for your custom space, as well as specify the gamma, the white point, and the primaries. If you're not already intimate with these terms, then you should probably just skip down to "Choosing a CMYK Working Space."

Gamma. The Gamma field lets you enter a value for the gamma of your working space. This is completely independent of your monitor gamma—there's no reason to match your working space gamma to your monitor gamma, and there may be plenty of good reasons not to do so. To oversimplify (the long explanation would be very long), the gamma of the editing space controls the distribution of the bits over the tone curve. Our eyes don't respond in a linear fashion to changes in brightness: A gamma of 2.2 is generally reckoned to be more or less perceptually uniform, so we recommend using that value for your working space gamma. It has the

Figure 5-9
Custom RGB

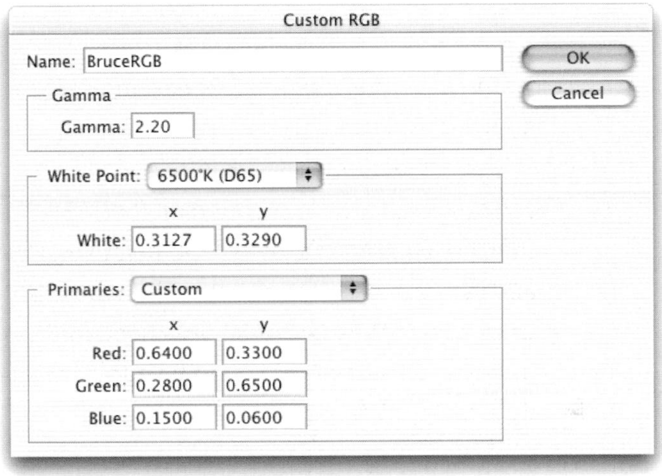

Custom RGB

Name: BruceRGB   OK   Cancel

Gamma
Gamma: 2.20

White Point: 6500°K (D65)
            x   y
White: 0.3127   0.3290

Primaries: Custom
            x   y
Red: 0.6400   0.3300
Green: 0.2800   0.6500
Blue: 0.1500   0.0600

The Custom RGB dialog box lets you define custom RGB working spaces by defining the gamma, white point, and primaries.

added benefit of devoting more bits to the shadows, which is where we find we usually need them during editing.

White Point. This setting defines the white point of the RGB working space. You can choose one of the ten built-in white points, or choose Custom to define a custom white point by entering xy chromaticities (the xy components of a color defined in CIE xyY). As with the gamma setting, the white point of the working space is quite independent of the monitor white point. It's also independent of the output white point. For a variety of reasons, we suggest using D65 as the white point for most RGB spaces. (For a more detailed discussion of white points, see the sidebar "How White Are Your Whites?" earlier in this chapter.) If you use one of the built-in spaces, this setting will be made for you automatically.

Primaries. The Primaries setting lets you choose from the Primaries menu, which contains six sets of phosphor-based primaries for common monitors and three sets of abstract primaries. Or you can enter custom xy values for R, G, and B to set the boundaries of the color gamut.

Tip: Finding the xy Values for Primaries. To find the xy chromaticities of the primaries for a chosen built-in space, first load that space from the RGB menu, and then choose Custom from the Primaries menu. The

Primaries dialog box appears, showing the xy chromaticities for the red, green, and blue primaries. If you wish, you can even plot them on a chromaticity chart like the one in Figure 5-10.

Figure 5-10
xy chromaticities

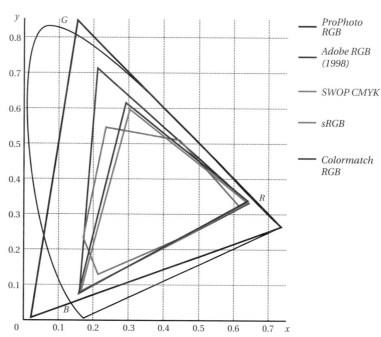

This figure shows the gamuts of several of Photoshop's working RGB working spaces and the gamut of SWOP CMYK, plotted in CIE xyY space. It illustrates the trade-off inherent in choosing an RGB space between clipping the gamut of CMYK and wasting bits on unprintable colors.

For example, here are the settings for BruceRGB:

▶ White point = 6500K

▶ Gamma = 2.2

▶ Red xy = 0.6400 0.3300

▶ Green xy = 0.2800 0.6500

▶ Blue xy = 0.1500 0.0600

Defining custom RGB spaces isn't for the faint of heart, and there are now so many RGB spaces available that relatively few people should need to build their own. But it's always nice to know that you can.

Tip: Custom RGB Settings and ICC Profiles. When you save custom RGB settings, you're actually creating an ICC profile. On Mac OS X, save them in the Library/ColorSync/Profiles folder. On Windows 2000/XP, save profiles in the WinNT/System/Spool/Drivers/Color directory. That way, the profile that describes your RGB working space will be readily available to other ICC-aware applications.

Figure 5-10 shows a chromaticity plot of some of Photoshop's built-in spaces, compared with the chromaticities of SWOP inks. A word of caution: color gamuts are complex three-dimensional objects, and a chromaticity plot is very much an abstraction. We include this figure primarily as a visualization tool to help you get your head around the implications of different RGB primaries, not as an exact comparison of their color gamuts.

RGB Output

It's possible to load an RGB output profile as your working space. This may even seem like a good idea if you're one of the many Photoshop users whose final output is a desktop inkjet printer. But even if you only ever print to an RGB printer, using your RGB output profile as your RGB work-

Mac OS X and Profiles

Mac OS X offers a bewildering variety of places to store profiles. You'll find them in the System/Library/ColorSync/Profiles folder, in the Library/ColorSync/Profiles folder, in the Library/ColorSync/Profiles/Displays folder, in the Library/Application Support/Adobe/Color/Profiles folder, in the Library/Application Support/Adobe/Color/Profiles/Recommended folder, in the Users/UserName/Library/ColorSync/Profiles folder, and in some cases, buried several levels deep in subfolders in the Library/Printers folder.

As David would say with characteristic understatement, "Oy!"

Here's the deal: There are really only three places where you probably want to store profiles.

If you want to make a profile available to everyone who uses the Mac, save it in the Library/ColorSync/Profiles folder. Don't try to put it in the System/Library/ColorSync/Profiles folder—a good rule of thumb is that the only thing that should mess with the OS X System folder is the OS X installer, or a hard-core UNIX geek who is comfortable driving the Mac from the Terminal window.

If you want to make a profile available only to you (or to someone else logged in as you), save it in the Users/YourUser Name/Library/ColorSync/Profiles folder. (If you're the only user, you may as well save all your profiles there.)

If you want to make a profile available from Photoshop's Color Settings dialog box when the Advanced checkbox is unchecked, save it in the Library/Application Support/Adobe/Color/Profiles folder.

ing space is a bad idea. RGB output spaces have two properties that make them very difficult to use as working spaces: They're rarely gray-balanced, and they're far from perceptually uniform.

You may find that you want to make small adjustments to your image after converting it to your RGB printer space, but with a good output profile you can obtain the same results more easily by keeping your image in the working space and using Photoshop's soft-proofing controls to provide an accurate simulation of your output on screen (see "Soft-Proofing Controls," later in this chapter).

To make the actual conversion from the working space to your printer's RGB output space, you have several choices as to where to apply your RGB output profile. (See "Print with Preview" and "Print," later in this chapter.) The one place you *don't* want to use your RGB output profile is as an RGB working space!

Choosing a CMYK Working Space

Unlike RGB working spaces, which may be entirely abstract and not based on any real device, CMYK working spaces always reflect some real combination of ink (or toner, or dye) and paper. The ideal situation is to have a custom ICC profile for the specific CMYK process to which you're printing, but in the real world that's still the exception rather than the rule. However, if you do have a custom ICC profile for your CMYK print process, or for an industry-standard proofing system such as Kodak Approval or Creo Spectrum, click the More Options button and load that profile into the CMYK menu in the Color Settings dialog box.

When Color Settings is in its abbreviated form, your choices of CMYK working space are limited to the press profiles that are installed by Photoshop, plus Custom CMYK, which users of older versions of Photoshop may recognize as the old "Built-in" panel of Photoshop 5's CMYK Setup (what we tend to call "Photoshop Classic"). Mac users also get the option to choose ColorSync CMYK, which with the advent of Tiger (Mac OS 10.4) is hardwired to "Generic CMYK," a profile that represents no printing condition known to mankind and is best ignored—see Figure 5-11.

In the absence of a custom profile, Adobe's press profiles are much, much better than the old Photoshop Classic mechanism. They typically

Figure 5-11
Photoshop's
CMYK profiles

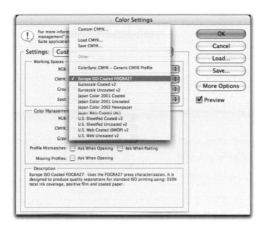

produce smoother gradations and better saturation than the old CMYK Setups, and the ink colors are more accurate.

If you're more comfortable with the old-style Photoshop CMYK setups, they're still available. Choosing Custom CMYK from the CMYK popup menu opens the Custom CMYK dialog box, as shown in Figure 5-12.

Figure 5-12
Custom CMYK

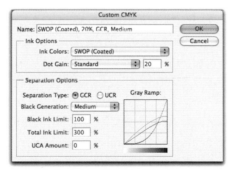

Should You Use Custom CMYK?

Before we get into the details of the Custom CMYK dialog box, a disclaimer is in order. The Custom CMYK feature in Photoshop CS was born at the introduction of CMYK capabilities in Photoshop 2.0 (which shipped in June of 1991, long before "color" and "management" were combined into a scary phrase, and before ColorSync was a twinkle in Apple's eye). The fact that it has persisted in one form or another through all subsequent revisions of Photoshop shows that it's perfectly possible to make great color separations using this mechanism, but nevertheless, terms like "ancient," "weird," and "junk" are more than slightly applicable.

If you're a relatively experienced Photoshop user and you're comfortable with defining CMYK settings this way, we have a few tricks that you may find useful. But if you're relatively new to the world of color and Photoshop, you'd be *much* better off spending your time and ingenuity investigating some of the many packages available for creating and editing ICC profiles (like GretagMacbeth ProfileMaker Pro or Monaco Profiler).

Ultimately, Adobe left Custom CMYK in Photoshop mostly for backward compatibility. ICC profiles are the wave of the future, and if you're at the beginning of your learning curve, you're better off concentrating on those instead. That said, there's still some life in the old dog, and we've even been able to teach it a couple of new tricks!

Editing Custom CMYK

The Custom CMYK dialog box has two sections: Ink Options, which lets you define the colors of your inks and the way they behave on your paper stock; and Separation Options, which lets you tell Photoshop how you want the inks to build color when converting to CMYK. Note that the Custom CMYK mechanism is entirely separate from Photoshop's (or anyone else's) ICC profiles—the SWOP definitions in Custom CMYK, for example, bear only a passing resemblance to those in the U.S. Web Coated (SWOP) v2 profile, or to the current SWOP specification. Custom CMYK is *not* a mechanism for editing ICC profiles!

Ink Colors. The Ink Colors setting tells Photoshop about the color of the inks you'll be using. You can create your own custom ink set or use one of Photoshop's built-in ink sets such as SWOP, Eurostandard, or Toyo, each of which has ink definitions for coated, uncoated, and newsprint stock (see Figure 5-13). The SWOP ink sets differ substantially from the current SWOP spec; but a great many Photoshop users have been using them for years, so you should talk to your commercial printer about which ink definitions to use.

Bear in mind that the built-in ink sets are paper-specific (that is, if you print cyan on a slightly pink paper, it'll look different than if you print it on a slightly blue paper). Unfortunately, no one seems to remember which paper stocks the built-in sets specify. Plus, even though there are rough standards for inks used on web presses, they actually vary widely, and a magenta on the West Coast might be different than one on the East Coast.

Figure 5-13
Preset ink sets

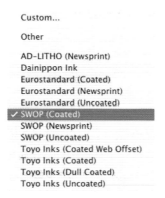

Custom...

Other

AD-LITHO (Newsprint)
Dainippon Ink
Eurostandard (Coated)
Eurostandard (Newsprint)
Eurostandard (Uncoated)
✓ SWOP (Coated)
SWOP (Newsprint)
SWOP (Uncoated)
Toyo Inks (Coated Web Offset)
Toyo Inks (Coated)
Toyo Inks (Dull Coated)
Toyo Inks (Uncoated)

The Ink Colors menu lets you choose one of Photoshop's built-in definitions for ink sets, or choose Custom to define your own.

You can generally produce good results using one of the built-in ink sets. We used to provide directions for measuring inks and plugging the measurements into the Custom Ink Colors dialog box, but quite honestly, if you have an instrument that can measure the inks, you almost certainly have accompanying profiling software that will do a far better job than Custom CMYK ever could, so we strongly recommend biting the bullet and building real profiles instead.

The Ink Colors dialog box (see Figure 5-14) lets you set the CIE xyY or CIE Lab values for the eight progressive colors (cyan, magenta, yellow, black, cyan+magenta, cyan+yellow, magenta+yellow, cyan+magenta+yellow), and the white of the paper stock. The only way to determine these accurately is to measure them from press output with a spectrophotometer, but as noted above, if you have a spectrophotometer, you probably have a profiling package too, so just use it instead.

Figure 5-14
Ink Colors
dialog box

	Y	x	y
C:	26.25	0.1673	0.2328
M:	14.50	0.4845	0.2396
Y:	71.20	0.4357	0.5013
MY:	14.09	0.6075	0.3191
CY:	19.25	0.2271	0.5513
CM:	2.98	0.2052	0.1245
CMY:	2.79	0.3227	0.2962
W:	83.02	0.3149	0.3321
K:	0.82	0.3202	0.3241

☐ L*a*b* Coordinates
☐ Estimate Overprints

Ink Colors

OK
Cancel

The Ink Colors dialog box lets you enter custom xyY or Lab values for your inks, or click the color swatches to open the Color Picker and choose an ink color by eyeball.

In truly dire emergencies, you can eyeball the ink colors. This technique isn't particularly accurate—in fact, it's a kludge—and we only recommend using it as a way to improve the color from desktop four-color inkjet and thermal-wax color printers driven by a CMYK RIP (though in a pinch we might use it for a digital press or direct-to-plate scenario too). It doesn't work with three-color CMY printers, or with inkjets that take RGB data and print through a Quickdraw or GDI driver, or on dye-subs—we've tried. But it doesn't require measuring equipment other than your eyeballs.

You need to print a set of color bars, which you must specify as CMYK colors (don't make them in RGB and then convert). Then, choose Custom from the Ink Colors popup menu to open the Ink Colors dialog box. Clicking on each color swatch opens the Color Picker dialog box. You can then edit each progressive color to match your printed output. Generally, desktop printers use colorants that are purer and more saturated than press inks, so head in that general direction.

Don't expect miracles from this technique—the results you get depend on your monitor calibration, your lighting, and your skill in matching colors by eye. It should get you into the ballpark, but given the amount of work involved and the uncertain quality of the results you get, we recommend that you investigate obtaining, building, or commissioning an ICC profile instead.

Tuning CMYK Previews. If you find that CMYK images don't look right on your screen (that is, they don't match what you're printing), there's a good chance your monitor profile isn't correct. However, if the problem doesn't lie with the monitor profile, you can try to create a custom CMYK ink set just for viewing your images. You can sometimes improve the accuracy of the CMYK Preview by fine-tuning the ink colors, then saving the result with a name that clearly indicates it's only to be used for viewing CMYK, not for creating it. The easiest way to do this is to open the CMYK image or images you're trying to match, make a Duplicate, and use Assign Profile to make it an Untagged CMYK image (see "Assign Profile," later in this chapter). Then go to Color Settings, turn on the Preview checkbox, choose Custom CMYK, choose Custom from the Ink Colors menu, and adjust the Ink Colors until you see the match you want. You may have to wait a second or two for the changes to show up in your image. Again, this technique is a kludge, and is no substitute for a good ICC profile, but in a pinch it can be better than nothing.

Printing to Desktop Printers

If you're one of the growing number of Photoshop users who print exclusively, or mainly, to desktop printers, rest assured that the vast bulk of the material contained in this chapter applies as much to you as it does to those whose printing is done on a commercial press. If you're printing to an inkjet printer, you'll have less variation to worry about on output since inkjet printers are stable, and inkjet inks are generally consistent from batch to batch. True photographic printers such as the Fuji Pictrography and the Durst Lambda also offer much better consistency than any printing press. So in some ways, your task is easier than printing on a press. But in other ways it's more complicated.

The main question you have to answer is whether you drive the printer as an RGB or a CMYK device. Photographic printers are true RGB devices—they expose photosensitive paper using red, green, and blue lasers or LEDs— so the CMYK color mode simply doesn't apply. Inkjet printers use cyan, magenta, yellow, and black inks (plus, sometimes, light cyan, light magenta, and even light black, which we used to know as gray), which in theory at least makes them CMYK devices. But in practice, unless you're printing through a PostScript RIP, desktop inkjet printers function as RGB devices because traditionally, the OS-level graphics languages have lacked any facility for pass-

ing CMYK to printers. Quartz, the graphics engine in Mac OS X, has the theoretical capability to hand off CMYK, but we've yet to see a printer driver that exploits it. Photoshop will let you send CMYK to these printers, but the printer driver will immediately convert it to RGB before doing anything else with it.

A PostScript RIP may seem to allow more control over the printing process by letting you control the individual inks, but that usually isn't the case. PostScript RIPs that use the printer's native screening algorithms usually send RGB to that part of the print process: Those that truly provide ink-level control use their own screening, which usually looks much worse than the printer's native screening. A PostScript RIP makes sense from a workflow standpoint if you're using a desktop printer as a proofer, but if your desktop print is your final output, we recommend using the RGB driver, or a specialized RIP designed for photo output, such as Colorbyte's ImagePrint.

RGB output. If you're printing RGB, you can skip the entire CMYK section in this chapter since it doesn't apply to you. You should, however, read the sections "Choosing an RGB Working Space," "Soft-Proofing Controls," and "Print with Preview" carefully. We recommend using ICC profiles for your printer. If you print us-

ing the printer vendor's inks and papers, the canned profiles that come with the printer work fairly well. If you're using third-party inks and papers, though, a custom profile will improve your output immensely. Inexpensive scanner-based profiling packages such as Monaco EZColor work very well with inkjet printers, and will likely pay for themselves quickly in savings on ink and paper. Don't use your RGB printer profile as an RGB working space, though, because RGB printer spaces aren't gray-balanced or perceptually uniform, making editing difficult. Instead, use a working space such as ProPhoto RGB, and fine-tune your image for output using Proof Setup to create a simulation of the printed output.

CMYK output. If you're printing CMYK through a PostScript RIP, almost everything we say in this chapter about press CMYK applies equally to desktop printers. Ideally, you should use a custom ICC profile for your inks and papers. If you always print using the same inks and paper, consider building a custom profile or commissioning one from one of the many companies and individuals offering such services. Or use some of the techniques we discuss in Custom CMYK to make a custom CMYK space for your printer in Photoshop, especially if you experiment with different inks and paper stocks.

To save this setting, select Save CMYK from the Color Settings CMYK menu. This saves the settings as an ICC profile. Remember to name it something that tells you that it's for viewing only; using this to convert RGB to CMYK could be disastrous. To use this profile for viewing, you'll load it into Proof Setup (see "Proof Setup Dialog Box," later in this chapter). When you're done making it, hit Cancel so you leave the dialog boxes without actually using this new setup.

Using Estimate Overprints for spot inks. The Estimate Overprints checkbox in Custom Ink Colors is primarily useful if you substitute Pantone spot inks (or other inks for which you have known CIE values) for CMYK—you can use Estimate Overprints to see how they'll interact with one another. Be aware that this is a highly experimental procedure, and the strongest possible, closed-track, professional-driver, don't-try-this-at-home caveats apply. But if you're in a situation where you're forced to do a job using spot inks instead of process, loading the spot inks into Custom Ink Colors and using Estimate Overprint will give you at least some idea of what'll happen when you overprint them (see Chapter 10, *Spot Colors and Duotones*). Using Estimate Overprints to save taking four measurements for the various CMY combinations is a very silly idea—the minimal savings of time simply aren't worth it.

Dot gain. When ink hits paper, it smooshes some, bleeds some, and generally "heavies up on press" (even if your "press" is a little desktop printer). That means that your 50-percent cyan halftone spot won't look like 50 percent when it comes off a printing press. It's your responsibility to take this dot gain into account when building your images, and if you don't, your pictures will always appear too dark and muddy. Custom CMYK gives you two methods to compensate for dot gain (see Figure 5-15). The simpler method, entering a single percentage value, is also the less accurate. Using individual dot gain curves for each ink will generally yield better results, but it takes a little more time and effort.

Tip: Where to Adjust Dot Gain. Photoshop automatically compensates for dot gain when it converts images to CMYK for printing. It's much less work to build the dot-gain compensation into the separation process than to try to compensate for it manually on an image-by-image basis. In a pinch, you can make slight compensations for dot gain in an already-

Figure 5-15
Dot gain compensation

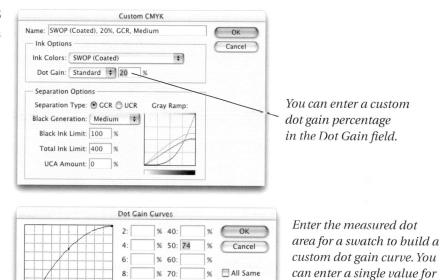

You can enter a custom dot gain percentage in the Dot Gain field.

Enter the measured dot area for a swatch to build a custom dot gain curve. You can enter a single value for the 50-percent dot, or take more measurements to increase accuracy.

separated CMYK file using Curves, but you'll generally get better results going back to the original RGB image, adjusting the dot-gain value in Custom CMYK, and generating a new CMYK file using the new settings. In

Canned vs. Custom Profiles

Canned profiles—profiles supplied by a third party that are based on something other than measurements of your specific device—have earned a bad reputation, often deservedly so. But under the right circumstances, generic ICC profiles can be very useful. It's true that each combination of printing press, ink, and paper is unique. However, virtually all press operators pride themselves on their ability to match a contract proof such as an Imation Matchprint or Fuji ColorArt—if

they couldn't, color printing would be almost impossible.

Proofer profiles. Proofing systems are generally very consistent from shop to shop. This makes them good candidates for canned profiles—stable, repeatable, consistent output processes like contract proofers simply don't need custom profiles. You need to make sure that the profile you choose has the correct ink limits, black generation, and substrate for your job, but as long as you pay attention to these

variables, you can produce excellent results using generic proofer profiles.

Sheetfed press. While sheetfed presses vary a little more than do proofing systems, we've seen excellent results from generic sheetfed press profiles too, providing the paper stock isn't too weird. Bear in mind that the press operator has a great deal of control over the final result—a profile only has to be a reasonable match to the press.

fact, one of the few advantages Custom CMYK has over ICC profiles is the ease with which you can adjust for minor variations in dot gain between different papers.

You'll hear all sorts of numbers bandied about with reference to dot gain, so it's important to be clear about what Photoshop means, and what your service providers mean, by a given dot gain percentage—they're often different (see the sidebar "Dot Gain: Coping with Midtone Spread"). All the built-in ink sets contain default dot gain values, but these shouldn't be considered as much more than a starting point. As we said earlier, the ink sets are paper-specific—the ink colors typically don't vary much from paper stock to paper stock (unless you're printing on puce, lime green, or goldenrod paper), but the dot gain can vary tremendously from one paper to another.

Table 5-1 shows some rough-and-ready numbers for typical dot gain, but they're guidelines, not rules. If you come up with values vastly different from these, double-check your calculations or measurements, reread the sidebar "Dot Gain: Coping with Midtone Spread," and talk to your service providers to make sure that there isn't some misunderstanding. Bear in mind that higher halftone screen frequencies have more dot gain than low ones. The values in the table are based on 133- to 150-line screens with the exception of newsprint, which is based on an 85-line screen.

	Press and stock	Typical dot gain
Table 5-1	Web press, coated stock	17–22%
Dot gain	Sheetfed press, coated stock	12–15%
settings	Sheetfed press, uncoated stock	18–22%
	Newsprint	30–40%
	Positive plates	10–12%

Dot Gain Curves. Single-value dot gains work reasonably well if you're using one of the built-in ink sets—the differential gain for each ink has already been factored in—but Photoshop CS2 offers an easy, unambiguous way to define the anticipated dot gain in the form of the Dot Gain Curves feature.

The only disadvantage to using Dot Gain Curves is that you need to use a densitometer (or a colorimeter or spectrophotometer that can read dot area) to read printed swatches. (You can often piggyback the swatches

Dot Gain: Coping with Midtone Spread

Dot gain is the name given to the tendency for halftone dots to increase in size from film to press. The biggest cause is the ink spreading as it hits the paper—the more absorbent the paper, the greater the dot gain—but some dot gain occurs when the ink is transferred from the ink roller to the blanket roller on press, and some may even creep in when the film is made into plates. Because dot gain makes your images print darker than anticipated, compensating for it is essential.

Photoshop's dot gain is always measured at the 50-percent value, because that's where its effect is greatest. The larger the circumference of the halftone dot, the more it's subject to dot gain; but above 50 percent the dots start to run together, so they don't gain as much. For the same reason, high screen frequencies are more prone to dot gain than low screen frequencies, because there's more circumference to the dots.

The subject of dot gain attracts more than its share of confusion because people measure different things under the name "dot gain." Then, to make matters worse, they have different ways of expressing that measurement.

Photoshop's dot gain. The Photoshop documentation states that Photoshop's dot gain value is the dot gain from film to press. However, since Photoshop also assumes that it's printing to a linearized platesetter—one that will produce a 50-percent dot when asked for one—we think it's less confusing to say that Photoshop's dot gain is really talking about the difference between the digital data and the final printed piece.

Photoshop's reckoning of dot gain is the absolute additive amount by which a 50-percent dot increases. So if a 50-percent dot appears on the print as 72 percent, Photoshop would call this a 22-percent dot gain.

When you ask your printer about the dot gain anticipated for your job, he may give you the gain from color proof to final print. There's a simple way to remove this ambiguity. Ask your printer, "What will happen to the 50-percent dot in my file when it hits the press?" If the response is that it will print as a 78-percent dot, that's 28-percent dot gain as far as Photoshop is concerned, and that's the number you should use for your Dot Gain setting in Custom CMYK.

But Photoshop CS2 offers an even simpler way to remove the ambiguity: just measure the dot area of the 50-percent dot, then simply plug that value into the 50-percent field in Dot Gain Curves—that way, no guesswork or arithmetic is involved.

Who makes the proof? Many service bureaus will sell you a proof such as a Kodak Approval, but it's unlikely that their proofing system is set up to match the press and paper stock on which your job will run. If you give this proof to your printer, he may tell you he can match it, but he's guessing. If the printer makes the proof, there's no guesswork involved, and responsibility is clear.

onto another job by printing them in the trim area, and if you don't have one of these devices, your printer or service bureau probably does.)

Choosing Curves from the Dot Gain popup menu opens the Dot Gain Curves dialog box (see Figure 5-15). It allows you to enter the actual dot values measured from 2, 4, 6, 8, 10, 20, 30, 40, 50, 60, 70, 80, and 90 percent patches for each ink. Measuring all the patches is probably overkill. At a pinch, you can simply measure the 50 percent dot and type in the measured value, but we recommend taking measurements of at least the

4, 6, 8, 10, 40, 50, and 80 percent swatches for each ink. Don't be tempted by the All Same checkbox—it's very unusual to find exactly the same dot gains on all four inks.

Separation Options. The Separation Options section is where you tell Photoshop how you want to use the inks you've defined in the Ink Options section (see Figure 5-16). It lets you control the total amount of ink you'll put on the paper, as well as the black generation—the relationship between black and the other colors. Note that unlike the Ink Options settings, the Separation Options have no effect on the display of CMYK images—these only control how colors will convert to CMYK.

Figure 5-16
Separation
Options

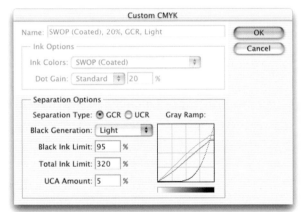

Separation Options lets you specify a total ink limit, a black ink limit, and a black generation method.

The decisions you make in Separation Options can make or break a print job, and there's no single correct answer, no hard-and-fast rules—every combination of press, ink, and paper has its own optimum settings. When it comes to determining what these are, there's no substitute for experience. But understanding the way the Separation Options work is key to making sense of your own experience, and even if there are no rules, there are at least some valuable guidelines.

Rules, guidelines, and caveats. It's important to remember that these guidelines are useful starting points, nothing more. You'll hear all sorts of recommendations from experts; most are valid, but it's unlikely that any of them will apply perfectly to your particular situation. Just how far it's worth going to optimize your color seps for a specific press depends in part on the economics of the situation, and in part on the degree of process control used by the commercial printer. It's the exception rather than the rule for every impression in a print run to be identical, but the amount of variation within a press run varies widely from shop to shop—typically, the less variation, the higher the prices.

Creating ideal separations for a given press is often an iterative process—you run press proofs and measure them, then go back to original RGB files, reseparate them, and repeat the whole process until you arrive at the optimum conditions. This is both time-consuming and expensive, and for most jobs the economics simply don't justify it. If you're willing to dedicate a print run to testing, you're better off ignoring the whole Custom CMYK mechanism and building (or commissioning) a good ICC profile instead.

Tip: Testing on a Budget. Remember that a printer can sometimes piggyback a test onto someone else's print job, particularly if you show that you can offer them a significant amount of business. Preparing several different versions of an image (and a few color bars, too) and ganging them on a page can tell you a lot when they're printed.

UCR vs. GCR. The Photoshop Classic separation engine offers two different methods of black generation: UCR (Undercolor Removal) and GCR (Gray Component Replacement). Both reduce the total amount of ink used to compensate for ink-trapping problems that appear when too much ink is applied to the page. (In this context, *trapping* is the propensity for one ink to adhere to others—it has nothing to do with building chokes and spreads to compensate for misregistration on press.)

▶ UCR separations replace cyan, magenta, and yellow ink with black only in the neutral areas. This uses much less ink in the shadows.

▶ GCR extends into color areas of the image as well—it replaces the proportions of cyan, magenta, and yellow that produce neutral gray with a corresponding percentage of black ink.

GCR separations are generally considered easier to control on press than are UCR separations, at least by the theoreticians. The downside of GCR is that it can make the shadow areas look flat and unsaturated since they're being printed only with black ink, so many commercial printers distrust GCR separations. UCA (Undercolor Addition) allows you to compensate for flat shadows by adding some CMY back into the neutral shadow areas (see "Undercolor Addition (UCA)," later in this chapter).

Some experts contend that UCR separations are better for sheetfed presses and that GCR is better for web presses, but we just don't buy it. We almost always use GCR separations with some UCA. But we've found that UCR sometimes works better than GCR when printing to newsprint with a low total ink limit—say, 220 to 240 percent. We suspect that many printers who profess to hate GCR seps often run them unknowingly, usually with good results, as long as the black generation amount isn't too extreme.

Black generation can be image-specific: If we take the extreme examples represented by two images—one, a pile of silver coins, the other, a city skyline at night—the first is an ideal candidate for a fairly heavy black plate using Medium or Heavy GCR, since there's little color, and carrying most of the image on the black plate improves detail and makes it easier to maintain neutral grays on press. The second image, though, will have significant color and detail in the deep shadows, and too heavy a black will make it flat and lifeless.

Black Generation. The Black Generation popup menu is available only when Separation Type is set to GCR. This feature lets you control the areas of the tonal range that Photoshop replaces with black (see Figure 5-17). For the vast majority of situations we prefer a Light black setting, in which Photoshop begins to add black only after the 40-percent mark. Often, however, a Medium black (where black begins to replace colors after only 20 percent) may work better for newsprint. We almost never use the Heavy or Maximum black settings, but Maximum black can do wonders when printing images that were captured from your screen (like the screen shots in this book), and is also useful when printing to color laser printers.

Custom black generation. The Custom option allows you to create your own black generation curve. This isn't something you should undertake lightly—the black plate has an enormous influence on the tonal reproduction of the image. However, if you want to make slight modifications to one of the built-in black generation curves, you can—choose the curve you want to view, then choose Custom. The Black Generation dialog box appears with the last selected curve loaded (see Figure 5-18).

Figure 5-17
Black generation

A UCR separation uses black ink only in the neutral areas. It produces rich shadows but can be difficult to control on press because it uses a lot of ink compared to GCR separations.

A Light GCR setting replaces slightly more CMY with K than does a UCR separation. In this image, Light GCR puts slightly more black into the sky and the water than does the UCR separation.

Maximum GCR replaces all neutral components of the CMY inks with black. It's easy to control on press because the black plate carries most of the image, but it can make shadow areas look flat.

Figure 5-18
Custom Black
Generation dialog box

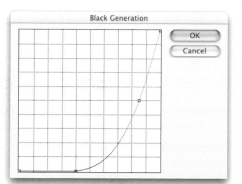

Choose Custom to create a custom black generation curve.

If your printer asks for a "skeleton black," you can use the Custom option to create a skeleton black curve—a very light black setting that still extends high up into the tonal range, typically to 25 or 30 percent. You should attempt to do this only if the printer demands it, and even then only if you have considerable experience in evaluating images by looking at the individual color plates.

Black Ink Limit. Black Ink Limit does just what it says—it limits the amount of black ink used in the deepest shadows. The Photoshop Classic mechanism seems to get less happy the further away this is set from 100%, so we generally recommend using 95–100% as a starting point. Below 95%, you get progressively less black ink than you requested, with how much less depending on the total ink limit.

Tip: Check Black with the Color Picker. The easiest way to check what values you'll actually get from a given setup is, with no documents open, set the foreground and background colors to default, then click the black swatch to open the Color Picker. The CMYK percentages shown in the Color Picker are the ones the current setup will generate for black.

Total Ink Limit. Total Ink Limit also does what it says—it limits the total amount of ink used in the deepest shadows. The ideal value depends on the combination of press, ink, and paper, but bear in mind that it isn't necessarily desirable to use the maximum amount of ink that the printing process can handle. It's generally true that more ink will yield a better image (within the limits of the press), but it also creates more problems with ink trapping and drying, show-through, and offsetting, and (for printers) it costs more because you're using more ink. Your printer will know, better than anyone else, the trade-offs involved.

For high-quality sheetfed presses with coated stock, a total ink limit of 300 to 340 percent is a good starting point—you may be able to go even higher with some paper stocks. For newsprint, values can range from 220 to 280 percent (see the next section, "Typical Custom CMYK Setups").

Undercolor Addition (UCA). UCA is used with GCR to compensate for loss of ink density in the neutral shadow areas. Using UCA lets you bring back richness to the shadows, yet still retain the benefits of easier color-ink balancing on the press that GCR offers.

The need for UCA is image-dependent. If your shadows look flat, the image can probably benefit from modest amounts of UCA. We rarely use more than 10 percent, and typically use less. (Because David doesn't like to think a whole lot, he usually sets this to 5 percent and forgets about it.)

Typical Custom CMYK Setups

Table 5-2 gives some general guidelines for different types of print jobs. The dot-gain values are based on 133- to 150-line screens, except for newsprint, which assumes an 85-line screen. If you use these values, you should get acceptable separations; but every combination of press, ink, and paper has its own quirks, and your printer should know them better than anyone else. View these values as useful starting points, and get as much advice from your printer as you can.

Tip: Creating ICC Profiles from Custom CMYK Settings. Once you've made a Custom CMYK setting, you can save it as an ICC profile by choosing Save CMYK from the Color Settings CMYK menu. Photoshop saves the settings as an ICC profile that you can use in any ICC-aware application. Profiles made this way support only relative and absolute colorimetric renderings, not perceptual or saturation, so they're more limited than profiles produced by full-blown profiling packages.

More Options. When you click the More Options button in Color Settings, you can choose any CMYK profile installed on your system as the CMYK working space. Bear in mind that the Convert to Profile command lets you convert images to any CMYK profile, so it isn't necessary to load a particular CMYK profile as the CMYK working space. It's simply more convenient to load the CMYK profile you're going to use most as the CMYK working space.

Tip: Adding Profiles to the Recommended List. You can easily add profiles to the Recommended list (the list that appears in the CMYK menu when the Advanced Mode checkbox is turned off) by storing the profile, or an alias to the profile, in the right place. In Mac OS X, the right place is inside the Library/Application Support/Adobe/Color/Profiles/Rec-

Table 5-2	Press and paper	Inks	Dot gain
Suggested separation settings	Sheetfed Coated	SWOP (Coated)	12–15%
	Sheetfed Uncoated	SWOP (Uncoated)	17–22%
	Web Coated	SWOP (Coated)	17–22%
	Web Uncoated	SWOP (Uncoated)	22–30%
	Newsprint 1	SWOP (Newsprint)	30–40%
	Newsprint 2	SWOP (Newsprint)	30–40%

ommended folder. In Windows, it's inside the Program Files/Common Files/Adobe/Color/Profiles/Recommended folder. This lets you access your favorite profiles without having to keep More Options displayed in Color Settings, so you don't have to wade through the entire list of profiles installed on your system, or deal with all the extra controls.

Press Profile Families

The main reason that some people continue to use the Photoshop Classic mechanism is that they're stuck with one ICC profile with a single black generation. When you build your own CMYK profiles for a press or proofer, it's always a good idea to build a family of profiles with different black generations—some profiling tools will even let you take an existing profile and regenerate it with new black generation settings.

Photoshop Classic is very old technology with rather more than its fair share of quirks. We debated leaving it out of this edition entirely, but we recognize that too many people still rely on it. If you're one of them, we gently suggest that you investigate 21st-century profiling technology. It has evolved a great deal more in the past 15-odd years than has Photoshop Classic, and will let you produce better results with less work.

Choosing a Gray Working Space

Grayscale is a first-class citizen in Photoshop CS2, with its own profiles independent of RGB or CMYK. However, note that grayscale profiles only contain tone reproduction information; they have no information about the color of the black ink or of the paper.

Black generation	Black limit	Total ink	UCA
GCR, Light	100%	320–340%	0–10%
GCR, Light	100%	270–300%	0–10%
GCR, Light	100%	300–320%	0–10%
GCR, Light	100%	280–300%	0–10%
GCR, Medium	95–100%	260–280%	0–10%
UCR	70–80%	220–240%	

WhenColor Settings is displayed with Fewer Options, you can choose among grayscale dot gains of 10, 15, 20, 25, or 30 percent, depending on your printing conditions. You can also choose either gamma 1.8 or 2.2, which are good choices for grayscale images destined for the screen, or for unknown printing conditions. Of course, there's nothing to prevent you from using these gamma values for print images, or the dot gain curves for onscreen use, but generally speaking, gammas are designed for on-screen and dot gain curves are designed for print.

Custom Gray

When you click the More Options button in Color Settings, you gain access to all the grayscale profiles installed on your system, as well as the ability to define custom grayscale working spaces (which you can then save as Grayscale ICC profiles, if you want).

Custom Dot Gain. If you print a lot of grayscale work on the same sort of paper stock, it may well be worth it to build your own custom dot gain (remember, the more you customize, the better results you'll get). You can define a custom dot gain by choosing Custom Dot Gain from the Gray menu in the Color Settings dialog box. The Custom Dot Gain dialog box (see Figure 5-19) lets you plug in values for the 2, 4, 6, 8, 10, 20, 30, 40, 50, 60, 70, 80, and 90 percent dots. You can enter a single value for the 50-percent field (for example, to define 18-percent dot gain, you'd enter 68 in the 50-percent field), but you'll get much better results if you first print a ramp with patches for all the values in the dialog box, then measure the actual dot area for each one, and enter them all in the dialog box. This gives you a very accurate grayscale profile.

Figure 5-19
Custom Dot Gain for
grayscale

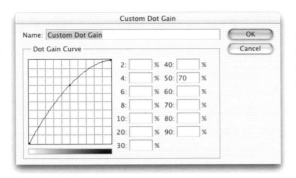

*The Custom Dot Gain
dialog box lets you
specify a precise dot
gain compensation for
grayscale images.*

Of course, it's not absolutely necessary to measure every single patch, but we strongly recommend that you at least measure the highlight (2, 4, 6, 8, and 10 percent) patches plus the 40- and 80-percent patches. Obtaining accurate measurements for the highlights lets you set your all-important highlight detail quickly and easily.

Custom Gamma. Grayscale gamma settings are designed primarily for on-screen images. We can't envisage too many situations where you'd need to define a gamma other than the gamma 1.8 and gamma 2.2 built into Photoshop, but if for some reason you need to do so, choose Custom Gamma from the Color Settings Gray menu. Permissible values range from 0.75 to 3.0 (see Figure 5-20).

Figure 5-20
Custom Gamma for
grayscale

Custom Gamma	
Name: Gray Gamma 2.2	OK
	Cancel
Gamma	
Gamma: 2.20	

*The Custom
Gamma dialog
box lets you create
a custom gamma
setting for grayscale
images.*

Tip: Create a Gamma 1.0 Profile to Help Understand Digital Raw. One of the biggest differences between shooting digital and shooting film is the camera's tone response curve, which unlike film or eyeballs has a gamma of 1.0. Making a black-to-white gradient and assigning a gamma 1.0 profile helps you understand how the camera sees light.

CMYK black channel. If you need to mix grayscale and color images in the same job, you might find it useful to simply load the black channel of your CMYK profile as your Gray working space. To do so, choose Load Gray from the Gray menu, then select the CMYK profile you wish to load from the dialog box and click Load. The profile appears in the Gray menu as Black Ink—ProfileName. Note that the Black Ink Limit in a CMYK profile has no effect on grayscale images (because Black Ink Limit only applies when you convert to CMYK). The grayscale setting uses the dot gain of the black ink, letting you use the entire dynamic range of the black channel.

Save Gray. To use a custom grayscale setting elsewhere in Photoshop (for instance, in the Proof Setup, Assign Profile, or Convert to Profile dialog boxes) and in other ICC-savvy applications, you need to save your grayscale setting as an ICC profile. To do so, choose Save Gray from the Color Settings Gray menu, browse to the appropriate folder or directory for your platform, and click Save. Your grayscale profile will now be available for use in any application that understands grayscale ICC profiles.

Spot Spaces

The Spot feature in the Color Settings dialog box lets you specify a dot gain for spot colors. As with grayscale settings, spot color settings know nothing about the actual color of the ink and paper, and they contain no information about the way the spot ink interacts with other inks. Spot settings essentially behave identically to grayscale ones.

The Spot popup menu in the Color Settings dialog box contains dot gain settings for 10, 15, 20, 25, and 30 percent dot gain. When you click the More Options button in Color Settings, you can also define a Custom Dot Gain, choose a custom grayscale profile, or load the black channel of a CMYK profile. The procedure for doing any of these is identical to that for Grayscale mode. But spot inks differ widely in how they behave on paper, and the only way to know what will happen is to print a tint build.

Loading the black channel of a CMYK profile for Spot is primarily useful if you need to use black as a spot color in a CMYK image: making type, callouts, or drop shadows print with only black ink are good examples. But using tints of spot colors, which spot dot gains seem to invite, is a very uncertain process. The dot gain curve ensures that the tint you request is the one you'll get, but the only way to find out how the spot color interacts with the process inks is, unfortunately, to print it.

Color Management Policies

If you ever got stuck trying to figure out what those dang "Profile Mismatch" or "Missing Profile" alerts were saying in Photoshop 5, you might appreciate the relative simplicity of the Photoshop CS2 Color Management Policies feature. While the working space definitions allow you to tell Photoshop what colors the various numbers in your images represent, the Policies and Warnings sections of the Color Settings dialog box (see Figure 5-21) do something quite different: They let you tell Photoshop how to use the interpretations of the numbers.

The policies control how Photoshop handles several aspects of color management. When you open a document with an embedded profile, the policies tell Photoshop to do one of the following.

▶ Use the embedded profile instead of the working space, opening the document as a Tagged document in its own "document space" (which may or may not be the same as the current working space).

▶ Convert the image from the document space represented by the embedded profile to the current working space.

▶ Ignore the profile and treat the document as Untagged (in which case the numbers in the file are interpreted according to the current working space).

▶ Ignore the profile and treat the document as a Tagged document in the working space.

When you create a new document, the policies tell Photoshop to treat it as an Untagged document, or as a Tagged document in the working space.

When you move pixels between documents (by copying and pasting or by dragging), the policies tell Photoshop to move either the numerical values of the pixels or the colors those numerical values represent.

When you save a document, the policies tell Photoshop whether or not to embed the profile currently associated with the document. You can override the policy's setting for profile embedding in the Save As dialog box, but the policy dictates whether the Embed Color Profile checkbox is turned on or off when the dialog box appears.

Figure 5-21
Color Management
Policies

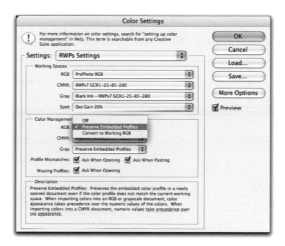

*Color Management
Policies let you tell
Photoshop how to
manage your color.*

You can set individual policies for RGB, CMYK, and grayscale images, but the policies themselves behave almost identically in each color mode. The thumbnail characterizations of the three policies are:

▶ Off means "behave like Photoshop 4."

▶ Convert to Working Space means "behave like Photoshop 5."

▶ Preserve Embedded Profiles means "behave sensibly."

If this characterization displays some bias on our part, we admit to it cheerfully. Nevertheless, there are some situations where one of the less-sophisticated policies make sense, as you'll soon see.

Off. The Off choice is somewhat misleadingly named, as there's really no way to turn color management entirely off in Photoshop CS. It is, however, pretty close to the way Photoshop behaved prior to version 5. When you set the policy for a color mode to Off, Photoshop behaves as follows:

▶ When you open a file that contains an embedded profile, Photoshop discards the embedded profile and treats the image as Untagged, *unless* the embedded profile happens to match the current working space. In that case, the image is treated as a Tagged document in its own document space, which in this case happens to be the same as the working space. If you change the working space in the Color Settings dialog box, all your Untagged images will change, taking on the new working space definition, but the Tagged images keep the old working space definition, now acting as a document space. (If you find this confusing and counterintuitive, you're not alone. We think it would be a lot simpler if Off simply treated all your documents as Untagged.)

► When you save the document, no profile is embedded (unless you turn on Embed Profile in the Save As dialog box, in which case the current working space profile is embedded), *unless* Photoshop is handling the document as a Tagged document because its embedded profile matched the working space that was in effect when it was opened. In that case, the profile that was embedded in the file when it was opened is re-embedded when you save, unless you turn off the Embed Color Profile checkbox in the Save As dialog box (see Figure 5-22).

Figure 5-22
The Embed Color Profile checkbox

You can control whether or not Photoshop embeds a profile by checking or unchecking the Embed Color Profile checkbox in the Save As dialog box. Photoshop always tells you which profile will be embedded (if you choose to embed a profile).

► When you open a file that has no embedded profile, Photoshop treats it as Untagged. When you save the document, no profile is embedded (unless you turn on Embed Color Profile in the Save As dialog box, in which case the current working space profile is embedded).

► When you create a new document, Photoshop treats it as Untagged. When you save the document, no profile is embedded (unless you turn on Embed Color Profile in the Save As dialog box, in which case the current working space profile is embedded).

► When you transfer pixels between images in the same color mode by copy and paste or by drag-and-drop, the numerical values get transferred. That means if the two documents are in different color spaces, the colors change even though the numbers are preserved. (If the two images are in different color modes—CMYK and RGB, for instance—the color appearance is always preserved.)

Off is the policy you want if you're a dyed-in-the-wool, by-the-numbers type who has been cursing at Adobe for years for stuffing color management down your throat. Of course, you don't have to set all the policies to Off. If you're in an all-CMYK, by-the-numbers workflow, you can set the policy to Off just for CMYK, and still get the benefits of color management in the other spaces. Similarly, if your work is mostly for the Web, and you need Photoshop's RGB to behave the same as RGB in the vast majority of Web browsers, you can set the policy to Off for RGB. (Well, actually, as we noted earlier in the chapter, on the Mac you may also want to set your RGB working space to Monitor RGB to ensure that RGB in Photoshop matches RGB in your other, non-color-managed applications.)

However, if you want to use color management in Photoshop, you'll want to choose one of the other policies and simply untag documents that need to be untagged on a case-by-case basis (see "Assign Profile," later in this chapter).

Preserve Embedded Profiles. This is the third-millennium, industrial-strength color management approach. Preserve Embedded Profiles is the "safe" policy, in that it makes sure Photoshop doesn't do color conversions when you don't want it to. With this policy, the working spaces in Color Settings are there only as a convenience because each image can live in its own document space. On the other hand, it can also be the "dangerous" policy because if you're not at least a little careful, you can wind up editing images in color spaces that are wildly inappropriate for editing. For instance, if your scanner software embeds its own profile in an image, this policy might mean you're editing the image in the scanner's space, which is significantly less than optimal. Overall, though, it's the policy that we typically use.

▶ When you open an image that contains an embedded profile, Photoshop preserves the profile and treats the image as Tagged, using the embedded profile as the document space (which may or may not be the current working space). When you save the document, the document space profile (the profile the image had when you opened it) is once again embedded in the saved file.

▶ When you open an image with no embedded profile, Photoshop treats the image as an Untagged image (it preserves the lack of an embedded profile, if you will). When you save the document, no profile is embedded (unless you turn on Embed Color Profile in the Save As dialog box, in which case the current working space profile is embedded).

▶ When you create a new document, Photoshop treats it as a Tagged document and assigns the current working space profile as the document space. When you save the document, Photoshop embeds the document space profile (even if you change the working space in the Color Settings dialog box, it has no effect on the image, which stays in the document space).

▶ When you transfer pixels between two RGB or two grayscale images (by copy and paste or drag-and-drop), the actual color gets transferred. If the two images are in different color spaces, the numbers change even though the color appearance is preserved.

▶ When you transfer pixels between two CMYK images, the numerical values get transferred. If the two CMYK documents were in different CMYK spaces, the color appearance changes even though the numbers are preserved. While this routine is the reverse of what happens with RGB and grayscale files, it is actually more logical and useful.

We believe quite strongly that Preserve Embedded Profiles is the best policy for the vast majority of Photoshop users. It keeps track of color for you and rarely performs any conversions that aren't explicitly requested (and *never* does so if you keep the Profile Mismatch—Paste warning turned on). If you have to deal with files from many different sources, this is almost certainly the policy you want to use. It does a good job of keeping color management out of your face, but it also offers tremendous power and flexibility for hard-core color geeks.

Convert to Working Space. Convert to Working Space tells Photoshop CS to behave very much like Photoshop 5, converting everything into your working RGB, CMYK, or Gray space. It tells Photoshop to convert images from their own space into the current default working space automatically. We find this method a bit too authoritarian, though if your workflow relies on picking a single RGB, CMYK, or grayscale color space and normalizing alll your images into it, you'll almost certainly want to use this policy. But we think it's best thought of as an automation feature: If it does something you wanted done with no intervention, that's great; on the other hand, if it does something unexpected behind your back, it's not so great!

▶ When you open a file that already has the current working space profile embedded, Photoshop preserves the profile and treats the image as a Tagged image, using the embedded profile as the document space. When you save the document, the document space profile (the profile the image had when you opened it) is once again embedded in the saved file, even if you change the working space in the Color Settings dialog box when the image is open.

▶ When you open a file that has an embedded profile different than the current working space, Photoshop converts the image from the embedded profile's space to the current working space. From then on, it treats the image as a Tagged image, with the working space profile that was in effect when it was opened as the document space.

▶ When you open an image with no embedded profile, Photoshop treats the image as Untagged. If you change the working space, Photoshop keeps the numbers in the file unchanged and reinterprets them as belonging to the new working space (so the appearance changes). When you save the document, profile embedding is turned off by default (though you can turn it on in the Save As dialog box).

▶ When you create a new document, Photoshop treats it as a Tagged document in the current working space. If you later change the working space, Photoshop preserves the working space profile that was in effect when the document was created. When you save the document, that same profile is also embedded.

▶ When you transfer pixels between two images (whether it's RGB-to-RGB, RGB-to-CMYK, or whatever), the color appearance gets transferred, even if that means Photoshop changes the numbers (which it'll have to do if the files are in different color spaces).

Convert to Working Space is a useful policy when you need all your images in the same space, such as when you're compositing RGB images or repurposing CMYK images from several different sources for a single output. It's a handy automation feature when you need to convert a bunch of pictures quickly. But unless you're very sure about what you're doing, it's safer to use Preserve Embedded Profiles instead, and perform the conversions manually whenever you need to change an image's working space (see "Applying Profiles Outside Color Settings," later in this chapter).

Profile Warnings

Although they appear in the Color Management Policies section of the Color Settings dialog box, the Missing Profile and Profile Mismatch warnings operate independently from the policies. (You can think of it this way: The policy determines the initial default setting of some of the warnings.) Unless you're adamantly opposed to the use of color management, we suggest you turn all the warning checkboxes on and keep them on until you decide you don't need them. They offer choices, letting you override the default behavior of the policy you've chosen for a specific color mode, though we'd find them even more useful if they didn't demand clairvoyance on our part and let us see the image before making decisions.

Profile Mismatch: Ask When Opening. When Profile Mismatch: Ask When Opening is turned on, Photoshop alerts you when you open a document with an embedded profile that's different from the current working space (see Figure 5-23). Even better, this Embedded Profile Mismatch dialog box offers you three choices for handling the profile mismatch.

Figure 5-23
Embedded Profile
Mismatch dialog box

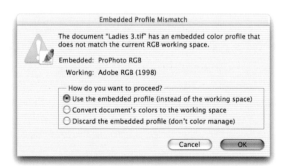

The Embedded Profile Mismatch warning offers three choices for handling images whose embedded profile differs from the working space.

► **Use the embedded profile (instead of the working space)** tells Photoshop to keep the embedded profile, treating the document as a Tagged image in the embedded profile's space. The embedded profile is then used to display the image, and is also used as the source profile for any subsequent color conversion. This is typically what you'd want to do.

► **Convert document's colors to the working space** does what it says: It performs a conversion from the embedded profile's space to the current default working space. This makes sense if you need several images in the same working space (for example, to composite them).

▶ **Discard the embedded profile (don't color manage)** strips off the embedded profile and opens the document as an Untagged image. The numbers in the document are left unchanged and are interpreted according to the current working space definition. You might use this if you know you're going to significantly edit the color and tone of the image and you don't care about any color interpretations that were already assigned. Similarly, this might be appropriate for an image destined for the Web, especially if you'll be saving it in the sRGB space.

The Embedded Profile Mismatch dialog box chooses one of these three as the default (the one that you'll get if you just hit the Enter key). The default it picks depends on the policy you've chosen for that color mode. Of course, the dialog box always allows you to override the default behavior for the policy on an image-by-image basis.

Profile Mismatch: Ask When Pasting. The second checkbox, Ask When Pasting, comes into play when you move pixels between two images that are in the same color mode, but in different color spaces (like sRGB to AdobeRGB, or from one CMYK setup to another). When this is on, Photoshop asks you whether you want to paste the numerical values or the color appearance (see Figure 5-24). Note that when you copy and paste or drag and drop between images that are in different color modes (like RGB to CMYK), this alert doesn't do anything because Photoshop only lets you paste the color appearance.

Figure 5-24
Paste Profile Mismatch
dialog box

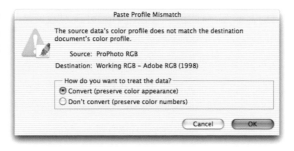

The Paste Profile Mismatch warning lets you choose whether to paste the numerical values or the perceived color those values represent.

Just to be clear: In this dialog box, "Convert (preserve color appearance)" tells Photoshop to change the numbers in the image so that you get roughly the same color. It's like doing a profile-to-profile conversion. We add the caveat "roughly" just in case a color in one profile simply cannot be represented in the gamut of the target profile. The "Don't convert (preserve color numbers)" option simply copies the numbers from the source file into the target file, without worrying about color changes. As with Profile Mismatch: Ask When Opening, the default option (the one you get if you just press Enter) is set to match the current policy for the color mode.

Missing Profile: Ask When Opening. The third warning, Missing Profile: Ask When Opening, comes into play when you open a document with no embedded profile. When this is turned on, Photoshop lets you choose how you want it to interpret the numbers in documents with no embedded profiles (see Figure 5-25).

Figure 5-25
Missing Profile
dialog box

The Missing Profile warning offers four choices for handling Untagged images.

▶ **Leave as is (don't color manage)** tells Photoshop to treat the file as an Untagged document. The numbers in the file are preserved and interpreted according to the current working space (which means that the appearance may change radically).

▶ **Assign working space** tags the document with the current working space profile. As with the previous option, the numbers in the file are preserved, and interpreted according to the current working space. The difference is that the document is treated as Tagged, so it keeps that profile if you subsequently change the working space.

▶ **Assign profile** lets you tag the document with a profile other than the working space profile. Again, the numbers in the file are preserved, but in this case they're interpreted according to the profile you choose.

▶ **Assign profile and then convert document to working space** lets you assign a source profile to the document, and then convert it to the working space. This is the only option of the four that actually changes the numbers in the file.

If you're in a workflow in which you know where images are coming from and you know where they're going, you can probably turn off the warning dialog boxes off. When you don't need them, they do get kind of annoying after a while.

Color Settings with More Options

When you click the More Options button in the Color Settings dialog box, you gain access to the Conversion Options and Advanced Controls, as well as to a wider range of profiles (we've discussed that earlier in the chapter). The Conversion Options can be useful in typical workflows, but the Advanced Controls are a grab-bag of options that may be useful to a very small number of serious players, and are "hurt-me" buttons for almost everyone else.

Conversion Options

The Conversion Options section of the dialog box lets you control useful things like Photoshop's default rendering intent and color management engine (CMM)—things you probably won't need to change very often, but might want to occasionally (see Figure 5-26).

Figure 5-26
Conversion Options

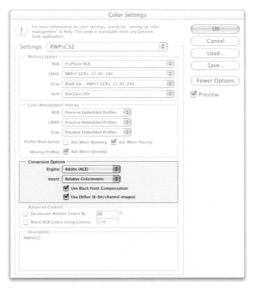

The Conversion Options let you choose the color Engine, the default Rendering Intent, and settings for Black Point Compensation and dithering in 8-bit/channel conversions.

Engine. The Engine popup menu lets you select the CMM that Photoshop uses for all its color space calculations. The options that appear on the menu depend on which CMMs are installed on your system. Unless you have really pressing reasons to use a different CMM, we recommend sticking with the Adobe (ACE) engine. Bruce has found bugs in all the other CMMs he's tried (though they're pretty dang obscure), and has yet to find any in ACE. Of course, no complicated software is entirely without bugs…. When the engines work correctly, there is only a tiny change in pixel values with the different engines; except for the bugs, we've never noticed a visual difference.

Mac users will notice separate entries for the Apple CMM and Apple ColorSync. Apple CMM means that the Apple CMM will always be used. Apple ColorSync uses whatever CMM is set in the ColorSync System Preferences (which have disappeared in Tiger).

Intent. The Intent popup menu is significantly more useful for the average user. Intent lets you choose the default rendering intent that Photoshop uses in any of the following color space conversions:

▶ Converting documents on opening

▶ Converting documents by choosing a different mode from the Mode menu (like separating RGB to CMYK)

▶ Calculating the numbers that appear on the Info palette for color modes other than the one the document is in

▶ Calculating the numbers that appear in the Color Picker for color modes other than the one the document is in

Every other feature in Photoshop that lets you convert colors from one profile's space to another has its own rendering intent controls. Photoshop's default rendering intent is relative colorimetric with Black Point Compensation. These defaults are always the subject of some pretty heated debate. We offer three observations:

▶ While some users may prefer perceptual rendering as the default choice, rendering intent is best treated as an image-specific and conversion-specific decision. Relative colorimetric renderings may actually do a better job than perceptual rendering when your images don't have a lot of significant out-of-gamut colors.

▶ Photoshop's color conversions have always been relative colorimetric in the past.

▶ It's just a default. Don't get your knickers in a twist; you can always override it to suit the needs of the image at hand.

Since Photoshop CS2 makes it very easy to both preview and apply different rendering intents for each image, the rendering intent setting here is more a matter of convenience than of necessity.

Use Black Point Compensation. Use Black Point Compensation, when turned on, maps the black of the source profile to the black of the target profile, ensuring that the entire dynamic range of the output device is used. In many cases you'll find no difference whether it's turned on or off, because it depends on the contents of the particular profiles involved. See the sidebar "Black Is Black (or Is It?)" for a detailed look at the Black Point Compensation feature.

While in earlier versions of Photoshop we offered a complex set of rules about when to turn this on and off, we now recommend that you just leave Use Black Point Compensation turned on at all times.

Use Dither (8-bit/channel images). The Use Dither feature is somewhat esoteric. All color space conversions in Photoshop are performed in a high-bit space. When Use Dither is turned on, Photoshop adds a small amount of noise when the 8-bit channels are converted into the high-bit space. This makes banding or posterization much less likely to occur (that's a Good Thing). But if your final output is JPEG, this tiny dithering is likely to produce a larger file size (because it introduces more discrete colors into the image), and if you're using Photoshop for scientific work, where you need to perform quantitative analysis on colors, you should turn this off, as it will introduce noise in your data. Otherwise, leave it on.

Advanced Controls

The Advanced Controls are aptly named. We recommend leaving them alone unless you have a pressing need to do otherwise, but in the interest of full disclosure, here's what they do.

Desaturate Monitor Colors By. The Desaturate Monitor Colors feature attempts to solve a problem with large-gamut working spaces: Rendering

Black Is Black (or Is It?)

We usually think of black as being "just black," but of course black on different devices appears differently (solid black on newsprint is much grayer than solid black on glossy sheetfed stock, for instance). Photoshop's Black Point Compensation forces us to think about this fact. The information here is fairly complex, but the basic principle is simple. When you transform from one color space to another, there are two ways of transforming the black point: absolute and relative.

Transformations involve first mapping the source gamut to the reference color space (also known as the Profile Connection Space, or PCS), which in most cases is Lab, and then mapping the Lab values to the destination space. In a relative black-point transformation, the source black is mapped to a L^* value of 0 in the PCS, but in an absolute black-point transformation, it's mapped to the actual L^* value that the source device can produce, which is usually substantially higher than zero. (A zero L^* value represents the total absence of any reflected light, which is blacker than anything other than a black hole can reproduce.) The ICC profiles themselves specify whether the transform should be absolute or relative.

This can lead to undesirable results. For example, Radius Color-Match RGB profiles map RGB 0,0,0 to $L^*a^*b^*$ 3,0,0 in the PCS. A CMYK profile that uses absolute black transformation may map to a black value in the PCS of $L^*a^*b^*$ 7,0,0. If you convert an RGB image to CMYK using this pair of profiles, your shadow detail will get clobbered because the first few levels in the RGB document will convert to L^* values in the PCS between 3 and 7. Since these are all darker than the output device can produce, they'll be clipped to black, and your shadow detail goes bye-bye.

If the same RGB profile is used with a CMYK profile that maps device black to $L^*a^*b^*$ 2,0,0, you'll get very different, equally undesirable results. The RGB black will convert to $L^*a^*b^*$ 3,0,0, which is lighter than the black the output device can produce. The resulting image will appear slightly washed out because it contains no true blacks.

If you want a transform that uses the entire dynamic range of the output device, you need a relative black transform both from source to PCS and from PCS to output. Photoshop's Black Point Compensation forces this to happen, no matter what the profiles say. It works by estimating the black point for the source and the target.

If they're the same, as they would be if both profiles use relative black encoding, the feature does nothing. But if the black levels are different, it adds an extra processing step: After the source color is converted into the PCS, Black Point Compensation adjusts the PCS to map the source profile's black to the destination profile's black via a straightforward linear transformation of the L^* values in the PCS. This ensures that the entire dynamic range of the source is mapped into the entire dynamic range of the target, without shadow clipping or washed-out blacks. Again, we now turn this on and leave it on.

to the monitor is always relative colorimetric, so colors in the working space that lie outside the monitor gamut get clipped to the nearest equivalent the monitor can display. You can think of desaturating the monitor as the poor man's perceptual rendering. Unless you're working with a very large space like Kodak's ProPhoto RGB, don't even think about messing with this. Even then, we don't use it—we find that the problem is much less severe than theory would lead one to expect.

For those brave (or foolhardy) souls who want to experiment with it, a setting in the 12 to 15 percent range seems somewhat useful for Kodak ProPhoto RGB, and 7 to 10 percent seems good for EktaSpace. If you're working with one of these spaces, try turning the feature on and off to see if it's doing anything useful for you. Whatever you do, don't forget to turn it back off before you try to do any normal work; otherwise you'll find yourself producing excessively colorful imagery!

Blend RGB Colors Using Gamma. The Blend RGB Colors Using Gamma feature controls how RGB colors blend together. To see its effect, try painting a bright green stroke on a red background with the checkbox turned off, and then again with the checkbox turned on and the value set to a gamma of 1.0. With the checkbox turned off, the edges of the stroke have a brownish hue, as they would if you were painting with paint. With it turned on, the edges are yellowish, as they would be if you were painting with light. You can think of the behavior with the checkbox off as artistically correct, and with it turned on as colorimetrically correct. Permissible values are from 1 to 2.2.

The Color Picker

Why are we talking about the Color Picker in this chapter? Simply, a great many people overlook the fact that the Color Picker is subject to the choices you make in Color Settings, because the numbers that appear in the Color Picker for all the color modes other than the current documents' mode are the product of color space conversions made using the default profiles, engine, and rendering intent.

We've lost count of the number of emails we've received from confused puppies who tried to specify black as 0C 0M 0Y 100K in an RGB document and then got bent out of shape because:

▶ The resulting color was dark gray.

▶ It picked up a bunch of C, M, and Y on conversion to CMYK.

Well, 100K isn't black because black ink isn't perfectly black or perfectly opaque—if it were, we'd never need to lay down more than 100% total ink. If you specify 0C 0M 0Y 100K in the Color Picker, then look at the RGB values, or the Lightness value in Lab, you'll find that they aren't zero. And unless your CMYK working space uses Maximum GCR, 0C 0M 0Y 100K isn't a "legal" value for a converted RGB 000 black—we almost always want to add some amount of CMY to increase the density.

The Color Picker is governed by two simple rules.

▶ The "real" color being specified is represented by the numbers pertaining to the color mode of the current document, which may not be the numbers you're entering. If you enter CMYK numbers while working on an RGB document, the color you're actually specifying is represented by the numbers that appear in the RGB fields, and vice versa.

▶ When you specify color in a mode other than the document's, the actual color is calculated by taking the color values you entered, then converting them to the document's mode using the working space profile for the mode you specified as the source profile, the document's profile as the destination profile, and the rendering intent specified in Color Settings.

When you think about it, it's hard to envisage how this could work any other way, but how may of us think about what we're doing when we work in the Color Picker?

Applying Profiles Outside Color Settings

The settings in the Color Settings dialog box represent the "fallback" position for performing color conversions. But two commands on the Edit menu (they've been moved from the Mode submenu under the Image menu in CS2—some of the deckchair rearranging on the *Titanic* that Bruce mutters about) offer much more flexibility for applying profiles and performing conversions on an image-by-image basis. In fact, Bruce hardly ever converts colors (like from RGB to CMYK) using plain ol' Mode changes, because he likes to be able to preview and select the rendering intent that does the best job on the image at hand.

Assigning and Converting

We still encounter many users who get confused as to when they should assign and when they should convert. Back at the beginning of this chapter, we told you that color management does only two things:

► Associate a specific color appearance with a set of otherwise-ambiguous RGB or CMYK numbers.

► Maintain that color appearance in a new context by changing the numbers to make the new device or process produce the desired color appearance.

Assign Profile is the mechanism for associating a color appearance with the RGB or CMYK numbers. Normally, you only have to do this with untagged images. Convert to Profile is one of the mechanisms for calculating a new set of numbers that maintain that color appearance, such as when you convert an RGB image to CMYK.

Assign Profile

Assign Profile lets you tag an image with a specified profile, or untag an image by removing its profile. It doesn't do any conversions; it simply attaches a description (an interpretation, as it were) to the numbers in the image, or removes one (see Figure 5-27).

Figure 5-27
Assign Profile
dialog box

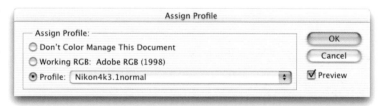

We mainly find Assign Profile useful when we're trying to decide what profile should be attached to an Untagged document. Unlike the profile assignment in the Missing Profile dialog box, Assign Profile lets you preview the results of applying various profiles. This gives you the opportunity to make an educated guess rather than a blind one.

The Assign Profile dialog box offers three options, which are identical to the first three options in the Missing Profile warning (see "Color Management Policies," earlier in this chapter).

Don't Color Manage This Document. Don't Color Manage This Document tells Photoshop to treat it as an Untagged document. The numbers in the file are preserved and are interpreted according to the current working space, and the embedded profile is stripped out. If you're delivering final CMYK to shops that are scared or confused by color management, if you're delivering images in sRGB for the Web, or if you've inadvertently embedded a profile in a calibration target, you can use this option to strip out the profile.

Assign Working Space. Assign Working Space tags the document with the current default working space profile (whatever is set in the Color Settings dialog box). As with the previous option, the numbers in the file are preserved, but reinterpreted according to the current working space. The difference is that the document is treated as Tagged, so it keeps that profile if you later change the working space. If you've opened an Untagged document and decided that it really does belong in the working space, use this option to make sure that it stays in the working space.

Assign Profile. Assign Profile lets you tag the document with a profile other than the default working space profile. Again, the numbers in the image are preserved, but in this case they're interpreted according to the profile you assigned. If you have a profile for your scanner, but the scanner uses an Acquire plug-in (so the image just shows up right in Photoshop), then you can use Assign Profile to assign color meaning to the image you've just scanned. You'll then probably want to use Convert to Profile (see below) to move the image into a more reasonable editing space, like AdobeRGB.

The Preview checkbox lets you preview the results of applying or removing a profile (it's rare that we turn this off—the preview is pretty fast, even on a 2.5 GB file). That's all there is to Assign Profile—it's a handy tool that's simple to use and doesn't involve much in the way of mysteries.

Convert to Profile

Convert to Profile, as its name suggests, lets you convert a document from its profile space (or, in the case of an Untagged document, the current working space) to any other profiled space, with full control over how the conversion is done (see Figure 5-28).

Figure 5-28
Convert to Profile
dialog box

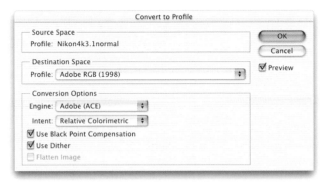

*The Convert to
Profile dialog
box gives you
full control over
conversions,
allowing you
to choose the
destination space,
engine, and
rendering intent.*

The Convert to Profile dialog box displays the source profile and lets you specify a destination profile, engine, and rendering intent. It also allows you to turn black point compensation on and off, decide whether or not to use dithering for 8-bit-per-channel images, and specify whether to flatten the image. Best of all, it lets you preview the results of the conversion correctly while the dialog box is still open, so you can see the effect of the various options.

The engine, rendering intent, black point compensation, and dithering options all work identically to those in the Conversion Optons section of the Color Settings dialog box (see "Conversion Options," earlier in this chapter).

The Flatten Image option is there as a convenience, when you want to produce a final flat file for output. When we use Convert to Profile, we usually make a duplicate of the layered file first (choose Duplicate from the Image menu), and then run Convert to Profile on the duplicate, with Flatten Image turned on—that way we keep our layered master files intact.

Bruce uses Convert to Profile instead of Mode change for most of his conversions (whether it's RGB-to-CMYK, cross-rendering CMYK-to-CMYK, or whatever), because it offers more control, and especially because it allows him to preview different rendering intents. Rendering intents only know about the color gamut of the source color space—they don't know anything about how much of that gamut is actually used by the source image—so applying perceptual rendering to an image that contains no significant out-of-gamut colors compresses the gamut unnecessarily. With Convert to Profile, you can see how the different rendering intents will affect a particular image, and choose accordingly.

Soft-Proofing Controls

If you're sane, you probably want to get some sense of what your images are going to look like before you commit to the $50,000 print run. There are three ways to proof your pictures: traditionally (print film negatives and create a laminated proof like a Matchprint), on a color printer (like one of the new breed of inkjet printers), or on screen. On screen? If you've been paying attention during this chapter, you know that you can set up your system well enough to start really trusting what you see on screen. Proofing images on screen is called *soft-proofing*, and Photoshop CS2 offers soft-proofing capabilities whose accuracy is limited only by the accuracy of the profiles involved.

In Photoshop CS2, soft-proofing has its own set of controls, separate from the Color Settings dialog box. These allow you to preview your output accurately, whether it's RGB or CMYK. This is a huge advantage for those of us who print to RGB devices like film recorders or to those photorealistic inkjet printers that pretend so assiduously to be RGB devices that we're forced to treat them as such. But soft-proofing is a big improvement for those of us who print CMYK too, because we can soft-proof different conversions to CMYK while we're still working in RGB, and have them accurately depicted on screen. (For example, you can quickly see how the same image would look on newsprint and in your glossy brochure.)

The Proof Colors command on the View menu lets you turn soft-proofing on and off. It even has the same keyboard shortcut, Command-Y, as the old CMYK Preview it replaces. But the real magic is in the Proof Setup submenu, which governs exactly what Proof Colors shows you (see Figure 5-29). The settings you make in Proof Setup are specific to the image window that's in the foreground when you make the settings, not to the image itself. This means that you can create several views of the same image (by choosing New View from the View menu), and apply different soft-proofing settings to each view, letting you see how the image will work in different output scenarios.

The default setting for Proof Colors (what you get if you don't change anything in the Proof Setup dialog box) works as follows:

▶ It first simulates the conversion from the document's space to working CMYK, using the rendering Intent and Black Point Compensation settings specified in Color Settings.

Figure 5-29
Soft-proofing controls

The Proof Setup menu lets you choose a wide variety of soft-proofing options, including your own custom settings.

▶ It renders that simulation to the monitor using relative colorimetric rendering. If Black Point Compensation is turned on in Color Settings, it's also applied to the rendering from the proof space to the monitor.

This essentially duplicates the behavior of the old CMYK Preview, except that it's a bit more accurate (because it doesn't use an intermediate transformation from CMYK to working RGB; instead, it goes straight from working CMYK to the monitor).

However, to really unleash the power of the new soft-proofing features, you need to visit the Proof Setup dialog box, which gives you an unprecedented degree of control over your soft proofs.

Proof Setup Dialog Box

Proof Setup lets you independently control the rendering from the document's space to the proof space, and from the proof space to the screen. Ultimately, it allows you to preview accurately just about any conceivable kind of output for which you have a profile. You can open the Customize Proof Condition dialog box by choosing Custom from the Proof Setup submenu (under the View menu; see Figure 5-30).

Figure 5-30
Setting up your soft proof

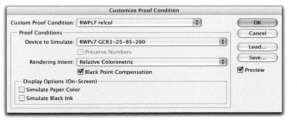

You can control conversions from document space to proofing space, and from proofing space to the monitor.

Custom Proof Condition. The Custom Proof Condition menu lets you recall setups that you've saved in the special Proofing folder. (On Mac OS X, this is the Library/Applications Support/Adobe/Color/Proofing folder. In Windows, it's in the Program Files/Common Files/Adobe/Color/Proofing folder.) You can save proof setups anywhere on your hard disk by clicking Save, and load them by clicking the Load button, but the setups you save in the Proofing folder appear on the list automatically. (Even better, they also appear at the bottom of the Proof Setup submenu, where you can choose them directly.)

Device to Simulate. The Device to Simulate menu lets you specify the proofing space you want to simulate. You can choose any profile, but if you choose an input profile (for a scanner or digital camera), the Preserve Color Numbers checkbox becomes checked and dimmed, and all the other controls become unavailable. (We're not sure why you would choose an input profile, but we suppose it's nice to have the option.) Generally, you'll want to choose an RGB, CMYK, or grayscale output profile.

Preserve RGB/CMYK/Gray Numbers. The Preserve Numbers checkbox, when on, tells Photoshop to show you what your file would look like if you sent it to the output device without performing a color space conversion. It's available only when the image is in the same color mode as the selected profile (as when both are in RGB); when you turn it on, the Intent menu becomes unavailable, since no conversion is requested.

We've found that this feature is particularly useful when you have a CMYK file that was prepared for some other printing process. It shows you how the CMYK data will work on your output, which can help you decide whether you need to edit the image, convert it to a different CMYK space, or just send it as is. It's also useful for seeing just how crummy your image will look if you send it to your desktop inkjet printer without converting it to the proper profile (see "Converting at Print Time," later in this chapter).

Rendering Intent. The Rendering Intent popup menu lets you specify the rendering intent you want to use in the conversion from the document's space to the proof space. This is particularly useful for helping you decide whether a given image would be better served by perceptual or relative colorimetric rendering to the output space. It defaults to the

Color Settings default rendering intent until you change it, whereupon it remembers what you last used. However, when you save a proof setup, your selected rendering intent is saved with it; so, if you find that you're continually being tripped up by the wrong intent, you can just save a proof setup with your preferred rendering intent.

Black Point Compensation. The Black Point Compensation checkbox lets you choose whether or not to use black point compensation in the conversion from the document's space to the proof space. You almost invariably want to keep this turned on, but you can always uncheck it and see the effect to make sure.

Display Options (On-Screen). The checkboxes in the Display Options section—Simulate Paper Color and Simulate Black Ink—control the rendering of the image from the proofing space to the monitor. When both Simulate Paper Color and Simulate Black Ink are turned off, Photoshop does a relative colorimetric rendering (with black point compensation if that option is turned on in Color Settings). This rendering maps paper white to monitor white and ink black to monitor black, using the entire dynamic range of the monitor. If you're using a generic monitor profile, this is probably as good as you'll get (of course, with a canned monitor profile, you can't trust anything you see on screen anyway). With a good monitor profile, though, you should check out the alternatives.

▶ When you turn on Simulate Black Ink, it turns off black point compensation in the rendering from proof space to the monitor. As a result, the black you see on the monitor is the actual black you'll get on output. (Within limits—most monitor profiles have a "black hole" black point. The black ink simulation will be off by the amount that real monitor black differs from the monitor profile's black point. On a well-calibrated monitor, the inaccuracy is very slight.) If you're printing to a low-dynamic-range process like newsprint, or inkjet on uncoated paper, Simulate Black Ink will give you a much better idea of the actual blacks you'll get in print.

▶ Turning on the Simulate Paper Color checkbox makes Photoshop do an absolute colorimetric rendering from the proof space to the display. (Simulate Black Ink becomes checked and dimmed, since black point compensation is always disabled in absolute colorimetric conversions.)

In theory at least, turning on Simulate Paper Color should give you the most accurate soft-proof possible.

In practice, the most obvious effect of turning on Paper White isn't that it simulates the color of the paper, but rather that you see the compressed dynamic range of print. If you look at the image while turning on Simulate Paper Color, the effect is dramatic—so much so that Bruce looks away from the monitor when he turns on Simulate Paper Color, and waits a few seconds before looking at the image to allow his eyes to adapt to the new white point. More importantly, he also makes sure that he hides all white user interface elements, so that his eyes *can* adapt.

Obviously the quality of the soft-proofing simulation depends on the accuracy of your monitor calibration and on the quality of your profiles. But we believe that the relationship between the image on screen and the final printed output is, like all proofing relationships, one that you must learn. We've never seen a proofing system short of an actual press proof that really matches the final printed piece—laminated film proofs, for example, often show greater contrast than the press sheet, and may have a slight color cast too, but most people in the print industry have learned to discount the slight differences between proof and finished piece.

It's also worth bearing in mind the limitations of the color science on which the whole ICC color management effort is based. We still have a great deal to learn about color perception, and while the science we have works surprisingly well in many situations, it's only a model (see the sidebar "CIE Limitations and Soft Proofing"). The bottom line is that each of the different soft-proofing renderings to the monitor can tell you something about your printed images. We recommend that you experiment with the settings and learn what works for you and what doesn't.

Proof Setup Submenu

The Proof Setup submenu (under the View menu) contains several other useful commands that we should discuss. For instance, when you're viewing an RGB or grayscale image, you can view the individual CMYK plates (or the CMY progressive) you'd get if you converted to CMYK via the Mode submenu (in the Image menu). You can also use these commands to view the individual plates in CMYK files, but it's much faster and easier to use the keyboard shortcuts to display individual channels, or click on the eyeballs in the Channels palette.

CIE Limitations and Soft Proofing

All ICC color management is based on the system of mathematical models developed by the Commission Internationale de L'Éclairage (CIE), starting with CIE XYZ (1931), and including later variants such as CIE Lab and CIE xyY. These models were all developed with a very specific purpose in mind, which was to predict the degree to which two solid swatches of reflective material of a specific size on a specific background at a specific distance under a known illuminant would appear to match.

By design, the CIE models ignore many of the contextual effects that modulate our color perception, such as surround color, simultaneous contrast, and the dozens of effects named after the color scientists (Abney, Hunt, Stevens, Bezold-Brücke, and Bartleson-Breneman, to name but a few) who documented them. For solid colors viewed under tightly controlled conditions, these effects don't matter much, but for pixels in images, they almost certainly come into play. Moreover, the CIE models were never designed for cross-media comparisons like that between a monitor and hard copy.

We know quite a lot about white point adaptation—the tendency of our perceptual system to see the brightest thing in the scene as white—but science knows relatively little about black point adaptation, which is very likely equally important in soft-proofing. It's not that CIE colorimetry is wrong, just that we've taken to applying the CIE models to situations for which they weren't designed. With our current understanding of color perception, it's probably unrealistic to expect an exact match between an image on a monitor and a hard copy of that same image, because we experience them differently. But Photoshop's soft proofs are better than any other we've seen, and with a little experience, we believe you'll be able to make important judgments about your printed images based on what you see on your monitor with Proof Colors turned on.

The next set of commands—Macintosh RGB, Windows RGB, and Monitor RGB—is available only for RGB, grayscale, and indexed color images, not for CMYK or Lab. They show you how your image would appear on a "typical" Macintosh monitor (as defined by the Apple RGB profile), a "typical" Windows monitor (as defined by the sRGB profile), and on your personal monitor (as defined by your monitor profile) if you displayed it on these monitors with no color management. These might be useful when producing Web graphics, for instance. The rest of the menu lists custom proof setups saved in the Proofing folder.

Photoshop's soft-proofing features let you see how your image will really appear on output, so you can optimize the image to give the best possible rendition in the selected output space. They also help you to be lazy by letting you see if the same master file can produce acceptable results on all the output conditions to which you plan on sending it, relying on color management to handle the various conversions. So whether you're a driven artist seeking perfection, or a lowly production grunt doing the impossible on a daily basis, Photoshop's soft-proofing tools will become an invaluable addition to your toolbox.

Converting at Print Time

Photoshop lets you perform color conversions as it sends the data to a printer—converting from the working space to a selected printer profile using a selected rendering intent, or from the document space to your Proof Setup space using the rendering intent in Proof Setup, and then to the printer profile using the intent you specify while printing.

The latter lets you print an RGB file to a composite printer and make it simulate the CMYK output you've been soft-proofing—that is, it gives you a hard copy of your soft-proofed image without your having to first convert the image to final output CMYK. The Print with Preview command lets you exercise either of these options. If you're familiar with Print with Preview in previous versions of Photoshop, you'll notice that the *Titanic*'s deckchairs have been rearranged once more, but no functionality has been added or taken away.

Print with Preview

We cover most of the cool new features in Print with Preview (choose Print with Preview from the File menu, or press Command-Option-P) in Chapter 13, *Image Storage and Output;* however, we'll cover the color management aspects of the dialog box here. These features let you use color management to control the color that gets sent to the printer.

To use the color management features in the Print with Preview dialog box, click the More Options button and choose Color Management from the unnamed menu that appears immediately below the image preview (see Figure 5-31).

The color management options let you control the data that's sent to the printer, choosing whether or not to let Photoshop do the conversion to printer space (we invariably let Photoshop do the conversion).

Print. The Print radio buttons let you choose the Document space (to reproduce the image as well as your printer allows) or the Proof space (to produce a hard copy of your soft-proof simulation). If the image window

Figure 5-31
Print with Preview Color
Management controls

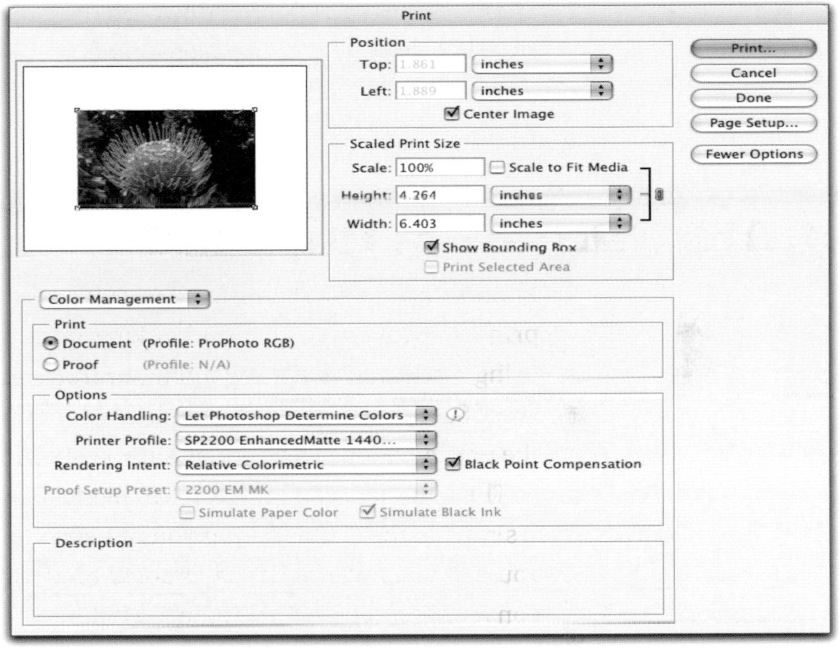

The dialog box is titled Print, but it's really Photoshop's Print with Preview...

from which you're printing has a custom proof setup, it will appear as the Proof option; otherwise the choice reads Profile N/A. This is slightly misleading, because if you click the Proof radio button, it actually enables the Proof Setup Preset menu in Options, described below.

Options. The Options popup menus let you choose whether or not Photoshop sends converted data to the printer, and if it does, how the conversion is performed. The Color Handling menu is new in Photoshop CS2—it contains options that previously appeared on the old Print Space menu (see Figure 5-32).

Figure 5-32
The Color Handling menu

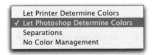

► **Let Printer Determine Colors** sends the source data unconverted. Use this option if you want to let the printer driver do the color conversion to printer space (which we don't really recommend). Color-managing CMYK images on PostScript printers requires PostScript 3—on a Post-

Script Level 2 printer, choose Lab Color instead—and PostScript color management varies enormously. Use it at your own risk.

▶ **Let Photoshop Determine Colors** enables the Printer Profile menu, and makes Photoshop convert the data that gets sent to the printer to the profile space described by the profile chosen from the Printer Profile menu, using the rendering intent specified in the Rendering intent menu. If you're trying to replicate the old behavior of choosing a printer profile in Print with Preview to make Photoshop do the conversion, you need to select this option first.

▶ **Separations** is only available for CMYK documents. It sends the individual plates to the printer, unmodified, as four separate pages.

▶ **No Color Management** is almost the same as Let Printer Determine Colors—it sends the numbers in the document to the printer, but it doesn't include the profile that describes them. We use this option for printing profiling targets, and precious little else.

Printer Profile. The Printer Profile menu is only enabled when you choose Let Photoshop Determine Colors from the Color Handling menu. Choose the profile that describes the printer to which you're printing, and the paper and ink the printer is using.

Rendering Intent. The Rendering Intent menu is enabled when you choose either Let Printer Determine Colors or Let Photoshop Determine Colors from the Color Handling menu, but in our experience it behaves reliably only in the former case. Choose the Rendering Intent that works best for the image by previewing the print using Proof Setup. (The Black Point Compensation checkbox is only enabled when Let Photoshop Determine Colors is selected in the Color Handling menu—as previously noted, we leave it turned on.)

Proof Setup Preset. The Proof Setup Preset menu is available with all choices except Separations in the Color Handling menu, and is enabled when you click the Proof radio button in the Print section. It makes Photoshop execute the conversion specified in the selected Proof Setup preset before sending the data to the printer using the options controlled by the Color Handling menu.

It disables the Rendering Intent menu. The rendering of the simulated proof space to printer space is controlled instead by the Simulate Paper Color and Simulate Black Ink checkboxes. When both are unchecked, Photoshop converts the simulated proof data to printer space using Relative Colorimetric rendering with Black Point Compensation. Checking Simulate Black Ink turns off the Black Point Compensation, while checking Simulate Paper Color makes Photoshop use Absolute Colorimetric rendering instead, forcing the printer to reproduce the actual paper white and actual ink black of the simulated proof.

In our experience, this feature works very well when Let Photoshop Determine Colors is selected in the Color Handling menu, and produces essentially random results when any of the other alternatives are selected in the Color Handling menu. By all means experiment, but don't say we didn't warn you!

Print

All the color management options you set up in Print with Preview are applied by Photoshop to the data that gets sent to the printer driver. You won't see any trace of them in the Print dialog box. If you use Print with Preview to convert the image for output, make very sure that you don't have another conversion specified in the Print dialog box—otherwise you'll get a double correction and a nasty print. Look for color management options like None, or No Color Adjustment, in the printer driver, and choose them to make sure that the driver doesn't sabotage you by throwing an extra conversion into the mix.

The print color management features allow you to control your printing precisely—whether you're trying to reproduce an original image as exactly as possible, or to make your printer simulate all sorts of other output conditions—from a single master RGB source file. This helps you by saving time and by cutting down on the number of different versions you need to prepare for a given image.

Isolating Variables

The information in this chapter may seem insanely complex, but it's really just insanely detailed. Remember, color management only does two things—if you can't remember what they are, go back to the beginning of this chapter! A good many color management problems are due to operator error. If you don't push the right buttons in the right sequence, you won't get the expected results, so it's important to keep track of the details.

All color management operations are dependent on a minimum of two profiles—just viewing a document involves the profile that describes the document and the profile that describes the display on which it's being viewed—and many involve three or even more profiles. If you run into issues that don't appear to be a result of operator error, it's likely that one or more of the profiles involved is a weak link. If you approach the requisite debugging methodically, testing each profile in isolation, and changing one thing at a time, you're likely to find the culprit much quicker than you will by flailing around and changing multiple parameters willy-nilly.

Color management isn't a panacea, and it doesn't remove the need for intelligent human color correction. It's just a useful tool that provides a solid floor for you to stand on when you make your (hopefully intelligent, certainly human) corrections.

6
Image Adjustment Fundamentals

Stretching and Squeezing the Bits

Tonal manipulation—adjusting the lightness or darkness of your images—is one of Photoshop's most powerful and far-reaching capabilities, and at first it may seem like magic. But there's nothing magical about it. Once you understand what's happening as you adjust the controls—it all comes back to those ubiquitous zeros and ones—it starts to look less like magic and more like clever technology. But your increased understanding and productivity should more than make up for any loss of the sense of wonder, and besides, you'll have more time to play.

Tonal manipulation makes the difference between a flat image that lies lifeless on the page and one that pops, drawing you into it. But the role of tonal correction goes far beyond that. When you correct color in an image, you're really manipulating the tone of the individual color channels.

In fact, just about every edit you make in Photoshop involves tonal manipulation. In Chapter 7, *The Digital Darkroom*, we'll show you some more esoteric techniques for getting great-looking images, but in this chapter we'll concentrate on the fundamentals—the basic tonal manipulation tools and their effects on pixels. Much of this chapter is devoted to two tools—Levels and Curves—because until you've mastered these, you simply don't know Photoshop! But we also cover the considerable number of other useful commands found on the Adjustments submenu in the Image menu.

Stretching and Squeezing the Bits

Every tonal edit you make causes some data loss. The purpose of this bald statement isn't to scare you, but simply to make you aware that like most things in digital imaging, editing tone and color involves a series of trade-offs. Photoshop's tools let you make the proverbial silk purse from a sow's ear, but they also let you do reverse!

Losing data is a natural and normal component of image editing. The trick is to throw away what you don't need, and to keep what you do need, and teaching you that valuable trick is one of the goals of this book.

When you work with images in Photoshop, they're often made up of one or more 8-bit channels, in which each pixel is represented by a value from 0 (black) to 255 (white). Grayscale images have one such channel, while color images have three (RGB or Lab) or four (CMYK). If you're more adventurous, you may work with *high-bit* images, where each channel uses 16 bits per pixel to represent a value from 0 (black) to 32,768 (white).

The key point is that when you use Photoshop's tonal controls, you're stretching and squeezing various parts of the tonal range, and in doing so, you inevitably lose some information. You lose a great deal more information in 8-bit-per-channel files than you do in high-bit ones, simply because you have much less data to start with. Here's a worst-case scenario that you can try yourself.

1. Create a new grayscale file in Photoshop, 7 inches wide by 5 inches tall, at 72 dpi, in 8-bit mode.

2. Use the Gradient tool to create a horizontal gradient from black to white across the entire width of the image (it's the third gradient in the default Gradients palette in the Options bar).

3. Choose Levels (from the Adjust submenu under the Image menu), change the gray input slider (the middle Input setting) to 2.2, and click OK (see Figure 6-1). You'll notice that the midtones are much lighter, but you may already be able to see some banding in the shadows.

4. Choose Levels again, and change the gamma to 0.5. The midtones are back almost to where you started, but you should be able to see that, instead of a smooth gradation, you have some distinct bands in the image (see Figure 6-2).

Figure 6-1
Adjusting
the gamma

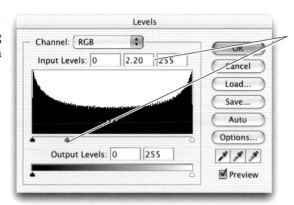

While it's not labeled as such, the gray Input slider applies a gamma correction, which adjusts the midtone values in an image.

What happened here? With the first midtone adjustment, you lightened the midtones—stretching the shadows and compressing the highlights. With the second midtone adjustment, you darkened the midtones—stretching the highlights and compressing the shadows.

Figure 6-2
Data loss due to
tonal correction

While the effect of successive tonal-correction moves on images may be subtle, the effect on the data within the image—as expressed in the histogram—is profound.

Histogram for the gray wedge at the right side of the image

Before tonal correction   *After two gamma moves*

But with all that stretching and squeezing, you lost some levels. Instead of a smooth blend, with pixels occupying every value from 0 to 255, some of those levels became unpopulated—in fact, if we're counting right, some 76 levels are no longer being used.

If you repeat the pair of midtone adjustments, you'll see that each time you make an adjustment, the banding becomes more obvious as you lose more and more tonal information. Repeating the midtone adjustments half a dozen times produces a file that contains only 55 gray levels instead of 256. And once you've lost that information, there's no way to bring it back.

Now repeat the experiment, but create a 16-bit-per-channel file instead of an 8-bit one (in the New dialog box, choose 16-bit from the menu to the right of the Color Mode popup menu). The difference in the result is dramatic, as shown in Figure 6-3.

Figure 6-3
Data loss due to tonal correction

With a high-bit file, you still lose some data, but the effect is much less drastic, as shown by the histogram of the edited image. The lesson is that high-bit files give you much more editing headroom than do 8-bit-per-channel ones.

Histogram for the gray wedge at the right side of the image

 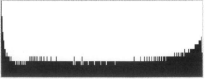

Before tonal correction   *After two gamma moves*

This set of adjustments represents, as we noted earlier, a worst-case scenario. No one with any significant Photoshop experience would make edits like this, with one edit attempting to undo the effect of the previous one. (And now that you've read this, you won't either!) The two immediate lessons to be drawn are:

▶ Successive edits that counteract each other should always be avoided.

▶ Data loss is much less of an issue with 16-bit/channel files than with 8-bit/channel ones.

But all edits lose data in one of two ways:

▶ When you stretch a tonal range, pixels that formerly had adjacent values may now differ by several levels. When you stretch the data too far, you lose the illusion of a continuous gradation, and you start to see distinct jumps in tone or color.

▶ When you squeeze or compress a tonal range, pixels that formerly had different values are now compressed to the same value. If you compress the range too much, you may lose desirable detail.

In short, whenever you edit tone and color, something has to give. See the sidebar, "Difference Is Detail: Tonal-Correction Issues," on the next page.

Data Loss in Perspective

Photography has always been about throwing away everything that can't be reproduced in the photograph. We start with all the tone and color of the real world, with scene contrast ratios that can easily be in the 100,000:1 range. We reduce that to the contrast ratio we can capture on film or silicon, which—if we're exceptionally lucky—may approach 10,000:1. By the time we get to reproducing the image in print, we have perhaps a 500:1 contrast ratio to play with.

This loss of image information may seem scarier than it really is. Nonetheless, we should hammer home the following lessons and the ensuing pieces of advice.

▶ All tonal manipulations incur some data loss.

Difference Is Detail: Tonal-Correction Issues

What do we mean when we talk about image information? Very simply, adjacent pixels with different values constitute image detail. If the difference is very slight, you won't be able to see it (especially in shadows); but it's there, waiting to be exploited. You can accentuate those differences—making those adjacent pixels *more* different—to bring out the detail.

The color of noise. Difference isn't always detail, though. Low-cost scanners, and digital cameras shot at high speeds, introduce spurious differences between pixels. Those differences aren't detail, they're just noise (like the static on the radio that drowns out the traffic report), and they're one of our least favorite things. Photoshop can't tell the difference between genuine image information and device-induced noise. You need to decide what is desirable detail and what's noise, accentuating the detail while minimizing the noise.

Posterization. Noise isn't the only problem to deal with when you're doing tonal correction, though. There's also *posterization*—the stair-stepping of gray levels in distinct, visible jumps rather than smooth gradations (see Figure 6-4). Unless you're working with a high-bit image, Photoshop gives you only 256 possible values for a gray pixel.

Posterization manifests itself in two ways. When you start making dark pixels more different, you eventually make them *so* different that the image looks splotchy—covered with patches of distinctly different pixels rather than smooth transitions. But posterization can also wipe out detail and turn smooth gradations into flat blobs.

Lost detail. When you accentuate detail in one part of the tonal range, making slightly different

▶ Once the data is gone, you can't bring it back.

▶ You lose much less data making corrections in high-bit mode.

▶ Successive tonal manipulations lose data at an increasing rate.

Get good data to begin with. If you've got a high-bit capture device, (which you almost certainly do), it's better to get the image as close to "right" as you possibly can while the image is in high-bit form. The whole point of high-bit capture is to let you manipulate the high-bit data, so that you get the *right* 8-bit data when you downsample to 8 bits per channel.

Use adjustment layers. You can avoid some of the penalties incurred by successive corrections by using an adjustment layer instead of applying the changes directly to the image. Adjustment layers use more RAM and create bigger files, but the increased flexibility makes the trade-off worthwhile—especially when you find yourself needing to back off from previous edits. But since the various tools offered in adjustment layers operate identically to the way they work on flat files, we'll discuss how

Figure 6-4 The effects of posterization

Figure 6-5 Loss of highlights

Before tonal correction

After tonal correction

pixels more different (*expanding the range*), you lose detail in other areas, making slightly different pixels more similar (*compressing the range*).

For instance, when you stretch the shadow values apart to bring out shadow detail, you inevitably squeeze the highlight values together (see Figure 6-5). If you make two different pixels the same, that detail is gone forever. That's what we mean when we say that information is "lost."

the features (Curves, Levels, Hue/Saturation, and so on) work on flat files first. For a detailed discussion of adjustment layers, see Chapter 7, *The Digital Darkroom*.

Use high-bit data. If your scanner or camera allows it, you can bring the 10-, 12-, 14-, or 16-bit-per-channel data directly into Photoshop—you are, in effect, telling your capture device "just give me all the data you can capture"—and then edit it in Photoshop. In the 16-bit-per-channel space, you have much more editing headroom before you run into posterization. Photoshop CS2 lets you do just about anything to a high-bit file that you can do to an 8-bit one, so the main reason for downsampling is to keep file sizes managable. If you bring digital captures into Photoshop using Camera Raw, note that Camera Raw always operates on the high-bit data, and offers the option to bring the edited high-bit data into Photoshop.

Minimize tonal correction. Small tonal moves are much less destructive than big ones. The more you want to change an image, the more compromises you'll have to make to avoid obvious posterization, artifacts due to noise, and loss of highlight and shadow detail.

Be decisive, or use adjustment layers. If you push an edit too far, don't try to correct it with a second edit—go back and fix the problem instead. You can use History to step back before the edit, or if you use adjustment layers, you have the freedom to keep changing your mind right up to the point where you flatten the image.

Cover yourself. Since the data you lose is irretrievable, leave yourself a way out by working on a copy of the file, by saving your tonal adjustments in progress separately (without applying them to the image by applying your edits using adjustment layers), or by using any combination of the above. Or you can use the History feature to leave yourself an escape route—just remember that History only remembers the number of states you specify in the Preferences dialog box, and it can consume mind-boggling amounts of scratch disk space.

Data loss can be good. Sometimes you want to throw away information. For example, none of these restrictions applies when you're working on masks or alpha channels—in fact, you usually *want* to throw away data on those, since you're often trying to exaggerate a feature or isolate it from its background. (See "Step-by-Step Silhouettes" in Chapter 8, *Making Selections.*)

With all these caveats in mind, let's take a look at Photoshop's tonal-manipulation tools.

Tonal-Correction Tools

Two Photoshop tools, Levels and Curves, let you address almost all tonal issues, and mastering them is a basic necessity for productive Photoshop work. As you'll find out later in this book, Levels and Curves aren't always necessarily the easiest way to correct tone, but until you've learned what they can do, you just don't know Photoshop.

However, two additional Photoshop features, the Histogram and Info palettes, provide information that can help guide your corrections. They let you analyze both the unedited image and the effect of your tonal manipulations. So before plunging into the Levels and Curves dialog boxes, both of which are quite deep, let's look at the analytical tools: the Histogram palette and the Info palette.

The Histogram Palette

A *histogram* is a simple bar chart that plots the tonal levels from 0 to 255 along the horizontal axis, and the number of pixels at each level along the vertical axis (see Figure 6-6). If there are lots of pixels in shadow areas, the bars are concentrated on the left; the reverse is true with "high-key" images, where most of the information is in the highlights. The height of the bars is arbitrary—they're simply comparative indicators of how many pixels have a given tonal value.

Some of the information offered by the Histogram palette may not seem particularly useful—for most image reproduction tasks you really don't need to know the median pixel value, or how many pixels in the image are at level 33. But histograms show some useful information at a glance.

Figure 6-6
Histogram
palette

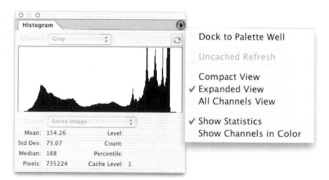

Endpoints

With a quick look at the histogram, you can see if the image has suffered clipping in the highlights or shadows (see Figure 6-7). If there's a spike at either end of the histogram, the highlight or shadow values are almost certainly clipped—we say "almost" because there are some images that really do have a very large number of pure white or solid black areas. But they're pretty rare.

You can also see if the image covers the whole dynamic range (see Figure 6-8). If the data stops a long way south of the white point or a long

Figure 6-7
Highlight and
shadow clipping

Clipped highlights and shadows

Figure 6-8
Limited dynamic range

No blacks or whites

way north of the black point, you'll usually need to stretch the data out so that it occupies the whole dynamic range. There are exceptions, but the vast majority of images need a few pixels that are very close to pure white and a few pixels that are very close to solid black if they're going to have decent contrast on output.

How Much Information Is Present?

The overall appearance of the histogram also gives you a quick, rough-and-ready picture of the integrity of your image data (see Figure 6-9). A good

*The combing in the histogram is a
sign that the image has already been
manipulated (but it looks better than
the unedited version in Figure 6-8).*

capture uses the entire tonal range, and has a histogram with smooth contours. The actual location of the peaks and valleys depends entirely on the image content, but if the histogram shows obvious spikes, you're probably dealing with a noisy capture device. If it shows a comb-like appearance, it's likely that the image has already been manipulated—perhaps by your scanning software or camera firmware.

The histogram also shows you where to examine the image for signs that you've gone too far in your tonal manipulations. If you look at the histograms produced by the earlier experiment in applying gamma adjustments to a gradient, you can see at a glance exactly what each successive adjustment did to the image—spikes and gaps start to appear throughout the histogram.

Note that a gap of only one level is almost certainly unnoticeable in the image—especially if it's in the shadows or midtones—but once you start to see gaps of three or more levels, you may begin to notice visible posterization in the image. The location of the gap gives you a good idea of where in the tonal range the posterization is happening.

Histograms Are Generalizations

Once you've edited an image, the histogram may look pretty ugly. This is normal; in fact, it's almost inevitable. The histogram is a guide, not a rule. Histograms are most useful for evaluating images before you start to edit. A histogram can show clipped endpoints and missing levels, but a good-looking histogram isn't necessarily the sign of a good image. And many good-looking images have ugly histograms.

Fixing the histogram doesn't mean you've fixed the image. If you want a nice-looking histogram, the Gaussian Blur filter with a 100-pixel radius will give you one, but there won't be much left of the image! The Histogram is just a handy way of looking at the data so that you can see how it relates to the image appearance. The image is what matters—take what useful information you can from the histogram, but concentrate on the image.

Tip: Don't Forget to Refresh the Histogram. For performance reasons, while you work on an image, the Histogram palette shows you values based on the antialiased screen display of your image. This view can hide posterization, giving you an unrealistically rosy picture of your data. Photoshop warns you of this by displaying a warning icon when the histogram is showing you an approximation of your data. To see what's really going on, click the Refresh button in the Histogram palette. (See Figure 6-10.)

Figure 6-10
Histogram
warning

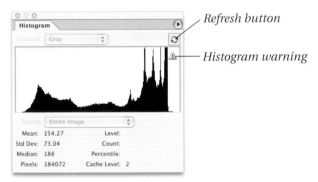

Refresh button

Histogram warning

The Info Palette

Like the Histogram palette, the Info palette is purely an informational display. It doesn't let you do anything to the image besides analyze its contents. But where the Histogram palette shows a general picture of the entire file, the Info palette lets you analyze *specific* points in the image.

When you move the cursor across the image, the Info palette displays the pixel value under the cursor and its location in the image. More important, when you have one of the tonal- or color-correction dialog boxes (such as Levels or Curves) open, the Info palette displays the values for the pixel before and after the transformation (see Figure 6-11).

Figure 6-11
Info palette

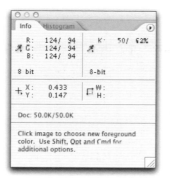

When you're working in one of the Adjust dialog boxes, such as Levels or Curves, the Info palette shows the pixel value before and after the correction.

Tip: Look for Differences. The Info palette lets you sample the actual values of different pixels, but it also lets you hunt down hidden detail, particularly in deep shadows and bright highlights where it can be hard to see on the monitor. Move the cursor over a deep shadow, and watch the Info palette. If the numbers *change* as you move the cursor, there's difference lurking in there—it may be detail waiting to be exploited or it may be noise that you'll need to suppress, but *something is* hiding in there.

Palette Options

You can control what sorts of information the Info palette displays in one of two ways. First, you can select Palette Options from the Info palette's popout menu (see Figure 6-12). The second method is to use the Info palette's hidden popup menus (see Figure 6-13). We have several different palette setups that we use for different kinds of work, and we use the Workspace feature, which captures the Info palette settings in addition to all the other palette locations, to load them as needed (see "Workspaces" in Chapter 2, *Essential Photoshop Tips and Tricks*).

For grayscale, duotone, or multichannel images, we generally set the First Color Readout to RGB, and the Second Color Readout to Actual Color. (Actual Color causes the readout method to change, depending on what type of image you're viewing.) We just about always display the mouse coordinates as pixels, because it makes it easier for us to return consistently to the same spot in the image.

Figure 6-12
The Info palette options

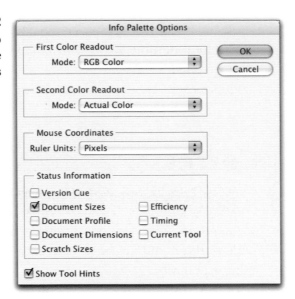

Figure 6-13
The Info palette's popup menus

Click the tiny black arrows to display the hidden menus

Why display RGB values for a grayscale image? Simply for the precision. Grayscale and Total Ink show percentages instead, on a scale of 100 instead of 255. For outrageous precision, Photoshop can also display 16-bit values—ranging from 0 to 32,768—when you work on high-bit files. (If these numbers make your head explode, you're not alone! We'd really like to be able to see the 8-bit and 16-bit values side by side, at least until we get used to thinking of midtone gray as 16,384. Photoshop CS2 introducues support for High Dynamic Range images with 32-bit floating point values per channel, and the Info palette displays those too.

The numbers for R, G, and B are always the same in a grayscale image, so the level just displays three times. Setting the second readout to Actual

Color lets you read the dot percentage, so you can display levels and percentages at the same time. We use different setups for color images, which we cover later in this chapter.

Now let's look at the tools you can use to actually change the image.

More Tonal-Correction Tools

Levels and Curves are the two fundamental Photoshop tools for global tonal and color correction. Levels is the easier of the two for beginning Photoshop users, and (in some situations) for experienced ones, too. Curves is a little more difficult to master, but a lot more powerful. We liken Levels to an automatic transmission and Curves to a stick shift. Levels is quick and easy. Curves lets you do all the same things (and more), but it demands a bit more skill, coordination, and experience.

Levels and Curves let you change existing (input) pixel values to new (output) pixel values—but they offer different ways of controlling the relationship between input and output. They share an important property that differentiates them from the Brightness and Contrast controls: They let you apply nonlinear transformations, instead of the linear transformations applied by the Brightness and Contrast controls (see the sidebar "The Nonlinear Advantage," later in this chapter).

Levels

Photoshop's Levels command opens a tonal-manipulation powerhouse (see Figure 6-14). This deceptively simple little dialog box lets you identify the shadow and highlight points in the image, limit the highlight and shadow dot percentages, and make dramatic changes to the midtones, while providing real-time feedback via the on-screen image and the Info palette. For more detailed tonal corrections, we use the Curves command; but there are a couple of things that we can do in more easily in Levels, and for a considerable amount of grayscale work, it's all we need.

The Levels dialog box not only displays a histogram of the image, it also lets you work with the histogram in very useful ways. If you understand what the histogram shows, the workings of the Levels controls suddenly become a lot less mysterious.

Figure 6-14
How Levels works

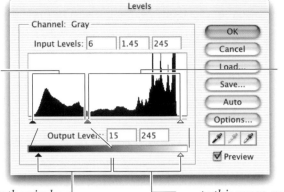

This tonal range is being expanded...

This tonal range is being compressed...

...to this range, spreading the pixels out and making them more different, so detail is more apparent.

...to this range, making the pixels more similar (and in some cases, identical), so detail is less visible or completely lost.

Input Levels

The three Input Levels sliders let you change the black point, the white point, and the midtone in the image. As you move the sliders, the numbers in the corresponding Input Levels fields change, so if you know what you're doing, you can type in the numbers directly. But we still use the sliders most of the time, because they provide real-time feedback—by changing the image on screen—as we drag them. Here's what they actually do.

Black- and white-point sliders. Moving these sliders in toward the center has the effect of stretching the dynamic range of the image. When you move the black-point slider away from its default position at 0 (zero) to a higher level, you're telling Photoshop to turn all the pixels at that level and lower (those to the left) to level 0 (black), and stretch all the levels to the right of the slider to fill the entire tonal range from 0 to 255.

Moving the white-point slider does the same thing to the other end of the tonal range. As you move it from its default position at level 255 (white) to a lower level, you're telling Photoshop to turn all the pixels at that level and higher (those to the right of the slider) to level 255 (white), and stretch all the levels to the left of the slider to fill the tonal range from 0 to 255 (see Figure 6-15).

Gray slider. The gray slider lets you alter the midtones without changing the highlight and shadow points. When you move the gray slider, you're telling Photoshop where you want the midtone gray value (50-percent gray, or level 128) to be. If you move it to the left, the image gets lighter, because you're choosing a value that's darker than 128 and making it 128. As you do so, the shadows get stretched to fill up that part of the tonal range, and the highlights get squeezed together (see Figure 6-16).

Conversely, if you move the slider to the right, the image gets darker because you're choosing a lighter value and telling Photoshop to change it to level 128. The highlights get stretched, and the shadow values get squeezed together. (David likes to think of this as grabbing a rubber band

Figure 6-15 Black- and white point tweaks

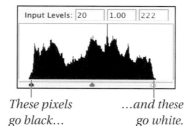

These pixels go black…   *…and these go white.*

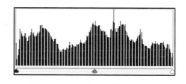

Postcorrection histogram, displaying some black- and white-point clipping

Figure 6-16
Gamma tweak

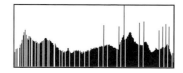

Adding a gamma adjustment of 1.2 to the image in the previous figure brings out some shadow detail, though highlight detail is lost, and the histogram displays some additional combing.

on both ends and in the middle, and pulling the middle part to the left or right; one side gets stretched out, and the other side gets bunched up.)

The number that appears in the slider's edit field is a *gamma* value—the exponent of a power curve equation, if that means anything to you. Values greater than 1 lighten the midtone, values less than 1 darken it, and a value of 1 leaves it unchanged. If you only adjust the midtone slider, you really are applying a pure gamma correction to the image, but if you also move the endpoints, you aren't: instead, you're applying an arbitrary three-point curve correction. If you want a more detailed mathematical understanding of gamma encoding and gamma correction, a good place to start is *http://chriscox.org/gamma/*, written by Adobe's own Chris Cox.

Output Levels

The Output Levels controls let you compress the tonal range of the image into fewer than the entire 256 possible gray levels. In the days before ICC profiles, we used to use these controls to make sure that our highlights didn't blow out and our shadows didn't plug up on press—the sliders let you limit black to a value higher than zero and white to a value lower than 255. Good ICC profiles tend to make this practice unnecessary, since they take the minimum and maximum printable dot into account.

However, even though grayscale is a first-class citizen in good color-management standing in Photoshop, very few other applications recognize grayscale profiles. When we have grayscale images with no specular highlights (the very bright reflections one sees on polished metal or water), we still use the output sliders in levels to limit our highlight dot, and—in images with very critical shadow detail—our shadow dot. For images with specular highlights, we use Curves instead (we discuss that later technique in this chapter).

We also use the output sliders when we're preparing images for slide shows that we burn to DVD and play on TV sets, and for producing "ghosted" images. And on those rare occasions when we're forced to deal with old-style legacy CMYK setups that use a single dot gain value, we may still use the output sliders to make sure that we don't force our highlight or shadow dots into a range that the output process can't print.

Black Output Levels. When this slider is at its default setting of 0, pixels in the image at level 0 will remain at level 0. As you increase the value of the slider, it limits the darkest pixels in the image to the level at which it's set, compressing the entire tonal range.

White Output Levels. This behaves the same way as the black Output Levels slider, except that it limits the lightest pixels in the image rather than the darkest ones. Setting the slider to level 240, for instance, will turn all the pixels at level 255 to 240, and so on (see Figure 6-17).

You might think that compressing the tonal range would fill in those gaps in the histogram caused by gamma and endpoint tweaks, and to a limited extent it will; but all that number crunching introduces rounding errors, so you'll still see some levels going unused.

Tip: Leave Some Room When Setting Limits. Always leave yourself some room to move when you set input and output limits, particularly in the highlights. If you move the white input slider so that your highlight detail starts at level 254, with your specular highlights at level 255, you run into two problems.

▶ When you compress the tonal range for final optimization, your specular highlights go gray.

▶ When you sharpen, some of the highlight detail blows out to white.

Figure 6-17
Output levels

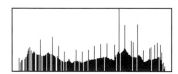

Compressing the tonal range with the Output sliders to the limits of the printing process (we used 12 and 243—about 5 and 95 percent) makes the darkest shadow detail more visible while reducing contrast overall.

It also points out the limitations of this targeting approach with images that include specular highlights (or headlights). They go gray.

The Nonlinear Advantage

Linear transformations (such as those applied by Brightness/Contrast) discard your image's information, and they do so in a pretty dumb way. They're called linear transformations because they do exactly the same thing to each pixel in the image. If you're trying to modify the brightness or contrast of an image, using Brightness/Contrast is a bad idea, because you lose detail at one or both ends of the tonal range and probably do severe violence to the image in the process.

For example, the Brightness control simply shifts all the pixel values up or down the tonal range. Let's say you increase Brightness by 10. Photoshop adds 10 to every pixel's value, so value 0 becomes 10, 190 becomes 200, and every pixel with a value of 245 or above becomes 255 (you can't go above 255). This is called "clipping the highlights" (they're all the same value, so there's no highlight detail). Plus, your shadows go flat because you lose all your true blacks.

The Contrast control stretches the tonal range as you increase the contrast, throwing away information in both the highlights and the shadows (and potentially posterizing the tones in between); and it compresses the tonal range when you reduce the contrast, so either way, you lose gray levels.

Don't use the Brightness and Contrast controls on images! You can use them to good effect with channels and masks, but that's another story.

The nonlinear transformations applied by Levels and Curves throw away some image information too (losing some highlight detail, in most cases), but they don't discard nearly as much, and they do it in a more intelligent way (see Figure 6-18). They let you adjust the values in the middle of the tonal range without losing the information at the ends, so you can improve your images dramatically while still preserving vital highlight and shadow detail.

Figure 6-18 Linear versus nonlinear correction

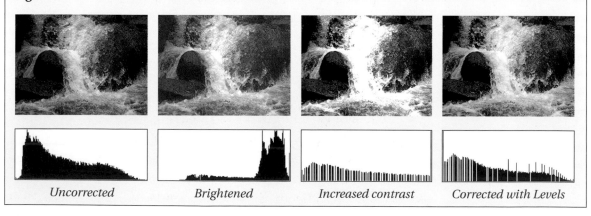

Uncorrected   Brightened   Increased contrast   Corrected with Levels

To avoid these problems, try to keep your significant highlight detail below level 250. Shadow clipping is less critical, but keeping the unoptimized shadow detail in the 5 to 10 range is a safe way to go.

Likewise, unless your image has no true whites or blacks, leave some headroom when you set the output limits. For example, if your press can't hold a dot smaller than 10 percent, don't set the output limit to level 230. If you're optimizing with the output sliders in Levels, set it to 232 or 233 so you get true whites in the printed piece. If you'll be optimizing later with the eyedroppers or Curves, set it somewhere around 237 or 240. This lets you fine-tune specular highlights using the eyedroppers or Curves, but brings the image's tonal range into the range that the press can handle. Again, we should emphasize that if you have a good ICC profile for your output, you don't need to compress the dynamic range using the output sliders because the profile will take care of it for you.

Levels Command Goodies

There are a few very useful features in the Levels dialog box that aren't immediately obvious. But they can be huge time-savers.

Preview. When you turn on the Preview checkbox in the Levels dialog box, Photoshop redraws the image—or the part of the image that is selected—to reflect any Levels tweaks you've made, so you can see the effect before you click OK.

Instant before-and-after. In any mode, you can see instant before-and-afters by turning the Preview checkbox on and off. (This is true in any Photoshop dialog box that has a Preview checkbox.)

Black-point/white-point clipping display. Black-point and white-point clipping is the one feature that keeps us coming back to Levels instead of relying entirely on Curves to make tonal adjustments. It doesn't work in Lab, CMYK, Indexed Color, or Bitmap modes—just Grayscale, RGB, Duotone, and Multichannel—but it's immensely useful.

When you set the black and white points, you typically want to set the white point to the lightest area that contains detail, and the shadow to the darkest point that contains detail. These aren't always easy to see. Hold down the Option key while moving the black or white Input Levels sliders to see exactly which pixels are being clipped (see Figure 6-19).

Tip: Look for the Jumps When Clipping. When you're Option/Alt-dragging the input sliders to view the clipping display, watch out for big clumps of pixels turning on or off. You generally want to stay outside of

Figure 6-19
The clipping
display in Levels

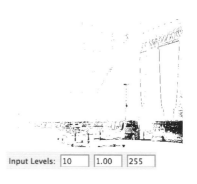

Holding down Option as you move the left and right input sliders shows which pixels are being clipped to white or (in this illustration) black. The display is really handy for setting white and black points, but it's useful in many other situations as well.

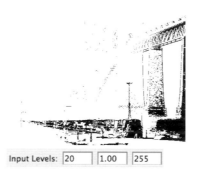

these clumps of image pixels, because moving past them removes a lot of detail.

These types of jumps are also what we look for when we're evaluating scans and scanners. A good scan gives you a smooth growth of pixels as you Option-move the sliders. Lesser-quality scanners tend to provide scans with distinct jumps between gray levels.

Auto. Auto Levels and Auto Contrast work identically on grayscale images, though they differ in their handling of color ones. For grayscale, we advise avoiding both unless you want to auto-wreck your images. They automatically move the black and white input sliders to clip a predetermined amount of data separately on each channel. If you have a large number of images that you know will benefit from a preliminary round of black and white clipping, you *may* want to consider running Auto Levels, but you'll probably want to reduce the default clipping percentages from 0.50 percent to something lower (the minimum is 0.01 percent). To change the clipping percentage, click the Options button, and enter your desired percentages in the dialog box that appears.

Auto Color, however, is one of Photoshop's more useful features for making quick fixes to *color* images (see "Auto Color," later in this chapter).

Auto-reset. If you hold down the Option key, the Cancel button changes to Reset (if you click this, all the settings return to their default states).

Levels in Color

When you work on color images, Levels lets you work on a composite channel (all colors) or on the individual color channels in the image (see Figure 6-20).

When you work in the composite (RGB, CMYK, or Lab) channel, Levels works very much the same way it does on grayscale images. It makes the same adjustment to all the color channels, so in theory at least it only

Figure 6-20
Levels in color

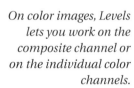

On color images, Levels lets you work on the composite channel or on the individual color channels.

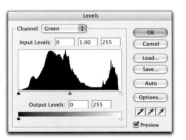

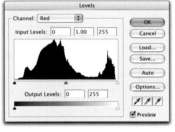

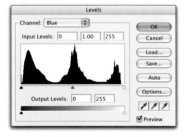

The image

The red channel

The green channel

The blue channel

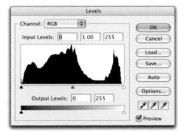

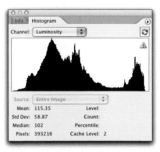

The composite RGB channel

The luminosity histogram

affects tone. In practice, it may introduce some color shifts when you make big corrections, so we tend to use Curves more than Levels on color images. But Levels is useful on color images in at least two ways.

▶ As an image-evaluation tool, using both the histograms and clipping display.

▶ When we have a color image that has no problems with color balance, but needs a small midtone adjustment. Often, a move with the gray slider is all that's needed.

We also use Levels' Auto Color feature to make quick major corrections (see "Auto Color," later in this chapter).

The Levels composite histogram. Like the Histogram palette, Levels displays the histogram for an individual channel when you're viewing a single channel, and offers a Channels menu when you're viewing the composite image. The composite histogram it displays (labeled RGB, CMYK, or Lab, depending on the image's color space) is the same as the default composite histogram in the Histogram palette, but different from the Histogram palette's Luminosity histogram.

In the Luminosity histogram, a level of 255 represents a white pixel. In the RGB and CMYK histograms in Levels, however, a level of 255 *may* represent a white pixel, but it could also represent a fully saturated color pixel—the histogram simply shows the maximum of all the individual color channels. Fortunately, the Levels dialog box's clipping display makes this clear (see Figure 6-21).

Note that saturation clipping isn't necessarily a problem. It's simply a signal that you should check the values in the unclipped channels to make sure that things are headed in the right direction. If you're trying to clip to white and the unclipped channel is up around 250, or you're trying to clip to black and the unclipped channel is under 10, you don't really have a problem. But if the values in the unclipped channels are far away from white or black clipping, respectively, you may actually be creating very saturated colors that you didn't want.

How Levels works on color images. As the composite histogram implies, any moves you make to the Levels sliders when you're working in the composite channels apply equally to each individual color channel.

Figure 6-21
Levels color
clipping display

*When you Option-drag
the white input slider, the
colors indicate:*

*Black = no clip
Red = red clip at 255
Green = green clip at 255
Blue = blue clip at 255
Cyan = green and blue
clip at 255
Magenta = red and blue
clip at 255
Yellow = red and green
clip at 255
White = all channels
clip at 255.*

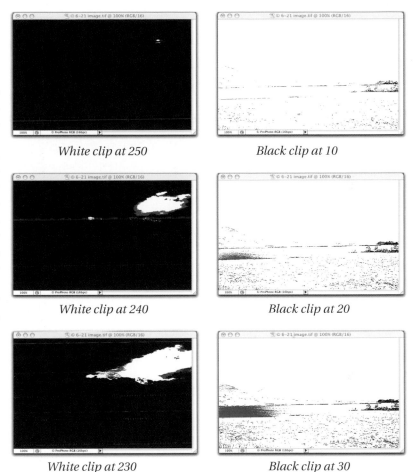

White clip at 250   *Black clip at 10*

White clip at 240   *Black clip at 20*

White clip at 230   *Black clip at 30*

*When you Option-drag the black input slider, the colors indicate the following:
White = no clip; Cyan = red clip at 0; Magenta = green clip at 0;
Yellow = blue clip at 0; Red = green and blue clip at 0;
Green = red and blue clip at 0; Blue = red and green clip at 0;
Black = all three channels clip at 0.*

In other words, you get identical results applying the same move individually to each color channel as you would applying the move once to the composite channel.

However, since the contents of the individual channels are quite different, applying the same moves to each can sometimes have unexpected results. The gray slider and the black and white Output sliders operate straightforwardly, but the black and white Input sliders require caution.

The white Input slider clips the highlights *in each channel* to level 255. This brightens the image overall, and neutral colors stay neutral. But it can have an undesirable effect on non-neutral colors, ranging from over-saturation to pronounced color shifts. The same applies to the black Input slider, although the effects are usually less obvious. The black Input slider clips the values in each channel to level zero, so when you apply it to a non-neutral color, you can end up removing all trace of one primary from the color, which also increases its saturation.

Because of this behavior, we use the black and white Input sliders primarily as image-evaluation tools in conjunction with the Option-key clipping display. They let you see exactly where your saturated colors are in relation to your neutral highlights and shadows. If the image is free of dangerously saturated colors, you can make small moves with the black and white Input sliders; but be careful of unintentional clipping, and keep a close eye on what's happening to the saturation—it's particularly easy to create out-of-gamut saturated colors in the shadows.

The image shown in Figure 6-22 is a good candidate for correction using Levels. It has no real color problems, and no dangerously saturated colors, but it's washed-out and flat. The Levels clipping displays reveal that the only data above level 232 is a tiny specular highlight, and clipping the shadows at level 10 introduces a hint of true black. A midtone adjustment with the gamma slider completes the job—three quick moves make an immense difference to the image.

We usually use Levels to make only relatively small corrections like the one in Figure 6-22, because compared to curves, it's something of a blunt instrument. But some situations call for a sledgehammer rather than a scalpel, and Levels' Auto Color feature is a case in point.

Auto Color

The Auto Levels feature in the Adjustments submenu (in the Image menu) generally wrecks color images, causing huge color shifts. Its younger sibling, Auto Contrast, while less of a blunt instrument than Auto Levels, still leaves a great deal to be desired. However, the Auto Color feature can be very useful indeed for making major initial corrections, particularly on scans of color negatives or on images that need major adjustments in color balance and contrast.

Figure 6-23 shows a pretty desperate situation. (This is what happens when your bags get lost by the airline and your undeveloped film goes through numerous baggage scanners as it chases you around the world!)

Figure 6-22
A quick fix with Levels

Original image

White clip at 232

Levels edit

Black clip at 10

Edited image

If you simply use Auto Color's default settings (for example, if you simply chose Auto Color from the Adjust submenu), you'll typically get a less-than-desirable result. With very little help, though, Auto Color can quickly get you a lot closer to where you need to be. Here's how we use it.

► We always launch it by opening the Levels dialog box and clicking the Options button.

► We click the Find Dark and Light Colors button to get Auto Color rather than Auto Contrast, which for some annoying reason is the default.

► We enable the Snap Neutral Midtones checkbox.

Figure 6-23
Auto Color

This image is need of serious help!

original image

Auto Color at default settings produces the cold, over-contrasty rendering at right. Reducing the clipping percentages for highlight and shadow, and choosing a warmer midtone color, produces the much more pleasing version shown below right.

Auto Color default settings

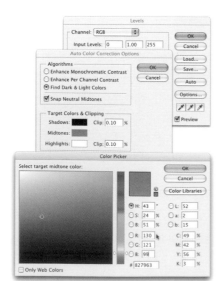

The Auto Color settings at left produce this result.

▶ We adjust the clipping percentages from the ridiculously high default value of 0.50 percent to a much lower value, typically in the range of 0.00 to 0.05 percent, depending on the image content.

▶ When necessary (that is, more often than not), we click the Midtones swatch to open the color picker, and adjust the midtone target value.

In the example shown in Figure 6-23, we reduced the default clipping percentages to a lower value to avoid blowing out the highlights in the sky and plugging up the shadows. The default midtone color setting made the image too cold, so we chose an amber warming filter color, and adjusted it by dragging the target circle in the Color Picker. The image updates as you change the target values, so the process is quick and interactive.

You can adjust the midtone swatch color by changing the numbers in the Color Picker, or simply by dragging the target indicator in the color swatch. Neither method is better than the other—use whichever you find more convenient.

Tip: Save as Defaults. When you dismiss the Levels dialog box, you're prompted to save the new settings as defaults. You may be tempted not to do so since the corrections are almost always image-specific. Save them anyway, because that way, the next time you click the Options button in Levels, it should be set to Find Light and Dark Colors with Snap Neutral Midtones turned on. You'll still probably want to adjust the clipping percentages and midtone target color, but you'll save yourself some time.

Tip: If Things Aren't Working Right. For some strange reason, the Options button in Levels sometimes defaults to Enhance Per Channel Contrast (Auto Contrast), and when you switch it to Find Light and Dark Colors (Auto Color), the Snap Neutral Midtones checkbox is turned off. If you're like us, you'll find yourself diving right in and adjusting the midtone target value, then wondering why nothing's happening. Don't forget to turn on that checkbox!

Other than in the situations covered by the two preceding tips, we don't usually bother saving the settings as defaults when prompted unless we're processing a bunch of images that need the same correction. More often than not, the settings are image-dependent. But we find that simply adjusting three values—the highlight clipping percentage, the shadow clipping percentage, and the midtone target color—lets us carry out powerful initial corrections with a minimum of fuss. We don't aim for perfection; rather, we use Auto Color to get the image into the ballpark, and fine-tune the results using the Curves dialog box.

Curves

As we said earlier, if Levels is an automatic transmission, Curves is a stick shift. It's indispensable when you're stuck in the snow or mud, but it takes a bit more effort to master. The Curves command offers a different way of stretching and squeezing the bits, one that's more powerful than Levels. But it also uses a different way of looking at the data.

When you use Levels, the histogram shows you the shape of the data you're working with. Curves doesn't do that (except through the Histogram palette). Instead, it displays a graph that plots the relationship between input level and output level (unaltered and altered). Input levels run along the bottom, and output values run along the side. When you first choose the Curves command, the graph displays a straight 45-degree line—for each input level, the output level is identical (see Figure 6-24).

Curves versus Levels. With the exception of the clipping display, anything you can do in the Levels dialog box, you can also do with Curves (see Figure 6-25). When you move the middle input slider in Levels to adjust the gamma, for instance, it's almost the same as moving the midpoint of the curve right or left. Setting the other four sliders is equivalent to setting the endpoints of the curve.

Tone curves are probably the most useful global image-manipulation tool ever invented—they're indispensable for color correction, but they're also very useful for fine control over grayscale work. Gamma corrections like the one in Levels let you change the broad distribution of midtones, but they only let you create very basic curves ("move the 50-percent point to here") with two endpoints and a single midpoint. Curves lets you make very precise adjustments to specific parts of the tonal range.

You change the relationship between input level and output level by changing the shape of the curve, either by placing points or by drawing a curve freehand (with the pencil tool). We almost always place points on

Figure 6-24
Curves dialog box

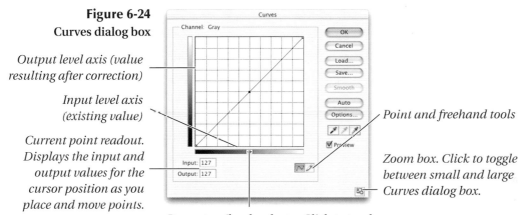

Output level axis (value resulting after correction)
Input level axis (existing value)
Current point readout. Displays the input and output values for the cursor position as you place and move points.
Point and freehand tools
Zoom box. Click to toggle between small and large Curves dialog box.
Percentage/levels selector. Click to toggle between black on the left, with level readouts (0–256), and black on the right, with percent readouts (0–100).
Curves
Channel: Gray
OK
Cancel
Load...
Save...
Smooth
Auto
Options...
Preview
Input: 127
Output: 127

Figure 6-25
Levels and Curves

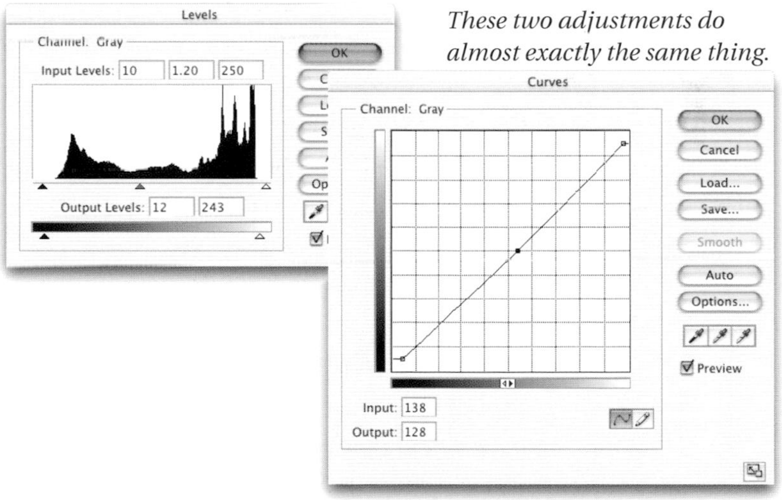

These two adjustments do almost exactly the same thing.
Levels
Channel: Gray
Input Levels: 10 1.20 250
Output Levels: 12 243
OK
Curves
Channel: Gray
OK
Cancel
Load...
Save...
Smooth
Auto
Options...
Preview
Input: 138
Output: 128

the curve because it's much easier to be precise that way. All the settings you can make with Levels—white point, black point, midtones, maximum shadow, and minimum highlight—you can make with Curves too, but the way you go about it is slightly different.

Before we get into adjusting curves, though, there are a couple of ways to customize the Curves dialog box to your preferred way of working.

Tip: Customizing the Curves Dialog Box. Some people are happy thinking of tone in terms of levels from 0 to 255. Others want to work with dot percentages. The Curves dialog box allows you to switch from one to the other by clicking the arrowheads in the middle of the gray ramp.

When you display levels, the 0,0 shadow point is at the lower left and the 255,255 highlight point is at the upper right. When you display using percentages, the 0,0 highlight point is at the lower left and the 100,100 shadow point is at the upper right. You can switch freely between the two modes at any time.

Tip: Change the Grid. You can also change the gridlines of the Curves dialog box. The default displays gridlines in 25-percent increments, but if you Option-click anywhere in the graph area, the gridlines display in 10-percent increments instead (see Figure 6-26). The 25-percent grid lets prepress folks think in terms of shadow, three-quarter-tone, midtone, quarter-tone, and highlight, while the 10-percent grid provides photographers with a reasonable simulation of the Zone System.

Figure 6-26
Changing the grid
in Curves

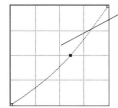

Option-click anywhere in the grid area to toggle between 25-percent and 10-percent gridlines.

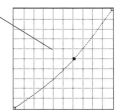

The curve. The great power of the Curves command comes from the fact that you aren't limited to placing just one point on the curve. You can actually place up to 16 curve points, though we rarely need that many. This lets you change the shape of the curve as well as its steepness (remember, steepness is contrast; the steeper an area of the curve, the more definition you're pulling out between pixel values).

For example, an S-shaped curve increases contrast in the midtones, without blowing out the highlights or plugging up the shadows (see Figure 6-27). On the other hand, it sacrifices highlight and shadow detail by compressing those regions. We often use a small bump on the highlight end of the curve to stretch the highlights, or on the shadow end of the curve to open up the extreme shadows.

The info readout. Whenever you move the cursor into the graph area, the Input and Output levels display (at the bottom of the dialog box) changes

Figure 6-27
S-curves

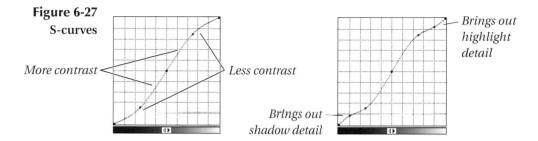

More contrast

Less contrast

Brings out highlight detail

Brings out shadow detail

to reflect the cursor's x,y coordinates on the graph. For example, if you place the cursor at Input 128, Output 102 and click, the curve changes its shape to pass through that point, and the readouts become editable fields. All the pixels that were at level 128 change to level 102, and the rest of the midtones are darkened correspondingly (see Figure 6-28).

Taking the midpoint of the curve and moving it left or right is analogous to moving the gamma slider in Levels. You can follow the shape of the curve with the cursor, and watch the info readout to determine exactly what's happening to each level.

Figure 6-28
The numeric entry fields

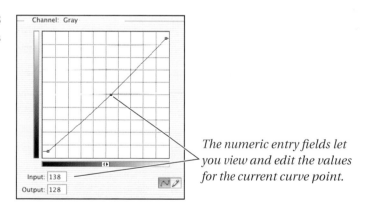

The numeric entry fields let you view and edit the values for the current curve point.

Handling black and white points. You can clip the black or white points by moving the endpoints of the curve horizontally toward the center of the graph (just like moving the input sliders in Levels; see Figure 6-29). For instance, if you move the black end of the curve directly to the right so that the info readout reads Input 12, Output 0, you've clipped all the pixels at level 12 or below and made them all level 0. This is exactly the same as moving the black input slider in Levels from 0 to 12.

You can also limit the highlight and shadow dots by moving the endpoints of the curve vertically toward the center of the graph (like moving

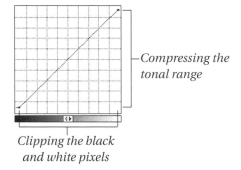

Figure 6-29
Clipping and
compressing
in Curves

Compressing the
tonal range

Clipping the black
and white pixels

the output sliders in the Levels dialog box). For example, to limit the highlight dot to 5 percent, move the highlight end of the curve until the Output level displays as 243—or (if you're displaying percentages) 5 percent.

The eyedropper. While the Curves dialog box lacks the black and white clipping displays of Levels, it has an extra cool feature that shows you at a glance where any point in the image lies on the tonal curve. When the Curves dialog box is open, the cursor automatically switches to the eyedropper when you move it over the image. If you hold down the mouse button, the info display in the Curves dialog box shows the input and output levels of the pixel(s) under the eyedropper, and a hollow white circle shows the location of that point on the curve (see Figure 6-30). This makes it very easy to identify the levels in the regions you want to change, and to see just how much you're changing them.

For some reason the eyedropper feature doesn't work when you're adjusting the composite (CMYK) channel in a CMYK image, though it does when you're adjusting individual channels.

Automatic curve point placement. A nifty feature in Curves is automatic curve point placement. When you Command-click in the image, Photoshop automatically places a point on the curve for the input value of the pixel on which you clicked. When you're working in the composite channel of a color image, you can place curve points in the individual channels by Command-Shift-clicking. Once the point is placed, you can adjust it by dragging, by pressing the arrow keys, or by making use of the following tip.

Tip: Numeric Curve Entry. An equally nifty feature in Curves is that you can specify curve points numerically. We use this in two ways:

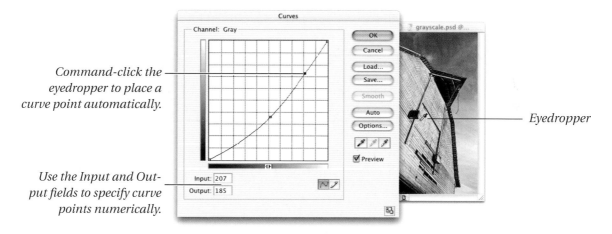

Figure 6-30
Curves dialog box
with eyedropper

*The circular marker shows
the position on the curve of
the current pixel value.*

*Before-and-after values are
displayed in the info readout.*

*Command-click the
eyedropper to place a
curve point automatically.*

*Use the Input and Output fields to specify curve
points numerically.*

Eyedropper

Eyedropper

▶ When we know the input and output values we want, we place a curve point by clicking anywhere on the curve, type in the input value, press Tab to move to the Output field, and type in the output value.

▶ When we want to set a specific point in the image to a specific output value, we Command-click on the image to place the curve point, and then we press Tab and type in the output value.

Other Curves command goodies. Like Levels, Curves has some hidden goodies. The Preview feature and the instant before-and-after work exactly the same as in Levels, as do the Auto and Options buttons, and the Option/Alt key provides the same auto-reset feature—Option-click Cancel to reset the curve. Press Control-Tab to cycle through the points on the curve, selecting the next one with each press, or reverse direction by pressing Control-Shift-Tab.

Dragging curve points with the mouse is almost always the least efficient way to proceed. Once you master the various shortcuts, you'll find that Command-clicking to place points, and then adjusting them using the keyboard, lets you make very precise edits very quickly.

Color Concerns

Editing grayscale is relatively straightforward—it's basically concerned with making pixels lighter or darker to improve the image appearance. Color, however, is considerably more complex. As with grayscale, the basic mechnisms let you make pixels lighter or darker, but depending on whether you do so in the composite channel or in individual color channels, the primary effect may be on tone or on color appearance.

As a result, even though the tools are the same whether you're editing grayscale or color, we use them somewhat differently depending on the image's mode. We'll point out the special concerns in context in the next section, "Hands-On Levels and Curves." But before we look at typical uses of the tools, there's one more topic we should address.

RGB or CMYK?

The debate over whether to work in RGB or CMYK has been the subject of countless magazine articles, several online flame wars, and even a book or two. Of course, if your work is destined for a film recorder, the computer screen, or videotape, then CMYK is quite irrelevant; but if you're working in the print medium, it's very important indeed.

There are still people who continue to maintain that if your work is destined for print, you should work exclusively in CMYK. When confronted, they usually give four reasons for this.

▶ It's the only color space that matters.

▶ RGB is meaningless.

▶ Monitor calibration is inherently impossible.

▶ All that matters are the CMYK dot percentages.

While all these points have some validity, we beg to differ with the philosophy as a whole. As we've noted before, when all you have is a hammer, everything starts to look like a nail. People who tell you to do everything in CMYK may have excellent traditional prepress skills and a deep understanding of process-color printing, but they just don't realize how much image information Photoshop loses during the conversion, and they probably are not comfortable working in RGB.

As a result, they convert unedited scans (or even worse, JPEGs from consumer digital cameras) to CMYK immediately, damaging the image irretrievably. Then they make huge corrections in CMYK, trying to salvage a printable image from what's left. Once they're done, they congratulate themselves on their exquisite skills while pointing out the limited quality you can obtain from tools like Photoshop.

These limits are self-imposed and largely illusory. If you follow these people's recommendations, you too will throw away about a third of your image right off the bat; then you'll be able to labor mightily, use all sorts of nifty tricks, and be rewarded with mediocre results for your efforts.

We have a very simple rule: *Don't change color modes unless or until you have to, and do as much of your correction as possible in the image's original color mode. The ideal number of color-mode conversions is one or none.*

All images ultimately come from an RGB source, so even if the desired end result is a set of CMYK separations, you should do as much of your image correction as possible in the RGB file. This is not a universally accepted view, but we believe that the arguments in its favor are compelling. When you prematurely convert to CMYK, you restrict yourself in at least four ways.

▶ You lose a great deal of image information, making quality tonal and color correction much more difficult.

▶ You optimize the image for a particular set of press conditions (paper, press, inks, and so on). If press conditions change, or if you want to print the image under various press conditions, you're in a hole that's difficult to climb out of.

▶ You increase your file size by a third, slowing most operations by that same amount.

▶ You lose some convenient Photoshop features that work only in RGB, like the Levels clipping display (see "Levels Command Goodies," earlier in this chapter).

More important, correcting images in RGB prior to CMYK conversion just plain works.

For the vast majority of Photoshop users, that means working in RGB for as long as possible, and converting your image to CMYK only after you're finished with your other corrections and you know the printing conditions. It's useful to keep an eye on the CMYK dot percentages while you work, but you don't need to work in CMYK to do that—they're always available in the Info palette, even when you're working in RGB.

We're not saying that you should never make corrections in CMYK—far from it. Your CMYK separations will often benefit from fine-tuning. Editing the black plate is a particularly powerful technique, but it's most effective as a fine-tuner, making small moves. Similarly, Hue/Saturation changes in CMYK are generally more delicate than in RGB. If you work in print, you must learn to edit in CMYK. But it isn't the only game in town.

When to Use CMYK

If your images come from a traditional drum scanner in CMYK form, it makes no sense to convert them to RGB for correction. You should stay in CMYK. If you find that you have to make major corrections, though, you'll almost certainly get better results by rescanning the image instead of editing it in Photoshop. In high-end prepress shops, it's not unusual to scan an image three times before the client signs off on it.

Tip: Ask for RGB. Color houses are so used to providing CMYK scans that they sometimes forget that their high-end drum scanners actually create RGB values, which an internal color computer then converts to CMYK on the fly. These color computers use essentially the same kinds of conversion algorithms as Photoshop, so productivity, not quality, is the main reason color houses use them.

But if you plan to manipulate the image yourself in Photoshop, or need an image that can be repurposed for multiple devices or press conditions, ask the shop to save the image in RGB format. They may tell you it can't be done, but most color houses are now RGB-capable. Of course, you're then responsible for the conversion to CMYK.

Certain kinds of fine-tuning, such as black-plate editing, can *only* be done on the separated CMYK file. But if you find you need to make large moves in CMYK after a mode change, it's time to look at your CMYK settings in Color Settings, because the problem probably lies there—a wrong profile, incorrect settings in Custom CMYK, or color management policies that weren't set the way you thought they were (see Chapter 5, *Color Settings*). In that case, it makes more sense to go back to the RGB original and reseparate it using new settings that get you closer to the desired result.

If all you have is a CMYK file, work in CMYK if at all possible. In dire emergencies, such as when you have a CMYK file separated for newsprint and you need to reproduce it on glossy stock, you *may* want to take the desperate step of converting it back to RGB, correcting, and reseparating to CMYK; but in general, treat RGB to CMYK as strictly a one-way trip.

Tip: CMYK to RGB. We can think of two reasons to convert a CMYK image to RGB: you need an image for the Web or multimedia, and a CMYK scan is all you have, or you need to repurpose the CMYK image for a larger-gamut output process. In either case, you need to expand the tonal range and color gamut—if you just do a mode change from CMYK to RGB, you'll get a flat, lifeless image with washed-out color, because the tonal range and color gamut of the original were compressed in the initial RGB-to-CMYK conversion, and the mode change reproduces the compressed gamut and squashed tonal range faithfully in RGB.

Instead, use the Convert to Profile command to do the transformation, using perceptual intent, with black point compensation and dither turned on. Then, open Levels, and click Auto. If this makes the image *too* saturated, back the black and white point sliders off a few levels. You'll find it works surprisingly well (see Figure 6-31). That said, this is a last-resort technique. Work on a copy of the file, and watch for color shifts and posterization.

When to Use RGB

If your image comes from an RGB source, such as a desktop scanner or a digital camera, you should do as much of your work as possible in RGB. The files are smaller, so your work goes faster, and you have the entire tonal range and color gamut of the original at your disposal, allowing you to take full advantage of the small differences between pixels that you want

Figure 6-31 Repurposing an image that's been prepared for reproduction on newsprint

The image above left was separated for newsprint. The separation settings resulted in a flat image that would reproduce well in that medium, but that had lost a great deal of its tonal and color range.

For the image above, we started with the newsprint-targeted CMYK file, pulled it back into RGB, made a Levels tweak, then reseparated for this book's wider gamut. The results aren't great, but as we said, it's a last-resort technique.

The image at left was created from the original RGB file, and separated using the proper settings for these printing conditions.

to emphasize in the image. It's also much easier to repurpose RGB images for different kinds of output than it is to do so with CMYK.

RGB has less-obvious advantages, as well. Some features (such as the clipping display in Levels) are available only in RGB, not in CMYK. And when you work in RGB, you have a built-in safeguard: It's impossible to violate the ink limits specified by your CMYK profile or Custom CMYK settings (because they'll always be imposed when you convert to CMYK).

When you edit CMYK files directly, you have no such constraint—you can build up so much density in the shadows using Levels or Curves that you're calling for 400-percent ink coverage. On a sheetfed press, this will create a mess. On a web press, it will create a potentially life-threatening situation! In any case, it's something to avoid unless you're printing to the rare desktop color printer that can handle 400-percent total ink.

CMYK Myths

One of the reasons we wrote this book was to dispel a number of the myths that have cropped up since the advent of desktop prepress (and some others that have been around even longer)—especially those regarding CMYK and RGB issues. Here are our answers to two areas that people often find confusing.

CMYK has more colors (false). We've heard experts deride the notion that CMYK contains fewer colors than RGB. "Do the math, stupid," they say. "CMYK has 256⁴, or more than 4 *billion* colors." We wish that were the case. CMYK has more than 4 billion color *specifications*, but a large number of them are simply alternate ways of specifying the *same* color using

a different balance of black to CMY inks. And many of them (for example, 90C 90M 90Y 100K) are "illegal" specifications that would turn the paper into a soggy mess scattered all over the pressroom floor. When you also take into account the constraints imposed by the black-generation curve and the total ink limit, you end up with far fewer colors than RGB.

CMYK is more accurate (true, sort of). Other experts say, "CMYK may have a narrower gamut, but the data points in CMYK are packed much closer together than they are in RGB, so CMYK specifies colors *more accurately* than RGB."

Here they have a point. You *can* specify smaller differences

between colors in CMYK than you can in RGB, because the same number of bits is being used to describe a smaller color gamut. (Whether these smaller color differences are detectable by the human eye is a question we'll leave to someone willing to carry out the empirical research.)

But this is relevant only if your RGB original is being converted to CMYK from high-bit RGB. The CMYK conversion can't be any more accurate than the RGB scan, and even in high-bit mode your image will still suffer from rounding errors. You can and very likely should fine-tune your CMYK after conversion, but you're *much* better off doing the heavy lifting on source RGB, preferably high-bit RGB.

Hands-On Levels and Curves

Armed with all the preceding information, let's look at some practical examples of working with Levels and Curves. We'll look at several different scenarios, because we have two different reasons for editing images—see the upcoming sidebar, "Why We Edit."

The classic order for preparing images for print is as follows.

▶ Spotting, retouching, and dust and scratch removal

▶ Global tonal correction

▶ Global color correction

▶ Selective tonal and/or color correction

▶ Optimization (resizing, sharpening, handling out-of-gamut colors, compressing tonal range, converting to CMYK)

We loosely adhere to this, but a great deal depends on the image and on the quality of the image capture. For instance, you often have to lighten an image before you can even consider removing dust and scratches.

And sometimes it's impossible to separate tonal correction and color correction. Changes to the color balance affect tonal values, too, because you're manipulating the tone of the individual color channels. For example, if you add red to neutralize a cyan cast, you'll also brighten the image because you're adding light. If you reduce the green to neutralize a green cast, you'll darken the image because you're subtracting light.

Image Evaluation

Before we edit an image, we always spend a few moments evaluating the image to see what needs doing and to spot any potential pitfalls that may be lying in wait. We check the Histogram palette to get a general sense of the image's dynamic range: If shadows or highlights are clipped, we can't bring back any detail, but we may still be able to make the image look good. If all the data is clumped in the middle, with no true blacks or whites, we'll probably want to expand the tonal range.

We also check the values in bright highlights and dark shadows on the Info palette, in case there's detail lurking there that we can exploit. We're pretty good at identifying color casts by eye, but we still check the Info palette—a magenta cast and a red cast, for example, appear fairly similar but the prescription for fixing each is quite different.

Fix the biggest problem first. The rule of thumb we've developed over the years is simple: Fix the biggest problem first. This is partly plain common sense. You often have to fix the biggest problem before you can even see what the other problems are. But it's usually also the most effective approach, the one requiring the least work, and the one that degrades the image the least.

Tip: Look at the Image Before You Start. This may seem obvious, but stop for a moment. Look at the image carefully. Zoom to 100 percent (Actual Pixels) and look at every pixel. Have you missed dust or scratches? Are there particularly noisy areas that might cause problems? Look at each

Why We Edit

When we break it down, we have two different reasons for editing images, though in some situations we may address both reasons with a single round of edits.

▶ We edit to get images into the best shape possible, without regard to any specific output process. The goal is to create a "use-neutral" master image.

▶ We edit to optimize the image for a specific output process. The goal is to render the image in the best possible way given the limitations imposed by the output process.

If you're a photographer, you probably hope that the image will have multiple uses, so it makes sense to produce a master version that doesn't make compromises to fit any specific output. If you're working in prepress, on the other hand, it's likely that you only care about the specific output process at the end of your production chain.

Of course, at some point all images that get reproduced will require optimization for the reproduction process, so the two approaches are not mutually exclusive.

We always edit our use-neutral color images in an RGB working space, because RGB working spaces are designed to provide an ideal environment for editing—CMYK is inherently use-specific, so we avoid working in CMYK except for final optimizations for known output processes. For grayscale use-neutral edits, we use the Gray Gamma 2.2 working space, because it's close to being perceptually uniform.

When we optimize color images for specific outputs, we still prefer to do as much of the work as possible on the RGB image, but we view it through Proof Setup, configured to represent the final output space (see "Proof Setup" in Chapter 5, *Color Settings*).

For CMYK output, we may do some required fine-tuning after conversion to CMYK. For RGB output, we've never seen any advantage to working directly in the output space—RGB output spaces are generally nonlinear with poor gray balance, so it's hard to edit in them.

For grayscale optimization, we use a measured dot gain curve where possible, or failing that, a single dot gain value. In the latter case, we pay attention to setting endpoints manually since we have no ICC profile to do so for us.

If you only care about a single use of the image, you can combine both sets of edits into a single operation. But in this case too, we recommend doing as much work as possible in RGB viewed through Proof Setup. RGB files are smaller than CMYK because they contain one fewer channel, so your work goes faster. We reserve CMYK editing for small black channel tweaks and for fine adjustments using Hue/Saturation, which is a much more sensitive tool in CMYK than in RGB.

channel individually. Are there details (or defects) lurking in one channel that are absent from others? Is noise concentrated in one channel? (It's usually most prevalent in the blue.) Look at the histogram. Is the image using the full tonal range? If not, should it? A few minutes spent critically evaluating the image can save hours later on. Develop a plan, and stick to it unless it obviously isn't working (in which case, see below).

Tip: Leave Yourself an Escape Route. The great Scots poet Robert Burns pointed out that the best-laid schemes o' mice and men gang aft agley. He didn't have the benefit of the History palette, or the Undo and Revert commands, but you do. History is a great feature, but it eventually it starts dropping states, so foster good habits. If a particular move doesn't work, just undo (Command-Z)—you can reload any of the commands in the Adjustments submenu (in the Image menu) with the last-used settings by holding down the Option key while selecting them either from the menu or with a keyboard shortcut. If a whole train of moves has led you down a blind alley, revert to the original version.

If you're working on a complex or critical problem, work on a copy of the image. When you apply a move using Levels, Curves, or Hue/Saturation, save the image before you apply it. That way, you can always retrace your steps up to the point where things started to go wrong.

Photoshop's Adjustment Layers feature lets you avoid many of the pitfalls we've just discussed. You don't need to get your edits right the first time because you can go back and change them at will. You automatically leave yourself an escape route because your edits float above the original image rather than being burned into it.

But sometimes it's impractical to use adjustment layers because of file size constraints, particularly with high-bit files, and to use adjustment layers effectively, you need to know how the various controls operate on a flat file. So even if you plan to use adjustment layers for as much of your editing as possible—and we encourage you to do so—you still need to master the techniques we discuss in this chapter, and the pitfalls they entail. For a much deeper discussion of adjustment layers, see Chapter 7, *The Digital Darkroom*.

Evaluation Examples

Figures 6-32 through 6-35 show several unedited images, and the conclusions we draw as to what we need to do to them. We'll execute the edits later in this chapter.

The evaluation process only takes a few seconds, and it's time well spent. We may encounter other problems that aren't obvious on the initial examination, but it's relatively rare that we'll encounter something that causes us to rethink the entire edit (and for those rare occasions, we always leave ourselves an escape route).

In the following examples, we'll apply the edits directly to the image, but the edits are exactly the same when applied with adjustment layers.

(None of these edits are likely to exceed the default 20 History States that Photoshop remembers, so we still have an escape route even though we're burning changes directly into the files—see "History and Virtual Layers" in Chapter 7, *The Digital Darkroom*.) So, armed with a plan, let's proceed to the edits.

Figure 6-32
A dark, muddy image

The histogram shows no serious clipping. We may want to finesse the endpoints a little with Levels, but the biggest problem is that the image needs a serious midtone adjustment. We'll start with Levels, then fine-tune the contrast with Curves.

Figure 6-33
A washed-out image

The histogram shows some highlight clipping, but the main problem is the lack of contrast. Again, we'll start with Levels, making black point and mid-tone adjustments, then we'll fine-tune the contrast with Curves.

Figure 6-34
A severe color cast

The biggest problem is the color cast. When we check a spot that should be approximately neutral (we used the highlights on the metal wheel) we find that red is much lower and blue is a little higher than green, indicating a cyan-blue cast. The histogram shows that the image is also quite underexposed. We'll use a single round of Curves adjustments to kill the color cast and fix the contrast

Figure 6-35
A flat image

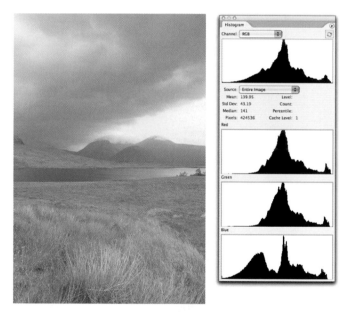

This is a good example of how the RGB histogram can mislead. It shows data all the way down into the shadows, but the image contains nothing resembling black. In fact, most of that data is from the yellow-greens, which are close to zero in the blue channel. We'll move the black point and midtone with levels, then fine-tune contrast with Curves.

Getting a midpoint fix. Figure 6-36 shows a simple Levels move. The Levels tweak makes a huge improvement, but we can improve matters even more by applying the Curves adjustment shown in Figure 6-37.

We started by placing points that corresponded to the light, middle, and dark tones on the main tree trunk (points 4, 5, and 6, counting from

Figure 6-36
A Levels fix

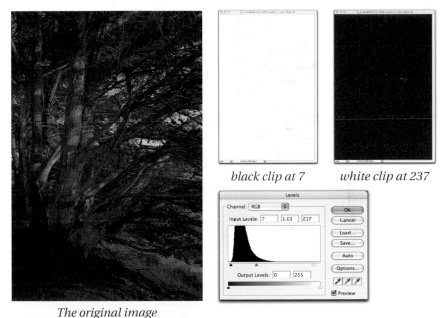

black clip at 7   *white clip at 237*

The original image

When we check the endpoints with the clipping display, we see that we can lighten the image without losing any important detail by reducing the white input slider value to 237, and we can add a little snap to the shadows by raising the black input slider value to 7. Adjusting the gray slider to 1.69 lightens the midtones. We'll fine-tune the contrast with Curves, but we've already made a huge improvement.

the shadow (0,0) point), and adjusted them to increase the contrast. This cause both ends of the curve to clip, so the additional points were added to fine-tune the highlight and shadow contrast.

We could have made the entire set of adjustments using Curves, but we find that Levels' clipping display is often helpful in setting the end-points—in this case we wanted to make sure that we were getting hints of pure white and solid black without clipping any detail.

Figure 6-37
Fine-tuning with Curves

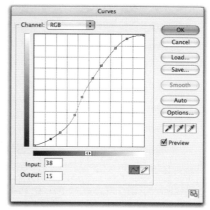

The image (left) after application of the Curve shown above. We placed the curve points by Command-clicking in the image, then adjusted them using the arrow keys.

We deliberately left a very little headroom to accommodate sharpening. As you'll learn in Chapter 9, *Sharpness, Detail, and Noise Reduction*, the process of sharpening images is really about adding contrast along edges, so sharpening always adds a little apparent contrast, and drives more pixels towards levels 255 and 0.

The significance of this depends on the output process for which you're preparing the image. Individual pixels being driven to black and white usually isn't a concern—unless you're printing at resolutions below 100ppi you're unlikely to see them on output. For Web work you may need to be a little more conservative. Figure 6-38 shows the sharpened image.

Washed out, not washed up. Our next image, shown in Figure 6-39, suffers from essentially the opposite problem from the one we've just edited. It's washed-out and too light. As with the previous example, we could go ahead and try to fix everything with a single Curves adjustment, but again we find that the clipping display in Levels provides sufficient reason to stop there before going on to the Curves command.

In this case, there's no headroom, though no serious clipping either, at the highlight end—just a few white pixels around the high-contrast edge of the bridge against the bright cloudy sky. At the shadow end, we can safely bring up the black input slider without clipping any significant

Figure 6-38
The sharpened image

*The image
after sharpening*

Figure 6-39
Initial fix with Levels

black clip at 9

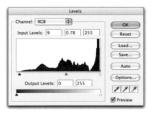

The original image   *After Levels adjustment*

*Checking the endpoints with the clipping display reveals that we have
no headroom in the highlights, but we can increase the black input slider value
to 9 without losing any important detail.*
*Adjusting the gray slider to 0.78 darkens the midtones, but fails to provide
enough contrast. If we darken the midtones further with the gray slider, the
highlights go too gray, so again we'll fine-tune the contrast with Curves.*

detail. We complete the Levels adjustment by darkening the midtones with the gray input slider.

Then we fine-tune contrast with Curves. As we did on the previous image, we place the curve points by Command-clicking in the image on areas whose contrast we want to enhance, then adding points as needed to stop the ends of the of the curve from blowing out highlights or plugging up shadows.

The second curve point (the first is the shadow 0,0 point) darkens the bridge piers and adds contrast to the ripples in the foreground. Points 3, 4, and 5 address the dark, middle, and light tones of the main span of the bridge, while point 6 adds contrast to the brighter areas in the water. Figure 6-40 shows the image after the Curves edit, with sharpening applied.

Figure 6-40
Final contrast
with Curves

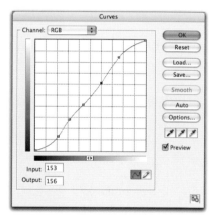

The image (left) after application of the Curve shown above. We placed the curve points by Command-clicking in the image, then adjusted them using the arrow keys.

Cast away that color. Moving on to color, we'll use Curves to neutralize the nasty color cast in the image from Figure 6-34. Obeying our maxim to fix the biggest problem first, we'll start by tackling the color cast, then, since we're already working in Curves, we'll improve the contrast there.

Using the technique described in the above tip, we use Curves to neutralize the color cast, as shown in Figure 6-41.

Tip: Look For Grays to Neutralize Color Casts. Possibly the easiest way to eliminate color casts is to look for something in the image that should be approximately neutral, then use Curves to make it so. One of the more useful features of Photoshop's RGB working spaces is that they're gray-balanced, so equal R, G, and B values always produce a neutral gray. Check the values on a should-be-neutral area with the Info palette, then use Curves to adjust the highest and lowest values to match the middle one. Nine times out of ten, the rest of the color simply falls into place.

Tip: Placing Curve Points in Color Channels. Command-clicking in the image places a point on the composite curve, but in this situation we want a point on each of the individual channel curves. Command-Shift-clicking the point we sampled in the Info palette places a point on each of the channel curves, ready for quick adjustment. The following tip makes the adjustments even faster.

Figure 6-41
Killing a color cast
with Curves

When we sample a spot from the highlights on the metal wheel we see the values shown in the Info palette.

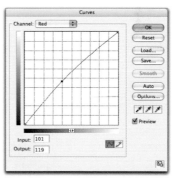

We adjust the red and blue curves to neutralize the point we sampled. In the red curve, we place a point at input value 101 (the value we sampled), and set the output value to 119 (the value we sampled from the green channel). We repeat the process for the blue curve, making a point with input value 138, output value 119, producing the image at right.

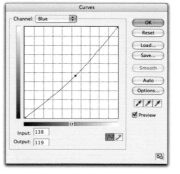

Tip: Use the Number Fields in Curves. In a situation like the one shown in Figure 6-37, where you're dealing with a known input and output value, the quickest way to adjust the points is to use the numeric entry fields. In each channel, press Control-Tab twice to highlight the point placed using the tip above, then press Tab twice to highlight the output field, and enter the value. Boom, you're done.

This simple tweak removes the worst of the color cast, allowing us to turn our attention to the tonal issues. Figure 6-42 shows a tweak to the composite RGB curve that spreads the data across the entire dynamic range. We don't have the Levels clipping display to rely on here, so we keep a watchful eye on the Histogram palette as we move the black and white points on the curve. Then we add a couple of points to improve the contrast.

Now we can see that our first approximation at removing the color cast was less than totally successful—the image is pretty green. We return to the individual color channels and tweak the existing points with the arrow keys to produce the result shown in Figure 6-43.

Note that we made all these edits without closing the Curves dialog box, so they're applied as a single pass, avoiding any unneccessary image degradation. In this case we decided to use Curves for the extra control it offers over contrast. But it's instructive to compare the Curves rendering with alternate results produced by our other favorite technique for killing color casts: Auto Color. Figure 6-44 shows the results produced by the various Auto options.

You need to be comfortable with both techniques to decide which approach makes sense, taking into account both the quality requirements and the time you can afford to spend. Photoshop offers several ways to accomplish any given task, and as we've mentioned, when all you have is a hammer, everything tends to look like a nail. You don't have to learn every single Photoshop feature—we doubt that's possible—but if you master the techniques in this book, you'll have strong Photoshop skills.

Figure 6-42
Setting endpoints and
contrast with Curves

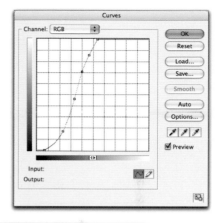

*The composite curve adjustment
at right spreads the data across the
whole dynamic range and increases
contrast.*

Figure 6-43
Fine-tuning the color
balance with Curves

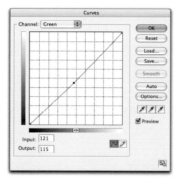

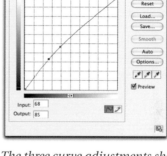

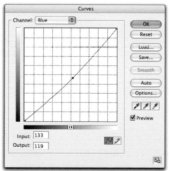

*The three curve adjustments shown
here produce the final image shown
below. We started with the green
curve since the color cast was
predominantly green, then we
adjusted the red curve, adding a
point to put more red into the rusty
metal. We finished by tweaking the
blue curve to put a little blue back
into the image.*

Figure 6-44
Auto options

The original image

Enhance monochromatic contrast (equivalent to choosing Auto Contrast)

Enhance Per Channel Contrast (equivalent to choosing Auto Levels)

Enhance Per Channel Contrast with Snap Neutral midtones

Find Dark and Light Colors with Snap Neutral midtones (equivalent to choosing Auto Color)

Make it pop. In the next example, we'll use both Levels and Curves to correct the tone on a color image. Figure 6-45 shows the original image, and the Levels correction. This is an improvement, but we can make matters still better with judicious use of Curves, as shown in Figure 6-46.

Figure 6-45
Setting endpoints
and midtone with Levels

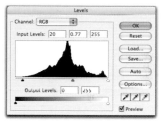

original image

black clip at 20

We set the black input slider value to 20, which darkens the shadows and increases the saturation of the yellow-green vegetation by clipping the blue channel to zero.

Then we darken the midtone by setting the gray input slider to 0.77. We'll fine-tune the contrast with Curves.

after Levels

Figure 6-46
Final contrast
with Curves

The image (left) after application of the Curve shown below. The points at the top of the curve bring detail into the bright sky; those on the lower end of the curve add contrast on the hillside.

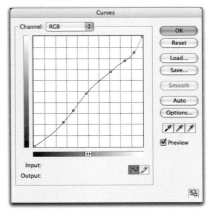

The remaining problem is that pulling the detail out of the sky turned it red, as we can see from the Info palette. Tweaking the extreme highlight ends of the red and blue curves produces the result shown below.

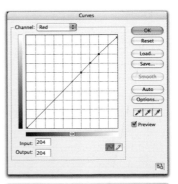

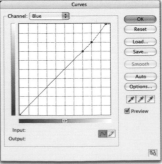

Info Palette for Color

The Info palette is a vital tool for working in color, particularly when you work in RGB. It lets you read the RGB values under the cursor, and equally important, it can show you the approximate CMYK values that you'll get when you do a mode change to CMYK. We say "approximate" because if you examine the CMYK values for an RGB file, then convert to CMYK and examine the values again, they may differ by a percentage point in one channel (which is a closer match than many production processes can consistently hold).

So, you can work on RGB images in their native color space, and still keep an eye on the CMYK values Photoshop will produce when you make color separations. You get the best of both worlds.

When you're working on an RGB file, the CMYK values displayed by the Info palette are governed by the settings in the Color Settings dialog box. If these preferences are set correctly, you should have to do little or no work on the CMYK file after you've converted from RGB to CMYK. See Chapter 5, *Color Settings,* for strategies for setting up these key preferences.

We prefer working visually—relying on a well-calibrated monitor—rather than going strictly by the numbers, but even the best monitor and the best calibration have inherent limitations. Some things are hard to detect visually. For example, without looking at some kind of printed reference under controlled lighting, it's very difficult to tell from the monitor whether or not a gray is really neutral. But the numbers in the Info palette provide an infallible guide. Without a well-calibrated monitor, they're your only real guide to what's going on.

Likewise, it's very hard to see differences of one or two levels between adjacent pixels, but the Info palette lets you find these differences, and as we've pointed out, difference is detail. Overly macho prepress guys will tell you that you can do color correction using a black and white monitor. This is true only if you have a good sense of the target values you're aiming for, which comes only with experience. But a big part of gaining that experience comes from examining the values on the Info palette for key areas of your images.

Info palette setup. For color work, we use the same Info palette setup more than 90 percent of the time. We set the first color readout to RGB, the second color readout to CMYK, and the mouse coordinates to pixels. You can set all these options with the Palette Options menu on the Info palette, or you can set individual readouts using the individual popup menus.

Setting eyedropper options. You can set the Info palette to show the values of the individual pixels under the cursor, a 3-by-3-pixel average, or a 5-by-5-pixel average, by setting the options for the Eyedropper tool to Point Sample, 3-by-3 Average, or 5-by-5 Average from the Sample Size menu in the Options bar. David chooses 3-by-3 Average unless he's working with a very high-resolution image, in which case he might go to 5-by-5. Bruce sticks with point sample, with the realization that he's only sampling single pixels at 100-percent view. When he zooms out, he's reading an average.

Tip: Use the Average Filter for Bigger Eyedropper Apertures. If you need a sample bigger than 5-by-5 pixels, make a marquee selection of the required size, choose Average from the Blur submenu (under the Filter menu), and read the result from the Info palette. Just don't forget to undo the filter once you've read the values!

Subtle curves. The image in the previous example had only one small color problem—the adjustments we made were essentially about contrast, though they had the desirable side effect of increasing saturation. Figure 6-47 shows a tougher example. The color is off, but only by a little. Small adjustments can have a big effect on the image, so in this exampe we'll look at more subtle problems.

First, the Levels adjustment adds some contrast. The white clipping adjustment produced clipping in the blue channel only in the brightest part of the clouds, while the smaller black clipping adjustment produced a true black on the backlit post in the foreground. The midtone adjustment was mainly done to compensate for the fact that we clipped white slightly more than black, lightening the image—the gray slider adjustment counteracted the lightening.

The color, however, is a little off—it has a cyan/green cast in the midtones, and the shadows on the snowbank in the foreground are a bit *too* blue (shadows on ice and snow are often blue, but they seem exaggeratedly

Figure 6-47
Endpoint adjustments
in Levels

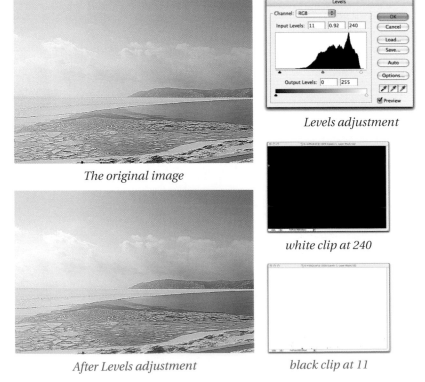

Levels adjustment

The original image

white clip at 240

After Levels adjustment

black clip at 11

so here). So we'll make a Curves edit, first to fix the color balance, then to fine-tune the contrast and bring some detail into the clouds. Figure 6-48 shows the Curves edits for color, then tone.

Figure 6-48
Endpoint adjustments
in Levels

The image at right is the result of the individual channel curves shown here. The lower point on the red and green curves fixes the blue shadows in the foreground snowbank; the upper point on the red and green curves addresses the darker clouds. On the blue curve, the lower point pulls blue out of the shadows. The remaining points anchor the rest of the curve, preventing the shadow move from turning the whole image yellow.

After per-channel curve adjustments

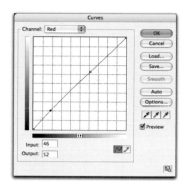

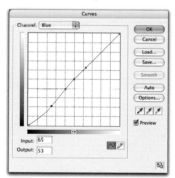

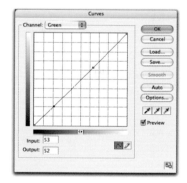

The image at right is the result of the tone curve shown at far right. The point on the upper part of the curve pulls some detail back into the bright clouds, while the point that is selected in the illustration adds some contrast to the background hills. The remaining points are anchor points.

After composite curve adjustment

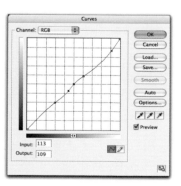

Levels and Curves Compared

The only thing you can do in Levels that you can't do in Curves is to see the black and white clipping displays. The clipping display is the feature that keeps us coming back to Levels.

We don't check the clipping on every single image. We do so only when there's a real question of what to clip and what not to clip. In the example shown back in Figure 6-49, for example, we just used Curves to set the clipping by eye. The clipping display is most useful when there's important detail near the highlight or shadow points, and particularly the highlight point—it's usually much harder to see details close to white on the monitor than it is to see details close to black.

Clipping isn't necessarily bad, either. We keep using the qualifier "important detail" because sometimes the detail can be distracting, and we want to do away with it, as in the example shown in Figure 6-45.

In cases like this, we don't really need to check the clipping display, so we just went ahead and used Curves.

Tip: When All Else Is Equal... If it's a wash as to whether to use Levels or Curves, use Curves because it's faster. When you use Levels, Photoshop has to spend time building the histogram (on large layered files this can take a significant amount of time), while the Curves dialog box just pops up, ready for immediate use.

The various Auto options (see Figure 6-44, earlier in this chapter) are available from either Curves or Levels, but despite the preceding tip, we usually invoke them from Levels, because the settings of the clipping percentages is quite critical, and we often want to check the result with the clipping display before we dismiss the Levels dialog box.

The Eyedroppers

Also common to both the Levels and Curves dialog boxes are the black, white, and gray eyedropper tools. Back in the days before color management these were mission-critical tools. Nowadays, we rely on them much less than before, but they still warrant a mention.

The black and white eyedroppers let you force the image pixel on which you click to the target value set for the eyedropper, adjusting all other pixels accordingly. (If you want to know exactly what they do, see the sidebar, "The Math Behind the Eyedroppers" later in this chapter.)

Figure 6-49
Clipping unwanted detail

The out-of-focus blobs in the background are simply distracting. The Curve shown below gets rid of them, and produces a more appealing image. The point near the midtone counteracts the darkening effect of the black clipping move.

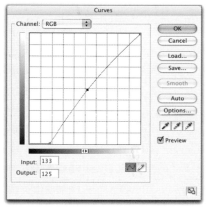

Setting minimum and maximum dots. In pre-color-management days, we always used to set our minimum highlight dot with the white eyedropper, and more often than not we set our maximum shadow dot with the black one. Good ICC output profiles make this practice unneccessary, because the profile has a detailed understanding of the tonal behavior of the output device, but we still use the eyedroppers for unprofiled grayscale

The Math Behind the Eyedroppers

For the terminally curious, or for those who want to know exactly what will happen to each value in the image, this is what the two eyedroppers do.

White eyedropper. The white eyedropper simply multiplies all the pixels in the image by *target value ÷ source value*. For example, if we choose a target value of 243 (a 5-percent dot) and click the tool on a pixel with a value of 248, all pixels at level 248 are turned to level 243. All the other values in the image are multiplied by 243 ÷ 248, or approximately 0.98.

So pixels with an input value of 255 produce an output value of 250, because 255 × 0.98 = 249.85. Pixels with an input value of 128 produce an output value of 125, and so on down the tonal range until you get to level

25, which remains unchanged (because 25 × 0.98 = 24.5, which gets rounded back up to 25).

If you make a much smaller move by choosing a source value of 246 and a target of 243, the multiplier is 0.99, so an input value of 255 produces an output value of 253, 128 produces an output value of 127, and values below 50 remain unchanged.

Note that you can use the white eyedropper to stretch the highlights (rather than compress them) by choosing a source color that's darker than the target color. This produces a multiplier with a value greater than 1, so the pixel values are increased rather than decreased.

Black eyedropper. The black eyedropper essentially does the reverse of the white eyedropper,

but the arithmetic is a little more complicated. To limit the effect to the shadows, the algorithm uses the inverse brightnesses of the input value and of the difference between source and target color—the inverse brightness of any value x is 255-x.

If we call the difference between source and target values y, then for each pixel value x, the output value equals:

$$((255\text{-}x) \div (255\text{-}y)\, 2\, y) + x.$$

If this makes your head hurt, don't worry—the net result is very similar to that produced by the white eyedropper, only in reverse. The source value is changed to the target value, and all other values in the image change proportionally, with the change becoming progressively smaller as you go toward the highlights.

output, or in those increasingly rare situations where we're forced to rely on an old-style Custom CMYK setting with a single dot gain value.

Unlike the output sliders in Levels, which simply compress the entire tonal range to minimum and maximum values, the eyedroppers let us set a specific value for minimum highlight and maximum shadow dots. If we want to preserve specular highlights, we can set the white eyedropper to the minimum printable dot value, then click on a diffuse highlight. This pins the diffuse highlight to the minimum dot, while allowing the brighter specular highlights to blow out to paper white.

Figure 6-50 shows a case in point. We want to hold a dot in the diffuse highlights while allowing the speculars to reach paper white. Here we're aiming for a 3 percent dot. Depending on the printing process you're targeting, you may want to set a lower or higher value. To translate Levels to

Figure 6-50
Setting a highlight
dot with the white
eyedropper

original image

We double-click the
white eyedropper to
open the color picker,
and set the target
color to Brightness
97 (equivalent to a 3
percent dot).

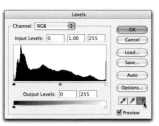 

We click the white eye-
dropper on the brightest
pixel value that we want
to hold a dot on press.

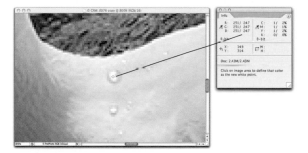

After the adjustment, the
water droplet holds a dot,
but the specular highlights
still go to paper white.

dot percentages, divide the levels value by 2.55, then subtract the result from 100 to get the dot percentage (but see the following tip).

Tip: Use Brightness for Faster Figuring. The fastest way to load the eyedroppers with a dot percentage is to use the Brightness field. Subtract the desired dot percentage from 100, then enter the result in the Color Picker's Brightness field.

As previously mentioned, we only use this technique when we don't have a good ICC output profile available. Essentially, that boils down to three situations:

▶ Grayscale images

▶ Custom CMYK with single dot gain values rather than dot gain curves

▶ RGB for television display on DVD (we set highlights to 235 and shadows to 15)

The rest of the time, we let the profile handle the minimum dot (though when highlight detail is critical, we always check the numbers in the Info palette).

Killing color casts. We also use the eyedroppers on occasion as a quick way to eliminate color casts. The black and white eyedroppers force the pixel on which they're clicked to the target values you set for the tools (the defaults are RGB 255 and RGB 0, respectively), scaling the individual color channels to meet the target value.

This behavior can cause some confusion. While the eyedroppers appear in two nonlinear editing tools (see the sidebar "The Nonlinear Advantage," earlier in this chapter), their effect is a linear adjustment. So if you labor mightily in Levels or Curves, then apply the black or white eyedroppers to the image, they promptly wipe out any adjustments you'd already made—see Figure 6-47. This behavior makes us use the eyedroppers only when there's a heavy cast near the shadows or highlights, and we've planned the correction.

The gray eyedropper. The gray eyedropper behaves quite differently from the black and white ones. It forces the clicked pixel to the target hue,

Figure 6-51
Removing color casts with
the eyedropper tools

*The image from Figure 6-46 with
the red sky.*

*If we click the white eyedropper to
neutralize the sky, it wipes out the
curves we've already applied, and
introduces a cyan cast to the clouds.*

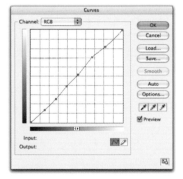

*The image with a new tone
curve, and color cast correction
applied with the gray
eyedropper.*

while attempting to preserve brightness. By default the target is set to
RGB 128 gray, since the the tool was designed for gray-balancing. Unlike
its black and white counterparts, it doesn't undo other edits you've made
in Levels or Curves, though it may change their effect.

We still use the gray eyedropper occasionally for gray-balancing (as in the example shown in Figure 6-47), but we're much more likely to use Auto Color and tweak the target midtone swatch, because it's more controllable. The results produced by the gray eyedropper depend critically on where you click in the image, while Auto Color responds in a much more predictable fashion while you tweak the target midtone color swatch (see Figure 6-24, much earlier in this chapter). In the example shown in Figure 6-47, we were already in the Curves dialog box, and the gray eyedropper was right there, so it made sense to try it, and in this case we obtained a good result. Figure 6-48 shows a more typical scenario where the gray eyedropper proves to be less useful than Auto Color driven manually.

The eyedroppers are pretty old technology, and have largely been superseded by newer additions to Photoshop's Adjustment menu, but occasion-

Figure 6-48
The gray eyedropper
versus Auto Color

The original image

Gray eyedropper clicked here

Clicking the gray eyedropper produces different results depending on the color of the pixel on which you click. With Auto Color, we can drive the color exactly where we want it to go by adjusting the midtone target swatch.

Gray eyedropper clicked here

Gray eyedropper clicked here

Gray eyedropper clicked here

Auto Color

ally they're just what you need. So investigate them, learn their behavior, and use them, but be aware of their limitations.

Freehand Curves

We'd be remiss if we didn't mention the freehand (pencil) tool in the Curves dialog box, which lets you draw freehand curves rather than bending the curve by placing points. We really have only one use for this, but when we need it, nothing else does the job. We use the freehand tool to handle specular highlights on printing processes where the minimum highlight dot is relatively large, such as laser printer or newsprint output.

Trouble in the transition zone. If you're dealing with newsprint or low-quality printing, the transition zone—that ambiguous area between white paper and the minimum reliable dot—can make your specular highlights messy. Some may drop out, while others may print with a visible dot. The solution is to make a curve that sets your brightest highlight detail to the minimum highlight dot value, and then blows everything brighter than that directly out to white. This is a two-step process.

1. Select the highlight point, then use the numeric fields to set your input point to a value corresponding to your brightest real detail, and an output value corresponding to your minimum printable dot. Figure 6-49 shows a point that sets the input value at 253 and the output value at 231, corresponding to a 10-percent dot. This sets all the pixels with a value of 253 to 231. But it also sets pixels with values of 253 through 255 to 231, which isn't what you want. You want them to be white.

2. Select the pencil tool, and *very carefully* position it at the top edge of the curve graph, until the input value reads 253 and the output value reads 255, then click the mouse button. (See Figure 6-49.) This keeps pixels with an input value of 252 set to an output value of 231, but blows out pixels with a value of 253 through 255 to white paper. Your highlight detail will print with a reliable dot, and your specular highlights will definitely blow out.

If this is something you have to do at all often, click the Save button to save the curve. Don't click the Smooth button, because it will smooth the curve—which in this case is not what you want. You can load the saved curve whenever you need it, or even create an action that you run as a batch to process multiple images.

Figure 6-49
Blowing out
the specular
highlights

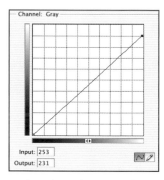

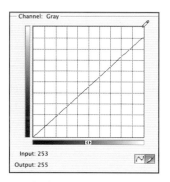

A curve point at 253 in,
231 out compresses the image
to the printable range.

A little touchup with the
pencil tool makes all the
white pixels white.

Levels and Curves Redux

Mastery of Levels and Curves is key to being productive in Photoshop, and these two tools can help you solve many image problems. Working on real images is a great way to learn the tools, but here's a simple exercise we keep coming back to.

Make an RGB gradient from white to black. The size isn't critical, but you want to have at least a couple of pixels at each level, so somewhere between 512 and 1024 pixels wide is good. Make sure that you can see the Info palette.

Use the Color Sampler tool to place color samplers—we suggest you start at approximately the midtone, quarter tone, and three-quarter tone areas. Then simply watch what happens to the numbers as you manipulate both the composite channel (all three RGB values will change equally) and the individual color channels (one value will change while the rest stay the same).

Levels and Curves have a very clear and direct relationship with the numbers we use to represent images, and the better you get to know that relationship, the less mysterious the tools' workings appear. But Levels and Curves aren't the answer to every image problem, and many people try to use them for things that they shouldn't, perhaps simply because the relationship with the numbers is so direct.

A very obvious case is attempting to use Curves or Levels to address problems with hue or saturation. Adjusting either hue or saturation means that you have to adjust at least two channels, and possibly three. It's extremely difficult to do so with any significant degree of precision, and just about impossible to affect hue without also affecting saturation. Which leads us to what is probably the most underused feature in Photoshop's arsenal: the unsung hero, Hue/Saturation.

Hue, Saturation, and Lightness

When we see people trying to make skin tones less red or skies less purple with Curves, we have to roll our eyes and bite our tongues, which is uncomfortable to say the least! The best tool for addressing issues with hue and saturation is, believe it or not, the Hue/Saturation feature.

However, Hue/Saturation is a tad more mysterious than Levels and Curves for at least three reasons.

▶ The relationship between the controls and the numbers that represent the image is much less obvious than with Levels and Curves.

▶ Much of the power of Hue/Saturation is hidden—you have to dig to find it.

▶ Unlike Levels and Curves, which are global adjustments (though we'll show you how to turn them into local ones in Chapter 7, *The Digital Darkroom*), Hue/Saturation is at heart a localized correction tool.

But Hue/Saturation isn't hard to master, and once you've done so, you'll find it's indispensable. The basic Hue/Saturation dialog box appears deceptively simple—see Figure 6-50.

Unfortunately, the Master panel of Hue/Saturation is of limited use. It does provides one of many ways of converting color images to grayscale (just reduce the Saturation slider all the way down to -100); it lets you produce colorized versions of color images using the Colorize checkbox; and it lets you produce "postcard" color by boosting saturation with the Saturation slider. The real power is hidden a little deeper, but let's deal with Colorize first.

Figure 6-50
The Master panel of the
Hue/Saturation
dialog box

Colorize

Figure 6-51 shows various treatments of an image with Colorize. The appearance is similar to a duotone, but the images are color images, and editable as such—you can run Hue/Saturation only on color images, while you can create duotones only from grayscale ones.

You can use Colorize for fast-and-dirty simulations of sepiatones, cyanotypes, selenotypes, bromide prints, and the like, as well as creating images that were impossible by traditional darkroom methods.

When the Colorize checkbox is checked, the Hue slider sets the dominant hue (the number is the hue angle, the same as the Hue field in the Color Picker); the Saturation slider sets the saturation on a scale from 0 to 100, with 0 being grayscale (completely unsaturated) and 100 being fully saturated; and the Lightness slider lets you darken or lighten the image on a scale of -100 to 100, with the default center point at zero. If you experiment, you'll find that the same settings produce different results depending on both the color mode (RGB, CMYK, or Lab), and the specific RGB or CMYK color space.

The Master Panel Controls

When the Colorize checkbox is disabled, the Lightness slider's behavior doesn't change, but that of the Hue and Saturation sliders does.

The Hue slider. The Hue slider shifts all the colors in the image by the specified hue angle. Small shifts are sometimes useful, but shifting hue by more than 5 or so degrees usually produces effects that can charitably be described as "creative"—see Figure 6-52. The top color bar shows the original color, the bottom color bar shifts to show the resulting color.

Global hue shifts are rarely useful except for creative effects (for which they can be quite useful), so we rarely use the Master Hue slider—instead, we adjust the hue of individual colors (see the next section, "The Color Panel Controls").

Figure 6-51
Colorize

Figure 6-52
Master Hue slider

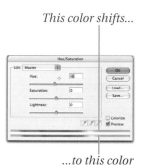

This color shifts...

This color shifts...

...to this color

6-degree hue shift   *180-degree hue shift*

...to this color

The Saturation slider. As with the Hue slider, the master Saturation slider is more chainsaw than scalpel. Boosting the Master Saturation value can work in small doses, but it's easy to drive your color into postcard territory (which is fine if you're in the postcard business)—see Figure 6-53.

We're much more likely to adjust the hue and saturation of individual color ranges separately (which we'll show you how to do shortly), because with the Master panel sliders, when we get one color right, we've typically pushed another too far, and yet another not far enough.

Figure 6-53
Master Saturation slider

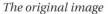

The original image   *Saturation +15*

Saturation +30   *Saturation +50*

We also, on occasion, use the Master Saturation slider to convert color images to grayscale—Photoshop offers half-a-zillion ways to do this, and they all produce subtly different results—see "The Color of Grayscale" in Chapter 12, *Essential Image Techniques*.

Figure 6-54 shows the same image converted to grayscale by choosing Grayscale from the Mode submenu (under the Image menu) and by adjusting the master saturation to -100. Note that the result you get from desaturating varies depending on which RGB or CMYK color space the original color image lived in.

Figure 6-54
Converting to grayscale
by mode change versus
by desaturating

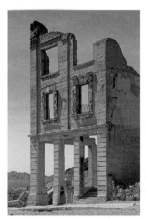  

The original color image   Grayscale by mode change   Grayscale by desaturation

The Lightness slider. We never use the Master panel's Lightness slider—it works exactly like the Brightness slider in Brightness and Contrast, simply shifting all the values, and usually clipping either highlights or shadows as a result. We do use it for individual color panels, however; see below.

The Color Panel Controls

The real power of Hue/Saturation is inside the individual color panels. When you open the Edit menu in the Hue/Saturation dialog box, you can choose Reds, Yellows, Greens, Cyans, Blues, or Magentas. At first glance, the controls offered in the individual color panels may seem identical to those in the Master panel—there's a Hue slider, a Saturation slider, and a Lightness slider. These work the same way as the Master panel's sliders, only they're constrained to operating on the selected color. What's much less obvious is that the named color ranges are simply preset starting points that you can adjust to affect exactly the color range you want. The controls operate the same way in all the other color panels—the only difference between the panels is the menu name and the preset range of color they affect.

The non-obvious controls are at the bottom of the dialog box. In between the two color bars are two inner vertical sliders and two outer triangular sliders. These define the range of color affected by the sliders (see Figure 6-55).

Figure 6-55
Color panels and
color range controls

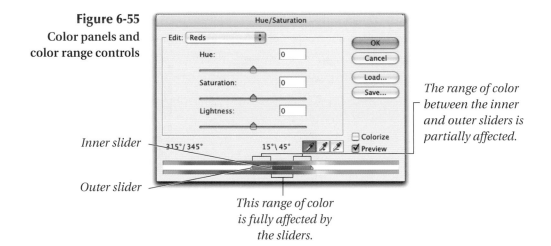

The range of color between the inner and outer sliders is partially affected.

Inner slider

Outer slider

This range of color is fully affected by the sliders.

For additional feedback, the numbers above the color bar show you the hue angles of the four slider positions. You can adjust the range of color that's fully affected by dragging the dark gray bar between the inner sliders, or by adjusting the inner sliders individually, and you can adjust the "feather"—the range of colors that's partially affected—by dragging the outer sliders.

You can also adjust the range by selecting the three eyedropper tools located above the color bars by clicking them in the image. The left eyedropper centers the range of fully affected colors on the hue of the pixel on which you click; the center eyedropper (with the plus sign) extends the range of fully selected colors to include the hue of the pixel on which you clicked; and the right eyedropper (with the minus sign) excludes the hue of the pixel on which you clicked from the fully affected range of colors. The size of the feather doesn't change with the eyedroppers, but it moves as the fully affected color range expands and contracts. Essentially, the controls provide a color-range selection with a controllable feather. The following two tips make using these controls a great deal easier.

Tip: Use Modifier Keys with the Eyedropper. We never go to the bother of choosing the different eyedropper tools. The left eyedropper is always selected by default. To use it to expand the color range, simply Shift-click; to eliminate colors from the color range, Option-click. The modifiers are just temporary overrides—they don't actually switch the selected tool—so you can just use them when you need them.

Tip: Use the Hue Slider for Visual Feedback. The biggest problem with the color range controls is that they don't provide any visual feedback as to which colors are affected. A simple trick lets you see clearly the range of selected colors—move the Hue slider all the way to the right or left before you start adjusting the color range sliders, then set it back to zero once you've adjusted the range (see Figure 6-56).

It's a very simple trick, but an invaluable one. It makes it easy to target the exact range of colors you want to tweak rather than the preset ranges Photoshop offers.

Figure 6-56
Adjusting the color
range controls
(continued on next page)

*We want to adjust
the darker, slightly bluish
greens without affecting
the yellow-greens, so we
start by clicking the eyedropper on the dark greens,
as shown at immediate
right. The problem is that
there's no way to see which
colors are affected.*

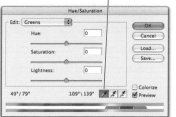

Moving the Hue slider all the way to the right, as shown above right, makes it obvious which colors are affected.

Figure 6-56
Adjusting the color
range controls
(*continued from
previous page*)

*We adjust the color range
sliders until only the darker
greens are fully affected, as
shown at immediate right.
We allow the adjustment
to feather slightly into the
lighter greens to avoid
creating a sharp unnatural
transition.*

With the color range tweaked as we wanted it we make the actual edit, as
shown above right.

It's also worth noting that the preset ranges are simply arbitrary labels.
There's nothing to prevent you from tweaking six different ranges of reds,
or greens, or yellows—though we find we rarely need more than three.

Skin tone adjustments. Hue/Saturation is invaluable for adjusting skin
tones. It's a great deal easier to adjust the red-yellow balance of Caucasian
skin with the Hue slider than it is to do so with Curves—in Curves you usually have to adjust all three color curves to obtain the correct hue, where
the Hue slider lets you do so in a single move.

Figure 6-57 shows an image of Bruce shot by our friend and colleague
Jeff Schewe. The unusally ruddy skin tones were likely caused by the excellent bottle of 1978 Masi Amarone we'd just consumed with dinner.

Jeff insists that Bruce looks "particularly Scottish" in this image. But
while Bruce is proud to be a Scot, he is reluctant to be thought a sot. So
we'll use Hue/Saturation to make his complexion a little less florid.

Figure 6-57
A skin tone problem

*The skin tones
are much too red.*

Making these kinds of adjustments with Curves is akin to medieval torture! In RGB, you'd have to manipulate at least two, and probably all three
color curves plus the composite, and you'd probably have to bounce back
and forth between the individual curves several times, since each move
affects the others. In CMYK, a curve edit is even more complex since you
have four color channels plus the composite rather than than three.

Hue/Saturation is useful in both RGB and in CMYK, but it lends itself
to much finer adjustments in CMYK than in RGB. In RGB, it manipulates
light, while in CMYK it manipulates ink percentages. Those of you with
sharp eyes will have noticed that we made the edits to this image in RGB
with CMYK soft-proofing turned on.

When we're preparing images for a CMYK destination, we always soft-
proof, especially on Hue/Saturation adjustments, but even with good
output profiles and a well-calibrated display, we're likely to make small
adjustments after conversion to CMYK, though we try to get as close as
possible to the desired result in RGB. When we looked at proofs of the
final results from Figure 6-58, we felt that the skin tone was just a hair too
yellow-green. Figure 6-59 shows the image after CMYK correction, along
with the correction itself.

Figure 6-58
Skin tone adjustments

We start by targeting the
very red areas, using the
Hue slider to make the
selected range obvious.

We tame the screaming
reds by shifting the hue
slightly and lightening.

The first adjustment lets us apply a huge tweak to all the skin tones, but we made sure that we excluded the yellow stars on the waistcoat from the color range.

A smaller hue shift with further lightening, accompanied by a saturation boost to counteract the lightening, produces the result shown right.

Figure 6-59
Hue/Saturation
correction in CMYK

The effect of the Saturation
slider in CMYK is much
more subtle than in RGB.
We also made a very small
Hue adjustment.

Matching hues. Another common task for which Hue/Saturation is well suited is matching hues across images. The light may change during an event, or you may simply have to force two disparate images to match.

Figure 6-60 shows a typical hue-matching challenge. Bruce stumbled across this wedding procession in La Paz, Bolivia, and had to switch from slide to color negative film halfway through. (The lack of oxygen at the 13,000-foot altitude made it somewhat miraculous that he managed to load *any* kind of film in the camera!)

The red shirts are rendered as a magenta-red by one film stock and as an orange-red by the other. And just to make things a little more challenging, one image is in ProPhoto RGB, the other is in Colormatch RGB, so the RGB numbers are of little help. Fortunately, the Info palette lets us display Lab values, so we'll use these as a guide—on a well-calibrated system you can make the match by eye, but the numbers always provide a useful reality check, and Lab numbers act as a universal translator, letting you match colors in different color spaces, or even different color modes.

Figure 6-60
Matching hues

The red shirts don't match!

We set the eyedropper tool to 5 x 5 average, then placed a color sampler set to read Lab color in each image, taking care to choose spots with the same luminance.

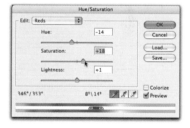

After refining the color range to focus on the red of the shirts and hatbands, we adjusted hue, saturation, and lightness to get a close match—we're one level off in b*, which isn't a visually significant difference.

The red shirts match!

While Photoshop's Adjustment submenu offers a command labeled "Match Colors," we confess that we've yet to find a way to make it produce predictable results, though it can make for some interesting creative effects. Hue/Saturation is quick and controllable.

Gamut mapping. One further task for which we rely on Hue/Saturation is gamut-mapping—controlling the rendering of colors present in the source image that are outside the gamut of the output process. In theory, perceptual rendering is supposed to take care of this for you. In practice, though, it sometimes fails. All profile-creation tools make assumptions, almost invariably undocumented, about the source space they attempt to map into the gamut of the device being profiled, and when the source space doesn't match the undocumented assumption, you can wind up with solid blobs of saturated color.

Sometimes the fix is as simple as just desaturating the color while looking at a soft-proofed version of the image. In other cases, you may be able to improve the rendering by adjusting hue and/or lightness too. You have to make the fix before converting to the output space, because after the conversion is done, all you can do is make the blobs more or less saturated—you can't recover the differences that represented detail.

We can't show you the out-of-gamut RGB colors in this book, because the CMYK print process won't let us. What we can do is to show you the unadjusted profile conversions of some problem images, the fixes we applied, and the results.

Figure 6-61 shows some problem images. The unadjusted versions are darn close to what we saw in the soft proofs that alerted us to the potential problems. In all these instances, something—hue, lightness, or saturation—has to give. There's an element of subjectivity in these decisions—we can't get the color we really want, so we have to settle for something else. There's no objectively correct answer as to what that something else is, but in all three cases, we feel that our choices are improvements over the straight, unadjusted profile conversions.

Figure 6-62 shows the adjusted images, along with the Hue/Saturation moves we used to make them. Only one of the examples—the red shirts in the last image—was fixed by a simple desaturation. The other fixes all involved changes to lightness and to hue, and in some cases the hue and lightness moves allowed us to boost saturation rather than decrease it.

Printing blues with CMYK inks is always tricky, because CMYK spaces contain so few of them! In most other color ranges, desaturation is our first line of defense for out-of-gamut colors. However, in the blue regions, lightness moves are often more effective, as shown in the middle image in Figure 6-62.

Figure 6-61
Gamut problems

The red gloves have plugged up into solid blobs with no detail.

The more saturated greens have turned into featureless blobs.

The darker blues in the ocean are washed-out with poor contrast.

The red shirts and green sleeve are plugged up with little or no detail.

Figure 6-62
Gamut fixes

A combined desaturation, hue shift, and darkening puts detail into the gloves.

We improved the problem greens by desaturating, darkening, and shifting slightly towards yellow.

We improved the blues by darkening, boosting saturation, and shifting the hue slightly.

We replaced the unprintable green with a lighter one.

We introduced detail into the shirts by desaturating.

Tip: Color Picker's Gamut Warning. Photoshop's Gamut Warning (it lives on the View menu—press Command-Shift-Y) isn't something we find terribly useful on images. It shows us which RGB or Lab colors are outside the gamut of our CMYK working space, but it doesn't show how far out of gamut they are, nor does it show us where the nearest in-gamut colors lie.

However, if you turn on the Gamut Warning while you're in the Color Picker, you can see exactly where the gamut boundary lies at different hue angles and lightness—see Figure 6-63.

Figure 6-63
Gamut Warning
in the Color Picker

When you turn on the Gamut Warning in the Color Picker, it shows you the gamut boundary for all lightness levels at a single hue angle. Use the Hue slider to see different hues.

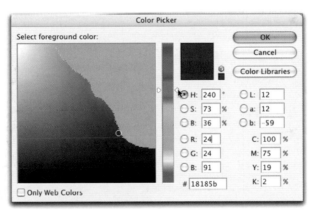

Bear in mind that the Gamut Warning always shows you the gamut of your current CMYK working space—see "CMYK Working Space" in Chapter 5, *Color Settings*—so make sure that you have the correct CMYK profile loaded before you try to use this tip!

Other Methods. Levels, Curves, and Hue/Saturation are *the* fundamental tools for adjusting global tone and color (we'll show you to apply them as selective local adjustments in Chapter 7, *The Digital Darkroom*). But several of the other commands on the Adjustments submenu are extremely useful, albeit in fewer situations.

You *must* master Levels, Curves, and Hue/Saturation to consider yourself any kind of Photoshop user. But the more specialized tools—to which the remainder of this chapter is devoted—can save you time and let you produce better-quality work, which is, after all, the object of the whole exercise. Photoshop always offers multiple ways to do just about anything, but one way is usually better or faster than the others.

Replace Color

Replace Color is really a shortcut. It's the equivalent of making a Color Range selection (see "Color Range" in Chapter 8, *Making Selections*), then performing a Hue/Saturation tweak.

Replace Color doesn't let you do anything you couldn't do with Hue/Saturation, but if you only need to adjust a single color, it's sometimes more convenient to use Replace Color. To emphasize the point that Photoshop always offers multiple methods of achieving the same goal, Figure 6-64 shows how we'd do the correction shown in Figure 6-60 using Replace Color instead of Hue/Saturation.

Figure 6-66
Replace Color

We want to match the red shirts.

We start by making the color range selection. Typically, we click the eyedropper in the image to get a starting point, then build up the selection by Shift-clicking. Then we adjust the color, either by the numbers from the Info palette or by eye.

This time we achieved an exact by-the-numbers match according to the Info palette.

Selective Color

Selective Color mimics the "system color" or "color-in-color" controls found in most traditional prepress drum scanners. We use Selective Color as a fine-tuning tool on images that have already been converted to CMYK—it works, after a fashion, in RGB, but it doesn't really do anything there that can't be done as easily with Hue/Saturation. In CMYK, it's a precision instrument for fine-tuning color.

Selective Color lets you increase or decrease the percentage of Cyan, Magenta, Yellow, and Black in the nine preset color ranges that appear on the Colors menu. Selective Color has two operating modes, Relative and Absolute (see Figure 6-67).

Figure 6-67
Selective Color

These color ranges are hard-wired—you can't change them. In Absolute mode, Selective Color adds or subtracts the specified percentages of each ink from colors in the center of the color range.

So, for example, if you ask for -20% magenta from reds, in Absolute mode, a 100M 100Y red becomes an 80M 100Y red, an 80M 80 Y red becomes 64M 80Y, a 60M 60Y red becomes 48M 60Y, and a 40M 40Y red becomes 32M 40Y. As you move away from the pure red axis, the percentage by which magenta is reduced lessens in proportion to how far off the red axis the color lies.

In the bad old pre-color-management days of trial-and-error color correction, when we burned film to make plates and a nominal 4% dot could reproduce as anything from paper white to around 7%, we'd sometimes use Absolute mode on Whites and Neutrals, making small moves to finesse the gray balance. Modern color management combined with direct-to-plate printing makes these remedies largely unnecessary today.

In Relative mode, Selective Color looks at how much of the specified ink is present in each pixel in the color range, how close it is to the center of the named color range, and how saturated the color is, so the effect is gentler than Absolute mode on everything except the fully saturated colors corresponding to the named color ranges.

It's hard to predict the final numbers from the numbers you plug in—it's a complex formula—so use the Info palette if you need numeric feedback. Figure 6-68 shows one of the images from Figure 6-62, before and after fine-tuning with Selective Color.

Figure 6-68
Selective Color

Intensifying the light blues in the ocean

Before Selective Color

After Selective Color

Intensifying the dark blues in the ocean

Brightening the reds

Shifting the yellow-greens slightly away from yellow

Making the bluer greens more yellow

The before-and-after differences are quite subtle, though they're obvious when it's pointed out. Relative mode is much more useful than Absolute for making fine adjustments to CMYK images, and these are the kinds of small but useful moves at which Selective Color excels.

Channel Mixer

The Channel Mixer does what it says—it lets you mix the channels, combining content from one or more channels and feeding it into another. We find it useful for getting grayscale images out of color ones (see "The Color of Grayscale" in Chapter 12, *Essential Image Techniques*), but its usefulness as a color-correction tool is less obvious.

We don't use Channel Mixer as a global correction tool on RGB images, though we sometimes use it to make local corrections, typically to bring out highlight or shadow detail that's only present in one channel.

On CMYK files, it's useful for tweaking the black plate in specific color ranges. We show one such scenario in Figure 6-69. The original separation setup added black into the skin tones, making them muddy. We'd rather fix this by going back to the RGB original and reseparating the image, but that's not always possible. Lightening the black plate in Levels or Curves would destroy the contrast—we only want to change the skin tones—and the Channel Mixer provides an easy means of doing so, with better feedback and finer control than Selective Color. We set the output channel to black; then we subtract some of the magenta and yellow channels from the black, and boost the black so that we preserve the black values in the shadows.

Figure 6-69 Removing black from skin tones

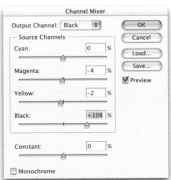

The image at left has black in the skin tones. We subtract some yellow and rather less magenta (the pink background relies on magenta), and boost the black slightly to produce the result at right.

Photo Filter

The Photo Filter command is designed to simulate traditional over-the-lens warming and cooling filters, though it actually lets you choose custom colors in addition to the presets. Its effect is similar to that of a solid color layer set to Color Blend mode, but the Photo Filter is easier to set up, and hence a bit quicker.

We find that the default 25-percent intensity is usually about twice what we need, and we often disable the Preserve Luminosity checkbox because it tends to exaggerate the effect in the highlights. Nevertheless, Photo Filter offers a quick and easy way to make images more appealing by warming them, or to make them more disturbing by cooling them. Figure 6-70 shows some Photo Filter warming and cooling adjustments.

Figure 6-70
Warming and cooling
with Photo Filter

The original image

Warming adjustment

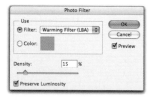

Cooling adjustment

Figure 6-70
Warming and cooling
with Photo Filter,
(*continued*)

The original image

Cooling adjustment

Warming adjustment

You can also achieve many different creative effects using either the stronger preset colors, or by creating your own filter color—just double-click on the color swatch to open the Color Picker.

Photo Filter is particularly effective at low intensity settings—the examples shown in Figure 6-70 are a bit stronger than the Photo Filter edits we usually make, which typically use intensities in the 3–12 percent range—we emphasized these to make the effect obvious in print.

Shadow/Highlight

The Shadow/Highlight command, which debuted in Photoshop CS, is probably the single most useful addition to Photoshop's Adjustment sub-menu since version 1.0. Unlike all the other commands on that menu, all of which treat each pixel the same way, Shadow/Highlight is an adaptive command that evaluates and adjust each pixel differently depending on the values of its neighboring pixels. (That's why it isn't available as an Adjustment layer—Shadow/Highlight has to calculate the value for each pixel, and it would have to recalculate not only whenever you changed the Shadow/Highlight settings but also when you changed any layers underneath, leading to agonizing slowdowns!)

Shadow/Highlight is a contrast-reducing tool: It lets you recover detail from nearly-blown highlights and nearly plugged shadows in a way that Curves or Levels just can't do, because where Levels and Curves shift all pixels at the same level by equal amounts, Shadow/Highlight evaluates local contrast and preserves it by making adaptive, context-sensitive adjustments.

In its default form, the Shadow/Highlight dialog box is very simple—frankly, too simple to be of real use. Turn on the More Options checkbox to reveal the full capabilities of Shadow/Highlight (see Figure 6-71).

Figure 6-71
Shadow/Highlight
dialog box

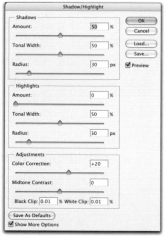

In its simple form, above, Shadow/Highlight offers two Amount sliders that control the strength of the Shadow and Highlight corrections. Click Show More Options to unlock its full power.

In its expanded mode, Shadow/Highlight offers Amount, Tonal Width, and Radius sliders for Shadows and for Highlights; a Color Correction slider (on grayscale images, it's replaced by a Brightness slider); a Midtone Contrast slider; and clipping percentage fields for black and white. The interaction between the controls is fairly complex, so let's look at them in turn.

Amount. The Amount sliders for Shadow and Highlight control the strength of the correction—they're the "volume knobs."

Tonal Width. The Tonal Width sliders dictate how far up the tonal range from black the Shadow correction applies, and how far down the tonal range from white the Highlight correction applies. They let you constrain the correction to the tonal range that needs it.

Radius. The Radius slider dictates the neighborhood that the command evaluates for each pixel, thereby affecting local contrast. A good rule of thumb is to set the Radius to the size of the features you're trying to emphasize. If you set too large or too small a radius, you tend to lose detail rather than emphasizing it. The easiest way to master the Radius slider is to experiment with it.

Color Correction. The Color Correction slider is a saturation control, but it operates only on the corrected colors, not on colors that are unchanged by the correction. Increasing its value saturates the corrected colors; reducing it desaturates them. We generally find that the default value of +20 is usually about right, but don't be afraid to experiment.

Brightness. On grayscale images, the Brightness slider replaces the Color Correction slider. It lightens or darkens the image—unlike the Color Correction slider, it affects the entire image, not just the pixels that are affected by the Shadow and Highlight adjustments.

Midtone Contrast. The Midtone Contrast slider adjust contrast—negative values decrease contrast; positive ones increase it. While its effect is most pronounced on the midtones, it affects the entire image, so use it carefully—if you push it too far, you might just end up undoing most of the effect of the Shadow and Highlight adjustments.

Black Clip/White Clip. The clipping percentages dictate how many of the corrected pixels are mapped to black (0) and white (255), so these controls let you adjust the contrast of the pixels close to black and white. Note that unlike the clipping percentage fields in Levels, these use three decimal places. Use them to fine-tune the contrast near the endpoints— when they're set too low, the image can turn muddy.

Figure 6-72 shows a step-by step Shadow/Highlight correction of an image with blown highlights and plugged shadows. The result would be impossible to obtain with Curves or Levels!

Figure 6-72
Shadow/Highlight
adjustment

The unadjusted image

*At the default settings,
Shadow/Highlight applies a
fairly strong shadow correction
with no highlight correction
(shown above right).*

*But we can push the
adjustments further.
We increase the Shadow
amount while reducing
the Radius, to emphasize
the fine details; add a
Highlight correction to
darken the sky; add a
slight boost to the Color
Correction so the image
doesn't turn gray; reduce
the Midtone Contrast to
preserve detail; and add
some punch back to the
shadows by raising the
Black Clip value.*

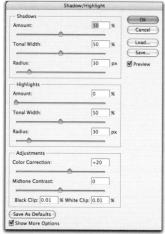

Shadow/Highlight is an amazingly flexible tool. Figure 6-73 shows some additional examples of its power.

Figure 6-73 Shadow/Highlight adjustments

Tools We Don't Use

We've covered most of the tools on the Adjustments submenu, but we've left a few out for the simple reason that we never use them. That said, we feel that a few words of explanation are in order, so here, briefly, are the tools we don't use, and our reasons for avoiding them.

Don't feel that you have to do as we do, or even do as we say—if you find any of the following tools useful, you know something we don't, and you can be proud of your hard-won knowledge. But first take a moment to ponder our critiques in case *you* are missing something.

Color Balance

The Color Balance command lets you make separate adjustments for red/cyan, green/magenta, and blue/yellow to three arbitrary tonal ranges labelled Highlights, Midtones, and Shadows. The problem is that these ranges overlap, and are never quite where we need them.

Nowadays, color crossovers are relatively rare—some early '90s desktop flatbed scanners were rather notorious for producing them, but when we see them now they're usually caused by shooting under mixed lighting, and the required corrections are usually selective rather than global. In any case, we find that it's easier to tweak the color balance of different tonal ranges using Curves.

Brightness/Contrast

Go back and read the sidebar, "The Nonlinear Advantage," much earlier in this chapter. If you actually *want* to blow out your highlights while washing out shadows, or gray your highlights while plugging up shadows, the Brightness slider is the perfect tool. The Contrast slider is likewise great for simultaneously blowing out highlights and plugging up shadows.

We suspect that the only reason that Brightness/Contrast still appears on the Adjustments submenu is that the Photoshop team never removes features (though they did take away the keyboard shortcut a few versions ago). There is simply nothing you can do with Brightness/Contrast that you can't do as easily, with more control, using Levels or Curves.

Match Color

Match Color sounds like a great idea. We've just never been able to get it to work with any significant degree of reliability. Match Color can produce some interesting creative effects, particularly when you use a source image with a completely different color palette from the one you're adjusting, but the results depend a great deal on any selection you make in the source image, and if you want to tweak that selection, you have to Cancel out of Match Color to do so.

We find that we can create color matches a great deal quicker using either Hue/Saturation or Replace Color. Match Color is just too fickle wand unpredictable for our taste.

Gradient Map

Gradient Map is useful for making custom graycale conversions and for creating truly wacky color effects. It's low on our list of grayscale conversion methods because it takes a lot of work—you have to edit the gradient to get the results you want, then use Gradient Map to actually get them—and we don't really do wacky color effects, though we have nothing against folks that do.

Exposure

The Exposure command is really designed for working with HDR (High Dynamic Range) images. On those, it's pretty useful—see "HDR Imaging" in Chapter 12, *Essential Image Techniques*—but on 8-bit or 16-bit/channel images, it doesn't do anything useful that you can't do just as easily with the gray input slider in Levels. Worse, the Exposure and Offset sliders basically replicate the behavior of the Brightness slider in Brightness/Contrast.

Invert, Equalize, Threshold, and Posterize

We often use Invert on masks (when we masked the area we wanted revealed and vice versa), but it's not something we'd ever do to an image. We never use Equalize—it redistributes the tonal values so that the brightest pixels are white, the darkest pixels are black, and the intermediate values are evenly distributed across the tonal range. We've yet to find a use for that, though we try to stay open-minded.

Threshold is useful for turning images into 1-bit black and white bitmaps. We use it when we scan line art, but not as an image correction tool. Posterize does something we generally struggle to avoid!

Variations

Variations is a nice tool for learning to distinguish different color casts, but a very blunt instrument indeed for correcting them, and it's limited to 8-bit/channel images. It doesn't do anything that can't be done with a great deal more control and precision using Hue/Saturation. If you're still uncertain of your ability to distinguish a red cast from a magenta one, or a cyan cast from a blue one (and it does take practice), a quick look in Variations can help you make the call, but we don't recommend using it to take whatever remedial action the image needs.

Mastering the Tools

You can do almost everything that most images need in terms of global corrections to tone and color using Levels, Curves, and Hue/Saturation. But sometimes none of these tools offers the quickest or best solution. We've emphasized them in this chapter because mastery of them really is part of the core of Photoshop skills. But if you ignore the other tools, you may create extra work for yourself. Knowledge of the tools helps you identify image problems, but equally important, that knowledge helps you come up with a plan to fix those problems.

In this chapter, we've concentrated on the basic functionality of the image adjustment tools to make global edits to entire images. In the next chapter, we'll show you how to use these tools, and some others, in more nuanced ways to make both global and local corrections.

7 The Digital Darkroom

Layers, Masks, Selections, Channels, and More

What would you say if we told you that you could perform color correction, use dodging and burning, build up density in overexposed areas, open up underexposed areas, and more—all with a minimum of image degradation and with an unlimited number of undos? You'd probably just laugh at us. But in this chapter we'll show you how.

You can do a lot using the controls we've already covered, but you can go much further, with more freedom to experiment, when you apply them as adjustment layers rather than simply burning the changes into your image. The controls in adjustment layers behave just as they do on a flat file, but with far more freedom and flexibility. You can change your adjustment settings at any time, and vary their strength globally by changing the adjustment layer's opacity. Even better, you can turn global corrections into local ones by painting on the adjustment layer's layer mask. In effect, you have not just unlimited undo, but selective, partial undo.

The techniques in this chapter can help you get a better image with little or no degradation and unprecedented control. But just as important, they're designed to give you maximum flexibility so that you can experiment and play with your images more, while still having an escape route back to safe territory if you push things too far. Making mistakes is one of the surest ways to learn lessons—we're living proof—so an environment where you can make mistakes safely is a great learning tool.

Why Use Adjustment Layers?

Whenever you apply a Curves or Levels tweak (or even a Hue/Saturation adjustment) to an image, you're degrading it a little by throwing away some image data. Once that data is gone, you can't get it back. In the digital darkroom, this degradation is no longer an issue because you make edits to layers above the image rather than to the image itself.

If you're a photographer, think of it this way: Your unedited image is like a negative that you can print through many different filter pack combinations on many different contrast grades of paper. You can make huge changes from print to print, but the negative itself doesn't change. If the unedited image is analogous to a negative, adjustment layers are like enlarger filter packs on steroids. You can change the color balance as you would with a filter pack, but you can also change the contrast and do local, selective editing akin to dodging and burning. However, unlike their analog counterparts, you can always undo digital dodging and burning.

There are several other reasons why we love working in Photoshop's digital darkroom.

▶ **Changing your mind.** Adjustment layers give you the freedom to change your mind. If you make successive edits with Curves or Levels on a flat file, your image will quickly degrade. With adjustment layers, you can go back and change your edits at any time without further degrading the image. This gives you endless freedom to experiment, and because you can fine-tune your edits with no penalty, you're more likely to get the results you want.

▶ **Instant before-and-afters.** You can always tell exactly what you're doing when you use adjustment layers. Because all your edits are on layers, you can easily see "before and after" views by turning off the visibility for the layer you're working on, and then turning it back on again (by clicking on the eyeball in the left column of the Layers palette).

▶ **Variable-strength edits.** The Opacity slider in the Layers palette acts as a volume control for your edits (this is similar to using the Fade feature; see Chapter 2, *Essential Photoshop Tips and Tricks)*.

▶ **Applying the same edits to multiple images.** You can use the same adjustment layer on a number of different images, and even script the layer with actions to batch-apply the effect to a folder full of images.

▶ **Brushable edits.** You can make selective, local edits to a particular area of an adjustment layer. This means you not only have essentially unlimited undo, but also *selective and partial* undo.

▶ **Doing the impossible.** You can use adjustment layers in conjunction with blend modes to do things that are usually extremely difficult, if not impossible—such as building density in highlights or opening up shadows without posterizing the image.

You can use adjustment layers as effectively on CMYK or Lab images as on RGB (though we still typically work with RGB images when we can). If you prefer to work by the numbers, the Info palette shows before-and-after values while you're working an adjustment layer's controls, and you can place color samplers to track key values just as you can on a flat file. If you'd rather work visually, you can use Proof Colors to see how your edits will work on the printed result. In fact, Photoshop even lets you preview the individual CMYK plates while working in RGB.

Adjustment layers and high-bit images. One of the biggest changes in Photoshop CS was the ability to use layers, including adjustment layers, on high-bit files. We love this capability and use it extensively, but we'd be remiss if we didn't point out that doing so can create extremely large files—think gigabytes rather than megabytes.

In Chapter 11, *Building a Digital Workflow*, we discuss strategies for dealing with ballooning file sizes in much more detail. For now, a relatively simple rule of thumb is to make your biggest corrections on the high-bit data. After that, we suggest staying in high-bit mode until it hurts, or until you need to do something that you still can't do in high-bit mode, such as running Extract, or some of the more esoteric filters.

The techniques in this chapter work in both high-bit and 8-bit modes. You need to make your own call on when to downsample to 8 bits per channel based on the quality needs of the job at hand, how much time you're willing to spend on an image, and the capabilities of your hardware. You may elect to downsample to 8 bits right in the camera by shooting JPEG, or you may decide to preserve your high-bit data all the way to the output process. However, unless you're shooting JPEG (in which case, you have no high-bit data to start from), we strongly recommend that you make your big initial edits in high-bit mode, and save the high-bit file. That way, if you run into the wall in 8-bit mode, you'll still have a fallback position.

Why Not Use Adjustment Layers?

With all these advantages, why not use adjustment layers for all your edits? The two reasons we consider reasonable are file size and file complexity.

Adjustment layers and file size. Adjustment layers use more RAM and hard drive space, both for scratch space and storage, than simply burning edits into a flat file. Adjustment layers themselves add very little to the RAM requirements because they contain almost no data, but painting on the Layer mask adds pixels that take up space.

Even if using an adjustment layer exceeds your available RAM, you may not see any slowdown because of the way Photoshop handles its image cache and scratch space. As Photoshop keeps getting smarter about the way it handles memory, it becomes more and more possible to do the seemingly impossible; so don't assume that you don't have enough horsepower to use adjustment layers—try it and see. (See Chapter 1, *Building a Photoshop System*, for more information on memory and scratch space, and Chapter 2, *Essential Photoshop Tips and Tricks,* for a more detailed discussion of the image cache.)

Adjustment layers and complexity. If you open a file you made a year ago, and it contains 20 layers with names like Curves 13 and Hue/Saturation 5, you may have to spend quite a bit of time remembering what all these layers did! Naming your layers, and organizing them into (informatively named) layer groups helps a lot.

All things considered, the disadvantages to using adjustment layers are minimal. We believe that most people will get better results faster using them. However, once you're happy with the edits, you may want to flatten the image to save storage space.

Adjustment Layer Basics

Before adjustment layers, our digital darkroom techniques involved duplicating the Background layer to use as an editing layer. Since all the edits were made to the duplicate, the original image was never damaged. Adjustment layers do the same thing, but they do it automatically, and with a much smaller RAM footprint. We mention this because it's much easier to get your head around what happens with an adjustment layer if you think of it as a copy of the base image, particularly when you start using adjustment layers in conjunction with blending modes.

The controls in adjustment layers work exactly as they do in flat files. The only features from the Adjustments submenu (under the Image menu) that you can't apply as an adjustment layer are Match Color, Replace Color, Shadow/Highlight, Exposure, Equalize, and Variations. We use Levels, Curves, Hue/Saturation, and Photo Filter far more often than the others, but we encourage you to experiment.

You *can't* do any harm, because your original image stays intact on the Background layer until you flatten it. However, there's no free lunch. When you flatten the image, the adjustment layers are calculated one by one, so you should still avoid successive edits that go in the opposite direction from one another—don't apply a Curve layer that darkens the image, and another that lightens it, for example.

Creating Adjustment Layers

The first step in working with adjustment layers is (obviously) to create one. Photoshop offers two different methods for creating an adjustment layer.

▶ **The Layer menu.** You can create an adjustment layer by choosing an adjustment layer type from the New Adjustment Layer submenu (under the Layer menu; see Figure 7-1).

▶ **The Layers palette icon.** You can choose an adjustment layer type by clicking on the Layers palette's New Content Layer icon. One method isn't better than the other—we use whichever one is closest to the mouse. Most often, though, we rely on the following tip.

Figure 7-1
Creating an
adjustment layer

Photoshop offers two different methods for creating an adjustment layer.

Tip: Adjustment Layer Actions. If you're going to be making a number of adjustment layers, you'll do yourself a favor by creating a "Make Adjustment Layers" action in the Actions palette (see "Actions and Automating Photoshop" in Chapter 12, *Essential Image Techniques)*. Bruce runs raw images through a Batch action that adds Levels, Curves, and Hue/Saturation layers so that he can get to work quickly as soon as the image opens.

Controlling Adjustment Layers

The big difference between using adjustment layers and editing a flat file is that adjustment layers give you much more freedom to control and refine your edits. You have four ways to control your editing when using an adjustment layer that you don't have with a flat file.

Variable strength. You can control the opacity of the adjustment layer by changing the Opacity slider in the Layers palette. This lets you change the intensity of the adjustment globally. We often make edits that are slightly more extreme than we really want, then back off the opacity of the editing layer to reduce the effect to just where we want it. We find this faster than trying to fine-tune the adjustment in the adjustment layer's dialog box.

Fine-tuning. Whenever you want to make a change to the adjustment layer, you can edit it (changing the curve or choosing other options) by double-clicking on the adjustment layer thumbnail in the Layers palette (see Figure 7-2). When you do this, Photoshop displays the settings you last used in the adjustment layer's dialog box. Not to beat a dead papaya, but you can do this as often as you want without degrading the image, because the edits aren't actually applied until you flatten the file.

Figure 7-2
Editing an adjustment layer

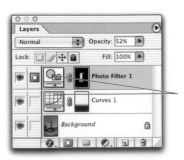

Double-click the adjustment layer thumbnail to change the adjustment layer's settings.

Multiple edits. You don't have to limit yourself to a single adjustment layer. You can have as many as you want, each stacked on top of the next to make successive edits. This technique is particularly useful when you want one curve to correct the image globally while another curve edits the image in selective places. However, if one adjustment counteracts another, you'll suffer the same amount of image degradation you'd get if you applied the edits successively to flat files.

Note that adjustment layers apply to all visible layers beneath them. As a result, the stacking order makes a difference, since each layer's result depends on the layers underneath it. Sometimes the differences are fairly subtle—you may need to check the numbers in the Info palette to see them—but occasionally the difference can be significant.

While you can't merge adjustment layers together, you can merge them into regular, raster layers. If you want only one layer, you can flatten the whole image or select Merge Visible from the Layer menu (Merge Visible retains any transparency in the image). We don't recommend doing this unless it's necessary, since you lose all the advantages of adjustment layers, and they take up very little space. Instead, keep all your adjustment layers live until you're finished with the project. Then, to save a flattened version of the image, choose Save As, and in the Save As dialog box turn on the As a Copy checkbox, and turn off the Layers checkbox.

Selective editing. While the Opacity slider applies to the entire adjustment layer, you can vary the opacity of the layer locally by painting on the adjustment layer's layer mask. To paint on the layer mask, simply click on the adjustment layer tile in the Layers palette and paint; the paint automatically goes on the layer mask. Black paint hides the effect of the adjustment layer; white paint reveals it; gray paint applies the effect partially (25-percent black ink applies 75 percent of the adjustment layer's effect). By varying the brush opacity in the Options bar, you can achieve precise control over the adjustment layer's opacity in specific areas.

Note that a new channel is automatically added to the Channels palette whenever you select an adjustment layer in the Layers palette. This is the channel that you're actually drawing on. You can use all the usual layer mask tricks, like Shift-clicking on the layer mask (in the Layers palette) to turn the mask on or off, and Option-clicking to view or hide the layer mask (see "Selections, Masks, and Channels," later in this chapter).

Tip: Use Painting Shortcuts. There are some little shortcuts that we use so often, we need to mention them again here. When painting on the layer mask, don't forget that you can press X to switch the foreground and background colors. Press the number keys (0–9) to set the opacity of the paintbrush—for instance, 0 sets the opacity to 100 percent, 9 sets it to 90 percent, 45 to 45 percent, and so on.

Saving adjustment layers. You can save an adjustment layer separately from an image. We find this most useful when we want to apply the same color- and tonal-correction edits to multiple images.

Here's how to save an adjustment layer into either a new or a different document.

1. Select the adjustment layer you want to save.

2. Choose Duplicate Layer from either the Layer menu or the Layers palette popout menu.

3. Pick a file in the Duplicate Layers dialog box to save the adjustment layer into. If you choose New for the destination, Photoshop creates a new document for you; if you choose an existing document, Photoshop copies the adjustment layer into that image.

4. Click OK.

The ability to copy adjustment layers also opens up some new workflow possibilities. Before we had adjustment layers, we always took care of retouching our image (dust and scratches, and so on) before we did any editing for tone or color. However, with adjustment layers, the order of these tasks doesn't matter. Two people can even work on the same image at the same time—one doing the retouching while the other edits tone and color—then later, you can apply the adjustment layer(s) to the retouched image.

Another workflow option is to make your color- and tonal-correction edits on a low-resolution version of a large image. The edits may go faster on the low-resolution version, and when you're done you can apply the adjustment layers to the monster 500 MB high-resolution version of the image. Of course, if you've done any painting on the layer mask, that won't translate properly when placed into the high-resolution file (see "Tip: Making Masks Meet," on the next page).

Tip: Copying Adjustment Layers Quickly. The Duplicate Layer feature is useful, but we find it faster to copy an adjustment layer simply by dragging it from the Layers palette in one image on top of another image. Again, if the two images have different pixel dimensions, any layer mask will probably transfer incorrectly (see the next tip).

Even better, you can use actions to script the creation of adjustment layers, and then apply exactly the same edits to a whole folder of images using Photoshop's batch processing features (see "Actions" in Chapter 12, *Essential Image Techniques)*. The only limitation is that you can't script edits that you've made by brushing on the layer mask.

Tip: Making Masks Meet. Trying to match an adjustment layer's layer mask in one image to its layer mask in another image is easy, as long as the pixel dimensions of the two images are the same. When you use the Duplicate Layer command to move an adjustment layer to a different document, Photoshop centers the layer mask in the new document. If the two documents have the same pixel dimensions, this works great; if they don't, you'll have problems.

When you drag an adjustment layer from one document into another, any pixels on the layer mask are placed exactly where you drop the layer (where you let go of the mouse button). This is almost never where you want them to be. Instead, as long as the two images have the same pixel dimensions, you can hold down the Shift key while dragging the layer; this way, Photoshop pin-registers the layer to the target image.

Remember, to match the pixel dimensions of an image, open the Image Size dialog box in the target image (the one you want to change), then select the source image (the one you're copying) from the Window menu.

Tip: Adjustment Layers and Disk Space. At first glance, adding one or more adjustment layers to your image seems to double its size when you save it to disk in the Photoshop format, even though the adjustment layer is essentially an empty layer. The key is to turn off "Always Maximize Compatibility for Photoshop (PSD) Files" in the Saving Files Preferences dialog box (under the Edit menu). As we noted in Chapter 2, *Essential Photoshop Tips and Tricks,* few workflows need this feature turned on. Turn it off, and your Photoshop files get much, much smaller.

Photoshop also lets you save layered files as TIFFs or PDFs, which are readable by other applications, up to a point. What they're really reading is the flattened composite. We haven't seen any credible reports of other applications or RIPs having trouble with layered files, but the trade-off you make when you use them is that you get to keep a single, round-trippable file that contains all your edits, at the expense of slinging more data around over your network. If a single-file workflow appeals to you, by all means go for it, but make sure your network and servers can handle the traffic.

Otherwise, you can save a flat version of the image using Flatten Image (from the Layer menu). Or, to save a flattened file without damaging your original layered document, choose Save As, and then in the Save As dialog box, turn on the As a Copy checkbox and turn off the Layers checkbox.

Simple Adjustment Layers

In their simplest form, adjustment layers work just like the similarly named commands on the Adjustments submenu (under the Image menu) that we discussed at length in the previous chapter. However, there are two important differences:

▶ You can go back and readjust the settings at any time.

▶ You can vary the strength of the effect by changing the layer's opacity.

Figure 7-3 shows a simple set of adjustment layer edits using one Levels and one Curves layer. We start by adding a Levels layer, which we use to adjust the color balance—the image is a little blue-green—and to make a small midtone lightening. We add a Curves layer to increase the shadow and midtone contrast, then we go back to the Levels layer and tweak the black point. It was easier to get the shadow contrast with the Curve when the shadow detail was left open, then go back and tweak the black point in Levels, than to set the black point and then try to tweak the contrast.

The ability to go back and refine previous edits is one of the strong points of adjustment layers. But what really floats our boat (or "snaps our bellybutton" or whatever your local colloquialism is) is the ability to turn global corrections into local ones using layer masks. But we've seen brain surgeons and physicists blanch at the terms "mask" and "alpha channel," so a little explanation is in order.

Figure 7-3
Simple Adjustment
Layers
(part 1)

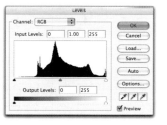

When we add a Levels layer, we're presented with the Levels dialog box.

We click Options to open the Auto Color Correction Options dialog box, choose Find Dark & Light Colors and Snap Neutral Midtones, then we adjust the target midtone color to give a warming effect.

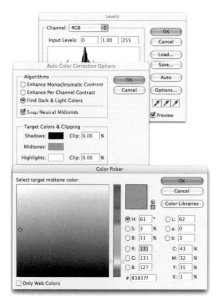

We complete the Levels tweak by making a slight midtone lightening. We'll fine-tune the contrast with Curves next, so we deliberately leave the shadows open.

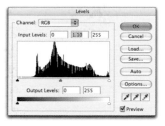

Figure 7-3
Simple
Adjustment
Layers
(part 2)

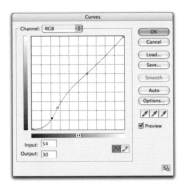

We add a Curves layer to increase the shadow contrast.

We finish by going back to the Levels adjustment and making a black point tweak that gives us true black while preserving detail in the brushes.

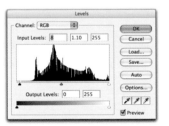

Selections, Masks, and Channels

The key to understanding selections, masks, and channels is to realize that deep down, they're all the same thing. No matter what kind of selection you make—whether you draw out a rectangular marquee, draw a path with the Lasso, or use the Magic Wand to select a colored area—Photoshop internally sees the selection as a grayscale channel. If you've ever carefully painted around a window (the kind in the wall of your house), you've probably used masking tape to mask out the areas you didn't want to paint. If you apply the masking tape to the window, you can paint right over it, knowing that the window remains untouched. Selections, masks, and channels are electronic forms of masking tape.

In Photoshop, the masking tape is typically colored black. Let's say you use the marquee to select a square. Behind the scenes, Photoshop sees this square as a grayscale channel. In this selection channel, the areas that you selected (the parts with no masking tape over them) are white, and the unselected areas (the parts with masking tape over them) are black. As our friend and colleague Katrin Eismann likes to intone, "Black conceals, white reveals."

Photoshop offers three ways of interacting with this selection information, but the relationship between them isn't always obvious.

▶ You can use the selection tools—marquee, lasso, magic wand, Color Range, and so on, to create a selection.

▶ When you save a selection (which you should do for any selection that takes more than 10 seconds to create), Photoshop saves the selection as an *alpha channel*, which is simply a regular grayscale channel. ("Alpha Channel" is, as we've mentioned, a scary term—whenever you see it, feel free to mentally substitute "saved selection," because that's all it really means!)

▶ To apply the selection information nondestructively to a layer (meaning that you can change or remove the selection), you use it as a *layer mask*—you're attaching the masking tape to just that layer.

We'll show you how to bounce the information back and forth between these three states a little later in this chapter, but first, let's take a look at the information, and how it manifests itself in each of these three forms. Selections can be very simple or extremely complex, but no matter how simple or complex they may be, they share the same behaviors.

We'll start with a very simple example, a rectangular marquee (see Figure 7-4). The rectangular marquee is a very simple bi-level selection—each pixel is either selected or unselected, and the channel that results when the selection is saved contains only black and white pixels. It works like real masking tape—the black pixels in the selection are the masking tape, protecting whatever's underneath, and the white pixels represent the area without masking tape, letting the paint (or the Curve, or Levels) pass through.

Why Digital Tape Is Better

There's reality, and there's Photoshop. In real life, you can't have partially opaque masking tape. The wood or window or whatever is either covered

pixels completely, affects the partially selected pixels in direct proportion to how selected they are, and doesn't affect the unselected pixels at all.

The ability to partially select pixels is insanely useful in all sorts of situations, many of which we cover in Chapter 8, *Making Selections*. For the purposes of this chapter, we'll focus on the role of partially selected pixels in layer masks. Layer masks let you apply local, rather than global, corrections—the mask lets you constrain the correction to the part of the image that needs it.

Unless you photograph outside the earth's atmosphere, you'll find that light never forms hard edges. There's always some transparency along edges, and the ability to create feathered (soft-edged) selections and masks is key to making localized corrections blend into the image in a way that seems natural.

Digital Tape Is Convenient

A second huge advantage of digital masking tape is that, unlike its real-world equivalent, you can easily copy it, move it, tweak it, or reuse it a year later. When you save a selection, you can recall it easily, and either reuse it as a selection, or apply it as a mask to a layer.

In fact, you can very easily bounce between selections, channels, and masks, which considering they're all the same thing, isn't surprising. The flexibility with which you can turn a selection into a channel or mask and vice versa is one of the major reasons why you should always get into the habit of saving any selection that's even slightly complex. A second reason is that if you fail to do so, you'll find that as soon as the selection becomes unavailable, you'll undoubtedly need it again!

Selections to channels. To turn a selection into a channel, you can use the slow method shown in Figure 7-3 and 7-4: choosing Save Selection from the Select menu and telling Photoshop where to save it. Alternately, you can use the much quicker method of clicking the "Save selection as channel" icon at the bottom of the Channels palette (see Figure 7-5).

Channels to selections. Photoshop offers three ways to load a channel as a selection. The slow way—which we typically use only when we've saved a channel outside the document on which we're working—is to choose Load Selection from the Select menu, choose the channel from the ensuing dialog box, and click OK.

A slightly quicker method is to select the channel we want to load in the Channels palette and click the "Load channel as selection" icon at the bottom of the Channels palette. However, this method isn't ideal because we have to go back to the Channels palette to select the channel (usually the composite) on which we want to use the selection. So we almost always use the third method, which is to simply Command-click on the channel we want to load as a selection in the Channels palette. Figure 7-6 shows all three methods.

Figure 7-5
Save selection as channel

Figure 7-6
Load channel as selection

Choose Load Selection from the Select menu, then choose the channel you want to load from the dialog box, or...

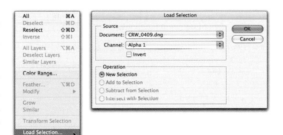

...click the Load channel as selection icon, or...

...Command-click the channel tile in the Channels palette.

Selections to masks. Photoshop always adds a layer mask when you create an adjustment layer. Even better, if you have a selection active when you add an adjustment layer, that selection is automatically used as the layer mask. So the easiest way to load a selection as a layer mask for an adjustment layer is simply to activate it before creating the layer.

For layer types other than adjustment layers, you can load a selection as a layer mask by choosing Reveal Selection from the Layer Mask submenu (under the Layer menu). Or, if you want to reverse the layer mask, choose Hide Selection from same submenu. Even easier: Click the Add Layer Mask icon at the bottom of the Layers palette (see Figure 7-7).

Figure 7-7
Load selection
as layer mask

With the selection active,
choose from the Layer
Mask submenu, or...

...click the Add Layer Mask
icon in the Layers palette

Selections to existing masks. Sometimes, of course, we add an adjustment layer without remembering first to load the selection we want to use as a mask. In this case, the procedure is a little trickier.

If the selection is saved as an alpha channel (remember, you can substitute the phrase "saved selection"), you can copy it into the mask channel. The trick is that you *must* make the respective channels visible before copying and pasting, otherwise you'll wind up with a new layer instead of the mask you wanted (this still trips us up). Click the alpha channel's tile in the Channels palette to make it selected and visible, choose Select All (Command-A), then Copy (Command-C). Then click the Layer mask tile in the Channels palette, click the eyeball to make it visible, and paste (Command-V; see Figure 7-8).

Or, if the selection is active, you can use the following method instead. Target the mask channel either by clicking its thumbnail in the Layers palette or by clicking its tile in the Channels palette. Make sure that Black is the Background color (press D to set black and white as foreground and background, respectively, then press X to switch them), and hit Delete to fill the selection with black on the Layer mask. This gives you the opposite selection from the one you want. To fix it, deselect the current selection (press Command-D), then invert the layer mask by pressing Command-I. It's a little fiddly but it takes longer to explain than to accomplish.

Figure 7-8
Copy channel
to Layer mask

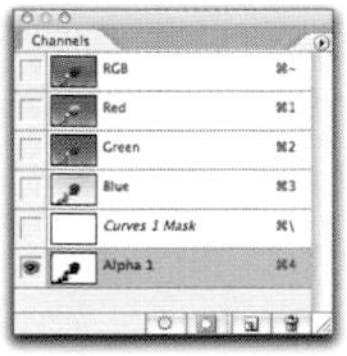

Click the alpha channel's tile in the Channels palette to select it and make it visible, Select All, and Copy.

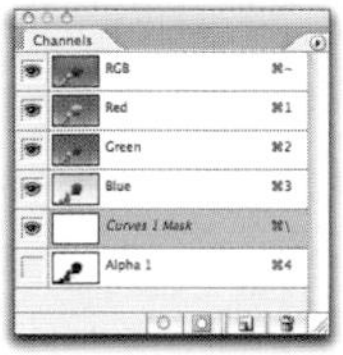

Click the layer mask's tile in the Channels palette to select it, and click the eyeball to make it visible.

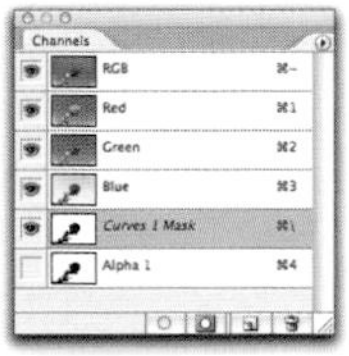

Choose Paste to paste the contents of the alpha channel into the layer mask.

Painting on the layer mask. Bruce has always felt that the process of first defining the area you want to change (by making a selection) and *then* changing it is fundamentally bass-ackwards. He much prefers to make the change, then apply it to the places that need it. With layer masks, he (and you) can do exactly that.

Typically, we make edits to a layer so that it affects the entire image (we ignore what's happening in the areas we don't want to change). Then, we'll edit the layer mask. Sometimes that means inverting the layer mask to turn it black, hiding the entire edit, and painting with white on the mask to reveal the edit where it's wanted. Sometimes it means painting with black to mask out the areas we want to leave unchanged—we'll use whichever method requires less brushwork. Quite often, we'll use a gradient fill to apply a graduated change across the image, and sometimes we'll even resort to using the selection tools! (Again, see Chapter 8, *Making Selections*, for more on selections and masking.)

So with all the aforementioned techniques under our belts, let's look at their application to actual images.

Advanced Adjustment Layers

The ability to mask adjustment layers is one of their most appealing features, but the ability to vary the opacity of the layer is also extremely useful. Figure 7-9 shows an image of a swan that needs a lighting tweak and how adjustment layers can save the day. (This is also a much safer technique than having your assistant chase a swan with a reflector!)

We started by applying a Curves adjustment layer to the entire image, which lightened the head and neck but blew out all the detail on the swan's back. So we chose the Gradient tool and applied a short white-to-black linear gradient to constrain the Curves adjustment to the area in shadow.

This gave us a big improvement over the original, but we can take it further. We duplicated the Curves layer, and reduced the layer opacity to

Figure 7-9
Masked adjustments

 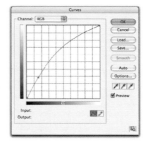

*The original image.
We want to get rid of the
shadow on the swan's
neck and head.*

*We applied the curve,
above, as an adjustment
layer, producing the result
shown at left.*

*We applied a gradient fill
to the layer mask using the
gradient tool, producing
the result shown right.*

*A gradient fill on
the layer mask*

*Painting on the
layer mask*

*We duplicated the Curves
layer and reduced the
opacity to 67 percent,
producing the result shown
near right. Then we painted
black into the duplicate
layer's mask to produce the
final result at far right.*

67 percent. This got the tonality we wanted on the swan's head and neck, but made the water a little too bright, so we painted the adjustment out with a soft-edged brush and black paint.

The whole process was very quick, with absolutely no time spent making painstaking selections. Painting on the mask with a soft-edged brush (light on planet earth just about *never* makes hard edges) is often the quickest and easiest way to constrain local adjustments. The following tips may make it even easier.

Tip: Enable and Disable the Layer Mask. Often, when you're editing a layer mask, it's useful to turn the mask off (and on again) to see your progress. You can make the lengthy trip to the Layer Mask submenu of the Layer menu and choose Enable or Disable there, but it's much quicker to Shift-click on the layer mask tile in the Layers palette. It's a toggle: When the mask is disabled, it shows a red X. Shift-clicking enables it, Shift-clicking again disables it, so you can see a quick before-and-after.

Tip: Show and Hide the Layer Mask. Most of the time, we just look at the layer mask's effect on the image, but sometimes it's useful to see the mask itself while you're editing it. Option-Shift-click on the Layer Mask icon in the Layers palette to display the mask *and* the layer, as though you were in QuickMask mode. Then, when you're ready to see the effects of your mask editing, Option-Shift-click on the icon again to "hide" it. (If you don't like the color or opacity of the layer mask, you can Option-Shift-double-click on the icon to change the mask's color and opacity.)

If you want to see *only* the layer mask (as its own grayscale channel), Option-click on its tile in the Layers palette. This is most helpful when touching up areas of the layer mask (it's sometimes hard to see the details in the mask when there's a background image visible).

Tip: Switch Foreground and Background Colors. When you paint on layer masks, you often need to switch between black and white paint. When you target a layer mask, Photoshop usually sets the Foreground color to black and the Background color to white (if it doesn't, press D.) Then, as we mentioned earlier, you can switch them quickly by pressing the X key.

Copying Layer Masks

In Photoshop CS2, copying layer masks has become even easier. Just Option-drag the layer mask thumbnail in the Layers palette to the layer to which you want to apply the mask. Quite often, the mask you want is already in the file (or its opposite is, in which case all you need to do is to copy and invert it), and other times it's often quicker to start from an existing mask and edit it than it is to start from scratch.

Figure 7-10 shows a series of local and global edits that include the use of a copied, then inverted, layer mask.

Figure 7-10
Local and global
adjustments

The original image. The sky is impossibly blue heading to purple, the contrast is flat, and the stone is magenta.

We applied the curve at far right as an adjustment layer, producing the result shown at near right. This improves the contrast on the pyramid, though it makes the sky worse.

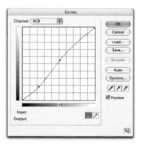

Working on the same Curves layer, we made a small move to the green channel to make the stone less magenta.

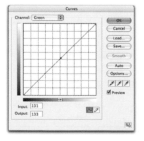

Figure 7-10
Local and global
adjustments, *continued*

*We masked the Curves layer by making
a Color Range selection on the blue,
and then painting over the clouds.*

*We added a Photo Filter
layer to warm the image
slightly. It shifted the sky a
little towards purple again,
but we'll fix that with its
own adjustment.*

*We added a Curves
adjustment layer to
increase the contrast
in the clouds. The curve
point that's selected in the
illustration is the one that
does the work—the others
are anchor points.*

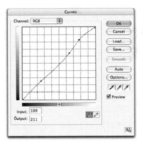

*Finally, we added a Hue/
Saturation layer to fix the
sky. Then we masked it
by duplicating the layer
mask from the first
Curves layer and inverting
it, to constrain the
adjustment to the sky.*

*We made the Hue/
Saturation layer mask
by Option-dragging the
Curves 1 mask onto the
Hue/Saturation layer, then
pressing Command-I
to invert it.*

Masking Techniques

Painting on the layer mask is often quick and effective, but it's not the only game in town. We always look for the way to accomplish the goal with the least amount of work. Figure 7-11 shows examples where we used several different masking techniques.

Remember that, because the mask is simply a channel, you can edit it using all the Photoshop tools you apply to images, including selecting specific areas of the layer mask.

Figure 7-11
Masking techniques
(part 1)

The original image.
The sky is a little magenta,
the contrast is flat, and the
foreground is oversaturated.

We Command-clicked to
place two curve points,
one for the medium sky
tones, another for the
darker shades in the ice
caps, and tweaked them
to increase the contrast.
Switching to the green
channel, we Command-
clicked the magenta part
of the sky and added green.
The remaining points are
anchors.

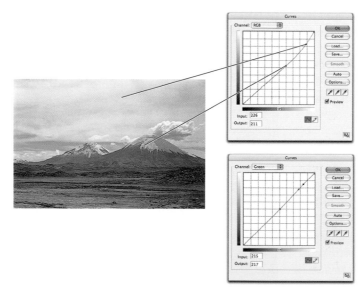

The Curves adjustment
improved the sky and
mountains, but made the
foreground too dark, so
we applied a gradient fill
to the layer mask, starting
above the mountains and
ending at their bottoms.

Figure 7-11
Masking techniques
(part 2)

Our next Curves layer focused on the mountains. We Command-clicked to place two Curve points, and increased the contrast.

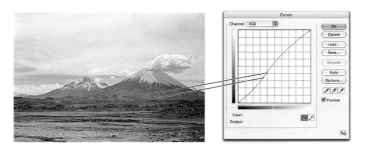

To constrain the Curves adjustment to the mountains, we inverted the layer mask, then painted the adjustment in by painting with white on the mask.

Next, we added a Hue/Saturation layer to desaturate the foreground, clicking on the brighter yellow-greens to center the yellow color range, then adjusting saturation and lightness.

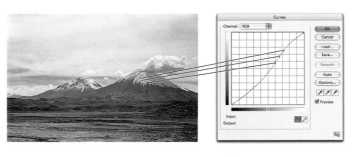

Another Curves layer increased contrast on the icecaps. We liked what it did to the mountains too, but it flattened the sky, made the foreground too contrasty, and the blue sky too saturated.

We duplicated the layer mask from our first Curves layer to mask the foreground.

Figure 7-11
Masking techniques
(part 3)

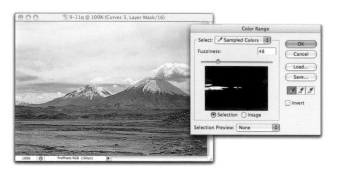

To take care of the oversaturated sky, we made a Color Range selection, then filled the selected area on the mask with black.

For our final edit, we put detail back in the sky by making a marquee selection that started at the top of the image and ended just above the blue sky, then we filled the selected area with a gradient fill.

Beyond Adjustment Layers

Applying Levels, Curves, Hue/Saturation, and the other adjustments as adjustment layers offers tremendous flexibility and power, but it isn't always the quickest or easiest way to fix your images. Also, while these tools are powerful (and essential to learn), they don't really relate to anything we did in the wet darkroom—they're much more akin to the controls on prepress scanners than to anything photographic.

The layer blending modes open up an entirely different way to edit images. Bruce likens use of the blending modes to making the images edit themselves—he actually spent the best part of a year eschewing the use of Curves layers as anything except a means of applying blending modes, just to see how far he could take this approach.

He concluded that Curves is indeed an indispensable tool, but nowa-days he's more likely to use it as a fine-tuning tool, doing the heavy lifting with blending modes.

Using Layer Blending Modes

When we started our blending mode experiments, we duplicated the Background layer, and applied the blending mode to the duplicate layer. We quickly found that we could obtain the same result by applying an adjustment layer—any kind of adjustment layer—without making any adjustments, and setting the blending mode of the adjustment layer rather than duplicating a pixel layer.

We quickly settled on using Curves layers to do this—Levels layers take longer to create because Photoshop has to build the histogram that appears in the Levels dialog box, and if we need to make actual adjust-ments, more often than not we need to do so with Curves. Applying blend-ing modes with Curves layers offers three advantages over doing so with pixel layers.

▶ The files are smaller than ones made with pixel layers when we save as Zip-compressed TIFF. (Uncompressed, they may be a little larger because the adjustment layer always has a layer mask. But if you apply a layer mask to the pixel layer, this difference goes away). In Photoshop CS, adjustment layers in 16-bit files didn't compress well—we're happy to report that CS2 does a much better job in this regard.

▶ Adjustment layers automatically come with a layer mask. Since much of the appeal of working with blending modes comes from painting adjustments in and out by painting on the layer mask, having one created automatically saves us time.

▶ If we need to make actual adjustments beyond just applying the blend-ing modes, we have Curves ready and waiting for our edits.

Before looking at actual examples, though, it's time to get your head around just what the blending modes do. They're sometimes referred to as "procedural blends" because they all use some arithmetical formula to calculate pixel values based on the values in the overlying and under-lying layer. (Of course, when we use adjustment layers without making actual adjustments, the overlying and underlying pixel values are the same, which actually makes things a little simpler to understand.)

Layer Blending Modes

The previous examples were relatively simple, using straightforward adjustment layers for global editing, with some painting on the layer mask for local corrections. However, when you combine adjustment layers with the power of blending modes, you open up a whole new world of possibilities.

One advantage of using blending modes rather than simply stretching and squeezing the bits with Levels and Curves is that blending interpolates tonal values, producing smoother results. We'll show you some examples of how we use some of the blendng modes, but we encourage you to experiment—there are plenty of new techniques waiting to be discovered.

The blending modes are arranged in logical groups, according to the way they function.

▶ **The Independent modes.** Normal and Dissolve both replace the underlying pixels with the overlying pixels (in the Normal or Dissolve layer) when the layer is at 100-percent opacity. At lower opacities, Normal blends the overlying pixels with the underlying ones according to opacity, while Dissolve replaces pixels randomly (see Figure 7-12).

Figure 7-12
Normal and Dissolve

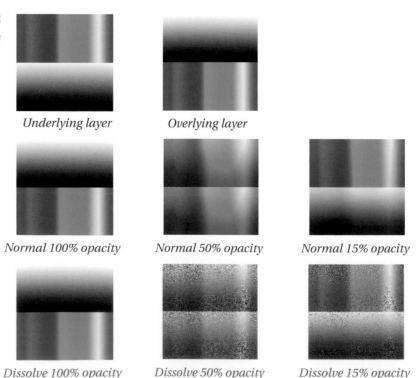

Underlying layer   *Overlying layer*

Normal 100% opacity   *Normal 50% opacity*   *Normal 15% opacity*

Dissolve 100% opacity   *Dissolve 50% opacity*   *Dissolve 15% opacity*

▶ **The Darken modes.** The neutral color for the Darken modes is white—white pixels on a layer set to a Darken mode leave the underlying pixels unchanged. Nonwhite pixels darken the result by varying amounts, depending on the blend mode and opacity (see Figure 7-13).

Figure 7-13
The Darken modes

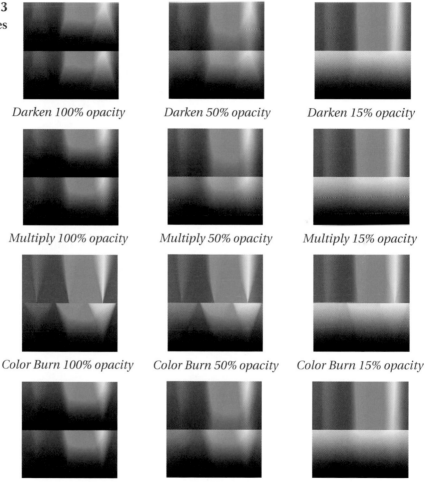

Darken 100% opacity   Darken 50% opacity   Darken 15% opacity

Multiply 100% opacity   Multiply 50% opacity   Multiply 15% opacity

Color Burn 100% opacity   Color Burn 50% opacity   Color Burn 15% opacity

Linear Burn 100% opacity   Linear Burn 50% opacity   Linear Burn 15% opacity

▶ **The Lighten modes.** The Lighten modes are the inverse of the Darken modes. The neutral color for the Lighten modes is black—black pixels on a layer set to a Lighten mode leave the underlying pixels unchanged. Nonblack pixels lighten the result by varying amounts, depending on the blend mode and opacity (see Figure 7-14).

Figure 7-14
The Lighten modes

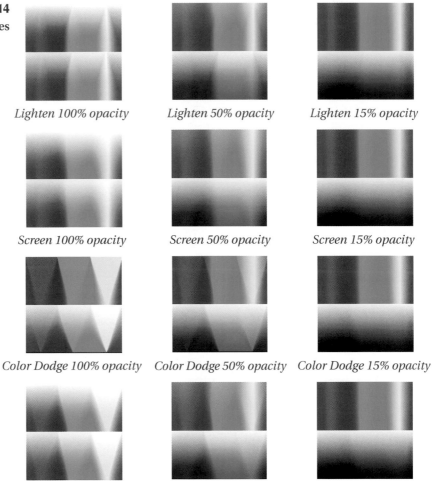

Lighten 100% opacity *Lighten 50% opacity* *Lighten 15% opacity*

Screen 100% opacity *Screen 50% opacity* *Screen 15% opacity*

Color Dodge 100% opacity *Color Dodge 50% opacity* *Color Dodge 15% opacity*

Linear Dodge 100% opacity *Linear Dodge 50% opacity* *Linear Dodge 15% opacity*

▶ **The Contrast modes.** The contrast modes combine corresponding Darken and Lighten modes. The neutral color for the Contrast modes is 50-percent gray—50-percent gray pixels on a layer set to a Contrast mode leave the underlying pixels unchanged. Lighter pixels lighten the result, and darker pixels darken the result, by varying amounts, depending on the blend mode and opacity (see Figure 7-15).

The odd man out is the new Hard Mix blend, which has no neutral color—but it doesn't really fit anywhere else either. It reduces the image to 8 colors—red, cyan, green, magenta, blue, yellow, white, or black—based on the mix of the underlying and blend colors, with a strength related to 50-percent gray.

Figure 7-15
The Contrast modes

Overlay 100% opacity   *Overlay 50% opacity*   *Overlay 15% opacity*

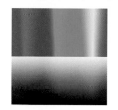

Soft Light 100% opacity   *Soft Light 50% opacity*   *Soft Light 15% opacity*

Hard Light 100% opacity   *Hard Light 50% opacity*   *Hard Light 15% opacity*

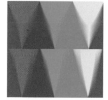

Vivid Light 100% opacity   *Vivid Light 50% opacity*   *Vivid Light 15% opacity*

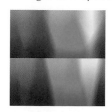

Linear Light 100% opacity   *Linear Light 50% opacity*   *Linear Light 15% opacity*

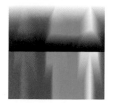

Pin Light 100% opacity   *Pin Light 50% opacity*   *Pin Light 15% opacity*

Figure 7-15
The Contrast modes,
continued

Hard Mix 100% opacity   *Hard Mix 50% opacity*   *Hard Mix 15% opacity*

▶ **The Comparative modes.** The neutral color for the Comparative modes is black. The Comparative modes look at each channel and subtract the underlying color from the overlying color or the overlying color from the underlying color, choosing whichever returns a result with higher brightness. Blending with white inverts the underlying color values (see Figure 7-16).

Figure 7-16
The Comparative modes

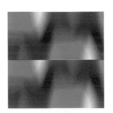 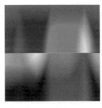 

Difference 100% opacity   *Difference 50% opacity*   *Difference15% opacity*

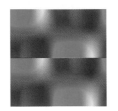  

Exclusion 100% opacity   *Exclusion 50% opacity*   *Exclusion 15% opacity*

▶ **The HSL modes.** While the members of the other groups do basically the same things in different strengths, the members of the HSL group each do something rather different, though they all operate on hue, saturation, and luminosity. Hence it makes sense to discuss them individually (see Figure 7-17).

Hue. Hue creates a result color with the brightness and saturation of the underlying color and the hue of the overlying color.

Saturation. Saturation creates a result color with the brightness and hue of the underlying color and the saturation of the overlying color.

Figure 7-17
The HSL modes

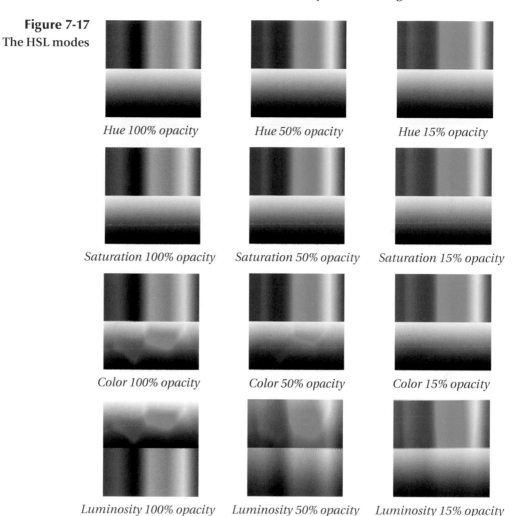

Hue 100% opacity   *Hue 50% opacity*   *Hue 15% opacity*

Saturation 100% opacity   *Saturation 50% opacity*   *Saturation 15% opacity*

Color 100% opacity   *Color 50% opacity*   *Color 15% opacity*

Luminosity 100% opacity   *Luminosity 50% opacity*   *Luminosity 15% opacity*

Color. Color creates a result color with the luminosity of the underlying color and the hue and saturation of the overlying color.

Luminosity. Luminosity is the inverse of Color. It creates a result color with the hue and saturation of the underlying color and the luminosity of the overlying color.

Layer Blending in Practice

If the preceding discussion has rendered you crosseyed, some less-abstract examples may be helpful. The blending modes we tend to use most are Multiply to build density, Screen to reduce it, Soft Light and Hard Light to increase contrast, Color to change color balance without affecting luminosity, and Luminosity to sharpen images without introducing color fringes (we discuss sharpening layers in much greater detail in Chapter 9, *Sharpness, Detail, and Noise Reduction*).

Tip: Stop-Based Corrections with Multiply and Screen. If you're more comfortable thinking in terms of f-stops than in levels or percentages, thank our friend and colleague Jeff Schewe for this insight. You can lighten and darken shadows by 1 stop by applying Screen and Multiply, respectively, at an opacity of 38 percent.

For a half-stop adjustment, use 19 percent. For a one-third stop, 13 percent seems to be slightly closer than 12, and for a quarter stop, 9 percent is the magic number. Multiply and Screen always affect the shadows more than the midtones and highlights, so the analogy with f-stops isn't perfect, but it's still a useful rule of thumb.

The practical examples that follow don't pretend to exhaust the power of blending modes. They're simply illustrative examples that we hope will fire your imagination and pique your curiosity. Remember—one of the huge benefits of working with layers is that you can't do any harm until you flatten the image, so feel free to experiment. Photoshop offers many ways to produce similar if not identical results, and we each find methods that work for us.

Building density with Multiply. The best analogy we've found for Multiply mode is that it's like sandwiching two negatives in an enlarger. Mathematically, Multiply takes two values, multiplies them by each other, and divides by 255. Practically speaking, this means the result is always darker than either of the sources.

If a pixel is black in the base image, the result after applying an adjustment layer with Multiply is also black. If a pixel is white in the base image, the adjustment layer has no effect (white is the neutral color for Multiply). We use Multiply with Curves adjustment layers to build density, particularly in the highlights and midtones of washed-out images like the one in Figure 7-18.

This image represents a scene with a huge dynamic range—a backlit boat against the sun rising over the Ganges—and thanks partly to the wonders of modern color negative film, partly to the filtration effect of the omnipresent smoke from the burning ghats, we were able to capture it. Our scan has detail in both the brightest part of the sun and in the darkest part of the boat, but the distribution of the midtones is quite wrong— they're much too light, rendering a potentially dramatic image merely pleasant. We can improve it very quickly with a single Curves adjustment layer, using the Multiply mode.

We create a new Curves adjustment layer, making no changes to the curve, and set the blend mode to Multiply by choosing it from the blend mode menu in the Layers palette. This is equivalent to duplicating the Background layer on top of itself and changing the new layer's blending mode to Multiply (see Figure 7-18).

Figure 7-18
Building density
with Multiply

The original image

We added a Curves layer, clicked OK to dismiss the Curves dialog box without making any adjustments, and set the blending mode to Multiply.

Adding Contrast with Hard Light. We use Soft Light, Hard Light, and Overlay to build contrast (since the overlying and underlying pixels are identical, Hard Light and Overlay produce exactly the same result). We use Soft Light for smaller contrast boosts, and Hard Light or Overlay for stronger ones. All three blend modes preserve white, black, and midlevel gray, while lightening pixels lighter than midlevel gray and darkening those that are darker. Figure 7-19 shows a contrast adjustment with hard light.

Figure 7-19
Increasing contrast
with Hard Light

*We added a second Curves
layer set to Hard Light to
increase contrast.*

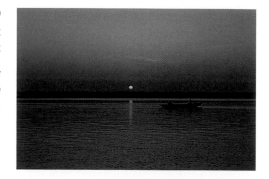

*This made the image too
dark, so we reduced the
opacity of the Multiply
layer to 80 percent.*

Adjusting color balance with Color. While we sometimes use Photo Filter adjustment layers for warming and cooling effects, we find that Solid Color layers set to Color blending with a low opacity offer more control—we can tweak the color by double-clicking on the layer without having to tunnel through the Photo Filter dialog box.

We start out by creating a Solid Color layer of approximately the color we want, then we reduce the opacity, typically to around 10–20 percent. Then we fine-tune the color to get the result we want—we usually tweak the Hue and Saturation fields of the Color Picker by placing the cursor in them and pressing the up and down arrows on the keyboard.

Figure 7-20 shows the process and the result of adding a Solid Color layer. We started out by picking the approximate color—the image is a little green, so we picked its opposite, magenta—then we used the color picker to fine-tune the solid color to get the result we wanted. Now the edited image does a much better job of conveying the oppressive heat, the omnipresent smoke and dust, and the languor of the millennia-old ritual that takes place at dawn on the Ganges.

Figure 7-20
Adjusting color balance
with Color

*The image is a little green,
so we added a Solid Color
layer using magenta, set
the blend mode to Color,
and reduced the opacity to
20 percent.*

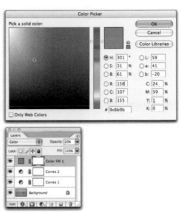
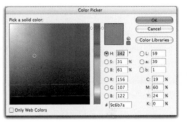

*This made the image a
little too blue-purple,
so we nudged the color
towards red by double-
clicking the adjustment
in the Layers palette to
open the color picker,
then adjusted the Hue by
selecting the Hue field and
pressing the arrow keys.*

Opening shadows with Screen. Screen is literally the inverse of Multiply. The best real-world analogy we've heard comes from Adobe's Russell Brown. Screen is like projecting two slides on the same screen. The result is always lighter than either of the two sources.

If a pixel is white in the base image, the result is white, and if it's black in the base image, the result is also black (black is the neutral color for Screen). Intermediate tones get lighter. We often use Screen to open up dark shadows.

If you're a techno-dweeb like we are, you probably want to know what Screen does behind the scenes. Photoshop inverts the two numbers (subtracts them from 255) before doing a Multiply calculation (multiplies them by each other and divides by 255); then the program subtracts the result from 255. That's it. Now, don't you feel better knowing that?

Bruce shot the image in Figure 7-21 from his deck, using a Canon EOS 1Ds, on a typically foggy San Francisco late afternoon. The image holds detail in both highlight and shadow, but the foreground is dark and muddy, an ideal candidate for opening up with Screen blending. We want to preserve the dark sky and hold the detail on the sunlit buildings across the bay, so we'll make the adjustment, then localize it using the layer mask.

Figure 7-21
Opening shadows
with Screen

The original image

We added a Curves layer set to Screen blending mode.

We added a layer mask to constrain the Screen blending adjustment to the dark foreground.

We wanted to open up the foreground a little more, so we duplicated the layer, including the mask, and reduced the opacity of the second layer to 40 percent.

Creating the mask. We could get a pretty good result by painting with a large soft-edged brush, but we found we could do even better by first making a marquee selection that covered the dark sky, filling the selection with black on the layer mask, and then making a second marquee selection on the bright area, and refining it with Color Range, as shown in Figure 7-22.

Figure 7-22
Building the layer mask

We start with a marquee selection that covers all the dark sky.

Making sure that the layer mask is targeted, we fill the selection with black.

We make a second marquee selection that encompasses all the bright areas, along with the skyline, then we target the Background layer and make a Color Range selection that picks up the skyline. Then, with the layer mask targeted, we again fill the selection with black.

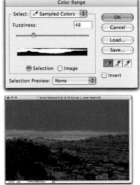

Complex Layer Blending

The preceding examples were relatively simple. While we always look for simple fixes, some images entail more complexity than others. The image in Figure 7-23 is a hardy perennial that we nevertheless continue to improve as both the tools and our understanding of them evolves.

This image has more than its share of problems—it's shot into the sun on color negative, and the scan is flat with a greenish color cast—but as is often the case in the real world, reshooting isn't an option!

Figure 7-23
An image with many problems

This image has a green cast, flat contrast, and a washed-out area from shooting into the sun.

One of our rules of thumb is to fix the biggest problem first, but in this case it's a toss-up as to whether the color or the contrast is the worse issue. Since we really dislike looking at green people, we'll address the color cast first, then the contrast hole caused by the lens flare, then the overall contrast and color balance. We won't be attempting perfection in the first round of edits—we're just putting building blocks in place that we'll tweak later.

Figure 7-24 shows our first stab at the color cast. When dealing with color casts, we usually try Auto Color's Find Dark and Light Colors with Snap Neutral Midtone, perhaps with manual adjustment of the target midtone color, but in this case it didn't do anything useful, so we applied a solid Color Fill layer with a purplish-magenta color, Color blend mode, and an opacity of 19 percent. The cast seemed stronger on the right side of the image than on the left, so we made a gradient fill in the layer mask from white to 25 percent gray.

Our next step was to fix the contrast hole caused by shooting into the sun. We created a Curves layer, and set it to Multiply. Then we applied a radial gradient to constrain the adjustment to the area suffering from flare, and tweaked the opacity until the adjustment blended in with the rest of the image, as shown in Figure 7-25.

Figure 7-24
Addressing the color cast

We start by applying a Color Fill layer set to Color blending, then we apply a gradient to the mask.

Figure 7-25
Fixing the lens flare

We create a Curves layer set to Multiply, apply a radial gradient to the layer mask, then fine-tune the opacity.

These two adjustments don't make the image look particularly good, but they lay the groundwork for the ones that follow, "normalizing" the image so that it can better take further edits. Our next edit adds contrast by applying a layer set to Hard Light. It blows out all the detail in the sky, so we make a Color Range selection and mask the sky.

This leaves the sky pink, so we load the sky selection by Command-clicking the layer mask tile in the Layers palette, press Command-Shift-I to invert it so that the sky is selected, target the Color Fill layer's mask, and fill the selected area with black so that the Color Fill no longer applies to the sky (see Figure 7-26).

Figure 7-26
Adding contrast
with Hard Light

We create a Curves layer set to Hard Light. Then we make a Color Range selection of the sky, and fill the selected area with black on the layer mask.

This leaves the sky quite pink, so we reuse the sky selection. We load it by Command-clicking the layer mask, invert it, target the Color Fill layer's mask, and fill the selection with black.

The top half of the image is still washed out, so we add a Multiply layer, then make a gradient fill on the layer mask so that it only affects the upper portion of the image—see Figure 7-27.

This leaves the image quite dark, so our next edit is a simple Levels adjustment—it's a good example of the kind of edit that drove Bruce to conclude that blending modes couldn't completely replace Levels, Curves, and Hue/Saturation. We could try to do something clever with Screen

Figure 7-27
Building density
with Multiply

*We add a Curves layer
set to Multiply, then we fill
the layer mask with a
gradient fill that
constrains the effect to
the upper portion of the
image to put detail
back in the sky.*

blending, Curves, and a layer mask, but we've learned to recognize the dangers of our own cleverness. so instead, we opt for the simple white point and midtone Levels adjustment shown in Figure 7-28.

Figure 7-28
Brightening the
image with Levels

*This simple Levels
adjustment makes the
image less murky.*

We'd like more contrast on the foreground figures, so we add a Curves layer set to Soft Light with a medium opacity. Then we invert the layer mask to hide the effect, and paint it in where we want it using a soft-edged brush set to 50% opacity. Using a medium opacity on the layer lets us fine-tune the effect later, if we need to, by adjusting the layer opacity. If we need still finer control, we can edit the layer mask itself using Levels, adjusting the midtone slider to reveal or conceal the effect. Figure 7-29 shows the edit before and after painting on the layer mask.

Figure 7-29
Adding local contrast
by painting in a
Soft Light layer

*We add a Curves layer set
to Soft Light, and invert
to hide the effect. Then we
paint it in with a
soft-edged, medium-
opacity brush.*

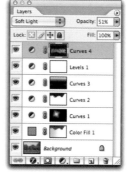

The overcast sky makes the image seem too warm, so we add a Photo Filter layer using a cooling filter, then reduce the layer opacity to get the strength we want. That way, if we need to increase or decrease the strength later, we can do so by adjusting the layer opacity directly from the Layers palette, without having to open the Photo Filter dialog box (see Figure 7-30).

Figure 7-30
A cooling adjustment
with Photo Filter

*We add a cooling Photo
Filter layer, deliberately
making it a little stronger
than we want, then we
reduce the layer opacity
so that we can decrease or
increase the effect without
going back into the Photo
Filter dialog box.*

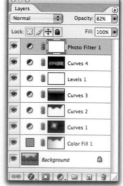

The image is still flat, so we add a Curves layer set to Soft Light, then reduce the opacity to 80 percent, as shown in Figure 7-31.

Figure 7-31
Adding global contrast
with a Soft Light layer

We add a Curves layer set to Soft Light, then reduce the opacity to 80 percent.

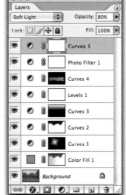

This improves everything except the skin tones. Bruce would admit that alcohol had been consumed, but the braw lads are looking a wee bittie too florid, so we add a Hue/Saturation layer, and adjust the Reds and Yellows, taming the skin tones and adding a little saturation to the grass, as shown in Figure 7-32.

Figure 7-32
Hue/Saturation
adjustments

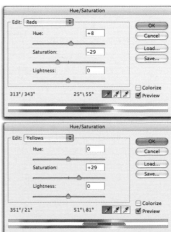

The Hue/Saturation adjustments shown at right tame the skin tones and add some saturation to the grass. We customized the color ranges by clicking in the image.

We have one remaining problem: The sky is still too pink. We already have a mask for the sky, so a localized adjustment is simple, and we could do it any number of ways, including using Curves or Hue/Saturation. We opted for a low-opacity Color Fill layer set to Color blend mode, with a layer mask to constrain it to the sky. We started by loading the mask from our second Curves layer as a selection, then we inverted the selection so that the Color Fill layer would pick it up and use it as a mask, then we chose the approximate color, set the blend mode to Color, and lowered the opacity. Figure 7-33 shows the result.

Figure 7-33
A Color Fill layer

The Color Fill layer, with the layer mask set to reveal only the sky, produces this result once the blend mode is set to Color and the layer opacity is reduced to 12 percent.

This sequence of edits may seem quite complex, but it took far less time to accomplish than it did to explain! However, it does serve to point out a major issue with making layered edits to images, whether using blend modes or simple adjustment layers.

Naming the layers. This image contains only 10 layers, not a huge number by any stretch of the imagination, but it isn't at all obvious what each layer does. We can glean a few clues by looking at the layer masks, but if we return to this image a year or two from now, we'll pretty much have to resort to turning the layers on and off to figure out what each one does.

It's a good idea to get into the habit of naming your layers informatively—just double-click on the layer name in the Layers palette, and type in a more informative name than "Curves 78" or "Color Fill 15." Figure 7-34 shows how we'd like the Layers palette to appear when we revisit the image.

Figure 7-34
Naming the layers

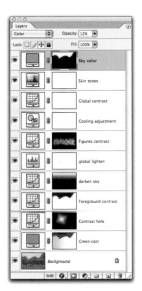

The small amount of time we invest in renaming the layers will be amply repaid should we have to revisit the image in the future. Instead of spending ten minutes trying to understand how the file is constructed, we can get a good idea of the role of each layer simply by looking at the Layers palette.

Letting the Image Edit Itself

We confess to being lazy. One of the ways that laziness manifests itself is that we're always looking for simpler solutions, which in the field of digital imaging can be difficult and occasionally dangerous. But using the contrast, darken, and lighten blend modes to adjust tonality is one of those few solutions that is both simple and safe.

Bruce calls this "letting the image edit itself" because rather than having to place curve points and carefully manipulate them, the image content does all the work. If you need more contrast, apply a Soft Light or Hard Light layer. The blending mode takes the contrast that's already in the image and increases it, with no danger of clipping, and no futzing around in the Curves dialog box. Likewise, when you need to lighten or darken an image, Screen and Multiply do those things proportionally, again with no danger of clipping. Moreover, the blend modes tend to introduce less hue-shifting than major tonal moves with Curves.

Each layer affects all the layers underneath it, so we often end up going back to a previous layer to tweak it to take account of the effect of the ones above it. Using the blend modes, we can simply adjust the layer opacity without having to open dialog boxes, or when we need to make localized changes, we edit the layer masks.

Once you get accustomed to working with the blend modes, you'll find that they're useful for many different kinds of edits. But it's important to remember that the conventional tools still work too!

Mixing and matching. The following example shows how we mix blending modes with "normal" techniques. A reasonable rule of thumb is that if a blend mode edit doesn't get you where you want to be fairly quickly, and it's not a masking issue—an edit that needs to be localized to a specific area in the image—it's probably time to go back to the "normal" Photoshop tools.

The image shown in Figure 7-35 is an unadjusted scan from a Kodak Portra 160 NC color negative. Two quick blend mode edits put it into a much better state for the subsequent fine-tuning.

Figure 7-35
Heavy tonal lifting
with blend modes

Two Curves layers, one set to Hard Light, the other set to Screen, quickly remap the tonal values in this image. Making extreme edits like these with Curves or Levels introduces hue shifts that may cause problems down the road.

Next, we shift the color balance—the image has a color cast that's basically cyan, as is common with scans from color negative. So we add red as a solid Color Fill layer, setting it to Color blend mode and 12-percent opacity. Then we go in and fine-tune the color (see Figure 7-36).

Figure 7-36
Fixing color balance with
a Color Fill layer

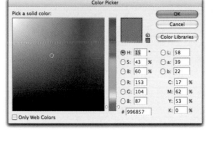

*We add a red Color Fill
layer, set the blend mode
to Color, and reduce the
opacity to 12 percent.
Then we double-click on
the layer's icon to open the
color picker, and fine-tune
the color.*

The Color Fill layer generally moves the color balance in the direction we want, but it's clear that the sky is going to need a localized correction. The blue sky is relatively easy to isolate, but we need to be careful, because the dark areas on the background hills are also blue, so we'll need to take that into account when we make the selection.

We're also faced with the question of how to edit the sky color. We could use a Hue/Saturation layer, or a Curves layer, or we could apply another solid-color layer set to Color blending. They all require approximately the same amount of work, but we opt for a solid-color layer because it's likely to be the easiest of the three to fine-tune afterwards.

If we used a Hue/Saturation layer or a Curves layer, we'd almost certainly apply it at 100-percent opacity, so if we needed to make the effect stronger, we'd have to tunnel into the dialog boxes. Color Fill layers, on the other hand, always use fairly low opacities, so we have an immediately available adjustment to make them weaker or stronger using the layer opacity—we only need to open the dialog box to adjust the actual color.

So we make a marquee selection that covers the sky blue areas, then refine it with Color Range. We add a Color Fill layer with a sky-blue color. The layer automatically uses the selection as a layer mask, so we set the blend mode to Color and reduce the opacity until it looks right, as shown in Figure 7-37.

Figure 7-37
A local correction with a
Color Fill layer

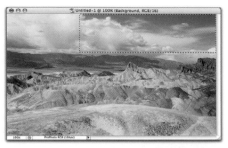

*We use Color Range to
select the sky, then add a
blue Color Fill layer. We set
the blend mode to Color
and reduce the opacity to
12 percent to produce the
result at near right.*

There is, however, the danger of falling in love with the techniques to the extent that you make extra work for yourself by overlooking the more conventional techniques—we learned this the hard way!

We want to make the background hills less blue (the dark areas are green vegetation), and we want to increase the saturation and the separation of the red and yellow tones in the foreground. We could do this with careful masking and two or three color fill layers, but since we're dealing with separate ranges of color, and we already have a mask that isolates the blue sky from the blue hills, it makes more sense to use a "conventional" Hue/Saturation layer with the blue sky masked out.

We start by Command-clicking on the Sky color layer's layer mask in the Layers palette to load it as a selection, then we press Command-Shift-I to invert the selection, leaving everything except the blue sky selected. When we add our Hue/Saturation layer, it automatically uses this selection as its layer mask.

We boost the saturation of the foreground yellows, and shift the hue of the background hills towards green. We have to darken the green to keep the same tonality, so we reduce the lightness as well as shift the hue—see Figure 7-38.

Our next problem is that the clouds are too cyan. They're relatively easy to select, so the simplest fix is a masked Color Fill layer using red to counteract the cyan cast. (Hue/Saturation doesn't work well on colors that

are close to neutral, and Curves would require quite a lot of fiddling—we'd need to adjust at least two points on the red curve, and possibly tweak green and blue too.) Figure 7-39 shows the fix.

Figure 7-38
A local correction with a
Hue/Saturation layer

We load the layer mask from our previous edit as a selection, then invert the selection so that the sky is masked rather than revealed. We click in the foreground of the image to center the Yellows color range on the foreground yellows and boost the saturation. Then we switch to the Blues tab, click on the background hills to center the color range, and make a major adjustment to both Hue and Lightness.

Figure 7-39
Warming the clouds with
a Color Fill layer

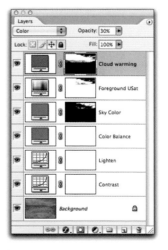

We make a quick Color Range selection of the clouds, then add a red Color Fill layer. We set the blend mode to Color and reduce the opacity to 30 percent to produce the result at near right.

Two simple blend mode edits let us adjust the final lightness and contrast. We add a Screen layer and a Soft Light layer, setting the opacities to 7 percent and 62 percent respectively. The Screen layer at 7 percent opacity provides a very gentle lightening, and the Soft Light layer at 62 percent gives a healthy contrast boost—see Figure 7-40.

Figure 7-40
Tonal fine-tuning
with blend modes

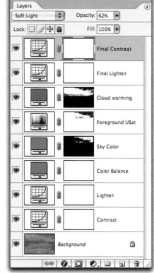

Two Curves layers, one set to Hard Light, the other set to Screen, quickly remap the tonal values in this image.

One of the biggest problems in digital imaging is knowing when the image is finished! We can't claim to do better than anyone else in that department, so we have two more edits. The first is to make the foreground a little warmer—we really want it to glow. We could use a Photo Filter layer, but we find Color Fill layers easier to control—there's one fewer dialog box to tunnel into if we need to tweak the color.

So we apply an amber warming color as a solid Color Fill layer, set the blend mode to Color, and reduce the layer opacity to 12 percent. This does wonders for the foreground but makes the clouds much too warm. So we select the Background layer, make a quick Color Range selection on the clouds, select the warming layer's layer mask, and fill the selection with black. (We had to target the background layer to make the Color Range selection because Color Range only works on layers that contain pixels, a quirk that has tripped us up more than once!) Figure 7-41 shows the image with the Color Fill layer applied, before and after masking.

Figure 7-41
Warming with
a Color Fill layer

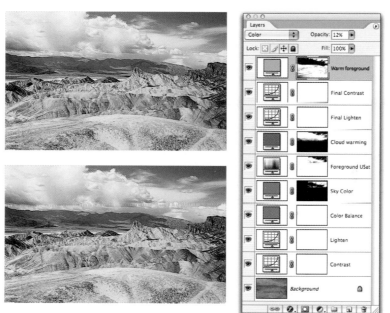

*We apply a warming color
as a Color Fill layer, then
mask the clouds using
Color Range.*

At this point, most of us would have the sense to leave well enough alone—we've come a long way since Figure 7-35—but the background hills aren't quite right, so we apply the Curves shown in Figure 7-42, invert the layer mask, and paint the final correction in with a soft-edged brush.

Figure 7-42
A masked Curves
correction

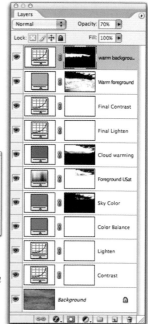

*We apply a Curves layer with the above Curves, then
we invert the layer mask, and paint the correction
in with a soft-edged brush.*

Beyond Adjustment Layers

Using "empty" adjustment layers to blend an image into itself is a very powerful technique, but sometimes, you may need to duplicate the image to a new layer, then edit the duplicate pixels themselves.

The image shown in Figure 7-43 is an old favorite that we've used in the past to demonstrate several different techniques. The big problems are that the main subject is dark, flat, and a little blue.

Figure 7-43
A problem image

We need to lighten, warm, and add contrast to the subject.

We can fix most of the problems using blend modes and layers masks as shown in Figure 7-44. We use Screen to lighten, Soft Light to add contrast, and a solid color fill set to Color for warming. All the masks were created using soft, low-to-medium-opacity brushes.

The first layer set to Screen lets us paint some virtual fill-flash that lightens the subject. The second layer set to Soft Light lets us add contrast to the face with a single dab of the brush. The third layer applies a solid amber fill set to Color blending with a low opacity, and warms the whole image. The fourth layer set to Screen softens the shadows on the left side of the face.

We're left with one remaining problem, the very bright highlight on the hair. If we simply add a masked adjustment layer set to Multiply, we

Figure 7-44 Blend mode corrections

1. Screen blending at 100 percent, brush at 20 percent opacity.

2. Soft Light blending at 100 percent, brush at 20 percent opacity.

3. Amber solid color fill set to Color blending at 11 percent opacity.

4. Screen blending at 45 percent, brush at 10 percent opacity.

5. Soft Light at 100 percent opacity, brush at 20 percent opacity.

can build density, but the result is also highly oversaturated. However, if we copy the actual pixels to a new layer set to Multiply, we can edit those pixels to produce a much more satisfactory result—see Figure 7-45.

Figure 7-45
A pixel layer
set to Multiply

We select the hair highlight, copy it to a new layer which we move to the top of the layer stack, and set the blend mode to Multiply.

The result is quite oversaturated, so we edit the pixels on the Multiply layer with the Channel Mixer and Hue/Saturation.

Editing the pixels lets us keep the Multiply layer at full opacity, so we get the maximum darkening effect without oversaturating the hair color.

We finish the image off with a Soft Light layer at 40 percent opacity to get the final contrast.

In this case, we use the Channel Mixer to exploit the detail in the blue channel by replacing some of the red and green channels with blue, then we use Hue/Saturation to desaturate the pixels. Then, with the highlight fix in place, we apply one more Soft Light layer to get the final contrast.

Advanced Pixel Blending

Blending pixel layers lets you do things that you simply can't do by adjusting a single image. One situation where we blend pixel layers is when we want to extend the apparent dynamic range of digital captures. Of course, the best way to do this is to take several bracketed exposures and merge them to a 32-bit floating point HDR (High Dynamic Range) image. But that requires planning, a hefty tripod, and a subject that moves little if at all.

It may seem that it's pointless to blend different renderings of a single digital capture. After all, all the data is in the capture, so why not simply edit it to get the results you want? We feel that there are two reasons.

▶ It's extremely difficult to get everything right from a single rendering of the image.

▶ Most cameras capture 12 bits of data. By blending multiple renderings of the 12-bit capture, you can populate more levels in 16-bit space than you can by stretching and squeezing the original 12 bits.

Figure 7-46 shows an "impossible" image produced just this way.

Figure 7-46
An impossible image

The sun is just outside the frame at the top of the image—we wouldn't even have attempted this with film!

Figure 7-48
Layer masking

Before layer masking

*Option-click
to "solo" the
Background
layer, then...*

*...Command-
click the RGB
tile or press
Command-
Option--(tilde).*

After layer masking

*Click the Add
layer mask
icon to load the
selection as a
layer mask.*

With less-challenging images, two layers masked this way may be all you need, but in this case, we need to add a third layer for the highlight detail. The procedure for adding the third layer and masking it is almost identical. We open the third rendering of the image, the one adjusted for highlight detail, Select All, Copy, and paste it into our layered document, where it becomes the third, topmost layer. (That's assuming that the top layer was selected when you pasted—if it wasn't, and the new layer comes in between the two existing ones, just drag it to the top of the layer stack.)

To make the mask for the third layer, click its eyeball icon in the layers palette, then load the combined Luminosity of the first two layers either by Command-clicking the RGB Channel thumbnail in the Channels palette, or by pressing Command-Option--(tilde)—remember, the selection that gets loaded is the luminosity of all visible layers. Then, select the third, topmost layer, click the eyeball to make it visible, and click the Add layer mask icon. The selection is added as a layer mask to the third (highlight) layer (see Figure 7-49).

The resulting image is pretty flat, but all the essential components are now in place. We can improve matters somewhat by tweaking the layer opacities—see Figure 7-50.

Figure 7-49
Adding and masking
the third layer

Before layer masking

Click to hide the new layer, then...

...Command-click the RGB tile or press Command-Option-~(tilde).

After layer masking

Click the Add layer mask icon to load the selection as a layer mask.

Figure 7-50
Tweaking the
layer opacities

Adjusting the layer opacities as shown in the Layers palettes at far right produces this result.

Producing the final image. To get from here to the result shown back in Figure 7-46, we used masked layers set to Multiply to darken, Screen to lighten, and Soft Light to add contrast. We left all the layers at 100 percent opacity and used the layer masks to control them.

On this image, the process was iterative, bouncing back and forth between the layers, and in all honesty it's unlikely that we'd be able to produce absolutely identical results twice in a row, though we'd come pretty close. Figure 7-51 shows the almost-final image, with layers applied to add contrast (Soft Light), lighten (Screen), and darken (Multiply).

Figure 7-51
Fine-tuning with
blend modes

The image adjusted
with masked layers set
to Soft Light, Screen, and
Multiply, respectively

We started by adding a layer set to Soft Light to increase contrast. We left the layer mask white while we added two more layers, one set to Screen, the second to Multiply. On those layers, we inverted the layer mask (target the mask and press Command-I) to hide the effect, then we painted the lightening and darkening into the image by painting on the masks with a soft-edged brush at opacities between 10 and 20 percent. Then we returned to the Soft Light layer, and painted out some of the contrast in the foreground trees.

While we didn't in this case resort to doing so, we'd be remiss if we failed to mention that it's also possible to edit the layer masks using Levels or Curves. To lessen the strength of a layer, you can use the white Output Levels slider in Levels to turn the white (fully revealing) areas of the mask to a light gray, or to let just a little of the effect show through fully masked areas, you can use the black Output Levels slider to turn the black (fully concealing) areas of the mask to a dark gray.

We finished off the image by adding a fully masked Soft Light layer, then painting the additional contrast in with a 5-percent-opacity brush to get the final result shown back in Figure 7-46.

Alternative workflows. In this example, we created three separate DNG files by saving them from Camera Raw with their respective settings, then opened them in Photoshop and copied-and-pasted to get them all into the same document. But there other useful ways to handle the task of combining multiple renderings of the same raw image.

▶ **Edit and Open in Camera Raw without saving settings.** If the edits needed to produce the different renderings are simple enough, it's probably not worth saving them as separate settings. Instead, you can open the raw file in Camera Raw hosted by Photoshop (this doesn't work when Camera Raw is hosted by Bridge), and Option-click the Open button (it changes to Open a Copy when Option is pressed) to open a copy of the image *without updating the Camera Raw settings*.

This technique is useful when you want to produce a few different renderings quickly without altering the "master" settings for a raw file. Once the images are open in Photoshop, the techniques for combining them are the same as in the example we've just covered.

▶ **Place Smart Objects.** Another alternative is to place the raw file multiple times into a Photoshop document as Smart Objects. That way, you can edit the settings for each rendering by simply double-clicking the layer thumbnail for the raw-place-as-Smart Object—it opens the the image up in Camera Raw and lets you edit the settings, which are applied only to that specific Smart Object.

Our enthusiasm for this workflow is tempered by two considerations, though. You have to create a Photoshop document with the correct dimensions before you start placing the Smart Objects, and while you can edit the images in place, you don't see them in the context of the other layers. So it makes changing the individual renderings a little quicker than going back to the raw file, editing it, and opening a new version, but it doesn't make getting the settings right any easier.

One of the most appealing aspects of layer-based editing is its non-destructive nature—the edits aren't committed until you flatten the file—but sometimes, you can take nondestructive editing so far that you create extremely complex files that are both large and hard to understand. So don't be overly afraid to mix a little destructive editing in with the non-destructive stuff. Remember that you can edit pixel layers directly, and sometimes, it's a good idea to do so. If you're nervous about making edits without an escape route, there's one more Photoshop feature that provides a handy fallback position—the History palette.

History and Virtual Layers

Layer-based edits offer great freedom and flexibility, but they have one major disadvantage—they make large files that can also be dauntingly complex. It's often a sobering exercise to return to a layered file you created months or years ago and try to figure out what each layer was supposed to do. Layer naming helps, but only up to a point.

We confess that when the History feature first appeared in Photoshop, we saw it as little more than a massively overengineered multiple undo. But our friend and colleague Jeff Schewe, who has probably had more influence on the History feature's development than anyone outside of Adobe, dropped some hints that made us realize the error of our ways.

History certainly gives you many levels of Undo—up to 1,000—but it does much more besides. When you use History in conjunction with blending modes and the History Brush, you have something that lets you apply very similar effects to those you can achieve with layers and masks.

Virtual Layers

We like to think of History as providing "virtual layers" because it lets us do many of the things we can also do with layers. But let's look at the important ways in which History's virtual layers differ from real ones.

- ► History is ephemeral. It's only around as long as your file is open. Once you close the file, its history is gone forever, giving a whole new twist to the old adage that those who can't remember history are doomed to repeat it. You can't save History with the file, so you have to get your edits right before you close. (You can save a history log, either in the file's metadata or in a text file, but the log doesn't let you re-create previous states of the image.)

- ► History is easier than layers when you know exactly what you're doing and can get things right on the first (or possibly second) try, but if you're less decisive than that, it quickly becomes more work than using layers to achieve the same effects.

- ► History can be even more demanding on your hardware than adjustment layers. It requires plenty of scratch space, and the faster the disk, the better.

Nevertheless, History is a powerful feature for making quick, effective, dare we say gonzo, edits.

History Tools

History works using just a handful of tools. The History palette lets you set the source for your History-based edits—the pixels that you'll apply to the image (see Figure 7-52).

Figure 7-52
The History palette

Click this column to set the History source.

This icon indicates the current History source.

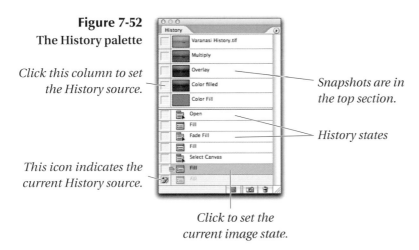

Snapshots are in the top section.

History states

Click to set the current image state.

The History palette. The History palette lets you click in the left column to set the History source to a History state or snapshot (the paintbrush icon indicates the current History source), or click on a snapshot or History state's tile to set the current state of the image.

The three icons at the bottom of the palette let you create a new document from the current History state, create a new snapshot, and delete the current History state, respectively. Snapshots are a convenience feature—they're usually easier to track than History states, and unlike History states, you can name them.

Applying History. You can apply History using either the History brush tool or the Fill command from the Edit menu. Fill is easier when you have a selection or you want to affect the entire image. The History brush is useful for actually brushing in edits. When you use either one, you can immediately use the Fade command (on the Edit menu) to adjust the edit's opacity (and hence its strength).

Figure 7-53 revisits the image from Figure 7-18, but this time we'll make the edits using History instead of layers. No masking is involved, so we simply use Fill from History to make all the edits.

Figure 7-53
Simple History edits

The unedited image

We set the History source to the current state.

We choose Fill, History, Multiply, and 83 percent.

We set the History source to the current state.

We choose Fill, History, Overlay, and 100 percent.

For the next edit, the History source is irrelevant, so we leave it alone.

We set the background color, then choose Fill, Background Color, Color, and 20 percent.

The process is very simple. Our first edit was a layer set to Multiply with an opacity of 83 percent, so we set the History source to the current image state (actually, since the image is newly opened, it's already set that way), and choose Fill from the Edit menu. In the Fill dialog box, we choose History from the Use menu, Multiply from the Mode menu, and 83 percent for the opacity.

Our second edit was an Overlay layer set to 100 percent. Again, we set the History source to the current image state—otherwise the Overlay blend would use the original image rather than the image after Multiply, and hence wouldn't match the layered version. Then we choose Fill, and the dialog box choose History, Overlay, and 100 percent.

Our final edit was a solid color layer set to Color blend mode with an opacity of 20 percent. For this, we don't need to use a History state. We simply set the background color (or foreground color, if you prefer) to our desired color (in ProPhoto RGB it was R 156, G 107, B 123), then we choose Fill, and in the dialog box, we choose Background color from the Use menu, Color from the mode menu, and 20-percent opacity.

The result is pixel-for-pixel identical to the layered version we produced earlier in the chapter. We don't have any layers to tweak, but we could, if we wished, fine-tune by continuing to blend the different History states.

Combining Blend Modes with History

History also lets you do things that you can't do as easily with layers. One trick we often use is to make a basic setup of three snapshots, one for the original image, a second darkened with Multiply, and a third lightened with Screen. Then we apply the darkened and lightened versions using Soft Light or Hard Light/Overlay to darken or lighten while adding contrast.

Figures 7-54 and 7-55 show a quick set of edits performed entirely with History. We don't necessarily advocate using this approach for all, or even most, edits, but it's one more useful set of techniques to get under your belt—the more techniques you master, the easier it is to pick the one that will get you the results you want with the minimum of effort in any given situation.

In this case, the unedited image is flat, so we want to pump up the contrast. Specifically, we want to darken the sky, then add contrast to the sagebrush while brightening the highlights. To do so, we first set up a series of snapshots that lighten and darken the image using Screen and Multiply, as shown in Figure 7-54.

Figure 7-54
Setting up Snapshots

We set the initial snapshot as source...

...then choose Fill, with History, Multiply, and 60 percent opacity, and save the result as a new snapshot.

Keeping the initial snapshot as the source, we repeat the process using Screen instead of Multiply as the blending mode for the Fill.

We save the result as a new snapshot, so that we now have a darkened version using Multiply and a lightened version using Screen, in addition to the original image.

Next, we apply the edits. We make a selection of the sky and fill it from the Multiply snapshot. Then we invert the selection, and use the History brush to paint the Screen snapshot into the sagebrush, using Overlay blending to increase contrast, as shown in Figure 7-55.

The trick here, of course, is that you can create a snapshot using one blend mode, then apply it using a different mode either by choosing it in the Fill dialog box, or by setting the blend mode for the History Brush.

Figure 7-55
Applying the edits

We make a quick Color Range selection of the sky and save it as a snapshot in case something goes wrong. Then we set the History source to the Multiply snapshot.

With the selection active, we Fill from History, using the Multiply layer as source, with Normal blending.

We invert the selection, then...

...we choose the History Brush with a large brush size, 60 percent opacity, and Overlay blending...

...we set the History source to the Screen snapshot...

...and use it to brush increased contrast into the sagebrush, as shown in the final image, right.

Print Optimization

As with the wet darkroom, the goal when working in the digital darkroom is often to make prints—otherwise the digital darkroom wouldn't be worthy of the name. But the digital darkroom offers a key advantage over its analog counterpart: Thanks to the wonders of color management, it lets you see what will happen in the print before you make it.

The naïve view of color management is that it makes your prints match your monitor. If you've read this far, you've probably realized that this is an impossible goal—printers simply cannot print the range of color a good display can display. Instead, color management tries to reproduce the image as faithfully as the limitations of the output process will allow.

But color management knows nothing about images; it only knows about the color spaces in which images reside. So no output profile, however good it is, does equal justice to all images. When you convert an image from a working space to the gamut and dynamic range of a composite printer, the profile treats all images identically, using the same gamut and dynamic range compression for all.

But thanks to Photoshop's soft-proofing features, you can see ahead of time exactly how the profile will render your images, allowing you to take the necessary corrective action. If you want great rather than good, you need to optimize images for different output processes, because something always has to give, and each image demands its own compromises.

Adjustment layers provide a very convenient method for targeting images for a specific output process. You can use adjustment layers grouped in layer sets to optimize the same master image for printing to different printers, or to the same printer on different paper stocks. The following technique uses three basic elements.

▶ **A reference image.** Create a duplicate of the image, with Proof Colors turned off, to serve as a reference for the image appearance you're trying to achieve.

▶ **A soft proof.** Use the Proof Setup command to provide a soft proof that shows how the output profile will render the image.

▶ **A layer set containing adjustment layers.** Group each set of optimizations for a specific output condition (printer, paper, ink) into a layer set, so that you can turn them on and off conveniently when you print to one or another device.

Making the reference image. Choose Duplicate from the Image menu to make a duplicate of the image. The duplicate will serve as a reference for the appearance you're trying to achieve on the print.

You need to make a duplicate rather than simply open a new view because you'll be editing the master image to optimize it for the print, and the edits would show up in a new view. The duplicate isn't affected by the edits you make to the master file, so it can serve as a reference—a reminder of what you want to achieve in the print.

Setting the soft proof. Choose Custom from the Proof Setup submenu on the View menu to open the Proof Setup dialog box. Load the profile for your printer, and check Paper Color to make Photoshop use absolute colorimetric rendering to the monitor (see Figure 7-56). We find that all the soft-proof views (using the different combinations of Paper Color and Black Ink) tell us something useful, but the absolute colorimetric rendering produced by checking Paper Color is, in theory at least, the most accurate.

Figure 7-56
Setting the soft proof

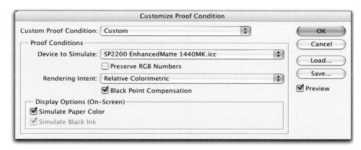

Load the profile for your output device, and turn on Simulate Paper Color.

However, the first thing you'll notice is that checking Paper Color makes the image look much worse. Sometimes it seems to die before your eyes. At this point, a good many people think Photoshop's soft proof must be inherently unreliable and give up on the whole enterprise. What's really going on is that Photoshop is trying to show you the dynamic range compression and gamut compression that will take place on printing.

The reason the soft proof looks bad at first glance is that Photoshop can only show you the gamut and dynamic range compression within the confines of your monitor space, and it can only do so by turning things down, so white in the image is always dimmer than your monitor white.

A second problem is that the vast majority of monitor profiles have a "black hole" black point (a black with a Lightness of zero in Lab). Real monitor black typically has a Lightness of 3 or higher, so the soft proof typically shows black as slightly lighter than it will actually appear on the print.

Typically, in the soft proof you'll see washed-out shadows, compressed highlights, and an overall color shift caused by the difference between the white of your working space and the white of your paper. Some images are only slightly affected by the conversion to print space, while with others the change can be dramatic. As with just about any proofing method we've encountered, you need to learn to interpret Photoshop's soft proofs. You may find the following tips helpful in doing so.

Tip: Look Away When You Turn On Paper White. Much of the shock you feel when you see Photoshop's absolute colorimetric rendering to the monitor stems from seeing the image change. If you look away from the monitor when you turn on Paper White, your eyes will be able to adapt to the new white point more easily.

Tip: Use Full-Screen View to Evaluate Soft Proofs. Your eyes can't adapt to the soft-proof white point unless you hide Photoshop's user interface elements, a good few of which are still pure white. Press F to switch to full-screen view with a neutral gray background, then press Shift-F to hide the menu bar. Press Tab to hide all the palettes. Now you can see the soft-proofed image on a neutral background with no distracting elements to bias your vision.

A further problem, particularly with vendor-supplied profiles for older printers, is that they weren't built with soft-proofing in mind. They do a good job of converting the source to the output, but they don't do nearly as good a job of "round-tripping"—converting the output back to a viewing profile. That said, all the profiles we've built with current third-party profiling tools make the round-trip very well.

If all this seems discouraging, take heart. Soft-proofing for RGB output may have passed its infancy, but it hasn't yet reached adolescence. And problems with profiles aside, the soft proofs offered by Photoshop are not, in our experience, any less accurate than those offered by traditional proofing systems. You simply need to learn to "read" them. Figure 7-57 shows some examples.

Figure 7-57
The soft proof and the
reference image

*The soft proof shows
reduced contrast and
a slight blue shift
when compared to
the reference image.*

The soft proof

The reference image

*The soft proof, left, shows a color shift in addition to the reduced dynamic
range when compared with the reference image, right.*

Make your edits. We suggest starting out viewing the soft proof and the reference image side-by-side. Once you've edited the soft-proofed image to get it back to where you want it to be, fine-tune your edits looking at the soft-proofed image in full-screen view.

Some images need minimal editing; others may require significant reworking. We start by applying adjustment layers to get the soft-proofed image to match the reference (the duplicate) as closely as possible. Then we group these adjustment layers in a layer group named for the print process it addresses. That way, we can easily optimize the master image for different print processes by turning the layer sets on and off, without having to create a new file for each print condition. Figure 7-58 shows the edited and reference images with the individual edits and their accompanying layer sets.

Figure 7-58
The edited image and the reference image
(part 1)

The Hue/Saturation layer shifts the blue of the sky slightly toward magenta.

We edited the soft-proofed image, left, to match the reference image, below.

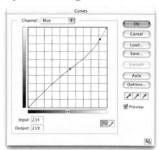

The blue curve removes the blue cast.

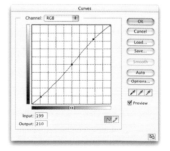

The RGB curve restores contrast.

Figure 7-58
The edited image and
the reference image
(*part 2*)

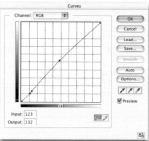

*The Curves adjustment
layer adds contrast
using the RGB curve.*

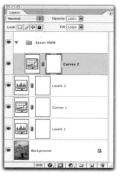

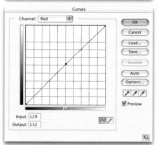

*We added small
amounts of red and
green, and reduced
blue, to remove the
color cast in the sky
and on the building.*

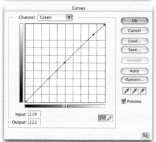

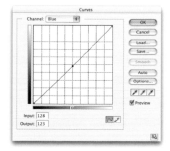

This technique is particularly useful when printing to inkjet printers directly from Photoshop—we can keep a single RGB master file, with built-in optimizations for each print condition, and let Photoshop do the conversion from RGB working space to printer space at print time. But it's also valuable when preparing images for CMYK output, which often involves, if anything, greater compromises. We may do final fine-tuning on the converted CMYK image, but we make heavy use of soft-proofing to get the RGB image into the best possible state to withstand the conversion before we actually make it.

Once we've edited the soft-proofed image to match the reference image, we use full-screen view to take a final look at the soft-proofed image prior to printing. (We prefer the gray background, with the menu bar hidden—the black background makes the shadows look too light.) In the majority of cases we find that no further editing is necessary, but occasionally we'll fine-tune highlight and shadow detail.

The final step is, of course, to print the image. See "Imaging from Photoshop" in Chapter 13, *Image Storage and Output*.

Darkroom Experiments

Don't get the idea that you have to work exclusively using adjustment layers, layer masks, blending modes, and the History Brush. Photoshop offers multiple methods of doing just about anything, so we present these as interesting and often useful approaches—it's up to you to decide whether and when to use them. You can mix and match the techniques in this chapter with the more conventional techniques described in the previous one.

Nonetheless, working with these techniques offers a huge amount of freedom to experiment. You can take chances, drive your images to extremes, and generally do things you couldn't do using the more conventional techniques.

Making Selections

Getting Just What You Need

You love the painting and retouching tools that Photoshop offers; you love layers; you even love all the options it gives you for saving files. But as soon as someone says "alpha channel" or "mask," your eyes glaze over. And when someone strings together a sentence like, "Edit your selection in Quick Mask mode and then intersect it with the eighth alpha channel," you drop your mouse and head for the door.

It doesn't have to be this way. Masks, channels, and selections are actually really easy once you get past their bad reputation. Making a good selection is obviously important when silhouetting and compositing images—two of the most common production tasks. But perhaps even more important, selections are also a key ingredient for nondestructive tonal corrections, color corrections, sharpening, and even retouching. We discussed some of these in the previous chapter, and we'll explore them further in later chapters—but before we get there, we must first make you a mask maven and a channel champion!

Note that in this chapter we're only talking about pixel-based selections; we'll discuss sharp-edged vector clipping paths and masks in Chapter 12, *Essential Image Techniques.*

Masking-Tape Selections

Back in Chapter 7, *The Digital Darkroom*, we introduced a few concepts that are crucial to becoming a selection expert.

▶ Selections, channels, and masks are actually all the same thing in different forms. And you can convert one to another easily.

▶ A channel is a saved selection and looks like a grayscale image where the black parts are fully deselected ("masked out"), the white parts are fully selected, and the gray parts indicate partially selected pixels.

▶ A layer mask is a selection or channel applied to a layer so that the black areas of the mask fully hide the layer and the white areas of the mask are transparent (they show the layer's pixels). If an area in a layer mask (or channel) is 25-percent gray, then that area is 75-percent visible. Remember: "Black conceals, white reveals," and the lighter the gray, the more selected or visible the area.

▶ Smooth transitions between selected (white) and unselected (black) areas are incredibly important for compositing images, painting, correcting areas within an image—in fact, just about everything you'd want to do in Photoshop.

Selection Tools

Although there are a mess o' ways to make a selection in Photoshop (we'll look at just about all of them in this chapter), there are three basic selection tools in the Tool palette: the Marquee tool, the Lasso tool, and the Magic Wand (see Figure 8-1). While some people eschew these tools for the more highfalutin' selection techniques, we find them invaluable for much of our day-to-day work.

The important thing to remember about these selection tools (and, in fact, every selection technique in Photoshop) is that they can all work in tandem. Don't get too hung up on getting one tool to work just the way you want it to; you can always modify the selection using a different technique (this idea of modifying selections is very important, and we'll touch on it throughout the chapter).

Figure 8-1
Selection
tools

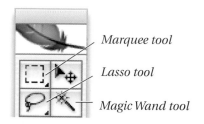

Marquee tool

Lasso tool

Magic Wand tool

Tip: You Can Always Move Your Selection. One of the most frequent changes you'll make to a selection is moving it without moving its contents. For instance, you might make a rectangular selection, then realize it's not positioned correctly. Don't redraw it! Just click and drag the selection using one of the selection tools. The selection moves, but the pixels underneath it don't. Or, press the arrow keys to move the selection by one pixel. Add the Shift key to move the selection ten pixels for each press of an arrow key.

Tip: Moving a Selection While Dragging. One of the coolest (and least known) selection features is the ability to move a marquee selection (either rectangular or oval) while you're still dragging out the selection. The trick: hold down the Spacebar key while the mouse button is still held down. This also works when dragging frames and lines in Adobe InDesign and Adobe Illustrator.

Tip: Adding to and Subtracting from Selections. No matter which selection tool you're using, you can always add to the current selection by holding down the Shift key while selecting. Conversely, you can subtract from the current selection by holding down the Option key. Or, if you want the intersection of two selections, hold down the Option and the Shift keys while selecting (see Figure 8-2). If you don't feel like remembering these keyboard modifiers, you can click on the Add, Subtract, and Intersect buttons on the far-left side of the Options bar instead.

Tip: Select It Again. While Bruce is the steady-and-sure type, David tends to rush through Photoshop like a madman. One result is that David often deselects a selection without having thought through the implications (like "will I need this again?"). Fortunately, when he finds he does need that old selection again, he can recall it by pressing Command-Shift-D (or choosing Reselect from the Select menu).

Figure 8-2
Adding, subtracting, and
intersecting selections

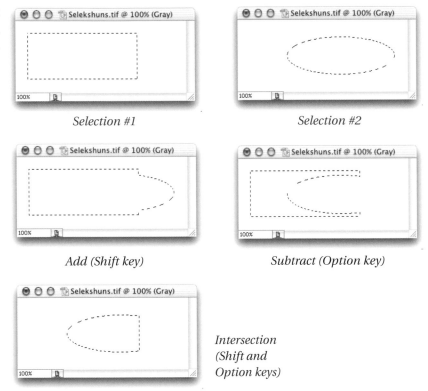

Selection #1

Selection #2

Add (Shift key)

Subtract (Option key)

Intersection
(Shift and
Option keys)

Tip: Transforming Selections. When you choose Transform Selection from the Select menu, Photoshop places the Free Transform handles around your selection and lets you rotate, resize, skew, move, or distort the selection however you please. When you're done, press Enter or click the Checkmark button in the Options bar.

Even less obvious is that after you choose Transform Selection, you can pick options from the Transform submenu (under the Edit menu) or type transform values into the fields in the Options bar. For example, if you want to mirror your selection, turn on Transform Selection, drag the center point of the transformation rectangle to the place around which you want the selection to flip, then choose Flip Vertical or Flip Horizontal from the Transform submenu (see Figure 8-3).

Marquee

The Marquee tool is the most basic of all the selection tools. It lets you draw a rectangle or oval selection by clicking and dragging. If you hold down the Shift key, the marquee is constrained to a square or a circle, depending

Figure 8-3
Transforming a selection

*We select the type by Command-clicking on
the type layer, then choose Transform Selection.*

*You can skew a selection
by Command-dragging
one of the side handles.*

*By dragging the
center point to here,
the transformation
is centered at this
location.*

*We skewed and scaled the selection by dragging
and typing in the Options bar. You can also
select items from the Transform submenu
(under the Edit menu).*

*After pressing Enter (to set the transform), we added a Levels adjustment
layer and moved the midpoint slider to darken the "shadow."*

on whether you have chosen Rectangle or Ellipse in the Marquee Options
bar. (Note that if you've already made a selection, the Shift key adds to
the selection instead.) If you hold down the Option key, the selection is
centered on where you clicked.

Tip: Pull Out a Single Line. If you've ever tried to select a single row of pixels in an image by dragging the marquee, you know that it can drive you batty faster than Mrs. Gulch's chalk scraping. The Single Row and Single Column selection tools (click and hold the mouse button down on the Marquee tool to get them) are designed for just this purpose. We use them to clean up screen captures, or to delete thin borders around an image. They're also useful with video captures, because each pixel row often equals a video scan line.

You can cycle through the rectangular, elliptical, single row, and single column selection tools by choosing from the Tool palette, but it's faster to press M once to select the tool, then press Shift-M to cycle through the tools (Option-clicking on the Marquee tool in the Tool palette also cycles through them).

Tip: Selecting Thicker Columns and Rows. If you want a column or row that's more than one pixel wide/tall, set the selection style to Fixed Size on the Options bar, and type the thickness of the selection into the Height or Width field (note that you have to type a measurement value, like "px" for pixels, or "cm" for centimeters). In the other field, type some number that's obviously larger than the image, like 10,000px. When you click on the image, the row or column is selected at the thickness you want.

Tip: Selecting that Two-by-Three. You've laid out a page with a hole for a photo that's 2 by 3 inches. Now you want to make a 2-by-3 selection in Photoshop. No problem: Choose Constrained Aspect Ratio from the Style popup menu in the Options bar (when you have the Marquee tool selected). Photoshop lets you type in that 2-by-3 ratio.

If you're looking to select a particular-sized area, you can select Fixed Size from the Style popup menu, and type any measurement you want ("in" for inches, "px" for pixels, and so on).

Lasso

The Lasso tool lets you create a freeform outline of a selection. Wherever you drag the mouse, the selection follows until you finally let go of the mouse button and the selection is automatically closed for you (there's no such thing as an open-ended selection in Photoshop; see Figure 8-4).

Figure 8-4 Lasso selections

Beginning the selection   *End of (very rough) selection*   *Closed on mouse release*

Tip: Let Go of the Lasso. Two of the most annoying attributes of selecting with the Lasso are that you can't lift the mouse button while drawing, and you can't draw straight lines easily (unless you've got hands as steady as a brain surgeon's). The Option/Alt key overcomes both these problems.

When you hold down the Option key, you can release the mouse button, and the Lasso tool won't automatically close the selection. Instead, as long as the Option key is held down, Photoshop lets you draw a straight line to wherever you want to go. This solves both problems in a single stroke (as it were).

The folks at Adobe saw that people were using this trick all the time and decided to make it easier on them. Photoshop includes a Straight-line Lasso tool that works just the opposite from the normal Lasso tool—when you hold down the Option key, you can draw nonstraight lines. If you press the L key once, Photoshop gives you the Lasso tool; then press Shift-L, and you get the Straight-line Lasso tool. (Of course, the Shift key trick won't work if you've turned off the Use Shift Key for Tool Switch option in the Preferences dialog box.)

In order to close a selection when you're using the Straight-line Lasso tool, you have to either click at the beginning of the selection or double-click anywhere.

Tip: Select Outside the Canvas. You may or may not remember at this point in the book that Photoshop saves image data on a layer even when it extends past the edge of the canvas (out into that gray area that surrounds your picture). Just because it's hidden doesn't mean you can't select it. If you zoom back far enough, and enlarge your window enough (or switch to full-screen mode) that you can see the gray area around the image canvas, you can hold down the Option key while using the Lasso tool to select into the gray area. (Ordinarily, without the modifier key, the selections stop at the edge of the image.)

Magnetic Lasso. The Magnetic Lasso tool (it, too, is hiding in the Tool palette behind the Lasso tool) lets you draw out selections faster than the regular Lasso tool. This tool can seem like magic or it can seem like a complete waste of time—it all depends on three things: the image, your technique, and your attitude.

To use the Magnetic Lasso tool, click once along the edge of the object you're trying to select, then drag the mouse along the edge of the selection (you don't have to—and shouldn't—hold down the mouse button while moving the mouse). As you move the mouse, Photoshop "snaps" the selection to the object's edge. When you're done, click on the first point in the selection again (or triple-click to close the path with a final straight line).

So the first rule is: Only use this tool when you're selecting something in your image that has a distinct edge. In fact, the more distinct the better, because the program is really following the contrast between pixels. The lower the contrast, the more the tool gets confused and loses the path.

Here are a few more rules that will help your technique.

▶ **Be picky with your paths.** If you don't like how the selection path looks, you can always move the mouse backward over the path to erase part of it. If Photoshop has already dropped an anchor point along the path (it does this every now and again), you can remove the last point by pressing the Delete key. Then just start moving the mouse again to start the new selection path.

▶ **Click to drop your own anchor points.** For instance, the Magnetic Lasso tool has trouble following sharp corners; they usually get rounded off. If you click at the vertex of the corner, the path is forced to pass through that point.

▶ **Vary the Lasso Width as you go.** The Lasso Width (in the Options bar) determines how close to an edge the Magnetic Lasso tool must be to select it. In some respects it determines how sloppy you can be while dragging the tool, but it becomes very important when selecting within tight spots, like the middle of a "V". In general, you should use a large width for smooth areas, and a small width for more detailed areas.

Fortunately, you can increase or decrease this setting while you move the mouse by pressing the square bracket keys on your keyboard. (For extra credit, set Other Cursors to Precise in the General Preferences dialog box; that way you can see the size of the Lasso Width.) Also, Shift-[and Shift-] set the Lasso Width to the lowest or highest value (one or 40). If you use a pressure-sensitive tablet, turn on the Stylus Pressure checkbox on the Options bar; the pressure then relates directly to Lasso Width.

▶ **Sometimes you want a straight line.** You can get a straight line with the Magnetic Lasso tool by Option-clicking once (at the beginning of the segment) and then clicking again (at the end of the segment).

▶ **Occasionally, customize your Frequency and Edge Contrast settings.** These settings (on the Options bar) control how often Photoshop drops an anchor point and how much contrast between pixels it's looking for along the edge. In theory, a more detailed edge requires more anchor points (a higher frequency setting), and selecting an object in a low-contrast image requires a lower contrast threshold. To be honest, we're much more likely to switch to a different selection tool or technique before messing with these settings.

The last rule is patience. Nobody ever gets a perfect selection with the Magnetic Lasso tool. It's not designed to make perfect selections; it's designed to make a reasonably good approximation that you can edit. We cover editing selections in "Quick Masks," later in this chapter.

Tip: Scrolling While Selecting. It's natural to zoom in close when you're dragging the Magnetic Lasso tool around. Nothing wrong with that. But unless you have an obscenely large monitor, you won't be able to see the whole of the object you're selecting. No problem; the Grabber Hand works just fine while you're selecting—just hold down the Spacebar and drag the image around. You can also press the + and - (plus and minus) keys to zoom in and out while you make the selection.

Magic Wand

The last selection tool in the Tool palette is the Magic Wand, so-called more for its icon than for its prestidigitation. When you click on an image with the Magic Wand (dragging has no effect), Photoshop selects every neighboring pixel with the same or similar gray level or color. "Neighboring" means that the pixels must be touching on at least one side (see Figure 8-5). If you want to select all the similar-toned pixels in the image, whether they're touching or not, turn off the Contiguous checkbox in the Options bar before clicking.

How similar can the pixels be before Photoshop pulls them into the selection? It's entirely up to you. You can set the Tolerance setting on the Options bar from 0 to 255. In a grayscale image, this tolerance value refers to the number of gray levels from the sample point's gray level. If you click on a pixel with a gray level of 120 and your Tolerance is set to 10, you get any and all neighboring pixels that have values between 110 and 130.

Figure 8-5
Magic Wand
selections

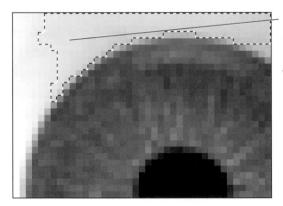

We clicked here with the Magic Wand tolerance set to 18.

In RGB and CMYK images, however, the Magic Wand's tolerance value is slightly more complex. The tolerance refers to each and every channel value, instead of just the gray level.

For instance, let's say your Tolerance is set to 10 and you click on a pixel with a value of 60R 100G 200B. Photoshop selects all neighbors that have red values from 50 to 70, and green values from 90 to 110, and blue values from 190 to 210. All three conditions must be met, or the pixel isn't included in the selection (see "Grow," later in the chapter for more info).

Bruce almost never uses the Magic Wand; he finds it too limiting, so he uses Color Range instead (which we talk about later in this chapter). David finds himself using the Magic Wand frequently. However, he almost never gets the selection he wants out of it, so he uses other features (such as Quick Mask) to fine-tune the selection.

Tip: Select on a Channel, Not Composite. Because it's often difficult to predict how the Magic Wand tool is going to work in a color image, we typically like to make selections on a single channel of the image. The Magic Wand is more intuitive on this grayscale image, and when you switch back to the composite channel (by pressing Command-~ (tilde, to the left of the 1 key on your keyboard) or clicking on the RGB or CMYK tile in the Channels palette), the selection's flashing border is still there.

 Tip: Sample Small, Sample Often. The Magic Wand tool can be frustrating when it doesn't select everything you want it to. When this happens, novice users often set the tolerance value higher and try again. Instead, try keeping the tolerance low (between 12 and 32) and Shift-click to add more parts (or Option-click to take parts away).

Tip: Sample Points in the Magic Wand. Note that when you select a pixel with the Magic Wand, you may not get the pixel value you expect. It all depends on the Sample Size popup menu on the Options bar (when you have the Eyedropper tool selected). If you select 3 by 3 Average or 5 by 5 Average in that popup menu, Photoshop averages the pixels around the one you click on with the Magic Wand. On the other hand, if you select Point Sample, Photoshop uses exactly the one you click on.

Bruce prefers Point Sample because he always knows what he's going to end up with. David only uses Point Sample when using the eyedropper tools in Levels or Curves (see Chapter 6, *Image Adjustment Fundamentals*); when he's just trying to pick up a color, he uses 3 by 3 Average.

Tip: Reverse Selecting. One simple but nonobvious method that we often use to select an area is to select a larger area with the Lasso or Marquee tool and then Option-click with the Magic Wand tool on the area we don't want selected (see Figure 8-6).

Floating Selections

We need to take a quick diversion off the road of making selections and into the world of what happens when you move a selection. Photoshop has

Figure 8-6
Reverse selecting

In order to select the green leaf, we first draw a marquee around the whole area.

By Option-clicking with the Magic Wand tool twice (once on the background and once on the yellow), our selection is almost complete.

Now the rough selection can be cleaned up with the Lasso tool or in Quick Mask mode.

traditionally had a feature called floating selections. A floating selection is a temporary layer just above the currently selected layer; as soon as you deselect the floating selection, it "drops down" into the layer, replacing whatever pixels were below it. When you move a selection of pixels within an image, Photoshop acts as though those pixels were on a layer. Unfortunately, while these floating selections act like layers, they don't show up in the Layers palette.

The Photoshop engineering team has been trying to get rid of floating selections for years, but there are still a few instances where they appear. In general, however, we prefer to avoid floating selections and instead move pixels to a real layer for accurate positioning.

Tip: Forcing a Float. If you want to cut out the pixels and float them (so that a blank spot remains where the pixels were), you can drag the selection with the Move tool. (You can get the Move tool temporarily by holding down the Command key.) If you'd rather copy the pixels into a floating selection, you can hold down the Option/Alt key while dragging. Note: The floating selections doesn't appear on the Layers palette.

Tip: Floating Selections Are Layers, Too. You can change the mode of a floating selection to Multiply, Screen, Overlay, or any of the others. You can even change its opacity. But if the floating selection doesn't appear in the Layers palette, how are you to make these changes? After floating the pixels, select Fade from the Edit menu. (Nonintuitive, but true.) However, as soon as you try to paint on it, or run a filter, or do almost anything else interesting to the floating selection, Photoshop deselects it and drops it back down to the layer below it. That's one reason we would rather just place pixels onto a real layer before messing with them.

Quick Masks

When you select a portion of your image, you see the flashing dotted lines—they're fondly known as *marching ants* to most Photoshop folks. But what are these ants really showing you? In a typical selection, the marching ants outline the boundary of pixels that are selected 50 percent or more. There are often loads of other pixels that are selected 49 percent or less that you can't see at all from the marching ants display. Very frustrating.

Tip: Hide the Marching Ants. The human eye is a marvelous thing. Scientists have shown us that one of the things the eye (and the optical cortex in the brain) is great at is detecting motion (probably developed through centuries of hunting and gathering in the forests). However, evolution sometimes works against us. In Photoshop, the motion of a selection's marching ants is so annoying and distracting that it can bring production to a halt.

Fortunately, you can hide those little ants by turning off Extras from the Select menu (or pressing Command-H). We do this constantly. In fact, we almost never apply a filter or do much of anything in Photoshop while the ants are marching.

The only problem is that you actually have to use your short-term memory to remember where the selection is on screen. With complex operations, you also have to remember that you have a selection—we've lost count of the number of times we've wondered why our filter or curve was having no visible effect on the image, only to remember belatedly that we had a 6-pixel area selected, usually one that currently wasn't visible.

However, seeing a cut-and-dried marching ant boundary is often not helpful. So Photoshop includes a Quick Mask mode to show you exactly what's selected and how much each pixel is selected. When you enter Quick Mask mode (select the Quick Mask icon in the Tool palette or type Q), you see the underlying selection channel in all its glory. However, because the quick mask is overlaying the image, the black areas of the mask are 50-percent-opaque red and the white (selected) areas are even more transparent than that (see Figure 8-7). The red is supposed to remind you of rubylith, for those of you who remember rubylith.

Figure 8-7
Quick Mask mode

The marching ants show some of the selected areas of the image.

The quick mask shows all the selected pixels (fully and partially selected).

You can change both the color and the transparency of the quick mask in the Quick Mask Options dialog box (see Figure 8-8)—the fast way to get there is to double-click on the Quick Mask icon in the Tool palette. If the image you're working on has a lot of red in it, you'll probably want to change the quick mask color to green or some other contrasting color. Either way, we almost always increase the opacity of the color to about 75 percent, so it displays more prominently against the background image.

Note that these changes aren't document-specific. That is, they stick around in Photoshop until you change them.

Figure 8-8
Quick Mask
Options dialog box

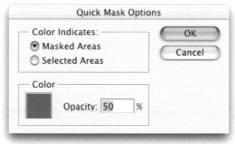

Tip: How Selected Is Selected? Even when you're in Quick Mask mode it's difficult to see partially selected pixels (especially those that are less than 50-percent selected). Note that the Info palette shows grayscale values when you're in this mode; those gray values represent the "percentage selected" for each pixel. It's just another reason always to keep one eye on that palette.

Editing Quick Masks

The powerful thing about quick masks isn't just that you can see a selection you've made, but rather that you can edit that selection with precision. When you're working in Quick Mask mode, you can paint using any of Photoshop's painting or editing tools, though you're limited to painting in grayscale. Painting with black is like adding "digital masking tape" (it subtracts from your selection), and painting with white (which appears transparent in this mode) adds to the selection.

If the element in your image is any more complicated than a rectangle, you can use Quick Mask to select it quickly and precisely. (We do this for almost every selection we make.)

1. Select the area as carefully as you can, using any of the selection tools (but don't spend too much time on it).

2. Switch to Quick Mask mode (press Q).

3. Paint or edit using the Brush tool (or any other painting or editing tool) to refine the selection you've made. Remember that partially transparent pixels will be partially selected (we often run a Gaussian Blur filter on the quick mask to smooth out sharp edges in the selection).

4. Switch out of Quick Mask mode by pressing Q again. The marching ants update to reflect the changes you've made (see Figure 8-9).

Figure 8-9 Editing quick masks

Original, quick-and-dirty selection with the Lasso tool

In Quick Mask mode, you can clean up the selection using any tool, including the brushes.

When you leave Quick Mask mode, the selection is updated.

Note that if you switch to Quick Mask mode with nothing selected, the quick mask will be empty (fully transparent). This would imply that the whole document is selected, but it doesn't work that way.

Tip: Filtering Quick Masks. The Quick Mask mode is also a great place to apply filters or special effects. Any filter you run affects only the selection, not the entire image (see Figure 8-10). For instance, you could make a rectangular selection, switch to Quick Mask mode, and then run the Twirl filter. When you leave Quick Mask mode, you can fill, paint, or adjust the altered selection.

Tip: Reversal of Color. Some people are just contrary. Give it to them one way, and they want it the other. If you're the kind of person who likes the selected areas to be black (or red, or whatever other color you choose in Quick Mask Options) and the unselected areas to be fully transparent, you can change this in Quick Mask Options. Even faster, you can Option-click on the Quick Mask icon in the Tool palette. Note that when you do this, the icon actually changes to reflect your choice.

Figure 8-10
Filtering
quick masks

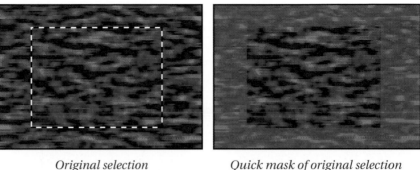

Original selection   *Quick mask of original selection*

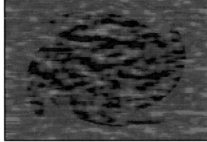

Quick mask after Twirl filter applied   *Post-Twirl selection*

If you do change the way that Quick Mask works, you'll probably want to reverse the way that channels and layer masks work, too (double-click on the channel in the Channels palette). Otherwise, you'll have a hard time remembering whether black means selected or unselected. Bruce doesn't worry about keeping these things straight—he just uses Inverse (from the Select menu, or press Command-Shift-I) when the selection winds up being the opposite of what he wants.

Anti-Aliasing and Feathering

If you've ever been in a minor car accident and later talked to an insurance adjuster, you've probably been confronted with their idea that you may not be fully blameless or at fault in the accident. And, just as you can be 25-percent or 50-percent at fault, you can partially select pixels in Photoshop. One of the most common partial selections is around the edges of a selection. And the two most common ways of partially selecting the edges are anti-aliasing and feathering.

Anti-Aliasing

If you use the Marquee tool to select a rectangle, the edges of the selection are nice and crisp, which is probably how you want them. Crisp edges around an oval or nonregular shape, however, are rarely a desired effect. That's because of the stair-stepping required to make a diagonal or curve out of square pixels. What you really want (usually) is partially selected pixels in the notches between the fully selected pixels. This technique is called *anti-aliasing*.

Every selection in Photoshop is automatically anti-aliased for you, unless you turn this feature off in the selection tool's Options bar. Unfortunately, you can't see the anti-aliased nature of the selection unless you're in Quick Mask mode, because anti-aliased (partially selected) pixels are often less than 50-percent selected. Note that once you've made a selection with Anti-aliased turned off on the Options bar, you can't anti-alias it—though there are ways to fake it (see below).

Feathering

Anti-aliasing simply smooths out the edges of a selection, adjusting the amounts that the edge pixels are selected in order to appear smooth. But it's often (too often) the case that you need a larger transition area between what is and isn't selected. That's where feathering comes in. *Feathering* is a way to expand the border area around the edges of a selection. The border isn't just extended out; it's also extended in (see Figure 8-11).

To understand what feathering does, it's important to understand the concept of the selection channel that we talked about earlier in the chapter. That is, when you make a selection, Photoshop is really "seeing" the selection as a grayscale channel behind the scenes. The black areas are totally unselected, the white areas are fully selected, and the gray areas are partially selected.

When you feather a selection, Photoshop is essentially applying a Gaussian Blur to the grayscale selection channel. (We say "essentially" because in some circumstances—like when you set a feather radius of over 120 pixels—you get a slightly different effect; however, there's usually so little difference that it's not worth bothering with. For those technoids out there who really care, Adobe tells us that a Gaussian Blur of the quick mask channel is a tiny bit more accurate and "true" than a feather.)

There are three ways to feather a selection.

Figure 8-11
Feathering

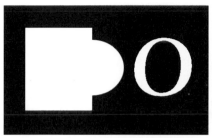

Original selection (no feather)   *Feather: 5 pixels*

Feather: 15 pixels

▶ Before selecting, specify a feather amount in the Options bar.

▶ After selecting, choose Feather from the Select menu (or press Command-Option-D).

▶ Apply a Gaussian Blur to the selection's quick mask.

Tip: Tiny Feathers. You don't need to use whole numbers when feathering. We find we often need a value of only .5 or .7 to get the effect we're looking for (a nice, subtle blend from what is selected to what's not). Let's say that after you've spent five minutes making a complicated selection, you realize that Anti-aliased was turned off on the Options bar. You can fake the anti-aliasing by feathering the selection by a small amount, like .5. This blurs the selection slightly (the edges contain partially selected pixels), giving an anti-aliased look.

Tip: Feathering a Portion of a Selection. When you choose Feather from the Select menu, your entire selection is feathered. Sometimes, however, you want to feather only a portion of the selection. Maybe you want a hard edge on one half of the selection and a soft edge on the other. You can do this by switching to Quick Mask mode, selecting what you want feathered with any of the selection tools, and applying a Gaussian Blur to it. When you flip out of Quick Mask mode, the "feathering" is included in the selection.

Note that if you want a nice, soft feather between what is feathered and what isn't, you first have to feather the selection you make while you're in Quick Mask mode (see Figure 8-12).

Figure 8-12 Feathering part of a selection

Original image   *Anti-aliased selection*   *After Gaussian Blur*   *Mustache and neck "feathered"*

Channels

Back in "Masking-Tape Selections," we told you that selections, masks, and channels are all the same thing down deep: grayscale images. This is not intuitive, nor is it easy to grasp at first. But once you really understand this point, you've taken the first step toward really surfing the Photoshop big waves.

A *channel* is a solitary grayscale image—each pixel described using either 8 bits or 16 bits of data, depending on whether or not it's a high-bit image. You can have up to 56 channels in a document—that includes the three in an RGB or four in a CMYK image. (Actually, there are two exceptions: First, images in Bitmap mode can only contain a single 1-bit channel; second, Photoshop allows one additional channel per layer to accommodate layer masks, which we'll talk about later in this chapter.)

But in the eyes of the program, not all channels are created equal. There are three types of channels: alpha, color, and spot-color channels (see Figure 8-13). We discuss the first two here, and the third in Chapter 10, *Spot Colors and Duotones*.

Figure 8-13
The Channels
palette

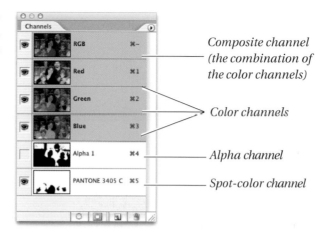

Composite channel
(the combination of
the color channels)

Color channels

Alpha channel

Spot-color channel

Alpha Channels

People get very nervous when they hear the term "alpha channel," because
they figure that with such an exotic name, it has to be a complex feature.
Not so. An *alpha channel* is simply a grayscale picture. Alpha channels let
you save selections, but a solid understanding of these beasts is also crucial
to tackling layer masks. Note that since Photsoshop CS, 16-bit images are
first-class citizens: You can make, save, and load any sort of selection or
channel in high-bit images.

Saving selections. Selections and channels are really the same thing
down deep (even though they have different outward appearances), so
you can turn one into the other very quickly. Earlier in this chapter we
discussed how you can see and edit a selection by switching to Quick Mask
mode. But quick masks are ephemeral things, and aren't much use if you
want to hold on to that selection and use it later.

When you turn a selection into an alpha channel, you're saving that
selection in the document. Then you can go back later and edit the channel, or turn it back into a selection.

As we pointed out in the last chapter, the slow way to save a selection
is to choose Save Selection from the Select menu. It's a nice place for
beginners because Photoshop provides you with a dialog box (see Figure
8-14). But pros don't bother with menu selections when they can avoid
them. Instead, click the Save Selection icon in the Channels palette. Or, if
you want to see the Channel Options dialog box first (for instance, if you
want to name the channel), hold down the Option key while clicking the

icon (see Figure 8-15). Of course, you can also assign a keyboard shortcut to the New Channel feature if you use this a lot.

Figure 8-14
Save Selection
dialog box

Figure 8-15
Saving a selection

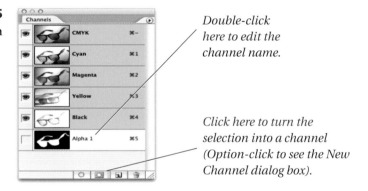

Double-click here to edit the channel name.

Click here to turn the selection into a channel (Option-click to see the New Channel dialog box).

Tip: Loading Selections. Saving a selection as an alpha channel doesn't do you much good unless you can retrieve it. Again, the slowest method is to use the Load Selection item from the Select menu (though there are benefits to this method; see "Tip: Saving Channels in Other Documents," later in this chapter).

One step better is to Command-click on the channel that you want to turn into a selection. Even better, press Command-Option-#, where the number is the channel you want. For instance, if you want to load channel six as a selection, press Command-Option-6. Note that if you press Command-Option-~ (tilde), you load the luminosity mask. This isn't really the "lightness" of the image; rather, it's like getting a grayscale version of your image.

Tip: Be a Packrat! Every time it takes you more than 10 seconds to make a selection in your image, you should be thinking: Save This Selection. We try to save every complex selection as a channel or a path until the end of the project (and sometimes we even archive them, just in case). The reason? You never know when you'll need them again.

Tip: Channels in TIFFs. If you're saving a mess of channels along with the image you're working on, and you want to save the file as a TIFF, you should probably turn on LZW compression in the Save as TIFF dialog box. Zip compression is even better, though QuarkXPress and most other programs can't read Zip-compressed TIFFs yet. However, Adobe InDesign can, and of course you can always reopen Zip-compressed TIFFs in Adobe Photoshop. Whatever the case, use some kind of compression—otherwise, the TIFF will be enormous. Of course, you could save in the native Photoshop format, but we find that a Zip-compressed TIFF file is almost always smaller on disk (see Chapter 13, *Image Storage and Output*).

Tip: Adding, Subtracting, and Intersecting Selections. Let's say you have an image with three distinct elements in it. You've spent an hour carefully selecting each of the elements, and you've saved each one in its own channel (see Figure 8-16). Now you want to select all three objects at the same time.

In the good old days, you would have sat around trying to figure out the appropriate channel operations (using Calculations) to get exactly what you wanted. But it's a kinder, gentler Photoshop now. After you load one channel as a selection, you can use Load Selection from the Select menu to add another channel to the current selection, subtract another channel, or find the intersection between the two selections.

Even easier, use the key-click combinations in Table 8-1. Confused? Don't forget to watch Photoshop's cursor icons; as you hold down the various key combinations, Photoshop indicates what will happen when you click.

Table 8-1
Working with selections

Do this to the channel tile...	...to get this result
Command-Shift-click	Add channel to current selection
Command-Option-click	Subtract channel from selection
Command-Shift-Option-click	Intersect current selection and channel

Figure 8-16 Adding, subtracting, and intersecting selections

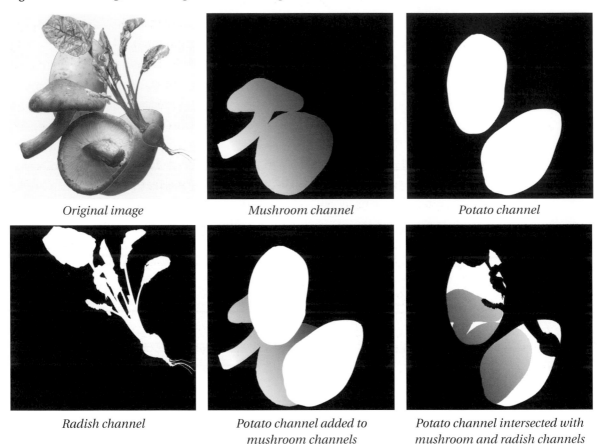

Original image	*Mushroom channel*	*Potato channel*

Radish channel	*Potato channel added to mushroom channels*	*Potato channel intersected with mushroom and radish channels*

Multidocument Channels

As we said earlier, your alpha channels don't all have to be in the same document. In fact, if you've got more than 56 channels, you have to have them in multiple documents. But even if you have fewer than 56, you may want to save off channels in order to reduce the current file's size. Here are a bunch of tips we've found helpful in moving channels back and forth between documents.

Tip: Saving Channels in Other Documents. As long as another file is currently open, you can save a selection into it using Save Selection, or load a selection (from a channel) from the file using the menu items. You can even save selections into a new document by selecting New from the Document popup menu in the Save Selection dialog box.

If you have two similar documents open and you've carefully made and saved a selection in one image, you might want to use it in the other image. Instead of copying and pasting the selection channel, take a shortcut route and use the Load Selection dialog box. You can load the selection channel directly by choosing it from the Document and Channel popup menus.

The catch here is that both documents have to have exactly the same pixel dimensions (otherwise, Photoshop wouldn't know how to place the selection properly).

Tip: More Saving Off Channels. If you've already saved your selection into a channel in document A, how can you then get that channel into document B? One method is to select the channel and choose Duplicate Channel from the Channel palette's popout menu (see Figure 8-17). Here you can choose to duplicate the channel into a new document or any other open document (as long as the documents have the same pixel dimensions).

Figure 8-17
Duplicating a channel to another document

Tip: Copying Channels the Fast Way. When it comes right down to it, the fastest way to copy a channel from document A to document B is simply by dragging the channel's tile (in the Channels palette) from document A onto document B. It's nice, quick, simple, and elegant. The problem is that the two documents have to be the same size, or else Photoshop won't align the channels properly.

We hear you asking, "Why not just copy and paste the channel from one document into another?" The answer is that copy and paste can really bog down in large files. ("Large" means different things to different people; Bruce counts in gigabytes!) In smaller files, however, copy and paste works just as well.

Selections from Channels

Why would you go through all the trouble of creating a selection if the selection was already made for you? More often than not, the selection you're looking to make is already hidden within the image; to unlock it you only have to look at the color channels that make up the image (see "Color Channels," on the next page).

Here's one good way to tease a selection mask out of an image (see Figure 8-18). We demonstrate these techniques in more detail in the step-by-step examples at the end of this chapter.

1. Switch through the color channels until you find the one that gives the best contrast between the element you're trying to select and its background.

2. Duplicate that channel by dragging the channel tile onto the New Channel icon in the Channels palette.

3. Use Levels or Curves to adjust the contrast between the elements you want to select and the rest of the image.

4. Clean up the mask manually. We typically use the Lasso tool to select and delete areas, or the Brush tool with one finger on the X key (so you can paint with black, then press X to "erase" with white, and so on).

Using Levels and Curves. The real key to this tip is step number 3: using Levels or Curves. With Levels, concentrate on the three Input sliders to isolate the areas you're after.

In the Curves dialog box, use the Eyedropper tool to see where the pixels sit on the curve (click and drag around the image while the Curves dialog box is open, and watch the white circle bounce around on the curve). Then use the Pencil tool in the dialog box to push those pixels to white or black. The higher the contrast, the easier it is to extract a selection from it.

Some people use the Smooth button after making these sorts of "hard" curve maps. But in this case, we often run a small-value Gaussian Blur after applying the curve, so we just don't bother with smoothing the curve.

Using RGB. It's usually easier to grab selection masks from RGB images than from CMYK images. However, if you're going to switch from CMYK to RGB, make sure you do it on a duplicate of the image, because all that mode switching damages the image too much.

Figure 8-18 **Starting with a channel**

Red channel

Green channel

Blue channel (best contrast)

Quick and dirty Levels adjustment to blue channel

Fine-tuned version of blue channel

Tip: Dragging Selections. Photoshop is full of little, subtle features that make life so much nicer. For instance, you can drag any selection from one document into another document using one of the selection tools. (The Move tool actually moves the pixels inside the selection; the selection tools move the selection itself.)

Normally, the selection "drops" wherever you let go of the mouse button. However, if the two documents have the same pixel dimensions, you can hold down the Shift key to pin-register the selection (it lands in the same location as it was in the first document). If the images aren't the same pixel dimension, the Shift key centers the selection.

Color Channels

When a color image is in RGB mode (under the Mode menu), the image is made up of three channels: red, green, and blue. Each of these channels is exactly the same as an alpha channel, except that they're designated as color channels. You can edit each color channel separately from the others. You can independently make a single color channel visible or invisible. But you can't delete or add a color channel without changing the image mode.

The first tile in the Channels palette (above the color channels) is the composite channel. Actually, this isn't really a channel at all. Rather, the composite channel is the full-color representation of all the individual color channels mixed together. It gives you a convenient way to select or deselect all the color channels at once, and also lets you view the composite color image even while you're editing a single channel.

Selecting and Seeing Channels. The tricky thing about working with channels is figuring out which channel(s) you're editing and which channel(s) you're seeing on the screen. They're not always the same!

The Channels palette has two columns. The left column contains little eyeball checkboxes that you can turn on and off to show or hide individual channels. Clicking on one of the tiles in the right column not only displays that channel, but lets you edit it, too. The channels that are selected for editing are highlighted. The two columns are independent of each other because editing and seeing the channels are not the same thing.

Tip: Keystroke Channels. When you're jumping from one channel to another, skip the clicking altogether and use a keystroke instead. Command-# displays the channel number you press; for instance, Command-1 shows the red channel (or whatever the first channel is), and Command-4 shows the fourth channel (the first alpha channel in an RGB image or Black in a CMYK image). Sorry, there's no way (that we know of) to select channels above number nine with keystrokes.

In ancient versions of Photoshop, Command-0 would select the color composite channel (deselecting all other channels in the process). Now, the keystroke is Command-~ (tilde).

You can see as many channels at once as you want by clicking in the channel's eyeball checkboxes. To edit more than one channel at a time, Shift-click on the channel tiles.

Note that when you display more than one channel at a time, the alpha channels automatically switch from their standard black and white to their channel color (you can specify what color each channel uses in Channel Options—double-click on the channel tile).

The Select Menu

If making selections using lassos and marquees, then saving or loading them, were all there was to selecting in Photoshop, life would be simpler but duller. Fortunately for us, there are many more things you can do with selections, and they all—well, almost all—help immeasurably in the production process.

You can find each additional selection feature under the Select menu: Grow, Similar, Color Range, and Modify. Let's explore each of these and how they can speed up your work.

Grow

Earlier in the chapter, when we were talking about the Magic Wand tool, we discussed the concept of tolerance. This value tells Photoshop how much brighter or darker a pixel (or each color channel that defines a pixel) can be and still be included in the selection.

Let's say you're trying to select an apple using the Magic Wand tool with a tolerance of 24. After clicking once, perhaps only half of the apple is selected; the other half is slightly shaded and falls outside the tolerance range. You could deselect, change the tolerance, and click again. However, it's much faster to select Grow from the Select menu.

When you choose Grow, Photoshop selects additional pixels according to the following criteria.

1. First, it finds the highest and lowest gray values of every channel of every pixel selected—the highest red, green, and blue, and the lowest red, green, and blue of the bunch of already-selected pixels (or the highest cyan, magenta, yellow, and black, and so on).

2. Next, it adds the tolerance value to the highest values and subtracts it from the lowest values in each channel. Therefore, the highest values get a little higher and the lowest values get a little lower (of course, it never goes above 255 or below 0).

3. Finally, Photoshop selects every adjacent pixel that falls between all those values (see Figure 8-19).

In other words, Photoshop tries its hardest to spread your selection in every direction, but only in similar colors. However, it doesn't always work the way you'd want. In fact, sometimes it works very oddly indeed.

For instance, if you select a pure red area (made of 255 red, and no blue or green), and a pure green area (made of 255 green, and no red or blue),

Figure 8-19
The Grow
command

After Magic Wand click   *After Grow*

then select Grow, Photoshop selects every adjacent pixel that has any red or green in it, as long as the blue channel is not out of tolerance's range. That means that it'll pick out dark browns, lime greens, oranges, and so on—even if you set a really small tolerance level (see Figure 8-20).

If you switch to a color channel (like red or cyan) before selecting Grow, Photoshop grows the selection based on that channel only. This can be helpful because it's much easier to predict how the Magic Wand and Grow features will work on one channel.

Figure 8-20
Anomalies with the
Grow command

When the two center squares are selected, Grow selects all the bottom squares and none of the top squares. Why? Because of slight blue "contamination" in the top squares.

Many of these colors are selected unexpectedly with Grow.

Tip: Instead of the Magic Wand. While the Magic Wand tool is pretty cool and provides a friendly point-and-click interface, it's often not very useful because colors in a natural image (like a scan) are typically varied. Instead, try selecting a larger representative area with the Lasso or Marquee tool. Then, select Grow or Similar from the Select menu (see below for a discussion of Similar). Bruce maintains that the best method is just to use Color Range instead (see "Color Range," on the next page).

Similar

The Grow feature only selects contiguous areas of your image. If you're trying to select the same color throughout an image, you may click and drag and grow yourself into a frenzy before you're done. Choosing Similar from the Select menu does the same thing as choosing Grow, but it chooses pixels from throughout the entire image (see Figure 8-21).

Note that Similar and Grow are both attached to the settings on the Options bar when you have the Magic Wand selected; Photoshop applies both the Wand's tolerance and its anti-alias values to these commands. We can't think of any reason to turn off anti-aliasing, but it's nice to know you have the option.

Figure 8-21
The Similar
command

Selection made with Magic Wand.
A Tolerance setting of 24 manages to
avoid the shadows and green areas.

After Similar is selected. Some
brighter areas of the apples
are still not selected.

Color Range

One of the problems with Similar and Grow is that you rarely know what you're going to end up with. On the other hand, Color Range lets you make color-based selections interactively, and shows you exactly which pixels will be selected. But there's one other advantage of Color Range over the Magic Wand features (we think of Similar and Grow as extensions of the Magic Wand).

The Magic Wand–based features either select a pixel or they don't (the exception is anti-aliasing around the edges of selections, which only partially selects pixels there). Color Range, however, fully selects only a few pixels and partially selects a lot of pixels (see Figure 8-22). This can be incredibly helpful when you're trying to tease a good selection mask out of the contents of an image.

There are four areas you should be aware of in the Color Range dialog box: selection eyedroppers, the Fuzziness slider, canned sets of colors, and Selection Preview.

Adding and deleting colors. When you open Color Range, Photoshop creates a selection based on your foreground color. Then you can use the eyedropper tools to add or delete colors in the image (or, better yet, hold down the Shift key to get the Add Color to Mask eyedropper, or the Option key to get the Remove Color from Mask eyedropper). Note that you can always scroll or magnify an area in the image. You can even select colors from any other open image.

Figure 8-22 Magic Wand versus Color Range

While you can make similar selections with the Magic Wand and Color Range, each is more efficient in particular situations. Magic Wand is faster for big, consistent areas, while Color Range excels for finer details.

The original image. It is photographed on a good, uniform white background, and includes an area of relatively solid color (the reds) that is an obvious target for change.

Three quick Shift-clicks with the Magic Wand yield a very serviceable silhouette mask. A bit of feathering or a Gaussian Blur on the mask (combined with a Levels tweak to adjust the blur) deals with the hard edges.

Because the object is hard-edged to begin with, the Magic Wand's inability to partially select pixels doesn't pose much of a problem in compositing.

A mask created with Color Range (here with few sample points and a high Fuzziness setting) is more appropriate for subtle selections.

A detail of the mask shows that there are partially selected pixels (the gray areas).

This more subtle mask is just the ticket for a Hue/Saturation tweak, changing the red areas to blue without an artificial look.

The Fuzziness factor. The Fuzziness slider in the Color Range dialog box is *not* the same as the Tolerance field on the Magic Wand Options bar. As we said earlier, pixels that fall within the tolerance value are either fully selected or not; pixels that fall on the border between the selected and unselected areas may be partially selected, but those are only border pixels. Color Range uses the Fuzziness value to determine not only whether a pixel should be included, but also how selected it should be. We're not going to get into the hard-core math (you don't need to know it, and we're not entirely sure of it ourselves), but Figure 8-23 should give you a pretty good idea of how fuzziness works.

Figure 8-23   Fuzziness versus sample points for Color Range

Four selections created with Color Range. At right is the result of a Hue/Saturation move on the selection.

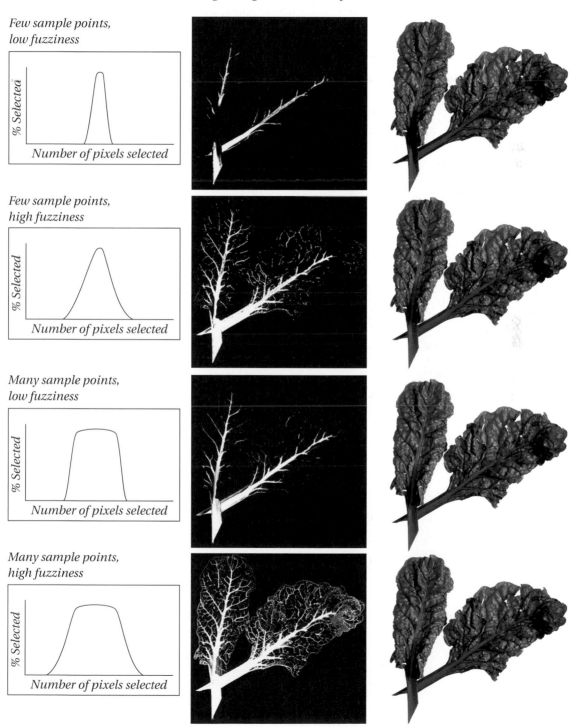

*Few sample points,
low fuzziness*

*Few sample points,
high fuzziness*

*Many sample points,
low fuzziness*

*Many sample points,
high fuzziness*

Tip: Avoid Sample Merged. Color Range is always in Sample Merged mode. It sees your image as though all the visible layers were merged together. If you've got an object on a layer that you don't want included in the selection mask, hide that layer before opening Color Range.

Tip: Sampling vs. Fuzziness. Should you use lots of sample points or a high Fuzziness setting? It depends on the type of image. To select large areas of similar color, tend toward a lower Fuzziness (10–15) to avoid selecting stray pixels. For fine detail, you need to use higher Fuzziness settings, because the fine areas are generally more polluted with colors spilling from adjacent pixels. Either way, try adding sample points to increase the selection range before you increase fuzziness.

Tip: Return to Settings. If you want to return to the Color Range dialog box with exactly the same settings as you last used, hold down the Option key when selecting Color Range from the Select menu.

Canned Colors

Instead of creating a selection mask with the eyedroppers, you can let Photoshop select all the reds, or all the blues, or yellows, or any other primary color, by choosing the color in the Select popup menu (see Figure 8-24). The greater the difference between the color you choose and the other primaries, the more the pixel is selected. (To get really tweaky for a moment: The percentage the pixel is selected is the percentage difference between the color you choose and the primary color with the next highest value.)

Do you really need to know any of this? No. Probably the best way to use these features is just not to use them at all (we almost never do).

On the other hand, you can also choose from Highlights, Midtones, or Shadows—which we find a bit more useful. When you choose one of these, Photoshop decides whether to select a pixel (or how much to select it) based on its Lab luminance value (see Table 8-2 and Chapter 5, *Color Settings*, for more information on Lab mode).

We find selecting Highlights, Midtones, and Shadows most useful when selecting a subset of a color we've already selected (see "Tip: Color Range Subsets," next).

Figure 8-24
Color Range
dialog box

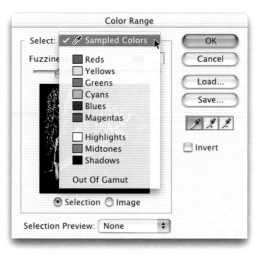

Table 8-2	Select name	Fully selected pixels	Partially selected pixels
Ranges for Color Range	Shadows	1–40	40–55
(L value in Lab mode)	Midtones	55–75	40–55 and 75–85
	Highlights	80–100	75–85

Tip: Color Range Subsets. If you're trying to select all the green buttons on a blouse using Color Range, you're going to pick up every other green object throughout the image, too. However, you can tell the Color Range feature to only select green items within a particular area—the blouse, for instance—by making a selection first. Draw a quick outline of the area of interest with the Lasso tool, then choose Color Range. Photoshop ignores the rest of the image. Similarly, you could select all the green items in the image, then go back to Color Range again and select only those greens that are in Highlight areas.

Tip: Invert the Color Range Selection. Do you often find yourself following up a Color Range selection with an Invert from the Select menu? If you are trying to select the opposite of what's selected in the Color Range dialog box, you can remove that extra step by turning on the Invert checkbox in the Color Range dialog box; Photoshop automatically inverts the selection for you. If you already have a selection made when you invert the Color Range selection, Photoshop deselects the Color Range pixels from your selection.

Selection Preview. The last area to pay attention to in the Color Range dialog box is the Selection Preview popup menu. When you select anything other than None (the default) from this menu, Photoshop previews the Color Range selection mask.

The first choice, Grayscale, shows you what the selection mask would look like if you saved it as a separate channel. The second and third choices, Black Matte and White Matte, are the equivalent of copying the selected pixels out and pasting them on a black or white background. This is great for seeing how well you're capturing edge pixels. The last choice, Quick Mask, is the same thing as clicking OK and immediately switching into Quick Mask mode.

Because the Selection Preview can slow you down, we recommend turning it on only when you need to, then turning around and switching back to None. It can be really helpful in making sure you're selecting everything you want, but it can also be a drag on productivity.

Tip: Changing Quick Mask Options. If you're a hard-core Color Range user, you may one day have the strange desire to change your Quick Mask options settings while the Color Range dialog box is open. You can do it (believe it or not). Hold down the Option key while selecting Quick Mask from the Selection Preview popup menu. Don't say we don't strive to give you every last tip!

Tip: Forget the Color Range Radio Buttons. If you frequently use the Image and Selection radio buttons in the Color Range dialog box, stop! Instead, press the Command or Control key—either one works on the Mac—on your keyboard. This toggles between the Selection and Image Previews much faster than you can click buttons. This is sometimes helpful if you need a quick reality check as to what's selected and what's not.

Modify

When you think of the most important part of your selection, what do you think of? If you answer, "what's selected," you're wrong. No matter what you have selected in your image, the most important part of the selection is the boundary or edge. This is where the tire hits the road, where the money slaps the table, where the invoice smacks the client. No matter what you do with the selection—whether you copy and paste it, paint within it, or whatever—the quality of your edge determines how effective your effect will be.

When making a precise selection, you often need to make subtle adjustments to the boundaries of the selection. The four menu items on the Modify submenu under the Select menu—Border, Smooth, Expand, and Contract—focus entirely on this task.

Border. Police officers of the world take note: There's a faster way to get a doughnut than driving down to the local Circle K. Draw a circle using the Marquee tool, then select Border from the Modify submenu under the Select menu. You can even specify how thick you want your doughnut (in pixels, of course). Border transforms the single line (the circle) into two lines (see Figure 8-25).

The problem with Border is that it only creates soft-edged borders. If you draw a square and give it a border, you get a soft-edged shape that looks more like an octagon than a square. In many cases, this is exactly what you want and need. But other times it can ruin the mood faster than jackhammers outside the bedroom window.

Tip: Level Borders. If selecting Border gives you a super-soft edge when what you want is a harder, fatter edge, try this quick-mask trick. Switch to Quick Mask mode (press Q), then use the Levels or Curves dialog box to adjust the edge of the selection (see "Tip: Finer Spreads and Chokes,"

Figure 8-25
Border

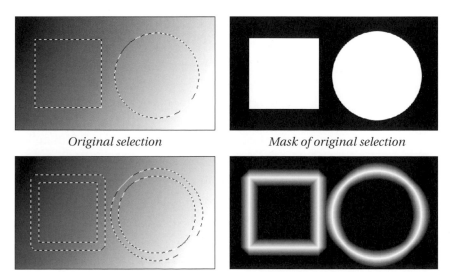

Original selection

Mask of original selection

After Border (20 pixels)

Mask of post-Border selection

later in this chapter). If you find that the edge of the selection becomes too jaggy, you can always apply a .5-pixel Gaussian Blur to smooth it out. Remember that when you're in Quick Mask mode, you can select the area to which you want to apply the levels or blur.

Tip: More Border Options. Here's one other way to make a border with a sharper, more distinct edge.

1. Save your selection as an alpha channel.

2. While the area is still selected, choose Expand from the Modify submenu under the Select menu.

3. Save this new selection as an alpha channel.

4. Load the original selection from the alpha channel you saved it in.

5. Choose Contract from the Modify submenu.

6. Mix the two selections (expanded and contracted) together by Command-Option-clicking on the other channel.

You can save this selection and delete one or both of the other alpha channels you saved. Note that you don't have to expand *and* contract the selection; this method also lets you choose to only contract or expand.

Note that we also discuss another way to make borders (edge masks) in Chapter 9, *Sharpness, Detail, and Noise Reduction*.

Smooth. The problem with making selections with the Lasso tool is that you often get very jaggy selection lines; the corners are too sharp, the curves are too bumpy. You can smooth these out by selecting Smooth from the Modify submenu under the Select menu. Like most selection operations in Photoshop, this actually runs a convolution filter over the selection mask—in this case, the Median filter. That is, selecting Smooth is exactly the same thing as switching to Quick Mask mode and choosing the Median filter.

Smooth has little or no effect on straight lines or smooth curves. But it has a drastic effect on corners and jaggy lines (see Figure 8-26). Smooth (or the Median filter, depending on which way you look at it) looks at each pixel in your selection, then looks at the pixels surrounding it (the number of pixels it looks at depends on the Radius value you choose in

Figure 8-26
Smooth

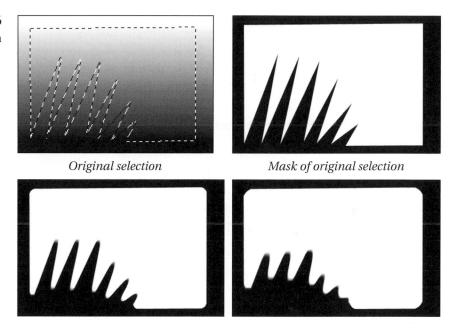

Original selection   *Mask of original selection*

After Smooth with 10-pixel radius   *After Smooth with 16-pixel radius*

the Smooth dialog box). If more than half the pixels around it are selected, then the pixel remains selected. If fewer than half are selected, the pixel becomes deselected.

If you enter a small Radius value, only corner tips and other sharp edges are rounded out. Larger values make sweeping changes. It's rare that we use a radius over 5 or 6, but it depends entirely on what you're doing (and how smooth your hand is!).

Expand/Contract. The Expand and Contract features are two of the most useful selection modifiers. They let you enlarge or reduce the size of the selection. This is just like spreading or choking colors in trapping (if you don't know about trapping, don't worry; it's not relevant here).

Once again, these modifiers are simply applying filters to the black-and-white mask equivalent of your selection. Choosing Expand is the same as applying the Maximum filter to the mask; choosing Contract is the same as applying the Minimum filter (see Figure 8-27).

Note that if you enter 5 as the Radius value in the Maximum or Minimum dialog box (or in the Expand or Contract dialog box), it's exactly the same as running the filter or selection modifier five times. The Radius value here is more of an "iteration" value; how many times do you want the filter applied at a one-pixel radius?

Figure 8-27
Expand and Contract

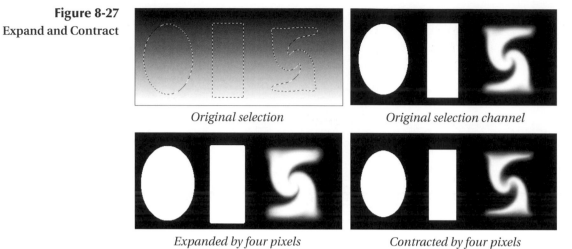

Original selection   *Original selection channel*

Expanded by four pixels   *Contracted by four pixels*

While we frequently find these selection modifiers useful, they aren't very precise. You can only specify the radius in one-pixel increments (see "Tip: Finer Spreads and Chokes," next).

Tip: Finer Spreads and Chokes. You can make much finer adjustments to the size of a selection by using Levels rather than Expand or Contract from the Select menu. Here's how.

1. Once you have your selection, switch to Quick Mask mode.

2. Apply a Gaussian Blur to the area you want to expand or contract (if it's the whole selection, then blur the whole quick mask). We usually use a low Radius value, such as .5 or 1.

3. In Levels (Command-L), adjust the middle (gamma) slider control to make the area darker or lighter. Making it darker contracts the selection; lighter expands the selection (see Figure 8-28 and, later in the chapter, Figure 8-34).

What's nice about this tip is that it's a very gentle method of expanding or contracting the selection. Instead of "Wham! Move one pixel over," you can say, "Make this selection slightly bigger or smaller."

Figure 8-28
Precision control
over expanding
and contracting

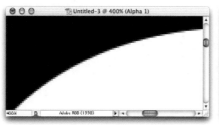

Original selection channel

*Selection channel after
Gaussian Blur and Levels*

*The gamma slider controls the
expansion or contraction of
the mask channel's gray levels—
hence the abruptness of the blur.*

Selections and Layers

We've talked about making selections; we've talked about saving channels; now it's time to delve into masks—specifically: transparency masks, layer masks, and using layers as a mask. But as you read the following pages, don't forget that masks are just channels, which are 8-bit (or 16-bit) gray-scale images. (Photoshop also lets you build a hard, vector-edged mask that is *not* based on a channel, called a *layer clipping path*; we'll discuss this in "Paths," in Chapter 12, *Essential Image Techniques*.)

Transparency Masks

Most of the time when you create a new layer, the background is transparent. When you paint on it or paste in a selection, you're making pixels opaque. Photoshop is always keeping track of how transparent each pixel is—fully transparent, partially transparent, or totally opaque. This information about pixel transparency is called the *transparency mask* (see Figure 8-29).

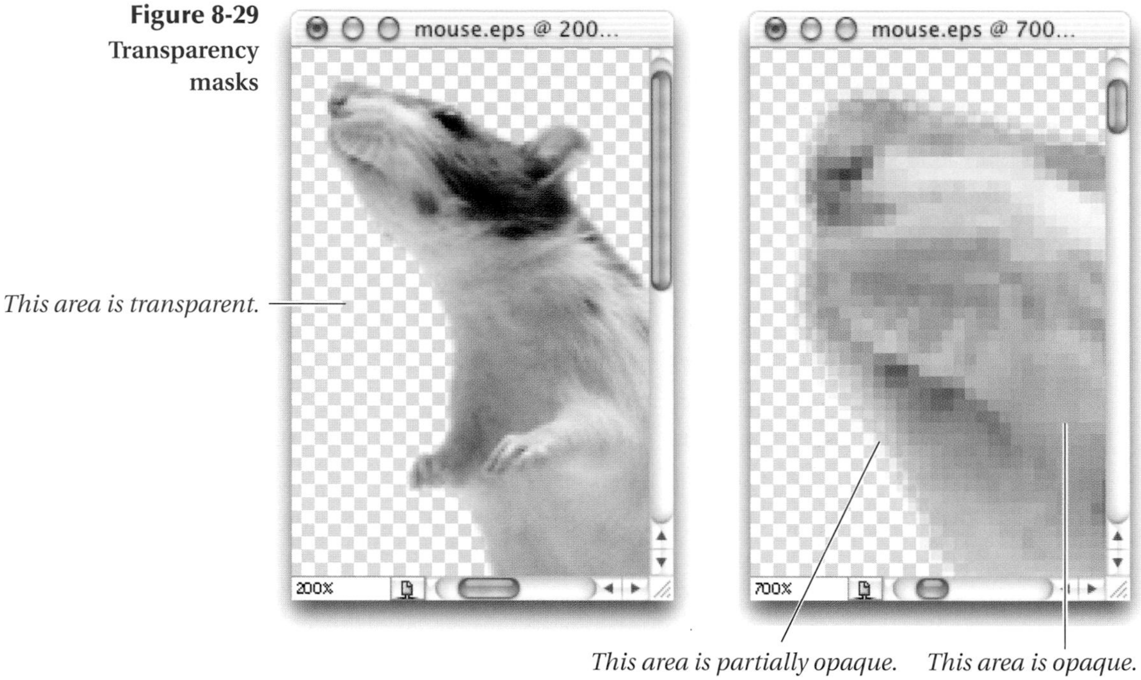
mouse.eps @ 200...
200%
mouse.eps @ 700...
700%
This area is transparent.
This area is partially opaque.
This area is opaque.

Figure 8-29 Transparency masks

Remember the analogy we made to masking tape earlier in the chapter? The selection/channel/mask (they're all the same) acts like tape over or around your image. In this case, however, the mask doesn't represent how selected a pixel is; it's how transparent (or, conversely, how visible) it is. You can have a pixel that's fully selected but only 10-percent opaque (90-percent transparent).

Tip: Load the Transparency Mask. You can load the transparency mask for a layer as a selection in the Load Selection dialog box, but it's much faster to Command-click on the layer's tile in the Layers palette. For instance, if you have some text on a type layer and you want to make a selection that looks exactly like the type, Command-click on the type layer's thumbnail. This loads the selection, and you're ready to roll.

Layer Masks

It's hard to emphasize in print just how important nondestructive editing is in our workflow. (A future MTV adaptation of this book will show us jumping up and down, rapping, "Yo, this is life-changing!") Perhaps you're compositing several images on a background, or you're retouching an image, or you're adjusting the hue and brightness of a photograph. Whatever the case, you know that after hours of sweat and mouse-burn, when you show the result to your art director, she's going to say, "Move this over a little, and we need a little more of this showing here, and you shouldn't have changed the color of this part . . . ."

Fortunately, you can use layer masks to avoid this sort of nightmare in your work. Layer masks are just like transparency masks—they determine how transparent the layer's pixels are—but you can see layer masks and, more importantly, edit them (see Figure 8-30). If you had used nondestructive layer masks in the example above instead of erasing or editing your original pixels, you would have smiled at your art director and made the changes quickly and painlessly. Here's how you do it.

Creating and editing layer masks. You can apply a layer mask to a layer by selecting Add Layer Mask from the Layer menu. When a layer

Figure 8-30 Layer masks

The earth is on a separate layer above the background image of the car.

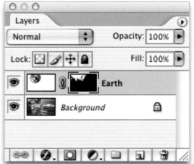

The layer mask   *After the layer mask is applied to the Earth layer*

has a mask, it can have only one (or two, if you include layer clipping paths)—the Layers palette displays a thumbnail of the mask (see Figure 8-31).

Figure 8-31
Adding a
layer mask

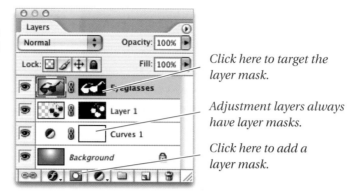

Click here to target the
layer mask.

Adjustment layers always
have layer masks.

Click here to add a
layer mask.

Tip: Faster Layer Masks. While there's no built-in keyboard shortcut to add a layer mask (you can assign one if you want), it is a little faster to click on the Add Layer Mask icon in the Layers palette. If you Option/Alt-click on the Add Layer Mask icon, Photoshop inverts the layer mask (so that it automatically hides everything on the layer).

Note that you can make a selection before clicking on the icon. In this case, the program "paints in" the nonselected areas with black for you (on the layer mask). This is usually much easier than adding a layer mask, then using the paint tools to paint away areas. (Of course, Option-clicking on the icon with a selection paints the selected areas with black, so that whatever was selected "disappears.")

At first, it's difficult to tell whether you're editing the layer or the layer mask. But there are two differences: The layer mask thumbnail has a dashed border around it (on a high-resolution screen, the two borders look about the same) and the document title bar says "Layer *x* Mask." We typically glance at the title bar about as often as we look in our car's rearview mirror; it's a good way to keep a constant eye on what's going on around us.

Editing a mask is as simple as painting with grays. Painting with black on the layer mask is like adding masking tape; it covers up part of the adjoining layer (making those pixels transparent). Painting with white takes away the tape and uncovers the layer's image. Gray, of course, partially covers the image.

Tip: Paint It In Using Masks. Layer masks let you paint in any kind of effect you want. For example, duplicate the Background layer of an image in the Layers palette, apply a filter to the new layer (like Unsharp Mask), then Option/Alt-click on the Add Layer Mask icon to mask out the entire effect. Now you can paint the effect back in using the Brush tool and non-black pixels. If you change your mind, you can paint away the effect with black pixels. This flexibility is addictive and you'll soon find yourself using this technique over and over, whether it's painting in texture or sharpening or blurring or whatever.

Tip: Use Gradients for Masks. Another trick you'll find us using daily is placing gradients on a layer mask. Whether you use a linear or radial blend, adding a gradient is a great way to affect just part of an image. For example, on a partially cloudy day, the lighting of a scene may be uneven. You can apply a global tonal adjustment on a separate layer and then draw a gradient across the layer's mask to affect just the part of the image that needs it (we discuss this in detail in the next chapter). If the gradient isn't quite right, open the Levels or Curves dialog box and make adjustments to the layer mask itself—these tonal adjustments to the mask give you almost infinite control over how your effect is applied.

Tip: Getting Rid of the Mask. As soon as you start editing layer masks, you're going to find that you want to turn the mask on and off, so you can get before-and-after views of your work. You can make the mask disappear temporarily by selecting Disable Layer Mask from the Layer menu. Or, if you need to get your work done quickly, do it the fast way: Shift-click on the Layer Mask icon.

If you want to hide the mask with extreme prejudice—that is, if you want to delete it forever—select Remove Layer Mask from the Layer menu (or, faster, drag the Layer Mask icon to the Trash icon). Photoshop gives you a last chance to apply the mask to the layer. Note that if you do apply the mask, the masked (hidden) portions of the layer are actually deleted.

One last way to get rid of a mask: All layer masks go away when you merge or flatten layers.

Tip: Layer Mask Keystroke. When you're working on a layer, you can jump to the layer mask (making it active, so all your edits are to the mask rather than the image) by pressing Command-\ (backslash). When you're ready to leave the layer mask, press Command-~ (tilde) to switch back to the layer itself.

If you Option-Shift-click on the Layer Mask icon in the Layers palette (or just press the \ key—that's the backslash), Photoshop displays the mask *and* the layer, as if you're in QuickMask mode. If you don't like the color or opacity of the layer mask, you can Option-Shift-double-click on the icon to change the mask's color and opacity. Then, when you're ready to see the effects of your mask editing, Option-Shift-click on the icon again to "hide" it (or press backslash again). If you want to see only the layer mask (as its own grayscale channel), Option-click on its icon. This is most helpful when touching up areas of the layer mask (it's sometimes hard to see the details in the mask when there's a background image visible).

Tip: When Masks Move. The layer mask is tied to its layer, so when you move the layer with the Move tool, the layer mask moves, too. While this is usually what you'd want, you can stop it from happening by clicking on the Link icon that sits between the layer and layer mask previews in the Layers palette. When the Link icon is on, the layer and layer mask move together; when it's off, the layer and layer mask can be moved independently.

Layers as Masks

Layers not only have masks, but they can act as masks for other layers. The trick is to use *clipping groups*. For instance, if you place a circle on a layer with a transparent background, then make a new layer and fill it entirely with some bizarre fractal design, the strange texture totally obliterates the circle. However, if you group the two layers together, the lower one acts as a mask for the higher one, and the fractal design only appears within the circle (see Figure 8-32).

You can group layers together in one of two ways.

▶ Select Create Clipping Mask from the Layer menu (or, even faster, press Command-G).

▶ Option-click between their tiles in the Layers palette (the layers have to be next to one another in any of these cases).

You don't have to stop with grouping two layers. You can group together as many as you want, though the bottommost layer always acts as the mask for the entire group (see Figure 8-33). No, you can't group a layer with a layer set—only individual layers.

Figure 8-32
Grouping layers together to make a layer mask

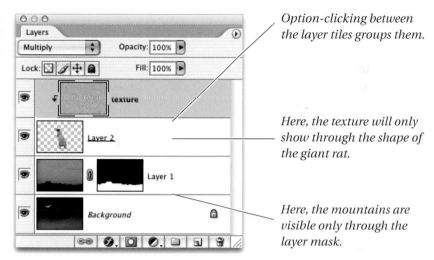

Option-clicking between the layer tiles groups them.

Here, the texture will only show through the shape of the giant rat.

Here, the mountains are visible only through the layer mask.

Figure 8-33
Layers as masks

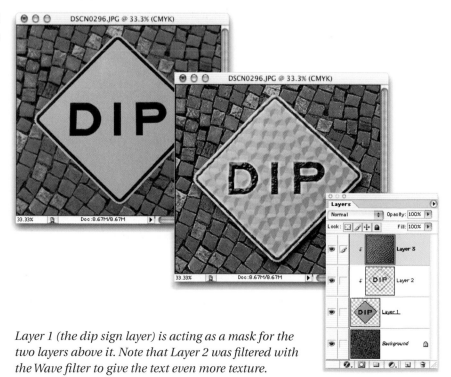

Layer 1 (the dip sign layer) is acting as a mask for the two layers above it. Note that Layer 2 was filtered with the Wave filter to give the text even more texture.

Step-by-Step Selections

Now that we've gone through all of Photoshop's tools for working with selections, channels, and masks, it's time to bring all those tools to bear. We'll start by showing how to create a simple silhouette, and work our way up to difficult image masks.

If there's one thing that makes silhouettes difficult, it's the edge detail. In most cases (especially when you're trying to select fine details), some of the color from the image background spills over into the image you want. So when you drop the silhouetted image onto a different background (even white), the spill trips you up, making the image look artificial and out of place.

A Simple, Hard-Edged Silhouette

When the image you're trying to select has been photographed on a white background with good studio lighting (so the background's free of colors that contaminate the edges), your selection is relatively easy. We typically jump in with several clicks of the Magic Wand along with Grow or Similar. We almost never get a perfect fit, however, so we usually clean up the edges in Quick Mask mode. In Figure 8-34, we use Gaussian Blur and Levels to choke the edges of the selection mask. That way, we can be sure no background color spills over in our final composited image.

Pulling Selections from Channels

Trying to build a selection mask for the tree in Figure 8-35 with the basic selection tools would drive you to distraction faster than having to watch Barney reruns with your four-year-old. Instead, we found the essence of a great selection hiding in the color channels of the image. While you can often pull a selection mask from a single channel, in this case we made duplicates of both the blue and green channels. Then, using Levels, we pushed the tree to black and the background to white. After combining the two channels, it took only a little touch-up to complete the mask.

Removing Spill with Preserve Transparency

Edge spill is insidious, and—as you saw in the last example—it can be a disaster when compositing images. Here's one more method of removing spill that we like a lot. If you place the pixels on a transparent layer, you

Figure 8-34 Silhouetting a hard-edged element

The original image. Our goal: to select the object from its background.

The Magic Wand, Grow, and Similar get us most of the way there.

We switch to Quick Mask mode and lasso the areas that should be excluded from the selection.

After fixing the edge detail, we incorporate a new background into the image (see below).

The original selection left some edge pixels unselected, causing edge spill.

We apply a small-radius Gaussian Blur to the quick mask, which appears to worsen the edge spill.

A radical Levels gamma shift on the mask makes the edge pixels darker.

When the mask is partially transparent, the dark areas around the edge tell us that there will be no edge spill.

can make use of the Preserve Transparency feature in the Layers palette to "paint away" the edge spill.

In the example in Figure 8-36, the color from the blue sky is much too noticeable around the composited trees. So we place the trees on a layer and build a selection that encompasses just their edges. This step is really just a convenience—it makes our job of painting out the edge spill easier. With Preserve Transparency turned on, we select the Rubber Stamp tool and clone interior colors over the blue edge pixels. In some areas, we also use Curves to pull the blue out (because our border selection is feathered, these moves affect only the pixels we're after).

This is a trick you can use with all sorts of variations. If the edge color is relatively flat, you might be able to use the Brush tool (we usually add a little noise after painting in order to match the background texture); this

Figure 8-35 Creating subtle masks from multiple channels

The original. Our goal: to select the tree and make it more green.

The blue channel has the best contrast between sky and tree.

The green channel has the best contrast between tree and grass.

We copy the blue channel, and force the sky to white and the tree to black with the Levels dialog box.

A similar move on the green channel creates a mask for the lower part of the tree.

We delete the "garbage" areas from each mask with the Brush and Lasso. To edit the channels better, we make the mask and the color channels visible at the same time.

We use Calculate (Add) to merge the two channels into one, providing the final mask.

After loading the selection mask, we use Curves to brighten and saturate the greens in the tree, and we pull back the reds and blues slightly.

Figure 8-36 Painting out edge spill using layers, a border mask, and Preserve Transparency

The original image

A mask created using Color Range

The trees are copied onto a layer above the sunset image. The blue spill ruins the compositing effect.

A closeup of the composited image shows the blue edge spill from the original sky.

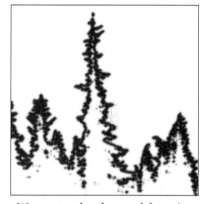

We create a border mask by using Border on the transparency mask, then running a Gaussian Blur.

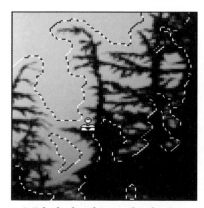

With the border mask selection loaded and Preserve Transparency turned on, we rubber stamp dark interior pixels over the blue pixels.

The final image after the blue edge spill has been removed

A closeup of the final image

is also an area where it behooves you to test out different Apply modes (Lighten, Multiply, and so on).

Tip: Enhancing Edges with Filters. We're naturally wary when it comes to using Photoshop filters; while very powerful, they're almost always used to create funky effects. However, every now and again we see how we can use the same filters to increase our productivity and enhance our work life. Here's one such application: using filters to get better selections.

The two filters that we use most often for this sort of thing are the High Pass and the Find Edges filters (usually one or the other; not both at the same time). We typically duplicate the image we're working on, then use one or more filters on the copy to extract the selection we want.

Find Edges is a very blunt instrument when it comes to making selections, but it can often draw out edges that are very hard to see on screen.

The trick to using High Pass is to use very small values in the High Pass dialog box, usually under 1 or 2 pixels. Then, you can use the Levels or Curves dialog box to enhance the edges in the mostly gray image.

Tip: Complex Masks with Plug-Ins. After working with Photoshop's selection tools for a while, you begin to know instinctively when you're up against a difficult task. For instance, trying to create a selection mask for a woman in a gauzy dress, with her long, wispy hair blowing in the wind, could be a nightmare. And if you have to perform 20 of these in a day . . . well . . . 'nuf said. It's time to plunk down some cash for one of the several masking programs on the market—for instance, Mask Pro from OnOne Software or KnockOut from Corel.

We're not saying that these plug-ins are perfect. In fact, far from it. But they can often get you 90 percent of the way to a great selection in 10 percent of the time it would take you with Photoshop's own tools.

Enhancing Edges with Adjustment Layers

Adjustment layers are almost always used for tonal or color adjustments (we talk about adjustment layers in quite some detail in Chapter 7, *The Digital Darkroom*). But here's a method that Greg Vander Houwen showed us that uses adjustment layers to help make selections. This is particularly useful when you're trying to select a foreground image out of a background, and the two are too similar in color (see Figure 8-37).

First, add an adjustment layer above the image (Command-click on the New Layer icon in the Layers palette). The type of adjustment layer you choose depends on what you're trying to achieve. You can make a

Figure 8-37 Using adjustment layers to emphasize elements and build masks

The original image

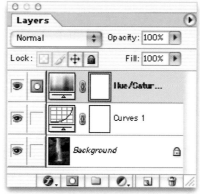

We add two adjustment layers: a Curves layer that drastically increases the image contrast, and a Hue/Saturation layer that desaturates the image slightly.

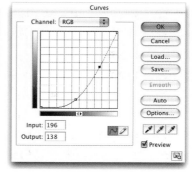

The Curves dialog box of the Curves adjustment layer. Note that the shadows have been completely blown out to black. The curve has also been tweaked on the red, blue, and green channels.

After these extreme adjustment layers are applied, the image looks almost unrecognizable.

We duplicate one of the channels of this "extreme" image and clean it up for our water mask. Now we can throw away the adjustment layers (they've done their job).

Finally, we load our new mask into the layer mask of a new, more subtle Hue/Saturation adjustment layer. This way, the effect only affects the water.

radical adjustment in this layer, knowing that you're not actually hurting your original image data. Use the adjustment layer to boost the contrast between the foreground and background, so that you can make a better selection.

Masks, Channels, and Life

While you can get by with performing global manipulations on images, the vast majority of images you'll work with require making a selection. We hope that after almost 60 pages we've done more to allay your fears than to cause you panic when selecting pixels in your image. Remember the two golden rules of selections:

▶ Masks, channels, and selections are all the same thing.

▶ You can (and often should) edit a selection after you've made it.

With those firmly planted in your mind, you'll have no problems as you tackle the techniques in the rest of this book.

9

Sharpness, Detail, and Noise Reduction

Getting an Edge on Your Image

The human visual system depends to a great degree on edges. Simply put, our eyes pass information to our brain, where every detail is quickly broken down into "edge" or "not edge." (Thousands of years of evolution have developed our brains to ignore most of what's going on in our field of vision and instead focus immediately on moving edges that might turn out to be a hungry tiger.) An image may have great contrast and color balance, but without good edge definition, we simply see it as less lifelike.

No matter how good your camera or scanner and how crisp your original may be, you always lose some sharpness when an image is digitized. Images from scanners and digital cameras always need a considerable amount of sharpening, though high-end scanners may sharpen as part of the scanning process. Even a high-resolution digital camera back mounted on a finely focused view camera produces images that will benefit from sharpening. You *cannot* solve the problem of blurry scans by scanning at a higher resolution. It just doesn't work that way.

Your images also lose sharpness in the output process. Halftoned images (almost anything on a printing press) and dithered ones (such as those printed on inkjet printers) are by far the worst offenders. But even continuous-tone devices such as film recorders and dye-sublimation printers lose a little sharpness.

Detail and Noise

In addition to detail, images contain *noise*—digital captures have camera noise, film scans have film grain that may be exacerbated by scanner noise. We only want to sharpen the detail, not the noise.

We have various tricks for sharpening detail without making the noise worse. And Photoshop CS2 introduces a new Reduce Noise filter that's quite effective, particularly with noise from digital captures. However, as with all noise reduction solutions, Photoshop's Reduce Noise filter also compromises detail. When we try to improve images, we always have to walk the fine line between increasing edge detail and decreasing noise.

We generally use noise reduction in Photoshop only on very noisy images—scans of color negatives and digital captures at ISO 800 and up are prime candidates. (We do, however, make full use of Camera Raw's noise reduction features when working with digital raw captures.) Otherwise, we prefer to concentrate on sharpening the available detail while protecting the noisy areas, partly because we don't want to soften the image unnecessarily with noise reduction, partly to avoid another step in the workflow.

When we do perform noise reduction—either Photoshop CS2's Reduce Noise filter or a third-party plug-in such as Noise Ninja, Grain Surgery, or Neat Image—we always do so before sharpening, for the simple reason that it works better than doing so afterwards. We'll cover noise reduction further later in this chapter.

Lens Defects

Lenses introduce their own quirks into the mix. Some lenses are simply sharper than others. (The new Smart Sharpen filter in Photoshop CS2 contains a routine that specifically addresses lens softness.) A second lens problem, which we encounter a great deal more with digital capture than we did with film, is chromatic aberration, where the lens fails to deliver the red, green, and blue wavelengths to the same plane of focus, producing color fringing. It's a particular problem towards the wide end of wide-angle zooms, which is where we see it most often.

We suspect that we see chromatic aberration in digital capture more than in film simply because digital is much less forgiving to lenses. Film grain and interlayer scattering of the light tend to mask chromatic aberration where digital capture reveals it quite brutally—shooting film and digital with the same lens tend to bear this out. Camera Raw's Lens tab has controls for addressing chromatic aberration in digital raw captures, while a second new filter in CS2, Lens Correction, addresses it in Photoshop.

We'll cover noise reduction and lens corrections in the course of this chapter, but while only some images need noise reduction or lens fixes, *every* image needs sharpening, so that's where we'll start.

Sharpening

To counteract the blurries in both the input and output stages, you need to sharpen your images. Photoshop offers several sharpening tools, but Unsharp Mask and Smart Sharpen are the only ones that really work as production tools. The Sharpening tool and the other sharpening filters may be useful for creative effects (and even then, we prefer other approaches), but they'll wreck your images very quickly if you use them to compensate for softness introduced during either acquisition or output.

Smart Sharpen is the new kid on the block, and it's pretty interesting, but if you want to understand sharpening, the place to start is the Unsharp Mask filter. It's easier to understand, and faster to execute, than Smart Sharpen.

Unsharp Masking

Unsharp masking (often abbreviated as USM) may sound like the last thing you'd want to do if you're trying to make an image appear sharper, but the term actually makes some sense; it has its origins in a traditional photographic technique for enhancing sharpness.

The things we see as edges are areas of high contrast between adjacent pixels. The higher the contrast, the sharper the edges appear. So to increase sharpness, you need to increase the contrast along the edges.

In the traditional process, the photographic negative is sandwiched in the enlarger along with a slightly out-of-focus duplicate negative—an unsharp mask—and the exposure time for printing is approximately doubled. Because the unsharp mask is slightly out of focus and the exposure time has been increased, the light side of the edges prints lighter and the dark side of the edges prints darker, creating a "halo" around objects in the image (see Figure 9-1).

As you'll see throughout this chapter, this halo effect is both the secret of good sharpening, and its Achilles' heel—depending on the size and intensity of the halo, and where it appears in the image. Photoshop lets you control the halo very precisely, but there's no single magic setting that

Figure 9-1 Edge transitions and sharpening

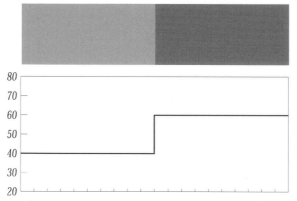

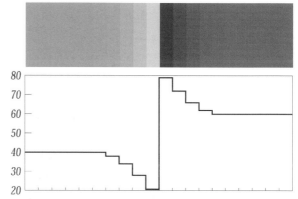

This image and graph depict an edge transition—from 40 to 60 percent. Each tick mark across the bottom of the graph represents a column of pixels.

After sharpening, the transition is accentuated—it's darker on the dark side, and lighter on the light side, creating a halo around the edge.

Unsharpened   Sharpened

The effect on images ranges from subtle to impressive to destructive. This image is somewhat oversharpened to make the effect clear.

These samples are darker after sharpening.

These samples are lighter after sharpening.

The net result is a sharper-looking image.

works for all images; so you need to know not only how the controls work, but also what you're trying to achieve in the image.

How the Unsharp Mask Filter Works

The Unsharp Mask filter operates pixel by pixel, which explains why it takes so long, even on a very fast machine. It compares each pixel to its neighbors, looking for a certain amount of contrast between adjacent pix-els—which it assumes is an edge. It then increases the contrast between those pixels according to the parameters you set. This creates a halo that, at normal viewing distances, increases apparent sharpness.

But Photoshop can't actually detect edges—it just looks at contrast dif-ferences (zeros and ones again). So unsharp masking can also have the undesired effect of exaggerating texture in flat areas and skin tones, and emphasizing any noise introduced by the scanner in the shadow areas.

You need to walk a fine line, sharpening only where your image needs it. The filter itself has few controls to adjust what gets sharpened (see Figure 9-2). So, we much prefer running sharpening through a mask. But to do so, you still need to understand the settings you can control in Photoshop's Unsharp Mask filter, what they do, and how they interact.

Figure 9-2
The Unsharp
Mask filter

Amount

We think of Amount as the volume control—it adjusts the intensity of the sharpening halo (see Figure 9-3). High Amount settings—you can enter up to 500 percent—produce intense halos with many pixels driven to pure white or solid black); low Amount settings produce less intense ones. Amount has no effect on the width of the halos—just on their contrast.

As you increase the Amount setting, the blips around big tonal shifts (edges) can be pushed all the way to white and black. At that point, increas-ing Amount has no effect whatsoever—you can't get more white than white! Worse, the all-white halos often stand out as artifacts and can look really dumb.

We almost always start out by setting Amount much higher than we'll eventually want it—between 400 and 500—until we set the Radius. Then

Figure 9-3
Varying the USM
Amount setting

Image resolution: 266 ppi
Radius: 0.5
Threshold: 0

Amount: 65   *Amount: 175*   *Amount: 350*

we adjust downward from there, depending on the image (see "Working the Controls," later in this chapter).

Radius

Radius is the first thing to consider when you're setting up sharpening; it sets the width of the halo that the filter creates around edges (see Figure 9-4). The wider the halo, the more obvious the sharpening effect. Choosing the correct Radius value is probably the most important choice in avoiding an unnaturally oversharpened look, and there are several factors to take into account when you choose, starting with the content of the image itself, the output method, and the intended size of the reproduction (see the sidebar "Image Detail and Sharpening Radius," later in this chapter).

Note that a Radius value of 1.0 does not result in a single-pixel radius. In fact, the halo is often between four and six pixels wide for the whole

Figure 9-4
Varying the USM
Radius setting

Image resolution: 266 ppi
Amount: 250
Threshold: 0

Radius: 0.4   *Radius: 0.9*   *Radius: 1.6*

light and dark cycle—two or three pixels on each side of the tonal shift. However, it varies in width depending on the content of the image.

Threshold

Unsharp Mask only evaluates contrast differences: it doesn't know whether those differences represent real edges you want to sharpen, or areas of texture (or, even worse, scanner noise) that you don't want to sharpen. The Threshold control lets you specify how far apart two pixels' tonal values have to be (on a scale of 0 to 255) before the filter affects them (see Figure 9-5). For example, if Threshold is set to 3, and two adjacent pixels have values of 122 and 124 (a difference of two), they're unaffected.

Figure 9-5
Varying the USM
Threshold setting

Image resolution: 266 ppi
Amount: 350
Radius: 0.7

Threshold: 0   *Threshold: 6*   *Threshold: 12*

You can use Threshold to make the filter ignore the relatively slight differences between pixels in smooth, low-contrast areas while still creating a halo around details that have high-contrast edges. And, to some extent at least, you can use it to avoid exaggerating noisy pixels in shadow areas.

Low Threshold values (0 to 4) result in a sharper-looking image overall (because fewer areas are excluded). High values (above 10) result in less sharpening, but often produce unnatural-looking transitions between the sharpened and unsharpened areas. We typically start out with a zero Threshold value, and then increase it only if necessary.

Tip: The Preview Checkbox. The Preview checkbox applies the Unsharp Mask filter to the entire image or selection on the fly, but we often keep this turned off. Even on fast machines, the preview can take a long time on large files, and every time you change the filter settings, Photoshop has to

▶ Capture sharpening is like converting from the source profile to the working space—it compensates for the quirks of the source and puts the image in a good state for editing.

▶ Creative sharpening is like doing color correction, using creative skills to make the image do what you want it to.

▶ Output sharpening is like converting to an output profile, creating a device-specific version of the image that is designed to work only for the designated output process.

Essentially, the capture and creative sharpens make a file that is repurposable (our mothers always taught us to keep our options open as long as possible), and responds well to resizing and final output sharpening.

Of course, if approached carelessly, this workflow can create some very ugly images. Just hitting the image with three rounds of Unsharp Mask using different radii is a recipe for certain disaster. Instead, retaining optimum quality requires finesse and some fairly advanced sharpening techniques. We look at individual sharpening techniques in detail later in this chapter, but here's the 30,000-foot overview.

Capture sharpening. The first round of sharpening in the workflow must be done very gently indeed; otherwise the result is likely to be a hideously oversharpened mess. It's often helpful to sharpen through an edge mask—so that only the high-contrast edges get sharpened—and to focus the sharpening on the midtones, protecting highlights and shadows so that they don't get driven to solid black and solid white.

With very grainy or noisy originals such as high-ISO digital capture or fast color negative, you may first want to apply some noise reduction (essentially *un*sharpening) using the Reduce Noise filter or a third-party noise reduction plug-in.

Creative sharpening. For creative sharpening, you can build "sharpening brushes" to paint your sharpening just where you want it. As you'll see, you do this by creating a new merged layer, setting the layer's blending mode to Luminosity (to avoid color-fringing), applying a global Unsharp Mask to the layer, then adding a layer mask set to Hide All. As you paint on the layer mask, Photoshop adds or removes the sharpening.

Creative sharpening effects are really only limited by your imagination. For example, one way to make an object appear sharper is to blur its surroundings—you can create "smoothing brushes" using the same techniques as sharpening brushes, but substituting a blur for the sharpen.

Output sharpening. Since the image-specific and source-specific concerns were already addressed in the capture and creative sharpening phases, output sharpening can concentrate solely on the output process.

Note that you can only sharpen the image's pixels—Photoshop has no control over how those pixels are rendered to ink on paper (or any other output process). So the key factor in output sharpening is the relationship between the pixels and the resulting hard copy. Hence output sharpening must be done at the final size and resolution, often as the last step before converting an RGB file to CMYK and saving the file to disk. Note that unlike capture and creative sharpening, output sharpening is something we always apply globally. Here are a few other considerations:

▶ A rule of thumb that has served us well is to aim for a sharpening halo of approximately $\frac{1}{50}$- to $\frac{1}{100}$-inch (.5 to .25 mm) in width, the thinking being that at normal viewing distances, a halo this size falls below the threshold of human visual acuity, so you don't see the halo as a separate feature—you just get the illusion of sharpness that it produces.

A good starting point for the Unsharp Mask filter's Radius setting is image resolution ÷ 200. (Remember: we're talking about final image resolution, after it has been placed on a page and scaled to fit.) Thus, for a 300-ppi image, you'd use a Radius of 1.5 (300 ÷ 200). For a 200-ppi image, you'd use a Radius setting of 1. This is a suggested starting point, not a golden rule. As you gain experience, you'll find situations where the rule has to be bent. When sharpening using methods that don't involve Unsharp Mask, you'll have to look closely and do some math yourself.

▶ Of course, there's really no way to get an accurate on-screen representation of how a sharpened halftone output will look—the continuous-tone monitor display is simply too different from the halftone. An image well-sharpened for halftone output will typically look "crunchy" on screen. And the monitor resolution and view percentage can help or hinder your appraisal of an image's sharpness. See the sidebar "Sharpening and the Display" for more on the subject.

Sharpening and the Display

Back in the days when all our monitors were CRTs, we thought we had a good idea of how to judge sharpness from the screen. But the vast differences in apparent sharpness between LCD and CRT monitors, and the research we've undertaken in applying output sharpening, have caused us to reevaluate that position.

LCD monitors are much, much sharper than CRTs at any given display resolution. Moreover, an image will appear quite different in terms of sharpening at a lower display resolution than it will at a higher one.

So where color management lets us compensate for a huge range of different display behaviors, we have no such solution for sharpening.

What we do have is a new set of very general rules of thumb. Use these with caution: You need to learn the relationship between what you see on your particular display at your preferred resolution and the resulting output (just as you had to do with color in the days before color management). With that caveat in mind, here are some very general guidelines.

Zoom percentage. We believe it's a good idea to look at the Actual Pixels view to see what's happening to the actual image pixels, but unless your output is to a monitor, Actual Pixels view may give a fairly misleading impression of the actual sharpness on output.

For halftone output, bear in mind that each halftone dot may be comprised of four image pixels. Viewing at 25-percent or 50-percent view may give a truer impression of halftone sharpness. Avoid the "odd" zoom percentages—33.3, 66.6, and so on, because Photoshop applies fairly heavy anti-aliasing to those views. For inkjet output, the key factor is the resolution you're sending to the printer. Look at the even-divisor zoom percentage that comes closest to reproducing the image at actual print size on the display.

How sharp is sharp? For the first two passes of sharpening—capture and localized creative—our general rule of thumb is to apply sharpening that looks good on a CRT display, or very slightly over-sharpened on an LCD display.

For output sharpening, you can really push the sharpening far beyond what looks acceptable on the monitor at Actual Pixels view, particularly when you print at higher resolutions (like 350 ppi for a 175-lpi halftone or 360 ppi for an inkjet print).

The key here is bear in mind the actual size of the pixels on output. At 360 ppi, each pixel is only $1/360$ of an inch, so to produce a $1/50$ of an inch halo, you'd need a dark contour approximately 3.6 pixels wide ($1/100$ of an inch) and a light contour the same size.

▶ On very large prints, you may have to use a slightly larger sharpening halo—if the resolution is below 100 ppi, the halo will be larger than $1/50$-inch because it takes at least two pixels, one light, one dark, to create the halo. But large prints are generally viewed from further away, so the longer viewing distance tends to compensate for the larger halo.

Someday, RIPs and printers may even be able to apply output sharpening on the fly, particularly if things like color conversions and trapping are also going to occur there. But for such an approach to succeed, the device will somehow need to know the state of the incoming images (what kind of sharpening has already been performed, and so on).

The Sharpening Workflow

We'll be the first to admit that taking a workflow approach to sharpening is a fairly radical idea, but the more we use it, the more we find that it makes sense. We've done a great deal of testing—Bruce reckons he sharpened about 5,000 images to build and fine-tune PhotoKit SHARPENER—but plenty of work remains to be done.

The results of two- or three-pass sharpening often justify the extra pains, especially with images we plan to reuse for several different types of output. However, if you're in a hurry, and you're preparing an image for one-off reproduction (particularly with a low screen frequency that can only show a limited amount of detail anyway), one-pass sharpening may make just as much sense.

We don't claim to have solved every conceivable sharpening problem. The techniques that follow are ones that we use every day in our sharpening workflow, and as we describe them, we'll tell you how we use them. But feel free to pick and choose, and to adapt them to your own work.

Sharpening Techniques

We use a host of techniques in the sharpening workflow—some obvious, others less so. Some attempt to avoid accentuating dust and scratches, noise, and film grain by sharpening through a mask. Others seek to make sharpening nondestructive, and editable after the fact, by applying the sharpening on a layer, and still others use localized sharpening applied with a brush, to pick out specific details in the image. In practice, we often mix these techniques into a single sharpening move, and we'll provide some examples. However, it's easier to digest the various techniques separately, so that's how we'll present them.

Sharpening Layers

We prefer to do most of our sharpening on layers, for much the same reasons we prefer using adjustment layers to burning Curves or Levels directly into an image—it's nondestructive, it affords us control after the fact, and it allows us to use masking when we need to. In the first stage of the sharpening workflow, layer-based sharpening also provides an easy way to concentrate the sharpening in the midtones through the Blend If sliders in the Layer Options dialog box.

Figure 9-8 shows the steps for creating a sharpening layer on a flat file, or on a layered one. The layer is set to Luminosity mode to avoid any color shifts or color fringes—it produces essentially the same result as converting the image to Lab and sharpening the Lightness channel. You can then run the Unsharp Mask filter globally on the layer, or apply Unsharp Mask through an edge mask.

Figure 9-8 Creating a sharpening layer

On a flat file, simply duplicate the Background layer, then set the blending mode to Luminosity.

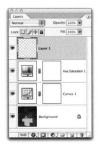

On a layered file, create a new layer, then choose Option-Merge Visible (or press Command-Option-Shift-E) to merge the visible layers into the new one...

...then, set the new layer's blending mode to luminosity, to avoid color-fringing.

Tip: Use Fade to Luminosity. If you really don't want to create a sharpening layer, but you want the benefit of sharpening in Luminosity mode, you can run the Unsharp Mask filter, then choose Fade from the Edit menu, and set the blending mode to Luminosity in the Fade dialog box.

Edge Masking

Edge masks are an indispensable tool for both sharpening and noise reduction. When sharpening, we use an edge mask to concentrate the effects of the sharpen on the edges, so that flat areas such as skies, and textured areas such as skin tones, don't get oversharpened. For noise reduction, we use the same kind of mask, but inverted, so that the edges are protected from the noise reduction.

Figure 9-9 shows the steps for building an edge mask. The first step is to create a channel that has good contrast between the edges and the non-edges. Sometimes one of the existing color channels will work—simply duplicate the channel to serve as the basis for the edge mask—but often

Figure 9-9 Building an edge mask

Add a new channel, either by duplicating an existing color channel, or by using the channel mixer to create a grayscale version of the image. Then run the Find Edges filter to isolate the edges.

The raw image

The new channel

The new channel after Find Edges

A Gaussian Blur softens the transitions and blurs the noise.

Inverting the image creates white edges where we want sharpening.

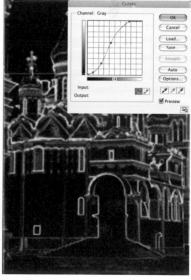
A Curves move controls the contrast between edges and non-edges.

you can achieve better results by using Channel Mixer or Calculations to create the channel. See "The Color of Grayscale" in Chapter 12, *Essential Image Techniques,* for a slew of methods for creating a grayscale version of the image.

Once you have a grayscale version of the image, run the Find Edges filter to locate the edges, then use a combination of blurring and contrast adjustments to control the relationship of the edges and non-edges. Once you've created the edge mask, you can load it as a selection through which you apply the sharpening, or you can add it to the sharpening layer as a layer mask. Each approach has advantages and disadvantages.

Edge mask as selection. To load the edge mask as a selection, Command-click on the channel's tile in the Channels palette. We suggest hiding the selection's marching ants (Command-H). Then, with the sharpening layer targeted, you can run Unsharp Mask. The white areas in the edge mask get fully sharpened, the black areas are fully protected from sharpening, and the gray areas receive sharpening proportional to the gray value.

The disadvantage is that you have no control over the transition between sharpened and unsharpened areas once you've applied the sharpening.

Edge mask as layer mask. Instead of sharpening through the mask as a selection, you can sharpen the layer globally, then add the edge mask as a layer mask: Load the edge mask as a selection, target the sharpening layer, and then click the Add Layer Mask icon in the layers palette (see Chapter 8, *Making Selections*).

Once you've added the layer mask, you can tweak the contrast of the layer mask with Levels or Curves to fine-tune the relationship between the sharpened and unsharpened areas. The downside to using the edge mask as a layer mask (rather than just sharpening the selection) is simply that it creates a larger file. Figure 9-10 shows the steps for applying the edge mask as a selection, or as a layer mask.

Edge mask for noise reduction. You can use approximately the same edge-masking technique to apply noise reduction instead of sharpening. Invert the mask (or omit the inverting step when creating the mask), leaving the edges black (so that they're protected from the noise reduction), and the non-edges white (so that they receive the full benefit of noise reduction). It's usually a good idea to use a slightly different blur, as well as different contrast, on the noise mask than on the edge mask—if you simply invert them you can exaggerate the transition between the edges and non-edges in both the noise reduction and sharpening layers. Making the masks slightly different helps a great deal.

Figure 9-10
Applying the edge mask

—*Command-click on the edge mask channel's tile to apply the edge mask as a selection.*

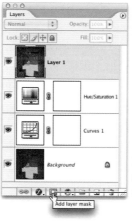

To apply the edge mask as a layer mask, first load it as a selection, then target the sharpening layer, and click the Add Layer Mask icon.

We find that the Despeckle filter does a great job of minimizing film grain and digital noise, but we generally apply it separately to each color channel, because typically one channel will need more applications than another. With film or print scans, the blue channel is almost invariably the noisiest, so we may run Despeckle once on the red channel, twice on the green, and three or more times on the blue. On digital images captured as JPEG, we look at each channel to determine where the noise lies, and Despeckle accordingly. With digital raw images, unless they're extremely noisy, we rely on Camera Raw's noise reduction features (see "The Detail Tab" in Chapter 11, *Building a Digital Workflow*).

If the noise is primarily in luminosity, as it is with transparency film, we prefer to carry out noise reduction on a layer set to Luminosity blending. Using separate layers for sharpening and noise reduction offers more control, but at the cost of a larger file size.

We also use masks with the new Reduce Noise filter, especially on higher-resolution film scans, where the filter seems to want to preserve the grain as well as the detail. The ability to edit the layer mask adds a level of post-filtering control that we often find useful.

Controlling the Tonal Range

One of the keys to a successful multipass sharpening workflow is to concentrate the first round of sharpening on the midtones while protecting the extreme highlights and shadows. It's so much easier to do this using a sharpening layer that we don't even try to use a nonlayered sharpen. The trick to controlling the tonal range is to use the Blend If sliders in the Layer Style dialog box—choose Layer Style>Blending Options from the Layer menu, or double-click the layer's tile in the Layers palette (see Figure 9-11).

The Blend If sliders let you control which tonal values in the overlying (sharpening) layer get applied to the underlying layer (and, conversely, which tonal values in the underlying, unsharpened layers are affected by the sharpening layer). Bruce thinks of the overlying layer as a ton of bricks suspended over a basket of eggs (the underlying layers). The top Blend If slider controls which bricks fall, and the bottom Blend If slider dictates which eggs receive the impact. (If this makes no sense to you, don't worry—Bruce often thinks of things in weird ways.)

Figure 9-11 shows some typical settings for the Blend If sliders for initial midtone sharpening. Depending on the image source (film or digital), and the amount of noise present, you may find that the shadow values need to be set higher or lower, but the basic principle is to set the bottom sliders to protect extreme highlights and shadows, and the top sliders to apply most of the sharpening in the midtones.

Sharpening Brushes

For localized creative sharpening, nothing beats painting with a brush. We have two methods that we use to make a "sharpening brush," one using a layer, the other using History. Layer-based brushes offer more control because you can control the local opacity of the layer mask by brushing with different opacities, and you can control the global strength of the sharpen by varying the opacity of the layer itself. However, layers increase your file size. Using the History brush is less controllable (because your only control is through the brush opacity itself) but doesn't add to the size of the file. Keeping your file size down is important when you're working with huge files.

Layer-based sharpening brush. To create a layer-based sharpening brush, first make a sharpening layer as we showed earlier in Figure 9-8. It's

Figure 9-11 Controlling the tonal range

The Blend If sliders let us focus sharpening on the midtones.

Unsharpened   *Before blending tweak*   *After blending tweak*

Here, the top sliders fully apply tonal values between level 65 and 200, and gradually feather values from 65–20 and 200–245.

The bottom sliders protect the underlying values below 20 and above 245, and feather the adjustment to values between 20 and 40, and 230 and 245.

The result is that the contrast of the dark and light sharpening halos is reduced, allowing headroom for subsequent creative or output sharpening.

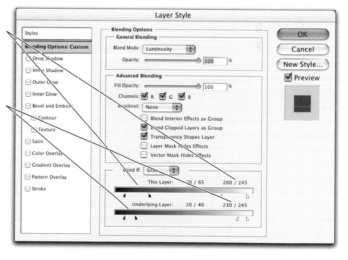

usually a good idea to apply slightly more sharpening to the layer than you ultimately desire, because that way you have more control after the fact. Next, add a layer mask set to Hide All. To brush in the sharpening, make sure that the layer mask is targeted, then choose the Brush tool, set the foreground color to white, and simply brush the sharpening in as desired. We prefer to use a brush set to substantially less than 100 percent opacity, because the lower opacity allows us more control. Figure 9-12 shows the results of a sharpening brush.

Figure 9-12 A layer-based sharpening brush

The unsharpened image

The unmasked sharpening layer
(before choosing Hide All)

The sharpening brushed
in locally on the mask

The unmasked sharpening layer

The brushed layer mask

History Brush sharpening. If you're too lazy to create masks, you're in a RAM-limited situation, or if you just want more interactivity than a mask offers, you can use the History Brush to paint sharpening into the image. This is a particularly handy technique with a pressure-sensitive stylus, because you can set the pressure-sensitivity to Opacity, and achieve fine control over both the strength of the sharpening, and exactly where it's applied.

The basic technique is a simple three-step process:

1. Apply the Unsharp Mask filter.

2. Set the History state to the step before you applied Unsharp Mask, and the source for the History brush to the Unsharp Mask step.

3. Paint the sharpening into the image as desired.

Or, if you prefer, you can *reduce* the sharpening with the History Brush by leaving the History state at the Unsharp Mask step, and then loading the step before it as the History Brush source. We typically choose the method that will require least brushwork on the image at hand.

The unsharpened image in Figure 9-13 is quite soft. (No, this isn't David or Bruce's child!) If we apply enough sharpening to pick up the texture in the fabric, it leaves the skin crunchy, which is bad at the best of times, but particularly so on babies!

Figure 9-13 Global sharpening makes crunchy skin.

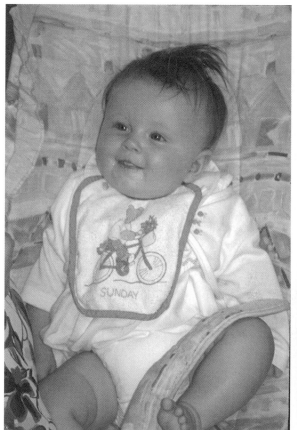
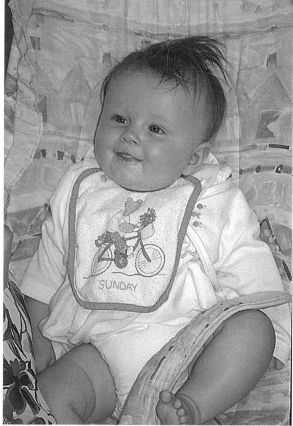

| *The unsharpened image* | *The image sharpened globally* |

In this case, it's much less work to set the History Brush source to the unsharpened state, and brush out the crunchies than it would be brush them in. A few quick strokes with a soft, low-opacity History Brush produce the much more pleasing rendition shown in Figure 9-14.

Figure 9-14 History Brush sharpening

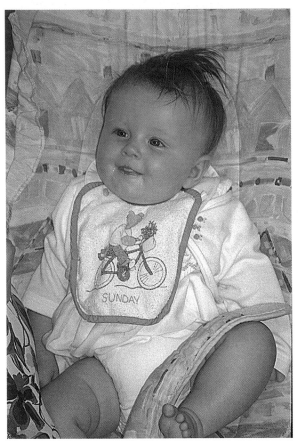

Taking the globally sharpened image as the starting point, we set the source for the History Brush to the unsharpened state, and brush out the crunchies.

The image after History brushing

Tip: Luminosity Sharpening with History. Earlier you saw that you can perform luminosity sharpening by selecting Fade from the Edit menu after running the Unsharp Mask filter (and setting the blending mode in the Fade dialog box to Luminosity). If you're brushing sharpening in rather than out, you can do the same thing by setting the blending mode for the History Brush to Luminosity using the Mode popup menu in the Options bar (see Figure 9-15).

Sharpening Without Unsharp Mask

Unsharp Mask is the Swiss Army Knife of sharpening tools, but it's not the only way to sharpen images. One technique that we often use, par-

Figure 9-15
Luminosity sharpening
with History

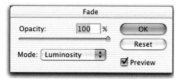

You can run Unsharp Mask, then choose Fade Unsharp Mask (from the Edit menu) and set the blending mode to Luminosity...

...or you can run Unsharp Mask, set the History state to the unsharpened image, set the History Brush source to the sharpened image, then set the blending mode for the History Brush to Luminosity.

ticularly when sharpening for output, is to make a duplicate layer, using the techniques we described earlier in this chapter under "Sharpening Layers." But rather than setting the blending mode to Luminosity and running Unsharp Mask, we use one of the contrast-increasing blending modes such as Soft Light or Hard Light, then we run the High Pass filter on the layer.

High-Pass Sharpening

The High Pass filter (in the Other submenu, under the Filter menu) is a simple way to create an edge mask, but in this case we don't use it as a layer mask. Instead, we simply create a duplicate of the background layer (or create a new merged layer if we have more than one layer in the Layers palette), apply the High Pass filter to it, and then set the layer's blending mode to Soft Light or Hard Light—which increases the contrast around the edges, effectively sharpening the image.

As with the other layer-based sharpening techniques, you can use a whole bag of tricks to refine the sharpening—like blurring noise in the mask, or painting on the layer itself with 50-percent gray (the neutral color for both the Hard Light and Soft Light blending modes) to erase the sharpening in local areas. You can apply a layer mask to confine the sharpening to a specific area, and you can stack multiple sharpening layers to apply selective sharpening to different areas of the image.

The critical parameter in using this technique is the Radius setting for the High Pass filter. If it's too small, you'll get little or no sharpening. If it's too big, grain and noise will appear in the image as if by some evil magic. However, for optimum output sharpening, we often need to produce a result that appears very ugly on screen (see the sidebar, "Sharpening and the Display," earlier in this chapter). Figure 9-16 shows the application of this technique and the resulting image—it looks fine in print, but the on-screen appearance is downright scary! When you look at the actual pixels on screen, bear in mind the size at which they'll reproduce in print—a 6-pixel-wide halo, with 3 pixels in the light contour, and 3 in the dark, will produce an "ideal" sharpening halo when you print at 300 ppi, even if it looks downright hideous on screen. The only way to really judge print sharpness is to make a print!

Figure 9-16 Sharpening with High Pass/Hard Light

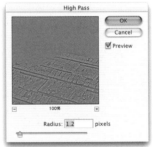

We create a sharpening layer and set the blending mode in the Layers palette to Hard Light, then run the High Pass filter.

The filtered layer set to Hard Light creates an unsharp mask very similar to a photographic unsharp mask. You can vary the character of the sharpening by using different radius settings in High Pass, and you can vary the strength of the sharpening by adjusting the layer's opacity.

On soft subjects and skin tones, Hard Light can give too strong a sharpening effect. On these types of image, or in any case where we want a more gentle sharpening effect, we often use Soft Light instead of Hard Light to avoid oversharpening the skin texture, as shown in Figure 9-17. You can switch between Hard Light and Soft Light after running the High Pass filter to see which rendering you prefer.

Figure 9-17 Sharpening with High Pass/Soft Light

Starting with the unsharpened image, left, we create a sharpening layer, and set the blending mode to Soft Light; then we run the High Pass filter to produce the result shown below.

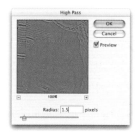

Setting the blending mode before running the High Pass filter lets us see the effect of different Radius settings on the image—the proxy window in the High Pass filter only shows the duplicate layer on which the filter is operating.

The image is now acceptably sharp with no exaggerated noise pixels, but the eyes could benefit from a little extra sparkle.

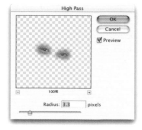

We quickly use the Lasso tool with Feather set to around 5 pixels to select the eyes. Then we target the Background layer, and use Command-J to copy the eyes to a new layer, which we set to Hard Light. We then run High Pass on the new layer to produce the result shown at left.

Techniques in the Workflow

In our sharpening workflow, we use combinations of all the techniques covered in the previous section. In this section, we'll describe briefly how we incorporate these techniques into a sharpening workflow.

If we're working on images from scratch—either from a film scan or from a digital capture—we use two or three sharpening passes, as described in "When We Sharpen," earlier in this chapter. When we have to deal with files that already have had some sharpening applied, we deal with them on a case-by-case basis. If we feel that they're adequately sharp, we may do no additional sharpening, or we may apply localized creative sharpening. If we have to resize the image for output, we'll almost certainly do a global sharpen after resize, tailored to the output process.

The First Sharpening Pass

Our first sharpening pass aims to compensate for the shortcomings of the capture in a way that's sensitive to the image content. We do so by creating a sharpening layer, applying an edge mask, sharpening with a radius that matches the image content, then constraining the tonal range to the midtones using the Blend If sliders in Layer Style.

The result is a subtle sharpen that makes the image behave better through resizing and through the subsequent sharpening phases. If the image has already had sharpening applied, we omit this step. We usually apply this sharpen after we've made our initial global adjustments for tone and contrast, because major contrast moves afterwards may defeat the sharpening. If file size is a concern, we may flatten the image after we've fine-tuned the initial sharpen.

If noise reduction is required, we'll do it before sharpening, either running Despeckle through a mask, or running Reduce Noise on its own merged layer. When extreme noise reduction is required, we'll apply a mask to the noise reduction layer to protect the edges.

Creative Sharpening

For localized creative sharpening, we generally use some variant of the sharpening brush techniques. We apply creative sharpening after we've fine-tuned the tone and color both globally and locally, because changes to contrast and color can easily affect the perceived sharpness.

Output Sharpening

We apply output sharpening globally, using a sharpening layer with no layer mask. For halftone and inkjet outputs, we often use the Hard Light/ High Pass sharpening technique. Output sharpening *must* be done at final output resolution. If you think it's likely the image will be resized after it leaves your hands, we advise omitting the output sharpening step—anyone who resizes the image will probably resharpen anyway, and if you've done a reasonably good job in the capture and creative phases, the final result will still be sharp.

The key difference between output sharpening and the earlier phases is that more often than not we produce a result that looks downright scary on the monitor. Keep in mind the physical size of the sharpening halo on output. Light and dark contours that are 3 pixels wide may look hideous on the monitor; but if you're printing at 300 ppi, they'll translate into contours (light and dark parts of the sharpening halo) that are only $\frac{1}{100}$ of an inch wide, so they won't be obvious on the final print.

Attempting to show the apparent on-screen sharpness in print is a very uncertain endeavor. What we've attempted to do in Figure 9-18 is to show the image pixels at 200-percent view through the various phases of sharpening, along with the final printed image at print size, in the hope that doing so will give you some idea of the relationship between what happens to the pixels themselves and the influence on the final printed result.

Obviously, the on-screen appearance at Actual Pixels will vary dramatically over different display types and resolutions, but as you zoom in, the differences between display types become much less significant. We hope that the figure at least demonstrates the dramatic differences in halos created by the capture and creative sharpening phases, and those created by the final output sharpening. To help understand what you're seeing, we've also noted the sharpening settings we used for each step of the sharpening process, from capture through to final output.

Output sharpening is the only phase that easily lends itself to a formula, because once the image has been sized and the output process chosen, the physical size of the pixels, and hence of the sharpening halos, is a known quantity. For the capture and creative phases of the sharpening workflow, common sense, good taste, and in the long run, experience are the best guides!

Figure 9-18 The sharpening workflow

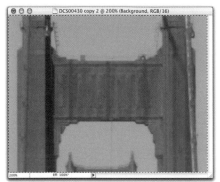

The first pass: Capture sharpening applied on a layer (with an edge layer mask) set to the Luminosity blend mode, at 66-percent opacity. Unsharp Mask applied at Amount 100, Radius 0.8, Threshold 0.

The unsharpened image pixels at 200 percent view

Capture sharpening at 200 percent view

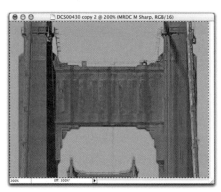

Creative sharpening applied on layer set to Overlay at 50-percent opacity, Unsharp Mask applied at Amount 500, Radius 0.6, Threshold 0, then High Pass filter applied at Radius 5. Sharpening brushed in with a brush at 33-percent opacity.

Creative sharpening at 200 percent view

The image was downsampled from its native 3072 by 2048 pixels to 488 by 732 pixels using Photoshop's Bicubic Sharper interpolation. Then final output sharpening was applied on a layer set to Luminosity at 66-percent opacity, with Unsharp Mask at Amount 187, Radius 1.3, Threshold zero to produce to the result at right. A zoomed detail is shown below.

Downsampled to print size, then sharpened for output, at 200-percent view

The final image

Noise Reduction

Any attempt at reducing noise will also soften the image. Noise reduction has not traditionally been Photoshop's forté, as evidenced by the healthy sales of dedicated third-party plug-ins such as Noise Ninja, Neat Image, and Grain Surgery. We've been known to use all of these in various situations, but since this is a Photoshop book, we've always felt bound to develop Photoshop noise reduction techniques that don't rely on third-party add-ons.

Until the Reduce Noise filter appeared in Photoshop CS2, we generally relied on the Despeckle filter, applied separately to individual channels multiple times, through an edge mask. We wish we could say that the Reduce Noise filter renders such kludges unnecessary, but unfortunately we encounter two major problems with Reduce Noise:

▶ The Preserve Detail feature really doesn't know the difference between detail and digital noise or film grain, so we still need to use masks.

▶ Even on fast machines, Reduce Noise is slow. Agonizingly, mind-numbingly slow. And not just when executing on a large file, but even simply to refresh the proxy image in the filter window. (And don't even think about turning on the Preview checkbox to preview the entire image!)

However, even with these problems, when we encounter *really* noisy images we will use Reduce Noise rather than despeckling.

Light Noise Reduction with Despeckle

When all we need is relatively light noise reduction, we still resort to the Despeckle filter. A typical case is noisy skies from a transparency scanner. We generally run Despeckle first on the red channel, then we run it a few more times on the green channel, and run it even more times on the blue channel, which tends to be the noisiest.

Figure 9-19 shows an image shot on Kodak EPP transparency film and scanned on an Imacon Flextight 848. The sky is quite a bit grainier than we'd like, so we tried both methods (Despeckle and Reduce Noise). Both filters required masking, so we made a quick Color Range selection of the sky and used it as a mask for the Noise reduction layer.

The Despeckled result has some slight mottling, but it's relatively clean and responds well to subsequent sharpening. The version that uses Reduce

Figure 9-19 Despeckle or Reduce Noise?

The image above has had noise reduction and final sharpening applied. The red box shows the area of detail we're examining for noise reduction.

The detail at Actual Pixels view before noise reduction

Even at the extreme settings we used, the version with Reduce Noise contains artifacts that are emphasized by subsequent sharpening that the Despeckle version lacks.

Despeckle at 400%

Reduce Noise at 400%

Noise reduced by Despeckle, four times on the red channel, six times on the green, ten on the blue

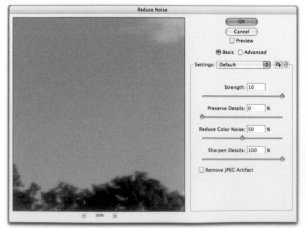

Noise reduced by Reduce Noise, settings shown at left

Noise—even when cranked all the way up, retains characteristic "wormy" dark artifacts that get much worse with output sharpening, as shown in the 400% blowups in Figure 9-19. Reducing the strength of Reduce Noise actually creates worse results, and moving the Preserve Detail control away from zero makes it preserve the noise we're trying to eliminate.

Moreover, even though we ran Despeckle 20 times in all, it still took less time than setting, previewing, and running the Reduce Noise filter, and we could easily see what happened each time we ran Despeckle, while with Reduce Noise we have to wait each time we move a control for the proxy to be updated, which even on fast machines typically takes several seconds. So for moderate luminance noise, like the example shown in Figure 9-19, we'll continue to use Despeckle with a mask.

The Reduce Noise Filter

We don't, however, mean to suggest that Reduce Noise is useless—far from it. But you *do* have to be careful, tune the subsequent sharpening to the noise reduction to avoid exaggerating the characteristic artifacts that Reduce Noise produces, and (in some cases) you may want to mask edges and important textural detail so that Reduce Noise doesn't destroy them. Figure 9-20 shows the Reduce Noise dialog box.

Figure 9-20
The Reduce Noise filter

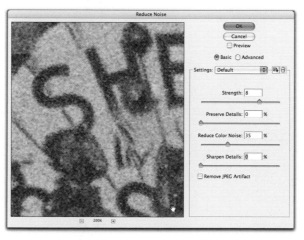

In Basic mode, Reduce Noise offers four slider controls, and a checkbox for reducing JPEG artifacts. The four sliders operate as follows.

Strength. The Strength slider controls the strength of the luminance noise reduction effect—it's not an overall strength control. Permissible values range from zero to 10. (At zero, you can still apply color noise reduction, or use the Advanced options on the individual channels.)

Preserve Details. The Preserve Details slider (permissible values are from 0 to 100 percent) attempts to do what it says—preserve details. Unfortunately, on anything except very low-resolution files, it also seems to preserve the noise you're presumably trying to eliminate. We find that the useful range is between 1 and 5—beyond that, it's difficult to get rid of the noise (See Figure 9-21).

Figure 9-21 Preserve Details

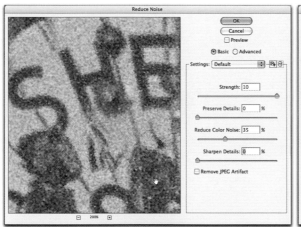

The unadjusted image

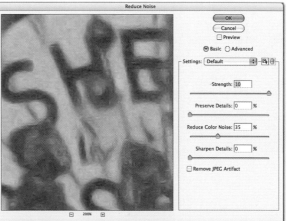

Preserve Details at zero

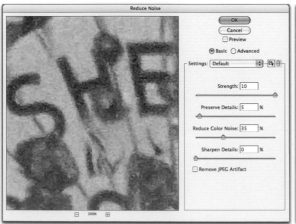

Preserve Details at 5

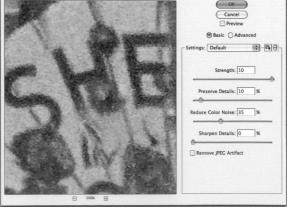

Preserve Details at 10

The Preserve Details and Sharpen Details controls seem designed to sharpen and reduce noise in one swell foop. On Web-resolution images, this works reasonably well. But if you plan on sharpening later, you need to keep the Preserve Details slider at a very low (or zero) value.

Reduce Color Noise. The Reduce Color Noise slider (permissible values are from 0 to 100 percent) reduces color noise independently of luminance noise. Transparency film has little or no color noise, negative film typically has more, while digital captures often have color noise reduced in the raw converter or the camera. At very high settings, Reduce Color Noise can lose saturation, but settings of 35–50 percent work well (see Figure 9-22).

Figure 9-22 Reduce Color Noise

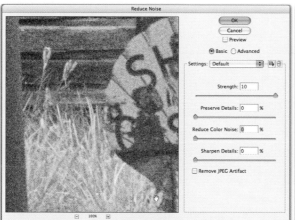

The unadjusted image

Reduce Color Noise at zero

Reduce Color Noise at 50 percent

Reduce Color Noise at 100 percent

Sharpen Details. While the Sharpen Details slider works independently of Preserve Details, its effect depends very much on that slider's value (whose effect depends—as we said a moment ago—on the image resolution). Feel free to try reducing noise *and* sharpening with Reduce Noise, but we suggest you only attempt to do so on low-resolution images—the significant lack of speed with which the filter updates the proxy on higher-res images doesn't really invite experimentation!

If you plan on sharpening the image after running Reduce Noise, we recommend leaving Sharpen Details at zero, otherwise you'll wind up with artifacts that are almost impossible to deal with.

Remove JPEG Artifact. The Remove JPEG Artifact checkbox attempts to remove the characteristic 8-by-8-pixel artifacts caused by heavy JPEG compression. Sadly, we haven't enjoyed much success with it.

Advanced Mode. In Advanced Mode, Reduce Noise lets you set values for Strength and Preserve Details for each channel individually. The effect is cumulative with the settings you make in the main panel of the dialog box. If this feature were ten times faster, we might find it useful, but currently we can't really recommend it in a production situation—if you need to handle the channels differently, we think you're better off running Despeckle through a mask.

Using Reduce Noise

We use Reduce Noise on very noisy images, as a precursor to sharpening. But we prefer to run it on a layer made by merging the visible layers, usually through a light edge mask (that is, a mask with no solid blacks, that de-emphasizes rather than fully protects the edges). Since we only use Reduce Noise on extremely noisy images, we tend towards extreme settings.

The degree to which we feel comfortable reducing noise depends in part on the eventual use of the image. While we like the idea of creating "use-neutral" master images (which is one of the goals of the sharpening workflow), we also recognize that there's a limit to the size at which images, and in particular, noisy images, can be reproduced. With noisy 35 mm images, for example, we may scan at 6300 ppi, perform noise reduction and sharpening, then downsample to 4000 ppi to create a smaller but cleaner master image. Figure 9-23 shows a noisy 35 mm color negative scan that lends itself well to this approach.

Figure 9-23 Reduce Noise in action

The image above has had noise reduction and final sharpening applied. The detail views show actual pixels before noise reduction, right; after noise reduction, below left; and after capture sharpening, below right.

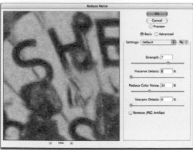

To reduce the noise, we ran Reduce Noise, using the settings shown at left.

Smart Sharpen

The new Smart Sharpen filter is a fascinating piece of work. Unfortunately, it shares with Reduce Noise a significant lack of speed, both in execution and, worse, in updating the proxy image when you change settings. For Web-resolution images, it's just about the greatest thing since sliced toast, but for high-resolution images its usefulness is much more debatable.

We suspect that somewhere inside Smart Sharpen lies the algorithm that lets the CSI team read that suspect's driver's license from a convenience store security camera frame grab—the catch is that this filter would have to run for about six months to produce the result.

If you need to make low-resolution images look good on screen, Smart Sharpen is great. If the idea of making sharpening masks fills you with terror, Smart Sharpen does a fairly good job of differentiating edges from non-edges. It's quite useful for capture sharpening, though on the whole we still prefer our tried-and-true techniques. On the other hand, it's a very slow and difficult way to do output sharpening.

Smart Sharpen Remove Modes

Smart Sharpen is really three sharpening filters in one. You select which one you want to use by choosing an option from the Remove menu (see Figure 9-24).

Figure 9-24
The Smart Sharpen filter

Gaussian Blur. The Gaussian Blur mode is—ironically—the Unsharp Mask with a new user interface. If you turn on the More Accurate option (when would you want "less accurate"?) the result is a good deal gentler than Unsharp Mask at the same Amount and Radius, but it's basically the same type of sharpening. We don't see any compelling reasons to use it.

Lens Blur. In Lens Blur mode, Smart Sharpen is a whole different animal than Unsharp Mask. Lens Blur uses much more sophisticated algorithms than Unsharp Mask (or Smart Sharpen in Gaussian Blur mode) to detect edges and detail, and hence typically produces better sharpening with less-obvious sharpening halos.

Motion Blur. In Motion Blur mode, Smart Sharpen tries to undo the effects of blurring caused by either camera or subject movement. If the movement is truly unidirectional, it does a surprisingly good job, but camera shake rarely happens in all directions, and subject movement is often quite complex, so don't expect blurred subjects to be rendered razor-sharp by the filter. We typically apply Smart Sharpen's Motion Blur on small areas of images rather than globally—few images benefit from global application.

Advanced Mode

When you choose Advanced mode by clicking the Advanced radio button, two additional tabs, labeled Shadow and Highlight, become available. They offer controls very similar to those offered by the Shadow/Highlight command found in the Adjust submenu (under the Image menu)—see "Shadow/Highlight" in Chapter 6, *Image Adjustment Fundamentals*.

Each tab provides three sliders for Fade Amount, Tonal Width, and Radius. They let you reduce the strength of the shadow and highlight sharpening contours, allowing stronger sharpening of the midtones.

▶ Fade Amount controls the strength of the fade from 0 to 100 percent.

▶ Tonal Width controls how far up from the shadows or down from the highlights the adjustment extends into the tonal range.

▶ Radius controls the size of the neighborhood used to decide whether a pixel is in the shadows or the highlights. A useful rule of thumb seems to be to set the Radius in the Shadow and Highlight tabs to double the Radius setting in the main panel.

Thus far, our use of Smart Sharpen is confined to the Lens Blur and Motion Blur modes, and we always use the Advanced setting with the More Accurate option turned on.

Smart Sharpen in Action

As with the Unsharp Mask filter, the key parameter is Radius. While you can obtain some interesting contrast effects with very high Radius settings (just as you can with Unsharp Mask), you typically need to match the Radius to the image content to obtain good sharpening. But as you'll see, you need very different Radius settings for the Lens Blur and Motion Blur modes.

We start out by setting the Amount all the way to 500 percent, in Basic mode, while we find the correct Radius setting (see Figure 9-25).

Figure 9-25 Setting the Radius

The unadjusted image

Radius at 1

Radius at 5

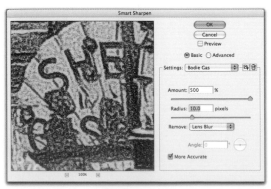

Radius at 10

At a Radius setting of 1, this high-resolution image barely looks different from the unsharpened version, even with the Amount cranked all the way up. At a Radius setting of 5, we see sharpening starting to happen, but it's emphasizing the film grain and the artifacts left by Reduce Noise rather than sharpening the image details. A Radius of 10 matches the image content nicely, though the Amount is obviously now far too high.

We proceed by bringing the Amount down to 50 percent, then we switch to Advanced mode and further soften the Shadow and Highlight contours (see Figure 9-26).

Figure 9-26
Setting the Amount and
Advanced settings

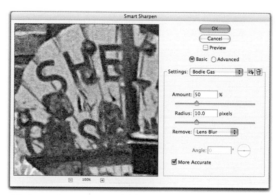

Reducing the Amount to 50 percent eliminates the unnatural-looking halos, but is still stronger than we want.

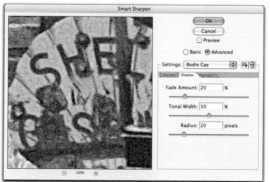

Switching to Advanced mode, we soften the Shadow contour. We set the Radius to 20, which is double the sharpening radius, then set the Tonal Width to 50 percent, and the Fade Amount to 20 percent, producing the result shown at left.

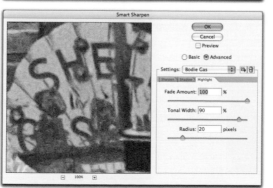

We finish sharpening by setting the Highlight tab. We use the same Radius setting as we did for Shadows, but this time we choose much higher settings for Fade Amount and Tonal Width, to produce the result shown at left.

Figure 9-28
Removing Motion Blur,
continued

The image with the adjustment applied globally

The image with the adjustment masked, then painted in on the fish

For reference, the image before we removed the motion blur—compare it with the one above. The difference is quite subtle, but useful.

Making the filter settings is only part of the process. After running the filter, we applied a solid-black layer mask, then we painted the filter effect into the image where we wanted it. Few if any images benefit from global application of Smart Sharpen in Motion Blur mode and this one is no exception.

In the example in Figure 9-28, we really needed to apply the filter globally, then mask it. But if you can isolate the area that needs the sharpening, you can make things go much faster if you make a rough selection, float the pixels to a new layer (by pressing Command-J), then load the layer's transparency mask as a selection. Loading the selection is key, because if you don't, the filter spends an inordinate amount of time trying to sharpen the transparent areas of the layer. Figure 9-29 shows a case in point.

Figure 9-29
Removing Motion
Blur on details

*We want to sharpen
the detail of the surfer
in this image.*

*We make a rough selection, copy the
pixels to a new layer, load the layer's
transparency as a selection, then run
Smart Sharpen. We start by determining
the radius and angle, above, then work
the controls in the Shadow and
Highlight panels, below.*

*The detail before
sharpening*

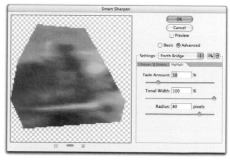

*The detail after
sharpening*

*We complete the process by masking the
layer, then painting the sharpening in by
painting white on the layer mask.*

When we run the filter on the entire layer, it takes *much* longer to execute than when we run it on the selection, even though most of the layer is empty!

Smart Sharpen is an intriguing piece of work that shows great potential, but until it gets a good deal faster and more interactive, we're likely to reserve its use for special cases such as Web or multimedia images, which are small and designed to be viewed on screen, or special cases such as removing motion blur. For most sharpening operations, we can obtain very similar results running Unsharp mask on masked layers set to Luminosity mode, and when we automate the process with actions, it's quite a bit faster than Smart Sharpen.

One final note: Those of you with sharp eyes may have noticed that many of the screen shots of Smart Sharpen use a named setting. It's great that Smart Sharpen lets you save settings, but in practice the mechanism doesn't seem to be at all reliable. If you load a saved setting, change it, and simply run the filter without renaming the saved setting, the new settings overwrite the old ones, so the next time you call up your carefully constructed saved setting, it doesn't contain the values you expect. We suspect that this isn't the intended behavior!

Lens Correction

One more new addition to Photoshop CS2 deserves mention here. While the Lens Correction filter (yes, this feature appears in the Filter menu, too) doesn't do noise reduction or sharpening as such, it does have an impact on detail, especially when it's used to correct chromatic aberration, and also to a lesser extent when you perform perspective corrections.

In our testing so far, it's become clear that Lens Correction should be run before you do any sharpening—you definitely don't want to sharpen the color fringes caused by chromatic aberration, but even the more innocuous-seeming perspective and distortion corrections are better performed before sharpening than afterwards. The relationship to noise reduction is less clear: If pressed we probably have a slight preference for doing noise reduction before running the Lens Correction filter, but if you prefer doing the lens corrections first, we won't quibble.

The Lens Correction filter lets you address barrel and pincushion distortion, chromatic aberration, vignetting, and perspective errors (see Figure 9-30). It's a very powerful tool with what at first glance may seem an overwhelming number of options, but they're arranged in a logical fashion.

Figure 9-30
The Lens Correction filter

Tool palette

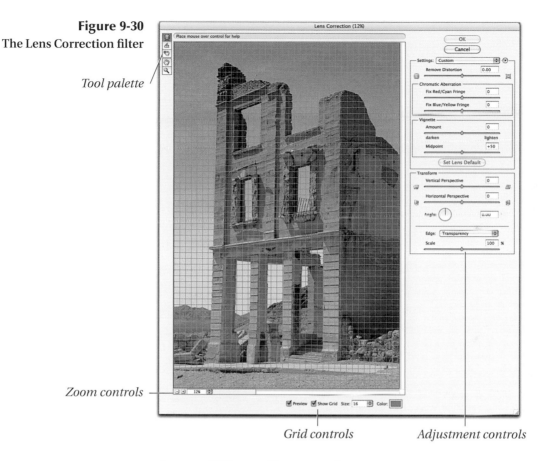

Zoom controls

Grid controls   Adjustment controls

Lens Filter Controls

The Lens Filter controls are arranged in five groups: the Tool palette, the zoom controls, the grid controls, the main control buttons and Settings menu, and the actual filter adjustment controls.

Tool palette. The Tool palette contains five tools. The Remove Distortion tool is rather a blunt instrument—we can make much finer adjustments using the slider control—but we use the Straighten tool to set horizontals or verticals to rotate and straighten the image because it's often easier than typing in an angle. The Move Grid tool lets us adjust the position of the alignment grid, which is particularly useful when adjusting distortion or perspective. But we never choose the Zoom and Hand tools from the palette, preferring to use the keyboard shortcuts—Option to zoom out, Command to zoom in, and spacebar to scroll.

Zoom controls. You can change the preview zoom by pressing the zoom in (+) or zoom out (-) buttons, or by choosing a zoom percentage from the zoom menu. In addition, Command-0 (zero) enlarges the filter dialog box to fill the screen, then zooms the image to fill the preview area, while Command-Option-0 (zero) displays the image at 100 percent view.

Grid controls. The grid controls let you show and hide the grid, and control its size and color. Also in this cluster is the Preview checkbox, which lets you toggle between previewing the adjusted and unadjusted image.

Main control buttons. The OK button commits the changes, and returns you to Photoshop. The Cancel button cancels the changes, and dismisses the filter, returning you to Photoshop. When you click Option, the Cancel button changes to Reset, which resets all the controls to their initial values, undoing any changes you've made, but leaving the filter dialog box open.

The Settings menu lets you choose saved settings that were saved in the filter's Settings folder, while the unlabeled menu immediately to its right lets you load settings saved anywhere on disk, save new settings, or delete settings.

The remainder of the dialog box is devoted to the image preview, and to the filter's meat and potatoes, the adjustments themselves. These are arranged in two groups—Settings and Transform.

Lens Default. The first group contains the Remove Distortion, Chromatic Aberration, and Vignetting corrections, which (for digital captures, at least) you can save as defaults for a specific camera, lens, and focal length by clicking the Lens Default button. Then, when the filter detects other images shot with the same camera, lens, and focal length by reading the image metadata, the Lens Default setting becomes available in the Settings menu, and choosing it applies those settings.

The Transform settings can't be saved as part of the lens default because they depend on the angle between the camera and subject, and hence are image-dependent. You don't have to save Lens Default settings (and unless the image contains the necessary metadata, which means either a digital capture or a very assiduous photographer, you can't), but they can be a huge time-saver. Let's look at the individual adjustments in turn.

Remove Distortion. The Remove Distortion slider lets you remove pin-cushion or barrel distortions, which bow straight lines inward and outward, respectively. Figure 9-31 shows an image before and after correction for moderate barrel distortion.

Figure 9-31
Remove Distortion

The image before we correct for barrel distortion. The wall of the building on the left is slightly bowed outwards.

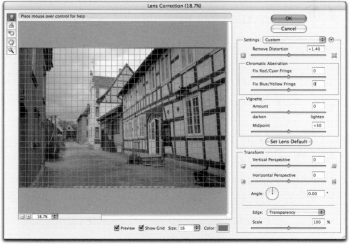

After correction, the wall is straight (though not quite vertical).

The grid is useful for checking barrel distortion, since it makes it easier to detect bowing of straight lines. You can drag the Remove Distortion tool towards or away from the center of the image to correct barrel and pincushion distortion, respectively, but we find it's easier to use the slider. The up and down arrow keys change the value by increments of 0.1; add Shift to change in increments of 1.

Chromatic Aberration. The Chromatic Aberration sliders work by changing the size of the red (for red/cyan fringing) and blue (for blue/yellow fringing) relative to the green channel. With digital raw captures, we prefer to fix chromatic aberration in the Camera Raw plug-in, because that way we only need to do it once, but sometimes we find we need to make different corrections on different parts of the image, and with film scans or JPEG, the Lens Correction filter is the only solution. Figure 9-32 shows a detail of the image before and after chromatic aberration correction.

Chromatic aberration is less common on film scans, though it happens with wide-angle zooms at the short end, But digital capture is brutal at showing the lens flaws that film masks. We see significant chromatic aber-

Figure 9-32
Chromatic aberration
correction

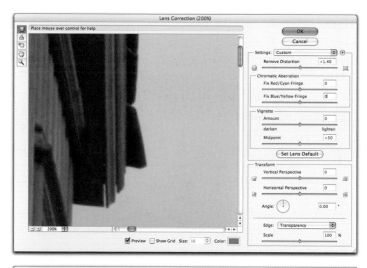

*The uncorrected image
shows color-fringing along
high-contrast edges.*

*After correction, the color
fringing is greatly reduced,
if not entirely eliminated.*

ration on digital captures with zooms shorter than 24 mm. You can go crazy trying to eliminate it entirely, but if you can render it unobjectionable at 200 percent view, you're unlikely to notice it in the final image.

Vignetting. Vignetting, where the lens illuminates the sensor or film plane unevenly, causing darkening in the corners, is most commonly seen when shooting at wide apertures. The Vignetting Amount slider controls the amount of lightening or darkening, while the Vignetting Midpoint slider controls how far from the corners the correction extends—lower values affect more of the image, higher ones confine the correction closer to the corners. Figure 9-33 shows a vignetting correction.

Figure 9-33
Vignetting correction

The uncorrected image shows slight vignetting in the corners.

After correction, the vignetting is eliminated.

The Remove Distortion, Chromatic Aberration, and Vignetting corrections can be saved for a particular camera, lens, and focal length combination. If you plan to do this, test the settings on more than one image—even then, you're likely to have to fine-tune the results for each image.

The Transform controls. The Transform controls are totally image specific. They allow you to reduce the perspective errors caused by tilting the camera, and while they do an impressive job, they don't turn an SLR into a view camera. But they do provide a reasonable substitute for 35 mm tilt/shift lenses. Figure 9-34 shows the image before and after perspective corrections.

Figure 9-34
Perspective correction

The uncorrected image has slanted verticals, and some horizontal perspective problems.

After correction, the perspective errors are greatly reduced.

Edge. When you make Distortion and Perspective corrections, you lose some of the image. The Edge menu lets you deal with the corrected edges, but the Edge Extension option rarely does anything useful, so we usually stick with Transparency. If we need to preserve the aspect ratio, we use the Scale slider to fill the image area (see Figure 9-35). When we want to keep as much of the image as possible, we crop in Photoshop instead.

Figure 9-36 shows the unadjusted image, and the image after lens corrections, noise reduction, and sharpening.

Figure 9-35 Scale

The Scale slider lets us enlarge the image to preserve the aspect ratio.

Figure 9-36 Before and after

Avoiding the Crunchies

The ability to sharpen your images is a powerful tool. Used well, it can give your images the extra snap that makes them jump off the page. Used badly, it gives images the unpleasant "crunchy" look we see in all too many Sunday newspaper color supplements. In overdoses, it can make images look artificial, or even blurry. With that in mind, we leave you with two final pieces of advice.

First, it's better to err on the side of caution. Despite what we've said about output sharpening, an image that's too soft will generally be less disturbing than one that's been oversharpened.

Second, always leave yourself an escape route. One of the great benefits of sharpening on layers is that you can always tweak the layer opacity to strengthen, reduce, or even eliminate the sharpening.

Sharpening is definitely one of those things that improves with experience, and a considerable part of that experience can be gained from revisiting your earlier efforts and figuring out what went wrong. If you save an unsharpened copy, or use layers to do your sharpening, you can always go back and refine your sharpening to get closer to the result you want.

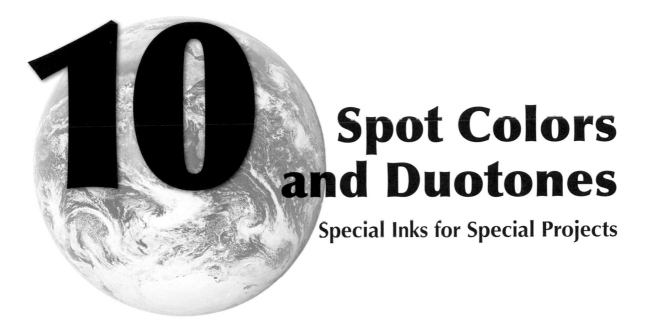

Spot Colors and Duotones

Special Inks for Special Projects

The fundamental problem with most printing presses is that they can only print one color at a time. It's like pixels on a black-and-white screen: The color is either on or off. You may have a gloriously rich full-color image on screen, but you've got to be mighty clever to get that image out the back side of a printing press, and no matter what you do, there will be trade-offs involved.

There are two methods for printing color on a press: spot color and process color. Both can give you a wide variety of colors. But they are hardly interchangeable.

Process color. As we've noted throughout the book, process color is the method of printing a wide range of colors by overlapping halftones (tints) of only four colors: cyan, magenta, yellow, and black. The colors themselves do not mix on paper. Rather, the eye blends these colors together so that ultimately you see the color you're supposed to.

Spot color. If you are printing only a small number of colors (three or fewer), you probably want to use spot colors. The idea behind spot color is that the printing ink is just the right color you want. With spot color, for example, if you want some type colored teal blue, you print it on a plate (often called an *overlay*) that is separate from the black plate. Your

511

commercial printer prints that type using a teal-blue ink—probably a PMS ink—and uses black for the rest of the job.

Because process colors simply cannot simulate some colors—like deep blues, and metallics like gold—spot colors are also used as *bump* plates and varnishes that print alongside or on top of process-color images. For instance, a picture of a fancy car might be printed with the four process colors, plus a spot red to highlight ("bump up") some areas of the car, plus a varnish over the image to make it glossy.

This is relatively easy to print on a six-color press. The hard part has always been building the spot color and varnish plates.

Spot Colors from Photoshop

"How can I print spot colors from Photoshop?" has long been one of the most common questions we hear. Remember that Photoshop was originally designed to do process-color work (or continuous tone RGB output), not spot color overlays. The process of getting spot colors out of Photoshop isn't difficult, though it's not as simple as it should be, even in CS2. There are three ways to do spot-color work in Photoshop:

▶ Use spot-color channels for all the spot-color image information, and save the file in DCS 2.0 or the native Photoshop (PSD) format. This feature lets you place spot colors in specific areas (like in text or in a logo).

▶ Use the Duotone mode. Duotones (or tritones or quadtones) are used to print neutral grayscale images with two or more colors (we'll discuss why you'd want to do this later in this chapter).

▶ Simulate spot colors in CMYK mode. You can use this technique for either duotones or specific-area spot colors.

Tip: Don't Pick Spot Colors. Note that choosing a Pantone (PMS) color from Photoshop's Color Picker and then painting with that color does *not* provide you with a spot-color ink. Rather, as you apply the "spot" color, it's actually being broken up into RGB or CMYK components. We've always felt that it was a particularly cruel joke by the programmers to offer people the chance to see and pick spot colors without also offering the opportunity to print these colors out on spot-color plates.

Tip: Bézier vs. Raster Spot Color. Photoshop can create vector artwork, but it can't yet apply spot colors to vectors, so any spot color you create here is going to be bitmapped. If you need crisp, high-resolution edges (like for text or a logo), you'll probably get a better result creating the spot-color art in a program like QuarkXPress, Adobe InDesign, Illustrator, or Macromedia FreeHand. (See Chapter 3, *Image Essentials*, for more on the difference between bitmapped and vector artwork.)

Spot-Color Channels

When you print color separations of a CMYK file, you get four plates—one plate per channel. So it's logical that if you want a spot color (or varnish or whatever) to print on its own plate, you have to add another channel to your image. Photoshop has a special kind of channel for spot colors called (you guessed it) a *spot channel*. Spot-color channels are, in most respects, identical to normal channels on the Channels palette. The primary difference is that they display on screen looking like spot colors—more or less. To create one of these beasts, select New Spot Channel from the popout menu on the Channels palette (or, faster, Command-click the New Channel button at the bottom of the palette).

The New Spot Channel dialog box offers you three controls for your new spot color: Name, Color, and Solidity (see Figure 10-1).

Name. You should generally leave the naming of the spot color up to Photoshop (it assigns one when you choose a color). The important thing is this: To ensure that your spot color appears on the correct plate when

Figure 10-1 Making a new spot-color channel

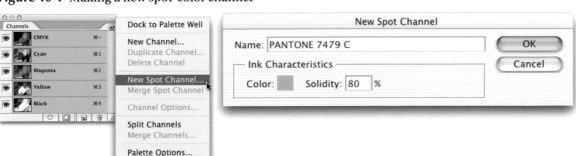

printing from a page-layout program, you must make sure the name of the spot channel matches the name of the same ink in the page-layout program.

Color. You can choose a spot color by clicking on the color swatch and then clicking on a color (if the Color Picker appears, click the Custom button to display the Custom Colors dialog box). The default color model here is Pantone Solid Coated, but you can choose a different swatch book type from the Book popup menu (see Figure 10-2). Curiously, the Book popup menu displays several process-color swatch books (like Trumatch and Focoltone) along with the spot-color swatch books (like Pantone and Toyo), even though the process-color books are meaningless here.

Actually, to be honest, all the colors here are meaningless, because they're used only for screen display. You can pick any color you want (even a regular RGB color, though for technical reasons we strongly encourage you not to spec spot colors using CMYK percentages), and as long as the name is right, it'll print fine. This is handy if you need to create an image even before you know what PMS color you'll be using on press. Just pick a color and name it "My Spot Color" (or whatever). Later, you can either change the name or just tell your printer that this piece of film should be printed with such-and-such a color.

Solidity. The Solidity feature lets you control how opaque the color is on screen (this is similar to the Opacity setting for regular alpha channels).

Figure 10-2
Picking a spot color

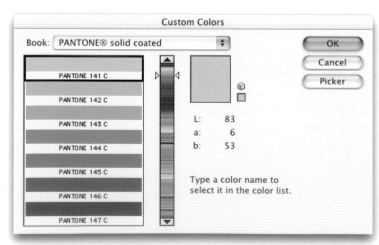

Again, like Color, this only determines your on-screen preview; it has no effect on the final printed image.

Picking the correct Solidity value for a spot color is almost impossible because every spot-color ink has a slightly different opacity, depending on how it was mixed, what colors it's printed over, and so on. In general, metallic inks are almost totally opaque, letterpress inks are usually more opaque than offset inks, and inks that include a good dose of Opaque White in their ingredients are less transparent than those without.

Ultimately, however, you just have to make up a number and move on, knowing that your screen display of the spot color will almost certainly be somewhat inaccurate. We almost always use a value of about 30 percent for spot colors. If we used 100 percent, we might forget that other colors might show through the spot color, causing mottling (see "Building Traps," later in this section). Of course, if the spot color is a varnish, we'd set the Solidity value to zero, because varnishes are almost transparent (here's one place that Solidity is not the same as Opacity—zero-percent Solidity can still be seen).

Applying Spot Colors

Spot-color channels appear on the Channels palette, though some people erroneously look for them on the Layers palette because spot colors always appear on top of the underlying original image. When you first create a spot-color channel, Photoshop automatically selects it for you; so if you start painting, the "ink" appears on this channel and not the RGB or CMYK channels. When you're finished working on the spot-color channel, you must manually switch to the RGB or CMYK channels. (The fastest way to do this is to press Command-~. That's the tilde character.)

Annoyingly, because spot colors appear on their own special channel, you cannot use the Layers feature with spot colors. In fact, even if you use the Type tool to place text on your spot-color channel, the text is automatically rendered and dropped into the channel, not on a layer. (You can still move it and adjust its mode and opacity by choosing Fade from the Filter menu while it's selected, but once you deselect it, it's rendered onto the layer.)

Remember that when you're painting on a spot-color channel, you're always painting in black, white, or gray, even when it looks like you're painting in color. Black is solid spot color; white is no ink at all; and gray is a tint of the spot color.

By the way, you can always change the spot-color channel's settings by double-clicking on its tile in the Channels palette.

Tip: Converting a Layer to a Spot-Color Channel. David finds the inability to use spot colors on layers frustrating at best (it's like going back to the Photoshop 2.x days). So he'll often lay out his spot colors on one or more layers first, using black rather than a color. Then this trick converts the layers into spot colors.

1. Load the "spot color" layer's transparency mask as a selection by Command-clicking on the layer's thumbnail image in the Layers palette.

2. Hide the layer (by turning off the Layer's visibility eyeball), or delete it if you don't think you'll need it again.

3. In the Channels palette, create a new spot channel, or select one you've already made. If you created a new spot channel, you're done; skip the next step.

4. If you picked a premade spot channel, fill the selection with black (usually the foreground color is black, so you can just press Option-Delete).

That's it! The information that was on the layer is now on your spot-color channel.

Tip: Converting Alpha Channels to Spots. If you find yourself wanting to convert a regular alpha channel into a spot-color channel, don't panic; just open the Channel Options dialog box by double-clicking the channel's tile (the little thumbnail preview, not the name of the channel). There you can select the Spot Color radio button. When you click OK, the channel is changed.

Tip: Building Bump Plates. Putting text or basic shapes on a spot-color channel is relatively easy. Creating quality bump plates for scanned images is much harder. One method is to use the Color Range feature (under the Select menu) to select the kinds of colors you're trying to enhance. For instance, if you're trying to bump up the color in a shiny red bicycle, you might use Color Range to select the reds in an image. When you create a spot-color channel after making your selection, Photoshop automatically converts the selection into spot color (the fully selected parts become solid spot color, and so on).

If you need to create a lot of bump plates or you need better precision, you might consider using The Imaging Factory's Color Correction Pro or Aurelon's CoCo plug-in, both of which let you build high-quality spot-color bump plates with better results than the one built into Photoshop.

Merge Spot Channel. Photoshop also lets you convert your spot-color channel into its RGB or CMYK color equivalents (choose Merge Spot Channel from the popout menu on the Channels palette). Generally, you only need to do this when sending an on-screen comp to a client or putting the image on the Web. (Make sure you save a backup of your file first!) Note that the Photoshop documentation implies that you have to merge spot colors before printing to a color printer, but this isn't necessarily true. Just make sure you choose Let Photoshop Determine Colors from the Color Handling popup menu in the Print with Preview dialog box; that way, Photoshop simulates the spot colors in the RGB it sends to the printer.

Knocking Out vs. Overprinting

As we said earlier, spot-color inks are rarely fully opaque, so if you try to print a solid PMS ink on top of your CMYK image, it'll probably look mottled. What's more, it may result in too much ink on the page, causing troubles at print time.

To avoid these overprinting problems, you'll need to manually knock out the parts of your image that lie underneath the spot colors. This knocking-out process is taken care of for you in other programs, such as when you place spot-color type over an image in QuarkXPress, Adobe InDesign, or PageMaker. Here's one way to do this in Photoshop. (Of course, if you're using a spot color as a bump plate or a varnish then you *don't* want to knock out the image behind it.)

1. Load the spot-color channel as a selection. (You can use Load Selection if you want, but we find it faster simply to Command-click on the spot-color channel's tile in the Channels palette.) You can now control color trapping by choking or spreading the selection (see the next section for more on this technique).

2. Create a new layer in the Layers palette.

3. Use the Fill command on the Edit menu to fill the selection on this new layer with white. (It may not look like much has changed, because the spot color is probably still overlapping the area you just filled with white. Try turning off the visibility of the spot-color channel to see the knocked-out area below.)

Creating a new layer is optional—you could just fill the background image with white—but we find it more flexible to knock out the portions of the image with a layer, just in case you have to make a change later. Of course, you'll still have to flatten the file when you save it in the DCS 2.0 format.

On the other hand, if you have two spot colors that overlap, and you want one to knock out the other, you won't be able to use this layer trick (because spot colors always sit on top of layers). In this case, you have to fill the selection with white on the lower spot-color channel.

Building Traps

There's only one problem with the knock-out steps outlined above: They don't take trapping into account. Trapping compensates for the slight paper misregistration that is inevitable on a printing press. For instance, if a cyan box abuts a magenta box, but the paper is slightly misregistered when the magenta plate is printed, there'll be a white sliver between the cyan and the magenta (see Figure 10-3).

Scanned images generally don't need trapping because there are gradual transitions between colors. For example, if you scanned a picture of a cyan box and a magenta box, the edge between the two would actually be made up of both cyan and magenta, creating a natural trap. If one plate misregisters, there's still enough overlap to avoid a white gap.

As soon as you knock out the background behind a spot color, however, you'll almost certainly need to think about trapping. There are three methods of trapping spot colors in Photoshop: choking the background, spreading the spot color, and the Trap feature.

Choking the background. The general rule of trapping is to spread the lighter color so that it slightly overlaps the darker color. If the spot color is dark, you can effectively spread the background colors "into" the spot color by making the area that you knock out (set to white) smaller. After loading the spot-color channel as a selection in the last step-by-step

Figure 10-3
Trapping colors

The image looks great on screen...   *...but if the press misregisters, an ugly gap appears.*   *A trap ensures that misregistration won't cause problems.*

 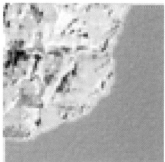

Scanned images rarely need trapping because shared colors usually mask press misregistration.

instruction, choose Contract from the Modify submenu (under the Select menu). A value of 1 pixel chokes the selection (shrinks it) by a single pixel, which is enough for most trapping problems. (A single pixel is about .25 point—.0033 inch—in a 300-ppi image.)

As it turns out, we often find ourselves using this method even when the spot color is lighter, especially when the spot-color channel contains type or other fine detail.

Spreading the spot color. If the spot color is lighter, you can spread it (make it bigger) so that it slightly overlaps the background. One way to do this is to select the channel in the Channels palette and choose the Minimum filter from the Other submenu on the Filters menu. Minimum spreads the image on a channel (makes it bigger), so that it slightly over-laps whatever is behind it. Again, a one-pixel value here should work well for most images. (Some printing processes—such as newsprint—require larger traps.) Watch out for muddying up the fine detail on the spot-color channel with this process, however.

Trap. While the previous technique works pretty well when you're trapping a spot color that is completely surrounded by other colors (because it spreads everything on the spot-color plate), it's not as effective when the spot color only partially overlaps another color. The Trap feature (under the Image menu; see Figure 10-4) lets you build some basic trapping between channels in your image, and traps only where two or more colors intersect.

To trap one spot-color channel, make sure both the background image and the spot-color channel are visible, but select the spot-color channel in the palette. To trap two channels, select them both (you can select multiple channels with the Shift key).

The Trap feature lets you specify a trap in millimeters, points, or pixels. Unfortunately, Photoshop currently seems to have some trouble interpreting these values, so you'll probably need to specify a trap significantly larger than your printer prescribes. For instance, a .25-point trap doesn't have any effect at all on most images; you need to use a value of 1 point to get even a negligible trap. Note that if you enter a value that's too small, Photoshop won't perform any trapping at all (it's as though you didn't even use the feature), so you should always check to make sure some trapping really occurred.

(To be honest, while we find the Trap feature occasionally useful, we use the "choking the background" method the most.)

Figure 10-4
Trap

Saving Images with Spot Colors

While we're going to hold off providing details about the various graphic file formats until Chapter 13, *Image Storage and Output*, when it comes to saving images that contain spot-color channels, the choice is currently pretty simple. If you're going to import the graphic into QuarkXPress, you should save it in the DCS 2.0 format. For Adobe InDesign CS or CS2, you can use either DCS 2.0 or the native Photoshop (.psd) file format. The PDF format should also work in most cases. In the future, we may have versions of XPress and InDesign that are able to better handle TIFF or PDF files containing spot colors, but at the time of this writing, it's safest to avoid them. We *do* know people who have made these formats work, but we know a greater or equal number who have not. DCS 2.0, however, is a sure thing.

Screen angles. When you print two colors on top of each other, and the colors are tinted, each halftone screen has to have a different angle or else you'll end up with distracting moiré patterns. (See Chapter 13, *Image Storage and Output*, for more on halftone screens and how to set them.) If your spot colors are solid (100 percent), then you don't have to worry about screen angles. If your spot colors are tinted but they don't overlap any other colors, you don't have to worry about it. But you'd better pay attention if you place 50 percent of some Pantone color on top of 20-percent black, or if you're building a spot-color bump plate to enhance a color in your image.

You can set the halftone screen angles in Photoshop (in the Print with Preview dialog box) or in your page-layout program. Generally speaking, halftone angles should sit either 45 or 30 degrees apart. (For more information, see the discussion on screen angles in "Saving and Outputting," later in this chapter.)

In the case of bump plates, all the available angles are typically taken up by the cyan, yellow, magenta, and black inks. You can either print the image with stochastic screens, or match the bump plate to one of the process-color inks. It's generally safe to match it to the closest color. For example, if you're printing a bright-red bump plate over a dull-red process-color image, you can probably get away with matching the bump plate's angle to the magenta screen (often 75 degrees). The two colors are similar enough, and the percentage of tint is high enough (almost solid) that you probably won't have any patterning.

Figure 10-5 Fake versus real duotones

Just dropping a flat magenta tint behind this grayscale image does little to enhance it.
Adjusting the curves for the two inks adds tonal range and depth.

The original grayscale   *Fake duotone*   *Real duotone*

In most color modes, each pixel's color is described with multiple channels—CMYK color is made of four channels, RGB is made of three. Multitones are different. In a multitone image, Photoshop saves a single grayscale image along with two or more curves—one for each color plate. These curves are just like those in the Curves and Transfer Function dialog boxes (see Figure 10-6). Note that you can only create a duotone from an 8-bit-per-channel grayscale image. (If you've got a color image, see "The Color of Grayscale" in Chapter 12, *Essential Image Techniques.)*

Because you're typically replacing a single gray level with two or more tints of ink, you almost always need to adjust the amounts of ink used by each channel. Otherwise, the image appears too dark and muddy (see Figure 10-7). For instance, if you replace a 50-percent black pixel with 50-percent black and 50-percent purple, it appears much darker. Instead, replacing that 50-percent black with something like 30-percent black and 25-percent purple maintains the tone of that pixel. On the other hand, if the second color were much lighter, like yellow, you'd need much more ink to maintain the tone. You might, for example, use 35-percent black and 55-percent yellow.

The duotone curves give you the ability to make these sorts of tonal adjustments quickly and with a minimum of image degradation because applying a duotone curve *never* affects the underlying grayscale image data. You can make 40 changes to the duotone colors or the curves and never lose the underlying image quality.

Note that we say the "underlying image quality" won't suffer. We're not saying that you can go hog-wild with the curves, and your final image will always look good. Far from it. In fact, duotones, tritones, and quadtones

Figure 10-6
Duotone curves

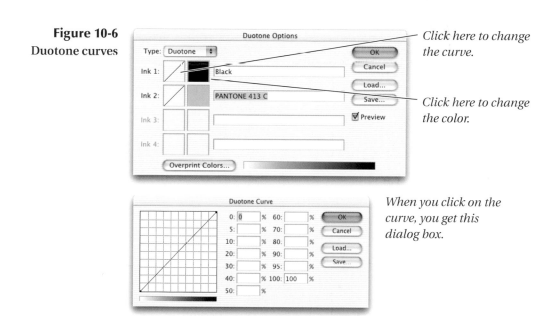

Click here to change the curve.

Click here to change the color.

When you click on the curve, you get this dialog box.

Figure 10-7 Adjusting multitone curves

The three inks are way too heavy, darkening the image considerably and obscuring shadow detail (far left).

These curves complement each other, maintaining and enhancing the tone of the grayscale image (left).

are often very sensitive and can quickly succumb to "lookus badus maximus." But the image data saved on disk is unchanged by adjusting these curves; they're like filters that are applied to the image data, but only when you view it on screen or print it out.

Tip: Use Stephen's Curves. Unless you really know what you're doing, just use the duotone curve sets built by photographer Stephen Johnson that ship with Photoshop. We almost never create a multitone image from scratch. Instead, we click the Load button in the Duotone dialog box, navigate to the Duotones folder (inside the Presets folder in the Adobe Photoshop folder), and pick one from there. Then we make small tweaks to the curves, depending on the image.

Most of the curves come in sets of four.

▶ The first and second colorize the image (the first does so more than the second).

▶ The third curve of the set affects the midtones and three-quarter tones primarily, and does very little to the highlights. The effect is to warm or cool the image significantly without colorizing it much.

▶ The final duotone curve makes the image slightly warmer or cooler (still mostly neutral), primarily affecting the three-quarter tones.

If we're using a Pantone color that's not included in the canned presets, we usually pick a canned set for a color that has similar brightness to the one we're using, and replace the color with ours. Then, depending on the two colors' tones, we adjust the curves accordingly.

Tip: Checking Each Duotone Channel. The biggest hassle with images in Duotone mode is that you can't see each channel by itself. If you make a tonal adjustment to an RGB or CMYK image, you can always go and see what that did to each channel. With a duotone, however, you're in the dark. Here's one way out: Convert the image to Multichannel mode.

While you're in Multichannel mode, you can view each channel of the multitone image. The first channel corresponds to the first ink, the second to the second ink, and so on. When you're done playing voyeur, select Undo (Command-Z), and you're back where you started.

Adjusting Screen Colors

No one is more aware than Adobe that colors on screen may not match colors on paper. Adobe tech support gets calls all the time from people screaming that they followed the manual's directions, but their images are always different from what they see on the screen.

Calibrating your system and adjusting your monitor is one way to get results that more closely match your display. But the Color Settings dialog box is really only designed to handle process-color printing and RGB monitors. Duotones, on the other hand, are often printed with spot-color inks such as Pantone or Toyo.

Fortunately, Photoshop not only lets you pick custom spot colors in the Color Picker (click the Color Libraries button), it also lets you adjust how they appear on screen. This is crucial for duotone work, where you want your monitor display to be as accurate as possible.

Note that your monitor simply cannot display many spot colors (including metallic and fluorescent inks) accurately, or even closely. If you want to produce metallic duotones, you have to use a great deal of imagination. A custom proof such as DuPont's Cromalin is a good idea, too.

Adjusting Colors

While Photoshop does a reasonably good job of representing spot colors on screen, we find that we occasionally want to make adjustments so that what we see on screen is closer to what we see in our swatch book. Once you've selected a spot color from the Color Picker's Custom dialog box, click the Picker button (see Figure 10-8). You can now adjust the RGB, HSB, or Lab values for that color to make it appear closer to your printed swatch.

If you use a spectrophotometer, such as X-Rite's Digital Swatchbook, you can read the Lab values directly from your printed swatch and type those into the Picker's Lab fields. However, if your screen isn't calibrated, then this representation may look even worse than Photoshop's.

Don't adjust the color's CMYK values, however. As soon as you change one value here, Photoshop assumes you want to adhere to the process-color gamut (not necessary for spot colors). For instance, if you adjust the color of a rich blue such as PMS 2738, making even a one-percent change to the CMYK values makes Photoshop snap the color to a pale imitation

Figure 10-8 The Color Picker and Custom Color dialog boxes

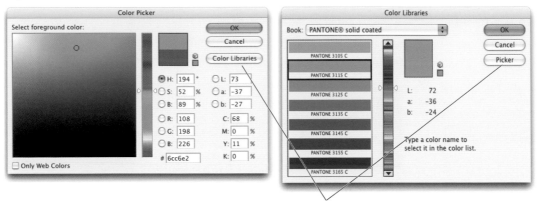

You can toggle between these two dialog boxes by clicking here.

of the blue. (It's in gamut, but who cares? This is for screen representation only; the real color will appear only when ink hits paper.)

Then, if you switch back to the Custom Color dialog box, Photoshop finds the closest match to this new, blah color: PMS 653. Again, it's just for on-screen display, but we're trying to get as close as we can.

Overprint Colors

Once you've told Photoshop how you want each of your colors to display individually in the multitone, you need to tell it how you want the colors to look when printed on top of each other. Duotones are easy, because most duotones are printed with black and another color. Overprinting these two colors results in a darker, richer black, but it's black nonetheless. Unfortunately, Photoshop won't distinguish between the two blacks.

However, when you add more colors to the image (as in a tritone or a quadtone), or don't use black in the mix, telling Photoshop how to display the overprinted colors becomes significantly more important. To set the overprint color, click the Overprint button in the Duotone dialog box (see Figure 10-9).

The basic advice for the Overprint dialog box is to leave it alone unless you have a printed sample of what the overprinted colors *should* look like, or you're really certain that Photoshop has built it wrong.

On the other hand, with some cajoling (and perhaps a pint of Häagen-Dazs sorbet or, for really big favors, Laphroiag), you can often get your printer to "draw down" a sample of the two colors overprinting. Place that under a 5,000-degree Kelvin light, and adjust away. Or, if you're using Pan-

Figure 10-9
Setting the
overprint color

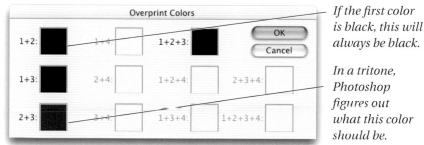

If the first color is black, this will always be black.

In a tritone, Photoshop figures out what this color should be.

tone inks, you may want to purchase the Pantone Tint Effects Color Suite, which shows various tint builds of Pantone inks, including 100-percent overprints (which is the relevant swatch here).

Changing the overprint colors has no effect on your printed output. It only affects how the colors appear on screen. It does affect mode changes, however; if you switch from Duotone mode directly to CMYK, RGB, or Lab, the overprint colors are taken into consideration. However, this conversion would be a silly thing to do unless you're printing to a color printer (see "Printing Proofs of Spot-Color Images," later in this chapter).

Setting Curves

Once you've specified the colors you want in your multitone image and adjusted the tonal range of the grayscale image, it's time to start adjusting your multitone curves. If you followed our advice in "Tip: Use Stephen's Curves," you may have already loaded a curve set that's somewhat appropriate for your image. However, we'd like to emphasize that every image (and every spot-color ink) is different, so your curves probably need some kind of tweaking. Whether or not you go through the trouble is up to you, but here are some things to think about if you want to give it a go.

Expanding Highlights and Shadows

There are two ways in which you can expand your tonal range with multitones: focusing inks and using ink tones.

Focusing inks. You can focus an ink plate on a particular area of the tonal scale by increasing the contrast in that area. Let's say you want to increase the detail in the shadows. From Chapter 6, *Image Adjustment Fundamen-*

tals, you know that you need to increase the slope of the tonal curve in the shadow areas. However, that means you have to decrease the slope (and therefore the contrast) in the highlights, so you lose detail there.

With one ink, that could be an unacceptable trade-off. But with two or more inks, you can use one to focus on the shadows—increasing the contrast there and bringing out detail—and use another to focus on the highlight detail (see Figure 10-10). When the page comes off press, you have greater detail in both areas. This is one methodology behind double-black duotones (where you print with black ink twice).

Tip: Save and Load Curves. As we said earlier, it's a hassle not being able to see how each "channel" of the image changes as you adjust its curve. This is especially frustrating to new users who have a difficult time picturing what the curves are doing without the visual feedback. Whether you're a beginner or a seasoned pro, you may find this technique useful.

1. Duplicate the image. (Remember that if you hold down the Option key while selecting Duplicate from the Image menu, Photoshop won't bother you with a superfluous dialog box.)

2. If the duplicate image isn't already in Grayscale mode, select Grayscale from the Mode menu. This simply throws away the duotone curves. It doesn't affect the image data.

3. Use Curves (Command-M) to create the curve you're trying to achieve for the duotone ink. You can use Preview or any of the other curve tricks we talk about in Chapter 6, *Image Adjustment Fundamentals*. You cannot, however, use arbitrary maps (curves made with the Pencil tool). Duotones don't understand those at all.

4. Save the curve to disk, then click OK or Cancel in the Curves dialog box. (It doesn't matter at this point; we usually cancel to save time.)

5. Switch back to the duotone image, open the Duotone dialog box (by selecting Duotone from the Mode menu again), and load the curve you've made into the ink's Curves dialog box.

If the curve you've made isn't quite right, you can always adjust it in the duotone image; or if you want to get visual about it, go back and load the curve into the grayscale image's Curves dialog box again.

Figure 10-10 Focusing inks on different tonal ranges

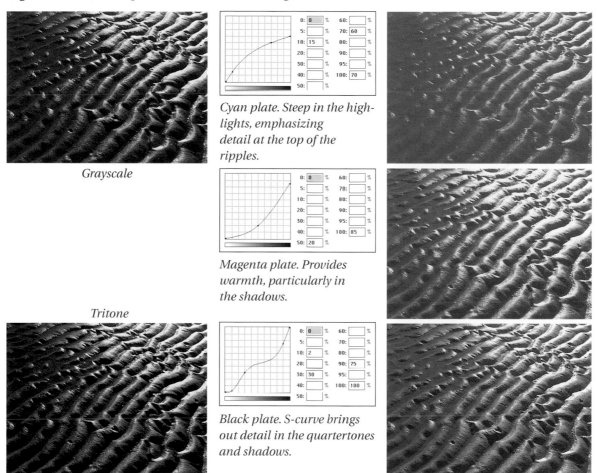

Grayscale

Cyan plate. Steep in the highlights, emphasizing
detail at the top of the
ripples.

Magenta plate. Provides
warmth, particularly in
the shadows.

Tritone

Black plate. S-curve brings
out detail in the quartertones
and shadows.

Ink tones. The second method of expanding your image's tonal range, ink tones, is almost always performed in conjunction with the first method, focusing inks. As we said earlier in the chapter, by printing with a gray ink along with black you immediately expand the tonal range, because a tint of gray is lighter than a tint of black; plus, gray printed over black is darker than black alone. Therefore, you can affect the tone of your image by picking appropriate second, third, and fourth colors.

For instance, printing with two dark colors may make less sense than printing with a dark and a light color. If you're printing with three colors, you may want to use black plus a lighter gray (to extend the highlights) plus a darker color (to enrich the shadows).

Curves Is Curves

If you're wondering about the difference between Duotone curves and regular curves (and transfer curves), the answer is: There's hardly any difference at all. It's mostly a matter of when the corrections are applied to the image.

When you use the Curves dialog box, the image data is affected immediately; you're actually changing the image. Curves also lets you use arbitrary maps (a fancy way of saying that you can draw a line with the Pencil tool).

Curves that you create in Duotone mode, on the other hand, don't get applied until you print the image. In fact, Photoshop just saves the grayscale image plus the curves. When you print, each curve is sent down along with the image data in the form of a transfer function. So you can always go back and change the curves without degrading the image.

Duotone curves have their pros and cons, though. You can't preview how a single channel changes as you move the curve; you can't even see how the mix of curves and inks looks on your image until you click OK in the Duotone dialog box. On the other hand, the Duotone Curves dialog box has an excellent feature: You can type in values instead of simply clicking on the curve. This is especially handy when it comes to targeting by compressing the tonal range.

Because a curve is a curve, you can save a curve from one dialog box and load it into another (see "Save the Curves" in Chapter 6, *Image Adjustment Fundamentals*). But you can't load curves with arbitrary maps into the Duotone or Transfer dialog box.

Creating the Curves

To ensure tonal consistency throughout the image, you need to think carefully about adjusting curves for each ink, depending on their relative tones. For example, let's say you're printing with black plus a PMS ink, Warm Gray 6 (which we can't show you, since we only have process inks to work with).

▶ The black is going to make up the skeleton of the image, with a lot of contrast in the shadows. To do this, we pull the black entirely out of the extreme highlights by setting the 5-percent field to zero. Then we compress the tonal range of the image slightly by setting the 100-percent black to 94 (that way, no pixels become totally black). Finally, to add even more contrast, we pull the 70-percent value down to 45.

▶ The warm gray will be the flesh of the image, holding the contrast in the midtones, and especially focusing on the highlights. To do this, we're going to boost the contrast in the highlights by raising the curve from 5 percent up to 9 percent. Next, we'll lower the 100-percent mark to 90 percent, so that the shadows don't get too dark when both inks print on top of each other. Finally, the curve in the highlights and midtones is steep, but we want it even steeper, so we'll raise the 50-percent mark to 75 percent.

While these adjustments flatten out the contrast in the shadows, we don't care, because the details there are handled by the black ink.

Note that this example is only that—an example. Change the ink, and you had better change the curve. Change one curve, and you had better change the other. Most of all, the curves you make and use must be dependent on the image you have, the data that makes up the image, and what you want to do with that data. Again, every image is different; so you should tailor the curves to bring out the detail where you want it most. (Fortunately, you can preview your duotone image as you adjust its colors and curves with the dialog box still open, making it easier to get it right the first time.)

The Info Palette

When we work on multitone images, we like to set up the Info palette so that the First Color Readout is Actual Color. This way, we can always see how much ink is being laid down in an area (see Figure 10-11). Then we set the Second Color Readout to Grayscale, which tells us what the original underlying grayscale data is. Finally, we set the Mouse Coordinates in the Info palette to Pixels (so that we can easily refer back to the same pixel coordinate if we need to).

Figure 10-11
The Info palette
for duotones

The Info palette shows how much ink is in each channel.

Tip: Make Gray Wedges Match. One of the most complicated challenges of creating multitone curves is maintaining the overall tone of the image while attempting to expand its tonal range. One method we use while adjusting multitone curves is to work with a gray wedge.

1.   Create a new grayscale document as wide as your duotone image and perhaps an inch or so tall.

Figure 10-13 Boosting depth by adding gray

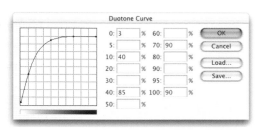

This curve can add depth to, or colorize, the entire image. (Of course, this strange-looking plate would be printed with a light color under black, so it wouldn't look so harsh.)

Original image   *After the curve is applied*

Figure 10-14 Adding ink in the highlights
It's usually better to extend an ink through the tonal range (top and left), rather than restricting it (bottom and right).

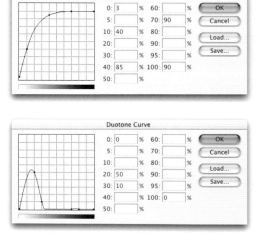

Compressing Tones for Targeting

There's no doubt that printing presses have difficulty printing extreme highlights or shadows—the tiny halftone spots disappear to white, and the white areas in the shadows fill in, resulting in solid ink. This is the reason we're so adamant about compressing the tonal range of your images so that all the gray values and details appear in a range that can successfully print on press (see "White Points and Black Points and Grays, Oh My!" in Chapter 6, *Image Adjustment Fundamentals*).

Nonetheless, one of the goals of multitone images is to expand the tonal range and recapture some of that highlight and shadow detail lost in the horrors of the printing process. If you compress the image data significantly before you start adjusting duotone curves, you've simply lost your chance to bring out those details.

We suggest avoiding the targeting step during tonal correction, and instead using the duotone curves to compress the data (see Figure 10-15 and Figure 10-16).

Figure 10-15
Examples of curves for
compressing data

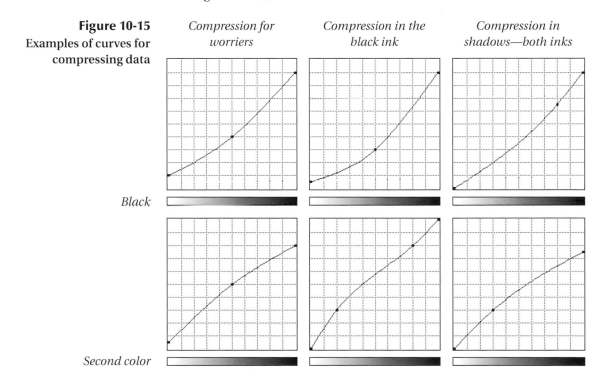

Compression for worriers

Compression in the black ink

Compression in shadows—both inks

Black

Second color

Turning Grayscale to Color

We've been exploring how to create multitones using the Duotone mode. But just because you want a multitone doesn't mean that you need to use the Duotone mode to get it. In fact, you can often get just as good results by manipulating the grayscale image in either the Multichannel mode or the CMYK mode. There are, however, pros and cons to each technique.

Figure 10-16 Creating curves for duotone and tritone images

By focusing inks on different tonal ranges, you can colorize a grayscale image, and emphasize otherwise-hidden details. The tables show the values entered in the Duotone Curves dialog box.

Cool neutral, details held with black

	20	50	70	100
Cyan	–	15	60	–
Black	10	–	60	–

Cyan holds highlights, magenta holds shadows.

	20	50	70	100
Cyan	36	67	–	–
Magenta	–	33	–	90

Cyan and yellow in the midtones, black elsewhere

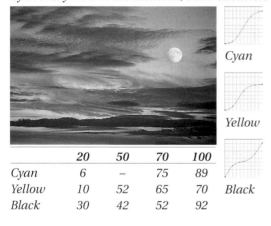

	20	50	70	100
Cyan	6	–	75	89
Yellow	10	52	65	70
Black	30	42	52	92

Magenta and yellow emphasize the shadows.

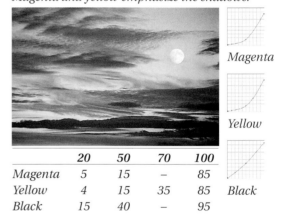

	20	50	70	100
Magenta	5	15	–	85
Yellow	4	15	35	85
Black	15	40	–	95

Magenta and yellow carry the highlights.

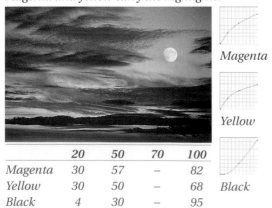

	20	50	70	100
Magenta	30	57	–	82
Yellow	30	50	–	68
Black	4	30	–	95

Cyan for the highlights, black for the shadows

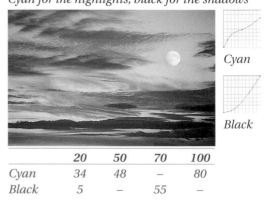

	20	50	70	100
Cyan	34	48	–	80
Black	5	–	55	–

▶ **File size.** An image in Duotone mode, whatever the number of inks, is saved as an 8-bit grayscale image along with curves. CMYK images, then, are four times the size, because each pixel is described with 32 bits of information, even if you're using only two channels. Similarly, a two-channel multichannel file is twice as large as a duotone.

▶ **Single-color areas.** In Duotone mode, there's almost no way to create a single area in which only one color is present. For example, it's a pain to make a 20-percent blue square in the middle of an image, without black also printing in it. However, this is easy to do in any other mode.

▶ **Blends.** There's also no way to create a gradient blend between two spot colors while in Duotone mode. In CMYK mode, it's easy.

▶ **Outputting images.** When you output a multitone image, the mode it's in may have an impact on your output process. For instance, you probably cannot transfer an image in Duotone mode to a high-end imaging system. Also, because duotone images must be saved in an EPS or PSD format (see "Saving and Outputting," later in this chapter), you cannot take advantage of any tricks your page-layout software may be able to do with TIFF images (see Chapter 13, *Image Storage and Output*).

▶ **Adjusting tone.** In Duotone mode, you can always change the duotone curves without affecting the underlying grayscale image data. That means you can quickly repurpose the image to a number of different output devices. Or, if your art director decides to print with green instead of yellow ink, you can quickly change the tonal curve to adjust for the difference in ink density.

   On the other hand, if you're creating multitones in CMYK mode, you may be changing the image data in each channel, so you want to minimize the number of adjustments you make to avoid image degradation (or use adjustment layers). Working in CMYK mode, however, gives you the chance to actually see (interactively) how your curves are affecting the image data. And you can use features like the white-and-black-point clipping display in Levels to make decisions about your curves. This can be very helpful, especially when making small tweaks to the curves (see Figure 10-17).

▶ **Screen representation.** Photoshop knows how to represent most spot colors reasonably well on screen when you're in Duotone mode. How-

Figure 10-17 Grayscale reproduction with the four process inks

The grayscale image

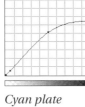

Cyan plate

Yellow plate

Magenta plate

Black plate

Printed using the four process inks

ever, if you're creating spot-color multitones rather than process-color multitones in CMYK mode, you'll either have to ignore the colors you see on the screen (which are RGB representations of CMYK colors) or look ahead in the chapter to "Simulating Spot Colors in CMYK."

Converting Grayscale Images to Color

Because a multitone image typically represents a grayscale image using color, you generally begin with a grayscale image. (If you've got a color image, see "The Color of Grayscale" in Chapter 12, *Essential Image Techniques*, for more on how to convert it to grayscale.) In this section we're discussing using CMYK to create duotones, so you'll want to switch your image from Grayscale mode to CMYK mode. You can use two methods—simple conversion, or copying into a new file.

Simple conversion. You can simply switch your image from grayscale to CMYK using the Mode menu. However, many people seem to think that this simply adds three new channels (cyan, magenta, and yellow), and leaves all the grayscale information in the black channel. Not so. Photoshop uses the color settings preferences (see Chapter 5, *Color Settings*) to convert the neutral grays into colors. The amount of black generation (based on the profile or Custom CMYK setting you've selected in Color Settings for CMYK) determines what appears in the Black channel.

You can use Custom CMYK as an equivalent to creating a quadtone using the Duotone dialog box. We rarely use this method; it's clunky and nigh-on impossible to make adjustments to each plate after the conversion. Plus, Photoshop's separation curves are not designed to expand the tonal range of a grayscale image, so you're losing the opportunity to enhance your image.

Nonetheless, if you *do* use this method, we strongly suggest you set Black Generation to Heavy in the Custom CMYK dialog box first. That way, the black channel contains more information, and small anomalies on press won't result in large color shifts.

The multichannel step. A second, more reasonable, way to convert your grayscale image into CMYK form is to convert the file to a Multichannel document first.

1.   Duplicate your image (select Duplicate from the Image menu).

2. Select Multichannel from the Mode submenu (under the Image menu). Notice that the Grayscale channel in the Channels palette has changed to "Black."

3. Duplicate the Black channel three times by dragging it on top of the New Channel button in the Channels palette. You should end up with four identical channels.

4. Finally, select CMYK from the Mode submenu. Photoshop assigns each channel to one of the colors (the first channel becomes cyan, the second channel is magenta, and so on).

Now it's time to start adjusting curves for each of the channels. This is a tricky proposition because, as we pointed out back in Chapter 6, *Image Adjustment Fundamentals*, you typically don't want to make tonal adjustments to a channel more than once or twice. You can work around this by using a Curves adjustment layer to tune the curves, and then flattening the image when the curves are the way you want them (see Figure 10-18).

Figure 10-18
Creating a tritone with
an adjustment layer

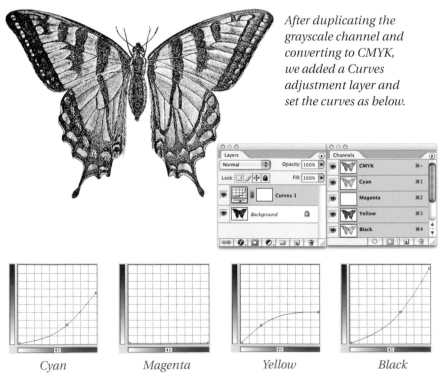

After duplicating the grayscale channel and converting to CMYK, we added a Curves adjustment layer and set the curves as below.

Cyan   Magenta   Yellow   Black

Simulating Spot Colors in CMYK

If you've decided to create or adjust your multitone in CMYK mode, you'll likely want to see a reasonable representation of the image on your screen. If the image is a process-color multitone, this isn't a problem at all. But if you're using one or more spot colors, Photoshop balks at the proposal—it thinks only in cyan, magenta, yellow, and black.

Fortunately, you can change Photoshop's thinking by creating a custom profile with your own definitions of CMYK, by choosing Custom CMYK from the CMYK working space menu in the Color Settings dialog box. As we discussed back in Chapter 5, *Color Settings*, Photoshop knows what color inks you're using by the ink set you've chosen from the Ink Colors menu in the Custom CMYK dialog box.

Here's how you can change these values to simulate spot colors and get a reasonably good on-screen representation of your image.

1. Find the Lab values for the inks you'll be printing with. (If you've already picked a Pantone or other spot color in the Duotone dialog box, click on the color swatch there. If you haven't picked one yet, you can find one by opening the Color Picker, clicking Custom, then clicking the Picker button to go back to the Color Picker.)

2. Note the Lab values for the color. (Yes, you have to write them down.)

3. Open Color Settings (Command-Shift-K) and choose Custom CMYK from the CMYK working space popup menu. Next, choose Custom from the Ink Colors popup menu (see Figure 10-19).

4. Click on the cyan color swatch and type in the Lab values for the spot color you chose. (If you have precise Lab or xyY values from a spectro-photometer, you can skip clicking on the color swatch and simply turn on the Lab Coordinates checkbox.) We suggest turning on the Estimate Overprints checkbox so you don't have to specify values for C+Y, C+M, and so on; this won't guarantee that the screen color will be any better, but other than using a spectrophotometer on an ink drawdown, it's about as good as it's going to get.

    Click OK to save the ink settings (or, if your image is a tritone or quadtone, change those inks first), then click OK again to close the

Figure 10-19

CMYK Setup and Ink
Colors dialog boxes

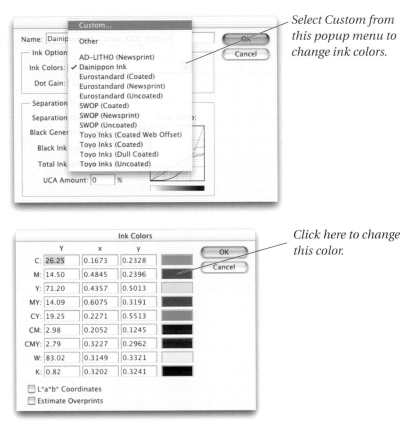

*Select Custom from
this popup menu to
change ink colors.*

*Click here to change
this color.*

Custom CMYK dialog box. If you want to save your custom settings
as an ICC profile, see "Tip: Creating ICC Profiles from Custom CMYK
Settings" in Chapter 5, *Color Settings.*

Photoshop now thinks of cyan as the spot color. However, if your image
already has an embedded profile, you'll have to select Assign Profile (from
the Edit menu) and choose either "Don't Color Manage This Document" or
the CMYK working space you just built. When you save this CMYK working
space, your multitone images should appear correctly—more or less—on
the screen.

Note that making changes in Color Settings has no effect on CMYK
image data. *It has a radical effect,* however, on any image that you convert
to CMYK mode, and on the way Photoshop displays CMYK images. Therefore, we strongly suggest you give the custom profile a name that clearly
indicates that it's for use with a nonstandard ink set, and switch back to
a standard SWOP ink set (or whatever you usually use) whenever you're
not working on your spot-color image.

Saving and Outputting

While we explore printing and saving from Photoshop in some depth in Chapter 13, *Image Storage and Output,* multitones have some specific requirements that we can better discuss in the privacy of this chapter. The two most relevant issues in getting a duotone out of Photoshop and onto paper or film are saving and screen angles.

The file format that you use when saving a multitone document depends entirely on the mode the image is in: Duotone or CMYK.

Duotone mode. You can save Duotone-mode images in four formats—Photoshop, EPS, PDF, and Raw. QuarkXPress users may use only the EPS file format; InDesign users can use EPS files, native PSD files, or PDF files (only InDesign CS or later).

To make the duotone separate properly from the page-layout program, however, you have to make sure that the color names in the duotone exactly match the names in your page-layout program's color list. For instance, if you used "Pantone 286 CVC" in your duotone, you should also have a color named "Pantone 286 CVC" in QuarkXPress, Adobe PageMaker, or InDesign. Fortunately, if you haven't defined the color name when you import the multitone, the latest versions of these programs add the name to the color list automatically on import.

CMYK mode. If you've created your multitone image in CMYK mode, you have a choice, just as with any other CMYK image, to save in either EPS or TIFF (or PDF or whatever other file format you normally use). However, if you need to specify particular halftone screen angles in your duotone—and you often do—you have to use EPS (TIFFs don't let you save that sort of information). Plus, if you've built custom ink colors, you may have to save as EPS in order to see the proper preview in your page-layout program. (If the program is smart enough to read and interpret an embedded ICC profile, TIFF files may work properly.)

The most important thing to remember when creating duotones, tritones, or quadtones in CMYK mode is this: If you're not intending to use process-color inks, be very careful at separation time. If you import a CMYK image into a page-layout program and print color separations, the cyan channel ends up on the cyan plate, the yellow channel ends up on

Converting from Duotone to CMYK Mode

While we wouldn't do this with most multitone images, we have occasionally found it helpful to convert our files from Duotone mode to either CMYK or Multichannel mode to take advantage of capabilities like solid color tints, blends, grayscale representations of each plate, and output benefits (see "Turning Grayscale to Color," earlier in this chapter). Of course the trade-off is that the file's size becomes much larger.

As in the conversion from Grayscale to CMYK mode, there are two methods for converting from Duotone mode to CMYK. The easiest method is simply to select CMYK from the Mode menu. Unfortunately, it's also the least useful, unless your art director just told you that you can only use process colors and have to do away with all spot colors. You're out of luck, however, if you want to change any of the multitone curves further.

If you're planning on converting the image in order to make further adjustments to it (add areas of solid color, and so on), it's much better to convert the image to Multichannel mode first. When you convert to Multichannel mode, Photoshop gives you two, three, or four spot color channels (depending on the number of inks you're using), each with the proper curve automatically applied to the original grayscale image. You can save multichannel images as DCS 2.0 files (see "DCS" in Chapter 13, *Image Storage and Output*).

You can also convert your file from Multichannel mode to CMYK mode, with two changes.

▶ If there are only two or three channels (if the image is a duotone or a tritone), add channels until you have four. We suggest naming them (double-click on the channel tile in the Channels palette) so you know which is which.

▶ Make sure the channels are in the correct order in the Channels palette. When you convert to CMYK mode, the first channel tile in the palette is always read as the cyan plate, the second as magenta, and so on. However, when you convert a quadtone into Multichannel mode, Photoshop makes black the first tile in the list. You have to drag it into its correct place, or the image will turn out incorrectly.

This, by the way, is how you can convert a duotone image into a CMYK format that old CMYK-only systems can read and use. Of course, unless you've changed the definitions of cyan, yellow, magenta, and black, the image may look very different than when it was in Duotone or Multichannel mode.

the yellow plate, and so on. This is what you'd expect and want if you were using process-color inks in your image; but if you're using spot-color inks (as in the earlier section, "Simulating Spot Colors in CMYK"), this could be a disaster.

Screen Angles

Every topic in digital imaging must have at least one controversy. One of the controversies surrounding duotones is what screen angles you should use when printing them. People fall into two camps: those who favor 30 degrees between inks, and those who favor 45. We are in the latter camp—

45 degrees between the halftone screens results in the least obvious patterns. (You always get *some* patterning when you overlap screens; the trick is to minimize it.) The angles you pick, however, may vary.

We typically print black ink at 45 degrees because people tend to "blur out" this angle the most (important for a dark color). But that leaves only zero degrees for the second ink. If that ink is very light, like yellow or a light gray, you can print it at zero degrees. With a darker color like burnt sienna, cyan, or dark gray, however, a zero-degree screen may appear too obvious. Our second choice is printing the inks at 30 and 75 degrees.

With these screen combinations, be aware that the RIP might think it knows better and substitute "optimized" process-color angles. Ask your output provider to turn off Balanced Screens, HQS, or whatever halftone substitution algorithms it may use.

The more traditional among us usually print with 30-degree offsets. We suspect there may be an element of superstition in this, but many people who've built more duotones than we've had hot dinners use angles 30 degrees apart. However, when pressed, most confess that they do so because that's what they were taught to do.

Conventional wisdom puts the strong color at 45 degrees and the weak one at 75 degrees. But this can have the effect of making one screen more obvious than the other, so in many cases, angles of 15 and 75 degrees are used instead.

In a tritone image, of course, we always revert to the second opinion: 30-degree offsets, usually using 15, 45, and 75 degrees (with 45 used for the ink/curve combination that is dominant—that has the greatest density). Finally, for quadtones, we use the four standard process-color angles: 0, 15, 45, and 75. (Note that many people state these angles as 45, 90, 105, and 165; they're the same thing, but three of them are rotated 90 degrees.) The lightest ink is always printed at zero degrees.

Printing Order

In order for the inks to match their proper halftone screen angles automatically, arrange them from darkest to lightest in the Duotone dialog box (bearing in mind the curves you've set up for each ink; a dark ink with a very light curve may not be terribly dominant on press).

If you want to specify angles manually, however, you can use the Screens button in the Print with Preview dialog box (see Figure 10-20 and "Imaging from Photoshop" in Chapter 13, *Image Storage and Output*).

Figure 10-20
Setting screens
for duotones

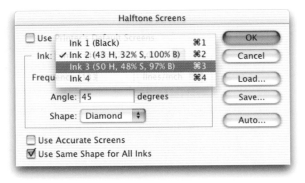

You usually can't do much about the order in which the inks are laid down, though, even though it may significantly affect the image. Discuss the topic with your printer, and rely on their experience with inks.

Printing Proofs of Spot-Color Images

Seeing spot colors on screen is one thing. Proofing them on paper is quite another. You really have only two choices when trying to proof your multitone images: custom inks and converting to process colors.

Custom inks. Some service bureaus provide proofing systems that attempt to match Pantone and other spot colors. For instance, the Cromalin system lets you build proofs using Pantone's spot colors (Matchprints cannot do this, by the way). This is certainly an expensive proposition, but it's the closest approximation you can get this side of a press check.

For this type of proofing, it doesn't matter whether you've used Duotone or CMYK mode to create your multitones, or what type of inks you'll finally be printing with. You're dumping a piece of black film for each ink color; the color (spot or process) appears only when the proofs are made.

Process colors. An alternative is to print proofs on a color printer with CMYK colorants. Most spot inks just can't be reproduced faithfully with CMYK, but with skill, luck, and a good dose of experience, you can get something meaningful out of these devices.

There are two ways to print a multitone image on a color printer:

▶ **Just print it.** If your image is in Duotone mode and you select Print with Preview from the File menu, Photoshop sends the grayscale image to the printer along with four transfer curves (one for each process color). Grayscale printers discard the transfer curves and just print the grayscale image. Color printers render the image as best they can.

The big problem with this approach is that Photoshop assumes that your multitone colors are spot colors—even if they're specced as process colors—so it pushes them through its color engine (see Chapter 5, *Color Settings*). This is more or less the same as converting to CMYK mode yourself and printing. If you have assigned the correct profiles and your system is well calibrated, there's a fair chance you'll get a nice-looking image. Otherwise, your image may look bizarre.

▶ **Convert to RGB.** A second method of printing multitone images is to convert them to RGB mode first (whether they're in Duotone or CMYK mode), and then tell Photoshop to send the RGB data to the printer (select RGB in the Print dialog box). Most desktop inkjet printers prefer to get RGB data like this, and as long as you apply the proper printer profile in the Print with Preview dialog box (see Chapter 13, *Image Storage and Output*), the image will probably come out okay. Remember though, that the inkjet is still just simulating your spot colors with its own inks.

Note that no matter which method you use, the color you see from a color printer is almost certainly going to be different from your final image, and no sane printer would take something like this as a contract proof. But it may be helpful in the process of creating good curves.

Tip: Be There During the Print Run. Stephen Johnson has made more duotones than anyone we know, and he maintains that even after printing hundreds of multitone images, he still doesn't know *exactly* what he's going to get until he shows up for the press run. Take his advice. If you're doing critical duotones, *be there* during the press run—the way the press operator controls the inks can make or break the final printed piece.

Billions of Shades of Gray

If the real world would simply perform as all the theories tell us, grayscale images would fly off the printing press with deep, rich tones and an incredible dynamic range, and CMYK images would simulate every color in the rainbow. But the real world doesn't pay much attention to theories, so we need to help the process along. Spot colors—whether in the form of bump plates, solid spot areas, or duotones—are great ways to do this. After all, if you're trying to faithfully reproduce an elephant, you want to listen to (or see) as many different perspectives as you can.

Building a Digital Workflow

Making Quick Work of Raw Images

Digital photography has been around in one form or another for well over a decade, but it's only recently that it has truly hit the mainstream. Today, the question is not whether, but when digital capture will replace film for the vast majority of uses.

That said, anyone who has made the switch from film to digital can tell you that one major—and usually unanticipated—bottleneck crops up as soon as it's time to choose the "keepers" from a day's shooting. With film, you can pay extra for rush processing, and sort the images on a light table. Digital captures, however, have to be transferred to the computer—and if they're saved in the camera's raw format, they must be converted to RGB images—before you even know what you've captured.

We've doubtless made some enemies by saying this, but the excellence of most camera vendors' hardware tends to be matched equally by the wretchedness of their software. Some photographers despair at the lengthy processing times for raw images, and opt to shoot JPEG instead, sacrificing both quality and flexibility in the interest of getting the work done quickly enough to allow them to have lives. Others rely on third-party conversion tools that complicate the workflow as well as cost extra money.

The Adobe Photoshop team delivered a set of powerful solutions in Photoshop CS, but Photoshop CS2 takes things even further. The old File Browser has been replaced by a new standalone application, Bridge, which acts as your virtual digital light table. Version 3 of the Camera Raw plugin, which ships with CS2 and can be hosted by Bridge *or* by Photoshop, adds important new functionality. Together, they form the building blocks for an efficient, speedy workflow using raw files. But before we get into strategies for this workflow, let's look at what a digital raw capture is.

Digital Raw Formats

Camera Raw appears as a file format in Photoshop's Open dialog box, but it isn't actually a single file format. Rather, it's Photoshop's catchall name for files that the Camera Raw plug-in can open, including Canon CRW and CR2 files, Nikon NEF files, and raw files saved as TIFF by various cameras.

A list of officially supported cameras appears on Adobe's Web site, currently at *www.adobe.com/products/photoshop/cameraraw.html*. The URL and the list may change during the lifetime of this book, so if you don't find the information there, keep digging. Camera Raw also offers "unofficial" support for many cameras that don't appear on the list. "Unofficial support" means that Adobe won't provide tech support and makes no guarantees about the quality of the conversions. We won't make any guarantees either, but we've been happy with the results from the unofficially supported cameras we've tried, and the unofficial support generally becomes official with the next dot release of Camera Raw.

What Is a Raw Capture?

One-shot digital cameras use color filters over each sensor in the area array to split the incoming light into its red, green, and blue components. So, each sensor captures only one color, depending on the filter that covers it. The actual capture is essentially a file that records the amount of light recorded by each element in the array.

Considerable processing is required to turn this raw capture into an RGB color image. When your camera is set up to save JPEG files (that's the default for most digital cameras), the conversion is performed by the camera's firmware, using the on-camera settings for white balance, tone, saturation, sharpness, and so on. However, when you tell your camera to save images in its raw format, the processing is deferred until you open the image on the computer using specialized software (like Camera Raw).

Why Shoot Raw?

Shooting raw images is much more flexible than shooting JPEG. When you shoot raw, the only on-camera settings that affect your capture are the shutter speed, aperture value, and ISO value. All other settings—white balance, tone curve, color space, contrast, saturation—are written into the capture as *metadata*—literally, data about data—that accompanies the raw information. Camera Raw may use this metadata as guidance for how to process the capture into an RGB image, but the settings have no effect on the actual capture of the image pixels.

So raw captures allow tremendous flexibility in postprocessing, letting you reinterpret white balance and exposure with no degradation to the image. Rather than stretching or squeezing levels, you're simply reinterpreting the way the captured photons get converted into an RGB image.

Raw capture offers other key benefits, too.

▶ It creates a smaller file on disk than an uncompressed RGB image.

▶ It allows you to capture a high-bit image from a one-shot camera.

▶ It allows you to convert the image into RGB spaces other than the ones supported by the camera.

There are several disadvantages to raw, too. Of course, the primary one is the need for processing the images, which takes time. But raw files are also larger than JPEG images, so it may take longer to save them to your camera's storage medium (which fills faster, too). However, we've struggled with most of the raw converters out there, and we're convinced that Camera Raw is one of the fastest available—fast enough to make shooting raw worthwhile for all but the most time-critical applications.

Moreover, Camera Raw starts working for you automatically as soon as you point Bridge at a new folder of raw images, quickly generating thumbnails and previews so you can see the raw images in enough detail to make a quick initial choice between the "hero" shots you plan to keep and the less-successful efforts you plan to discard (or revisit later).

If you want to simply jump in with both feet, take a quick look at Figure 11-1, then get to work. But the combination of Bridge and Camera Raw is complex enough that you'll probably want to read the rest of this chapter to get the rest of the juicy details! (Bruce has even written an entire book on the subject: *Real World Camera Raw with Adobe Photoshop CS2*—from which some of this chapter was taken.)

The Digital Raw Workflow Quick Start

Figure 11-1 A quick start to a digital raw workflow

Start by copying your raw images to a new folder (we strongly recommend that you never open images directly from the camera storage media). Point Bridge to the image folder using the Bridge's Folders panel. Bridge immediately starts generating thumbnails and previews, then it reads the metadata from each image. This not only gives you large-size previews—it also verifies that the raw images were transferred correctly to the computer.

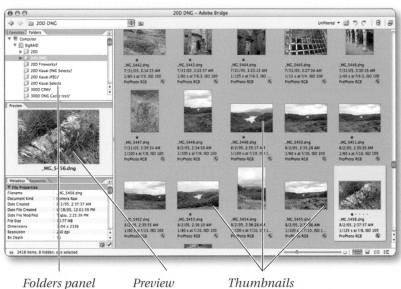

Folders panel   Preview   Thumbnails

Drag to resize

Drag the resizing controls to make the preview area large enough to allow you to see enough detail in your images that you can decide which ones you want to work with.

You can save different Bridge configurations by choosing Save Workspace from the Workspace submenu (under the Window menu). The saved workspaces then appear on the Workspace submenu for easy recall.

Double-click an image's thumbnail or preview to launch the Camera Raw plug-in, which allows you to control the conversion of the raw file into any of four preset RGB working spaces.

The histogram, preview, and RGB readouts all show the results of the conversion from the raw file to the designated working space.

To apply the settings without opening the image, click Done. The settings are remembered until you next open the file.

To apply the settings quickly to similar images, choose Apply Camera Raw Settings from Bridge's Edit menu, then choose Previous Conversion from the Apply Camera Raw Settings submenu.

The settings get recorded in the image's metadata, and are used when you open the image.

You can now process the images without revisiting the Camera Raw dialog box, either by Shift-double-clicking to open the selected images, or by choosing Batch from the File Browser's Automate menu to process the images automatically using Actions.

Camera Raw, Photoshop, and Bridge

If you're used to the old Camera Raw/File Browser combination in Photoshop CS, you'll notice that things have changed in several ways, all for the better. If you're new to Camera Raw, this section explains why the screenshots in this chapter may look different from your copy of Camera Raw when you launch it.

As we mentioned earlier, unlike the old Photoshop File Browser, Adobe Bridge is a standalone application. One of the many advantages that its standalone status confers is that it's capable of hosting Camera Raw when Photoshop is either not running, or—more likely—is busy doing something else. You can open Camera Raw in Bridge *or* Photoshop, whichever is the more efficient for the task at hand.

For example, if you want to edit the Camera Raw settings for one or more images, but don't plan on opening them in Photoshop, you can open Camera Raw in Bridge while Photoshop is busy (such as when it's running a batch process). Or you could edit an image in Camera Raw in Photoshop while Bridge is busy caching a folder full of images. You can even open one Camera Raw window in Bridge and another in Photoshop, though doing so has the potential to make you a very confused puppy!

The subtle clue as to which application is currently hosting Camera Raw appears in one button: When Camera Raw is hosted by Bridge, the default button is labeled Done (clicking it closes Camera Raw, applies the settings to the raw file, and returns you to Bridge). When in Photoshop, the button is labeled Open (clicking it closes Camera Raw, applies the settings to the raw file, and opens the converted image in Photoshop).

A second important workflow enhancement is the "filmstrip" mode of Camera Raw. Now you can open and edit multiple images in Camera Raw, transferring settings from one image to another inside the Camera Raw interface (see Figure 11-2 and "Filmstrip Mode," later in this chapter).

Turn off default auto-correction. Camera Raw now auto-corrects images by default. Some people seem to love this feature, while others (those who want to see the effects of exposure bracketing) hate it. Fortunately, the behavior is easily changed: Press Command-U to turn off the Auto checkboxes, make sure that White Balance is set to As Shot, then choose Save New Camera Raw Defaults from the Camera Raw menu. Note that the defaults are per camera model, so you'll need to do this for each camera model you use. You can still get an auto-correction for an individual image by pressing Command-U to toggle the Auto checkboxes on again. See "Use Auto Adjustments," later in this chapter, for more detail.

Figure 11-2
Camera Raw in
filmstrip mode

*When you open multiple
raw images in Camera
Raw, they appear in the
filmstrip at the left of the
Camera Raw window,
allowing you to work
with multiple images in
several useful ways.*

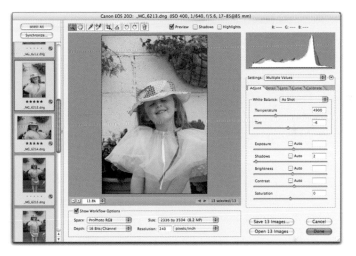

Camera Raw Anatomy

The Camera Raw dialog box offers two sets of controls; one static set that is "sticky" (the settings remain unchanged until you change them) and another dynamic, image-specific set that changes depending on which tab is currently selected (see Figure 11-3).

Figure 11-3
Camera Raw controls

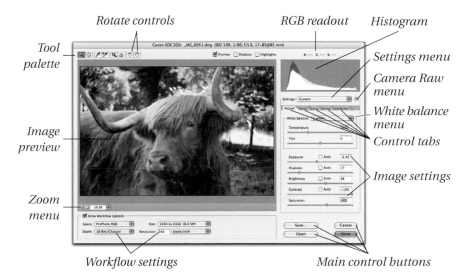

Rotate controls

RGB readout   *Histogram*

Tool palette

Settings menu

Camera Raw menu

White balance menu

Control tabs

Image preview

Image settings

Zoom menu

Workflow settings   *Main control buttons*

Camera Raw Static Controls

The static controls, which appear all the time in Camera Raw, fall into several groups: the Tool palette; the rotate buttons; the Preview controls; the main control buttons; the histogram; the RGB readout; the Settings menu; and the Camera Raw menu. Let's look at each of these in turn (see Figure 11-4).

Figure 11-4
Camera Raw
static elements

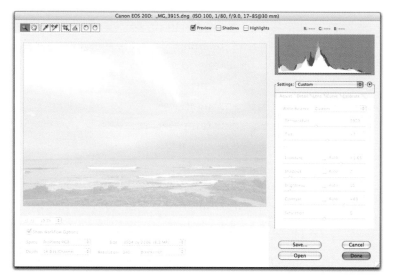

The Tool Palette

Camera Raw's Tool palette contains six tools, three from the previous version, plus three new ones (see Figure 11-5).

Zoom and pan. The zoom (magnifying glass) and pan (grabber hand) tools work just like their Photoshop counterparts.

Tip: Use Keyboard Shortcuts for Fast Navigation. All of Photoshop's navigation shortcuts work here, too: Hold down the Command key (Mac) or Ctrl key (Windows) to zoom in. To zoom out, add Option/Alt. For the Pan tool, hold down the spacebar. Or, press Z to choose the Zoom tool and H for the Hand tool. Command -+ zooms in, Command -- (hyphen) zooms out. Command-0 (zero) fits the entire image in the preview (as does double-clicking the hand tool), and Command-Option-0 (zero) or double-clicking the zoom tool zooms to Actual Pixels view.

Figure 11-5
Camera Raw Tool palette

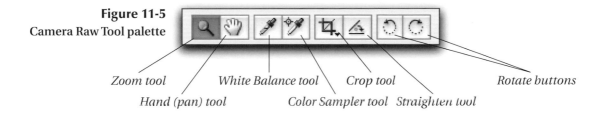

Zoom tool

Hand (pan) tool

White Balance tool

Color Sampler tool

Crop tool

Straighten tool

Rotate buttons

White balance. The White Balance tool lets you set the white balance by clicking on the image. Unlike the white eyedropper in Levels or Curves, it doesn't allow you to choose a source color, and it doesn't affect the luminance of the image. Instead, it lets you set the white balance—the color temperature and tint—for the capture by clicking on pixels you think should be neutral.

Click-balancing with the white balance tool provides a very quick way to set color temperature and tint simultaneously. You can always fine-tune the results using the individual Temperature and Tint controls in the Adjust tab, which we'll cover in due course.

Tip: Click-Balance on Diffuse Highlights. Camera Raw's White Balance tool works best on a light gray close to diffuse highlight, but one that still contains detail, rather than on a specular highlight that's pure white. The second-to-lightest gray patch on the old 24-patch Macbeth Color-Checker works well, as do bright (but not blown-out) clouds.

Color samplers. The Color Sampler tool (press S) lets you place up to nine individual color samplers, each of which gets its own readout, in the image (see Figure 11-6). Combined with the static RGB readout, the color sampler tool lets you monitor the values of up to 10 different locations in the image, which should be enough for any reasonable use.

Crop. The new Crop tool (press C) lets you drag out a cropping rectangle, choose one of several common predefined aspect ratios, or define your own custom aspect ratio from the tool's pull-down menu. The same menu allows you to clear the crop (see Figure 11-7). The Camera Raw preview always shows the crop in the context of the whole image, but you'll see the crop in filmstrip previews, Bridge previews and thumbnails, and of course to the image itself when you open it in Photoshop.

Figure 11-6
The Color Sampler tool

Color sampler readout

Color sampler

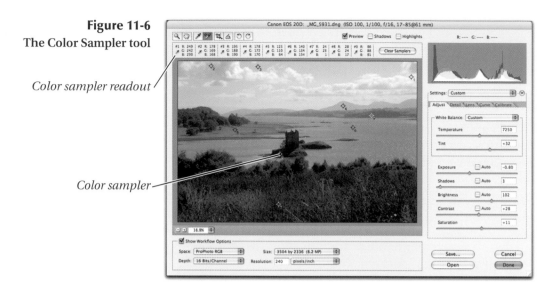

Figure 11-7
The Crop tool and menu

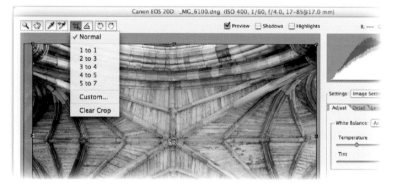

Tip: Crop to Up-Rez. The Custom setting on the Crop tool lets you specify pixel dimensions up to 10,000 by 10,000 pixels (see Figure 11-8). This feature offers a means of producing a much larger file than the sizes that appear on Camera Raw's Size menu. Of course, the pixels will be interpolated—it doesn't magically give you a 100-megapixel camera! But you can downsample to sizes other than those on the Size menu, too.

Straighten. The new Straighten tool (press A) is an enormous time-saver for those of us who sometimes fail to keep our horizons horizontal. It should really be called the "straighten *and crop*" tool because it also automatically applies the crop that maintains the maximum rectangular image when the Crop tool is set to Normal, or a straightened crop of the specified aspect ratio when the Crop tool is set to something else. If there's an existing crop, it's preserved and rotated. Compared to straightening and cropping an image in Photoshop using the Measure tool, Arbitrary Rotate, and the Crop tool, we much prefer the Straighten tool's speed and simplicity (see Figure 11-9).

Figure 11-8
Upsampling with
Custom Crop

Figure 11-9
Straighten and crop

Drag the Straighten tool to define a horizontal or vertical.

A rotated crop appears in Camera Raw. The cropping and rotation are applied to the Bridge thumbnail and preview (below) and to the image when it's opened in Photoshop.

The histogram can show you at a glance exactly what's happening to your exposure and clipping at the current image settings. For example, a white spike at both ends indicates clipping of shadows and highlights because the scene dynamic range was more than the camera could capture. Space at both ends of the histogram indicates that you've captured the entire scene dynamic range. A white spike at one end shows that you may need to adjust the Exposure or Shadows slider to avoid clipping. A colored spike at either end may indicate gamut clipping, or tonal clipping in one or two channels. Note that if the clipping disappears when you set the Space menu (in the Workflow Settings) to ProPhoto RGB, you can be certain that it's showing gamut clipping from a smaller output space.

A red, green, or blue spike indicates color clipping in that channel; a cyan spike indicates clipping in both green and blue; a magenta spike indicates clipping in both red and blue; and a yellow spike indicates clipping in both red and green.

RGB readout. The RGB readout shows the RGB values for the pixels under the cursor. The values are those that will result from the conversion at the current settings. The RGB readout always reads 5-by-5 *screen* pixels at zoom levels of 100% or less, so it may display different values at different zoom levels. When you fit the entire image into Camera Raw's preview, you're sampling an average of a fairly large number of pixels. At zoom levels greater than 100%, the sample size is always 5-by-5 *image* pixels.

The Settings Menu

The Settings popup menu lets you apply any saved Camera Raw settings (see Figure 11-12). The items that always appear are Image Settings, Camera Raw Default, Previous Conversion, and Custom.

Image Settings. Image Settings indicates that you've previously applied edits to the image. If you're working on an image, choosing Image Settings

Figure 11-12
The Settings menu

will show you the settings that were in effect before you started editing. If the image is brand-new and has never been edited, Image Settings is the same as the next item, Camera Raw Default.

Camera Raw Defaults. Camera Raw Defaults is what it says—it's the default setting that applies to all images unless and until you override it. It's also the setting used by Bridge to create the high-resolution previews when it sees a folder full of new raw images. If you find that the shipping default settings aren't to your liking, you can set your own Camera Raw Defaults for each supported camera model. If you get yourself in a mess by doing so, you can return Camera Raw to the shipping default settings using the appropriate commands from the Camera Raw menu.

Previous Conversion. Choosing Previous Conversion applies the settings from the last image you opened in Camera Raw to the current image.

Custom. Custom denotes the current settings you're applying in Camera Raw. As we mentioned previously, you can toggle between Image Settings and Custom to compare your current edits with the ones that were in effect when you opened the image in Camera Raw.

You can also save your own custom settings as presets, which then become available from this menu. It's easy to overlook the mechanism for doing so, though, because it lives on the Camera Raw menu, which—although it's one of the most important of the static controls—is unfortunately unlabeled. Let's take a look at this menu next.

The Camera Raw Menu

Cleverly hidden under the small unlabeled right-facing triangle is the Camera Raw menu, which allows you to load, save, and delete settings or subsets of settings, turn Camera Raw's Auto corrections on or off, set default settings for an individual camera model, restore Camera Raw's default settings for a camera model, and set Preferences (see Figure 11-13).

We'll start with Preferences, because until you understand the various behaviors controlled by Preferences, the other commands may not make a whole lot of sense. Camera Raw's Preferences are fairly simple, but they have far-reaching implications for your workflow.

Figure 11-13
The Camera Raw menu

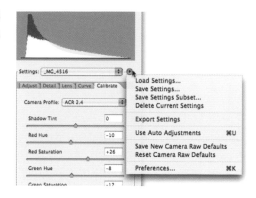

Preferences

Camera Raw's Preferences (see Figure 11-14) let you decide whether your raw edits are saved in the Camera Raw database or in "sidecar" .xmp files, and whether to apply sharpening to the converted image or to the preview only. It also allows you to choose the location and size of the Camera Raw cache, and lets you purge the Camera Raw cache. Camera Raw 3.1 and later adds settings that control the behavior of DNG files—they have no effect on other raw formats.

Save image settings in. Camera Raw treats the raw images as read-only, so your Camera Raw edits for the image get saved either in a sidecar .xmp file—a small file designed to travel with the image—or in the Camera Raw database. Each approach has strengths and weaknesses, and you can choose with the "Save image settings in" option in this dialog box.

Saving your edits in the Camera Raw database means that you don't have to keep track of sidecar files or worry about making sure that they get renamed along with the image—the Camera Raw database indexes the images by file content rather than name, so if you rename the raw file, the Camera Raw database will still find the correct settings. The major disadvantage is that when you move the images onto a different computer, or burn them to a CD or DVD, the edits won't travel with the images.

Saving your edits in sidecar files allows the edits to travel with the images. Adobe gives you a lot of help in handling the .xmp sidecar files. By default, Bridge hides them, and automatically keeps them with their respective images when you use Bridge to move or rename them. The only danger is that if you move or rename the images *outside* Bridge, you need to keep track of the sidecars yourself.

Figure 11-14
Camera Raw Preferences

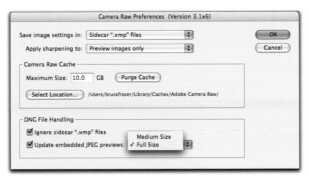

A solution to this potentially confusing issue is to convert your raw images to DNG format (see "The Main Control Buttons," later in this chapter for more on this). Camera Raw treats raw files as read-only because all the vendors' proprietary formats—Canon's .CRW and .CR2, Nikon's .NEF, Olympus' .ORF, and so on—are undocumented. Rather than taking the risk of messing up the file by writing metadata such as Camera Raw settings into it, Camera Raw uses sidecar files or its own database. But DNG is a completely documented, open format, so when you use DNG, Camera Raw settings and other metadata get written directly into the DNG file itself.

Apply sharpening to. The "Apply sharpening to" option lets you choose whether to apply sharpening to the previews *and* to the converted image, or to the previews only. Setting this option to "Preview images only" lets you enjoy reasonably sharp previews, but apply more nuanced sharpening to the converted images. Note that this preference only affects the Sharpness setting, not either of the noise reduction settings, which are found on the same Detail tab as the Sharpness control (see "The Detail Tab," later in this chapter).

Camera Raw cache. The Camera Raw cache holds pre-parsed raw data for the most recently used raw files, which is used to speed up the following operations:

▶ Opening the Camera Raw dialog box

▶ Switching between images in the Camera Raw filmstrip

▶ Updating the thumbnails in the Camera Raw filmstrip in response to settings changes

▶ Rebuilding the thumbnails/previews in Bridge in response to settings changes

The cache file sizes average about 5 MB, so at the default size limit of 1 GB, the Camera Raw cache will hold the pre-parsed data for about the 200 most recently accessed images. If you commonly edit folders with more than 200 raw files, you probably want to increase the Camera Raw cache's size limit. Nothing is stored exclusively in the Camera Raw cache, so purging it never loses data.

DNG File Handling. The two checkboxes under DNG File Handling control the behavior of DNG files. They have no effect on other raw formats.

▶ **Ignore sidecar ".xmp" files.** This preference addresses a relatively obscure situation that arises only when you have a DNG and a proprietary raw version of the same image in the same folder, and they're identically named except for the extension. If you edit the proprietary raw file, Camera Raw 3 also applies the edits to the DNG, to maintain compatibility with Photoshop CS and Photoshop Elements 3, both of which write sidecar files for DNG. The preference setting lets you tell Camera Raw 3.1 to ignore sidecar files and leave the DNG alone in this situation.

▶ **Update JPEG Previews.** This setting controls when the embedded JPEG previews in DNG files get updated. When it's turned on, Camera Raw updates the embedded preview as soon as you dismiss Camera Raw after editing a DNG file, thereby incurring a speed penalty since the previews take time to write and save.

You can defer the speed hit by turning this item off. Then, when you want to update the previews, choose Export Settings from the Camera Raw menu. You'll see the dialog box shown in Figure 11-15, which lets you choose the preview size. Or, to skip the dialog box, press Option while choosing Export Settings. Camera Raw will update the preview size you selected last time you opened the dialog box.

Figure 11-15
Export Settings for DNG

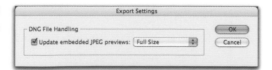

When you choose Full Size, Camera Raw embeds both Full Size and Medium Size previews. The downside is that Full Size previews take longer to build, and make a slightly larger file. Bear in mind, though, that you can choose which application, Photoshop or Bridge, gets tied up generating the previews so you can continue working in the other application while the one hosting Camera Raw builds the previews.

Loading and Saving Settings

The Load Settings, Save Settings, and Save Settings Subset commands let you load and save settings or settings subsets you make with any of the image-specific (Adjust, Detail, Lens, Curve, and Calibrate) controls. We find the Save Settings Subset command especially helpful. For example, you could create settings that adjust only the exposure value up or down in increments such as +0.25, +0.50, -0.25, -0.5, and so on (see Figure 11-16).

To make saved settings or subsets appear on the Settings menu automatically, save them in User/Library/Application Support/Adobe/Camera Raw/Settings (Mac), or Documents and Settings\User\Application Data\Adobe\Camera Raw\Settings (Windows). These saved settings also appear in the Apply Camera Raw Settings submenu on Bridge's Edit menu. If you save settings anywhere else, you can load them using Camera Raw's Load Settings command.

Figure 11-16
Loading and saving
settings subsets

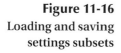

Export Settings

The Export Settings command offers a way to write a sidecar .xmp file when you have the Camera Raw Preferences set to save edits in the Camera Raw cache—it offers a way to produce sidecar files when you want to copy the images to removable media for use on another computer while preserving the edits. If the preference is set to use sidecar files, Export Settings will export a sidecar file only if no sidecar file already exists. If there's an existing sidecar file, Export Settings does nothing.

Use Auto Adjustments

When the Use Auto Adjustments feature is turned on, which it is by default, Camera Raw tries to come up with optimum settings for each image, essentially auto-correcting tone and exposure. While the word "auto" usually makes us squirm, this feature isn't as simple as it might seem at first glance.

However, keeping Use Auto Adjustments as part of the default setting makes it difficult to learn the behavior of a camera, because each image has been adjusted individually, so you don't get to see a consistent baseline interpretation. That's not a problem for everyone, and if it isn't a problem for you, then by all means leave the default settings alone. Beginners will likely find that Use Auto Adjustments provides a quick way to get decent results, but it also makes it much more difficult for them to learn the relationship between shutter speed, aperture setting, and the result.

Use Auto Adjustments isn't an all-or-nothing proposition, but the alternate methods of using it aren't terribly obvious. First, you can toggle Use Auto Adjustments on and off by pressing Command/Ctrl-U, but if you do so on an already-edited image, you may get some surprises. This feature is really designed to work on top of the default settings, so its algorithms ignore any adjustments you have made in the Curve tab, and also ignore any Vignetting adjustments you've made in the Lens tab. If you turn on Use Auto Adjustments when the values for Curve or Vignetting are significantly different from the default values, you won't get good results!

Auto adjustments for initial previews. The Command/Ctrl-U toggle is useful for comparing auto adjustments with a static baseline interpretation, either the old Camera Raw 2.4 defaults (which are what you get if you just turn Use Auto Adjustments off without doing anything else), or with your own customized camera defaults that don't use auto adjustments (see the next section, "Setting Camera Defaults"). If you want to take advantage of the auto adjustments to generate the initial previews and thumbnails in Bridge, just keep the Camera Raw defaults at their factory settings. Then you can either use the auto adjustments as a starting point for edits, or press Command/Ctrl-U to turn them off before you start editing.

Applying auto adjustments over baseline defaults. If you need to see a baseline interpretation of your images, but want to apply auto-corrections quickly as a reality check or starting point, you'll need to create a new camera default setting without auto adjustments (see the next section). Then you can simply use the Command/Ctrl-U toggle to switch the auto-corrections on after opening the dialog box.

Comparing auto adjustments with your own edits. This is a little trickier, because, as previously noted, if you simply toggle Use Auto Adjustments on top of edits that include Curve or Vignetting adjustments, you may get very nasty results.

If you've kept Use Auto Adjustments as part of your camera default settings, you can simply toggle between Camera Default and Image Settings (for a newly opened but already-edited image) or Custom (for edits in progress) by choosing them from the Settings menu.

If you prefer a baseline default that treats all images identically, create that default setting (see the next section), then open an unedited image and press Command/Ctrl-U to turn on the auto adjustments. Once you've done so, choose Save Settings from the Camera Raw menu, make sure that you're saving them in the appropriate folder for your platform, and name the setting Auto. It will then appear on the Settings menu, so you can toggle between Auto and Image Settings or Auto and Custom to compare the auto adjustments with your own edits.

Setting Camera Defaults

Camera Raw contains the factory settings for each supported camera model, and these are used as the default settings for images originated by that model of camera. But you can create your own defaults—the image metadata tells Camera Raw which default to use for each camera model.

To save a Camera Raw setup, choose Save New Camera Raw Defaults from the Camera Raw menu. For example, you may find the default Shadows setting of 5 a little too high or you notice that you consistently find yourself lowering the Color Noise Reduction slider. So set the controls the way you want them, then choose Save New Camera Raw Defaults from the Camera Raw menu.

Getting good default settings ("good default settings" means different things to different people) is generally an iterative process. Don't be afraid to experiment. It won't harm your raw files in any way, and if you get hopelessly messed up, you can easily set everything back to the shipping defaults and start over by choosing Reset Camera Raw Defaults from the Camera Raw menu.

No set of defaults will do equal justice to every image, so just try to find default settings that provide a good starting point for your images, and hence save you time.

The Main Control Buttons

The main control buttons let you specify the action that Camera Raw will perform on your raw image.

The Save button (Command-S) lets you save an image as a DNG, TIFF, JPEG, or Photoshop file directly from the Camera Raw dialog box without actually opening it in Photoshop. Clicking Save opens the Save Options dialog box, which lets you specify the destination, the file format, any format-specific save options such as compression, and the name for the saved file or files (see Figure 11-17). When you click Save in the Save Options dialog box, you're returned to Camera Raw, and the file gets saved in the background.

In single-image mode, this feature is only mildly useful. Its real power becomes apparent when you open multiple images in Camera Raw's "film-strip" mode, because the conversion from the raw to a saved RGB image happens in the background. That means that you can continue to edit other images while Camera Raw processes the ones you're saving.

It's also worth noting that Camera Raw is in itself a DNG converter. If you've decided that you want to stay with proprietary raws as your working files, but would prefer to hand off DNG files when you need to submit raw images (to make sure that your metadata gets preserved), it's much easier to save out DNG files as you need them from Camera Raw than it is to run them through the standalone Adobe DNG Converter.

The Cancel button (press Esc) does exactly what it says: It ignores any adjustments you've made since opening Camera Raw, dismisses the Cam-

Figure 11-17
Save Options dialog box

Save Options for DNG

Save Options for JPEG

Save Options for TIFF

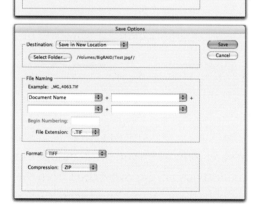

era Raw dialog box, and returns you to the host application, leaving the raw file settings unchanged.

The Open button (Command-O) dismisses the Camera Raw dialog box and opens the image in Photoshop, using the settings you applied in Camera Raw. These settings are written to the raw file's metadata, and Bridge's previews and thumbnails are updated to reflect the new settings. When Camera Raw is hosted by Photoshop, Open is the default button.

The Done button (or press Return or Enter) dismisses the Camera Raw dialog box, writes the settings you applied in Camera Raw to the raw file's metadata, and returns you to the host application. Bridge's previews and thumbnails are updated to reflect the new settings. When Camera Raw is hosted by Bridge, Done is the default button.

Alternate buttons. If you hold down the Option/Alt key, some of the buttons change to those listed below, depending on whether Bridge or Photoshop is the host application for Camera Raw.

▶ The Save button (or press Command-Option-S) saves the image, bypassing the Save Options dialog box, using the settings that were in effect the last time you saved. This keeps Camera Raw open.

▶ The Reset button returns all Camera Raw settings to the state they were in when you launched Camera Raw (either Image Settings, if the image had previously had its own Camera Raw settings applied, or Camera Raw Defaults if it hadn't), and keeps Camera Raw open.

▶ The Open a Copy button (Photoshop only; press Command-Option-O) dismisses the Camera Raw dialog box and opens a copy of the raw file *without writing the settings to the file's metadata.* This feature is especially useful when you want to blend different renderings of the same raw image in Photoshop, but it's also handy when you have a rendering of an image that you like but suspect is capable of improvement. You can quickly try different tweaks without losing the settings that gave you the rendering you liked, and without having to go to the trouble of saving those settings.

Camera Raw Workflow Controls

At the bottom of the Camera Raw dialog box, four controls let you set output parameters for the converted image (see Figure 11-18). The settings you make with these controls apply to the current image, or to all the images being converted in a batch process. Unlike the settings made with the image-specific controls, these settings aren't saved with images. This is useful, because you can set the workflow controls to produce large files in a large-gamut color space for print or final delivery, or change them to produce small files in sRGB for review on the Web or e-mail.

Space lets you choose the destination color space for the conversion from one of four preset working spaces: Adobe RGB (1998), Colormatch RGB, ProPhoto RGB, or sRGB IEC61966-1 (the last being the "standard" flavor of the sRGB standard). See the sidebar "Camera Raw and Color" for details on how Camera Raw handles the color management aspect of the conversion.

Figure 11-18
Camera Raw
workflow settings

Camera Raw and Color

One of the more controversial aspects of Camera Raw is its color-handling, specifically the fact that Camera Raw has no facility for applying custom camera profiles. Having tried most camera profiling software, and having experienced varying degrees of disappointment, we've concluded that unless you're shooting in the studio with controlled lighting and a custom white balance for that lighting, camera profiling is an exercise in frustration if not futility. So we've come to view Camera Raw's incompatibility with custom camera profiles as a feature rather than a limitation.

The way Camera Raw handles color is ingenious and, thus far, unique. For each supported camera, Thomas Knoll, Camera Raw's creator, has created not one but two profiles: one built from a target shot under a D65 (daylight) light source, the other built from the same target shot under an Illuminant A (tungsten) light source. The correct profiles for each camera are applied automatically in producing the colorimetric interpretation of the raw image. Camera Raw's White Balance (Color Temperature and Tint) sliders let you interpolate between, or even extrapolate beyond, the two built-in profiles.

For cameras that write a readable white balance tag, that white balance is used as the "As Shot" setting for the image; for those that don't, Camera Raw makes highly educated guesses. Either way, you can override the initial settings to produce the white balance you desire.

It's true that the built-in profiles are "generic" profiles for the camera model. Some cameras exhibit more unit-to-unit variation than others, and if your camera differs substantially from the unit used to create the profiles for the camera model, the default color in Camera Raw may be a little off. So the Calibrate controls let you tweak the conversion from the built-in profiles to optimize the color for your specific camera. This is a much simpler, and arguably more effective, process in most situations than custom camera profile creation.

Depth lets you choose whether to produce an 8-bit/channel image or a 16-bit/channel one. A 16-bit/channel file needs twice as much storage space as an 8-bit/channel one, but it provides *128 times* as many tonal steps between black and white, so it offers much more editing headroom.

Size lets you resample the image on the fly, or convert it at the native camera resolution. The actual sizes offered depend on the camera from which the image came, but they generally correspond to the native resolution; downsampling to 66 percent or to 50 percent; and upsampling to 133 percent, 166 percent, and 200 percent.

Resolution lets you specify a resolution for the converted image, in pixels per inch or pixels per centimeter, giving you the option to save yourself a trip to the Image Size dialog box once the image is converted. Unlike the Size control, it has no effect on the number of pixels in the converted image.

Camera Raw Image Controls

The image controls—the ones you're likely to change with each image—occupy the rest of the Camera Raw dialog box. The five control tabs are:

▶ Adjust, which deals with color balance and basic tone mapping.

▶ Detail, which deals with sharpening and noise reduction.

▶ Lens, which deals with chromatic aberration and vignetting.

▶ Curve, which lets you fine-tune the tone-mapping.

▶ Calibrate, which lets you fine-tune Camera Raw's built-in color profiles to better match the behavior of your specific camera body.

You can switch quickly between tabs by pressing Command-Option-1 through Command-Option-5. These image controls are really the meat and potatoes of Camera Raw, offering very precise control over your raw conversions. Some of the controls may seem to offer functionality that also exists in Photoshop, but there's a significant difference between editing the tone mapping in Camera Raw, which tailors the conversion from linear to gamma-corrected space, and editing the tone mapping by stretching and squeezing the bits in a gamma-corrected space in Photoshop.

The more work you do in Camera Raw, the less work you'll need to do afterwards in Photoshop. At the same time, if you get your images close to the way you want them in Camera Raw, they'll be able to withstand much more editing in Photoshop—which you may need to do to optimize for a specific output process, or to harmonize the appearance of different images you want to combine into a single one.

The Adjust Tab

The controls in the Adjust tab let you tweak the white balance, exposure, tonal behavior, and saturation (see Figure 11-19). It's the default tab in Camera Raw but you can always get to it by pressing Command-Option-1. Three controls in this tab deserve special attention: The Temperature, Tint, and Exposure controls let you do things to the image that simply cannot be replicated using Photoshop's tools after you convert the image.

The Contrast, Brightness, and Shadows controls provide similar functionality to Photoshop's Levels and Curves, with the important difference that they operate on the high-bit linear data in the raw capture, rather than on gamma-encoded data postconversion. If you make major corrections ("major" meaning more than half a stop) with the Exposure slider, you'll certainly want to use the Brightness, Contrast, and Shadows controls to shape the raw data the way you want it before converting the raw image. With smaller Exposure corrections, you may still need to shape the tone in Camera Raw rather than in Photoshop, especially if you want to avoid shadow noise in underexposed images.

Figure 11-19
The Adjust tab

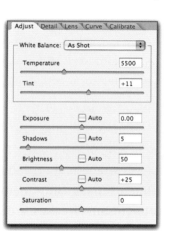

The Temperature and Tint sliders set the overall color balance.

The Exposure, Shadows, Brightness, and Contrast sliders shape the tone mapping.

The Saturation slider sets global saturation.

The white balance controls let you alter the color balance dramatically with virtually no image degradation, which you simply can't do once the image is converted and open in Photoshop. The freedom with which you can reinterpret the white balance is one of the main advantages of capturing raw rather than JPEG images.

Tone mapping controls. Learning how the four tone mapping controls—Exposure, Shadows, Contrast, and Brightness—interact is essential if you want to exercise control over the image's tonal values. It may not be obvious, but the controls work together to produce a five-point curve adjustment.

Exposure and Shadows set the white and black endpoints, respectively. Brightness adjusts the midpoint. Contrast applies an S-curve around the midpoint set by Brightness, darkening values below the midpoint and brightening those above. Figure 11-21 shows Brightness and Contrast adjustments translated approximately into Photoshop curves.

Let's go into even more depth on each of these controls.

▶ **Exposure.** While the Exposure slider controls the mapping of the tonal values in the image to those in your designated working space, it's first and foremost a white-clipping adjustment.

Large increases in exposure value (more than about 0.75 of a stop) will increase shadow noise and may even make some posterization visible in the shadows, simply because large positive exposure values stretch the relatively few bits devoted to describing the shadows further up the tone scale. If you deliberately underexpose to hold highlight detail, your shadows won't be as good as they could be. We certainly don't advocate overexposure—perfect exposure is always desirable—but *slight* overexposure is more often than not preferable to significant underexposure.

When set to negative values, the Exposure control offers the amazing ability to let you recover highlight information from overexposed

Figure11-21
Tonal adjustments
translated into (more or
less) equivalent curves

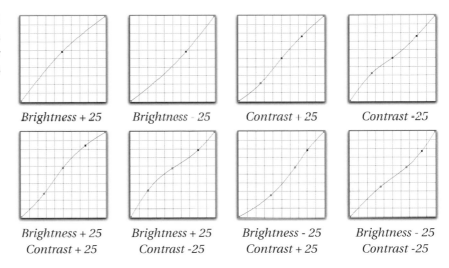

Brightness + 25   Brightness - 25   Contrast + 25   Contrast -25

Brightness + 25   Brightness + 25   Brightness - 25   Brightness - 25
Contrast + 25   Contrast -25   Contrast + 25   Contrast -25

images. Figure 11-22 shows a fairly typical example of highlight recovery—the actual amount of highlight data you can recover depends primarily on the camera model, and secondarily on the amount of compromise you're prepared to tolerate in setting white balance. But it's not at all unusual to recover two-thirds of a stop, and it's often possible to recover more.

By the way, when you use significant negative Exposure adjustments, the logic of how the tonal controls interact changes somewhat, because extended highlight recovery tries to undo some of the highlight compression applied by the Brightness slider. But the same general principles we mentioned earlier still apply.

When the Exposure field is selected, the up and down arrows on your keyboard change the exposure in increments of 0.05 of a stop. Adding Shift changes the exposure in increments of 0.5 of a stop.

▶ **Shadows.** The Shadows slider is the black clipping control. It works very like the black input slider in Photoshop's Levels dialog box, letting you darken the shadows to set the black level. But since the Shadows control operates on the linear-gamma data, small moves tend to make bigger changes than the black input slider in Levels. You may find the default value of 5 (when Use Auto Adjustments is off) a little too aggressive. See the following tip for checking black clipping. When the Shadows field is selected, the up and down arrow keys change the shadows in increments of 1; add the Shift key for increments of 10.

Figure 11-22
Highlight Recovery

With Exposure at zero, the
highlights are blown.

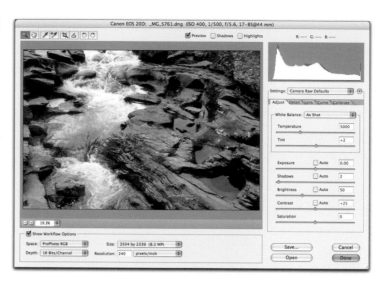

With Exposure at -0.60
and a little fine-tuning
with the Curve tab, the
highlight detail appears.

Highlight detail before recovery

Highlight detail after recovery

Tip: Use the Clipping Display in Exposure and Shadows. For years, we've relied on the threshold clipping display in the Levels dialog box to show us exactly what's being clipped in each channel as we adjust the black and white input sliders. Camera Raw offers the same feature for the Exposure and Shadows sliders. (We wish it offered it for Saturation, too.) Hold down the Option/Alt key as you move the Exposure or Shadows slider and you'll see the clipping display. White pixels indicate highlight clipping, black pixels indicate shadow clipping, and colored pixels indicate clipping in one or two channels (see Figure 11-23).

Figure 11-23
Exposure and Shadows
clipping display

The image

Exposure clipping display

Shadows clipping display

▶ **Brightness.** Unlike its image-destroying counterpart in Photoshop, Camera Raw's Brightness control is a non-linear adjustment that works very much like the gray input slider in Levels. It lets you redistribute the midtone values without clipping the highlights or shadows. Note, however, that when you raise Brightness to values greater than 100, you can drive 8-bit highlight values to 255, which looks a lot like highlight clipping, but if you check the 16-bit values after conversion, you'll probably find that they aren't clipped. See the previous tip for an easy way to check highlight clipping.

▶ **Contrast.** The Contrast slider also differs from the Photoshop adjustment of the same name. While Photoshop's Contrast is a linear shift, Camera Raw's Contrast applies an S-curve to the data, leaving the extreme shadows and highlights alone. Increasing the Contrast value from the default setting of +25 lightens values above the midtones and darkens values below the midtones, while reducing the Contrast value does the reverse. Note that the midpoint around which Contrast adds the S-Curve is determined by the Brightness value (see Figure 11-21, a few pages back).

Saturation. The Saturation slider acts like a gentler version of the Saturation slider in Photoshop's Hue/Saturation feature. It offers somewhat finer adjustments than Hue/Saturation. However, a Hue/Saturation Adjustment Layer allows you to fine-tune by varying the layer opacity, so it's pretty much a wash whether you make the adjustments in Camera Raw or in Photoshop. The up and down arrow keys change the saturation in increments of 1. Adding Shift changes the saturation in increments of 10.

Working in the Adjust Tab

All the controls in Camera Raw are useful, but the Adjust tab is where we spend the majority of our time. We use the Adjust tab controls to optimize our images for global tone and color, but we first use the Adjust tab controls to evaluate the exposure. Underexposed, overexposed, and normally exposed images each need their own handling. While it's possible to produce superficially similar renderings using very different combinations of settings, ascertaining the correct value for the Exposure slider is key to getting the best results from raw images.

Evaluating exposure. We always start with the Exposure slider. Half of the data in a raw capture is devoted to describing the brightest f-stop, so correct placement of the highlights is critical. So our first order of business is invariably to set the Exposure slider, holding down Option to see the clipping display, so that the only clipping is on specular highlights.

The order in which we adjust the remaining sliders depends largely on the image—we adhere to our tried and true maxim of fixing the biggest problem first. However, as we'll shortly see, the Contrast slider can be quite tricky, because its behavior is largely determined by the setting of the Brightness slider. Figure 11-24 shows a typical set of adjustments for a normally exposed image.

Figure 11-24
Adjusting a normally
exposed image
(part 1)

At our Camera Raw
Default settings, the
image is flat and gray.

Aided by the clipping
display, we set the
Exposure slider to +0.45.
Nothing clips, and the
adjustment lets us make
the best use of the data.

We add contrast by
increasing the Contrast
slider value to 90.

Figure 11-24
Adjusting a normally
exposed image
(part 2)

Figure 11-24
Adjusting a normally
exposed image
(part 2)

*Next, the Exposure and
Contrast adjustments
make the midtones too
light, so we reduce the
Brightness slider to 40. It
may seem odd to increase
Exposure and lower
Brightness, but doing so
makes the best use of the
plentiful highlight data.*

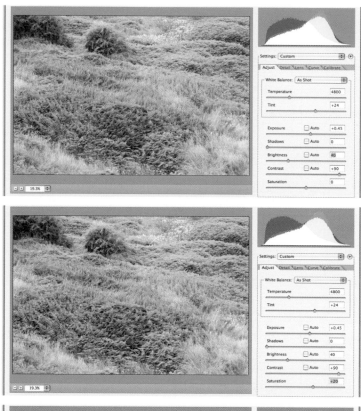

*A modest boost to the
Saturation makes the
image less gray.*

*The As Shot white
balance seems cold,
so we increase the
Temperature slider for a
gentle warming effect.*

The Exposure slider has more impact on the overall tone mapping than any of the others simply because raw captures contain much more data in the highlights than they do in the shadows. In Figure 11-24, we stretched the highlights by first increasing the Exposure, then reducing the Brightness. That way, the highlight region was spread over a wider range, reducing the likelihood of visible noise or posterization in the shadows. Figure 11-25 shows a more extreme example.

As in the previous example, the Exposure slider is the critical adjustment in the example shown in Figure 11-25—the other moves, while all constituting improvements, are relatively subtle by comparison.

Figure 11-25
Adjusting an
underexposed image
(part 1)

At Camera Raw Default settings, the image appears hopelessly underexposed.

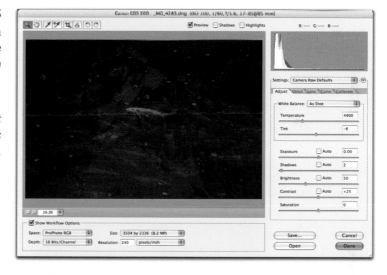

Increasing the Exposure value to +2.35 reveals that there is, in fact, an image!

A cooling adjustment to the Temperature, combined with a small Tint adjustment, reduces the glare on the water and reveals more detail.

Figure 11-25
Adjusting an
underexposed image
(part 2)

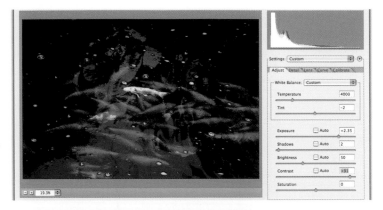

*Increasing the contrast
makes the subject pop.*

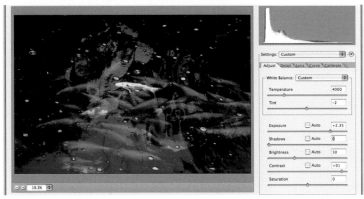

*Reducing the Shadows
value to zero reveals
some extra shadow
detail without
producing noise.*

Shadows, Brightness, and Contrast. While the Exposure slider is the most significant tonal adjustment in the Adjust tab, it would be a mistake to ignore the Shadows, Brightness, and Contrast sliders. Figure 11-26 examines the interplay of the Shadows, Brightness, and Contrast sliders in two different images. In each case, we show two superficially similar yet significantly different renderings of the same raw image. One uses the Contrast slider to add contrast, while the other uses the Shadows slider to add contrast. The point isn't that one is right while the other is wrong. Both are acceptable renderings, though both probably need some fine-tuning either with camera Raw's Curve tab, or postconversion in Photoshop. The point is that seemingly small differences in tone-mapping technique have a large impact on what you can do with the image.

White balance controls. As we saw earlier, the white balance controls can have an enormous impact on the emotional tone of an image. But they also have a significant, albeit more subtle effect on skin tones.

Figure 11-26
Shadows, Brightness,
and Contrast
(part 1)

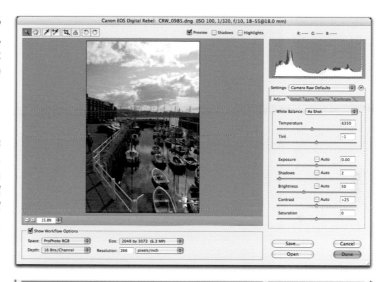

*The image at Camera
Raw Default settings.
To bring back detail in
the highlights, we need
to reduce Exposure and
increase Brightness.*

*After the Exposure and
Brightness adjustments,
this rendering backs
off the Shadows and
increases the Contrast.*

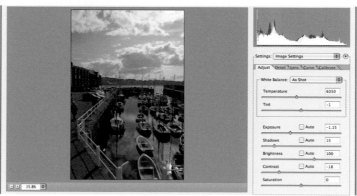

*This rendering has the
same Exposure and
Brightness adjustments
as the one above, but
with reduced Contrast
and increased Shadows
values. The differences
can be seen in the
quarter tones and
three-quarter tones.*

One of the common complaints voiced by those transitioning from film
to digital is overly red skin tones. It's certainly true that digital is much
more sensitive to red and infrared light than is film, which in turn is more
sensitive to blue and ultraviolet. The first place to address the camera's

Figure 11-26
Shadows, Brightness,
and Contrast
(part 2)

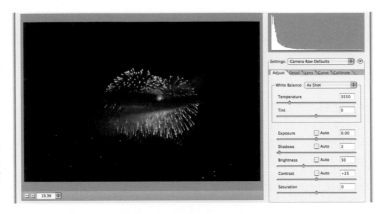

*The image at Camera
Raw Default settings. To
bring back detail in the
fireworks, we need to
reduce Exposure and
increase Brightness.*

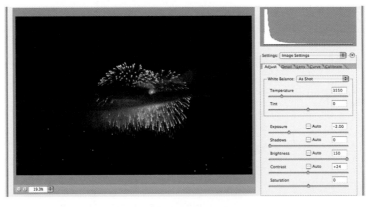

*Reducing Shadows to
zero while leaving
Contrast at its default
setting does very little
to open up the
three-quarter tones
and shadows.*

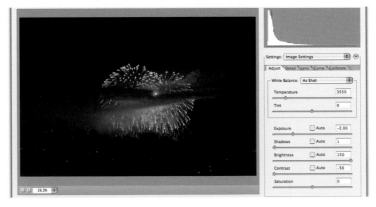

*Reducing the Contrast
value to -50 and raising
the Shadows value to
1 opens up the three-
quarter tones while still
producing solid blacks.*

color rendering is the Calibrate tab (see "The Calibrate Tab," later in this chapter), but even a well-calibrated camera can still err on the ruddy side in skin tones. Figure 11-27 shows how relatively small moves to the Temperature and Tint sliders can improve matters.

In fact, after Exposure, the white balance controls are the most critical in the Adjust tab. Like Exposure, the white balance controls let you do things to the image that you simply cannot do postconversion in Photoshop, so make friends with them, and don't be afraid to use them creatively!

Figure 11-27
White Balance and skin tones

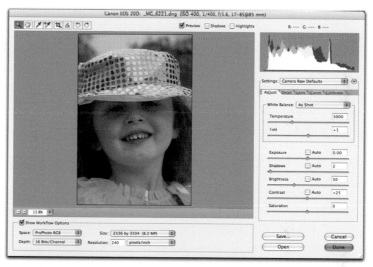

The image at Camera Raw Default settings

After tone-mapping, the skin tones are still a little red, partly from the light being filtered through a pink hat, partly from the camera's behavior.

Lowering the Temperature and Tint controls produces this more pleasing rendering.

Why use the Adjust tab? We see a distressingly large number of photographers who convert their raw images at Camera Raw default settings, then complain that Camera Raw produces flat, unsaturated results that require a lot of Photoshop work. Camera Raw's defaults tend to be more conservative than those of proprietary raw converters, which generally aim to match the in-camera JPEG. They often bury shadow detail to hide noise and produce a pleasingly contrasty result. Camera Raw, on the other hand, shows you everything the camera has captured, warts and all, and lets you work with all the bits. The controls are there for a reason. If you use them wisely, Photoshop becomes a tool for making localized edits that you can't do in Camera Raw. If you make your global edits in Camera Raw, you'll have much less work to do post-conversion, and you'll get better results.

The Detail Tab

The sliders in the Detail tab (press Command-Option-2) let you apply global sharpening and reduce noise in both luminance and color (see Figure 11-28). To see the effect of these controls, you need to zoom the preview to at least 100%—often 200% or higher is more useful—because while the Camera Raw preview tries to show their effect at 50% or higher zoom, they're hard to see until you zoom in. Pressing the up and down arrow keys moves the sliders in increments of 1. Adding Shift moves the sliders in increments of 10.

Most cameras need some amount of color noise reduction regardless of ISO speed. Each camera vendor makes its own compromise between image softness and color artifacting: If an image detail falls on only a red,

Figure 11-28
The Detail tab

only a green, or only a blue pixel, the demosaicing algorithm has to make some guesses to figure out what color the resulting image pixel should really be, and sometimes single-pixel color artifacts result. Color noise reduction can also eliminate rainbow artifacts in highlights and green-magenta splotches in neutral grays. The need for luminance noise reduction, though, is more dependent on ISO speed and image content.

Sharpness. The Sharpness slider lets you apply a variant of Unsharp Mask to the preview image or to both the preview and the converted image, depending on how you set Camera Raw Preferences (see "The Camera Raw Menu," earlier in this chapter). Unlike Unsharp Mask, Camera Raw's Sharpness only offers a single control—the Threshold value is calculated automatically based on the camera model, ISO, and exposure compensation values reported in the image's metadata.

We usually set the preference so that Sharpness only applies to the preview, and apply more controlled sharpening postconversion in Photoshop. But if we're simply trying to get a bunch of images processed for approval, trying to make them good rather than great, we may apply a quick sharpen here, knowing that we can reprocess the "hero" shots from the raw file with no sharpening once we've decided which ones they are.

Luminance Smoothing. The Luminance Smoothing slider lets you control grayscale noise that makes the image appear grainy—a typical problem when shooting at high ISO speeds. The default setting is zero, which provides no smoothing; but many cameras benefit from a small amount—say 2 to 4—of luminance smoothing even at slow speeds, so you may want to experiment to find a good default for your camera. At high ISO speeds—800 and up—you'll almost certainly need to apply luminance smoothing at even higher settings.

At very high settings, the Luminance Smoothing slider produces images that look like they've been hit with the Median filter, so always check the entire image at 100% view or above before committing to a setting.

Bear in mind that the controls in the Adjust tab can have a huge impact on the visibility of noise. Unlike many raw converters, Camera Raw gives you access to everything the camera has captured, including, sometimes, extremely noisy shadows that other converters may simply map to black. Attempting to pull shadow detail out of an underexposed image will almost certainly result in noisy shadows.

Color Noise Reduction. Color noise appears as random speckles of color rather than gray: In our experience, all cameras need some amount of color noise reduction (see Figure 11-29). While the visibility of color noise varies with ISO speed, the required correction seems to vary less

Figure 11-29
Noise reduction

The image at 200% view (right), and the entire image (below)

Color Noise Reduction set to 15 removes the color noise.

Luminance Smoothing set to 40 greatly reduces the luminance noise (higher settings softened the image without significantly helping the noise).

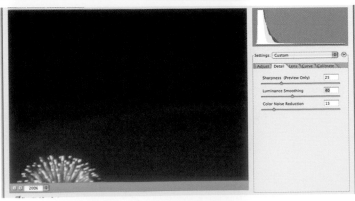

than is the case with luminance noise, so you can generally find a good default value for your camera, and deviate from it only when you see an obvious problem.

It's difficult to show typical noise scenarios in print—noise that looks objectionable on the displayed RGB file is often quite invisible by the time the image has been converted to CMYK and printed.

The Lens Tab

The controls in the Lens tab (press Command-Option 3; see Figure 11-30) let you address two problems that occasionally show up in digital captures, one much more common than the other.

Figure 11-30
The Lens tab

Chromatic aberration. Chromatic aberration is the name given to the phenomenon where the lens fails to focus the red, green, and blue wavelengths of the light to exactly the same spot, causing red and cyan color fringes along high-contrast edges. In severe cases, you may also see some blue and yellow fringing. It typically happens with wide-angle shots, especially with the wide end of zoom lenses, and is typically worse at more open aperture settings.

▶ **Chromatic Aberration R/C.** This slider lets you reduce or eliminate red/cyan fringes by adjusting the size of the red channel relative to the green channel. While the red/cyan fringes are usually the most visually obvious, chromatic aberration usually has a blue/yellow component too.

▶ **Chromatic Aberration B/Y.** This slider lets you reduce or eliminate blue/yellow fringes by adjusting the size of the blue channel relative to the green channel.

Figure 11-31 shows before-and-after versions of a chromatic aberration correction. As with the controls in the Detail tab, zoom the preview to 100% or more when making corrections with the chromatic aberration sliders.

Tip: Turn Off Sharpening. To see the color fringes clearly and to judge the optimum settings for the sliders, turn off any sharpening you've applied with the Sharpness slider in the Detail tab. The color fringes are usually

Figure 11-31
Chromatic aberration
correction

Detail from the image (below left) shown before chromatic aberration correction (right) and after chromatic aberration correction (below right). Note that before applying the correction, we set Sharpness in the Detail tab to zero to make it easier to see where the fringing starts and ends.

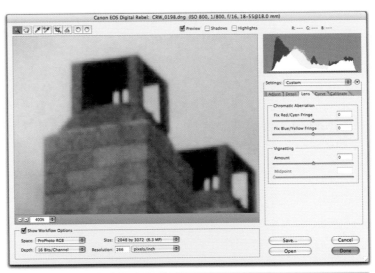

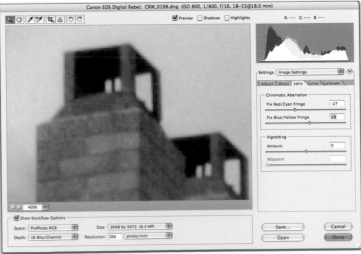

most prominent along high-contrast edges, and sharpening applies a halo to such edges that makes it harder to see exactly where the color fringes start and end.

Tip: Option-Drag the Sliders to Hide the Other Channel. Red/cyan fringing is usually much easier to see than blue/yellow fringing, but chromatic aberration is almost always a combination of both. Holding down the Option key as you drag either of the Chromatic Aberration sliders hides the channel that isn't being affected by the adjustment, making it much easier to apply exactly the right amount of correction to both channels.

Vignetting. Vignetting, where the lens fails to illuminate the entire sensor area, darkening the corners, is a problem you may encounter when shooting wide open (see Figure 11-32).

Figure 11-32
Vignetting correction

Vignetting often becomes objectionable when shooting a bright sky at wide apertures. The image before vignetting correction is shown above right; the corrected image is shown below right.

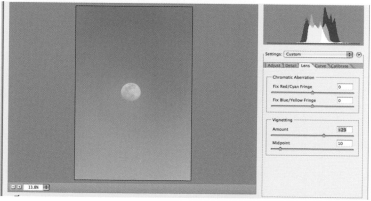

▶ **Vignetting Amount.** This slider controls the amount of lightening or darkening (negative amounts darken, positive amounts lighten) applied to the corners of the image.

▶ **Vignetting Midpoint.** This slider controls the area to which the Vignetting Amount adjustment gets applied. Smaller values reduce the area; larger ones increase it.

The Curve Tab

New to Camera Raw 3.0, the Curve tab (press Command-Option-4) offers a luminosity-based curve control that lets you fine-tune the image's tonality. If you're used to thinking of Photoshop's Curves command as the best way to edit images, you may be tempted to skip the slider controls in the Adjust tab and use the Curve tab for all your tone-mapping adjustments, but that's not a good idea. To understand *why* it isn't a good idea, you need to know a little about how the Curve tab actually works.

Like the sliders on the Adjust tab, the Curve tab operates on the linear capture—in fact, the slider adjustments and the curve adjustments get concatenated into a single operation during the raw conversion. But the user interface for the Curve tab makes it appear that the curve is operating on gamma-2.2-encoded data. (If the curve interface corresponded directly to the linear data, the midtone value would be around level 50, and the three-quarter tone would be all the way down at level 10 or so, which would make it pretty hard to edit!)

The key point is that the Curve tab works on top of the slider adjustments in the Adjust tab. You'll find that it's much easier to use the sliders for rough tonal shaping and the Curve tab for fine-tuning than it is to try to do all the heavy lifting in the Curve tab (see Figure 11-33).

Navigation. Camera Raw's Curve tab shares many features with Photoshop's Curves dialog box, but also contains a few subtle differences. When you press Command and mouse over the image, a small white circle appears on the curve showing where on the curve the pixels under the cursor lie. Command-clicking places a point on the curve at that location. To delete a curve point, Command-click it, select it and press the Delete key, or drag it over one of the adjacent curve points.

Control-Tab selects the next curve point, Control-Shift tab the previous point. To select multiple curve points, Shift-click on each one. The up,

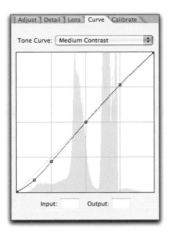

Figure 11-33
The Curve tab

down, left, and right arrow keys move the selected curve point by one level: add Shift to move in increments of 10 levels. You can also enter numeric values for the selected curve point in the Input and Output entry fields.

Tone Curve. The Tone Curve popup menu contains three preset curves—Linear, Medium Contrast, and Strong Contrast—and Custom, which indicates a tone curve you have edited. The default tone curve is Medium Contrast, but if you prefer a different default, you can change it, then save a new Camera Raw Default. In addition, you can save tone curves just like you can save any other custom subset of settings.

To make saved tone curves appear automatically on the Tone Curve menu, save them in User/Library/Application Support/Adobe/Camera Raw/Curves (Mac), or Documents and Settings\User\Application Data\Adobe\Camera Raw\Curves (Windows)—this is a different folder from the one for all other Camera Raw settings and subsets, but if you save a subset containing only a tone curve, it gets saved in this folder automatically. If you save tone curves anywhere else, you can load them using Camera Raw's Load Settings command (see "Loading and Saving Settings," earlier in this chapter).

Adjustments and previewing. One key difference between Photoshop's Curves and Camera Raw's Curve tab is that the latter doesn't offer a real-time preview. Photoshop's Curves simply adjusts pixel values directly, but Camera Raw's Curve tab controls have to do a lot more work in mapping the edits you've specified in the gamma 2.2 interface of the tone curve onto the linear data as modified by the sliders in the Adjust tab. Today's machines simply don't have enough horsepower to update the preview in real time.

The most practical way to adjust the curve is to place points on it by Command-clicking, then use the arrow keys to make an adjustment, wait for the preview to update, and continue to fine-tune using the arrow keys. Figure 11-34 shows a typical Curve tab adjustment.

Figure11-34
Adjusting contrast with
the Curve tab

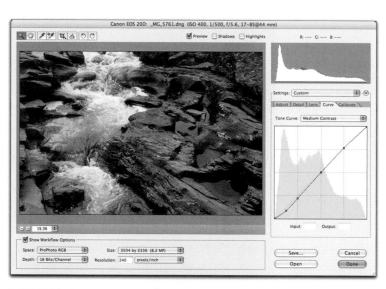

The Curve tab
adjustments add
highlight contrast to
the white water, and
put a little extra punch
in the shadows.

The curve is particularly effective for fine-tuning highlight detail, simply because in a linear capture, that's where most of the data lies. To shape the shadows, things go much more easily when you get as close as possible with the slider controls in the Adjust tab, and reserve the curve for small tweaks to the slider results.

The Calibrate Tab

As we explained earler in this chapter (see the sidebar "Camera Raw and Color"), Camera Raw contains two built-in generic profiles for each supported camera. The controls in the Calibrate tab (press Command-Option-5) let you fine-tune the behavior of the built-in camera profiles to tweak for any variations between *your* camera and the one that was used to build Camera Raw's built-in profiles for the camera model (see Figure 11-35).

Figure 11-35
The Calibrate tab

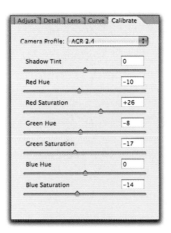

Camera Profile. For most cameras, the only choice on the Camera Profile menu is ACR 2.4, indicating that the built-in profiles used in Camera Raw 3.0 are the same as the ones in Camera Raw 2.4. For a few cameras, Camera Raw 3.0 offers new, improved profiles. If you have legacy images adjusted for the Camera Raw 2.4 profiles you can choose the ACR 2.4 profiles from this menu, while taking advantage of the new profiles for new images.

Using the Calibrate controls. By far the easiest way to get good Calibrate tab settings for your specific camera is to employ the free Colorbrator script written by our friend and colleague Thomas Fors. You can download the script, along with the instructions for using it, from this Web site: *www.chromoholics.com/Colorbrator.html.*

Besides the script, you'll need a GretagMacbeth ColorChecker—the old 24-patch ColorChecker, in either its full-sized or miniature form, is ideal, but you can also use the newer ColorChecker SG, which contains the old target. Tom's site provides good directions for lighting and shooting the target. Once you've done so, simply follow the instructions that accompany the script, and let it do its thing.

If you're a driven control freak who distrusts anything automatic (or you're simply deranged), Bruce has documented the manual process on which the script is based in *Real World Camera Raw with Adobe Photoshop CS2*, and at *www.creativepro.com/story/feature/21351.html*.

Filmstrip Mode

If you had to adjust every slider on every image, you might conclude that Camera Raw was an instrument of torture rather than a productivity tool. Fortunately, the combination of Camera Raw, Bridge, and Photoshop offers several ways of editing multiple images. One of these is built right into Camera Raw itself: When you select multiple images to open, either by selecting them in Bridge or in the Photoshop's Open dialog box, Camera Raw opens them in filmstrip mode (see Figure 11-36).

Figure 11-36
Filmstrip mode

When you select multiple raw files to open, Camera Raw presents them in filmstrip mode, with the thumbnails arranged vertically down the left side of the Camera Raw dialog box.

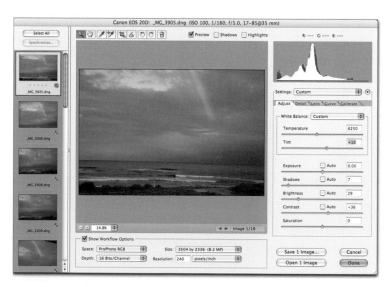

Camera Raw's filmstrip mode offers a great deal of flexibility when it comes to editing multiple images. You can select all the open images using the Select All button, which makes all your edits apply to all the selected images. You can also select contiguous ranges of images by Shift-clicking, or discontiguous by Command-clicking. When the focus is on the filmstrip, you can navigate through the images using the up and down arrow keys, or select them all by pressing Command-A.

Tip: Match Zoom Percentage. If you want to view the images at a zoom percentage other than Fit in View (the default view), select all the images in the filmstrip, then choose the desired zoom percentage from the zoom menu or using the zoom tool. Then as you navigate through the images, each one is displayed at the zoom percentage you specified.

Synchronize Settings

When you select more than one image, the Synchronize Settings button becomes available. Synchronize Settings lets you apply all the settings or any subset of the settings for the image that's currently being previewed, to all the selected images. This feature is of most use when you open a series of images that need similar corrections, but within that general mandate you have a great deal of flexibility in how you choose to work.

In Figure 11-37, we applied the same white balance to all the images in the series—the changing light and the varying amounts of whitecaps require different tonal adjustments. On a different series of images, we may synchronize the tonal adjustments, or the noise reduction, all the settings, or whichever combination of settings is most applicable. A general rule of thumb is to start out by applying the settings that are applicable to the largest number of images, then whittle them down to smaller groups that can take the same corrections.

If you're willing to spend a little extra time planning your corrections, consider sorting the images in Bridge so that images that require identical corrections are grouped in order. That way, you can very quickly zip through large numbers of images, applying general corrections quickly, and doing fine-tuning only on those that require it.

Filmstrip mode also offers a quick way to examine raw images at actual pixels view without performing conversions. And since Camera Raw can be hosted by both Photoshop and Bridge, you can even open two separate Camera Raw sessions, one in Photoshop, one in Bridge, for those times when you need to see two images side-by-side at actual pixels view. It's not a particularly elegant or intuitive solution, and in the longer term we'd much prefer it if Bridge could show images at full resolution, but it's certainly better than nothing.

Figure 11-37
Synchronizing settings

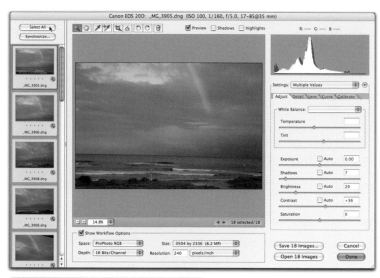

*When you select
multiple images, the
Synchronize Settings
button becomes enabled.
Clicking it opens the
Synchronize Settings
dialog box, below.*

*The Synchronize Settings
dialog box lets you apply
all the current image's
settings, a single setting,
or any combination of
settings to the selected
images. The menu offers
a quick way to select
commonly used subsets.*

Saving Images in the Background

One of the major enhancements to Camera Raw 3.0 is the ability to save
converted images directly to disk without having to first open them in
Photoshop. Notice that when you have more than one image selected,
Camera Raw's Open and Save buttons change to read "Open *x* images"
and "Save *x* images," (where *x* is the number of images).

When you click the Save *x* images button, the Save Options dialog box
appears (see Figure 11-38). Then, when you click Save, Camera Raw goes
to work processing the images. When Photoshop is hosting Camera Raw,
you can continue to work in the Camera Raw dialog box during the save.
But if you dismiss the dialog box, you'll see a Save Status dialog box, and
you won't be able to do anything else until the save is completed.

Figure 11-38
Save Options dialog box

The Save Options dialog box lets you specify a location, a naming convention, and a file format for the files you save out of Camera Raw.

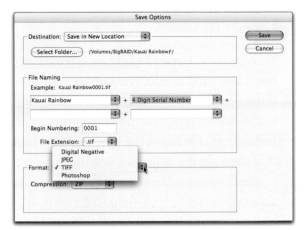

When Bridge hosts Camera Raw, the images are processed in the background. You can continue to work in the Camera Raw window, or you can dismiss it and do other work in a Bridge window (including launching a new Camera Raw session). While Camera Raw hosted by Bridge is saving files in the background, the only status message that appears is in the Camera Raw window itself (see Figure 11-39).

Figure 11-39
Camera Raw Save Status message

When Camera Raw hosted by Bridge is saving files, the only status message is in the Camera Raw window itself, just above the main control buttons.

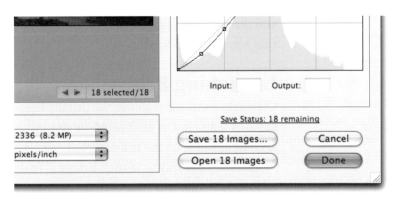

We'll discuss the workflow implications of Camera Raw's saving abilities under both hosts in more detail later in this chapter. For now, we'll simply point out that Camera Raw 3.0 offers much more workflow flexibility, with many more options, than did its predecessor.

Figure 11-41
Bridge window modes

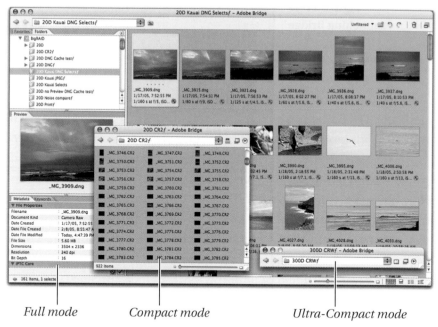

Full mode   Compact mode   Ultra-Compact mode

The icons in the
upper-right corner of the
window let you switch
between modes.

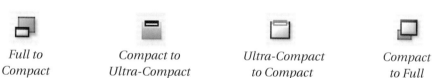

Full to   Compact to   Ultra-Compact   Compact
Compact   Ultra-Compact   to Compact   to Full

You can cycle through all the open Full-mode windows by pressing Command-~ (tilde) on the Mac and Alt-Tab on Windows, but the shortcut doesn't apply to Compact or Ultra-Compact windows, so it's just as well that they float by default. If the floating behavior annoys you, you can turn it off for individual Compact or Ultra-Compact windows from the flyout menu sported by those window modes (see Figure 11-42), but be warned that doing so can make your Compact and Ultra-Compact-mode windows hard to find.

You can toggle between Full and Compact modes by pressing Command-Return (Mac) or Ctrl-Enter (Windows). The shortcut toggles between Full and either Compact or Ultra-Compact modes, depending on which of the compact modes you'd last applied to the window.

Tip: Select to Ensure the Right Window. One curious side effect of the floating compact windows is that Bridge can have multiple windows as the foreground window, and sometimes simply clicking on the one you

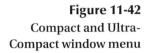

Figure 11-42
Compact and Ultra-
Compact window menu

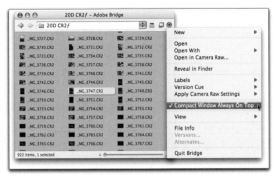

want to switch from compact to full or vice versa doesn't work. If you select one or more thumbnails in that window, though, keyboard shortcuts will then apply to that window.

Bridge Window Components

In Full mode, Bridge windows contains seven different areas, two of which, the tools and buttons, and the main window containing the thumbnails, are always visible. The five remaining components—the Folders, Favorites, Preview, Metadata, and Keywords palettes—are resizable and rearrangeable within the palette area at the left of the window (see Figure 11-43).

The main window holds thumbnails, which you can display at different sizes. The Folders palette lets you quickly browse through folders and also lets you move or copy files by dragging or Option-dragging their thumbnails to a folder icon in the Folders palette. The Preview palette shows a preview of the selected image. The Metadata palette shows the metadata associated with the selected image—you can control which fields are displayed. The Keywords palette lets you create keywords and sets of keywords, assign them to images, and perform searches.

Bridge Tools and Buttons

Bridge's tools and buttons are arranged in three logical groups. The navigation controls are at the upper left of the window, the content controls are at the upper right, and the display controls are at the lower right.

Navigation controls. The Back/Forward buttons work like those in Web browsers, letting you move backward and forward through recently visited folders. The Look In menu shows the current folder and its path, the number

Figure 11-43
Full window components

Back/Forward buttons   Up One Level button   Unfiltered menu   New folder   Rotate buttons   Delete button

Look In menu

Favorites panel tab

Folders panel

Preview panel

Size controls

Keywords panel tab

Metadata panel

Show/Hide panels toggle

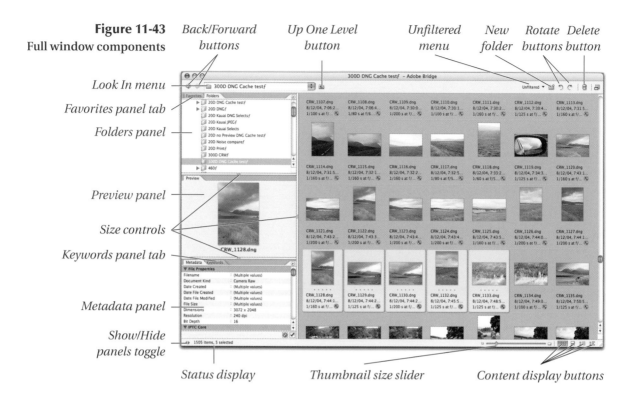

Status display   Thumbnail size slider   Content display buttons

of recently visited folders specified in Bridge's Preferences, and folders or Navigation controls. You can add items to this list by choosing Add Folder to Favorites from the File menu or by dragging a folder into the Favorites panel (see Figure 11-44). The Up One Level button lets you navigate upward through the folder hierarchy.

Content controls. The content controls are a somewhat loose logical grouping, but they all affect the main window content in some way. The Unfiltered/Filtered menu lets you choose which thumbnails are displayed based on their rank or label (but not both; see Figure 11-45). We'll discuss using ranks and labels later in this chapter.

The New Folder icon lets you create a new folder inside the folder you're currently browsing (you can do the same by pressing Command-Shift-N). The rotate left and rotate right tools (keyboard shortcuts are Command-[and Command-], respectively) rotate the selected thumbnails

Figure 11-44
Bridge Look In menu

Figure 11-45
Bridge Unfiltered menu

and previews, and instruct Bridge to apply the rotation to the file when it gets opened. The Trash icon (keyboard shortcut is the Delete key) moves selected items to the Trash/Recycle Bin, but doesn't actually empty it.

Display controls. The thumbnail size slider lets you control the size at which Bridge's thumbnails are displayed, with the long side at a minimum of 16 pixels to a maximum of 512 pixels. The remaining buttons let you switch quickly between Thumbnails view, Filmstrip view, Details view, and for VersionCue users, Versions and Alternates view (see Figure 11-46). VersionCue is outside the scope of this book and isn't readily applicable to a raw digital workflow.

Note that the view buttons apply only to the main window that shows the image thumbnails. They have no effect on the palettes—if the palettes are visible, switching views keeps the palettes visible, and if they're hidden, switching views keeps them hidden.

Figure 11-46
Bridge views

Note that all of Bridge's palettes are closed in these images.

Thumbnails view shows the image thumbnails with up to three lines of additional metadata.

Filmstrip view shows the image thumbnails arranged along the bottom of the window with a large preview of the selected image displayed above.

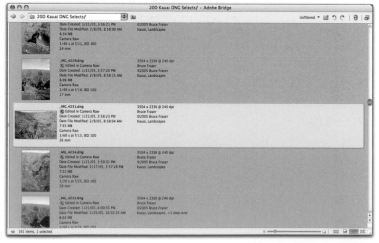

Details view shows the thumbnails as a list, along with additional metadata.

Bridge Palettes

The main window in Bridge—the one that displays thumbnails—lets you do a great deal of your work, but the other palettes are very useful for specialized tasks.

The Folders palette. The Folders palette displays the volume and folder hierarchy, allowing you to navigate to different folders (see Figure 11-47). Once you click on one of the folders, you can navigate up and down the folders list using the up and down arrow keys, and you can collapse and expand volumes or folders that contain subfolders using the left and right arrow keys. Command-up arrow moves you up to the next level in the folder hierarchy. The palette menu contains but one command, Refresh.

Figure 11-47
The Folders palette

The Favorites palette. The Favorites palette is a handy place for storing places that you often want to return to in a Bridge window (see Figure 11-48). In addition to actual volumes and folders, the Favorites palette can hold Collections, which are saved search criteria that act as "virtual" folders. You can configure the preset items from Bridge's Preferences (see "Bridge Menu Commands," later in this chapter), and you can add items to it by dragging or by menu command.

Figure 11-48
The Favorites palette

The Preview palette. The Preview palette displays a preview for the selected image. Like the other palettes, you can collapse it by double-clicking on its tab and resize it by dragging its size controls, but it has no menu and no secrets. (At least, none that we know of!)

The Metadata palette. The Metadata palette (see Figure 11-49) displays the metadata associated with the currently selected image or images (see the sidebar "All About Metadata"). When you have more than one image selected, many of the fields will likely read "Multiple Values Exist."

Metadata fields that are editable appear in the palette with a pencil icon next to the title. To edit these fields, select the images or images whose metadata you wish to edit, and then either click the pencil icon or click directly in the text area to enter the new metadata. To confirm entries, click the Apply checkbox at the palette's lower-right corner, or press Enter (Mac) or Alt-Enter (Windows). The only IPTC field that isn't editable here is the Keywords field—to edit keywords, you need to use the Keywords palette.

The Metadata palette's flyout menu lets you launch a search using the Find command (press Command-F), which is replicated in Bridge's Edit menu; increase or decrease the font size used in the palette; and append or replace metadata from saved templates, which appear in the menu. The Preferences command takes you directly to the Metadata panel of Bridge's Preferences. It's definitely worth taking the few minutes needed to decide which fields you want to display—very few Photoshop users need to see them all!

The Metadata palette contains two separate sets of IPTC metadata. The older IIM (Information Interchange Model) set is there for compatibility with legacy images—it has been superseded by the new IPTC Core schema for XMP metadata. You can find out more about the IPTC standards at *www.iptc.org*.

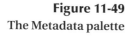

Figure 11-49
The Metadata palette

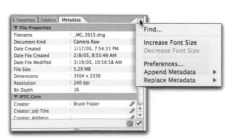

All About Metadata

Metadata (which literally means "data about data") isn't a new thing. Photoshop's File Info dialog box has allowed you to add metadata such as captions, copyright info, and routing or handling instructions, for years. But digital capture brings a much richer set of metadata to the table.

Most current cameras adhere to the EXIF (Exchangeable Image File Format) standard, which supplies with each image a great deal of information on how it was captured, including the camera model, the specific camera body, shutter speed, aperture, focal length, flash setting, and of course the date and time.

IPTC (International Press Telecommunications Council) metadata has long been supported by Photoshop's File Info feature, allowing copyright notices and the like. Other types of metadata supported by Photoshop CS include GPS information from GPS-enabled cameras (it's immensely cool that our good friend Stephen Johnson's stunning landscape images include GPS metadata that will allow people to identify where they were shot 10 or 100 years from now, and note how the landscape has changed). You apply Camera Raw settings as metadata to instruct Photoshop how you want the image to be processed before actually doing the conversion. You can even record every Photoshop operation applied to the image as metadata using the History Log feature.

Adobe has been assiduous in promoting XMP (eXtensible Metadata Platform), an open, extensible, W3C-compliant standard for storing and exchanging metadata—all the Creative Suite applications use XMP, and because XMP is extensible, it's relatively easy to update existing metadata schemes to be XMP-compliant. However, it will probably take some time before all the other applications that use metadata, such as third-party digital raw converters, get updated to handle XMP. But let's be very clear: XMP is not some proprietary Adobe initiative. It's an open, XML-based standard. So if you find that another application is failing to read XMP metadata, contact the publisher and tell them you need them to get with the program!

Right now, unless you're a programmer or a very serious scripting wonk, there may not be a great deal you can do with much of the metadata, at least, not automatically; but it likely won't be too long before you start seeing things like camera-specific sharpening routines that vary their noise reduction with ISO value and exposure time, to give just one example. The more information you have about an image, the better your chances of being able to do useful things to it automatically; and the more things you can do automatically, the more time you can spend doing those things that only a human can do, like exercising creative judgment.

The Keywords palette. The Keywords palette lets you create keywords (which you can group into categories called keyword sets), and apply them to a selected image or images. The keywords get written into the Keywords field of the IPTC metadata, so they're visible in the Metadata palette—you just can't edit or apply them there.

Keyword sets appear as folders—the triangle to the left lets you expand and collapse them. When they're expanded, you can see the list of keywords in the set (see Figure 11-50). To apply a keyword to selected images, click in the column at the left of the palette—a checkmark appears, indicating that the selected images contain this keyword. To apply all the keywords in a set,

Figure 11-50
The Keywords palette

click beside the set name rather than beside the individual keyword. Icons at the bottom of the palette let you create a new keyword set or keyword, or delete an existing keyword set or keyword. Deleting keywords removes them only from the list, not from any files that contain them. You can also move keywords to a different set by dragging.

The Keywords palette menu commands mostly replicate the functions of the control buttons, but the Rename command provides the sole path for renaming keywords or categories, and the Find command (which is only enabled when a keyword is selected) takes you to Bridge's Find dialog box with the selected keyword already loaded in the search criteria.

Bridge Menu Commands

Bridge serves not only Photoshop but the entire Creative Suite, so a good many of its menu commands aren't relevant to a digital raw workflow. Moreover, many of the menu commands offer relatively inefficient ways to accomplish tasks that can be performed more easily by other means, so we'll content ourselves with providing an overview of the menus, along with details about the commands we find particularly useful.

Preferences and the Bridge Menu

The Bridge menu, which is found only in the Macintosh version of Bridge, contains only one important command: Preferences (press Command-K). You can also get to the Preferences dialog box with the Camera Raw menu (see "The Camera Raw Menu" earlier in this chapter). On Windows, this also lives on the Edit menu. Bridge's Preferences dialog box contains six different panels, each governing a different aspect of Bridge's behavior.

General Preferences. The controls in the General panel let you set the shade of gray for the background on which thumbnails are displayed, hide or show tooltips, and specify up to three additional lines of metadata that are displayed under the thumbnail along with the filename (see Figure 11-51). It also lets you specify items that always appear in the Favorites panel, and offers two control buttons, one of which reveals scripts in the Finder (Mac) or Explorer (Windows).

Figure 11-51
Bridge Preferences,
General

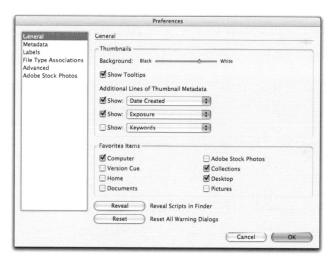

Metadata Preferences. These options let you specify which metadata fields are displayed on the Metadata palette. If you don't have a GPS-enabled camera, for example, you may as well hide all the GPS fields. This panel also offers the option to hide fields that are empty for the selected image or images automatically (see Figure 11-52).

Labels Preferences. These options let you associate text labels with the label colors (you can't change the colors) to something more useful than the color names (see Figure 11-53). The label text is searchable in Bridge, and can be displayed both in the Metadata palette and as an additional line of metadata accompanying the thumbnails if you choose that option in the General Preferences tab. If you change the label text in Preferences, images that have previously had labels applied lose the label color—it turns white—but the label text remains part of the image's metadata.

Figure 11-52
Bridge Preferences,
Metadata

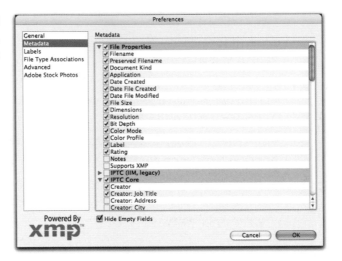

Figure 11-52
Bridge Preferences,
Metadata

Figure 11-53
Bridge Preferences,
Labels

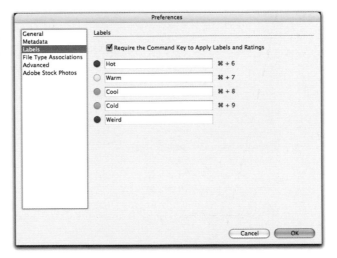

File Type Association Preferences. These options let you specify the default application for opening files from Bridge. They apply only to the behavior you get when opening files from Bridge, and have no effect on OS-level behavior (see Figure 11-54).

Advanced Preferences. This panel contains several unrelated but nevertheless important items (see Figure 11-55). The Miscellaneous preferences are largely self-explanatory, with the exception of "Double-click edits Camera Raw settings in Bridge." When this preference is turned off (which it is by default), double-clicking a raw's thumbnail opens it in Camera Raw hosted by Photoshop. When it's checked, doing the same thing opens the raw image in Camera Raw hosted by Bridge. This preference works as advertised, but has a non-obvious impact on some other file-opening keyboard shortcuts (see "File Info and the File Menu," on the next page). The other important setting in this panel is the choice of whether to use centralized or distributed cache files.

Bridge's cache holds the image thumbnails and previews, custom sort order, and—for file types that can't store metadata either in the file itself or in a sidecar .xmp file—label and rating information. For raw files, only the thumbnails, previews, and custom sort order are stored uniquely in the Bridge cache, but since the thumbnails and previews take some time to generate, they're pretty important.

Figure 11-54
Bridge Preferences,
File Type Associations

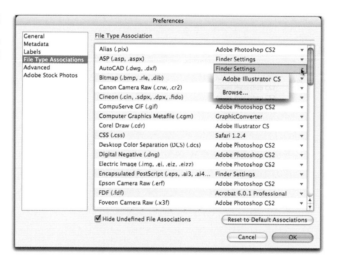

Figure 11-55
Bridge Preferences,
Advanced

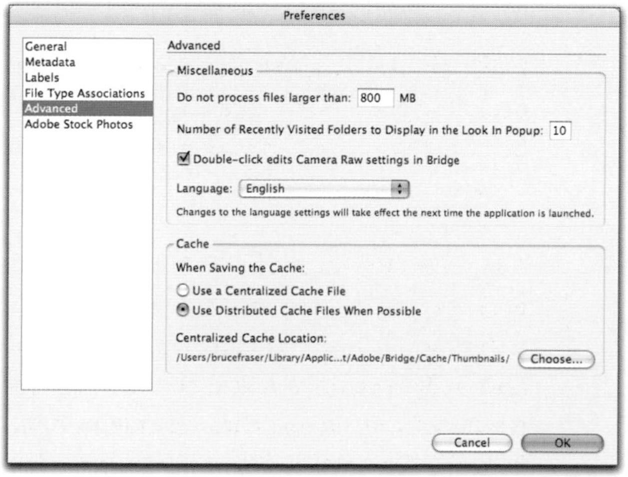

The only advantage offered by using a centralized cache is simplicity—you know where all your cache files are. The significant disadvantages of the centralized cache are:

▶ If you move or rename a folder outside Bridge, the connection to the cache files is lost.

▶ When you burn a folder full of images to a CD or DVD, you first have to go through the extra step of exporting the cache. If you don't, the recipient of the CD or DVD has to take the time to recache the folder, rebuilding thumbnails and previews, and any custom sort order is lost.

Using a distributed cache avoids both problems. The cache files are written directly into the folder to which they pertain, and travel with the folder even when it's renamed or moved. But note that if Bridge for some reason can't write a distributed cache (the volume may be read-only, or mounted on a server) it writes to the central cache instead.

The only real downside to using distributed caches is that every folder that Bridge has opened ends up with two files named Adobe Bridge Cache. bc and Adobe Bridge Cache.bct. By default, Bridge hides these files, but the Macintosh Finder and Windows Explorer do not. If this makes you squirrely, by all means use the centralized cache; otherwise it's well worth suffering the small inconvenience to obtain the benefits of distributed caching. (And besides, it's often useful to be able to see the cache files so that you can check that they're present and up-to-date.)

File Info and the File Menu

The bulk of the commands on the File menu let you do things that are better accomplished via keyboard shortcuts—opening images, creating new windows, and so on (see Figure 11-56).

In the case of raw images, the subtle difference between "Open" (Command-O) and "Open in Camera Raw" (Command-R) is that the former opens the raw image or images in Camera Raw hosted by Photoshop, while the latter opens the raw image or images in Camera Raw hosted by Bridge. There are several easier ways to open images than choosing the menu commands, including the aforementioned keyboard shortcuts, and the ones listed in Table 11-1.

Most of the other commands are self-explanatory. However, the File Info command, which opens the File Info panel, deserves a closer look (see Figure 11-57).

The first thing you'll notice when you open File Info in Bridge is that it's a modal panel (not a movable modal dialog box) that helpfully covers all the images. We find this behavior a bit south of being ideal!

Figure 11-56
Bridge File menu

File	
New Window	⌘N
New Folder	⇧⌘N
Open	⌘O
Open With	▶
Open in Camera Raw...	⌘R
Eject	⌘E
Close Window	⌘W
Move to Trash	⌘⌫
Return to Adobe Photoshop CS2	⌥⌘O
Reveal in Finder	
Reveal in Bridge	
Place	▶
Add to Favorites	
File Info...	⌥⇧⌘I
Versions...	⌥⇧⌘V
Alternates...	

Table 11-1
Opening raw images

To do this...	Press this
Open raw images in Camera Raw hosted by Bridge, leaving Photoshop unaffected.	Command/Ctrl-R
Open raw images in Camera Raw hosted by Photoshop, bringing Photoshop to the foreground, and leaving Bridge visible in the background.	Command/Ctrl-O, Return/Enter, or Command/Ctrl-down arrow
Open raw images in Camera Raw hosted by Photoshop, bringing Photoshop to the foreground, and hiding Bridge.	Option-Return/Alt-Enter, or Command-Option-down arrow / Ctrl-Alt-down arrow
Open raw images directly into Photoshop, bypassing the Camera Raw dialog box, bringing Photoshop to the foreground, and leaving Bridge visible in the background.	Shift-Return/Enter, or Command-Shift-down arrow / Ctrl-Shift-down arrow
Open raw images directly into Photoshop, bypassing the Camera Raw dialog box, bringing Photoshop to the foreground, and hiding Bridge.	Option-Shift-Return / Alt-Shift-Enter, or Command-Option-Shift-down arrow / Ctrl-Alt-Shift-down arrow

Figure 11-57
Bridge File Info

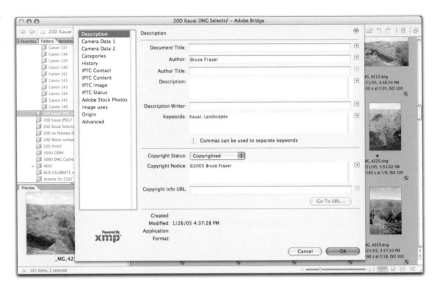

While Bridge allows you to open File Info when multiple images are selected (the old File Browser did not), it's a relatively inefficient way to apply keywords and other metadata when compared to the Metadata and Keywords palettes. Nevertheless, we use it in three ways:

▶ To add image-specific keywords that we don't want to save in a keyword set to small numbers of images.

▶ To examine metadata in something close to raw form—for example, to see exactly how the camera encodes things like shutter speed and aperture value, or the date and time shot—by looking in the Advanced panel of File Info under EXIF Properties.

▶ To save Metadata Templates that we can apply from the Metadata palette menu (see Figure 11-58).

Select, Find, and Edit with the Edit Menu

The Edit menu hosts Bridge's Preferences command on Windows. It also hosts the usual Copy, Paste, Cut, and Duplicate commands, as well as the Rotate commands (whose functionality is replicated by Bridge's Rotate buttons). The important commands for the raw workflow are the various Select commands, the Find command, and the Apply Camera Raw Settings commands (see Figure 11-59).

Figure 11-58
Save Metadata Template

To save a Metadata template, make the entries you want the template to contain in File Info, then choose Save Metadata Template from the File Info panel's flyout menu. This template applies the copyright flag and notice.

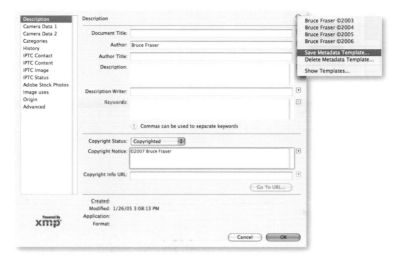

Figure 11-59
The Edit menu

Selection commands —

Find command —

Apply Camera Raw —
Settings command

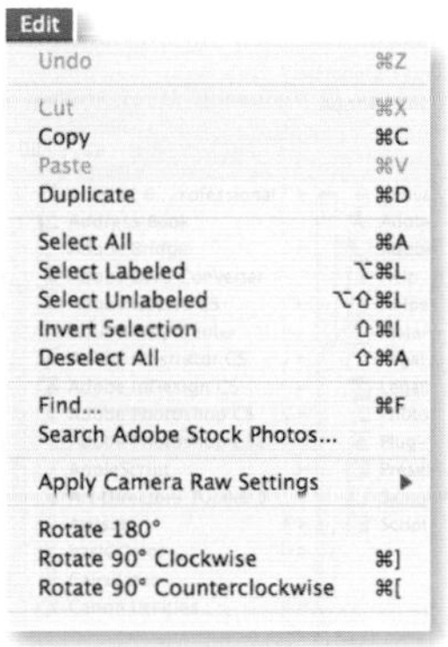

Selection commands. The Select commands offer quick ways to manipulate selections. Select All (press Command-A), Deselect All (press Command-Shift-A) and Invert Selection (press Command-Shift-I) do exactly what they say—Invert Selection deselects the files that were selected and selects those that weren't. The two remaining commands, Select Labeled and Select Unlabeled (press Command-Option-L and Command-Option-Shift-L, respectively), work in conjunction with Bridge's Label feature, which lets you apply one of five labels, or no label, to images. See "Labeling, Rating, and the Label Menu," later in this chapter.

Find command. The Find command lets you perform searches using up to 13 different search criteria (see Figure 11-60).

Figure 11-60
The Find dialog box

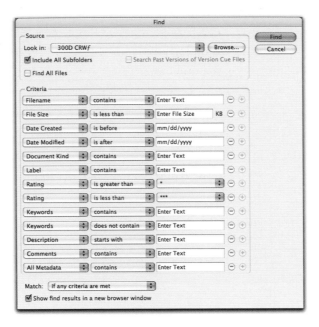

In addition to the criteria, the Find dialog box has the following important features.

▶ **Include All Subfolders** does what it says—it extends the search to include any subfolders in the folder specified in the Look In menu.

▶ **Find All Files** also does what it says (when you check this option, the selection criteria are grayed out). This feature is mostly useful in conjunction with the "Show find results in a new browser window" option when you've done a lot of work winnowing down files using ratings and labels, and you want to see all the images quickly in a new window.

▶ **The Match menu** lets you choose whether to find files if any criterion is met (equivalent to an "or" between the criteria), or to find files only if all criteria are met (equivalent to an "and" between the criteria).

▶ **Show find results in new browser window**... well, it's likely that you can figure that one out by y'self.

Save As Collection. When you perform a search, you have the option to save the search criteria as a "collection." Unfortunately, it's slightly confusing that the option doesn't appear in the Find dialog box, but rather in the results window (see Figure 11-61).

When you save a collection, you can save it as an "absolute" search or a "relative" search. Absolute searches always search the folder you specified in the Find dialog box's Look In popup menu when you performed the initial search that created the results; relative searches can be applied to any folder. Turning on the "Start Search From Current Folder" option in the Save Collection dialog box creates a relative search; leaving it turned off creates an absolute one. Collections are saved in User/Library/Application Support/Adobe/Bridge/Collections (Mac) or Documents and Settings\Username\Application Data\Adobe\Bridge\Collections (Windows).

Figure 11-61
Save As Collection

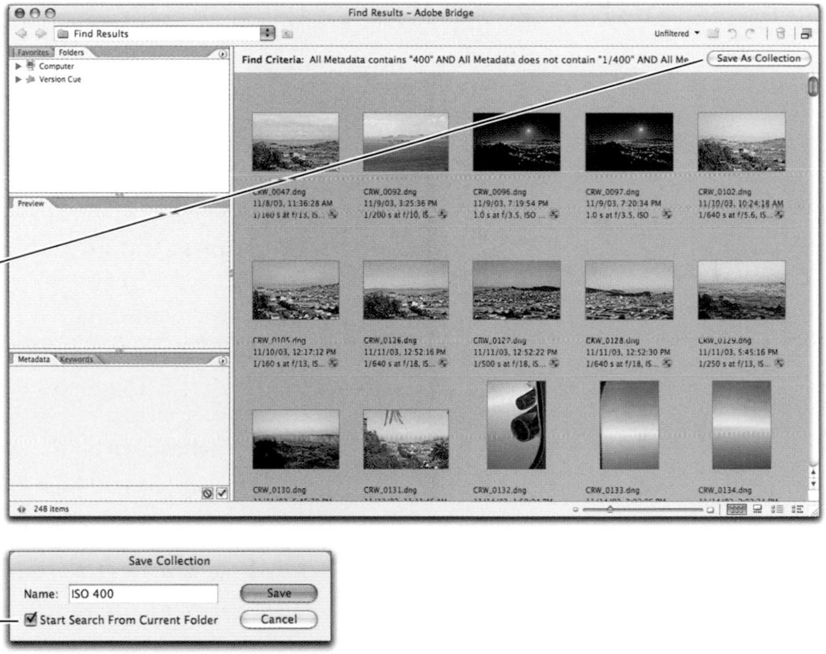

To save search criteria as a collection, click the Save As Collection button.

Turn on this option if you want to apply the search to any folder. Leave it off if you always want to search the same folder.

Apply Camera Raw Settings. The Apply Camera Raw Settings submenu lets you apply Camera Raw Defaults or Previous Conversion (the last-used Camera Raw settings) to selected images (see Figure 11-62). It also lets you copy settings from an image and apply them to others by pasting, or clear existing settings from an image. Finally, it lets you apply any saved settings that you've saved in Camera Raw's Settings folder (see "Loading and Saving Settings" earlier in this chapter).

The difference between applying Camera Raw defaults and clearing Camera Raw settings is rather subtle. The effect on the image is identi-

Figure 11-62
Apply Camera
Raw Settings

Saved custom settings
appear at the foot of the
Apply Camera Raw
Settings submenu.

cal in both cases, but Bridge offers a useful piece of feedback that shows whether or not an image has settings applied to it (see Figure 11-63). When you apply Camera Raw defaults, Bridge treats the image as having had settings applied; when you clear the settings, Bridge treats the image as having no settings applied.

Figure 11-63
Apply Camera Raw
Defaults and Clear
Camera Raw Settings

When you choose Apply Camera Raw
Defaults, Bridge indicates that the
image has settings applied.

When you choose Clear Camera Raw
Settings, Bridge indicates that the
image has no settings applied.

The Copy Camera Raw Settings command (Command-Option-C) copies all the Camera Raw settings from the selected image. When you choose Paste Camera Raw Settings (Command-Option-V), the dialog box shown in Figure 11-64 appears, giving you the opportunity to choose all the settings, any individual parameter, or everything in between, to apply to the image or images to which you're pasting the settings.

Pasting Camera Raw Settings to multiple images offers an alternative to working directly in Camera Raw in filmstrip mode.

Figure 11-64
Paste Camera
Raw Settings

The checkboxes let you
apply individual settings;
the menu lets you choose a
group of settings quickly.

Automation, the Cache, and the Tools Menu

The Tools menu provides access to several useful Photoshop-hosted automation features as well as Bridge's own Batch Rename feature, allows you to manipulate Bridge's cache files, and provides an alternative means of applying metadata templates if you don't want to use the Metadata palette menu (see Figure 11-65).

Figure 11-65
The Tools menu

Batch Rename. Bridge's Batch Rename feature looks nothing like Photoshop's, though it offers essentially the same functionality. The option to preserve the current filename in XMP metadata actually adds a custom metadata tag containing the filename. If you've already applied Camera Raw settings before renaming, you can skip this option because the Camera Raw settings metadata already contains the original filename, but if you're renaming otherwise-untouched raw files, and you want the original filename to be retrievable, it's a good idea to turn on this option.

Tip: Undoing Renaming. One of the useful things that the aforementioned "Preserve current filename in XMP Metadata" option allows is easy undoing of batch renaming. Simply choose Batch Rename, and specify Preserved Filename. Your files will get renamed to their original filenames.

You can add up to 10 different sets of data for inclusion in the filename. Since Bridge is eminently JavaScriptable, you can expect to see a variety of useful image-ingestion scripts, possibly including some from Adobe, that will likely include more flexible metadata-based renaming features, but Bridge's Batch Rename at least provides baseline functionality out of the box.

Photoshop. The Photoshop submenu (see Figure 11-66) provides access to several useful Photoshop automation features. If you want to run any of these automations using images selected in Bridge as the source, you *must* launch them from Bridge's Tools menu—if you try to launch them from Photoshop's Automate submenu (in the File menu), you'll find that Bridge is either grayed out or simply unavailable as the source.

Figure 11-66
The Photoshop submenu

To invoke any of the Automate features from Bridge, select the images you want processed through the automation, then choose that automation from the Photoshop submenu (in Bridge's Tools menu). Photoshop then goes to work, opening the images using the Camera Raw settings you've applied, or the camera-specific default settings if you haven't applied settings to the image, then processing them using the settings you've specified for the automation. You can continue to work in Bridge while Photoshop is processing the images.

Labeling, Rating, and the Label Menu

The Label menu offers a not-very-efficient alternative to the keyboard shortcuts for applying labels or ratings to your images (see Figure 11-67). The only things you can do from this menu that you can't do with keyboard shortcuts are to remove a label, and to apply the fifth label, which by default is called Purple (though you can change its name in Bridge's Preferences; see "Labels Preferences," earlier in this chapter).

Labels and ratings are entirely separate (see Figure 11-68). Labels apply the selected label color to the image thumbnail's label area, and write the label text into the image's metadata (in the Label field under File Properties). Ratings apply zero to five stars to the image thumbnail's rating area, and write the rating (from one to five) into the image's metadata (in the Rating field under File Properties).

You can search images by label and by rating, and sort images by label *or* by rating. Last but not least, you can use the Unfiltered/Filtered menu (on Bridge's toolbar, not on the menu bar) to filter which images are displayed in the Bridge window based on label, on rating, or by doing first one, then the other, on both.

Figure 11-67
The Label menu

Figure 11-68
Labels and ratings

Labels appear as colored swatches beneath the thumbnails. Ratings appear as stars in the label area. Both the label text and the rating appear in the File Properties metadata.

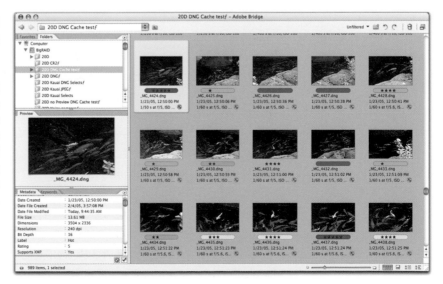

Labels and ratings are simply arbitrary flags that you can apply to images. It's entirely up to you to decide what they mean. Bruce dislikes the Label feature because he doesn't want extraneous color in his field of view when he's looking at images, but he admits that that's a personal bias—what's important is that you come up with a system that works for you. For some suggestions on how to use these features, see "Rating and Labeling," later in this chapter.

Applying labels and ratings. By far the easiest way to apply labels or ratings is to use the keyboard shortcuts (most of which also work in Camera Raw). To apply red, yellow, green, and blue labels, press Command-6 through Command-9, respectively. To apply the purple label, or to remove labels, you must use the menu commands. Inside Camera Raw, the purple label can be toggled using Command-Shift-0.

To apply ratings, press Command-1 through Command-5 to apply that number of stars, and press Command-0 to remove ratings. Inside Camera Raw, the shortcut is command-~ (tilde) because Command-0 fits the image in the preview. You can also press Command-. (period) to increase the rating by one star or Command-, (comma) to reduce it. A slower but sometimes convenient alternative is to click and drag in the rating area of the thumbnail—dragging to the right increases the rating, and dragging to the left reduces it. Last but not least, Command-' (apostrophe), toggles one star on or off.

Bridge Display and the View Menu

The commands on the View menu offer a variety of controls over the way Bridge displays both its windows and their contents. In the former category, several of the commands replicate the functionality of the control buttons in Bridge's windows—Compact Mode, As Thumbnails, As Filmstrip, As Details, and As Versions and Alternates (the last is relevant for VersionCue users only). Others toggle the visibility of the individual panels—Favorites, Folders, Preview, Metadata, and Keywords (see Figure 11-69).

Sort. You can sort the contents of the Bridge window based on the file properties listed in the Sort submenu. Or, if you sort images into a custom order by dragging their thumbnails around, you'll see a checkmark next to the "Manually" item—choosing this from the submenu has no effect unless

Figure 11-69
The View menu

you've previously sorted your images manually, in which case it switches to the last manual sort order you used.

Show Thumbnail Only. The Show Thumbnail Only command suppresses the display of the filenames and any other optional metadata displayed under the thumbnails. Press Command-T to toggle the metadata display on and off.

Note that despite its name, Show Thumbnail Only doesn't hide the other palettes. The easiest way to perform that trick is to click the Show/Hide panels button at the lower left of the window. Or, alternately, choose a Workspace that hides them from the Workspace submenu under the Window menu (see "The Window Menu and Bridge Configuration," later in this chapter).

Content filtering commands. Six commands on the View menu let you control the types of content Bridge displays in its windows.

▶ **Show Hidden Files** toggles whether or not Bridge displays sidecar .xmp files and Bridge cache files, as well as files that are normally hidden by the operating system, in its windows *and* in the Folders panel. By default, it's turned off.

▶ **Show Folders** toggles the display of subfolders. By default, it's turned on; we're not sure why you wouldn't want to see subfolders.

▶ **Show All Files** shows all file types *except* those that are governed by Show Hidden Files.

▶ **Show Graphic Files Only** shows most types of graphics files, including TIFF, JPEG, EPS, Photoshop, and Camera Raw. Curiously, it doesn't show PDF, even when the PDF is created by Photoshop.

▶ **Show Camera Raw Files Only** does exactly what it says. Use this when you only want to see raw files with no distractions from other file types—but don't forget that you've turned it on; otherwise you may waste some time in fruitless searches for your TIFFs and JPEGs!

▶ **Show Vector Files Only** shows Illustrator (.ai), EPS, and PDF files (sadly, including those PDFs that only contain pixels).

Slide Show. Slide Show (press Command-L) offers an alternative to Bridge's light table metaphor by presenting selected images as a slide show that also allows you to apply ratings and rotations while enjoying the benefits of a large image preview. Press H (with no modifier) to display all the keyboard shortcuts that apply in Slide Show mode.

You can run the slide show in a window, or in full-screen mode with the image either scaled to fit the screen (the entire image is displayed at the maximum size that will fit your screen) or scaled to fill your screen (the image is cropped to the aspect ratio of your screen and displayed at maximum size).

The Window Menu and Bridge Configuration

The one item in the Window menu you're likely to use again and again, besides simply choosing open windows, is the Workspace submenu. This lets you save and recall custom Bridge configurations. Bridge ships with four preconfigured Workspaces—Lightbox, File Navigator, Metadata Focus, and Filmstrip Focus—but if you're at all like us you'll probably find that none of them is exactly what you want.

Fortunately, Bridge windows are eminently configurable, and you can save your custom configurations as Workspaces too. You can dock the panels as you wish, resize them by dragging their borders, remove panels you don't need using the View menu commands, or hide all the panels using the Show/Hide panels toggle.

Saving Workspaces in Bridge is easy. Configure the window the way you want the Workspace to appear, then choose Save Workspace from the Workspace submenu. Enter a name (and, optionally, a keyboard shortcut), then click Save. Turn on the Save Window Location as Part of Workspace option if you always want the window to appear in the same place (very useful on dual-monitor setups). Your saved Workspace is then added to the Workspace menu (see Figure 11-70).

For those of you who have to know where all things get saved, Workspaces are stored in Users/username/Library/Application Support/Adobe/Bridge/Workspaces on Mac OS and in Documents and Settings\Username\Application Data\Adobe\Bridge\Workspaces on Windows.

Tip: Bridge Navigation. You can always navigate in Bridge with the mouse, but it's often more efficient to do so from the keyboard. Here's a list of most of our favorites.

Figure 11-70
Saving a Workspace

Configure the window the way you want the Workspace to behave. In this case, we're displaying two maximum-size thumbnails side by side with filename and metadata hidden.

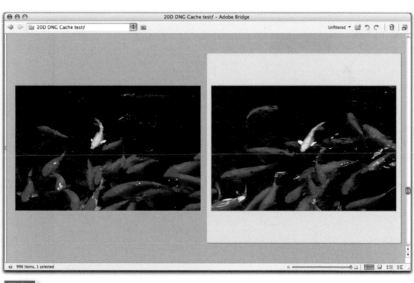

Choose Save Workspace from the Workspace submenu on the Window menu.

Name and save your Workspace.

In the Folders panel, the up and down arrow keys move up and down one folder at a time. Adding the Command key moves up one level in the hierarchy. The right arrow key expands folders containing subfolders; the left arrow key collapses them.

In the Metadata panel, Tab advances to the next editable field, Shift-Tab to the previous one, and Enter commits an entry. In the Keywords panel, the up and down arrows move up and down the keywords list.

In the main window, the up, down, left, and right arrows move the selection to the next thumbnail in their respective directions. Adding Shift extends the selection to include the next thumbnail in that direction. (You can't, however, make discontiguous selections from the keyboard—you have to Command-click the thumbnails to add noncontiguous images to the selection.) Home selects the first thumbnail, and End selects the last one. Command-A selects all thumbnails, and Command-Shift-A deselects all thumbnails. Command-Option-L selects all labeled images, while Command-Option-Shift-L selects all unlabeled images. Last but not least, Command-Shift-I inverts the selection, deselecting the selected images and selecting the formerly unselected ones.

Working in Bridge

Camera Raw is a wonderful raw converter, and Bridge is a pretty capable image manager, but what really makes Photoshop CS2 a compelling solution for a raw digital workflow is the integration between the two. As soon as Bridge encounters a folder of raw files, Camera Raw kicks in automatically, generating thumbnails and generous-size previews that allow you to make good judgments about each image without actually converting it, so that you can quickly make your initial selects.

Note that the previews are based on Camera Raw's default settings for your camera. If you find that they're consistently off, it's a sign that you need to change your Camera Default settings (see "Loading and Saving Settings" earlier in this chapter).

Then, when you've decided which images you want to work with, Bridge lets you apply conversion settings from Camera Raw by writing them to the image's metadata, again without doing an actual conversion, using either the Apply Camera Raw Settings command or—if you need to see larger zoomable previews—in Camera Raw itself.

Other than quick one-offs, we almost always do our conversions as batch processes, incorporating other actions—we may set up one batch to produce high-res JPEGs for client approval, another to produce low-res JPEGs for e-mailing, and still another to prepare images for localized editing in Photoshop, with adjustment layers already added so that much of the grunt work is already done.

However, before we look at any more details of how Bridge and Camera Raw work, or how you can automate your workflow, we want to focus on some theories and philosophies that we think are helpful.

Workflow Principles

There are likely as many workflows are there are photographers—maybe more! One of the wonderful things about Bridge, Camera Raw 3.0, and Photoshop CS2 is the incredible workflow flexibility that they offer. The price of this flexibility is, of course, complexity. There are multiple ways to accomplish almost any task, and it may not be obvious at first glance which way is optimal in a given situation. Understanding the different ways of accomplishing the basic tasks is the tactical level. But to make a workflow, you also need a strategy that tells you how and when to employ those tactics.

Even a single photographer may need more than one workflow. On the one hand, there's the workflow you need when you're on a shoot, the client is looking over your shoulder, and you need to agree on the hero shots before you strike the lighting and move on. On the other hand, there's the workflow you'd like to follow when you're reviewing personal work with no deadlines attached. These two scenarios represent extremes, and there are many points on the continuum between them.

We can't build your workflow for you, since we know neither your needs nor your preferences. Instead, we'll offer two key principles of workflow efficiency that should always guide you in how to employ them.

▶ Do things *once,* efficiently.

▶ Do things automatically whenever possible.

Doing Things Once

When you apply metadata such as copyright, rights management, and keywords to your raw file, the metadata is automatically carried through to all the TIFFs, JPEGs, or PSDs that you derive from that raw file, so you only need to enter that metadata once.

By the same token, if you exploit the power of Camera Raw to its fullest, many of your images may need little or no postconversion work in Photoshop, so applying Camera Raw edits to your images is likewise something that can often be done only once.

A key strategy that helps you do things once is: Start with the general and proceed to the specific. Start with the things that can be done to the greatest number of images, then make increasingly more detailed treatments of ever-decreasing numbers of images, reserving the full treatment—careful hand-editing in Camera Raw and Photoshop, applying image-specific keywords, and so on—to those images that truly deserve the attention.

Do Things Automatically

Automation is a vital survival tool for simply dealing with the volumes of data a raw workflow entails. Once you've told a computer how to do something, it can do that something over and over again. Photoshop actions are obvious automation features, but metadata templates and Camera Raw presets are important automations, too.

We rarely open a single image from Camera Raw directly into Photoshop unless we're stacking multiple renderings of the raw file into the same Photoshop image. Even then, we use the Option-Open shortcut to open the images as copies so that we don't have to rename them manually in Photoshop—that, too, is an automation feature!

In the vast majority of cases, we convert our raw images using either Batch or Image Processor, and we use actions to create adjustment layers so that the images are immediately ready for editing.

Be Methodical

Once you've found a rhythm that works for you, stick to it. Being methodical and sticking to a routine makes mistakes less likely, and allows you to focus on the important image decisions that only you can make.

For better or worse, computers always do *exactly* what you tell them to, even if that's jumping off a cliff. Established routines (and Actions) help ensure that you're telling the computer to do what you really want it to.

Planning and Strategy

An efficient workflow requires planning. You can flail around and try every-thing—it's actually not a bad way to get your feet wet—but at some point, you have to decide what works, and stick with it.

Among the things you need to decide, and stick with, are the following.

▶ **Bridge cache.** You can use a centralized cache, or use distributed caches. Each has its strengths and weaknesses, but your life will be simpler, and your workflow more robust, if you pick one approach and stick to it.

▶ **Camera Raw settings for individual images.** You can save the Camera Raw settings for each image in the Camera Raw database, in sidecar .xmp files, or in the case of DNG format, in the DNG file itself. It's slightly easier to switch from one approach to another in Bridge with Camera Raw 3 than it was with File Browser and Camera Raw 2, but doing so requires considerable work and a great deal of care.

▶ **File naming conventions.** If filenames like _MG_3672.cr2 drive you batty, you probably want to rename your raw files. If you do, pick a naming convention that makes sense to you, and stick with it.

▶ **Labels and ratings.** The labels and ratings you apply in Bridge or Camera Raw are simply arbitrary flags. Labels and ratings give you two sets of flags, each of which contains six possible values when you include no label and no rating. It's entirely up to you what they mean. Again, pick a system that makes sense to you, and stick with it!

You'll need to make plenty of decisions when you're working on your images. It's a Bad Idea to start making decisions about any of the aforemen-tioned when you're working on a deadline, because doing so introduces complexity (of which you already have enough) and increases the chance of unintended consequences (which you want to avoid).

Bridge Cache

As we mentioned in earlier in this chapter, Bridge's cache performs the important task of storing image thumbnails, previews, and sort order. (For file types that can't support sidecar .xmp files, it also stores keywords and metadata, but that doesn't apply to raw formats.) Bridge's Advanced Prefer-ences let you choose whether to use a central cache or distributed caches (see the Advanced Preferences section under "Preferences and the Bridge Menu" earlier in this chapter).

The only downside to using distributed cache files is that you end up with two cache files in every folder that Bridge ever sees. If that drives you crazy, by all means use a central cache instead, but do so with the clear knowledge that you run the risk of losing thumbnails, previews, and custom sort orders when you do any of the following:

▶ Rename a folder outside of Bridge.

▶ Copy a folder outside of Bridge.

▶ Burn a folder to removable media such as CD-ROM or DVD.

▶ Copy a folder to a different computer.

You can work around these limitations of the central cache by using the Export Cache command from Bridge's Cache submenu (in the Tools menu), but you're introducing complexity that is unnecessary with distributed caches, and hence creating more opportunities for operator error.

When you use a central cache, you're putting all your eggs in one basket. You can control where the central cache gets stored, so you don't have to store it in the default location on your startup drive where it's vulnerable to permissions issues and other ills. But like pets, all hard drives die eventually, and storing all your caches in one folder incurs the risk that you'll lose them all. With distributed caches, every folder contains a cache automatically, you can copy and rename your folders without having to think about it, and when the inevitable does happen, you've only lost what was on that drive. (Which was of course backed up, right?)

Strategies for Settings

You can save Camera Raw settings either in the Camera Raw Database or in sidecar .xmp files. The same arguments may seem to apply to the Camera Raw Database as apply to the centralized Bridge cache, but in fact it's not that simple.

The Camera Raw Database indexes images by their content, not by their filenames, so you can copy, move, or rename them willy-nilly without losing track of your raw settings—but only as long as the images remain on the same computer as the Camera Raw Database. Move them to another machine, and the settings are gone (or, rather, they're still on the originating computer where they'll do absolutely no good). If you always remember to use Camera Raw's Export Settings command to write out a sidecar .xmp file for the image, and you always remember to include the sidecar file with the image, there's no problem. But that's a lot of "always remembering."

Bridge does its best to keep track of sidecar .xmp files—as long as you only copy, move, and rename your raw files in Bridge, the sidecar files travel with them automatically. But if you copy, move, or rename your raw files *outside* of Bridge, you must keep track of your sidecar files and move them with the images manually. Again, it's not an ideal solution.

A third alternative is to use the DNG format instead. The convenience of having all the metadata, including Camera Raw settings, stored right in the file itself outweighs the one-time speed bump entailed in converting the raws to DNG. But if you want to use your camera vendor's converter, and your camera doesn't write DNG, you should stick with proprietary raws for your working files, at least for now.

What's in a Name?

If you want to make a practice of renaming your raw files, we suggest the following two simple rules:

▶ Adopt a naming convention that makes sense to you, and stick to it (in other words, be methodical).

▶ What's in a name? Anything you want, but if you want that name to be consistently readable across platforms and operating systems, stick to alphanumeric characters—no spaces (the underscore is a good alternative), and no special characters.

    The only place a period should appear is immediately in front of the extension—today's OSs tend to treat everything following a period as an extension, and promptly hide it, so periods in the middle of filenames often cause those filenames to be truncated. Many special characters are reserved for special uses by one or another operating system. Including them in filenames can produce unpredictable results.

Aside from these two simple rules, file naming conventions are limited only by your ingenuity. Don't overlook metadata as a source for naming elements, and expect to see ingestion scripts that offer more metadata-related naming features than Bridge's Batch Rename from both Adobe and third-party scripters.

Ratings and Labels

Bridge and Camera Raw offer two independent mechanisms, labels and ratings, for flagging images. Each mechanism offers six possible values: if you use them in combination, you can have 36 possible combinations of ratings and labels, which is almost certainly more than most people need!

If you think you can use a system with 36 values productively, knock yourself out. Otherwise, we suggest keeping things simple. The ratings system mimics the time-honored practice of making selects on a light table by marking the keepers from the first round with a single dot, adding a second dot to the keepers from the second round, and so on.

Bruce uses labels for various esoteric purposes. For example, he applies the purple label (renamed as "weird") to the ever-growing collection of high-ISO sodium-vapor-lit nighttime cityscapes he uses for testing noise reduction techniques, but hides them of the time. Labels are handy for this kind of use because they operate independently of the star-based rating system. If you can think of uses for them, go ahead and use them, but don't feel that just because a feature exists, you have to use it.

Simplicity Is Its Own Strategy

Camera Raw, Bridge, and Photoshop offer an amazing number of options. Only a genius or a fool would try to use them all. If, like us, you're neither, we recommend keeping things as simple as possible without making any overly painful compromises.

The four issues discussed in this section—Bridge cache, Camera Raw settings, naming conventions, and rating/labeling strategies—are things that can't be changed later without considerable pain. By all means spend some time trying out the options before setting your strategies in stone, but once you've found the approach that works best for you, don't change it arbitrarily. If you do, it's entirely likely that you'll lose work, whether it's Camera Raw edits, Bridge thumbnails, ratings, or simply winding up with a bunch of incomprehensibly named files. Any of these violates the first workflow principle—do things once, efficiently—and you pay for it with that most precious commodity, your time.

Workflow Phases

We've spent most of this chapter looking at the various tools offered by Bridge and Camera Raw. But knowing what buttons to push to get the desired result just means you know how to do the work. To turn that understanding into a practical *workflow*, you need to understand and optimize each part of the process.

There are four basic stages in a raw workflow. You may revisit some of them—going back and looking at the initial rejects, or processing the images to different kinds of output file—but everything you do falls into one of four stages.

▶ **Image ingestion.** You start by copying the raw images to at least one hard disk on the computer.

▶ **Image verification.** You point Bridge at the newly copied images and let it cache the thumbnails, previews, and metadata.

▶ **Preproduction.** You work with the images in Bridge, selecting, sorting, applying metadata, and editing with Camera Raw.

▶ **Production.** You process the raw images to output files.

In the remainder of this chapter, we'll look at each of these four stages, but our major emphasis lies in the preproduction stage—the work you do in Bridge—because about 80 percent of the actual work happens in this stage, even if it only takes about 20 percent of the time spent.

Image Ingestion

Transferring your images from the camera to the computer is one of the most critical yet often one of the least examined stages of your workflow. It's critical because at this stage, your images exist only on the camera media. Compact Flash, Secure Digital, and microdrives aren't dramatically more fragile than other storage media, but at this stage there's only one copy! Losing previews or camera raw settings is irritating, but you can redo the work. If you make mistakes during ingestion, though, you can lose entire images.

The following ground rules have thus far prevented us from losing even a single image.

▶ Don't use the camera as a card reader. Most cameras will let you connect them to the computer and download your images, but that's a bad idea for at least two reasons: Cameras are very slow as card readers, and when the camera is acting as card reader, you can't shoot with it.

▶ Never open images directly from the camera media. It's been formatted with the expectation that the only thing that will write to it is the camera. If something else writes to it, maybe nothing will happen, but then again, maybe something bad will.

▶ Don't rely on just one copy of the images—always copy them to two separate drives before you start working.

▶ Don't erase your images from the camera media until you've verified the copies (see "Image Verification," below).

▶ Always format the cards in the camera in which they will be shot, never in the computer.

Following these rules takes a little additional time up front, but much less than a reshoot (assuming that lost images can in fact be reshot).

Tip: When Disaster Strikes. If you wind up with a card that's unreadable but contains data you want to recover (it's rare, but it can be caused by doing things like pulling the card out of the reader without first ejecting it in software), *do not* format it! Doing so will guarantee that any data that was still on the card will be permanently consigned to the bitbucket. Major CF card vendors such as SanDisk and Lexar include data-recovery software with the cards. Before attempting anything else, try the recovery software. If that fails, and the data is truly irreplaceable, several companies offer data recovery from CF cards, usually at a fairly hefty price—a Google search for "Compact Flash Data Recovery" will turn up all the major players.

Image Verification

Once you've copied the raw files to your hard disk, the next thing to do is to point Bridge at the folder containing the raw images. Bridge is command central for dealing with hundreds of images. You'll use it to make your initial selects, to apply and edit metadata including Camera Raw settings, and to control the processing of the raw images into a deliverable form.

But before you start doing any of these things, give Bridge a few minutes to generate the thumbnails and previews and to read the image metadata. Photoshop's old File Browser was almost unusable while it was building previews. Bridge is much more responsive while building previews, but it's not exactly snappy; we think it's still a good idea to let it finish building the cache for the folder before starting work.

The reason is simple. While you can identify and open raw images as soon as the thumbnail appears, the thumbnails are generated by the camera and Bridge simply displays them. To build the high-quality previews, though, Camera Raw has to actually read the raw data.

If there's a problem reading the images, the problem will only show up on the high-quality thumbnail and preview. The initial thumbnails are the camera-generated ones, and they don't indicate that the raw file has been read successfully. The high-quality ones *do* indicate that the raw file has been read successfully, so wait until you see them before you erase the raw image files from the camera media.

If you see a problem at this stage, check the second copy (if you made one) or go back to the camera media. It's fairly rare for the data to get corrupted in the camera (though it does sometimes happen, particularly in burst-mode shooting), so the first suspect should be the card reader.

Feeding the Cache

Bridge's cache holds the thumbnails, previews, and sort order information for each folder at which you point it. (The cache may contain additional information for other file types, but with raw files the thumbnails, previews, and sort order are the only pieces of data that are uniquely stored in the Bridge cache.) With a brand-new folder of images, there's no custom sort order, so the caching process consists of reading the thumbnails and EXIF metadata, and building the high-quality previews.

This is a two-pass process. The first pass reads the thumbnails and metadata, the second pass actually uses Camera Raw to build the high-quality previews—it's this second pass that lets you verify the raw images.

When you point Bridge at a folder of raw images for the first time, it goes to work. You may see a message that reads "Examining folder contents." That's quickly followed by a second message, "Getting *filename* thumbnail." This pass extracts the camera-created thumbnail from the raw images (see Figure 11-71).

The last phase of the initial cache-building process is also the most crucial one—generating previews. In this phase, Bridge uses Camera Raw to build higher-quality thumbnails than the ones that appear initially. They're downsampled versions of the result you'd get if you processed the raw file using the current Camera Raw Default settings. If you look closely, you can see the thumbnails updating. (Even in print at this small size, you can probably see the difference between the thumbnails in Figure 11-71 and the ones in Figure 11-72.)

Figure 11-71
Getting thumbnails

Figure 11-72
Generating previews

Once Bridge has finished generating the previews, it displays a message showing the number of images in the folder, indicating that it's ready for you to move to the preproduction phase. Large previews appear instantly when you advance from one image to another, so you can work quickly.

Interrupting the Cache

In the real world, you might not have time to wait for the entire cache to be created. There are a couple of ways to start work while Bridge is still building its cache. You're still verifying the images, just not necessarily in the order in which Bridge loaded them.

If you need to start working with a specific image right now, you can force Bridge to read all the data and build the preview by selecting the thumbnail in the Bridge window. Bridge gives preference to that image, and generates a preview before moving on to the other images. Unfortunately, this approach doesn't work with multiple images—Bridge builds the preview for the first selected image, then carries on reading thumbnails. You can also scroll the Bridge window to give preference to a series of images—Bridge always builds previews for those images whose thumbnails are currently visible in the main window first.

But the most effective way of getting images while Bridge is still caching is to select the thumbnails, then press Command-O to open the images in Camera Raw filmstrip mode hosted by Photoshop. Camera Raw builds the previews very quickly, and because it's hosted by Photoshop, it has a minimal effect on Bridge's caching performance. You can apply ratings or labels in Camera Raw in addition to editing the images. The only thing you can't do is to apply keywords, or metadata other than labels, ratings, and Camera Raw settings.

Tip: Download to Your Fastest Drive. Cache-building is largely dependent on disk speed, so the faster the drive to which you download the raw images, the faster Bridge builds the cache. Consider dedicating a partition on your fastest drive, the same size as your camera media, for downloading and caching your raw images. If you use distributed caches in Bridge, you can then copy the folder to another drive without having to do anything else to keep your thumbnails and previews intact.

Caching Multiple Folders

Most cameras create subfolders on the camera media with 100 images in each. If you use larger-capacity cards, you may have three or four image folders. The fastest way to deal with multiple folders is to copy all the image folders to a single "umbrella" folder. Then, when the copy is complete, point Bridge at this folder and choose Build Cache for Subfolders from Bridge's Cache submenu (in the Tools menu). Bridge builds a cache for each subfolder in the enclosing folder, reading the thumbnails and metadata and generating previews for all the images contained in the subfolders. It displays a status message so you'll know when it's done.

The Preproduction Phase

Preproduction generally means doing the minimum number of things to the maximum number of images so that you can quickly get to the point where you can pick the "hero" images that are truly deserving of your time, while leaving the rejects ready for revisiting.

Because the order in which you perform preproduction tasks—such as selecting, sorting, renaming, keywording, and so on—isn't critical, the order in which we'll discuss them is arbitrary. In those cases where the result of one task depends on the prior completion of another, we'll point that out.

We do, however, offer one golden rule: Start with the operations required by the largest number of images, and complete these before you start handling individual images on a case-by-case basis. For example, the first thing we always do with a folder full of new raw images is to select all the images and enter our copyright notice by applying a metadata template.

Similarly, if you know that you want to add the same keyword or keywords to all the images in a shoot, do it now (see "Applying Keywords and Metadata," later in this chapter). But if you don't care about copyrighting or keywording your rejects, you can make your initial selects first.

Selecting and Editing

Some photographers like to do a rough application of Camera Raw settings on all the images before they start making selects by flagging or ranking. Then they look at a large preview for each image and apply a flag or rank accordingly. Others may take a quick scan of the thumbnails and weed out any obvious junk before proceeding.

Bridge can accommodate all these different styles. Start out by loading a Bridge workspace that works for the task you want to start with—if you need to refresh your memory on configuring Bridge's layout for different tasks and saving those layouts as workspaces, see "The Window Menu and Bridge Configuration" earlier in this chapter.

Selecting by thumbnail. If the thumbnail view lets you see enough detail to make initial selects, choose an all-thumbnail view, then click-select the keepers or the rejects, whichever is easier. Shift-clicking selects all contiguous files between the last-selected image and the one on which you click; Command-clicking selects noncontiguous images one at a time. You can apply a label or rating as you go (see "Rating and Labeling," a bit later).

Selecting by preview. To see more detail, you can look at each image's preview. Bridge's Filmstrip view lets you see a large preview with a single row of thumbnails. The left and right arrow keys let you navigate from one thumbnail to the next and display the corresponding preview (see Figure 11-73). With this method, it's easier to apply a label or rating as you go than to rely on selecting thumbnails.

Selecting in Slide Show. Bridge's Slide Show view lets you review images one at a time at up to full-screen resolution. Slide Show offers the largest preview you can get without opening the image in Camera Raw and zooming. Plus, it lets you apply labels or ratings.

Comparing images. When you're making selects, you often need to compare images. In Slide Show view you can see before-and-afters, but we offer two techniques for comparing images side by side.

▶ To compare using thumbnails, set your Bridge window to show two largest-size thumbnails side by side (see Figure 11-74). It's often easier to open a new Bridge window, and use another window with smaller thumbnails to navigate.

▶ To compare the images at full resolution, open the images in Camera Raw *twice*, with one Camera Raw session hosted by Photoshop and the other by Bridge. (Press Command-O to open the images in Camera Raw

Figure 11-73
Selects by preview

*Press right arrow to go to
the next image.*

*Press left arrow to go to
the previous image.*

Figure 11-74
Comparing thumbnails
in Bridge

hosted by Photoshop, then return to Bridge and press Command-R to open them again in Camera Raw hosted by Bridge.) Then arrange the two Camera Raw windows so that you can see the preview in each one. Figure 11-75 shows two simultaneous Camera Raw sessions.

If you use this technique, remember that the settings that get applied to the image are those written by the last copy of Camera Raw to touch it. We suggest making all your edits in one copy of Camera Raw, and closing the other copy first.

Figure 11-75
Simultaneous Camera
Raw sessions

*Camera Raw hosted
by Photoshop*

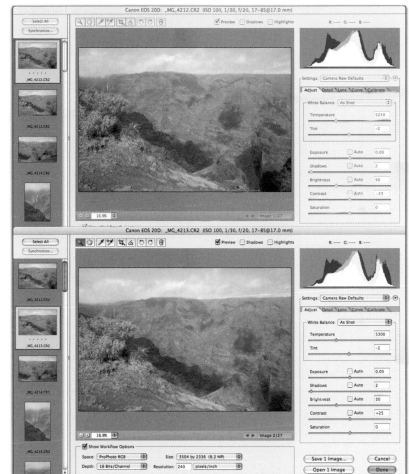

*Camera Raw hosted
by Bridge*

Rating and Labeling

Physically selecting thumbnails is one way to distinguish keepers from rejects, but it's ephemeral (you lose the selection as soon as you click on any other image). The better method is to assign ratings or labels. Ratings and labels become part of the image's metadata that you can use to search and to filter which images get displayed.

One-star rating for binary sorts. If you've become accustomed to using the old File Browser's flagging mechanism for binary, yes/no sorting and selecting, you'll be happy to find that the old keyboard shortcut, Command-' (apostrophe), lets you toggle a one-star rating on and off.

If you've selected a mixture of images, some with a one-star rating and some unrated, pressing Command-' first adds one star to the unrated images, preserving the one-star rating for those that already have it. If all the selected images have the same attribute (all rated with one star, or all unrated), the command acts as an off/on toggle instead.

However, if the selection also contains images rated with more than one star, pressing Command-' will apply a one-star rating to these images, so you need to be a little careful with your selections.

Command-1 applies a one-star rating to all selected images, and Command-0 removes the rating for all selected images. You can apply the rating to one image at a time (the most convenient method in Filmstrip view, and the only possible one in Slide Show view), or to multiple images (which is convenient in Thumbnails view). Once you've applied the one-star rating, you can segregate the rated and unrated images in any of three ways.

▶ Choose Show 1 or More Stars (press Command-Option-1) from Bridge's Unfiltered/Filtered menu (this also displays images that have more than one star rating, but if you're making an initial yes/no select, none of your images will have more than one star as yet).

▶ Choose Show Unrated Items Only from Bridge's Unfiltered/Filtered menu, then choose Invert Selection (press Command-Shift-I) from Bridge's Edit menu to invert the selection.

▶ Choose Find (press Command-F) from Bridge's Edit menu, then in the Find dialog box, choose Rating is equal to * (one star). If some of the images in the folder already have a rating of more than one star, this is the only way to display *only* those images that have exactly one star as their rating.

One-star is great for making quick, yes/no, binary decisions—keep or reject—but for more nuanced choices, you can add stars to the rating.

Multistar Ratings. The techniques for applying multistar ratings are the same as those for applying a single star. Command-0 removes the rating, and Command-1 through Command-5 apply one to five stars. Command-. (period) adds a star to the current rating, and Command-, (comma) reduces it by one star. There are basically two ways to approach rating your images.

▶ Make an initial one-star pass, then go through the one-star images and apply an additional star to those images that deserve it, then go through the two-star images, and apply a third star to those that deserve it. Many photographers find that four levels (unrated, one, two, or three stars) is enough, but you can go to five if you see the need.

▶ Apply all your ratings in a single pass.

If you're collaborating with others in determining the hero shots, the first approach is probably the more suitable. The second approach lends itself better to situations where you're the only person making the call.

Labels. The Label mechanism is less well suited to rating images than is the star-based ratings system. It's intuitively obvious that a five-star rating is either better or worse than one star, while there's no clear comparison between, say, yellow and green.

The stars are incremental, but the labels are not—they're simply arbitrary labels. You can apply any of the first four labels using Command-6 through Command-9, but there's no concept of promoting or demoting images from one label to another.

Labels are also less portable than ratings. Your labels will show up as white on any machine that uses a different label definition than yours, which is almost certain to happen if you use something other than the default label definitions (red, yellow, green, blue, and purple), and reasonably likely to happen even if you do use the default definitions, since the recipient may not. They can always search for your label text, but it's probably simpler just to use ratings.

Applying Camera Raw Settings

To work efficiently, look for and select images that require approximately the same edit. Once you've done so, you can apply the edits in any of the following three ways (or mix and match the techniques as required). Remember, at this stage in the workflow, you're simply aiming for good, not perfect. (Perfect comes later, when you've whittled the images down to the few you'll actually deliver.)

Edit by example in Bridge. Select the first of the images that need the same edit, then open it in Camera Raw. The choice of host application—Bridge or Photoshop—depends on what else is going on. If Photoshop is busy batch-processing files, host Camera Raw in Bridge. If Bridge is busy building the cache, host Camera Raw in Photoshop. If they're both busy, host Camera Raw in Bridge—Bridge's multithreading lets you work in Camera Raw even while Bridge itself is busy doing other tasks.

Make your edits—white balance, exposure, whatever the image needs—and then dismiss the Camera Raw dialog box by clicking Done (it's the default option in Camera Raw hosted by Bridge, but not in Camera Raw hosted by Photoshop).

Now, from the Apply Camera Raw Settings submenu (in Bridge's Edit menu), choose Copy Camera Raw Settings, or press Command-Option-C. Then select all the other images that need the same edit and choose Paste Camera Raw Settings (or press Command-Option-V). If necessary, select the combination of subsets or settings you want to apply from the Paste Camera Raw Settings dialog box first (see "Select, Find, and Edit with the Edit Menu," earlier in this chapter).

This approach works well when you need to apply the same settings to a large number of images that are identifiable by relatively small thumbnails, because you can select them quickly. But if you need to make small changes to the settings for each image, the following two approaches are better suited.

Edit by presets. If you've saved presets for Camera Raw in Camera Raw's Settings folder (see "Loading and Saving Settings" earlier in this chapter) you can apply them to all the selected images by choosing Apply Camera Raw Settings from Bridge's Edit menu, then choosing the settings or settings subsets from the submenu. Saving Settings Subsets as presets is particularly powerful, because you can simply choose them in succession. Each one affects only the parameters recorded when you saved it, so you can load a preset for white balance, followed by one for Exposure, for Brightness, for Contrast, for Calibrate settings, and so on.

Edit in Camera Raw. The method that offers the most flexibility is to open multiple images in Camera Raw. There's probably a limit to the number of images you can open simultaneously in Camera Raw, but we haven't yet found it—we've been able to open 1,500 images simultaneously in Camera Raw and while it took a couple of minutes to launch, it worked perfectly.

That said, it's more practical to work with smaller sets of images. If you open 10 or more images, you'll get a dialog box asking if you really want to open 10 files. We recommend clicking the Don't show again checkbox, and cheerfully opening as many images as your machine can reasonably handle without bogging down—if the hardware is at all recent, it's almost certainly a considerably larger number than 10.

When you open multiple images, Camera Raw works in filmstrip mode. The current image is always the one whose preview shows in the preview window. Camera Raw in filmstrip mode offers two basic methods for editing multiple images besides editing them one by one.

▶ **Select multiple thumbnails.** When you select multiple thumbnails in Camera Raw, only the first (chronologically) selected image shows in the preview, but any edits you make apply to all the selected images, so you are in effect editing multiple images simultaneously. You'll see yellow warning triangles appear on the thumbnails while Camera Raw is updating them to reflect the edits, then disappear when the new thumbnail is built.

When you work with multiple selected images in Camera Raw, the up and down arrow keys move through the selected thumbnails, ignoring the unselected ones. The current image has a slightly heavier border than the others, but the filename in the title bar is a more obvious guide as to which image is the current one (see Figure 11-76).

▶ **Use Synchronize.** Camera Raw's Synchronize feature is similar to copying and pasting Camera Raw settings. The Synchronize button lets you

Figure 11-76
Editing multiple images
in Camera Raw

Selected images

The current image

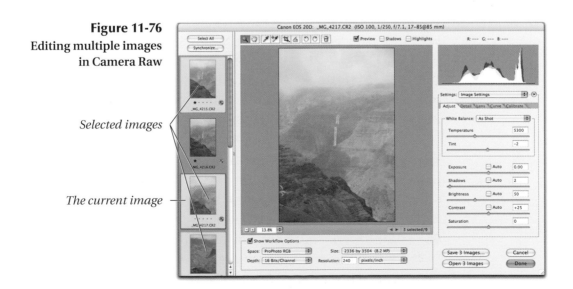

apply the settings of the current image to all the other selected images, so you need to pay attention to which image is in fact the current one!

When you click the Synchronize button, the Synchronize dialog box appears, allowing you to choose which settings will be applied to the selected images (see Figure 11-77). To skip the dialog box and apply all the settings, Option-click the Synchronize button.

You can mix and match both of these approaches, while enjoying the benefits of zoomable previews, and Undo. (And if you simply can't resist the temptation, you can fine-tune individual images too.)

Figure 11-77
Synchronize Camera
Raw setting

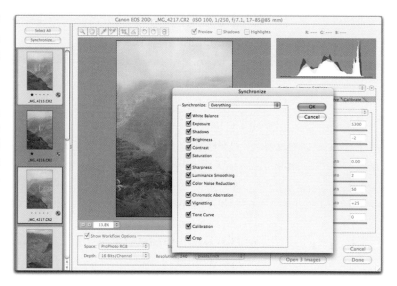

The Synchronize button and dialog box let you synchronize the selected images' settings to those of the current image.

Sorting and Renaming

By default, Bridge sorts images by filename, so new raw images appear in the order in which they were shot, because the camera applies consecutive numbering to each image. However, as we noted earlier, you can vary the sort order by choosing any of the options on Bridge's Sort submenu (in the View menu).

You can also create a custom sort order by dragging the thumbnails around, just as you would with chromes on a light table. When you do so, the Manually item on the Sort menu is checked. Your custom sorting order is stored only in the Bridge cache for the folder. If you use distributed caches, you can move or rename the folder and Bridge will still remember the sort order. But if you combine images from several folders into a different folder, you have in effect created a new sort order, and it may well not be the one you wanted. So a simple way to preserve that order is to use Batch Rename to rename the images including a numbering scheme that reflects your custom sort order (see "Automation, the Cache, and the Tools Menu," earlier in this chapter).

Applying Keywords and Metadata

The key to being efficient with keywords and metadata is the same as that for being efficient with applying Camera Raw edits: Look for and select images that need the same treatment, and deal with them all at once.

IPTC metadata. The only metadata that is editable in Bridge (or in Photoshop, for that matter) is the IPTC metadata. For recurring metadata such as copyright notices, metadata templates provide a very convenient way to make the edits (see "File Info and the File Menu," earlier in this chapter).

Alternatively, you can select multiple images and then edit the metadata directly in the Metadata palette. Click in the first field you want to edit, and type in your entry. Then press Tab to advance to the next field. Continue until you've entered all the metadata shared by the selected images, and then click the checkmark icon at the lower right of the palette, or press Enter or Return, to confirm the entries.

Keywords. Keywords show up in the IPTC section of the Metadata palette, but you can't enter or edit them there—you have to use the Keywords palette. The Keywords palette contains individual keywords grouped into sets (represented by the folder icons). The default keywords and sets are pretty useless unless you know a lot of people called Julius and Michael, but you can easily replace them with ones that are more useful for your purposes.

To apply a keyword, select one or more images and then click in the column to the left of the keyword. A checkmark appears in the column, and Bridge writes the keyword to each file's sidecar.xmp file. To remove a keyword, select the images and then turn off the checkmark.

Deleting a keyword from the Keywords palette doesn't delete the keyword from any images to which it has been applied; it only deletes it from the palette. So it makes sense to keep only keywords you know you'll use a lot stored in the palette. For keywords that apply only to the current session, we create them in a set called Temp and delete them when we're done, to keep the palette manageable.

Keyword sets let you organize keywords, but they also offer a very useful functionality: You can apply all the keywords in the set to selected images by clicking next to the set name rather than the keyword names. This is better than assigning keywords one at a time because when you click next to a single keyword to apply it, Bridge starts writing it to the selected images. If you then add another keyword, Bridge will write both keywords to the images it hasn't yet touched, but then it has to go back and add the second keyword to the images it had already processed.

Tip: Drag to Sets. Create one keyword set that serves to add multiple keywords. When you want to apply multiple keywords to a set of images, drag the keywords you want to use into this set, or create any new ones you want to apply inside this set. Now you can apply the entire set at once to all your selected images.

The Production Phase

The production phase is where you hand-polish the select images that deserve the bulk of your time and attention—hand-tuning the Camera Raw settings, and bringing the images into Photoshop for the kinds of selective corrections that Camera Raw simply isn't designed to do (all that stuff we talk about in the rest of this book).

The exercise of your creative judgment is one aspect of the workflow that you can't automate, but automation can and will speed up the execution of that creative judgment. When it comes to efficiency in converting raw images, actions are the key. We generally convert raw images in batches using actions rather than simply opening them in Photoshop.

Background Processing

One of the most useful additions to the raw workflow toolkit is the capability of Camera Raw 3.0 to save images in the background, hosted either by Photoshop or Bridge (see "Saving Images in the Background" earlier in this chapter). We use background saving for two distinct purposes.

▶ After initial rough edits, metadata addition, and keywording, we open the whole folder in Camera Raw, select all the images, click Save *x*

Images, and save them as DNG using the Compressed (lossless) option, with Full Size JPEG preview, to a new folder.

All the metadata, including Camera Raw settings and any keywords, are written into the DNG files, so we no longer need to worry about sidecar files. The choice of which application hosts Camera Raw for background saving depends entirely on which application we want to use while the files are being saved in the background.

▶ When we need to save a bunch of JPEGs or, less commonly, TIFFs without running any actions on them, we change the file format in camera Raw's Save Options dialog box to the one we need, and save the files in the background.

Bear in mind that when Camera Raw is tied up performing saves in one application, it's still available for use in the other.

Automated Conversions

Background saving is useful when you've done everything the image needs in Camera Raw, but images often need some postconversion work in Photoshop. The Photoshop submenu offers a variety of useful routines for creating images in a deliverable form, but by far the most powerful and flexible is the Batch command. That's what we'll tackle next.

Using Batch

The Batch command is one of Photoshop's most powerful features. It's conceptually very simple. You point it at a batch of images, it runs an action on them, it (optionally) renames the images, and then it does one of the following:

▶ Saves new files

▶ Delivers open images in Photoshop

▶ Saves and closes, overwriting the source files

As you'll see shortly, though, the devil is in the details, and some of the details in the Batch dialog box are distinctly counterintuitive. To open the Batch dialog box from within Photoshop, choose Batch from the Automate submenu (in the File menu). To batch process files from within Bridge, select the images you want to process and then choose Batch from the Photoshop submenu (in Bridge's Tools menu). Figure 11-78 shows the Batch dialog box before customizing any of the settings.

Figure 11-78
The Batch dialog box

The dialog box is split into four different sections, each of which controls a different aspect of the batch process's behavior.

▶ **Play** lets you choose an action from an action set that will be applied to all the images. Note that we discuss actions and how to create them in more detail later in this chapter, as well as in Chapter 12, *Essential Image Techniques.*

▶ **Source** lets you choose the images on which the batch will be executed, and also lets you pick some very important options which we'll explore in a moment. Your choices from this menu are: a folder full of images (click the Choose button to choose the specific folder); the currently open files; images imported through the Photoshop File menu's Import command; or—when running Batch from within Bridge—on the images that are currently selected in Bridge. For raw images, the source will invariably be a folder or the selected images in Bridge.

▶ **Destination** lets you control what happens to the processed images. Choose None to leave them open in Photoshop after processing. To save the changed files and close them, choose Save and Close (more on this soon); Folder lets you designate a folder in which to save the processed images. This section also includes the same renaming features offered by Batch Rename.

When you process raw images, you'll always choose either None or, much more commonly, Folder. Save and Close often ends up being a "hurt-me" button, because its normal behavior is to overwrite the source image. With raw files this is usually impossible and always undesirable. Photoshop can't overwrite files in formats it can't write, including most raw image formats; but if you use a camera that records its raw images as .tif, there's a real danger of overwriting your raws if you choose Save and Close—so avoid it!

▶ **Errors** lets you choose whether to stop the entire batch when an error is encountered or log the errors to a file. We usually stop on errors when we're debugging an action used in Batch and log them to a file when we're actually running a batch in a production situation. However, when processing raw files, the batch typically either works on all files or fails on all files.

Rules for Batching Files

The difficulties that users typically encounter in running Batch are in the way the selections in the Source and Destination sections interact with the action applied by the batch operation. Here are The Rules. (Note: these are our rules, and we swear by them. They don't represent the only possible approach, but by the time you're sufficiently skilled and knowledgeable to violate them with impunity you'll have long outgrown the need for a book like this one!)

Rules for opening files. To make sure that the raw files get opened and processed the way you want them in a batch operation, you need to record an Open step in the action. In the case of raw images, you'll want to make sure that Camera Raw's Settings menu is set to Image Settings so that it applies the custom-tailored Camera Raw settings you've made for each image, and you'll also want to make sure that Camera Raw's workflow settings—Space, Bit Depth, Size, and Resolution—are set to produce the results you want.

Now comes one of the counterintuitive bits. If you record an Open step in the action, you must turn on the Override Action Open Commands option in the Batch dialog box. If you don't, the batch will simply keep opening the image you used to record the Open step in the action. Override Action Open Commands doesn't override everything in the recorded Open command; it just overrides the specific choice of file to open, while ensuring that the Selected Image and workflow settings get honored.

Some people find this set of behaviors so frustrating and counterintuitive that they latch onto the fact that you can run Batch using an action that doesn't contain an Open step and hence doesn't require messing around with the checkbox. The problem with doing so is that you lose control over Camera Raw's workflow settings—the batch will just use the last-used settings. So you may expect a folder full of 6,144 by 4,096-pixel images and get 1,536 by 1,024-pixel ones instead, or wind up with 8-bit sRGB instead of 16-bit ProPhoto RGB. If you simply follow The Rules, you have complete control over the workflow settings.

Rules for saving files. To make sure that the processed files get saved in the format you want, you need to record a Save step in the action that will be applied in Batch. This Save step dictates the file format (such as TIFF, JPEG, or PSD) and options that go with that format (TIFF compression options, JPEG quality settings, and so on).

Now comes the second counterintuitive bit. You must turn on the option labeled Override Action "Save As" Commands in the Batch dialog box—otherwise the files don't get saved where you want them, don't get saved with the names you want, or possibly even don't get saved at all! When you turn on this option, the file format and file format parameters recorder in the action's Save step are applied when saving the file, but the name and destination are overridden by the options you specify in the Batch dialog box.

Rules for running a batch operation. Two other settings commonly trip people up. Unless you turn on the Suppress File Open Options Dialogs checkbox, the Camera Raw dialog box pops up whenever the batch opens a file, and waits for you to do something. Turning on this option just opens the image directly, bypassing the Camera Raw dialog box. The Camera Raw settings for each image are used, but the batch operation isn't interrupted by the appearance of the dialog box.

If the workflow settings recorded in the action result in an image in a color space other than your Photoshop working space, you should also turn on the Suppress Color Profile Warnings checkbox; otherwise the batch may get interrupted by the Profile Mismatch warning. The day always gets off to a bad start when you find that the batch operation you'd set up to generate 2,000 Web-ready JPEGs overnight is stalled on the first image with a warning telling you that the file is sRGB when your working space is ProPhoto RGB! (This feature didn't work in Photoshop CS. Fortunately, it's fixed in Photoshop CS2 and now works as advertised.)

Playing by The Rules. If you follow this relatively simple set of rules, your batch operations won't fall prey to any of these ills, and they'll execute smoothly with no surprises. If you fail to do so, it's very likely that your computer will labor mightily and then deliver either results that are something other than you desired or, even more frustrating, no results at all!

So with The Rules in mind, let's look first at creating some actions and then at applying them through the Batch command.

Recording Batch Actions

Writing actions for batch-processing raw images is relatively simple. You don't need to worry about making sure that the action can operate on files that already have layers or alpha channels, or that are in a color space other than RGB. You're always dealing with a known quantity.

Bear in mind that if your actions call other actions, the other actions must be loaded in Photoshop's Actions palette, or the calling action will fail when it can't find the action being called. An easy way to handle this is to make sure that any actions on which other actions are dependent are saved in the same set as the actions that depend on them.

Simple Action—Save as JPEG

Let's begin with a simple action that opens a raw image at its native resolution and saves it as a maximum-quality JPEG in the sRGB color space.

Creating an action and action set. Start out by creating a new action set called "Batch Processing" in which to save the actions you'll create in the rest of this section (see Figure 11-79 and "Actions, Automate, and Scripting," in Chapter 12, *Essential Image Techniques*.)

Figure 11-79
Creating an action set

To create a new action set, click the "Create new set" button...

...enter a name and click OK.

The new set appears in the Actions palette.

Creating a new action. Before creating the action, select a raw image in Bridge that has *already* had custom Camera Raw settings applied. That way, once you've created the action, you can start recording immediately without recording any extraneous steps, such as selecting a file, and you can correctly record the Camera Raw Selected Image setting.

Now click the "Create new action" icon in Photoshop's Actions palette, enter a name (such as "Save as JPEG") for the action, and then click Record to dismiss the dialog and start recording the action.

Recording the Open step. Now that you're recording, switch back to Bridge and open the image in Camera Raw by pressing Command-O (you must open the image in Camera Raw hosted by Photoshop). The Camera Raw dialog box appears (see Figure 11-80).

When you use the action in Batch, the Camera Raw dialog box won't appear, so it's essential to get the settings right when you record this step. You need to record several key settings for this action in the Camera Raw dialog box.

▶ Set the Settings menu to Image Settings to ensure that each image gets opened using its own custom settings, rather than the ones you choose for this particular image.

When you record an Open step, it's critical to make sure that the Settings menu is set to Image Settings and the workflow settings are set the way you want them for the batch operation.

▶ Set the Space popup menu to sRGB to produce a converted image that's already in sRGB, the standard color space for the Web.

▶ Set the Depth menu to 8 bits/channel, because you're simply saving JPEGs (which only support 8-bit channels), and this action won't include any operations that could benefit from a higher bit depth.

▶ Set the Size menu to the desired size (in this case, we chose 1536 by 1024).

▶ Set the Resolution field to 72 pixels per inch (to preserve the polite fiction that Web images are 72 ppi; see Chapter 14, *Multimedia and the Web*).

Then click OK to open the image. (If the Profile Mismatch warning appears, click OK to dismiss it. This doesn't get recorded in the action, and anyway, you'll suppress the warning when you use the action in Batch.) The image opens, and the Open step appears on the Actions palette.

Recording the Save step. To record the Save step, choose Save As from the File menu, or press Command-Shift-S. The Save As dialog box appears. The filename and the destination for saving that you enter here has no impact on the batch process—we tend to use an obviously silly name such as "foo.jpg"—and choose the Desktop as destination, to simplify cleanup.

In this example, make sure that the format is set to JPEG, and incorporate any other settings in this dialog box that you want to include in the action. Then click Save to proceed to the JPEG Options dialog box, set the desired quality, set the Format Options to Baseline (Standard) for maximum compatibility with JPEG-reading software, and then click OK. The file is saved on the Desktop as "foo.jpg," and the Save step appears in the Actions palette. Then close the open document so that a Close step appears in the Actions palette.

Stop and save. Finally, click the Stop button in the Actions palette to stop recording. Photoshop doesn't allow you to save individual actions to disk—only action sets. So if you want to save an action as soon as you've written it, you need to select the action set that contains it in the Actions palette and then choose Save Actions from the Actions palette flyout menu (see Figure 11-81).

Figure 11-81
Saving the action set

Tip: Go Ahead and Save Now. Note that until you save actions explicitly using the Save Actions command, they exist only in Photoshop's Preferences, and Photoshop's Preferences only get updated when you quit the application "normally" by using the Quit command. If Photoshop crashes, or you suffer a power outage, any unsaved actions will be lost. So if your actions are even slightly complex, it's a very good idea to save them before doing anything else. You can save actions anywhere, but if you want them to appear automatically in the Actions palette even after deleting Photoshop's preferences, save them in the Adobe Photoshop CS2/Presets/Photoshop Actions folder.

When you expand the steps in the Actions palette by clicking the triangles beside those that have them, you can see exactly what has been recorded for each step (see Figure 11-82). When you use this action in Batch with the appropriate overrides selected (see "Rules for Batch Processing," earlier in this chapter) the filenames and folder locations you recorded will be overridden by the settings in the Batch dialog box, and all the other settings you've recorded here—the Camera Raw workflow settings and the JPEG Save Options—will be honored.

Figure 11-82
Save as JPEG action

Variants. You can create variants of this action by recording different Open or Save steps. For example, you can create larger JPEGs by changing the Size setting in the Camera Raw dialog box to one of the larger sizes, and you can embed thumbnails or create lower-quality JPEGs by making those settings in the Save As and JPEG Options dialog boxes, respectively. To save in a different format, with different options, just choose the desired format and options when you record the Save step.

Complex Action—Save for Edit

Now let's try a more complex example: an action that produces 16-bit/channel TIFFs with adjustment layers set up ready for final editing in Photoshop. It's designed for use on "hero" images that merit individual manual edits in Photoshop. It doesn't actually *do* any of the editing, because the required edits will almost certainly be different for each image in a batch. Instead, it simply does a lot of the repetitive grunt work involved in setting up an image for editing, so that when you open the image, all the necessary adjustment layers are already there, waiting for you to tweak them. (Or, if you don't need them, you can throw them away later.)

Create the new action. You can record this action in the same set as the previous one, since it's also designed for raw processing. As before, select a raw image in Bridge that has had custom Camera Raw settings applied before you start recording the new action. Then click the "Create new action" icon in the Actions palette, enter a name (such as "Save for Edit") in the New Action dialog box, and then click Record to start recording.

Recording the Open step. As before, start by launching Camera Raw from Bridge by pressing Command-O. In the Camera Raw dialog box, again make sure that Settings is set to Selected Image. This time, though, you'll make some different workflow settings.

▶ In the Space menu, choose ProPhoto RGB, our preferred working space.

▶ Set the Depth menu to 16/bit channel, because you'll want to make the edits in Photoshop in 16-bit/channel mode.

▶ Set the Size menu to the camera's native resolution.

▶ Enter 240 pixels per inch in the Resolution field, because you'll almost certainly check your edits by printing to an inkjet printer at 240 ppi (see Chapter 13, *Image Storage and Output*).

Then click OK to open the image. The image opens, and the Open step appears on the Actions palette.

Adding the edits. This action adds three different editing layers to the image before saving and closing; a Levels adjustment layer; a Curves adjustment layer; and a Hue/Saturation adjustment layer, as follows.

▶ Add a Levels adjustment layer by choosing Levels from the New Adjustment Layer submenu (under the Layer menu). Just click OK to create a Levels adjustment layer that does not as yet apply any adjustments.

Remember, you'll make the adjustments on an image-by-image basis in Photoshop—the action just does the grunt work of creating the layers.

▶ Add two more adjustment layers—a Curves layer, then a Hue/Saturation layer—in both cases also clicking OK when the respective adjustment dialog boxes appear.

Recording the Save step. As before, choose Save As from the File menu, naming the file "foo" and save it on the Desktop for easy disposal after you're finished making the action. This time, choose TIFF as the format, make sure that the Layers and Embed Color Profile checkboxes are turned on (creating untagged ProPhoto RGB files is a Very Bad Idea). Then click Save to advance to the TIFF Options dialog box, and make your preferred settings. (Again, see Chapter 13, *Image Storage and Output,* for advice.)

Finally, close the image (so that the batch operation will do so, too), and click the Stop button in the Actions palette to stop recording. Figure 11-83 shows the resulting action in the Actions palette with all the steps expanded.

As with the earlier, simpler action, when you use this action in a batch process with the necessary overrides applied in the Batch dialog box, the filenames and locations will be overridden by the Batch settings, while everything else in the Open and Save steps will be honored.

Figure 11-83
Save for Edit action

Running Batch

Using the actions we've just shown you in Batch is really very simple—as long as you remember The Rules! (If you need to take another look, refer back to "Rules for Batching Files," earlier in this chapter.) Play by The Rules, and all will go smoothly. Violate them at your peril.

Common errors. Other than choosing incorrect settings in the Batch dialog box, there are three common situations that can cause a batch operation to fail.

▶ There isn't sufficient space on the destination volume to hold the processed files.

▶ No source files were selected in Bridge.

▶ Files with the same names as the ones you're creating already exist in the destination folder.

If these points seem blindingly obvious, we only mention them because they've tripped us up more than once. With those caveats in mind, let's look at setting up the Batch dialog box to run the Save for Edit action you built in the previous section. As we pointed out earlier, the key settings in Batch are the overrides in both the Source and Destination sections of the panel.

Source settings. Whenever you run a batch operation using an action that includes an Open step, you must check Override Action "Open" Commands in the Source section. To process raw images, you also need to turn on Suppress File Open Options Dialogs—otherwise the Camera Raw dialog will pop up for every image. And whenever you run a batch operation unattended, it's a good idea to check Suppress Color Profile Warnings so that the batch doesn't get stuck on a Profile Mismatch warning.

Destination settings. Similarly, whenever you run a batch operation using an action that includes a Save As step, you must turn on Override Action "Save As" Commands in the Destination section; otherwise the files won't get saved. Figure 11-84 shows the Batch dialog box set up to run the Save for Edit action.

Figure 11-84
Batch

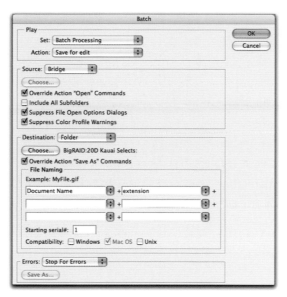

Make the Work Flow

Bridge, Camera Raw, and Photoshop are deep, complex, and very powerful tools that put you in charge of an even deeper, more complex, and more powerful workflow system. Bridge lets you do many things once, and once only, so that you don't need to keep doing them over and over again—whether it's applying Camera Raw settings, entering copyright notices, or rotating and cropping images. The time you spend in Bridge will be amply repaid further down the line.

Digital shooting inevitably entails processing mind-numbing quantities of data that only a few years ago would have made a NASA engineer blanch. If you want to survive, let alone enjoy the digital revolution, a streamlined, efficient workflow is an absolute necessity, and automation is a key technology. If you absorb the lessons of this lengthy chapter, you'll be able to spend less time sitting in front of the computer, and more time having a life!

12

Essential Image Techniques

Pushing Pixels into Place

The vast majority of Photoshop users stare at this program many hours a day, doing the same sort of image manipulation over and over again. Retouch the background of this photo; convert this color image to grayscale; add a drop shadow behind this car; silhouette this pineapple; put a new background behind this amazing kitchen aid; incorporate this logo into that image.

In this chapter we offer a whole mess of tips and tricks to make your images fly a little faster, and perhaps even make them a little more fun to manipulate, too. The chapter is split up into a hodgepodge of common Photoshop issues: retouching, grayscale conversions, working with vector graphics and text, and so on. Read 'em and reap!

Taking Care of the Basics

The two most important techniques in image editing are, in many respects, the simplest to accomplish:

▶ Look at every pixel.

▶ Build base camps.

Look at every pixel. Try to get in the habit of returning to 100-percent (Actual Pixels) view frequently, so you can get a sense of what's going on in your image. People often zoom in closer than this, thinking "the closer the better." Not so. Sure, you can see the pixels, but you're not really seeing the image. (Zen koan or sage advice? You be the judge.)

If you can't fit the image on your screen, start at the upper-left corner (press the Home key) and use the Page Down key to move down until you reach the bottom. Scroll once to the right (press Command-Page Down), and start over. We can't overstress the importance of this procedure.

If you like working zoomed in or out and can't be bothered with getting back to 100-percent view, check out "Tip: Use New Window" in Chapter 2, *Essential Photoshop Tips and Tricks*.

Build base camps. Our friend and colleague Greg Vander Houwen (you've probably read about him elsewhere in this tome) turned us on to the mountaineering phrase "base camp." The concept is simple: while you're working on an image, don't just save every now and again; instead, create an environment that you can return to at any time. That means taking snapshots in the History palette or—better yet—using Save As at strategic moments in your image manipulation. It also means saving your curves before applying them, and sometimes even writing down the various settings you use in dialog boxes (like Unsharp Mask).

When you've built a solid base camp, you can always return to it, get your bearings, and start up the hill again. As Greg noted, "I might build a few base camps along the way, depending on how high the mountain is."

The Color of Grayscale

Photoshop is a wonderful tool for handling color, but we don't live by color alone. Grayscale images have a magic all of their own, and many photographers—even those who print exclusively in grayscale—find that they can produce much better grayscale images from color captures than they can from black-and-white captures, whether they're shooting with film or digital cameras.

However, if you convert images by selecting Grayscale from the Mode menu, there's a good chance you're not getting the best-quality images you can. Many color images contain a great grayscale version, but you often have to wrestle to find it. The obvious method isn't always the best, so let's first take a look at the nonobvious ones too.

Tip: Scan in Color. Almost every scanner on the market these days is built to scan color images. If your original image is a color picture, you'll often get a better final result by scanning it in color and then converting it to grayscale in Photoshop using one of the techniques below—it's like using color filters when you shoot black-and-white film. If you're scanning a grayscale picture, you may also get a better result scanning in color; it depends on how neutral gray the image really is. For instance, we're more likely than not to scan an ancient yellowed black-and-white photograph as an RGB color image.

Convert to Grayscale. The most obvious way to convert an image to grayscale is simply to choose Grayscale from the Mode submenu (under the Image menu). When you do so, Photoshop mixes the red, green, and blue channels together, weighting the red, green, and blue channels differently (according to a standard formula that purports to account for the varying sensitivity of the eye to different colors). If that produces the result you want, great, but if it doesn't, there are many alternatives.

Take a channel, any channel. Look at the individual color channels in the image. Occasionally you'll find the grayscale image you want sitting in one of them. Then you can copy and paste it, or use Duplicate Channel from the Channel palette's popout menu to save it into a new document. Or you can just delete the other two channels by first displaying the channel you want, and then selecting Grayscale from the Mode menu.

Desaturate. You can select Desaturate from the Adjustments submenu (under the Image menu, or press Command-Shift-U). This is the same as reducing the Saturation setting in the Hue/Saturation dialog box to zero—it literally pulls the color out of each pixel in the document. The image is still RGB, but if you convert it to grayscale you'll get a different result than if you'd simply converted it to grayscale without desaturating first.

Convert to Lab. For a more literal rendering of the luminance values in an image, you can convert the image to Lab, then discard the color channels (a and b). This gives you yet another different rendering.

Load the luminance mask. One of David's favorite methods for squeezing a grayscale image out of a color photograph is to Command-click on the composite color channel (the RGB or the CMYK tile in the Channels palette), which loads the file's luminance map (this is different than the L channel of a Lab file). You can then tell Photoshop to save this selection as a new file by choosing Save Selection from the Select menu. We find that this often provides a much better grayscale image than simply converting to Grayscale mode.

Devious methods. Sometimes none of the above methods provides the grayscale image you want. Photoshop offers some more devious alternatives. In the past you had to use the dreaded Calculations dialog box to mix channels; we still use Calculations sometimes, because it lets you do things you can't do any other way, but the Channel Mixer feature offers an easier way to blend channels, so we often turn to it first.

The Channel Mixer dialog box is more utilitarian than you'd hope from a program like Photoshop (see Figure 12-1), but it lets you do one thing very well: mix the color channels of your image. You mix channels by percentage, and the result is a single channel (you can choose which channel the result will end up on in the Output Channel popup menu).

Figure 12-1
Channel Mixer dialog box

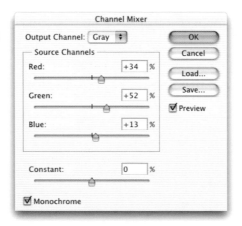

When converting an RGB image to grayscale, remember two things. First, the percentages in the dialog box should always add up to 100 percent to maintain the same overall tone of the image (though there may be situations where you don't *want* to maintain the overall tone of the image). Second, turn on the Monochrome checkbox to ensure that the result is neutral gray.

(Note that the Channel Mixer works fine with CMYK images, but it's much harder to maintain the image's tone. We prefer working from an RGB image when building grayscale images with the Channel Mixer, even if it means converting from CMYK to RGB first.)

Tip: Channel Mixer Adjustment Layers. We pretty much always use the Channel Mixer on an adjustment layer rather than applying the effect directly to an image, because the adjustment layer makes it very easy to edit—just double-click on the tile in the Layers palette, and you can change the Channel Mixer settings. Even better, you can combine a Channel Mixer adjustment layer with a Levels or Curves adjustment layer to really bring out your image's most important tones. (See Chapter 7, *The Digital Darkroom*, for much more on adjustment layers.)

Calculating images. Like the Channel Mixer, selecting Calculations from the Image menu lets you mix and match a new grayscale image from the existing channels, but with much more power and flexibility (see Figure 12-2). The options in the Blending popup menu are the same as the ones in the Layers palette, and the Opacity field serves the same function as the Layers palette's Opacity slider. Calculations lets you combine the channels in much more complex, albeit less-intuitive ways than the simple addition and subtraction offered by the Channel Mixer.

Figure 12-2
The Calculations
dialog box

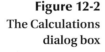

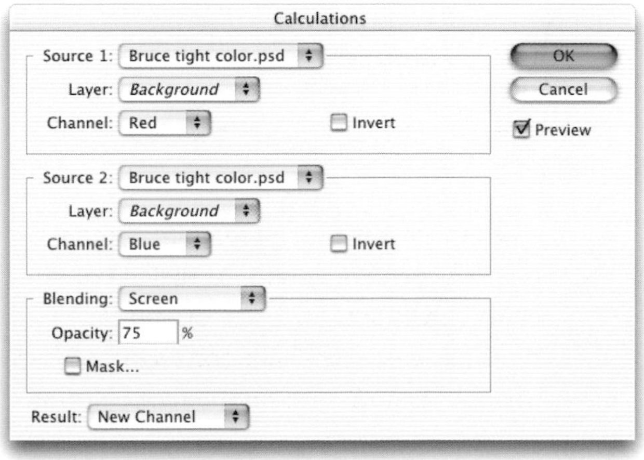

Tip: Use Preview in Calculations. At first glance, the Calculations dialog box seems a lot less interactive than the Layers palette. But it doesn't have to be that way. When you turn on the Preview checkbox, you can actually watch how the various combinations work in real time (or at least as fast as your machine can compute). For instance, when you change opacity with Preview turned on, you see the effect almost immediately. You can type a new Opacity setting almost as quickly as you can move the slider in the Layers palette.

Figure 12-3 shows the results of the various grayscale conversion techniques on a Macbeth Color Checker (so that you can easily see how the colors convert to tone), and on an actual image.

Figure 12-3 Finding the hidden grayscale

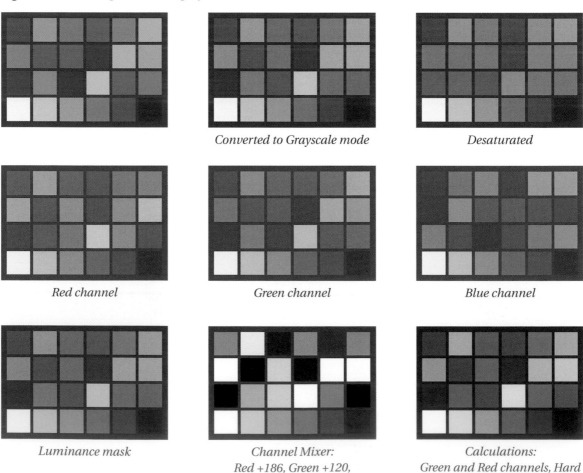

Converted to Grayscale mode

Desaturated

Red channel

Green channel

Blue channel

Luminance mask

Channel Mixer:
Red +186, Green +120,
Blue -200

Calculations:
Green and Red channels, Hard
Light blending, 100% opacity

Figure 12-3 Finding the hidden grayscale, *continued*

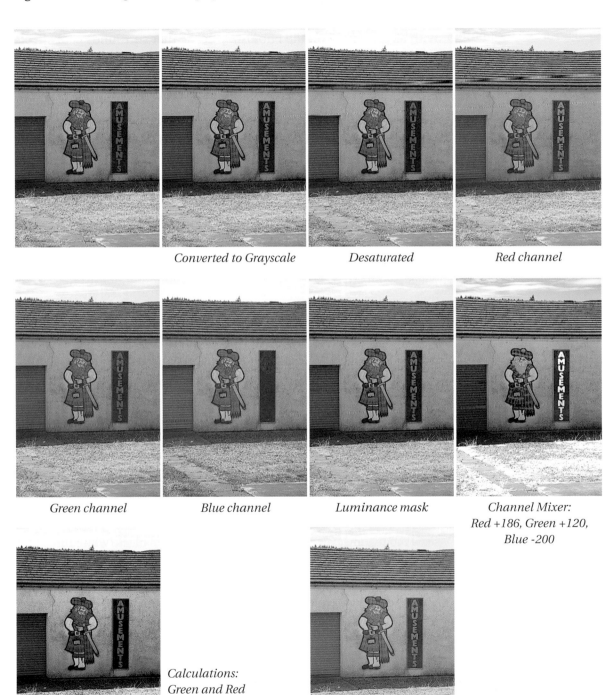

Converted to Grayscale   *Desaturated*   *Red channel*

Green channel   *Blue channel*   *Luminance mask*   *Channel Mixer: Red +186, Green +120, Blue -200*

Calculations: Green and Red channels, Hard Light blending, 100% opacity

Lightness channel from Lab

Of course, you never need image resolution higher than your output resolution. If you're printing your final artwork on a 600-dpi laser printer, for instance, you don't need more than 600-ppi image resolution. The additional data just gets thrown away.

Tip: Scan Big for High Resolution. "Great," you're saying. "They say we need 800-ppi images, but all we've got is a 600-ppi scanner. And they said back in the *Image Essentials* chapter that upsampling is useless. What are we supposed to do with this business card the client gave us?"

You've got two ways to get a higher resolution out of a low-resolution scanner. First, you can scan a large original at your scanner's highest optical resolution and scale it down, increasing resolution. If you reduce the image to 50 percent, for instance, you double the resolution.

You can either scale the image in a page-layout program, or adjust the size in Photoshop's Image Size dialog box while the File Size checkbox is turned on (see Chapter 3, *Image Essentials*).

If you don't have a larger version of the artwork, you can enlarge your small version on a quality photocopier, and scan that. You still get a higher-quality image because the optical enlargement doesn't cause pixelization (there may be some cleanup work involved after the scan, of course).

The second solution (which you can use in combination with this enlargement/reduction technique) is covered in the next tip.

Tip: Doubling Your Scanner's Line Art Resolution. The second method for going beyond your scanner's resolution essentially "steals" information from an 8-bit grayscale scan, converting that information into higher line art resolution.

1. Scan your artwork as a grayscale image at your scanner's maximum optical resolution (let's use 600 ppi for this example).

2. Double the image resolution (thus quadrupling the file size) using the Image Size dialog box (make sure the Resample Image checkbox is turned on with Bicubic as the resampling method). In our example, you'd upsample to 1,200 ppi. Note that if your scanning software can interpolate up to this same resolution, you can use that as you scan, and save yourself a step.

If you're yelling, "Hey! You said interpolation was useless," you're right—we did. This is an exception; upsampling here adds pixels where you need them, even though it doesn't add any detail.

3. Sharpen and threshold the image as outlined later in this chapter.

4. Switch to Bitmap mode at the same resolution (1,200 ppi in our example), with the 50% Threshold option selected (see Figure 12-5).

Figure 12-5
Converting to
Bitmap mode

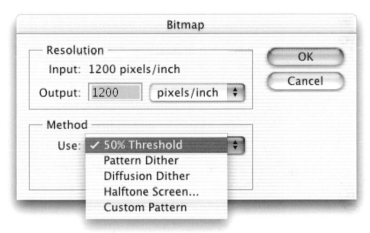

Voilà! A 1,200-ppi line art image from a 600-ppi scanner. While it isn't a true 1,200-ppi scan, it's so close that we dare you to find a difference. You may be able to raise the image's resolution above two times optical resolution, but that's pretty much the point of diminishing returns.

Note that you can use this tip alongside the previous one to res up to 1,800 ppi or higher.

Sharpening

Nothing will do more for the quality of your line art images than sharpening the grayscale scan (see Figure 12-6). 'Nuf said. We recommend running the Unsharp Mask filter twice with the settings 500/1/5. However, if the second USM makes the image look terrible (it often does if you're scanning poorly printed originals), undo it and stick with just one pass of unsharp masking. By the way, if your scanning software can sharpen, you may be able to save yourself a step, though most scanners' drivers don't do as good a job as Photoshop's Unsharp Mask filter.

Figure 12-6
Line art with and
without sharpening

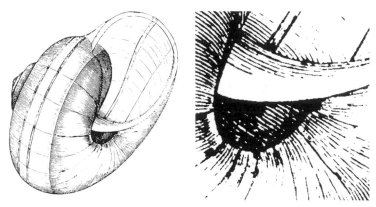

Without sharpening

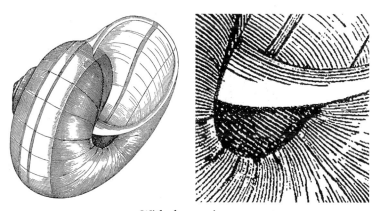

With sharpening

Thresholding

When you scan line art in Grayscale mode, lines aren't captured as hard lines, but as a collection of pixels with different values (see Figure 12-7). But although you scanned in grayscale, you ultimately want a straight black-and-white image. The way you get there is via the Threshold command (from the Adjust submenu under the Image menu). Threshold turns gray pixels above a certain value to black, and pushes all other pixels to white.

By adjusting the break point in the Threshold dialog box where pixels go to black or white, you can control the widths of lines in your scanned-as-grayscale line art image (see Figure 12-8).

For simple line art images that don't include very detailed and dense shadow areas, just set Threshold to 2 and press Return. With images that

Figure 12-7
Line art scanned
as grayscale

Scanned as line art   *400%*

Scanned as grayscale   *400%*

Scanned as grayscale with sharpening   *400%*
and thresholding applied

do include densely detailed shadows, try values up to about 55. As you move the slider to the left, you can see the fine lines start to break up. As you move right, the shadow areas start to clog. It's a lot like working the trade-off between shadow and highlight detail with the Levels dialog box on a grayscale image.

Figure 12-8
Threshold
settings for
line art

Threshold: 2

Threshold: 80

Threshold: 185

As we noted earlier, there are no grayscale pixels left in the file after you use Threshold, so you might as well convert the image to Bitmap mode (in the Mode submenu of the Image menu). Bitmap images are one-eighth the size of Grayscale images.

Rescreens

The problem with printed photos is that they've already been halftoned. That is, the grays or colors of the image are simulated with little dots, and while our eyes are easily fooled, scanners are not. If you scan these images in Grayscale or Color mode and print them, the PostScript printer rescreens them. The conflict between the original halftone screen and the output screen results in a real mess (see Figure 12-9).

The other problem is that in the original screening, a lot of the image detail is lost (the coarser the screen, the less detail remains). So when you scan the screened image, there's not a lot of detail there for the scanner to grab. The goal is to capture (and maintain) as much of that detail as possible, while avoiding the problems of overlapping screens. Don't expect miracles, though. Remember: garbage in, garbage out.

Figure 12-9
The problem with rescreens

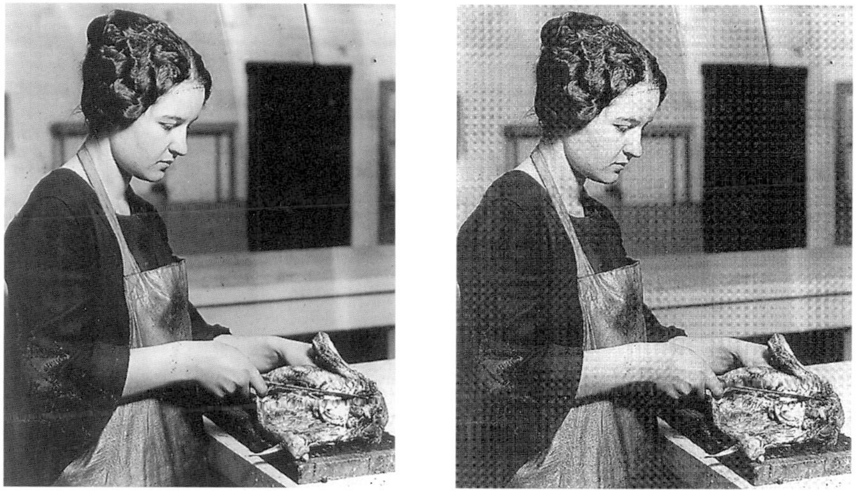

The original halftoned image *A halftoned halftone*

There are two basic approaches to working with screened images:

- **Line art.** Reproduce the image as black-and-white line art. This only works well with low-frequency images, under about 85 lpi. Note that you can't resize the image in a page-layout program later without making the image fall apart or creating moiré patterns. If your halftone was printed at 100 lpi or higher, it's probably better to convert it into a grayscale image using the techniques from the previous section.
- **Grayscale.** Scan in grayscale or color, then use filters to remove the halftone pattern while maintaining detail. The essential concept is "blur, then sharpen."

Tip: Make Rescreens Smaller. Since there's not much detail in screened images, you should generally plan on reproducing them at a smaller size than the original. You can use the techniques described here to break up the halftone pattern, and not suffer the loss of detail as much; because the image is smaller, less detail is needed.

Tip: Get Permissions First. This should be obvious, but all too often it is not: if the printed image isn't yours, you should always get permission to use it *before* you scan it in. Ethics aside, there are certainly copyright issues involved here. Most copyright violations in digital imaging occur when people scan pictures from magazines or books without thinking.

Frequency Considerations

One of the first things to consider when working with rescreens is the screen frequency of the printed images. Our techniques vary, depending on whether we're working with low-, mid-, or high-frequency halftones.

Low-frequency halftones. Low-frequency images are both hard and easy. They can be easy because you can reproduce them as line art, as mentioned above. But they're frustrating because there's so little detail; scanning as grayscale is almost always futile. If the line-art techniques aren't working for you, however, you can try using the methods for medium-frequency images described in the next section.

Medium-frequency halftones. Capturing medium-frequency halftones—80 lpi to 120 lpi—is perhaps the hardest of all. These halftone spots are too small to re-create in line art, but they're too large and coarse to blend together as a grayscale without blurring the image unacceptably (see "High-frequency halftones," later in this chapter). You know a halftone falls into this category if you can see the halftone dots when the paper is six inches away from your face, but you can't see them (at least, not clearly) when the paper is two feet away.

There are six techniques that we commonly use when scanning mid-frequency halftones (there are other techniques, but we usually find these ones effective). All five attempt to capture grayscale information and remove the moiré patterns that typically occur (see Figure 12-10).

▶ **Median, Despeckle, and Dust and Scratches.** The Median and Dust and Scratches filters are probably the most effective methods for removing dot patterning, but they work at a cost. Both filters average several pixels together to get a median value for the group. That means your image gets blurry. Often you can retrieve some of the edges with Unsharp Mask, but sometimes you have to apply the filters so much that the image is damaged. Nonetheless, even a one-pixel Dust and Scratches filter can smooth out many of the problem areas in an image.

If the resolution of the printed image is above 100 lpi, the Despeckle filter might work better than Median. We often try Despeckle first, and if it doesn't work well enough (or it damages the image in ways we don't like), we undo it and revert to Median.

Figure 12-10 Rescreening mid-frequency halftones often causes moirés.

A 400-ppi scan of the screened image printed with a 75-lpi screen   *After using the Despeckle, Median, and Unsharp Mask filters (75 lpi)*   *After downsampling (133 lpi)*

▶ **Downsampling.** Downsampling using bicubic sharper interpolation (see Chapter 3, *Image Essentials*) is one of the best ways we know to get rid of patterning, because Photoshop groups together a number of pixels and takes their average gray value. The problem, of course, is that you can also lose detail. Your goal is to downsample just enough to average out the halftone dot pattern, but not so much that you lose details in the image.

▶ **Upsampling.** After you downsample, you might need to upsample again to regain image resolution. You never get lost details back, of course, but sometimes sharpening the higher-resolution image can make it appear as though you did.

▶ **Rotating.** When you rotate an image in Photoshop, the program has to do some heavy-duty calculation work, and those calculations typically soften the image somewhat, breaking up the halftone pattern. If you have a very slight patterning effect after scanning a pre-halftoned image, you might try rotating the entire image 10 or 20 degrees, and then rotate the same amount back again. This double rotation can average out some patterning.

Once you've managed to break up the halftone pattern, you'll need to go after the image with the Unsharp Mask filter to give the impression of sharpness for the detail that remains. Since the image will probably be fairly blurry, you'll have to make the more extreme sharpening moves that we suggest in Chapter 9, *Sharpness, Detail, and Noise Reduction*, while being careful to avoid bringing the halftone pattern back out.

High-frequency halftones. Scanning pre-halftoned images with high screen frequencies—over 133 lpi—is often easier, because the dot patterns blur into gray levels while maintaining detail. You often need to use the techniques listed above, but you don't have to work as hard at salvaging the image. In fact, we often find that just scanning at the full optical resolution of the scanner and downsampling to the resolution you need is enough to get rid of patterning. Or, try placing the artwork at an angle on the scanner, then downsampling and rotating in Photoshop (the Cropping tool lets you do both at once).

Tip: Pay Attention to Actual Pixels. Remember that the most important magnification view in Photoshop is Actual Pixels (100-percent view). If you scan an image and you see horrible moiré patterns at 33-percent view, don't panic. Zoom in to 100-percent view and see what's really going on. The damage is often much less than you first thought. Even if you don't see patterning in the Actual Pixels view, you still may opt to do a little smoothing work (especially if you see patterning when zoomed in to 200- or 400-percent), but it's not essential.

HDR Imaging

If 16 bits per channel just isn't enough, Photoshop CS2 supports HDR (High Dynamic Range) imaging, which uses 32-bit floating point data per channel to record an *unlimited* dynamic range. Photoshop CS2 supports established HDR formats such as Industrial Light and Magic's OpenEXR and the Radiance format used by the open-source Radiance ray-tracing and rendering engine, in addition to Portable Bitmap Format (PBM), Large Document Format (.psb), Photoshop (.psd), and TIFF. The three lattermost formats allow profile embedding, but be aware that color-managing HDR data is an uncertain endeavor at best.

Thus far, HDR imaging has largely been confined to the movie industry, and to synthetic imaging produced by ray-tracing applications. Its applicability to "normal" photography is unclear, mainly because we lack any output methods that can handle the dynamic range. The only camera we know that can capture HDR images is SpheronVR's SpheroCamHDR, which is very much aimed at the 3D rendering market. Possibly the most interesting aspect of Photoshop's HDR support is that it allows you to create HDR images from bracketed exposures shot with normal cameras.

Merge to HDR

You can create HDR files using Merge to HDR with bracketed exposures in Camera Raw format, or from bracketed exposures shot as JPEG. You can also merge processed files saved in any of the formats Photoshop supports that allow EXIF metadata, but these only work if you haven't made any edits to the file, so using anything other than Camera Raw or camera-generated JPEGs just creates extra work.

Merge to HDR uses the EXIF metadata to determine the exposures and blend them accordingly. If you apply edits to Camera Raw files, they're simply ignored by Merge to HDR: If you apply edits to JPEGs (or to any of the other formats), you'll get really nasty results.

Shooting for HDR. We find that we get the best results when we bracket by one-third of a stop, though this may be overkill. Bracketing by 1 stop, using enough exposures to cover the entire dynamic range you're trying to capture, often works well. A heavy tripod, mirror lockup, and a static scene all help—Merge to HDR doesn't do well when objects in the scene move.

Using Merge to HDR. The process of creating an HDR file is quite simple. You start by shooting a series of bracketed exposures, varying only the shutter speed, that cover the dynamic range you're trying to capture. The easiest way to merge the images to an HDR file is to select them in Bridge, then choose Merge to HDR from the Photoshop submenu (in the Tools menu; see Figure 12-11). Or, if you want to do things the hard way, you can choose Merge to HDR from Photoshop's Automate menu, which produces the Merge to HDR dialog box shown in Figure 12-12.

The Merge to HDR dialog box lets you choose the source files, and gives the option of auto-aligning the source images. Don't expect miracles here—we find it's better to rely on a solid tripod.

Figure 12-11
Merge to HDR
from Bridge

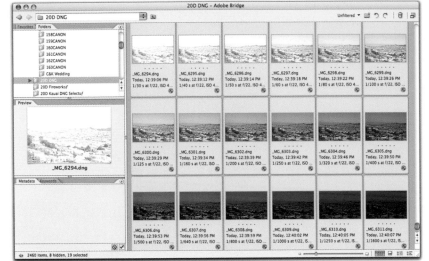

Select the source
images in Bridge.

Choose Merge to HDR

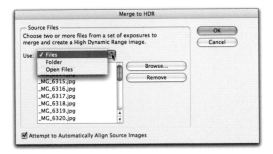

Figure 12-12
Merge to HDR
from Photoshop

When you click OK in the dialog box shown in Figure 12-12, or when you launch Merge to HDR from Bridge, you get the dialog box shown in Figure 12-13 (also, somewhat confusingly, named Merge to HDR). This dialog box shows thumbnails of the source files at the left, and a preview of the image. You can uncheck thumbnails to exclude them from the results—handy if something in the scene has moved to the extent that it causes artifacts—and set a white point for the image preview using the slider at upper right. The preview white point only affects the 8 bit/chan-

Figure 12-13
Merge to HDR
dialog box

nel preview on screen—it has no effect on the data in the HDR file itself. When you click OK, Photoshop dismisses the dialog box and opens the HDR file.

You can perform limited edits on the HDR file itself. The clone stamp tool lets you eliminate dust spots; you can run Channel Mixer, Photo Filter, and Exposure from the Adjustments menu; and you can use a variety of filters, the most useful of which are probably Smart Sharpen and Unsharp Mask. Figure 12-14 shows the HDR image before and after sharpening—we find we get significantly better results sharpening the HDR image than we do sharpening after we've downsampled to 16 bits or 8 bits per channel.

Note that there's an important difference between using the Exposure command from the Adjustments submenu (in the Image menu) and using the 32-bit Preview Options command from the View menu, even though the controls appear similar (see Figure 12-15).

The Exposure command actually remaps the 32-bit floating-point data (though it doesn't clip—it actually preserves blacker-than-black and whiter-than-white thanks to the magic of floating-point math), while the 32-bit Preview Options simply adjust the way the 32-bit data is displayed on your 8-bit display.

Figure 12-14
Sharpening the
HDR image

Figure 12-15
Exposure versus Gamma

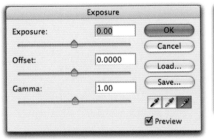

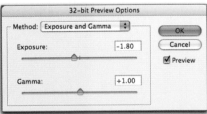

Downsampling HDR Images

To do just about anything else with an HDR image, including printing it, you need to downsample to 16-bit/channel or 8-bit/channel mode by choosing one of these options from the Mode submenu (in the Image menu). When you choose 8-bit or 16-bit/channel, the HDR Conversion dialog box appears (see Figure 12-16). It offers four ways of performing the conversion to a lower bit depth. Note that while you can display the

Figure 12-16
Downsampling
the HDR image

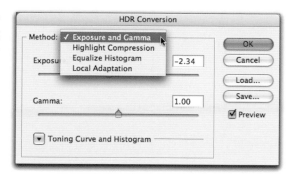

Toning Curve and Histogram at the bottom of the dialog box in all four methods, only Local Adaptation actually appears to do anything!

Exposure and Gamma. The default method, Exposure and Gamma, offers two slider controls. Exposure sets the white point, Gamma sets the midtone. Figure 12-17 shows the HDR image from Figure 12-13 converted to 16 bits per channel using Exposure and Gamma with Exposure set to -1.84 and Gamma set to 1.04.

Figure 12-17
Conversion using
Exposure and Gamma

Highlight Compression. There are no options for Highlight Compression—it simply is what it is. Figure 12-18 shows the result.

Equalize Histogram. As with Highlight Compression, there are no options for Equalize Histogram. Figure 12-19 shows the result.

Figure 12-18
Conversion using
Highlight Compression

Figure 12-19
Conversion using
Equalize Histogram

Local Adaptation. Local Adaptation offers the most control, but at default settings often produces the least encouraging results. Nevertheless, persistence is rewarded. Figure 12-20 shows Local Adaptation at default settings and the resulting conversion.

The default settings probably work well for some image somewhere, but we've yet to find it. Fortunately, the defaults are eminently tweakable. Local Adaptation is loosely akin to Photoshop's Shadow/Highlight command. The Radius setting adjusts the size of the neighborhood the algorithm uses to calculate the local adaptation, while the Threshold setting tells it how far apart two pixels' tonal values must be before they're no longer part of the same brightness region. Figure 12-21 shows the settings adjusted to more appropriate values for this image, and their result.

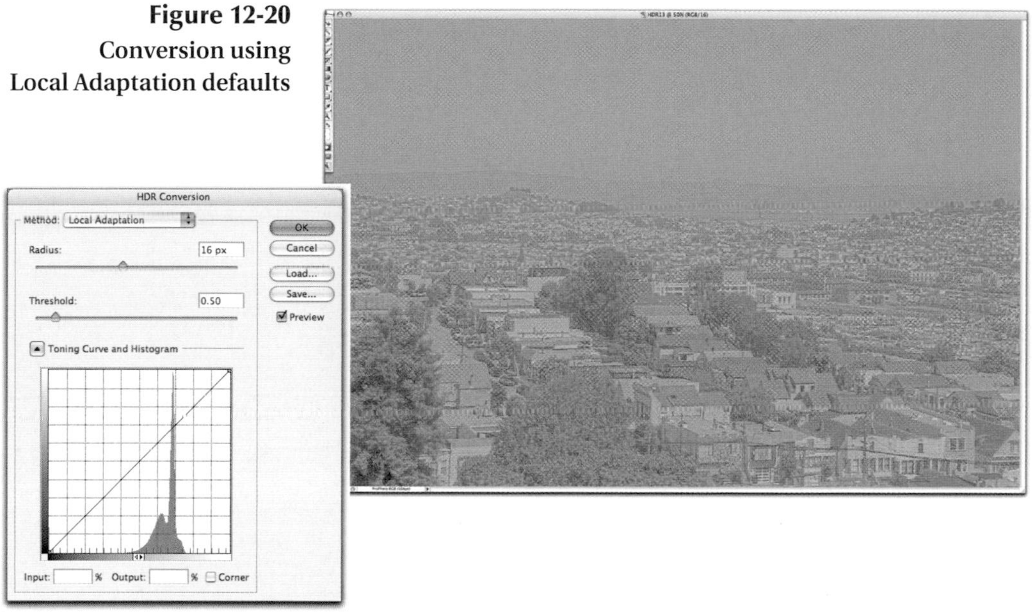

Figure 12-20
Conversion using
Local Adaptation defaults

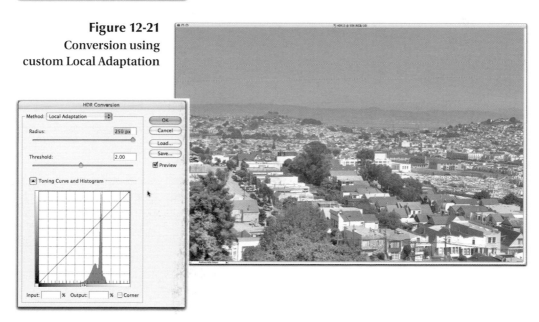

Figure 12-21
Conversion using
custom Local Adaptation

The Threshold setting essentially sets the local contrast, while the Radius setting controls the size of the local neighborhood to which that contrast applies.

For further control, Local Adaptation also offers the Toning Curve and Histogram. The Toning Curve differs from Photoshop's Curves in a couple of ways. First, the red tick marks on the horizontal scale represent 1 EV

(Exposure Value) increments—approximately 1 f-stop (remember that you're dealing with an unbounded dynamic range). The second difference is that you can place corner points on the curve (click the Corner checkbox to turn the selected curve point into a corner point), thereby creating a sharp tonal break. This can be useful for placing a diffuse highlight and ensuring that the specular highlights blow out.

As with Photoshop's Curves, you can click in the image to see where on the curve the pixels under the cursor lie, but unlike Photoshop's Curves, you can't place points by Command-clicking in the image. Figure 12-22 shows the image after editing with the Toning Curve.

Figure 12-22
Conversion using custom Local Adaptation and Toning Curve

We think it's great that Photoshop has started supporting HDR imaging, but given the considerable difficulties in capturing and processing multiple exposures into an HDR file, we confess to being uncertain of its applicability to mainstream photography. But it's fascinating, and once you've ascended the fairly steep initial learning curve, it's also addictive!

Retouching

Everyone has their own tolerance level of what can or should be changed in a photograph. We've heard photographers argue convincingly that each time you manipulate an image, especially when you add or remove real objects, it erodes the credibility of photography as a representation of the real. But we've heard other photographers argue equally convincingly that they've never seen a piece of reality they didn't want to improve. We don't have an answer to this debate, but we urge you to at least consider the question.

It's useful to make the distinction between "dust-busting" (removing specks of dirt, dust, mold, hair, and so on) and "retouching" (actually changing the content of an image). In many cases, the tools and techniques overlap, but dustbusting and retouching typically happen at different times—we prefer to do dustbusting early in the workflow, and whenever possible, do it once (since it's about as much fun as a root canal). In this section, we'll relay a few key pointers that we've learned over the years about both dustbusting and retouching images, in the hope that they'll make you more efficient in whatever work you're undertaking.

Dustbusting

While dust tends to be a bigger problem with film scans than with digital captures, the latter are by no means immune either. Images that don't require dustbusting tend to be the exception rather than the rule. We generally dustbust early in the editing process. We usually do any noise reduction and make basic global corrections to tone and color before dustbusting.

Tip: Retouch on a Layer. However you retouch your image—with the Clone Stamp tool, the Healing Brush, painting, copying pixels from other portions of the image, and so on—try to do the work on a separate layer. When your edits are on a separate layer, it's easy to erase a change, and it's easy to see "before-and-after" views by turning the layer's visibility off and on. Remember that if you're using the Clone Stamp tool or one of the Healing Brushes when painting on a separate layer, you need to turn on the Use All Layers checkbox in the Options bar.

An alternate method is to create a new layer containing merged copy of all the underlying layers by making a new layer and pressing Command-Option-Shift-E (or choosing Merge Visible from the Layer menu while holding down the Option key). That way we can turn off Use All Layers, which can speed things up slightly, at the cost of a larger file size.

The Healing Brushes and the Patch Tool

Photoshop introduced two new tools that should make even the most hardened retoucher crack a smile: the Healing Brush and the Patch tool. The Healing Brush (press J) is quite a marvel of modern science; you first pick a spot on your image from which you want to clone (like the Clone Stamp tool, you Option- or Alt-click to pick the source), and then you paint in the area you want to change (see Figure 12-23). While the mouse button is down, the screen looks as though you were using the Clone Stamp tool. However, when you let go of the mouse button, Photoshop uses a complicated algorithm to blend the image of the source layer with the tone and texture of the area you're painting. The result is a Clone Stamp tool that blends in better than the Clone Stamp tool ever could.

Figure 12-23
Painting with the
Healing Brush

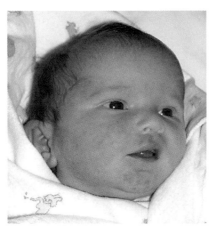

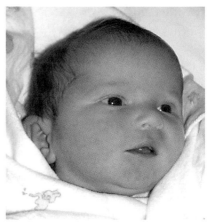

The original image.
Infants often have splotches and
scratches that pass in a day or two.

Here, the red marks and
other distractions have been
removed with the Healing Brush.

The lip, caught by
the camera at a bad
moment, was selected
with a feathered edge
and fixed with the
Liquify command.

Healing brush paint area ⎯⎯⎯

Source area (Option/Alt-click) ⎯⎯⎯

gabriel @ 200% ...

200%

In Photoshop CS2, things get even better thanks to the debut of the new Spot Healing Brush. The Spot Healing Brush does away with the pesky requirement to choose a source point—instead, it automatically samples the surrounding area. Figure 12-24 shows an image with its fair share of flaws—the typical dust, hair, and scratches that often bedevil film.

Figure 12-24
Using the Spot
Healing Brush

The red outline in the image above shows the area seen in detail, right.

Dust spot

Scratch

Hair

The Spot Healing Brush handles the dust spot flawlessly just by clicking—we used a small brush just big enough to cover the spot. For the hair, we simply painted over the hair by dragging the Spot Healing Brush, again using a brush just wide enough to cover the flaw. The scratch proved slightly more problematic: Often, we can fix scratches like this by clicking the Spot Healing Brush at one end of the scratch, holding down the Shift key, and clicking at the other end of the scratch to paint in a straight line with the Spot Healing Brush. This worked everywhere except where the scratch crosses the horizon (see Figure 12-25).

Figure 12-25
Spot Healing Brush
results

*The dust spot disappears
with a single click.*

*The scratch is a little more
problematic. Painting in
a straight line causes an
artifact where the scratch
crosses the horizon.*

*The hair disappears with a
single brush stroke.*

When a situation like this arises, our first instinct is often to hit Undo, but since the repair was good everywhere except on the horizon, a better starting point for the solution is to use the History Brush to paint out only that part of the repair that didn't work—we set the History Brush Source to the step before the scratch healing, then clicked with a History Brush sized to cover the artifact. In this case, we made the repair by zooming to 300% view, then painting with a very small (3-pixel) Spot Healing Brush (see Figure 12-26). In more difficult cases, we may use either or both of the following tips.

Tip: Watch Out for Edges. The main problem with the Healing Brush and the Patch tool is that they don't work particularly well along edges in your image. For instance, let's say you have a shot of a dark-haired model against a light backdrop. These tools work beautifully in the model's face, but they can cause a mess when used along the edge where the hair meets the backdrop. The reason? These tools rely on the pixels around the

Figure 12-26
Spot Healing fine details

Zooming in to 300% view, we painted out the bad repair with the History Brush.

Then we made the repair with a 3-pixel Spot Healing Brush.

brush stroke to blend in properly. Near high-contrast edges, the algorithm breaks—in this case, the dark pixels of the hair would smear into the lighter background pixels. The solution: make a soft-edged selection around the area you want to change; these tools won't take the areas outside the selection into consideration, so you won't get this smear effect.

Tip: Replace Mode. When you have the Healing Brush selected, you can select something called Replace from the Mode popup menu in the Options bar. The idea is simple: The Clone brush doesn't work particularly well with soft-edged brushes (the edges get too blurry). The Healing Brush set to Replace mode acts just like the Clone Stamp tool, but works much better if you have a hankerin' to use a soft-edged brush.

The Patch tool is like a combination of the Healing Brush and the Lasso tool. Drag the Patch tool around an area you want to fix like you would make a selection with the Lasso tool (Option-click to create straight-line segments). Then click inside this selection and drag it to the part of your image that you want to copy. When you let go of the mouse button, Photoshop clones that source area over the area you first selected, and then performs its "healing" algorithm to blend the source in properly (see Figure 12-27).

We find that the Patch tool rarely makes a perfect fix, and the results usually need to be cleaned up with the Healing Brush or Clone Stamp tool. But using it and then cleaning up the details is still significantly faster than not using the Patch tool at all.

Figure 12-27
Quick fixes with
the Patch tool

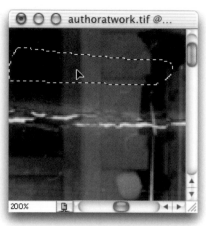

The original photograph has scratch-es and folds.

After dragging out a selection with the Patch tool, drag it on top of an area you want to copy (above). Here, we hold down the Shift key to constrain the drag vertically, ensuring the door frame will align properly when we let go (below).

The Patch tool fixes most of the heinous problems quickly, but the image still requires help, especially in the newly created anomalies in the window panes.

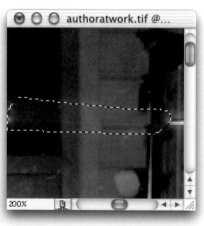

We use the Healing Brush to fix the details, including despotting.

Dust and Scratches

While the Dust and Scratches filter promises great things ("wow, a filter that dustbusts my image!"), you should be aware that this tool can do significant harm to the rest of your image, too. The Dust and Scratches filter is basically the same as the Median filter, but with a threshold feature (so that you have some control over what gets "median-ized"). That means that it removes all small details in your document, including film grain or other image details that might be important.

If, in fact, you're trying to smooth out a grainy image while dustbusting, Dust and Scratches might be just the ticket. In that case, make sure you set the Radius value as low as possible and the Threshold value as high as possible. (It'll take some trial and error to get it right, so that the dust and scratches are gone, but the image isn't too blurry.) Then, re-sharpen the image with Unsharp Mask to return some edge contrast.

Tip: Maintain the Texture. While the Healing Brush and the Patch tool are designed to maintain the original texture of the image (including film grain), the Clone Stamp tool, Dust and Scratches filter, and other tools tend to destroy texture, and hence appear unnatural. You can sometimes simulate texture that's been lost by running the Add Noise or Grain filter on the affected area at a low setting, but it's generally better to keep a close eye on what's happening to your texture as you retouch.

Tip: Snapshot Patterns. Sometimes it's nice to paint a texture or a pattern with one of the brush tools. For instance, instead of adding noise to a selection, you might want to paint noise selectively. The most flexible way to do this is to create a layer by Option-clicking on the New Layer button in the Layers palette (which brings up the New Layer dialog box). Choose Overlay from the Mode popup menu, and turn on the "Fill with Overlay-neutral color" checkbox. Now, run the Grain filter or Add Noise filter to this layer, and add a layer mask. When you paint on the layer mask with black and white pixels, you paint the effect on and off.

Tip: Use Feathering. Often, the smallest thing makes the biggest difference—feathering, for example (see Figure 12-28). When you're retouching a local, selected area—whether you're adjusting tone, painting, using a filter, or editing pixels—it's often important to feather the selection (see "Anti-Aliasing and Feathering" in Chapter 8, *Making Selections*).

Figure 12-28 Feathering as a retouching tool
This trick only works when covering an element with an area of uniform color and texture.

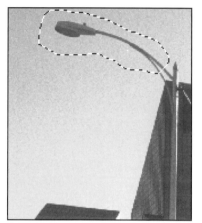
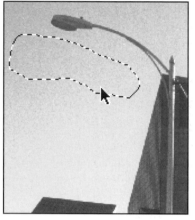
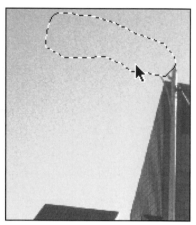

Make a loose selection with the Lasso tool and feather 4 pixels.

Drag the selection to another location.

Command-Option-drag back to cover the original. The feathering ensures a seamless edge.

Feathering is like applying a Gaussian Blur to the edges of a selection: it blends the selected area smoothly into the rest of the image. How much to feather depends entirely upon the image and its resolution, but even a little feathering (two or three pixels) is much better than nothing.

On the other hand, we find that using a soft brush when dustbusting often kills the grain or texture of an image, so we typically use a harder-edged brush or selection for this sort of work.

Tip: A Myriad of Small Spots. Mildew, dust, bugs, corrosives, abrasive surfaces, or even a mediocre scanner can cause hundreds or thousands of tiny white or black spots in an image. And after sharpening, these spots pop out at you like stars on the new moon. If you're like us, you're already cringing at the thought of spot-healing all those dots out.

Here's a technique that can stamp out thousands of dust spots in a single move. You still may have to use the Healing Brush tool to get rid of a few artifacts and some of the larger spots, but most of your work is already done (see Figure 12-29).

1. Select the area with the spots, and feather the selection.

2. Copy the selection to a new layer (Command-J).

Figure 12-29
Getting rid
of spots

The raw image

Setting the blending mode

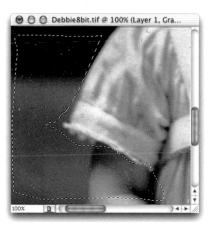

The dust spots copied to a new layer, and moved 4 pixels up and to the left

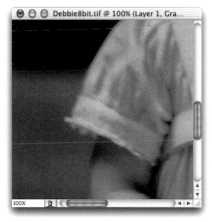

The final despotted image

3. If you're trying to remove white spots, set the blending mode in the Layers palette to Darken. If you're trying to remove black spots, set it to Lighten.

4. Use the Command and arrow keys to move the new layer left, right, up, or down by a few pixels—just enough that you see the dust spots disappear (if the spots are tiny, a one- or two-pixel move does the trick).

5. You can see a "before and after" by turning on and off the visibility of the new layer.

Figure 12-31
Stroking a path with the
Clone Stamp tool

Getting rid of the powerlines by hand would take forever.

We draw a path along the powerline. Then, with the Clone Stamp tool set to a small soft-edged brush, we carefully align the source point to the path.

 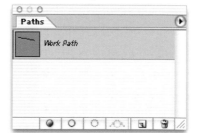

We Shift-click on the path in the Paths palette to hide the path, then drag the path over the Stroke icon at the bottom of the palette.

After repeating the process twice for the remaining powerlines, we arrive at the result shown at right. The critical parts of the operation are choosing the correct brush size, and setting the source point. In some cases, it's best to split the path into sections, choosing a different source for each one.

1. Draw the path using the Pen tool, keeping it as close to the center of the scratch (or powerline, or whatever) as possible. It's a good idea to save it (double-click on the Work Path in the Paths palette and name it).

2. Select the Clone Stamp tool, and click the Aligned button in the Options bar. To remove a light-colored scratch, set the mode to Darken; to remove a dark powerline, set the mode to Lighten.

3. Choose a soft brush a little wider than the widest point of the scratch.

4. Option-click beside the start of the path to set the source point for the cloning operation, just as you would if you were going to clone-stamp the scratch by hand.

5. Shift-click on the path in the Paths palette to hide it, then drag the path over the Stroke button at the bottom of the palette.

Presto, the scratch is gone. The keys to making this technique work are careful selection of the brush size and source point. If the brush is too big (or small), or your source point isn't aligned correctly, you may wind up duplicating the scratch instead of removing it. However, with a little practice you can make this work very quickly and easily.

Red-Eye

A common retouching task is removing red-eye—that devilish effect that appears when a camera flash reflects off the retina. Ideally, you'll avoid red-eye by using off-camera flash, but if your (or someone else's) photograph already has red-eye, you'll have to remove the red. The new Red Eye tool (it shares a tool palette slot with the Healing Brushes and the Patch tool) is by far the easiest way of doing so, but sometimes it removes the eye color too, so we still resort to the following techniques when necessary.

Hue/Saturation. Select the offending pupils with an oval marquee, feather the selection by a few pixels, copy the selection to a new layer (Command-J), and then use Hue/Saturation to shift the color, brightness, and saturation. Every image requires different values, but we usually start with Hue at +40 (for brown eyes) or −120 (for blue eyes), Saturation at −75, and a Lightness value of −50. The key is to remove the glaring color while still maintaining the specular highlights and color that make the eye look alive.

Color Replacement tool. The Color Replacement in Photoshop CS2 now shares a slot with the Brush in the Tool palette. It lets you change the color of pixels to the foreground color, but leave the pixels' saturation and brightness alone. In other words, it changes the color but retains the detail. We haven't found it useful for large areas, but it's quite good at fixing things like red-eye. Hold down the Option key and click on the darkest part of the eye (or some other dark area nearby), then let go of the Option key, adjust the brush size to slightly smaller than the pupil, and draw over the red portions. You may need to increase the Tolerance level in the Options bar to 35 or 40 percent.

Perspective Retouching

One of the whizzier new features in Photoshop CS2 is the Vanishing Point filter, which lets you clone while preserving perspective, a task that even the studliest pixel-pusher has long found daunting. Vanishing Point makes editing in perspective orders of magnitude easier than it used to be.

Vanishing Point is a very deep plug-in, and if you plan to use it a lot, we strongly recommend reading the online help and mastering the considerable number of keyboard shortcuts. Perspective cloning isn't something we do a lot, so we'll barely scratch the surface here, but we hope to at least give you an idea of the process and a hint of the power.

Tip: Clone to a Layer. If you create a new layer before running Vanishing Point with the new layer selected, Vanishing Point's results get returned to the new layer. This makes fine-tuning the results much easier.

Tip: Take Care of Lens Distortions First. Vanishing Point calculates mathematically perfect planes, so if your lens shows any barrel or pincushion distortion, the cloned results may be a little off. You can try fixing them post-Vanishing Point (the above tip makes doing so easier), but you'll get better results if you fix the distortion using the Lens Correction filter before running Vanishing Point (see "Lens Correction" in Chapter 9, *Sharpness, Detail, and Noise Reduction).*

Defining the planes. The first step in using Vanishing Point (after choosing the feature from the Filter menu or pressing Command-Option-V) is to define a perspective plane by clicking on four points (see Figure 12-32).

Figure 12-32
Defining a
perspective plane

*The Create Plane tool
lets you click to define
the corners of a
perspective plane.*

Figure 12-33
Enlarging the
perspective plane

*The Edit Plane tool
lets you scale the plane by
dragging the edge and
corner handles.*

Then enlarge the plane to cover the area you want to affect, as shown in Figure 12-33. Watch the color and size of the grid when dragging its corners or sides: Red means the grid is not a valid perspective; yellow is pretty close, and blue is good. But in general it's better to see a grid of bigger squares than smaller rectangles. Sometimes moving the grid corners by a pixel or two will make a big difference in the quality of the perspective.

Performing the cloning. Once you've defined the plane, you can use the marquee or clone stamp tool to clone regions in the image, or paste elements from other images. In this simple example, we used the marquee to select the light fixture, then Option-dragged it to create duplicates. Note that the selection created by the marquee automatically conforms to the perspective plane (see Figure 12-34).

In this simple example, we used a single perspective plane, but once you've defined the basic plane, you can automatically create perpendicular planes by Command-dragging an edge node. And while we generally find that it's easier to fine-tune the result on a layer after we've run Vanish-

Figure 12-34
Cloning with the marquee

We select the area we want to clone with the marquee, which automatically conforms to the perspective grid.

We Option-drag the selection to create duplicates in perspective.

ing Point, the Transform tool in Vanishing Point lets you transform float-ing selections.

For more complex cloning operations, we use Vanishing Point's Stamp tool, which works just like the Clone Stamp tool in Photoshop. Figure 12-35 shows before-and-after versions of Bruce's unsanctioned remodel of a listed building in the heart of mediaeval Edinburgh.

Figure 12-35
Before and after cloning

In this example we used the Stamp tool in Vanish-ing Point to clone to a new layer, then fine-tuned the result in Photoshop.

Compositing Images

The number one problem in making selections and compositing images together is edge spill, where some of the background color gets picked up as fringe along the edges of your selection. Of the considerable number of methods for getting rid of edge spill, most involve cutting away at the edge pixels rather than removing the background color from the mix.

Now, to the rescue, comes the Extract feature, which is designed to search out edges, erase pixels, and—most important—perform edge-color decontamination, where Photoshop distills out background colors while leaving the foreground colors. It's almost like magic, and would be extraor-dinary if it really worked for more than a handful of images.

Note that Photoshop also has a Magic Eraser and Background Eraser tools, which erase to transparency—the Magic Eraser is like clicking with the Magic Wand tool and then pressing Delete. But both of these tools are blunt instruments, so we just generally ignore them.

But Photoshop has other tools for compositing images together, from Layer Blending to the Photomerge feature (for creating panoramas). Let's take a look at just a few.

Tip: Layer Blending Is Fast Blending. One of our favorite compositing techniques doesn't involve making selections or using Extract. It's the little-known and less-understood Blending Options feature in the Layer Style dialog box. If your image stands out well from its background on any one channel, layer blending is often the fastest way to composite it into a different background (see Figure 12-36).

Figure 12-36
Compositing an image
with layer blending

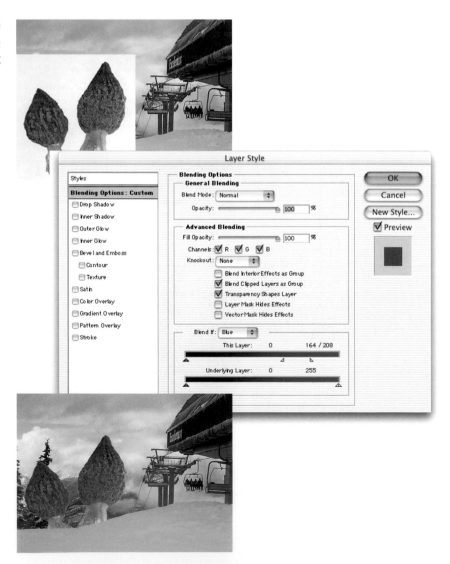

When you set the right "This Layer" slider in the Layer Style dialog box to 20 percent gray, you're telling Photoshop *not* to include any pixels in the layer that are lighter than 20 percent. The problem: this creates a hard edge, so you get a jaggy composite. The solution: Option-click on each of the sliders to break it into two half-triangles. This provides a smooth blend between what is included and what is not.

Tip: Alignment via Opacity and Mode. When compositing images together, we prefer to place selected pixels on a separate layer for accurate positioning (see Figure 12-37). You can do this by pressing Command-J (or choosing New Layer via Copy from the Layer menu). Say you're working on a group portrait of a family where everyone's expressions are great except the teenage son's, whose eyes are closed. You have another shot in the same basic pose where he looks good, so you decide to replace the head in image A with the one from image B.

Figure 12-37 Aligning floating selections

The original image

When the new selection is dropped over the original image, it's hard to see where it should be placed.

Opacity set to 60 percent so that positioning is easier

The final image

With this kind of massive editing, it's often difficult to align the new image with the old. One way is to change Opacity in the Layers palette to 50 percent or less, so you can see the image underneath. In this example, we align the new head's eyes with the original image's eyes (nudging one pixel at a time with the arrow keys). Finally, we set the Opacity to 100 percent, and retouch the overlying layer's edges.

Note that instead of changing the opacity, you can change the overlying layer's blending mode. When trying to align two objects in an image, we often set the mode to Darken or Lighten. Then we watch the pixels darken and lighten, to give us clues.

Extract: Quick 'n' Dirty Masking

The good news is that Adobe is listening to its customers: The People said that they were tired of buying plug-ins that built high-quality selections and masks, so Adobe created the Extract feature. The bad news is that you'll probably still want to go buy a plug-in.

Don't get us wrong: The Extract feature is reasonably good at what it does, but what it does is not nearly as powerful as most people want. Nonetheless, Extract is what we've got for now—assuming that you don't have another plug-in, such as OnOne's MaskPro—and so Extract is what we're going to talk about.

When to use Extract. There is a temptation to use Extract for any and every selection. Don't. Remember that Color Range or any of the other selection tools may provide a better, faster result. It depends entirely on the image and what you mean to do with it. Extract works best with images that display significant contrast between foreground object and background color, and where the edges aren't too detailed. For instance, your best friend photographed against a bright-blue sky would work well. On the other hand, you're going to have more trouble with an image of the typical blond model, hair shimmering against golden sand.

The best reason to use Extract is its edge-color-decontamination. If you're just trying to make a selection, and you're not planning on compositing an object on top of some other background (one with a very different tonal or color range than its original), then you'll probably find more peace of mind with another selection method.

Tip: Always Work on a Duplicate. Note that the Extract feature does not result in a mask or selection. Instead, it actually changes and deletes pixels in your image (it has to do this because of how it performs color decontamination). Because Extract is a relatively blunt instrument, you almost always have to clean up afterward. Therefore, before using Extract, it behooves you to work on a duplicate layer, or take a snapshot of your document, or save the document, or *something*, so that you don't mess up your original data. We tend to use a duplicate layer; then we can transform the result of Extract into a layer mask by loading the duplicate layer's transparency mask (Command-click on the layer), switching to the original layer, and clicking on the New Layer Mask button in the Layers palette. (Of course, if the original layer is a Background layer, you'll have to turn it into a regular layer first by double-clicking on it.)

Step-by-step extraction. Once you've identified an appropriate image, open the Extract dialog box by choosing Extract from the Filter menu (in earlier versions, it was in the Image menu). Better yet, just press Command-Option-X to open the Extract dialog box. The Extract interface is still pretty clunky and unlike the rest of Photoshop (see Figure 12-38). But it's not too bad once you know the steps you need to take.

Figure 12-38
The Extract dialog box

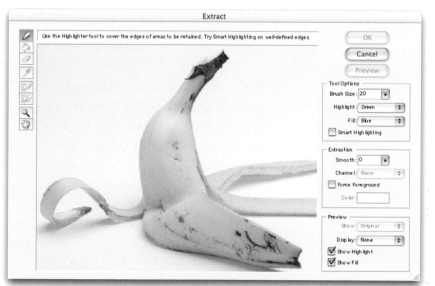

1. Use the Highlighter tool to paint a line along the edge of the foreground object (the thing you're trying to extract). The Highlighter should already be highlighted; if it's not, press B to select it. If you make a mistake, you can erase the "paint" with the Eraser tool (press E).

    When painting, you can press the bracket keys—[and]—to change the size of the highlighter brush. This is important because the brush size has a direct effect on the way Photoshop extracts the image. In general, you want a smaller brush around hard, defined edges, and a larger brush around soft, hairy, difficult edges. Note that you need to completely cover the edge transition with the highlighter, but you want the smallest brush you can get away with (see Figure 12-39). You also want to target the transition area, and stay away from the foreground object (the part you want opaque) as much as possible.

2. Now select the Paintbucket tool (press G) from the Extract dialog box, and click on the foreground object (inside the line you just drew). This tells Photoshop which side of the line is the stuff you want to keep. If the Paintbucket fills past the boundaries of your highlighter line, then there's a break in the line somewhere. In that case, simply select the Highlighter tool again, fill in the break, and then re-click with the Paintbucket tool.

3. Once you've specified what constitutes the edge (with the Highlighter) and what constitutes the inside of the object (with the Paintbucket), you must click the Preview button to see the result. If you don't like what you see, you can tweak the highlighter edge… but first turn on the Show Highlight checkbox, and set the View popup menu to Original.

4. Finally, when you have the effect you want, you can click OK. Photoshop deletes the background pixels, leaves the inside pixels, and "decontaminates" the pixels covered by the highlighter. The result is hardly ever perfect, so you must now use the History brush, the Clone Stamp tool, or any number of other methods to finalize the image.

Tip: Draw Faster Edges. Neither of us has particularly steady hands, so when it comes to drawing out the edge of the image with the Highlighter tool, we tend to use the Shift-click approach: Click once on the edge, then Shift-click someplace else, and Photoshop draws a straight line between

Figure 12-39
Extracting the
foreground object

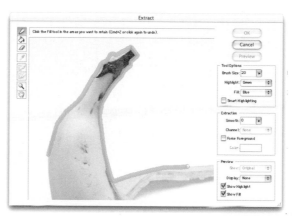

First, use the highlighter tool to define the edge of the object. Use as small a brush as you can while still overlapping the transition pixels.

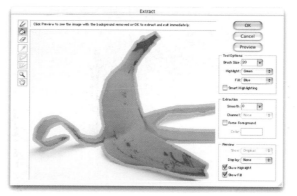

Click inside the object to tell the program what it should save.

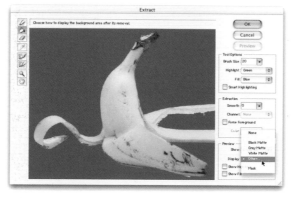

After you click Preview, you can change the matte color (here it's green) to see the image over different colors.

the two points. These straight lines are often perfect for tracing the edge of an image.

Tip: Use Prebuilt Channels. As we said earlier, the best thing about the Extract feature is its edge-color decontamination. Sometimes it's easier to select the object with other methods (the Magic Wand, the Channels trick we describe in Chapter 8, *Making Selections*, and so on). You can use these techniques together to get the best of both worlds.

1. First, make a selection around the foreground object. The selection should be relatively clean and well defined. (Of course, if you spent more than 15 seconds making this selection, it's a good idea to save it as a channel so you can recall it later if necessary.)

2. Choose Border from the Modify submenu (under the Select menu) and select a border width appropriate for the resolution of the image. For a low-res image, you can probably use 4 or 5 pixels; for higher-resolution images, you'll need to use a larger amount. The resulting selection should straddle the edge of the object (see Figure 12-40).

3. Invert this selection (press Command-Shift-I) and then save it in the Channels palette. The channel should appear black along the edge of the object and white everywhere else.

Figure 12-40
Making a border selection

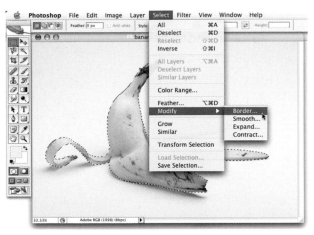

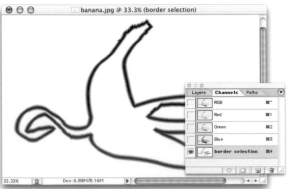

4. Now, when you open the Extract dialog box, choose this channel from the Load Highlight popup menu. This loads your "selection," so you don't have to draw one manually.

5. Finally, click on the inside with the Paintbucket tool and click Preview.

This still isn't a perfect system, but it's sometimes easier than drawing the outline yourself.

In our opinion, the Extract feature earns an "A" for effort, a "B" for final results, and a "C" for interface. Ultimately, however, no one ever said extracting images was going to be easy. Just easier.

Photomerge

Even the widest-angle lens can't capture every scene you'll ever want to capture; sometimes you need to shoot several photographs and attempt to match them up for a panorama. Enter the Photomerge feature. Technically this is an automation tool, but it has both brains and brawn behind it. To merge two or more images together, select Photomerge from the Automate submenu (under the File menu). You can choose which images to merge by picking from the Use popup menu: Open Files (if your images are already open), Files (to pick the files from disk), or Folder (to pick a whole folder of images). Note that after adding files to the list in the Photomerge dialog box, you can remove any of them by clicking the Remove button. You can also select two or more images in Adobe Bridge and select Photomerge from the Photoshop submenu (in the Tools menu).

When you click OK, Photoshop goes to work: It opens both images, resamples them if necessary to make them match, merges them as layers in a single file, and then opens the Photomerge dialog box (see Figure 12-41). Photoshop compares the edge detail to find matches, and then attempts to stitch the images together by blending from one into the next. Adobe's marketing team likes using the term "seamless," when describing Photomerge's results, but unless you were mighty careful about the lighting when you shot the images you'll almost certainly be able to find the seams where one image blends into the next. The seams are often at an angle, so they're less obvious to the eye. You can usually get a slightly better effect by turning on the Advanced Blending option in the Photomerge dialog box. Click the Preview button to see the difference between regular and advanced blending.

Figure 12-41
Photomerge

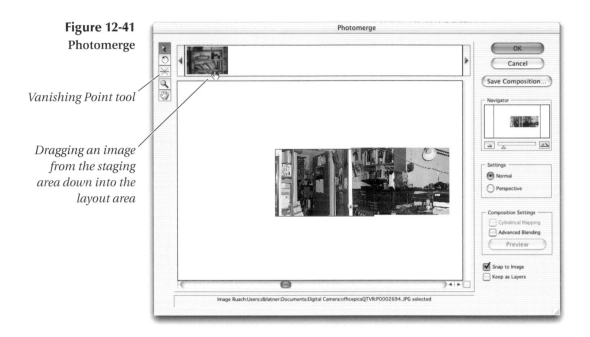

Vanishing Point tool

*Dragging an image
from the staging
area down into the
layout area*

Tip: Shooting Panoramas. When shooting images destined for Photomerge, try to capture each using the same exposure and the same lighting, using a tripod when possible to keep the camera level. With some point-and-shoot cameras, you may have to work a bit to ensure you're getting the same exposure.

Keep as Layers. The Keep as Layers checkbox tells Photoshop not to flatten the image when it's done compositing, so each image remains on its own layer. Unfortunately, it also removes all the blending from one image into the next, so you're forced to do that part yourself.

Manually compositing. If Photomerge fails to figure out how images should be stitched together, you can drag the images from the panel at the top of the Photomerge dialog box down into the main compositing area. Drag the images around in this window until you get a reasonably good overlap. If you need to, use Photomerge's Rotate tool to rotate each selected image for a better fit. We recommend leaving the Snap to Images checkbox turned on so that Photoshop will try to snap one image to the other. When you turn this off, Photoshop acts just as though you moved images around using the Move tool in a Photoshop document.

Perspective. The problem with panoramas is that they typically ignore perspective. For a more lifelike panorama, click the Perspective button. By default, Photoshop designates the middle image as the vanishing point and the images to the left and right (or above and below) splay out, as though the edges were closer to you, the viewer. You can override this by clicking on any other image with Photomerge's Vanishing Point tool (that's the third tool down; see Figure 12-42). Note that the vanishing point image has a blue outline when you click on it with the Select Image tool; non-vanishing point images have red outlines.

Saving Compositions. If it took you more than a minute or so to build your photomontage, it's probably worth saving the composition to disk by clicking (you guessed it) the Save Composition button. Compositions are very small files that reference the full-resolution files and how they're blended together. Later, if you decide to make changes, select Photomerge from the Automate submenu and click the Load Composition button instead of selecting files.

Figure 12-42
Photomerge
perspective

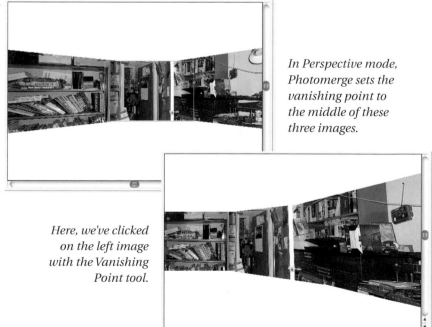

In Perspective mode, Photomerge sets the vanishing point to the middle of these three images.

Here, we've clicked on the left image with the Vanishing Point tool.

Vectors vs. Pixels

Wasn't it Robert Frost who said, "Pixels are pixels, and vectors are vectors, and never the twain shall meet"? They may not meet, but Photoshop brings them awfully close together. In ancient versions of Photoshop, vector information was limited to paths that you could convert to selections or clipping paths. Now, Photoshop offers layer clipping paths (also called, "shapes") and text based on vector outlines. Additionally, paths can affect the pixels around and inside them, especially when you use layer effects.

If you're a typical Photoshop user, you have likely focused most of your attention on pixels and let those wacky Illustrator users deal with the vectors. But Photoshop lets you perform many of the tasks for which you might use an illustration or page-layout program. Plus, its drawing tools can be very helpful even if you're a photographer or Web designer who usually ignores vector artwork, because vectors are infinitely modifiable, and they can easily be converted to bitmaps at the drop of a hat.

Photoshop CS2 offers a wide array of vector tools.

▶ Draw, edit, delete, and save paths

▶ Copy and paste paths between Photoshop and Adobe Illustrator or Macromedia FreeHand

▶ Convert paths into selections and *vice versa*

▶ Rasterize paths into pixels (stroking and filling)

▶ Create layer clipping paths (also called "shapes")

▶ Draw shapes that remain vectors through print time

▶ Convert text to shapes (so you can edit the outlines)

▶ Save EPS images with a path applied as a clipping path

▶ Maintain vector paths as a smart object layer

Photoshop also has very powerful tools for handling text (which by default are vectors), including placing text along a path. We cover the text features later in this chapter.

Strengths and weaknesses. Curiously, the primary strength and weakness of paths stem from the same attribute: Paths have no connection to the pixels below them; they live on a separate mathematical plane in Photoshop, forever floating above those lowly bitmapped images.

The strength of this is that you can create, edit, and save paths without regard for the resolution of the image, or even for the image itself. You can create a path in the shape of a logo (or better yet, import the path from Illustrator or FreeHand) and drop it into any image. Then you can save it as a path in Photoshop, ask the program to rasterize the path (turn it into a bitmapped image), drop it down into the pixel layers, convert the path to a selection, or just leave it as a path so that it prints with sharp edges (as high resolution as the PostScript device you print on).

The weakness of paths' separateness is that paths used as selections can't capture the subtlety and nuance found in most bitmapped images. A path can't, for instance, have any partially selected pixels or blurry parts; you can only achieve hard-edged selections (see Figure 12-43).

Figure 12-43 Paths versus channels

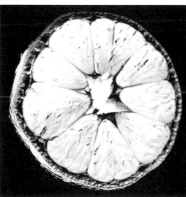

The original image

Selection masks can partially select pixels (here only selecting orange).

Paths are good at clean, sharp outlines, but they can't select image detail.

Open vs. Place

Many people don't realize that Photoshop has a built-in PostScript RIP that can read virtually any EPS or PDF file and convert it into pixels. Your client gave you their logo in a PDF and you need to use it in Photoshop? No problem! There are two ways to import EPS and PDF files: Open and Place.

Open. When you open an EPS or PDF file via the Open dialog box, Photoshop recognizes it as such and gives you additional options. The additional options you get with an EPS or PDF file let you specify the resolution and size of the final bitmap image. When you click OK, Photoshop makes a new document and rasterizes the EPS or PDF (turns it into a bitmap). Any areas of the EPS or PDF that don't have a fill specified come in transparent.

Tip: Forcing the EPS Point. If you can't see the EPS or PDF file in Photoshop's Open dialog box, it probably means that the file type, creator, or suffix is missing (depending on whether you're on a Macintosh or a PC). Your best bet is to try changing the file's name so that it ends in ".eps" or ".pdf". If this still doesn't work, the file may have become corrupted.

Tip: Opening Previews. You can, if you want, open the PICT or TIFF preview of an EPS file instead of rasterizing the EPS itself. This might come in handy if the whole EPS file is enormous and takes too long to rasterize. For example, if you want a thumbnail of your magazine's cover for your Web site, you could save the cover as an EPS, open it in Photoshop, and reduce it in size. However, you don't need all that high-resolution data, so you could just open the low-resolution preview and shrink that down instead. The trick is to choose EPS PICT Preview or EPS TIFF Preview from the Format popup menu in the Open dialog box. (In Windows, this is the Open As dialog box.) Now when you open the file, you only get the low-resolution preview.

Place. When you select Place rather than Open, Photoshop drops the EPS or PDF file into your current document and then lets you scale and rotate it to fit your needs (you can scale it by dragging a handle, rotate it by dragging outside the rectangle, and move it by dragging inside the rectangle). Hold down the Shift key while dragging a handle to constrain the width/height ratio (so it stays proportional).

When you have finished scaling the image, press Return or Enter. Photoshop doesn't rasterize the image into pixels until you do this, so scaling won't degrade the final image. (Note that you can always press the Escape key to cancel the Place command.) Like Paste, Place almost always creates a new layer for your incoming image (although it won't if you place an EPS or PDF on a spot color channel, for instance). Note that your new layer is automatically saved as a smart object in CS2. We'll cover smart objects and why they're so cool in the next section.

Tip: Colorizing Black and White Images. For some reason, David keeps finding himself in the position of opening a black-and-white EPS file (like a logo) in Photoshop and needing to colorize it. But the Colorize feature in Hue/Saturation—the tool he'd usually use for this sort of thing—doesn't work, because it doesn't colorize pixels that are fully black or fully white. There are many different ways to get around this, but our favorite is to add a Solid Color adjustment layer just above the logo's layer, set the adjustment layer's color to Screen, and then group it with the logo layer (Option-click between the layers in the Layers palette). Then, if you want to change the color, just double-click on the adjustment layer to edit it.

Smart Objects

Until CS2, Photoshop always rasterized placed or pasted graphics at the resolution of the current document. That means if you imported a vector graphic (such as something from Adobe Illustrator), Photoshop turned it into pixels and plopped them on a layer. Similarly, if you pasted a high-resolution image into a lower-resolution image, then scaled it down to fit, you lost much of your data. Try to scale the image up and you'd find that all those original pixels were gone, never to return (unless you paste the original graphic in again).

Now things have changed in CS2 with the advent of *smart object* layers. If you have used a page-layout application such as InDesign or QuarkXPress, you know how they link to high-resolution or vector files on disk and only access them at print time. A smart object layer does essentially the same thing—but in this case, Photoshop does not link to a file on disk; rather, it embeds the file inside your Photoshop document.

When you use the Place feature (from the File menu) to import a vector or image file, Photoshop automatically brings it in as a smart object layer. You can then move it or transform it (with scaling, warping, skewing, and so on) with the knowledge that Photoshop will automatically re-rasterize the data for you based on the original. That means you can scale it from 1,000 pixels tall down to 10 pixels tall, and then later scale it back up again and it will look just as good.

Creating a smart object. As we noted above, you can make a smart object layer by placing an external file—either a vector file (such as a PDF, EPS, or AI) or an image file (including TIFF, JPEG, or even Camera Raw). Here are some other ways you can make smart objects:

▶ When you copy-and-paste an object from Illustrator, Photoshop offers you the option to automatically convert the vector data into a smart object (see Figure 12-44).

Figure 12-44
Pasting Illustrator or
FreeHand paths

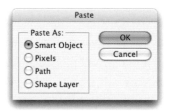

▶ You can select one or more layers in the Layers palette, then choose Group Into New Smart Object from the Smart Objects submenu (in the Layer menu). Photoshop creates a new Photoshop document with the selected layers and embeds it into the current document as a smart object layer.

▶ You can select an image in Adobe Bridge, and then choose "In Photoshop" from the Place submenu (in Bridge's File menu).

Smart object layers look and act the same as normal layers in the Layers palette, with one small difference: A small icon appears in the corner of the smart object layer's preview thumbnail (see Figure 12-45).

Figure 12-45
Smart Objects

Smart object layers
have a small icon
in the lower-right
corner of the preview
thumbnail.

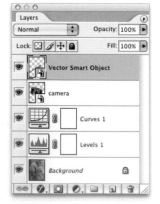

When you paste an Illustrator vector, the layer is named Vector Smart Object.

Editing smart objects. Once you create a smart object layer, you can transform it like any other layer (use the Move tool to drag it around, use Free Transform to scale or skew it, and so on). You can also adjust its blending mode, opacity, or layer style in the Layers palette. However, if you double-click on the layer's preview thumbnail in the palette (or take the long way and choose Edit Contents from the Smart Objects submenu), Photoshop opens the smart object in its own window, ready for you to edit. If it was a raw image, Photoshop launches Camera Raw (see Chapter 11, *Building a Digital Workflow*). Or, if it's vector data from Illustrator, Photoshop will launch Illustrator and open the file there.

When you edit a smart object layer, you're not editing the original file! Photoshop is actually writing the data to disk as a temporary, invisible file, then opening it. There is no link to the original file. After you make edits to the file, save it and close it. (And, if necessary, switch back to Photoshop.) Like magic, you'll see the smart object update, as Photoshop replaces the embedded smart object data with the new file.

Tip: Linking Smart Object Layers. Need more than one copy of the same smart object? For example, you might have a logo that appears in five places in the same image. You can duplicate a smart object layer by dragging it over the New Layer button in the Layers palette (or pressing Command-J). In this case, the new smart object layer points to the same embedded smart object; that is, the two layers are linked so that if you edit the smart object on one of the layers, all the layers change.

On the other hand, if you duplicate the layer by choosing New Smart Object Via Copy from the Smart Object submenu (under the Layer menu), the duplicate is not linked because this actually creates a new smart object and embeds it.

Replacing smart objects. You can replace a smart object with another smart object by choosing Replace Contents from the Smart Objects submenu, then choosing the new file you want. For instance, you might want to switch one image with another. When you replace an image, any scaling, warping, or effects you applied to the first image is maintained.

Exporting smart objects. Because a smart object is just a file embedded inside your Photoshop document, you can unembed it—saving it out to disk as a separate file. To do this, select the smart object layer in the Layer palette, then choose Export Contents from the Smart Objects submenu (under the Layer menu). You don't have a lot of control over the format of the export: Image smart objects are saved as a PSB (Photoshop Large Document) file and vector objects are saved as PDF files.

Rasterizing smart objects. When Photoshop embeds the smart object in your document, your file size grows accordingly. That is, if you place a Camera Raw file, your document grows the size of the raw image data, plus the normal amount the file would grow when you add an additional layer. If you know you no longer need to edit the smart object data, you might consider converting it to a normal layer (discarding the embedded data) at its current size, resolution, and so on. To do this, choose Convert to Layer from the Smart Objects submenu. Alternately, you can choose Smart Object from the Rasterize submenu (under the Layer menu).

Tip: Warping Text and Smart Object Layers. Sandee Cohen and Steve Werner (authors of *Real World Creative Suite 2*) alerted us to an interesting problem and its workaround. Photoshop won't let you apply the arbitrary Warp feature (from the Transform submenu, under the Edit menu) to a text layer. However, you can select one or more text layers into a smart object layer and then apply any warp you want.

Tip: Get It From the Context Menu. The commands on the Smart Object submenu (under the Layer menu)—such as those to create or export a smart object—also appear in the context menu when you right-click on one of the layer tiles (not the preview thumbnail) in the Layers palette. We find this much faster than using the Layer menu.

Creating and Editing Paths

If you've ever used Adobe Illustrator or Macromedia FreeHand, you're already familiar with drawing and editing paths in Photoshop. In fact, the paths interface is most similar to Adobe Illustrator's (no surprise there; see Figure 12-46).

Whether you're drawing a layer clipping path, a path to clip the entire document, or a path to help you select pixels, you have to use the same basic tools. Remember that paths are visible only when the path is selected in the Paths palette (or, for layer clipping paths, when its tile is selected in

Figure 12-46
Paths

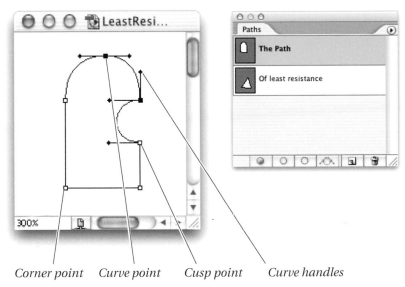

Corner point   Curve point   Cusp point   Curve handles

the Layers palette). The Paths palette displays all the paths in your document, and gives you some control over what to do with them. To draw a path, you must select one of the Pen tools or Shape tools in the Tools palette. There are seven Pen tools and six Shape tools, but we tend to use only two or three of the Pen tools, using modifier keys to get to the rest.

Pen tool. The Pen tool (press P) is the only tool we ever select to draw paths. Without modifier keys, you can draw straight-line paths by clicking, or curved paths by clicking and dragging. You can also easily access any of the other tools. For instance, if you move this tool over a point on a line, it automatically changes to the "delete point" tool. If you move the Pen tool over a segment, it lets you add a point (click or click-and-drag). If you're forever adding or deleting points when you don't mean to, just turn off the Auto Add/Delete checkbox on the Options bar.

Selection tools. As in Illustrator and InDesign, Photoshop has both a Selection tool and a Direct Select tool. You can press A (for "arrow") to jump to the selection tool in the Tool palette, and then press Shift-A if you want the other selection tool. However, if you want the Direct Select tool, it's much easier to hold down the Command key when any Pen tool or the Selection tool is active. These tools let you select a point or points on the path. For example, you can select points on a curve with the Direct Select tool by clicking on them or by dragging a marquee around them. To select all the points on a curve, use the Selection tool or hold down the Option key when you click on the path with the Direct Select tool (or, Command-Option-click with the Pen tool).

Once you've selected a point or a path, you can move it. As in most other programs, if you hold down the Shift key, Photoshop only lets you move the points in 90- or 45-degree angles. If you hold down the Option key when you click and drag, Photoshop moves a copy of the entire path.

Tip: Paths vs. Shapes vs. Pixels. Important note: Each time you use the Pen tools, you need to specify in the Options bar whether you want the Pen tools to create a path or a vector shape. When you select one of the Shape tools, you can choose path, vectors, or pixels (see Figure 12-47).

Figure 12-47 The Path and Shape tool's Options bar

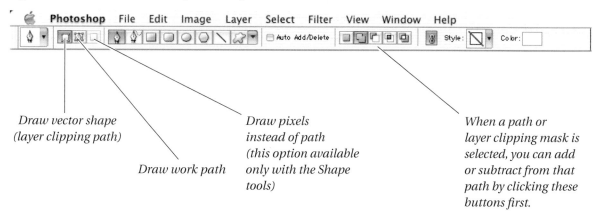

Draw vector shape (layer clipping path)

Draw work path

Draw pixels instead of path (this option available only with the Shape tools)

When a path or layer clipping mask is selected, you can add or subtract from that path by clicking these buttons first.

Convert Point tool. When you're working with the Pen tool, you can create a sharp corner by clicking, or a rounded corner by dragging. When you have two round corners on either side of a corner point, that corner point is called a *cusp* point. But what if you change your mind and want to make a corner into a curve, or a curve into a cusp?

The Convert Point tool lets you add or remove curve *handles* (those levers that stick out from the sides of curve or cusp points). If you click once on a point that has curve handles, the curve handles disappear (they get sucked all the way into the point), and the point becomes a corner. If you click and drag with the Convert Point tool, you can pull those handles out of the point, making the corner a curve.

Similarly, you can make a cusp by clicking and dragging on one of the control handles on either side of the point. If you select the Pen tool, you can get the Convert Point tool by holding down the Option key.

Tip: Use Cusp Points. Many folks tell us that they make all points cusp points while drawing paths. Here's how: To create the first point of the path, just click and drag to set the angle of the first curve. All subsequent points on the path are created by clicking, dragging to set the angle of the previous curve, and then Option-dragging from the point to set the launch angle of the next curve. Finally, to close the path (if you want it closed), Option-click—if you want the final segment to be a straight line— or Option-drag—if you want the final segment to be a curve—on the first point of the path. While it takes some getting used to and takes a bit more work, this technique gives you much more control over the angle and curve of each segment in the path because each point is independent of the ones on either side.

Freeform Pen tool. David got into this business because he can't draw worth beans, but if you've got a steady hand and a sure heart—and a graphics tablet wouldn't hurt, either—you might find yourself wanting to draw paths with the Freeform Pen tool. When you let up on the mouse button, Photoshop converts your loose path to a smooth path full of corner, curve, and cusp points. (Exactly how closely Photoshop follows your lead is up to the Curve Fit setting on the Options bar.)

Note that, like the Lasso tool, you can draw a straight line with the Freeform Pen tool by holding down the Option key and lifting the mouse button. Then you can either click to "connect the dots" or release the Option key to return to freeform drawing.

Magnetic Pen tool. Once the engineers at Adobe figured out how to make the Magnetic Lasso tool, it was a snap for them to add the functionality to the Pen tool, too. Thus, the Magnetic Pen tool was born. (Well, it's not really a separate tool; you get it by turning on the checkbox labeled Magnetic on the Options bar.) The Magnetic Lasso and the Magnetic Pen work so similarly that it's hardly worth discussing twice; instead go read that section in Chapter 8, *Making Selections*. Their similarity extends to producing a result that you will almost certainly have to finesse; the magnetic tools are not known for their precision.

Tip: Hide the Path. When you have a path selected in the Paths palette or a layer clipping path selected in the Layers palette, Photoshop displays the path on screen as a thin gray line. When you have a non-painting tool selected in the Tool palette (like the selection tools or the Move tool), you can deselect the path (make the line go away) by pressing the Enter key.

Tip: Arrow Keys and Paths. If you have one or more points on a path selected, you can move them one pixel at a time using the arrow keys—but only when the Pen or one of the Selection tools is selected in the Tool palette. Or, if you hold down the Shift key, the arrow keys move the path ten image pixels (*not* screen pixels). At 100-percent view, image pixels and screen pixels are the same thing, of course.

Tip: Drag Segments, Too. When editing your paths, don't get too caught up with having to move the paths' points and the curve handles around. As in FreeHand and Illustrator, you can also drag the path segment itself. If it's a curved segment, Photoshop adjusts the curve handles on either side of it automatically. If it's a straight-line segment (hence there are no curve handles to adjust), Photoshop actually moves the corner or cusp points on either side of the segment.

Tip: Connecting Paths. You've got two paths you want to connect? It's not as hard as you think.

1. Use the Path Selection tool to select one of the path's endpoints.

2. Switch to the Pen tool.

3. If you want that point to be a cusp, Option-drag out a handle.

4. Click and drag on the other path's endpoint. (Or alternatively, Option-drag to make it a cusp point.)

Tip: Flipping, Rotating, and Modifying Paths. At first glance, it doesn't appear that you can transform (rotate, scale, and so on) paths in Photoshop, but you can: Just select the path you want to edit in the Paths palette and choose Free Transform from the Edit menu (or press Command-T).

Similarly, you can select from the many options in the Transform submenu (under the Edit menu). You don't have to transform the entire path, either. If the path has several subpaths, you can select one of them (by Option-clicking on the subpath) before transforming. You can even select one or more points on the path; in this case, Photoshop only changes those points and the segments around them.

Paths to Selections

Once you have a path, you can convert it into a selection, rasterize it (turn it into pixels), or fill it with a color or adjustment. Let's look at converting to selections first. Photoshop makes this process easy for you: You can convert a path into a selection in one of four ways:

▶ Select Make Selection from the Paths palette's popout menu (or drag the path's tile on top of this button).

▶ Click on the Convert Path to Selection icon (see Figure 12-48).

▶ Command-click on the path's tile in the Paths palette.

▶ Press Command-Enter (in ancient versions, this was simply Enter).

If you hold down the Option key while dragging a path on top of, or clicking on, the Convert Path to Selection icon, Photoshop displays the Make Selection dialog box. This dialog box lets you add, subtract, or intersect selections with selections you've already made (if there is no selection, these options are grayed out). It also lets you feather and anti-alias the selections. The default for selections (if you don't go in and change this dialog box) is to include anti-aliasing, but not feathering.

Figure 12-48
Converting a path
to a selection

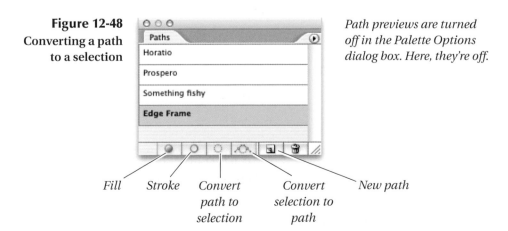

Path previews are turned off in the Palette Options dialog box. Here, they're off.

Fill Stroke Convert Convert New path
path to selection to
selection path

Alternatively, you can use these keystrokes instead of the Make Selection dialog box to add, subtract, or intersect paths:

▶ Command-Shift-Enter adds the path's selection to the current selection (if there is one).

▶ Command-Option-Enter subtracts the selection.

▶ Command-Shift-Option-Enter intersects the two selections.

Each of these works when clicking on the Make Selection icon or dragging the tile over the icon, too. But the Enter key is so much easier.

Selections to Paths

To turn a selection into a path, choose Make Work Path from the popout menu in the Paths palette. When you ask Photoshop to do this, you're basically asking it to turn a soft-edged selection into a hard-edged one. Therefore, the program has to make some decisions about where the edges of the selection are.

Fortunately, the program gives you a choice about how hard it should work at this: the Tolerance field in the Make Work Path dialog box. The higher the value you enter, the shabbier the path's representation of the original selection. Values above 2 or 3 typically make nice abstract designs, but aren't otherwise very useful.

There's one more way to convert a selection into a new path: Click on the Make Path icon in the Paths palette. Note that this uses whatever tolerance value you last specified in the Make Work Path dialog box, unless you hold down the Option key while clicking on the icon, in which case it brings up the dialog box.

Rasterizing Paths

As we said back in Chapter 3, *Image Essentials*, rasterizing is the process of turning an outline into pixels. Photoshop lets you rasterize paths in two ways: You can fill the path area and you can stroke the path.

Filling. To fill the path area with the foreground color, drag the path's tile to the Fill Path icon, or click on the Fill Path icon in the Paths palette. Or, better yet, Option-click the icon, and the Fill Path dialog box appears (this is the same dialog box you get if you choose Fill Path from the Paths palette's popout menu). The dialog box gives you options for fill color, opacity, mode, and so on.

Stroking. Stroking the path works just the same as filling: You can drag the path's tile to the Stroke Path icon, or simply click on the Stroke Path icon in the Paths palette (while a path is visible). You can change the tool it uses to stroke with by Option-clicking on the Stroke Path icon (or select Stroke Path from the popout menu in the Paths palette).

Tip: Stroking on Enter. When you have a painting tool selected in the Tool palette (like the Brush, Dodge, or Rubber Stamp tool), pressing Enter strokes the path with that tool (using the current brush size and blending mode). We like this because we almost always want a different painting tool than the one we used last time. (See "Retouching," earlier in this chapter, for a powerful retouching technique that uses the Clone Stamp tool and this "path stroking" tip.)

Tip: Rasterizing Paths Inside Selections. If you make a selection before filling or stroking your path, Photoshop fills or strokes only within that selection. This has tripped up more than one advanced user, but if you're aware of the feature, it can really come in handy.

Clipping Paths

The old art of cutting silhouettes out of paper is mostly gone now, though it lives on at street fairs and tourist spots. If you've ever seen someone cutting one of these, you know how painstaking a process it can be. We wonder why, then, people expect creating a silhouette in Photoshop to be as easy as snapping their fingers. Far from it: masking out the background of an image—leaving only the foreground object—is a difficult proposition. Unfortunately, it's something that many of us in production work have to do every day (see Figure 12-49).

The biggest problem is often not making a selection to silhouette (we cover a lot of selection and silhouetting techniques in Chapter 8, *Making Selections*). Rather, it's bringing that selection into a page-layout program without unnaturally harsh edges resulting. In this section we'll discuss getting silhouettes to print properly from InDesign, QuarkXPress, or Page-Maker.

Figure 12-51
Three ways to make a
layer clipping path

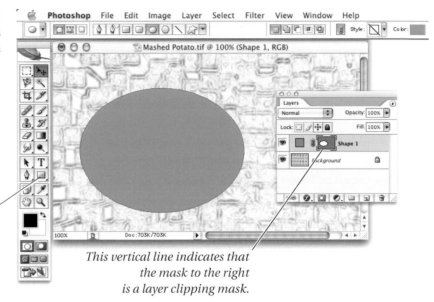

*The Shape tool always
makes or adds to a
layer clipping mask.*

*This vertical line indicates that
the mask to the right
is a layer clipping mask.*

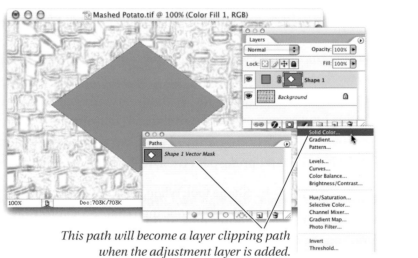

*This path will become a layer clipping path
when the adjustment layer is added.*

*You can add a layer
clipping path by
Command-clicking
on the Layer Mask
button.*

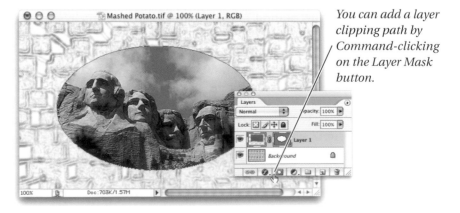

▶ **Add layer clipping path.** You can add a layer clipping path to any layer (except the Background layer) by selecting either Reveal All or Hide All from the Add Layer Clipping Path submenu (under the Layer menu). But that's slow; instead, just Command-click on the Add Layer Mask button in the Layers palette. (Command-Option-click adds a layer clipping path that "hides all.") If a path is already selected in the Paths palette, Photoshop automatically assigns it to the layer clipping path; otherwise, you can just start drawing a path with the Pen tool.

Tip: Adding and Subtracting Paths. If you use the Shape tool while a layer clipping path is selected in the Paths palette (if it's visible on screen), then Photoshop adds your shape to that layer clipping path. Before you draw the shape, you can tell the program how you want this new path to interact with the path already there by clicking on the Add, Subtract, Intersect, or Exclude Intersection button in the Options bar. If you forget to select one, don't fret: Command-click with the Shape tool on the shape you just drew (to select all its points), and *then* click the button in the Options bar.

Tip: Vectors for Web and Fine Art. Even if you don't print to a Post-Script printer, vector art (in the form of layer clipping paths) can be useful. For instance, let's say you want a grid of buttons for your Web page. You can make the buttons by painting pixels on a layer and then applying layer effects (such as Emboss) to them; but if you later need to change the buttons—perhaps make them all slightly smaller—it's going to be a real hassle because you need to actually edit the pixels. Instead, if you make each button with the Shape tool (or with the Pen tool on a layer clipping mask), the edits are simple: Just use the Path Selection tool or the Transform Path feature to reshape the paths on the layer clipping path (see Figure 12-52).

Tip: Invert the Path. One of the most annoying parts of making layer clipping paths is that there's no easy way to invert the path (making the clipped-out parts fall inside the path and *vice versa*). But there is *a* way.

1. Make sure the layer clipping path is visible (select the layer and then select the clipping path's tile in the Paths palette).

Figure 12-52
Quick edits with shapes

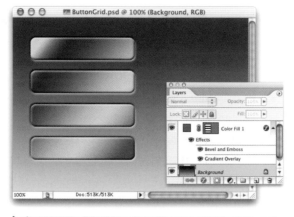

Vector-based layer clipping paths can easily be stretched and rotated.

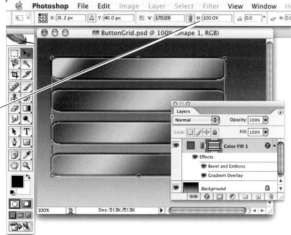

2. Select the path itself by either Command-clicking inside of it with the Shape tool or Option-clicking on its boundary with the Path Selection tool.

3. With either the Shape or Pen tool selected, click on either the Add or Subtract button in the Options bar. If one doesn't invert the path, then the other will.

Tip: Turn Off the Clipping Path. You can disable a layer clipping path (turning it off, so the whole layer is visible) the same way you turn off a regular layer mask: Shift-click on the layer clipping path's thumbnail on the Layers palette. (Or, the slow way: Select "Disable Layer Clipping Path" from the Layer menu.)

Making vectors and pixels interact. Putting vector artwork on a layer on top of pixels is no great feat; if that's all you want to do, you can do the same thing in Illustrator, FreeHand, QuarkXPress, InDesign, or whatever. The real value to Photoshop's layer clipping paths is in how pixels can blend together and still retain a sharp edge. For example, you can use the Shape tool to draw a solid black oval on top of your Background layer, and then change the opacity of that layer to 50 percent. Now, you can see the background image through your semi-transparent black oval. Of course, the vector artwork isn't really blending with the pixels beneath it. Rather, Photoshop is mixing the pixels on one layer with the pixels on another layer and then using the layer clipping path to define the edge between the two layers.

If you zoom in to magnify the edge of the oval, it appears as though the edge is anti-aliased with the background; however, when you print from Photoshop (or save the image as an EPS and print it from a page-layout program), you'll see that the edge is sharp (see Figure 12-53). Remember that what Photoshop is showing you on screen is what the image would look like if you flattened it (losing the vector paths).

Any layer can have a layer clipping path (even text layers), and you can change the opacity, blending mode, or layer effect of a clipped layer just the way you would ordinarily. So, if you want your shape layer to have a drop shadow, use the Overlay mode, and have a 75-percent opacity, you can change all that in the Layers palette.

Figure 12-53
Vectors fool the eye.

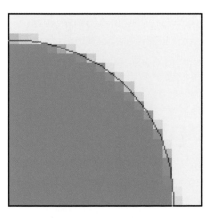

What the vector-based
"shape" looks like on screen

When you print to a PostScript
printer, it's much sharper.

Tip: Blending Into Vectors. How do those folks at *Sports Illustrated* do those covers anyway? You know the type: a photo of some sports star partially over and partially under the title of the magazine. It has always been very difficult to achieve this sort of look, because where the photograph overlaps the sharp, vector masthead, the pixels have to anti-alias into the text. Photoshop lets you create this kind of effect easily: Just put the text on one layer, and the cutout image on a different one (see Figure 12-54).

Tip: Don't Fill, Adjust! When you use a Shape tool, Photoshop automatically creates a Solid Color Fill layer and applies the shape to the layer clipping path. But you can change this from a Solid Color Fill layer to any other kind of adjustment layer in the Change Layer Content submenu (under the Layer menu). For example, you could change it to a Gradient Map, a Curves adjustment layer, or a Pattern layer. Then you can adjust the layer's opacity and blending mode to change how it interacts with the shapes and pixels on layers beneath it.

Tip: Saving Vectors. We cover how to save images in Chapter 13, *Image Storage and Output*, but in case you're in a rush, we'll let you in on a secret now: If you have used layer clipping paths, and you want to retain those sharp edges when you print your image from your page-layout application, you should probably save your file as either a PDF or an EPS file. If you are using a spot color, you'll have to use the DCS 2.0 format. Note that while the EPS format saves and prints the layers and clipping paths properly, when you reopen your EPS file in Photoshop, it automatically gets flattened. Very annoying. So, make sure you save the EPS as a copy, and archive your layered Photoshop file just in case you need to go back to edit it. PDF files don't have this problem.

Text and Typography

Photoshop gained typographic prowess late in its career; in fact, for a long time it was downright painful to get good-looking type out of it. But that's all changed now. It's like the folks on the Photoshop team took a look at the typography in InDesign and suddenly said, "Hey, we can do that!" Photoshop lets you tweak kerning, leading, color, hyphenation, and more

Figure 12-54
Vectors and pixels
together at last

Note that this vector text sits both behind and in front of the bit-mapped image.

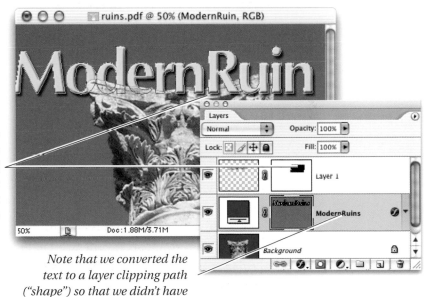

To achieve the effect, we copied some of the image onto a new layer, added a layer mask (which is invisible here), and put the text in between the two layers.

Note that we converted the text to a layer clipping path ("shape") so that we didn't have to send the font to the printer.

Once again, the screen can't be trusted. Here, the text is vector, but it appears to be soft-edged.

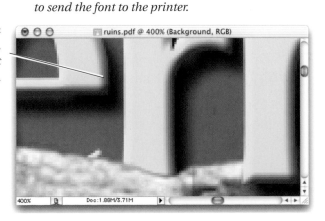

to your heart's content. You can set beautiful type in Photoshop... but that doesn't mean you should.

People who want to overlay text on top of pictures often ask us, "Should we use the Type tool in Photoshop, or the features in our page-layout or illustration program?" The answer, as always, is "it depends."

▶ If your final output is to a color printer such as an ink-jet or dye-sub printer, anti-aliased type within Photoshop's bitmapped image often looks better. The hard-edged type from a program such as QuarkXPress looks too jaggy off these low-resolution devices.

▶ If the text is integrated into your image—you want to apply a wacky filter to it, you want it to sit partially behind part of your image, or something like that—instead of being a separate element overlaying the image, there's a good chance that you'll need to create it in Photoshop. While QuarkXPress cannot create transparent text, Adobe InDesign can.

▶ If you want sharp vector (as opposed to anti-aliased) text, you need to be very careful of what file format you use when saving. In many cases (such as if you save as TIFF), the text gets rasterized—if you're working with a 225-ppi image, any text you add to that image in Photoshop is similarly 225 ppi. That's high enough for most images, but it looks crummy for hard-edged type. (See Chapter 13, *Image Storage and Output*, for more information about saving files with text layers.)

▶ Photoshop's text controls are cool, but they're not exactly speedy. In general, the more text you have, the more you should set it in some other program.

So, if you're setting more than a few words, you should probably set them in QuarkXPress, InDesign, PageMaker, Illustrator, FreeHand, or some other program. But if you're hell-bent on using Photoshop to lay out text, here are some tips and tricks to help you do so more efficiently.

Tip: Making Text Blocks. Most people who have used Photoshop for years use the Text tool by simply clicking on their image. That works, but if you're going to type more than one line's worth of text, the click-and-type procedure is a pain because you have to manually break lines by hitting Return. Instead, drag out a text *frame* with the Text tool before typing. Photoshop automatically wraps the text to fit that frame, and you can always reshape the frame by dragging its corner or edge handles, or rotate the text block by dragging outside of the frame.

By the way, keep your eye on the lower-right corner handle; when there's too much text to fit the frame, Photoshop places a little + sign there. It's subtle, so you have to look carefully.

If you want to create a new text block near or on top of another bit of text, you might have trouble because Photoshop will think you're trying to select the existing text. No problem: Shift-click or Shift-drag with the Text tool to force Photoshop to create a new text layer.

When you're done creating or editing text, press Enter on the keypad, or Ctl-Enter (Windows) or Command-Return (Macintosh).

Tip: Setting the Column Width. Do you need a text block exactly 144 points wide? No problem: Just Option-click with the Text tool, and Photoshop offers you a way to type in an exact size.

Tip: Editing Type Layers. Once you have created some text on a type layer, there are several ways to edit it:

▶ You can double-click on the type layer's thumbnail icon in the Layers palette. (Double-clicking on the tile instead opens the Layer Style dialog box or lets you edit the layer name.)

▶ You can click on top of the text with the Type tool. You know your cursor is in the right place when the Type tool's cursor changes to an "I-beam." However, if you click in the wrong place, Photoshop will create a new type layer; in this case, press the Escape key to cancel the new layer.

▶ Best yet, when you have both the Type tool selected in the Tool palette and the type layer selected in the Layers palette, you can choose Edit Type from the context-sensitive menu. On the Mac, Control-click anywhere on the image, or right-mouse-button click in Windows.

You can also format various aspects of a layer by selecting the layer in the Layers palette and changing values in the Options bar (when the Text tool is selected), Character palette, or Paragraph palette (see "Text Formatting," later in this chapter, for more on this). This changes the formatting (or color, or whatever) for all the text on the layer.

Tip: Rendering Type Layers. Type layers are special; you can't paint or run filters on them, or do anything else that relies on pixel editing. If you need to do something like that, you have to render them (turn them into pixels) by selecting Type from the Rasterize submenu (under the Layers menu) or from the context-sensitive menu you get with the Type tool (Control-click on Mac, right-click in Windows). But it's generally best to do all your transformations (rotating, scaling, positioning, skewing), and layer effects (drop shadows, and so on) that you need before rendering the type layer. That way, you can be assured of the highest-quality type.

Tip: Making Text Masks. There are two tools in the Tool palette that create text masks rather than text (that is, as you type, Photoshop makes a selection in the shape of text rather than text itself). However, when it comes to making selections in the shape of text, we would rather create a normal type layer and then Command-click on it in the Layers palette. By actually creating a type layer, we can preview it in the image before clicking OK, we can edit the text later, or use the type someplace else (even in another image). If we had simply used a Type Selection tool, we'd have nothing but an ephemeral group of marching ants.

Tip: Check Your Spells. No, the Check Spelling feature won't help you with your spells if you end up at Hogwarts School of Magic, but it might help if your Photoshop document has a lot of text in it. To check the spelling of a single word, select the word with the Text tool and choose Check Spelling from the Edit menu or the context-sensitive menu. If no word is selected, Photoshop checks the spelling of every text layer in your file.

We find this feature especially helpful with foreign words, which we often have no idea how to spell correctly. Photoshop ships with a number of different language dictionaries, such as Spanish and Swedish. However, in order for the Check Spelling feature to work correctly with foreign words, you must first select the words and choose the appropriate language from the Language popup menu in the Character palette.

Tip: Find and Replace Text. For those of you who use Photoshop to create advertisements or other materials more appropriate for page-layout applications, note that Photoshop has a Find and Replace Text feature that lets you search for simple text strings. This feature isn't nearly as powerful as those in other programs (for instance, there's no way to search for text formatting or special characters such as tabs). But if you're trying to find a word or phrase that has gone missing, it does the trick.

Tip: Text on a Path. Need to run text along a path? No problem. Simply draw a path with the Pen tools (see "Paths," earlier in this chapter) and then click on it with the Text tool. Note that the Text tool's cursor icon changes when it's on top of a path, and when you click and then start typing, the text begins from the point you clicked. To adjust the starting and ending points for the text on the path, switch to the Path Selection tool (press A); as you hover the cursor over the start or end point, the cursor changes to a vertical line with a thick black arrow. If you click and drag with this cursor, you adjust where the text begins or ends on the line.

The direction you draw your path determines how Photoshop draws the text. If you draw a path from left to right, the text flows on the top of the line; if you draw from right to left, the text flows from right to left—upside down. To flip the text over, use the Path Selection tool and drag the beginning or ending endpoint to the other side of the line.

Photoshop doesn't offer a lot of control over how the text flows along the line, but you can rotate the text so that it flows "vertically" along the line by clicking the "Change the text orientation" button on the far left of the Options bar.

Text Formatting

Placing text in your image is all very well and good, but you won't win design awards until you've figured out how to format your text. (Well, there might be a few other steps before you win awards, too. We make no guarantees.) There are two types of formatting: Character (which can apply to one or more characters) and Paragraph (which always applies to one or more paragraphs). You can find these settings in the Options bar (when the Text tool is selected in the Tool palette) or in the Character and Paragraph palettes (see Figure 12-55).

Tip: Hide the Selection. Formatting text is difficult when you have text selected, especially when you're trying to change the text's color. Don't forget you can press Command-H to hide the text selection; the text remains selected, but you can see the changes more easily as you make them.

Figure 12-55
Formatting text

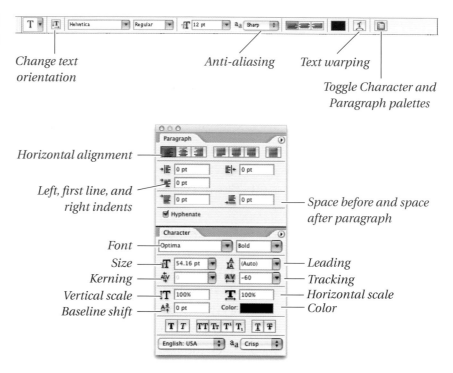

Change text orientation

Anti-aliasing

Text warping

Toggle Character and Paragraph palettes

Horizontal alignment

Left, first line, and right indents

Space before and space after paragraph

Font

Size

Kerning

Vertical scale

Baseline shift

Leading

Tracking

Horizontal scale

Color

Leading. Leading ("ledding") determines the amount of space between lines in a paragraph. Bruce, who is accustomed to PageMaker and InDesign, finds Photoshop's leading feature intuitive because in all three programs, leading is considered a character attribute. In QuarkXPress, however, leading is a paragraph attribute. If you're used to XPress (like David), you need to be extra careful when changing leading. If you want the leading to be consistent throughout a paragraph, you should either select every character in the paragraph *before* you set the leading in the Character palette, or you should apply the leading while the text layer is selected in the Layers palette (but no text on the layer is selected).

Kerning and tracking. Kerning determines the amount of space between each character. Tracking is the same thing, but over a range of text (which is why some folks call it "range kerning"). Photoshop lets you do both in the Character palette—if your cursor is placed between two characters, you can kern them; if you've selected more than one character, then you can track them. (Or, if the type layer is selected in the Layers palette but no text is selected, then tracking applies to every character on that layer.) Note that the kerning and tracking values in Photoshop are based on $1/1000$

em (one em in a 24-point font is 24 points wide; in a 50-point font, it's 50 points wide, and so on).

The default kerning value for text is Metrics—these are the kerning pairs built into the font. But we almost always select the type layer (with no text selected on it) and change the kerning to Optical in the Character palette, which tells Photoshop to use its very cool method of analyzing the shape of each character and adjusting the kerning accordingly. If it's small text, this sometimes makes it look really ugly, so we change it back to Metrics, or even possibly change it to 0 (zero).

Anti-alias settings. While some people recommend turning off anti-aliasing for very small text, we find that anti-aliasing almost always helps on-screen readability, so we generally leave it on. The problem is that in small text sizes, anti-aliasing sometimes leaves fonts looking a bit anemic. Fortunately, Photoshop lets you change the anti-aliasing style. We usually set the Anti-alias popup menu (in the Options bar or the context-sensitive menu when the Text tool is selected) to Crisp or Smooth (there's too little difference between the two to notice most of the time). However, when working with small text, we sometimes use the Strong option. It's entirely a judgment call—if Strong is too bold, then we'll switch back to Smooth.

Fractional Widths. Text characters rarely fit perfectly on a 72-dpi grid— for instance, a letter "A" might be 18.1 pixels wide. Photoshop offers you the choice of how to deal with these "fractional widths." When the Fractional Widths feature is turned on in the Character palette menu, Photoshop rounds the character widths to the nearest pixel, which usually results in some characters moving slightly closer together. In large point sizes, this is usually a good thing, but in small text sizes, the characters often run into each other and it looks dorky. Note that Fractional Widths affects the entire text block, not just selected characters.

Tip: Changing Text Color. The fastest way to change the color of one or more characters in a text block is by selecting them with the Text tool and then simply picking a color in the Options bar, or the Tool, Character, Swatches, or Color palette. Or, if you already have the color chosen as your foreground or background color, you can select the text and press Option-Delete (to apply the foreground color) or Command-Delete (for the background color). If you want to apply the same color to every character on a type layer, then select the layer in the Layers palette and press these same keystrokes. (Photoshop acts as though Preserve Transparency—what's now called Lock Transparent Pixels—is always turned on for text layers.)

Tip: Linking Text Layers. Do you want to change the font and size of six different text layers in your document? No problem: Just select all the layers in the Layers palette. (See Chapter 2, *Essential Image Techniques*, for more on selecting layers.)

Tip: Keyboard Type Shortcuts. There are a number of keyboard short-cuts that can help you speed up your text formatting (see Table 12-1). Remember that the extra time you take to learn these now will come back as time saved later.

	To do this...	...press this
Table 12-1	Show/Hide type selection	Command-H
Type tool	Move right one word	Command-Right arrow
keyboard	Move left one word	Command-Left arrow
shortcuts	Select right one word	Command-Shift-Right arrow
	Select left one word	Command-Shift-Left arrow
	Move to next paragraph	Command-Down arrow
	Move to previous paragraph	Command-Up arrow
	Increase size 2 points	Command-Shift-. (period)
	Decrease size 2 points	Command-Shift-, (comma)
	Increase leading 2 points	Option-Down arrow
	Increase leading 10 points	Command-Option-Down arrow
	Decrease leading 2 points	Option-Up arrow
	Decrease leading 10 points	Command-Option-Up arrow
	Increase kerning 2/100 em	Option-Right arrow
	Increase kerning 1/10 em	Command-Option-Right arrow
	Decrease kerning 2/100 em	Option-Left arrow
	Decrease kerning 1/10 em	Command-Option-Left arrow
	Increase baseline shift 2 points	Option-Shift-Up arrow
	Increase baseline shift 10 points	Command-Option-Shift-Up arrow
	Decrease baseline shift 2 points	Option-Shift-Down arrow
	Decrease baseline shift 10 points	Command-Option-Shift-Down arrow

Other character styles. Photoshop offers a number of other character styles to help make your award-winning text. Here are a few others you should know about:

▶ **Faux styles.** Want Hobo Bold? Or Zapf Dingbats Italic? Sorry, they don't exist (there are no outlines that describe them), so Photoshop won't let you use them. But Photoshop is ready and willing to fake them (see Figure 12-56). When you turn on Faux Italic in the Character palette menu, Photoshop obliques (skews) the font slightly. Faux Bold makes the font heavier. The effect is generally pretty good, and even lets you make a bolder bold and a more slanted italic face than might otherwise be available. (However, note that you can't embed Faux Bold fonts in PDF files and expect them to remain vector type.)

The Character palette's popout menu also offers the Underline and Strikethrough styles, which—true to their names—place a line under or through the selected text. No, you can't adjust the size, shape, color, or anything else of the underline or strikethrough line. Yes, we know you can do that in InDesign CS. Personally, we find these faux features particularly silly.

Figure 12-56
Faux Italic

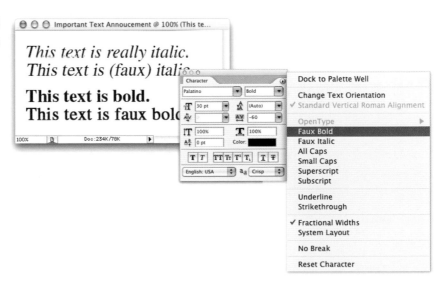

▶ **Scaling and moving.** You can scale individual characters (or all the words on a text layer) vertically or horizontally in the Character palette, though we find that many designers overuse this and create really far-out, stretched typefaces that are simply unreadable. Use with discretion. The Character palette also offers a Baseline Shift feature, which you can use if you want to move individual characters up or down (like in a math equation, the little ® symbol, and so on).

▶ **Case and caps.** Want to make your text REALLY SCREAM? Then turn on All Caps in the Character palette's popout menu. (Personally, we find All Caps rather annoying to look at.) There are other features in this menu, too: Small Caps, Super Script, and Subscript. Each of these applies to selected text unless no text is selected on a type layer. You can turn them off again by reselecting them from the popout menu. Note that unless you're using Open Type fonts, the Small Caps feature fakes the small caps (if you have an Expert font that contains the real small caps, you'll get better quality using that instead).

Hyphenation and justification. Hyphenation and justification (usually just called "H&J") are two methods of making text fit into a given space by controlling the amount of space between letters and words, and by breaking certain words at line endings with hyphens. Photoshop can also stretch text in order to help it fit a particular column width. If any one of these methods is used in excess, the results are awful. So it's important to find a good balance among them.

The H&J settings are only relevant when you have a paragraph or more of text—that is, when you've dragged out a text frame, rather than just clicked and typed (see "Tip: Converting Point Type to Paragraph Type," later in this chapter). And the H&Js are always paragraph-wide formats; you can't apply them to a single character or line within a paragraph. Let's look at the several features in Photoshop that relate to H&Js:

▶ **Hyphenation.** By default, Photoshop hyphenates words that fall near the end of a line of text if it thinks it will make the imaginary line down the right side of the text (sometimes called "the rag") look better. If you don't want a paragraph to have any hyphenated words, then turn off the Hyphenate checkbox in the Paragraph palette.

You have a significant amount of control over what sort of words get hyphenated in the Hyphenation dialog box (choose Hyphenation from the popout menu in the Paragraph palette; see Figure 12-57). Alas, there is no way to save these settings so you can later apply them to other paragraphs. If you want a whole text block to have the same hyphenation settings (rather than just the currently selected paragraph), then make sure the cursor isn't in the text block, but the text layer is selected in the Layers palette when you make the change.

▶ **No Break.** Sometimes Photoshop will hyphenate a word you don't want hyphenated. No problem: select the word in the text block and choose No Break from the Character palette menu.

▶ **Justification.** The paragraphs in this book are "justified," meaning that the right margin is carefully aligned in a straight line (this is sometimes called "flush left and right"). As we said earlier, this is pulled off by adding or removing space between characters and words. Photoshop offers one other control: stretching or compressing text. You can justify a paragraph by selecting it and clicking one of the Justified Text buttons in the Paragraph palette. (There are four, each of which handles the last line of the paragraph differently.)

 If you don't like the way that Photoshop justifies your text, you can alter its built-in settings by choosing Justification from the popout menu in the Paragraph palette. Most typographers agree that justified text should have little character spacing, a reasonable amount of word spacing, and no character ("glyph") scaling. However, in a pinch, you may need to bump up the character spacing and glyph scaling by one

Figure 12-57
Hyphenation and
Justification

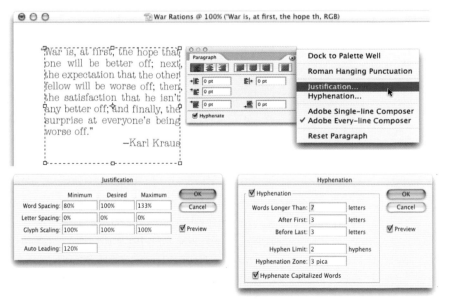

or two percent; just be careful that it doesn't make the text look too unnatural.

▶ **Composer.** Adobe InDesign shook the publishing world by packaging an old idea into new software: calculating the justification settings based on more than one line of text in a paragraph rather than just setting each line individually (like QuarkXPress and PageMaker have always done). You can now do this in Photoshop, too, by selecting Adobe Every-line Composer from the popout menu in the Paragraph palette. This almost always gives you tighter, better-looking paragraphs with more consistent spacing. We turn this on and leave it on.

▶ **Hanging punctuation.** Photoshop hangs small punctuation—such as periods, hyphens, quotation marks, commas, and so on—outside the text block, because the human eye tends to ignore these little extrusions and the text usually looks better. This is especially obvious in justified text. If you don't care for the look, you can turn it off in the popout menu in the Paragraph palette.

Ultimately, while it's cool that Adobe included all these typography features in Photoshop, we do find it a little absurd because it's so rare that you would ever want to set more than a few lines of text in Photoshop. The one exception is creating images for a PDF workflow. In fact, unless you save your files in the PDF format, the text will either be rasterized (anti-aliased into the background pixels) or it'll take forever to print and create enormous EPS files.

Tip: Converting Point Type to Paragraph Type. As we said earlier, you can create text in Photoshop by either clicking or dragging with the Text tool. If you drag, you get "Paragraph Type," which is a text block with text handles, that can reflow. If you click, you get "Point Type" which is text that starts at a point; all line breaks have to be made by hand, and you can't apply justification or hyphenation. You can change Paragraph Type to Point Type (and *vice versa*) by making sure no text or text blocks are selected (clicking on the text layer in the Layers palette will do this), then choosing Convert to Point Text or Convert to Paragraph Text from the Type submenu (under the Layer menu). You can also select this from the context-sensitive menu you get when Control- or right-button-clicking with the Type tool.

Filters and Effects

Sure, you can paint and retouch and composite within Photoshop, but you know as well as we do that the most fun comes from playing with filters. But if you're like most people, you could make filter fooling a lot more fun. Here are some methods we've found useful.

Tip: Float Before Filtering. Standard protocol leads people to make a selection, then choose a filter from one of the Filter submenus. We suggest adding one step to the process: copy the selection to a new layer first (Command-J). Doing so gives you much more flexibility in how the filter is applied. For instance, once the filter is applied on the new layer, you can move it, change its blending mode, run an additional filter, soften the effect by lowering the layer's opacity, and so on. Best of all, you don't damage your original pixels until you're sure you've got the effect exactly right. If you don't like what you've done, you can undo, or just delete the entire layer. Similarly, if you're going to run a filter on a whole layer, consider duplicating the layer first. It's safer, and much more flexible.

Tip: Filter Keystrokes. Like many other features of Photoshop, working with filters can be sped up with a couple of little keyboard shortcuts. You can tell Photoshop to run a filter again by pressing Command-F. However, this doesn't let you change the dialog box settings. If you want to follow this advice, press Command-Option-F; this reopens the dialog box of the last-run filter, so you can change the settings before applying it.

Tip: Fading Filter Effects. Most folks figure that once they run a filter, the choice is to either move forward or select Undo. But the Fade feature (in the Edit menu) allows you to take a middle path by reducing the opacity of a filter, or even changing the blending mode, immediately after running it. (As soon as you do anything else—even make a selection—the Fade feature is no longer available.) You can get to the Fade dialog box quickly by pressing Command-Shift-F (see Figure 12-58).

The Fade feature works not only with filters, but also with any of the features in the Adjustments submenu (under the Image menu) and almost every paint stroke. For example, you can run Hue/Saturation on an image, then reduce the intensity of the effect with Fade. We almost never use this,

Figure 12-58 Opacity changes how much a filter is applied

Filter applied with 100-percent opacity

Fade set to 60-percent opacity

Fade set to 20-percent opacity, and Mode set to Vivid Light

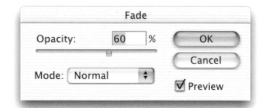

because we prefer to use adjustment layers, which are even more powerful (see Chapter 7, *The Digital Darkroom*).

Tip: Build Textures on Neutral Layers. Instead of burning filter effects directly into an image, you can filter a neutral-colored layer. Using filters in conjunction with neutral layers gives you much more freedom to change your mind later. When you select New Layer from the Layer menu or the Layers palette, Photoshop gives you the choice of filling that layer with the neutral color for the mode you choose for the layer. For instance, if you set the layer to Screen mode, Photoshop can fill the layer with black—screening with black has no effect on the image below, so it's "neutral." If you choose Overlay mode, then the neutral fill would be 50-percent gray.

Now, when you apply a filter to that layer, the parts that get changed are no longer "neutral." They change the appearance of the pixels below. Then you can run filters on this layer and they begin to affect the image below (see Figure 12-59). Of course, this primarily works with filters that add texture to an image, like the Texturizer feature. It typically won't have any effect at all with the Distort or Artistic filter.

Figure 12-59
Filtering on a layer

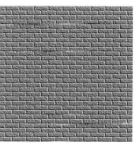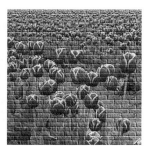

Original image *Texturizer filter applied* *Background image and*
to a neutral layer *neutral layer visible*
at the same time

Tip: Filtering Layer Masks. Katrin Eismann taught us that running a filter on a layer mask can offer powerful flexibility and cool effects, too.

1. Add a new layer and fill it with a solid color.

2. Select Add Layer Mask from the Layer menu, then choose Hide All.

3. Run the Add Noise filter on the layer mask. The more noise you add, the more the solid color layer shows. Try other filters for other effects.

Actions, Automate, and Scripting

The trick to being really productive and efficient with computer technology is being lazy. Yes, it's a paradox, but it's true—the lazier you are, the more likely you are to find the really efficient ways of doing things so you can get out of work faster and go to the beach. If you have an overzealous work ethic, you probably don't mind repeating the same mind-numbing tasks 400 times, but you won't be exploiting the power of the computer in front of you.

For example, Bruce works with a lot of digital cameras, and each digital camera's images need a particular kind of tweaking. Rotate the image 90 degrees, run this filter, use that Curves setting, resize the image to such-and-such…. Instead of performing each task one at a time, he can run through them all with a keystroke. Even better, Photoshop's automation features let you batch process all the images in a folder, so you don't even have to open them in Photoshop.

As Photoshop gets smarter with each new version, we can offload more busywork onto it while we take longer trips to the fridge for artichoke dip. (We're just hoping that Photoshop doesn't get too smart and starts making us do the work while it gets the dip.)

Photoshop offers four automation features: actions, Automate, Variables, and scripting. Actions are "macros" that live in the Actions palette and let you repeat a series of steps. Photoshop ships with a number of premade actions, and you can easily build your own (we'll show you how). Automate refers to the built-in tools in the Automate submenu (under the File menu). Variables is a way to create a template image that changes depending on data imported from a spreadsheet or a database. Scripting is a way to automate Photoshop from behind the scenes using AppleScript, JavaScript, or Visual Basic. We'll look at each of these techniques in turn.

Actions

In the last chapter, we discussed the basics of building actions—particularly actions that help in the processing of raw files. But Photoshop also comes with a number of premade actions that are not only useful, but educational, too, because you can look at them to see how they produce their magic. (You can load additional sets of actions by selecting Load Actions from the Actions palette's popout menu, or by choosing the presets that appear at the bottom the popout menu.)

The key is that you can only make an action for something you can do methodically, with no feedback from the program, and with little or no brain activity. For example, you can't record an action that says, "if the pixels in the upper-left corner of the image are sort of reddish, then do such-and-such." That would require Photoshop to be able to see and respond. No can do.

However, you can easily create an action that runs a particular set of Curves, adds a text layer, adds a layer effect, sharpens the background layer, and so on, because all these things are methodical.

Tip: Exporting Actions as Text. Trying to decode how other people made actions can be a hassle because the Actions palette is hard to read. Fortunately, you can export all the actions currently visible in the palette as a text file that you can open in a word processor: just hold down Command and Option while selecting Save Action from the Actions palette's popout menu.

Action limitations. Before you get too heady with your newfound actions power, you should know that Photoshop doesn't let you record everything you might want. While Photoshop can record blend modes, opacity, shapes, brush selections, and even pixel selections, you still cannot record paint strokes (like those made with the Brush, Airbrush, and Clone tools), zooms, switching windows, and scrolls. And there are many features that aren't necessarily recordable, but you can force them into an action (see "Editing Actions," later in this chapter). Last but not least, the whole Actions mechanism has a logic unto itself. If an operation isn't recordable by keyboard shortcut, it may be recordable by choosing the menu command instead, or vice versa.

Keep in Mind

Besides the limits of what you can and cannot record in the Actions palette, there are a few more things to keep in mind.

Difficulty. While recording and playing simple actions (those with only two or three steps) may be easy, trying to build complicated actions can be damaging to your head (and the wall you're banging it against).

Modularity. Rather than trying to make one big action that does everything you want, break it down into smaller steps that you can debug individually, then chain together to reuse in more complex actions.

Think it through. You should always think the action through completely before you start recording it. You might even write down each step on paper, and then record it after you're pretty sure everything will work out the way you think.

Generic actions. Try to make your actions as generic as possible. That means they should be able to run on any image at any time. Or, barring that, provide the user with a message at the beginning of the action noting what kind of image is required (as well as other requirements, such as "needs text on a layer" or "must have something selected"). This is a good idea even if you're the only one using your actions, because (believe us) after you've made a bunch of actions, you'll forget which action requires what (see "Tip: Talk to Your Users," later in this chapter).

There are a number of things to think about when making your actions generic. The following is a good place to start, but isn't necessarily a complete list:

▶ Never assume image mode. The image may be in RGB, CMYK, Grayscale, or even Indexed Color mode. This is very important when running filters, because some filters don't run in certain modes.

▶ Don't assume the image has layers (or doesn't have layers). Also, don't assume that if the image does have layers, the Background layer is selected (or even that there is a layer called Background). If you need the lowest layer selected, press Option-Shift-[.

▶ Avoid using commands that pick layers by name, unless the Action has already created and named the layer. For example, if you record clicking on a layer in the Layers palette, Photoshop records the click by layer name, not position. Instead, record pressing Option-[or Option-] to target the next layer down or the next layer up, respectively. Command-[and Command-] move layers up or down.

▶ If you're saving and loading channels, you'll almost certainly have to name the channels. Make sure you give them names that are unlikely to already be present in the image. *Do* name them, though, rather than leaving them set to the default names like "#4". If a document has two channels with the same name when you run an action, Photoshop always uses the first channel with that name.

Clean up. It's a good idea to make your actions clean up after themselves. In other words, if your action creates three extra channels along the way to building some other cool effect, the action should also probably delete them before ending. If the action hasn't cleaned up after itself and you run it a second time, those channels (or layers, or whatever) are still hanging around and will probably trip up the action.

Get more info. This section offers a quick overview of actions, but if you have Web access, check out one or more of the actions-oriented sites on the Internet like *http://share.studio.adobe.com*. You can also find more links from a site such as *www.photoshopnews.com*.

Actions Basics

Making an action is pretty straightforward:

1. Open the Actions palette (see Figure 12-60).

2. Click the New Action button (or select New Action from the palette's popout menu). Give the action a name (and a keyboard shortcut, if you want). If you have more than one set (see "Sets," later in this chapter), choose which set this new action will be part of. When you click OK, Adobe Photoshop begins recording automatically.

3. Perform the steps that you want the action to do.

4. Click the Stop button in the Actions palette (or select Stop Recording from the popout menu).

Then, to run the action, select the action's tile in the Actions palette and click the Run button (or, better yet, just Command-double-click on the action). If the action is relatively simple, it may perform perfectly the first time. But in most of the actions we make, we find that something goes wrong somewhere along the line, usually due to our performing a step that Photoshop can't record into an action (see "Troubleshooting Actions," later in this section).

Tip: Save Your Work First. If you run an action and then decide that you don't like what it did, you're in trouble because you cannot undo a full action, only the last step of an action. If the action used only a few steps,

Figure 12-60
The Actions palette

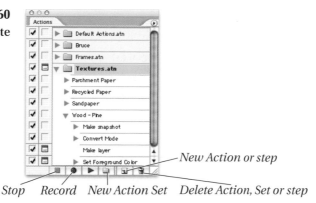

New Action or step

Stop   Record   New Action Set   Delete Action, Set or step

you might be able to use the History palette to return to a pre-action state, but this isn't always possible either, particularly if you ran the action as a batch process on multiple files. To guarantee an "undo" option, we're in the habit of saving a snapshot of our document in the History palette before running any action. That way, if something goes wrong or we don't like the effect, we can revert back to this snapshot. Another option is to simply save your document first, and then use the Revert command (in the File menu) to undo the action. Of course, neither of these techniques works with actions that save and close the file—we recommend always making actions that use Save As, rather than saving over the original.

Tip: Making Buttons. You can change the Actions palette into a palette full of buttons by choosing Button Mode in the palette's popout menu. When it's in Button mode, you only have to click once on a button to run it. Switch out of Button mode to create new actions or edit existing ones.

Sets. Photoshop lets you create sets of actions, a godsend to anyone who works with dozens of actions. Sets are pretty self-explanatory.

▶ You can create a new action set by choosing New Set from the Action palette's popout menu (or by clicking the New Set button in the palette). You can delete a set by selecting it and choosing Delete from the same popout menu, or by clicking the Delete button in the palette.

▶ You can move actions between sets by dragging them.

▶ You can rename a set by double-clicking on its tile in the Actions palette.

▶ You can show or hide the actions within a set by clicking on the triangle to the left of the set's name.

▶ You can also save sets (see "Saving actions," a bit later).

▶ You can play all the actions in a set (in order) by selecting the set and clicking the Play button.

Editing actions. Once you've built an action, you can edit it (in fact, you'll almost certainly want to edit it unless it worked perfectly the first time). If you want to record additional steps somewhere in the middle of the action (or at the end of the action), select a step in the action and click the Record button. When you're done recording actions, click the Stop button. All the new actions fall after the step you first selected.

If you want to add a step that cannot be recorded for some reason (perhaps it's an item in the View menu), you can select Insert Menu Item from the Action palette's popout menu. This lets you choose any one feature from the menus, and then inserts it into the action (after whatever step is currently selected).

To change the parameters of a step, double-click on it in the Actions palette. For example, if a step applies a curve to the image (using the Curves dialog box), but you want to change the curve, double-click on the step and choose a different curve. Note that when you do this, you may actually change the current image; just press Command-Z to undo the change (to the image, not to the action).

Annoyingly, some steps cannot be re-recorded. For instance, a step that sets the foreground color to red should be able to change so that it sets it to blue... but it can't. Instead, you have to record a new step, then delete the original.

If you want to change the action's name, its tile or button color, or its keyboard shortcut, just double-click on the action's name.

Tip: Duplicating Actions. Option-dragging a step duplicates it. For instance, if you want to use the same Numeric Transform step in two actions, you can Option-drag that step from one action into the proper place in the second action.

Tip: Stop Where You Are. Normally, Photoshop won't display any of the usual dialog boxes when you run an action. For instance, if you include a Numeric Transform step in an action, Photoshop just performs the transform without displaying the dialog box. But you can force Photoshop to display the dialog box, stop, and wait for the user to input different settings before continuing. To do so, click once in the second column of the Actions palette, next to the step. A black icon indicating a dialog box appears next to the step, and a red icon appears next to the action's name.

Don't click on a red dialog box icon! If you do, it turns black *and* Photoshop adds a black "stop here" icon next to every step in the action that can have one. There's no Undo here, so the only way to reset the little black icons to their original state is to turn them on or off one at a time. (You can, however, turn them *all* off by clicking the black icon next to the action's name.)

Note that if you insert a step using the Insert Menu Item command, Photoshop always opens the appropriate dialog box and doesn't even offer you the chance to turn this icon on or off (because steps inserted in this way are meant to simulate the user actually selecting the item).

Tip: Talk to Your Users. You can insert a command at any point in your action that stops the action and displays a dialog box with a message in it. This message might be a warning like, "Make sure you have saved your image first," or instructions such as, "You should have a selection made on a layer above the Background." To add a message, select Insert Stop from the Actions palette's popout menu. Photoshop asks you what message you want to appear and whether the message dialog box should allow people to continue with the action (see Figure 12-61).

Figure 12-61
Adding a message

If the message is a warning, you should turn on the Allow Continue option, but if the message consists of instructions, you may want to leave this checkbox off. When Allow Continue is turned off, Photoshop stops the action entirely. After the user clicks the OK button in the message dialog box, Photoshop automatically selects the next step in the Actions palette, so the user can continue running the action by clicking the Run button again (this works even if the Actions palette is in Button mode).

Saving actions. After you've created the world's most amazing action, you may want to share it with someone else. You can get actions out of your Actions palette and on to your hard drive by selecting Save Actions from the Actions palette's popout menu. Unfortunately, you cannot save a single action; the Save Actions feature only saves sets of actions. Fortunately, the workaround isn't too painful.

1. Create a new set (click on the New Set button at the bottom of the Actions palette), and name it something logical.

2. Either move or duplicate the action you want to save by dragging it or Option-dragging it into the new set.

3. Select the new set and choose Save Actions from the palette's popout menu.

4. If you want, delete the set you just created.

Of course, you can load sets of actions just as easily with the Load Actions and Replace Actions features in the palette's popout menu. Watch out for Replace Actions and its cousin Clear Actions; these replace or clear *all* the actions in the palette, not just the selected one.

Tip: Curves and Adjustments. We love the fact that Photoshop can record the exact settings of the Curves, Levels, and Hue/Saturation dialog boxes. Nonetheless, you should note that if you record loading a Curves file from disk (or a Levels or Hue/Saturation file, or any other adjustment), Photoshop records the name of the file rather than the curve itself.

The workaround: record loading the setting in the Curves dialog box (or whatever), then change the settings just a tiny bit before clicking OK. As long as there is a difference, Photoshop records the settings in the dialog box rather than the file's name. Remember that you can always go back and change the settings back to the way you want them.

Troubleshooting Actions

Sometime, somewhere, something will go wrong when you're building actions. That's where troubleshooting comes in. When troubleshooting (or debugging, as it's often called), the most important thing to keep in mind is that there *must* be a logical solution to the problem. (This isn't always true, but it's good to keep a positive attitude....)

Dummy files. The first thing you should do after building an action is not test it on some mission-critical image. Rather, try it on a dummy image. Even better, try it on several dummy images, each in a different mode

(RGB, CMYK, Grayscale, Indexed Color), some with layers, some without, some with selections made, others without, and so on. If it doesn't operate correctly on any one of these, you can decide whether to work at making it work or to add a message at the beginning of the action that says "don't try it on such-and-such-type of images" (see "Tip: Talk to Your Users," earlier in this section).

Step-by-step. You can force Photoshop to pause between each step and redraw the screen by selecting Step-By-Step in the Playback Options dialog box (you can choose this from the popout menu in the Actions dialog box). This is often useful, but the best troubleshooting technique in the Actions palette (in fact, probably the only troubleshooting technique) is to select the first item in the action and click the Run button while holding down the Command key. This plays only the first step. Now go check out all the relevant palettes. Is the Channels palette the way you expect it? What about the Layers palette? What are the foreground and background colors?

When you're convinced that all is well, press Command-Run again to check the second step in the action. And so on, and so on....

If at any time you find the palettes or colors set up improperly, now is the time to replace the last step or double-click on it to change its settings. If something is really messed up, then don't forget the Revert feature.

Tip: Use History. The History palette, when suitably configured, lets you step backwards through all the steps in an action, making it a great deal easier to figure out just where things went awry. So much so, in fact, that we wouldn't dream of trying to debug complex actions without it. The key is simply to make sure that you set Photoshop's Preferences to record a large enough number of History states to cover all the steps in the action.

Automated Workflows

Earlier we said that actions cannot perform any task that requires brain activity. However, Adobe's engineers have built some automation tools that do have some "smarts" and placed them in two places: in the Automate submenu (under the File menu) and in the Bridge's Tools menu. These menus are also home to the Batch feature, which lets you run an action on an entire folder of images. Let's take a quick look at some of these options.

(Note that we discuss one automation feature—Photomerge—in "Compositing," earlier in this chapter, and we cover a second automation feature—Web Photo Gallery—in Chapter 14, *Multimedia and the Web*. We also explore the Automate menu, and especially the oft-infuriating Batch command, in Chapter 11, *Building a Digital Workflow*.)

Tip: Making Droplets. We're not sure why the Make Droplet feature is hiding in the Automate submenu instead of the Actions palette, but that's where you can find this really awesome feature. You can use Make Droplet to save any Photoshop action to disk as a file. Then, when you want to process an image (or a folder full of images) with that action, you can simply drag the image (or folder) on top of the droplet file.

Bonus tip: If you work on both Macs and PCs, you can copy droplets from one platform to the other. On the PC you simply have to make sure the droplet has an *.exe* extension. When you bring a PC droplet to the Mac, you have to initialize it once by dragging it on top of Photoshop.

Picture Package. Picture Package is a boon to any photographer tired of duplicating, rotating, and scaling photos to fit pictures on one sheet of film. You can use Picture Package to lay out different versions of the same picture (like school photos, where you want so-many wallet-sized, and so on). Or you can use it to lay out different images together onto one page. The interface is simple enough to understand quickly (see Figure 12-62), though there are a few things to watch out for:

▶ First off, make sure you pay attention to the final resolution and final image mode setting. The default resolution, 72 dpi, leaves a great deal to be desired if you're planning to print your page.

▶ If you want all the images on the page to be the same, just select File from the Use popup menu and then click the Choose button to select your file. If you want different images, you can click on one or more of the preview images in the lower-right area of the dialog box.

▶ Photoshop lets you choose a label to add to the images. However, the choices are pretty slim. For instance, the label is always added on top of the image (there's no way to get it in a margin), the fonts are limited, and there are no options for styles (like drop shadows or glow around the label to make it stand out better).

Figure 12-62
Picture Package

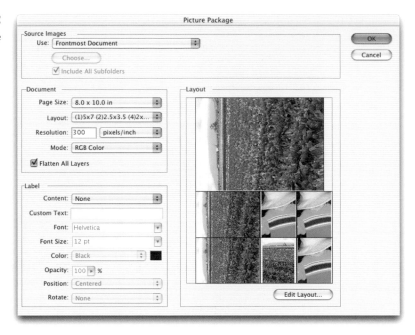

▶ If you choose more than one image (either by selecting Folder from the Use popup menu, or by selecting more than one image in Bridge and setting the Use popup menu to Selected Images in Bridge), Picture Package doesn't lay them out on the same page; it prepares one page for each image. Unfortunately, there doesn't appear to be any way to preview more than one page at a time, so we generally avoid selecting more than one image when using this feature.

▶ Note that the final result is not a flattened file, but rather all the images on a single floating layer. This means you can easily change the color behind the images, but it also means that you may need to flatten the file before printing or exporting the document.

Tip: Customized Package Pages. Photoshop offers about 20 different Picture Package layouts, but in case you just gotta' be you, you're welcome to create your own customized layouts, too. Photoshop sports a nifty layout editor (select an example template from the Layout popup menu and then click the Edit Layout button in the lower-right corner of the Picture Package).

The Edit Layout dialog box (see Figure 12-63) works like a basic drawing program: First choose a page size that corresponds to your printed

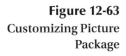

Figure 12-63
Customizing Picture
Package

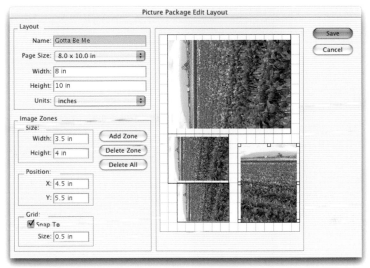

paper size in the Layout area. Then, click on a box (a "zone") to move it or change its size. You can remove a zone by clicking the Delete Zone button, or add one by clicking Add Zone. Unless you're really going wacky and wild, do yourself and everyone around you a favor and turn on the Snap To checkbox so that as you drag or resize a zone it snaps to a grid line; the grid is based on the value in the Size field.

When you're done, give your layout a name and click Save. Photoshop knows just where to save these files (in the Photoshop>Presets>Layouts folder), so you just need to name your file (probably something similar to your layout name) and click Save. The layout name is what appears in the Layout popup menu; the filename is just the on-disk filename.

Contact Sheet II. Contact Sheet builds pages of thumbnails from a folder full of images (see Figure 12-64). In ancient versions of Photoshop, Contact Sheet wouldn't actually label any of the images, making the contact sheet somewhat unusable. That has changed; on the other hand, Photoshop doesn't know what to make of long filenames, and usually truncates them. With any luck, Contact Sheet III will give you even more controls (though who knows when that will show up).

Crop and Straighten Photos. The Automate features are designed to save you from mind-numbing grunt work, and the Crop and Straighten Photos feature fits that bill exactly. If you throw four photos on a flatbed

Figure 12-64
Contact Sheet II

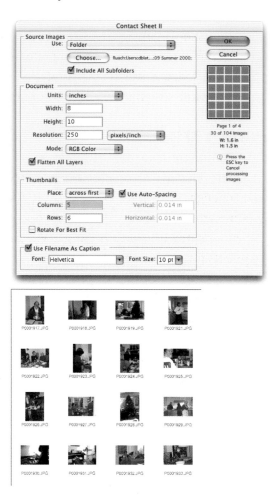

scanner, you can either scan four times (adjusting the scanning area each time) or scan once, duplicate the resulting file three times, and crop each one a unique image. Now you've got another choice: Scan once and choose Crop and Straighten Photos from the Automate submenu. This feature does the work for you by analyzing the image, duplicating it, cropping it, and rotating each one so that it sits straight. If you decide you only want a couple of the images on the page, draw selection marquees around the ones you want, and Photoshop will focus on them.

Obviously, the more clearer the boundaries are between the images the better the feature works. Crop and Straighten Photos usually works quite well, but we've found we sometimes still need to do a little cropping cleanup on some images (especially old photos that don't have clearly defined boundaries or in contact sheets with black borders). On rare occasions, Photoshop breaks an image into two or more pieces (if the colors in the image have areas that are too similar to the color around the images). In that case, make a selection around the image and then hold down Option/Alt while selecting the feature from the Automate submenu.

Using Variables

Most folks don't tend to think of Photoshop as a tool for making templates that will be filled in with content at a later date, but the Variables feature should change that. Variables lets you turn a static Photoshop document into a dynamic one that can change based on information stored in a database or spreadsheet. For example, you might have 300 photographs of products for your catalog and you want to place each product's price on top of its image. In addition, perhaps you want to place a starburst over the products that are new in this year's catalog. You can use variables to perform this task with no special scripting knowledge.

There are three kinds of variables in Photoshop: visibility (whether a layer is visible or not), text (the text that appears on a text layer), and picture (the image that appears on a layer). To set up the example above, you could make a four-layer Photoshop file: the blank background layer; another layer filled with white; a text layer with any random text on it in the size, style, and position you want the price to appear; and a layer with a "New!" starburst image on it. After you create this template:

1. Choose Define from the Variables submenu (under the Image menu; see Figure 12-65).

2. Choose the layer you want to define as a variable from the Layer popup menu.

3. In the Variable Type section, select either Visibility, Text Replacement (if it's a text layer), or Pixel Replacement (if it's a normal layer), and give the variable a name in the appropriate Name field.

4. Repeat steps 2 and 3 for each layer you want to be variable.

5. Choose Data Sets from the popup menu at the top of the dialog box. A data set is like a single record in a database—it provides the data for what to do with the variables. You can use the controls here to build your own data set, or you can click the Import button to load a set of records from a database or a spreadsheet. You can find the details for

Figure 12-65
Variables

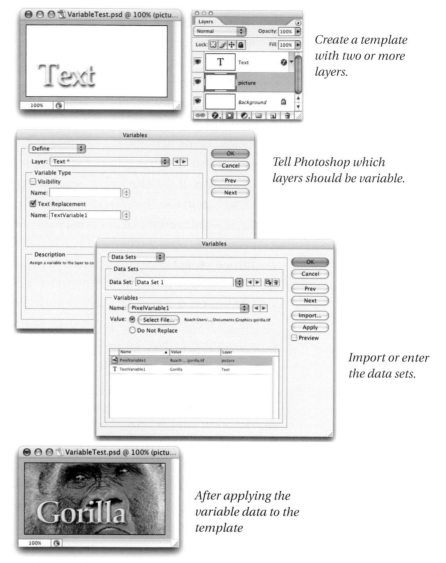

Create a template
with two or more
layers.

Tell Photoshop which
layers should be variable.

Import or enter
the data sets.

After applying the
variable data to the
template

how to build a file to import in the Photoshop help files. If you only
have a small number of data sets, you can create them manually by
clicking the New Data Set button and then choosing each variable in
order from the Variables section.

6. When you are done with the data sets, click OK. To load a single data set,
    choose Apply Data Set from the Image menu. If you want to create all
    the data sets, creating a new Photoshop PSD file for each one, choose
    Data Sets as Files from the Export submenu (under the File menu).

Scripting Photoshop

If actions and variables got you all excited about automating Photoshop, you're going to love scripting. Scripting is a way for one application (or your system) to talk to another application behind the scenes. For instance, in Mac OS X 10.3 or later, you can attach a script to a folder, so that as soon as you drop an image into the folder, your system launches Photoshop, performs several operations on it, saves the file, and then closes it again; it's all handled automatically.

Scripting is one of the coolest features in Photoshop, and it works on both the Macintosh and Windows platforms, but almost no one knows about it because Adobe doesn't advertise it well.

Scripting vs. actions. There are four basic differences between actions (which are also called macros) and scripts. First, actions are entirely dependent on the user interface—the menus, dialog boxes, keyboard shortcuts, and so on. Scripts, however, let you sneak in the back door of the program and control it from behind the scenes, almost like a puppeteer pulling the strings of a marionette. Second, scripts have flow control. *Flow control* is a programming term that means you can set up decision trees and loops, like "keep doing this until such-and-such happens." Third, scripts often contain variables, so you can save the value of something (like the color of a pixel) to use it later.

Last, scripting lets you control more than one program at time. For example, if you use QuarkXPress (which is also scriptable on the Macintosh) or InDesign (which is scriptable on both Macintosh and Windows), you could write a script that would automatically "see" how you've rotated, sized, and cropped images within your picture boxes. It could then open the images in Photoshop, perform those manipulations on the original images, resave them, and re-import them into the page-layout program. Powerful stuff!

Tip: Hiring a Scripter. Even though scripting is extremely powerful, it's just a fact of life that most people don't want to learn the ins and outs of scripting. Fortunately, there are a number of scripters for hire. You can find a good scripters on Adobe's scripting forum: *www.adobe.com/support/forums/*. If you're looking for a scripter for the Macintosh, there are also consultants listed at *www.apple.com/applescript/resources/*.

Scripting languages. You can script Photoshop using a number of different languages. On the Macintosh, you can use AppleScript or JavaScript. In Windows, you can use JavaScript, Visual Basic, or any other language that is COM aware, such as VBScript, Perl, or Python. Note that only JavaScript scripts can be used cross-platform. That would seem to make it the best option for scripting, but unfortunately, only a few other applications are JavaScript-aware—Adobe InDesign (CS and CS2) and Adobe Bridge are, but QuarkXPress is not.

First steps in scripting. We don't pretend that we can actually teach you how to script Photoshop in this book. Although we believe that almost anyone can learn how to write scripts (especially using AppleScript, which is much easier than other forms of scripting), scripting is still a form of computer programming and as such, it takes time and patience to learn. So where can you learn it?

▶ **Books.** Several good books have been published on scripting. Most are pretty general, such as Matt Neuburg's *AppleScript: The Definitive Guide*, the *AppleScript for Applications Visual QuickStart Guide*, and *Visual Basic Visual QuickStart Guide*—these don't discuss Photoshop's scripting, but they'll get you up to speed so that Adobe's own documentation makes a lot more sense. You might also look at Sal Soghoian's book *AppleScript 1-2-3*—Sal knows everything there is to know about the subject.

▶ **Examples.** The best way to learn how to script Photoshop is by first looking at and deconstructing other people's scripts. If you can find a script that already does what you want, then use it. If the script isn't quite right, then edit it to make it work for you. Adobe has provided a number of scripts to play with, including scripts that add text, warp it, and then convert the text to a selection. You can open AppleScripts in Script Editor (the free AppleScript editor that comes with the Macintosh), and Windows scripts in any Visual Basic editor in Windows to see how they work or edit them to suit your needs. JavaScripts are just text, so you can use any text editor to read or write them.

You can find even more scripts on Web sites, such as the Adobe Studio Exchange at *share.studio.adobe.com*.

▶ **Scripting dictionary.** On the Macintosh, all scriptable applications have a built-in scripting dictionary that outlines the various things that can be scripted in that program. One way to see this information is by choosing Open Dictionary in the File menu of the Script Editor utility. The dictionary is often most helpful as a quick reference when your books or documentation isn't around.

▶ **The Web.** The World Wide Web is, of course, one of the best sources for AppleScript, Visual Basic, and JavaScript information. There are a number of great sites out there that offer both tutorials on scripting and scripts that you can download, use, and learn from. If you want AppleScript information, the best place to start, of course, is Apple's own scripting site: *www.apple.com/applescript*. Another excellent place to learn about scripting is the Photoshop Scripting forum on Adobe's own Web site at *www.adobe.com/support/forums/main.html*, or here: *www.ps-scripts.com/*.

Running scripts. Even if you never find yourself writing scripts, you're missing out if you don't know how to run them—the example scripts that Adobe provides are extremely helpful. AppleScript and Visual Basic scripts must be run from outside of Photoshop, from a program like Script Editor (which ships free with all Macs).

JavaScript scripts are even more flexible: The easiest way to run a JavaScript from within Photoshop is to place it in the Photoshop/Presets/Scripts folder. Photoshop lists these files in the Scripts submenu, under the File menu (see Figure 12-66). If your script doesn't live in that folder, you can tell Photoshop where to find it by selecting Browse from the Scripts submenu.

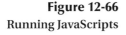

Figure 12-66
Running JavaScripts

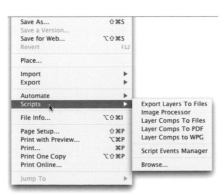

Here's a brief description of the five JavaScripts that Adobe ships with Photoshop:

▶ **Export Layers to Files.** This script saves each layer in your document as a separate, flattened file on disk. You get to choose what file format to save in.

▶ **Image Processor.** Formerly Dr. Brown's Image Processor, created by Russell Brown (if you look up "inimitable" in the dictionary, his picture should really be there), Image Processor lets you save multiple versions of your images—a high-resolution TIFF and a Web-resolution JPEG, for example—while also allowing you to apply an action in the process.

▶ **Export Layer Comps to Files.** When you have created one or more layer comps in the Layer Comps palette, this script saves each one as a flattened image. You can choose the file format and output options.

▶ **Export Layer Comps to PDF.** This script saves your layer comps in a single PDF file, one comp per page. We find this is a great way to send multiple comps to a client.

▶ **Export Layer Comps to WPG.** If you want to post your layer comps on a Web site, choose Export Layer Comps to WPG. *WPG* stands for "Web Photo Gallery." We cover these galleries in more detail in Chapter 14, *Multimedia and the Web*.

Tip: Running Scripts on Events. In the previous chapter, we described an action that would add several adjustment layers to a bunch of files in a batch process. Another way of going about this is to apply this action as an event script, which runs each time you perform a task such as opening a document. (Yes, event scripts work with both scripts and actions.) To create an event script, choose Scripts Events Manager from the Scripts submenu (under the File menu) and turn on the Enable Events to Run Scripts/Actions checkbox (see Figure 12-67).

Next, choose an event from the Photoshop Event popup menu—such as Open Document, Save Document, or Start Application. (You can also add your own events if you understand the Photoshop scripting model well enough.) Now choose a Script or Action at the bottom of the dialog box.

When you click Done, Photoshop starts "listening" for your event to take place. As soon as you perform the event, the action or script is trig-

Figure 12-67
Run a script on an event

gered. For example, you might have a script that opens a set of files each time you launch Photoshop and an action that creates a thumbnail and saves it as a JPEG each time you open a document. But remember to come back and turn off the checkbox at the top of this dialog box if someone else is going to use your copy of Photoshop. Otherwise, they'll be mighty confused as to why Photoshop is acting so oddly.

Tip: Hard-Core Scripting. If you really get into writing scripts, you will find yourself spending a lot of time writing or debugging scripts and you will want to take a look at some of the other scripting applications on the market. For instance, Late Night Software's Script Debugger is a full-featured tool that helps you write and debug AppleScripts, and is better than Apple's rather spartan Script Editor. Adobe's ExtendScript Toolkit (which ships with the Creative Suite), is very helpful when writing JavaScripts.

Also, the more complicated a script, the more it requires a way for the user to interact with it—buttons, text fields, dialog boxes, and so on. If you're interested in building user interfaces for your AppleScripts, take a look at Apple's own AppleScript Studio. In Windows, you can build interfaces using Visual Basic. For JavaScript scripts, see the *JavaScript Reference Guide* that comes with Photoshop for details.

Tip: Scripting the Unscriptable. Sadly, not everything in Photoshop is scriptable at this time, and some features are scriptable using JavaScript, but not via AppleScript or Visual Basic. This will change in time, but in the meantime, there are two options workaround. First, you can create an action in the Actions palette that performs that one step, and then trigger that action inside the script.

The second choice is to use the ScriptingListener plug-in, which comes with the Scripting Support files. When this plug-in is loaded, it can actually write a JavaScript of whatever you do in Photoshop. For instance, you can open a new document, make a selection, fill it with a gradient, and save the file to disk. The ScriptingListener writes the JavaScript for those commands to disk for you (Java Script files are just text files that can be edited in any text editor program). Then you can tell your AppleScript or Visual Basic script to run this little JavaScript code at the appropriate time.

New Techniques

Even though Photoshop is an amazing tool, it still won't do everything for you. Creating drop shadows, silhouettes, special edges, or text in Photoshop can be a chore. But we hope that with these new methods, your work will fly faster and you'll be able to focus on more fun stuff.

13 Image Storage and Output

Managing Files for Fast Production

We've filled the last few hundred pages with techniques for making great-looking images in Photoshop. What we haven't done yet is looked at how to get these images *out* of Photoshop. Perhaps you'll be printing your image directly from Photoshop. Or perhaps you're saving the file to be used in a page-layout application—such as InDesign or QuarkXPress—or on a Web page. How you save your image or how you print it is determined by what you want to do with it next.

In this chapter we're going to explore two key subjects: how to save your images to disk and how to print them. Along the way, we'll also discuss some of the concepts you'll need to be familiar with in order to make good decisions in Photoshop, including halftoning methods, metadata, clipping paths, and transparency.

Storing Images

When Photoshop writes an image to disk, it doesn't save the picture itself; rather, it just saves a bunch of zeros and ones. But the zeros and ones that one program writes to disk may not be readable by another program. The same data can be written to disk in a variety of ways, called *file formats*. Different file formats may be as different as two languages (like Spanish versus Chinese), or as similar as two dialects of the same language (like American versus British English).

The world would be a simpler place if everyone (and all software) spoke the same language, but that's not going to happen. Fortunately, programs such as Photoshop, QuarkXPress, and InDesign can read and sometimes even write in multiple file formats. The important thing, then, is not for us to understand exactly what makes one different from the others, but rather what each file format's strengths and weaknesses are, so that we can use them intelligently.

In the first part of this chapter, we're taking an in-depth look at each of the many file formats that Photoshop understands. (Note that we won't cover Camera Raw or DNG here, because Photoshop can't write these files—it can only read them; they're discussed in Chapter 11, *Building a Digital Workflow.*)

Tip: Hide Formats You Don't Use. Photoshop itself actually only knows how to read and write about half of the file formats we're discussing in this chapter. It can read and write the other types because of plug-ins that came with the program. For instance, when the CompuServe GIF and FilmStrip plug-ins are in Photoshop's Plug-ins folder, Photoshop can read and write in these "languages." But if you don't use these formats, you don't have to leave them cluttering up your Save As popup menu. Instead, move any formats that you don't want out of the File Formats folder (inside the Plug-ins folder in the Photoshop folder) into some other folder outside the Plug-ins folder. Don't just hide them inside another nested folder; Photoshop can still find them there.

However, before we get to our discussion of file formats and compression, we need to cover three sets of options that appear in the Save As dialog box: Save, Color, and Image Previews.

Save As Options

Over the years, the Save As dialog box has become pretty complex (see Figure 13-1). It offers a lot of different options, including the important ability to save a copy of your file (see sidebar "Saving and Opening Images"). Depending on the settings in the Preferences dialog box, you may have

Figure 13-1
The Save As
dialog box

The Save As dialog box allows you to decide which elements to save in your image. The Macintosh (upper left) and Windows (left) versions are similar.

If you choose a format that doesn't support one or more of the types of data in the image, Photoshop places a warning icon beside that data type and forces you to save a copy (above right).

even more options available to you. Note that the file format you choose (TIFF, PDF, EPS, and so on) determines which of these options are available. If you choose a format that doesn't support something in your file, Photoshop places a warning icon next to the offending option, and forces you to Save As a Copy.

Save Options

The five options in the Save section of the Save As dialog box are relatively self-explanatory, but when you want them turned on or off might not be as obvious.

Figure 13-3
Image preview options

force Windows to generate icons for PSD and other files, but we've never figured it out. Let us know if you can do it.

Thumbnail. The second preview, Thumbnail, is a slightly larger image that QuickTime-savvy applications can display in their Open dialog boxes. This way, you can see just what's in the image before you open it. Photoshop and InDesign don't require this (they'll create a thumbnail on the fly whether you save one or not). There are two choices: Macintosh Thumbnail and Windows Thumbnail. We turn both off.

Full Size. When Ask When Saving is turned on in Saving Files Preferences, Photoshop on the Mac gives you one additional choice: Full Size preview. This one adds a considerably larger JPEG-compressed 24-bit PICT resource to the file; its dimensions are the actual physical output size of the image, downsampled to 72 pixels per inch.

The primary benefit to Full Size preview is that it can be used by many third-party image browsers and databases. Unfortunately, it's ignored by InDesign, PageMaker, and QuarkXPress. We rarely turn on this option.

Note that there's no reason to select Full Size preview with an EPS file; it's equivalent to saving the EPS file with a Macintosh (JPEG) preview (see "Encapsulated PostScript (EPS)," later in this chapter).

Tip: Save Time Saving Previews. Saving an icon or thumbnail preview can considerably lengthen the time it takes to save your image (especially for very large files). But if you save one type of preview, saving the other type as well takes hardly any additional time—one or two seconds at most. Saving a full size preview takes still longer, so you should only do so if the image is going to an application that will benefit from it.

File Formats

You've probably noticed by now that a lot of this book focuses on prepress; nonetheless, we've done our best to include vital information for those whose output is continuous-tone film or the computer screen. Most people use Photoshop to prepare images that they're going to take elsewhere, be it PageMaker, Adobe InDesign, QuarkXPress, the Web, or whatever. The file format in which you save your file depends on where it's headed.

In the past, we've always advised that, while you're working on an image in Photoshop, you should save the file in Photoshop's native file format (PSD). But since few other applications besides Adobe's can read these files, you generally need to save your finished images in some other format before transferring them to a page layout, presentation, or multimedia application. Most people have developed the habit of keeping a layered version of the file in Photoshop format, and saving flattened versions in other formats to export to other applications.

You can still do that with Photoshop, but this workflow has become less convenient because Photoshop has made changes to how it handles PSD and TIFF formats. Plus, people are increasingly using Adobe InDesign or QuarkXPress 6.5—both of which can read PSD files. These changes open up some new workflow possibilities (see the sidebar "One File or Two?").

If your image is destined for a presentation program, a multimedia program, or another screen-based application, PICT and JPEG are probably the best formats to use. But if the image is going to a page-layout program, you should always use PSD (InDesign only), TIFF, EPS, PDF, or DCS.

Photoshop

The Photoshop file format—otherwise known as Photoshop's "native" format or PSD—used to be the only way to save everything that Photoshop is capable of producing: multiple layers, adjustment and type layers, layer effects, paths, multiple channels, clipping paths, screening and transfer settings, and so on. (Note that Undo states, histories, and snapshots are not saved in any file format.) We used to recommend it as the format for saving images that were being worked on, and for archiving finished layered images. However, today the Photoshop format is often much less necessary than it used to be. But there are still a few times when it trumps any other format.

The PSD file format is less necessary because almost anything you can save in a Photoshop file, you can now also save in either a TIFF or a PDF file. It's important to note, however, that other applications may not be able to read those formats properly (for instance, you can now save spot colors in a TIFF file, but no other programs currently handle those spot colors properly).

Saving a composite. By default, Photoshop pretty much insists on saving a flattened composite version of the image in every PSD file because it "maximizes file compatibility." As a result, those of us who have become accustomed to using PSD to save files that consist only of a Background layer and some adjustment layers get a rude shock when we find that our

One File or Two?

If you're like us, you probably have the ingrained belief that PSD always means the layered file, and TIFF always means the flat one. For better or for worse, this is no longer a tenable assumption because TIFF files can contain almost everything you can put into a PSD file, including layers. So you have a trade-off.

On the one hand, you can keep a single TIFF file with all your layers, which is fully editable in Photoshop, and place that same layered file in your page layout application. This gives you the convenience of dealing with one

file instead of two (no small issue in most people's workflows).

On the other hand, the file is going to be a lot bigger than a flat TIFF would have been, so it takes longer to transmit over e-mail or to download from your server. When your files are 50 MB layered TIFFs instead of 5 MB flat ones, you may have a real job of getting your file to your output provider.

The larger file has a negligible impact on print speed, because the page layout program simply ignores the extra data and sends only the part it can understand to the RIP. In Adobe InDesign and

QuarkXPress, it doesn't seem to have any effect on the speed of placing files. PageMaker, however, insists on reading the entire file before concluding that it doesn't understand most of it—so placing layered TIFFs in PageMaker is considerably slower than placing flat ones.

You can continue the practice of saving two files. Nevertheless, it's a sure thing that sooner or later, someone will (deliberately or inadvertently) send you a TIFF that contains layers, so you simply can't assume that TIFF is a print-ready flat file anymore.

Photoshop PSD files are about twice the size of the ones we saved from Photoshop 6 and earlier.

Fortunately, you can prevent Photoshop from saving flattened composites in two ways, each tied to the Maximize PSD and PSB File Compatibility popup menu in the File Handling panel of the Preferences dialog box. By default, this popup menu is set to Ask, which means that whenever you try to save a PSD file with layers you get to choose whether or not you want to "maximize file compatibility." Plus, you get a scary-looking warning that suggests turning off Maximize is a course of action that will result in The End Of The Universe As We Know It (see Figure 13-4).

Figure 13-4
The really annoying
"Maximize compatibility"
warning

The warning is there for two reasons.

▶ Several other applications claim to be able to read Photoshop files, and while a few can actually read layered files, most just read the flattened composite. Adobe Illustrator, Adobe InDesign, and QuarkXPress 6.5 will all attempt to read Photoshop files even if the composite is not present, so if you're using one of these, you can usually proceed without the composite—if your layered files are relatively straightforward. However, if your layers use any of the new blending modes such as Pin Light or Vivid Light, the layers will very likely not be read correctly, so it's safer to include the composite. Plus, while InDesign and Illustrator can read 8-bit layered PSD files without a composite, they can't handle 16-bit PSD files without one.

▶ Future versions of Photoshop may change the layer-blending algorithms, which means that when you opened a layered document it would look slightly different than it does now. Adobe reasons that with the flattened composite, you'll still be able to retrieve the correct image appearance in future versions. Of course, if you someday open the composite rather than the layered document, you lose all your layers, so the advantage over saving a flattened copy is questionable.

TIFF vs. EPS

As we travel around the world doing seminars and conferences, we are forever hearing people say things like "My service bureau told me to only use EPS files," or "I was told I'd get better images if I used TIFFs," or "Don't EPS files print better?" While we try to appear calm and collected, inside we're just waiting to scream, "Who told you this nonsense? Were they raised by wolves?"

While the confusion is understandable, we want to make a few points about TIFF and EPS that will, we hope, clear the air a tad.

For most images, TIFFs and EPSs contain *exactly the same image data*. The way in which it's written (encoded) may be somewhat different, but that doesn't change the image one iota.

The key differences between TIFFs and EPSs are not what they are or how they're written, but what other programs can do to them and what Photoshop features they can contain.

Encapsulated data. The entire philosophy behind EPS (Encapsulated PostScript) files is that they're little capsules of information. No other program should have to—or even be able to—go in and change anything about the data that's there.

EPS files were designed to be imported into other programs so that those programs wouldn't have to worry about what's in them at all. When it came time to print, that program would simply send the EPS down to the printer, trusting that the PostScript inside would image correctly. EPS files depend on a PostScript interpreter, so if you're using a non-PostScript desktop inkjet, you may have trouble printing them from a program like QuarkXPress.

Open TIFF format. TIFFs, on the other hand, were designed not only to be imported into other programs, but also to be exchanged among image editors.

That is, the program that imports the TIFF can actually access the information inside it and, potentially, change it.

Programs such as QuarkXPress, InDesign, and PageMaker have exploited this property of TIFFs by incorporating features that let you make changes to the TIFF image. On pages, for instance, you can apply a color to a grayscale TIFF image. When you print the page, the program changes the image data on its way to the printer. It almost never changes the data on your disk, but it changes it in the print stream. Other than InDesign's ability to alias one spot color to another, these programs can't really change EPS files at all.

Downsampling and cropping. More important, Adobe PageMaker, Adobe InDesign, and QuarkXPress all have the ability to downsample TIFF data at print time. If you import a 300-ppi TIFF into XPress and print it to a

Duotones. Because TIFF and PDF do almost everything that the native Photoshop file format does (and often do it better), we almost never use PSD files anymore. The exception is when using multitone images. Adobe InDesign CS (not InDesign 2) can import PSD files saved in Duotone mode, and these files are more flexible than PDF, EPS, or DCS files. (See Chapter 10, *Spot Colors and Duotones*, for more on spot colors and these file formats.)

desktop laser printer at 60 lpi (see "Contone vs. Halftone," later in this chapter, for more on halftone screen frequency), QuarkXPress automatically downsamples the image to 120 ppi (two times the halftone frequency).

QuarkXPress does this because it knows that sending the extra data is wasted time. The result is that your page prints faster. In PageMaker, you can achieve the same result by choosing Optimized in the Print: Options dialog box; in Adobe InDesign, choose Optimized Subsampling from the Send Data popup menu in the Print dialog box. There's no way we know of to downsample an EPS at print time.

Similarly, have you ever tried importing a full-page, 20 MB EPS file into one of these page-layout programs and cropping it down to a 1-by-1-inch square? The program is forced to send the entire 20 megabytes to the printer, even though all you want is a little bit of the image.

With a TIFF image, however, only the data needed to print the page at that screen frequency is sent to the printer, again saving printing time and costs.

Previews and separations. One of the biggest hassles of TIFF images, however, is that they can take a long time to import on slow machines, because the page-layout program has to read the entire file in order to create a screen preview for the image. EPS files can import quickly because Photoshop has already created a preview image.

On the other hand, CMYK TIFF files sometimes print separations much faster than EPS files because the data can be separated into discrete 8-bit chunks (only sending yellow data for the yellow plate, and so on). With EPS files, however, some programs (like PageMaker) have to send all 32 bits (cyan, yellow, magenta, and black) for each plate. This slows down printing considerably. Fortunately, QuarkXPress and InDesign both separate CMYK EPS files properly, so they print about as fast as TIFF files.

Workflow considerations. There are plenty of other differences between EPS and TIFF files—like the fact that you can save transfer functions, duotones, and halftone screening information in EPS files—but we're going to leave them for later in the chapter. Our purpose is simply to show that TIFF and EPS files are equal in stature if not in the goals they were designed to meet.

As for us, when we have a choice, we almost always use TIFF files; we prefer them for their flexibility, and we do a *lot* of page proofing with large grayscale images, so the downsampling at print time helps a lot. However, if we need fast importing of large files, or a duotone image, we switch to EPS. But don't listen to us. The most important reason why you should use one over the other is not "my consultant/service bureau/guru told me so," but your own workflow. The sorts of images you work with, the kind of network and printers you have, and your proofing needs all play a part in your decision.

Photoshop 2.0 format. No one we associate with still uses Photoshop 2.0. If you need to open your Photoshop documents in some really ancient version, you may be tempted to save your files in the Photoshop 2.0 format. Don't bother. We have not yet found any advantage of saving documents in this format. (Note that this format is not even available in Photoshop for Windows.) Instead, just save the file in Photoshop format, including the flattened composite.

File Formats for Print

If your image is destined for multimedia or the Internet, you may want to use the JPEG or GIF format. But if the image is going to a page-layout program, you should always use PSD, TIFF, PDF, EPS, or DCS.

Some page-layout programs will tell you that they can accept and print images in PICT, or BMP, or WMF, or various other weird formats. This may even be true on every third Tuesday of the month, when it coincides with the full moon, and the wind is coming briskly out of the southwest; but in general, using anything other than TIFF, PDF, PSD, EPS, or DCS in a print-based application is courting disaster. So these are the formats that we'll cover in detail first and foremost; then we'll look at formats appropriate for non-prepress applications.

TIFF

The Tagged Image File Format (TIFF, pronounced just as it reads) is the industry-standard bitmapped file format. Nearly every program that works with pixel-based images can handle TIFF files—either placing, printing, correcting, or editing the pixels. TIFF was once a very straightforward format—the only information it contained beyond the actual pixels themselves was the output size and resolution. But that's no longer the case. Photoshop's TIFF files can now contain just about everything you can put in a native Photoshop file, including vector data, clipping paths, transparency, spot color channels, annotations, and adjustment layers. The only exception is that you can't save a duotone as TIFF. But beware. Just because you can save something in a TIFF doesn't mean a program like InDesign or QuarkXPress can open or print it.

A Photoshop TIFF can be any dimension and resolution (at least we haven't heard of any limits). You can save it in Grayscale, RGB, CMYK, or Lab color mode with 8 or 16 bits per channel, as 8-bit RGB indexed color, or as a (1-bit) black and white bitmap. Before you get totally carried away, though, bear in mind that TIFF files have a permanent hard-coded size limit of 4 GB.

You can save adjustment layers, content layers, spot color channels, vector data, and screening and transfer-curve information in a TIFF, but they're all mostly ignored by applications other than Photoshop. Quark-XPress can read alpha channel information, but only as a method of building a clipping path (which we don't recommend). InDesign CS (and later versions) understand spot color channels in TIFF files, though InDesign 2 doesn't. Some applications are also unable to read high-bit TIFFs (though they're usually applications that are unable to handle high-bit data in *any* format). So while Photoshop can read everything it saves in a TIFF, the vast majority of applications can't. As a result, just because you can save a vector text layer or a spot channel in a TIFF, and your page layout application can read TIFFs, don't assume that you'll get a spot plate or vector text when you place the TIFF in your page layout app.

Photoshop's Preferences dialog box offers an option called "Ask Before Saving Layered TIFF Files." When you add layers to a TIFF that started out flat and try to save it, this option forces you to look at the TIFF Options dialog box (which we discuss below).

Again, even though you can save spot channels in a TIFF, we know of no application other than Photoshop that can print them properly from a TIFF. And even though you can save your vector data (type and layer clipping paths) in a TIFF, it will print as raster (pixels) from any application other than Photoshop, not vector. So you need to be careful.

When you save a layered TIFF, Photoshop always includes a flattened composite of the image. Applications such as QuarkXPress and InDesign import the flattened image (one of the nicer properties of TIFF is that it's designed in such a way that applications can simply ignore the elements they don't understand), but if you later open the TIFF in Photoshop, it reads the layers.

Some of us wish Adobe had been a little less aggressive in pushing what our friend and colleague Dan Margulis calls, in his inimitable fashion, "exploding TIFFs" on the world: Others of us are absolutely delighted that we can save disk space and simplify our workflow by saving high-bit layered TIFFs with very efficient ZIP compression and place them directly in InDesign. The bottom line: Determine the lowest-common-denominator TIFF settings that will work in your workflow, and use them.

When you save a TIFF, Photoshop lets you choose from among various options in the TIFF Options dialog box (see Figure 13-5).

Compression. Photoshop lets you save the composite (flattened) information in TIFF files with LZW or ZIP (lossless), or JPEG (lossy) compression. LZW may still give a few antediluvian applications some problems, but is generally well supported. However, LZW doesn't work well on high-bit

Figure 13-5
Saving TIFF files

files—it actually makes them bigger rather than smaller. The only program (besides Photoshop) we know of that can read TIFF files with ZIP or JPEG compression is Adobe InDesign.

If you save your TIFF with ZIP or JPEG compression, you do get a warning that these compression options "are not supported in older TIFF readers"—which really means that they're unsupported by any application *except* InDesign and Photoshop. We hope this changes, because ZIP compression is lossless, and highly efficient. With layered TIFFs, you have the option of applying ZIP compression only to the layers, while leaving the flattened composite uncompressed. We use this option a lot, because compressing the layers makes for a much smaller file, and the uncompressed flattened composite is still readable by other applications.

LZW compression is relatively inefficient, and useless on high-bit files, so we generally avoid it (David still uses LZW compression on screenshots, but when pressed will admit he does so largely out of habit). We use ZIP compression on flattened images destined for InDesign: If we don't know the final destination, we leave our flattened TIFFs uncompressed.

Pixel Order. Photoshop CS2 introduced a new TIFF option—Pixel Order—which lets you choose between Interleaved (known in Neolithic times as "chunky") or Per Channel (also known as "planar"). The difference has to do with how each channel of an image is saved: Interleaved saves a pixel's red channel value, then its green channel value, and then its blue channel value—repeating this cycle for each pixel in the image. That's how every version of Photoshop before CS2 saved TIFFs. Per Channel saves the entire red channel, followed by the green channel, and finally the blue channel.

Most older programs simply can't read Per Channel TIFFs, so we typically just stick with Interleaved. But if you're trying to make your file as small as possible, Per-Channel pixel order with ZIP compression produces the smallest file on high-bit images, and Interleaved pixel order with ZIP compression does so on 8-bit ones.

Byte Order. For some reason, Windows-based PCs and the Macintosh have different versions of TIFF. It has something to do with the file's byte order and the processing methods of Motorola versus Intel chips. Happily, programs like Photoshop, PageMaker, InDesign, and QuarkXPress on both Windows and Mac can import either Intel- or Motorola-type TIFFs, so saving in one format or the other is rarely crucial in the prepress world.

Image Pyramid. Photoshop's TIFF Options dialog box lets you save something called the Image Pyramid. This option is completely irrelevant for prepress work and was designed looking forward to a time when TIFFs might be used on the Web. The Image Pyramid is basically the contents of the Image Cache (see "Image Cache" in Chapter 2, *Essential Photoshop Tips and Tricks*). With the necessary support from a browser, it lets you download just the resolution you need. But since the necessary browser support is currently rarer than hens' teeth, we don't see any reason to turn on the checkbox.

Transparency. When your image has transparency (the file is not flattened, and has no "Background" layer), you can save the image transparency in the TIFF file by turning on the Save Transparency checkbox. At first, we thought that turning on this option would make the TIFF unreadable in old applications (such as QuarkXPress or PowerPoint). But oddly enough, it works: Programs that understand transparency (such as InDesign), can read the transparency in these TIFF files. Older programs import the file as though it had be flattened.

Layer Compression. Photoshop also always compresses the layers in a layered TIFF files using either RLE or ZIP. If we're saving layered TIFFs for placement in a page-layout application, we almost always leave the composite data uncompressed, but we choose ZIP compression on the layers (as we noted earlier). ZIP takes a bit longer to save, but it's a much more efficient compression algorithm than RLE so it results in significantly smaller files.

When we're saving layered TIFFs for further work in Photoshop (Bruce has started using TIFF instead of PSD as his archive format), we use ZIP compression on both the layers and the background. We do this only for TIFFs that we only ever plan to open in Photoshop, or place in InDesign. TIFFs with ZIP-compressed backgrounds aren't readable by XPress, Page-Maker, or any version of Photoshop earlier than 6.

Compatibility. TIFF is in many ways the ideal bitmapped file format, but it's become increasingly flexible over the years, and that flexibility comes at the price of compatibility. Prepress users tend to believe that there used to be something called a "standard TIFF" that contained pixels and resolution information. But TIFF has always had to serve the needs of communities as diverse as video (where RGB TIFF with alpha channels is a standard), digital camera vendors (where the raw capture is stored as a grayscale TIFF with all sorts of metadata, some of which pertains to converting the raw capture to color), and fax (where compressed bitmapped TIFFs have long been an international standard). JPEG compression and transparency, for example, have been part of the published TIFF specification since 1992, so while prepress folks may blame Adobe for screwing up the TIFF format, an equal number of people have been yelling at Adobe for the past 10 years to implement the features in Adobe's own published specification.

But whatever the politics of the situation, the bottom line is that in Photoshop it's very easy to save TIFFs that are either unreadable by other applications, or may not print as expected from other applications. Photoshop can read anything it can save in a TIFF, so TIFF is great as a work file format for Photoshop. But other applications generally ignore alpha channels (except when building clipping paths) and spot color channels (except for InDesign), and will print any vector data included in the TIFF as raster. The vast majority of TIFF-consuming applications don't understand ZIP or JPEG compression, or transparency.

Since Photoshop is the 800-lb gorilla, the TIFF-reading capabilities of other applications will almost certainly change during the useful life of this book, so it's pointless for us to try to provide chapter and verse on just what will and will not work when you place Photoshop TIFFs in other applications. Instead, we offer this rule of thumb: assume that anything consuming a Photoshop TIFF will read the flattened composite and ignore everything else, and assume that the only widely supported compression option for the flattened composite is LZW.

Tip: Color Management Systems. If you're relying on a color management system to control your color, it's generally a great deal easier to do so using TIFF than it is using EPS files, because as yet there's no widespread support for embedded profiles in EPS files, whereas there is for TIFFs. It's possible to build a color-managed workflow around EPS using commercial XTensions and utilities such as Color Solutions' Parachute (which intercepts all the color elements in a PostScript stream and applies color transformations based on rules that you set in advance), or PraxiSoft's ColorSyncXT for QuarkXPress (which allows you to apply profiles to imported EPS files). Technically, you can also force InDesign to color manage EPS files by setting the EPS to 99-percent opacity on the InDesign page, but that's a pretty unpleasant workaround. But InDesign, QuarkXPress, and PageMaker all include support for color-managing TIFF files with no additional software or icky extra steps.

Encapsulated PostScript (EPS)

As we said back in Chapter 3, *Image Essentials*, Encapsulated PostScript (EPS) is really an object-oriented file format, but Photoshop can save pixel-based and vector (like text) image data in the EPS format. There are two things you should remember about EPS:

- ▶ EPS files are only relevant when importing images into a page-layout program.

- ▶ EPS is a twentieth-century file format that is in the slow-but-steady process of being replaced by PDF. Old, "second millennium" software like PageMaker or QuarkXPress 4 handles EPS files better than PDF files, but for modern software (like InDesign CS2), PDF is the vector file format of choice.

Include Vector Data. If your image includes vector data—vector text or vector clipping shapes that haven't been rasterized into pixels—then you must turn on the Include Vector Data checkbox. If you turn it off, all that vector data gets rasterized upon saving. For more on vector data, see Chapters 3, *Image Essentials*, and 12, *Essential Image Techniques*.

Note that if you save vector data in your EPS file and then later open that EPS file in Photoshop, all the vectors get rasterized. This is a one-way street: Photoshop can export EPS files with vector data, but it cannot retain vectors when importing EPS files. Just another reason to use PDF instead of this ol' format when possible.

Image Interpolation. If you have a PostScript 3 printer, you might find the Image Interpolation feature intriguing: It smooths out low-resolution images, like Web graphics or screen captures, on the fly (in the printer). It also works when distilling PostScript files into PDF (so it's helpful for online documentation). It's not fabulous, but it's nice that Adobe gives us the option, just in case. We always leave this turned off for normal images (files with enough resolution so that you can't see the actual pixels).

DCS

DCS is a special case of the EPS file format. However, it's weird (and important) enough that Adobe added it as two separate file formats in the Save As dialog box: Photoshop DCS 1.0 and Photoshop DCS 2.0.

Originally, DCS was designed to separate the high-resolution image data from a low-resolution "preview" version. The DCS 1.0 format always results in five files: four with high-resolution data for each color plate (cyan, magenta, yellow, and black), and one—called the *master file*—is what you import into a page-layout program. The master file contains three things: a low-resolution screen preview of the image, a low-resolution composite CMYK version, and pointers to the other four files.

There are two problems with DCS 1.0. First, some people don't like to keep track of five files for each image (though to be fair, many other people think this is nifty because they can leave the high-resolution data on a server and just use the master file on their own systems). Second, there was no way to include spot colors.

Ultimately, we know of no good reason to use DCS 1.0, so we'll focus on version 2.0, which does everything that 1.0 does and more.

Of the various options in the DCS 2.0 Format dialog box (see Figure 13-8), most of them are equivalent to the ones in the EPS Options dialog box (which we discussed in the last section). For instance, Preview lets you determine the quality and kind of RGB screen preview; Encoding determines the format of the data within the file; and so on. The only new feature here is the DCS popup menu, in which you can choose whether you want one single file or multiple files on disk, and what sort of composite image you want.

Figure 13-8
Saving Desktop Color
Separation (DCS) files

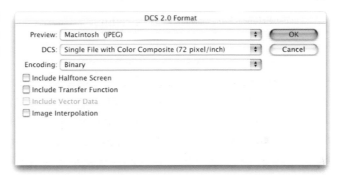

DCS composites. Many people confuse the DCS's composite image with the preview image. This is understandable, because they're almost exactly the same thing. Both are low-resolution (72 ppi) representations of the original image; and both can be used instead of the high-res image for proofing.

The real difference is in their uses. The preview image is always in RGB mode and is designed for screen use only. The composite image is saved in CMYK mode (it's the same as downsampling the high-res CMYK image to 72 ppi using Nearest Neighbor interpolation), and is meant for sending to a low-resolution color printer for use as a comp or a proof.

For color-proofing devices that require color separations, you can force XPress to send the high-resolution data with a third-party XTension. Adobe InDesign CS and CS2 can do this automatically (though InDesign 2 cannot). We don't know of any way to do this in PageMaker other than trying to get the color printer to recombine the separations. Honestly, though, we tend to think it's better to proof images before you save them as DCS files; once they're encapsulated like this, it's hard to get any really accurate proofs from them.

Multi-file or single file. Whether you tell Photoshop to write a single file or multiple files is up to you and your workflow. Probably the best reason to use multiple files is if you need or want to keep your high-resolution data in a separate place (like on a server or at your imaging bureau). This is especially helpful with very large files (we leave the definition of "very large" up to you).

On the other hand, keeping track of a number of files can be a pain in the left buttock, and the links to the high-res images can be "broken" if you rename or move those files (see "Tip: Recovering Lost Links in DCS," below).

Tip: Naming Spot Colors. As we explain later in this chapter, if your DCS file includes spot colors, your page-layout software must also have colors named exactly the same way (yes, PageMaker, InDesign, and XPress import these names automatically when you import a DCS 2.0 file).

Tip: Recovering Lost Links in DCS. Occasionally, when working with multi-file DCS files, the master file gets lost or the link between the master file and the high-res color files is broken (this can happen if you move or rename the high-res files). Fixing broken pointers is often easy: Just open the master file in a text editor like BBEdit or NotePad and edit the file names in the lines that begin with "%%PlateFile".

However, don't fear if you lose the master file entirely; you can always reassemble the separate DCS files in Photoshop.

1. Open each of the high-res images in Photoshop. They're all EPS files, and they're all in Grayscale mode. Of course, opening these files will rasterize any vector data. Make sure that each file is flattened.

2. When all four of the files are open, select Merge Channels from the Channels palette's popout menu.

3. Make sure the mode is set to CMYK and the Channels field is set to 4 (see Figure 13-9); click OK.

4. Photoshop is pretty good at guessing which file should be set to which color channel in the Merge CMYK Channels dialog box, but if it guesses wrong, set the popup menus to the proper files.

Figure 13-9
Merging channels

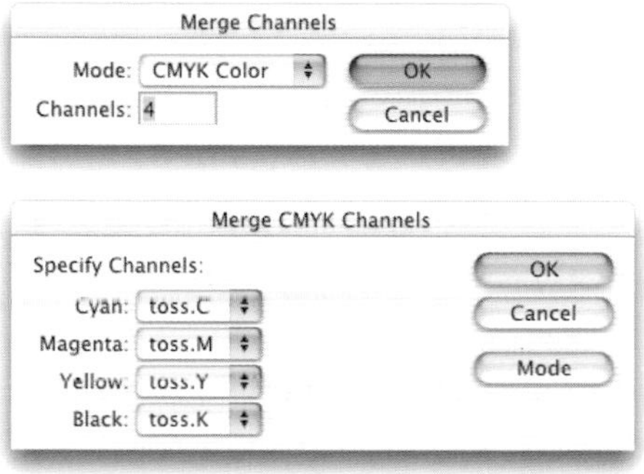

Merge Channels

Mode: CMYK Color

Channels: 4

OK

Cancel

Merge CMYK Channels

Specify Channels:

Cyan: toss.C

Magenta: toss.M

Yellow: toss.Y

Black: toss.K

OK

Cancel

Mode

When you click OK, Photoshop merges the four grayscale files into a single, high-resolution CMYK file. You can now create the five DCS files again, if you want. (Note that if you have spot colors in your DCS file, you'll have to add the additional channels manually, after you merge the CMYK channels.)

PDF (Portable Document Format)

We like to use the PDF file format whenever an image contains a significant amount of vector data (like text) that we want to maintain as sharp-edged vectors in the final output. While text is rasterized in TIFF files (making the edges pixelated) and converted to outlines in EPS files (making them slow to print if there's a lot of text), PDF files handle text beautifully. Best of all, you can embed a font into your PDF file, so it will display and print correctly wherever it goes.

PDF is also an excellent format for sending proofs or samples to clients. Not only can you include password protection, but you can create multi-page (multi-image) documents very easily; see "PDF Presentation," a bit later in this chapter.

But as much as we like PDF, it's not a perfect file format. Some programs still don't import Photoshop's PDF files very well. And note that Photoshop can save transparency in a PDF or spot colors in a PDF, but it can't yet handle both.

Round-tripping. When you save an image in the Photoshop PDF format, you're offered a whole mess o' options (see Figure 13-10). Some of these options actually override the options you chose in the Save As dialog box. For example, the Layers checkbox in the Save As dialog box normally

CompuServe GIF

The Graphics Interchange Format (commonly known as GIF, pronounced "jiff" or "giff," depending on your upbringing), was once the "house-brand" image file format of the CompuServe online information service. That's why this file format is listed as "Compuserve GIF" in Photoshop's Save As dialog box, even though GIF images have long since broken free of CompuServe's corporate walls and are now the industry standard across the Internet.

GIF files are designed for on-screen viewing, especially for images where file size is more important than quality, and for screens that only display 8-bit color (256 colors). Photoshop GIFs are always 8-bit indexed color images, making them quite reasonable for on-screen viewing, but totally unreasonable for printing. GIFs are automatically compressed using lossless LZW compression (see "Compressing Images," later in this chapter). But we never save a GIF file with the Save As dialog box; rather, we use the Save For Web feature (see Chapter 14, *Multimedia and the Web)*.

JPEG

Earlier in the chapter we talked about JPEG as a compression method within another file format—like JPEG DCS—but these days when most people say "JPEG" they're referring to the JPEG file format itself. While plenty of people use JPEG images for prepress work, the vast majority of JPEG images are found on the Web. The only problem with using the JPEG format for printing is that it's lossy (see "Compressing Images," later in this chapter). We recommend only using JPEG files in a prepress work-flow if it's essential that you drastically limit your file sizes (perhaps you have limited RAM or hard drive space, or your weekly rag has 800 images). Note that if you do save your files in a JPEG format, it's important not to open them and save them repeatedly—each time you save a JPEG file it further degrades.

Note that neither XPress nor PageMaker nor InDesign actually sends the JPEG information to the printer for decompression (as they do with JPEG-encoded EPSs). Instead, they decompress it and send it down just as they would a TIFF file. So you get the hard disk savings, but it actually takes longer every time you print the file because the printing program has to decompress the JPEG image each time.

JPEGs on the Web are a different matter. JPEGs are ubiquitous on the Internet because they're the only good way to display full color (24-bit) images in a Web page. We discuss JPEG images and how to make them in Chapter 14, *Multimedia and the Web.*

Niche File Formats

As we noted back in the Preface, this book only covers a fraction of the potential uses of Photoshop—those centered around production. People use this program for so many different things that we couldn't hope to cover them all here. In the last two sections, we discussed each of the file formats that are relevant for professionals who are putting images on paper, film, or the Web. You, however, might be doing something interesting, different, or just plain odd. Don't worry; Photoshop can probably still accommodate you.

While some of the following file formats appear in the Format popup menu in the Save As dialog box in the default shipping version of Photoshop, others are only available when you have loaded their plug-in from the Optional Plug-ins folder on the Photoshop or Creative Suite install discs (it's inside the Goodies folder).

Alias. Do you use Alias/Wavefront software for 3D rendering? Well, here's the file format for you: Photoshop can read the Alias .pix file format.

Amiga IFF. The Amiga computer story reads like that of the Tucker car or the PublishIt! desktop publishing software. Most people have never heard of these products, much less realized how great they were. Perhaps out of a sense of obligation to the would-be contender, or perhaps from a real need in the market (though we don't see it), Photoshop still lets you open and save in the Amiga IFF format. However, unless you really need it, or you want to see a format that features rectangular rather than square pixels, ignore it.

Cineon. Kodak developed the Cineon file format for handling high-bit images (it's actually a 10-bit format). We're told Photoshop can open Cineon files, though we've never tried. Photoshop offers you the Cineon file format when you save a 16-bits-per-channel image. But as far as we can tell, Cineon is a dying format, so we don't bother with it.

ElectricImage. ElectricImage is a powerful 3D rendering program. Photoshop can read these native files if you install the optional plug-in.

Filmstrip. Video, film, and animation all have a similar popular appeal, and the tools that let mere mortals create this sort of stuff (like Adobe Premiere or iMovie) are everywhere these days. But that doesn't mean that programs that create or edit still images will go away. For what is video but a bunch of still images strung together over time?

Adobe Premiere and AfterEffects let you save movies in a file format that Photoshop can open, called Filmstrip. You can then edit each frame individually in Photoshop, save the file out again, and import the clip in the video/animation program. This technique not only lets you make small retouching changes, but even perform rotoscoping (a form of animation), colorizing, or any number of other special effects.

When you open a Filmstrip file in Photoshop, it looks like a tall and narrow noodle. But when you double-click on the Zoom tool to scroll in to 100-percent view, you can see each image frame clearly, along with its time and frame code. Note that changing the file's size, resolution, or pixel dimensions may be disastrous, or at least unpredictable. Instead, constrain your edits to the pixels that are already there.

HDR file formats. When you're dealing with High Dynamic Range (HDR) files—which use 32 bits per channel—Photoshop can read and write several additional file formats:

▶ The LogLUV format, developed by Silicon Graphics (SGI)

▶ The Radiance HDR file format, used by the popular Radiance raytracing UNIX software

▶ The OpenEXR file format, which is the house-standard at Industrial Light & Magic for motion picture special effects

You can also save HDR files in the TIFF, Photoshop (PSD), Large Document Format (PSB), and Portable Bitmap (PBM) formats. We cover HDR in more detail in Chapter 12, *Essential Image Techniques*.

JPEG 2000. In the twilight years of the twentieth century, a bunch of smart folks got together to discuss the future of the JPEG file format. They came up with a new specification for JPEG—labeled JPEG 2000—that does a better job of compressing images (more compression, less image degradation). Plus, unlike JPEG, JPEG 2000 can handle high-bit files, grayscale files, full 8-bit transparency, and even an option for lossless compression.

Unfortunately, just because there's a better format available doesn't mean people will rush to use it. As we go to press, no page-layout application can import JPEG 2000 files (though we assume the next version of InDesign will), nor can any Web browser display them without a specialized plug-in.

Nevertheless, always ahead of the curve, Photoshop can read and write JPEG 2000 files. Actually, it can read and write a flavor of JPEG 2000 it calls JPF. But it can only do so when you have installed the plug-in, found in the Optional Plug-ins folder, inside the Goodies folder on the Photoshop install disc. JPF files aren't compatible with most other JPEG 2000 software (which usually reads a flavor called JP2), but JPF offers more compression options than JP2, including the ability to JPF files compatible with JP2 readers—at the expense of a slightly larger file size.

Once JPEG 2000 support is more widespread, we think this file format should replace the use of JPEG images in the prepress industry, where quality is key. (Note that we said it "should," as in "it ought to, if there's anyone out there who needs compressed files but still cares about quality.")

MacPaint. The MacPaint format is the most basic of all graphic formats on the Macintosh, but it's so outdated that there's almost no reason to use it anymore. Paint files (more rarely called PNTG, or "pee-en-tee-gee," files) are black and white (one bit per pixel), 72 pixels per inch, 8-by-10 inches (576-by-720 pixels). That's it. No more and no less.

PCX. Whereas many formats (such as TIFF) are industry standards, the PCX format was developed by ZSoft Corporation, the creators of Publisher's Paintbrush. It's a granddaddy of bitmapped formats, predating Windows 1.0 when it hit the streets as part of PC Paintbrush. The current version of PCX supports adjustable dimensions and resolutions, and 24-bit color, but only a 256-color palette (indexed to 24-bit color), up from earlier 4- and 13-color versions. We typically recommend using TIFF files instead of PCX whenever possible.

Portable Bitmap (PBM). Some Unix tweaks save their images in the Portable Bitmap format (.pbm, .pgm, .ppm, or .pnm). Even HDR files can be saved in the PBM format.

Pixar. To understand why Photoshop still saves and opens Pixar files, you have to understand that Photoshop was born from the minds of Thomas and John Knoll as a way to do some of the low-level grunt work that goes into the cool special effects produced at George Lucas's Industrial Light and Magic (ILM), which is a close cousin of Pixar. As far as we're concerned, someone should put this file format out of our misery.

Pixel Paint. David used Pixel Paint once, a very long time ago. On the odd chance that you have a Pixel Paint file sitting around, it's good to know that Photoshop can read it with the optional plug-in.

PSB (Large Document format). While early versions of Photoshop limited your images to 30,000 pixels per side (2.5 GB), Photoshop CS lifted this to 300,000 pixels per side (a whopping 251 GB file). We only know of a handful of people who need this, including our friends in the intelligence community (who are reading this book over your shoulder right now), and our friend Stephen Johnson, who is using a scanning back camera to make hyper-resolution panoramas at $7,500 \times 75,000$ pixels each. While the native Photoshop file format still tops out at 30,000 pixels per side, you can save these truly huge files as TIFF files (up to 4 GB), Photoshop Raw files (not to be confused with Camera Raw), or—the best option—in the Large Document (PSB) format.

To save a PSB file, turn on the Enable Large Document Format checkbox in the File Handling panel of the Preferences dialog box. (Perhaps PSB stands for "Photoshop Behemoth"?) Then, choose Large Document Format from the Format popup menu in the Save As dialog box. PSB files support layers, effects, and any other Photoshop feature. However, they can only be opened in Photoshop CS or later.

PNG (Portable Network Graphic). For a while there it looked like the GIF file format would take over the Internet, and therefore the world. Then, in early 1995, CompuServe and Unisys shocked the world by demanding that developers whose software wrote or read GIF files pay a royalty fee for the right to use the format. Legally, they were entitled; but no one had had to pay before, and it jarred the electronic publishing community enough that a group of dedicated individuals decided to come up with a new file format for Web graphics.

The result of their work is the PNG format (which is pronounced "ping," and officially stands for "Portable Network Graphic," though it unofficially stands for "PNG's Not GIF"). Not only is it a free format that any developer can use, but it does much more than GIF.

For instance, PNG can support both 8-bit indexed color and full 24-bit color. Where GIF can include 1-bit transparency (where each pixel is either transparent or not), PNG has full 8 bit transparency with alpha channels, so a graphic could be partially opaque in some areas. PNG also includes some limited ability to handle color management on the Internet, by recording monitor gamma and chromaticity. There are many other features, too (among which is the significant bonus of, unlike GIF, having a relatively unambiguous pronunciation).

Unfortunately, PNG has never been widely accepted by users or Web browsers, and the patents on GIF (which were based on GIF's LZW compression scheme) expired back in 2004. Our prediction is that PNG will slowly fade away over the next couple of years.

PICT Resource. Are you authoring multimedia or developing software on the Macintosh? If so, you may find yourself needing to save an image into the resource fork of a file. Here's where the PICT Resource file format comes in. To be honest, it's not really a different file format; the Macintosh lets you place PICT information in the data or resource fork of a file. Photoshop, however, is a convenient way to move the image from one to the other. (Windows programs don't have a resource fork, so PC users can ignore this file format.)

Note that Photoshop lets you open PICT resources in two different ways. First, if the file has a PICT resource numbered 256, Photoshop lets you open that particular resource directly from the Open dialog box. If there are multiple PICT resources, you can access them only by selecting PICT Resource from the Import submenu (under the File menu).

Raw. The last file format that we can even remotely recommend using is the file format of last resort: the Raw format. (Don't confuse this with the Camera Raw format, which Photoshop can read but not write. See Chapter 11, *Building a Digital Workflow*, for more on Camera Raw.) If you've ever traveled in a foreign country, you've probably found yourself in situations where you and the person in front of you share no common language. The answer? Reduce communication to gestures and sounds.

The Raw format is a way to read or write image data in a "language" that Photoshop doesn't know. It relies on the basics of bitmapped images (see Figure 13-12).

▶ All bitmapped images are rectangular grids of pixels.

▶ Some bitmapped images have header information at the beginning of the data.

▶ Color data is usually either interleaved (such as alternating red, green, blue, red, green, blue, and so on) or noninterleaved (such as all the red information, then all the green, and finally all the blue).

If you're trying to import from or export to some strange computer system, you may have to rely on the Raw format because that system might not know from TIFF, EPS, or any other normal, everyday file format. This is becoming less of a problem as most mainframe systems (especially the imaging systems that are used for scientific or medical imaging) learn the newer, better file formats we've been discussing up until now.

Note that Photoshop can only read data using the Raw data format if it's saved as binary data; hexadecimal is out.

Figure 13-12
Opening Raw data

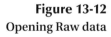

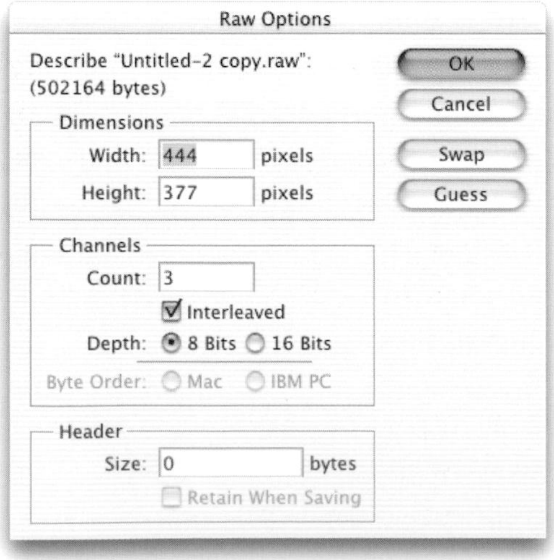

Raw Options

Describe "Untitled–2 copy.raw":
(502164 bytes)

OK

Cancel

Dimensions

Width: 444   pixels

Height: 377   pixels

Swap

Guess

Channels

Count: 3

☑ Interleaved

Depth: ⦿ 8 Bits ◯ 16 Bits

Byte Order: ◯ Mac ◯ IBM PC

Header

Size: 0   bytes

☐ Retain When Saving

Tip: Make Photoshop Guess for Raw Data. Okay, someone gives you a file and you find you can't open it using any of Photoshop's standard file format options. You decide to take a leap and attempt the Raw format. But when you ask your so-called friend about the file's vital signs—"What are the pixel dimensions? Interleaved or noninterleaved color? Is there a header?"—he just stares at you blankly.

Fortunately, Photoshop can do a little guessing for you. If you click the Guess button in the Open as Raw dialog box when the Width and Height fields are blank, Photoshop figures out a likely height/width combination for the image. If it's a color image, you need to know if it's RGB (three channels) or CMYK (four channels).

If there's a header and your friend doesn't know how big it is (in bytes), then it's probably a lost cause. On the other hand, if your friend knows the pixel dimensions but not the header, you can click the Guess button while the Header field is blank.

RLA. Wavefront software can also export in the .rla file format, which Photoshop supports.

Scitex CT. Whether to use the Scitex CT file format is a no-brainer: if you own a Creo Scitex system or are trying to output via a Scitex system, you may want to save your document in this format as the last stage before printing. If you don't have any contact with a Creo Scitex system, ignore this one.

It may be important to note that the Scitex CT format is not actually the CT ("continuous tone") format that Scitex folks usually talk about. It's actually the Handshake format, which is less proprietary and more common (even QuarkXPress can import these files). Scitex CT files are always CMYK or grayscale; however, Photoshop lets you save RGB images in this format, too. We don't know why. If you can figure out a good use for them, let us know.

SGIRGB. Yes, the SGI in the name SGIRGB is the SGI of the SGI computer company. We just like typing SGI. But we don't use this format. If you do, just make sure your files have one of these file name extensions: .sgi, .rgb, .rgba, or .bw.

ter compression at the cost of more intense calculation. However, other than JPEG 2000—which is based on wavelet compression—Photoshop doesn't support these compression schemes without a third-party plug-in. For example, the Genuine Fractals plug-in, originally developed by Altamira and currently sold by OnOne Software (after a long line of owners, including LizardTech). This has won a loyal following among the large-format print crowd for its ability to upsample files with noticeably less degradation than other methods. OnOne's pxl SmartScale does a similar thing—taking low- to medium-resolution images, compressing them, and then enlarging them with minimum visual degradation.

While these plug-ins' more aggressive compression is lossy, the artifacts that it creates are less objectionable to the eye than those created by JPEG, on the one hand, or overly aggressive upsampling on the other. A lossless compression method is also offered. However, while fractal compression artifacts look natural in images, they look strange on sharp synthetic edges such as type.

Bruce has used Genuine Fractals to upsample 75 MB scans to the 300+ MB required for a 30-by-40-inch print at 300 ppi, and he thinks the result looks more natural than using Photoshop's Bicubic interpolation. But while it can be very useful for this kind of upsampling, the lengthy compression times and relatively low compression ratios of Genuine Fractals make it less appealing as a general compression utility.

To Compress or Not to Compress

Over the years, we've found only a few universal truths. One of those is: "Fast, Cheap, or Good: you can have any two of the three." Compression is certainly no exception to this rule. Compressing files can be a great way to save hard drive space (read: "save money") and sometimes to cut down on printing times (read: "save more money"). But compressing and decompressing files also takes time (read: "lose the money that you just saved").

Optimally, if you have way too much hard drive space and you transfer your files from place to place on DVD discs, you may never need or want to compress your images. Otherwise, you may want to use a lossless compressed file format (Zip-compressed TIFF) for some of your images. If you really need to save space, you might choose a lossy file format (like JPEG).

Bruce uses ZIP-compressed TIFF (with compression on both the layers and the background) as his archival format, except for those relatively rare occasions when he's in too much of a hurry to take the speed hit. David still has restless dreams about fitting files on 400 K disks in 1985, so he tends to use lossless compression on all but the smallest files. When we absolutely need to save a file in a lossy compressed file format, we use JPEG, but we rarely use anything other than Maximum quality in JPEG—we find the increase in compression at Good, Medium, or Low simply isn't worth the degradation in quality (except for Web images). Ultimately, storage space is getting so inexpensive these days that it's almost silly to worry about compression. Writing 650 MB CDs or 5.2 GB DVDs is now so inexpensive that you might as well buy one and another for your dog. If time equals money, then time spent compressing and decompressing files (whether it's manual or automatic) is money down the big porcelain doughnut.

Archiving

You may have worked with programs such as StuffIt or ZipIt. These tools all have the same function: to compress files—any kind of files—and save space on your hard drive. This sort of compression is called *archiving* because people typically use it on files that they're not currently using.

Archiving a file is like folding up a piece of paper and putting it into an envelope. It takes a little time to fold it up (compress it) and a little time to unfold it (decompress it), and while it's in the envelope, you can't read it. The archive file (the "envelope" that contains the compressed file) takes up less room on your hard drive, but to work on the enclosed file, you have to decompress it. Both Mac OS X 10.3 (and later) and Windows XP have Zip compression built in.

All archival compression programs use lossless compression methods, so you never have to worry about degrading the image. However, that also means they may not compress down as much as you'd like. ZIP-compressed TIFFs, for example, generally won't get any smaller. If we need to send a number of images to someone via the Internet, we generally zip them first, but that's mostly to get them into one file, and to provide a degree of protection from the munging behavior that various Internet gateways are prone to exhibiting.

File Metadata

Remember the good old days, when you could jot down notes on the back of a photograph with a soft pencil? Storing information about your pictures is essential for a robust workflow, but where's the pencil in an all-digital world? It's called *metadata*—data about data—and in Photoshop it lives hidden inside or alongside image files in a format called XMP (eXtensible Metadata Platform).

(By the way, the word "Metadata" was coined and trademarked by Jack Myers in the early 1970s, back when the word didn't mean anything. However, many people argue that the word has since become part of common language, and is therefore no longer enforceable as a trademark. But if Jack ever prevails, we suggest people use the word "datad'data"—which is more fun to say anyway.)

File Info. Photoshop offers two paths to an image's metadata: the File Info dialog box (choose File Info from the File menu, or press Command-Option-I) and Adobe Bridge's Metadata palette (in earlier versions, this was in Photoshop's File Browser). Bruce likes the Metadata palette because it lets him see and edit information about his images without first opening them (we cover this palette in Chapter 11, *Building a Digital Workflow*). This makes it very easy to perform tasks like adding a copyright notice to 50 images in one fell swoop—it's the only way to add metadata to multiple images simultaneously. David likes the File Info dialog box because he likes the layout better (see Figure 13-14) and he tends to have images open while editing their metadata anyway.

By default, the File Info dialog box has seven panels of metadata, including two that display camera data, one that can capture the file's history, and some general information about the image (title, copyright information, keywords, and so on). The metadata in the Camera Data panels isn't editable (it's captured by the camera itself). Most of the other fields are editable.

If you need to store other sorts of specialized data (perhaps you want to store GPS data or model release information for each image), you can create custom File Info panels relatively easily by editing XML files (there's instructions on how to do this in the Goodies folder on the Photoshop install disc) or using Pound Hill Software's MetaLab utility.

Figure 13-14
File Info dialog box

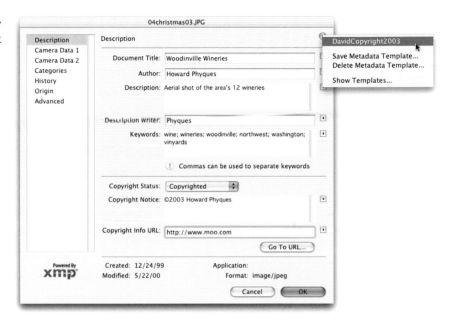

Tip: Move Data to the Page. If you use other Adobe products, you may notice that InDesign CS and Illustrator CS each have an identical File Info dialog box. InDesign CS also has a Info palette that can read the XMP data inside imported images. This means you can use Photoshop to insert metadata such as copyright, image description, and photographer, and then later retrieve that information from within InDesign. You know you're in a digital workflow when you no long receive e-mails or phone calls saying, "Hey, don't forget that the copyright notice for that picture of the girl on a bicycle should be . . . ."

See *Real World InDesign* for more information about using metadata in Adobe InDesign.

Metadata templates. Generally, much of the metadata you'll want to store in your images is repeated information—data that is the same for lots of different images. Fortunately, you don't have to type that stuff repeatedly. Photoshop remembers recently typed metadata for each field in the File Info dialog box. To recall something you typed recently, click on the little triangle to the right of the metadata field.

You can also save metadata templates that include a collection of metadata entries. (These aren't really "templates"; they're just a way to fill out a bunch of metadata fields automatically.) The most common example is a template for your copyright information where you want to change three fields: Copyright Status, Copyright Notice, and Copyright Info URL. To do this, set just these fields (leave the others in the dialog box blank), choose Save Metadata Template from the dialog box's popout menu, and give the template a name.

Later, when you want to apply these metadata to another image, just select the template's name from the top of the popout menu. Photoshop appends the metadata template to whatever is already in the File Info palette; it won't delete any data that is already there but it will replace data with the data from the template. (That is, if there was already copyright information saved in the file, the metadata template would replace it with the new data.)

History. Imagine if you took a picture with your digital camera and later had to admit the image as evidence in court. A lawyer might jump up and ask, "How do we know this file hasn't been digitally altered?" If you really care about recording everything that was done to your images, you can turn on the History Log checkbox in the General panel of the Preferences dialog box. You can tell Photoshop where to save the information (Metadata saves it in each file's metadata; Text File saves it to disk). You can also tell Photoshop what to remember.

▶ Sessions just saves when the image was opened and closed. We have no idea how this would be helpful for anyone.

▶ Concise saves the names of basic steps. So it records "Crop" or "Levels" but not how much was cropped or what got a levels tweak.

▶ Detailed records specific actions, such as "Levels Adjustment, Blue Channel, Gamma 0.82".

Generally, if you're going to turn on the History Log, we think it makes the most sense to set it to Detailed. However, if you're going to do a lot of work on a file, it could increase the file size a bit; so you might want to save the history in a log file rather than metadata. (On the other hand, if you're saving it for legal purposes, it probably makes much more sense to save it in the file's metadata.)

Metadata in PDF files. Earlier in this chapter we mentioned that when you save your image as a PDF file, you can give it password protection. If you choose Acrobat 6-level protection, you can choose whether or not you want the metadata to be secure. For example, you might want your PDF files to be password protected, but want to be able to search for them based on keywords or description from within the File Browser.

Output Methods

"The time has come," the Walrus paraphrased, "to speak of many things. Of zeros and ones, pixels and fun, and lastly, imaging." Though Lewis Carroll and his oysters never had to contend with such ephemeral things as pixels, we do. And, as you're probably aware, a pixel's greatest strength is also its greatest weakness: it doesn't really exist, except as electrical current in RAM or as magnetic force on disk. However, sooner or later, we all have to capture those wily devils in a more permanent form, such as paper or film. (We'll discuss multimedia and the Web in the next chapter.)

In the grand tradition of verbing nouns, the term used to include printing, exposing, displaying, or any other process of turning digital images into analog, static ones is *imaging*. The rest of this chapter is dedicated to issues specific to imaging your images, whether from Photoshop or another program, such as Adobe InDesign or QuarkXPress. But before we get into the nitty-gritty, we should cover a little background first: the distinction between contone and halftone output.

Contone vs. Halftone

We all live in an illusion (and not just the Buddhist *samsara* that Bruce keeps muttering about): when we see a leaf, our eye makes us think we see a continuous range of colors and tones, continuous lines, and continuous shapes. That's an illusion, because the eye simply doesn't work that way. Without going too far into visual physiology, suffice it to say that the eye works much like an incredibly high-resolution digital camera.

Rods and cones (each a distinct light sensor, like a CCD) cover the back of our eye (the retina), and convert the light that enters our eye into electrical signals. Our brain then—starting with the optic nerve—tries to make sense of all those impulses (you can think of them as zeros and ones). The end effect is that our brains fool us into thinking we're seeing a wash of colors and shapes, when in fact we're simply seeing over a hundred million pixels of information.

And it turns out that because the brain is already so good at fooling us into thinking that we're seeing detail where there is none, or continuous colors where there aren't any, we can fool it even more. The process of imaging data is inherently one of fooling ourselves, and some methods are better than others. The two primary methods of imaging are halftone and contone. Let's take a closer look at each of them.

Halftones

Printing presses, platesetters, inkjet printers, and laser printers all share one thing: they only print on or off, black or white. They can't print shades of gray. To print 15 different colors, you'd have to run the paper through the machine 15 times with different-colored inks, or toners, or whatever. However, lithographers figured out in the late nineteenth century that they could create a tint of a colored ink by breaking the color down into a whole bunch of little spots. Our brain plays along with the game and tells us that we really are seeing the shade of gray, not just spots (see Figure 13-15). These spots make up the *halftone* of the image.

There are a number of ways to halftone an image, but the most common is to combine printer dots—those tiny square marks that platesetters or laser printers make, sometimes as small as $\frac{1}{3,600}$ of an inch—together into larger spots (see Figure 13-16). The darker the gray level, the larger the spot—the more dots are turned on. Each spot sits on a giant grid, so the center of each spot is always the same distance from its neighbors. (The spots don't really get closer or farther from each other, just bigger and smaller; see Figure 13-17.)

You can print multicolor images by overlaying two or more color halftones (typically cyan, magenta, yellow, and black). Again, our eyes fool us into thinking we're seeing thousands of colors when, in fact, we're only seeing four.

David coauthored a book with Glenn Fleishman, Conrad Chavez, and Steve Roth, called *Real World Scanning and Halftones (3rd edition)*, that covers halftoning in much more detail than we can get into here. However, we should at least cover the basics. Every halftone has three components, or attributes: screen frequency, screen angle, and spot shape.

Figure 13-15
Halftoning

Figure 13-16
A representation of
digital halftone
cells (spots)

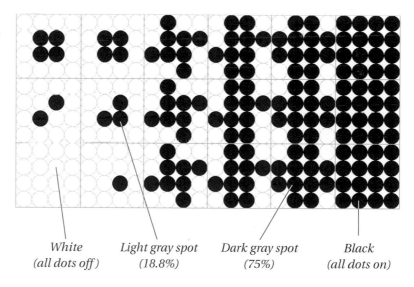

*White
(all dots off)*   *Light gray spot
(18.8%)*   *Dark gray spot
(75%)*   *Black
(all dots on)*

Figure 13-17
Tint percentages

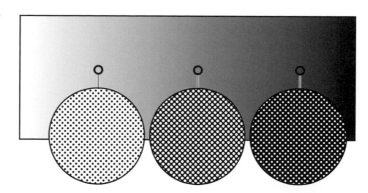

Screen frequency. Halftone spots on a grid are like bitmapped images; they have resolution, too. The more spots you cram together within an inch, the tighter the grid, the smaller the spots, and so on. The number of halftone spots per inch is called *halftone screen frequency*. Higher frequencies (small spots, tightly packed, like those in glossy magazines) look smoother because the eye isn't distracted as much by the spots. However, because of limits in digital halftoning, you can achieve fewer levels of gray at a given output resolution. Also, higher screen frequencies have much more dot gain on a printing press, so tints clog up and go muddy more quickly (see "Image Differences," later in this chapter).

Lower screen frequencies (as in newspapers) are rough-looking, but they're easier to print, and you can achieve many levels of gray at lower output resolutions. Screen frequencies are specified in lines per inch, or *lpi* (though we're really talking about "rows of spots per inch").

Screen angle. Halftone grids are not like bitmapped images; you can rotate them to any angle you want. (In a bitmapped image, the pixels are always in a horizontal/vertical orientation.) Halftones of grayscale images are typically printed at a 45-degree angle because the spots are least noticeable at this angle. However, color images are more complex.

When you overlap halftone grids, as in color printing, you may get distracting moiré ("mwah-RAY") patterns that ruin the illusion. In order to minimize these patterns, it's important to use specific angles. The greater

Overriding Screen Settings

When you send a grayscale or color bitmapped image to a PostScript printer, the computer inside the printer converts the image into a halftone. That means that the printer sets the halftone screen frequency, angle, and spot shape. Sometimes you might want to override the printer's default settings to use your own halftone screening information. Unfortunately, while most programs offer you ways to do this, many printers just ignore the application's halftoning instructions.

Instead, platesetters and imagesetters usually use screening "filters" that catch all screening instructions, and replace the frequency/angle combinations with similar (or not) built-in settings.

This is particularly important if you're trying to achieve a specialized spot shape. However, in most cases, you'd want to use a custom halftone spot shape for special effects at somewhat low halftone frequencies. In these cases, we recommend people simply create the halftone in Photoshop rather than relying on the output device for it. (See the sidebar "Making Halftones in Photoshop," later in this chapter, for information on how to do this.)

Figure 13-18
Spot shape

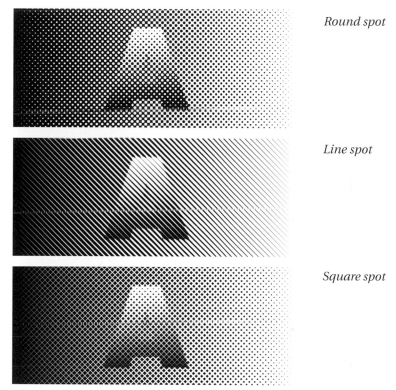

Round spot

Line spot

Square spot

the angle difference between overlapping screens (you can't get them any farther apart than 45 degrees), the smaller the moiré pattern. With four-color process printing, the screens are typically printed 30 degrees apart at 15, 45, and 75 degrees (yellow, the lightest ink, is generally printed at 0 degrees—15 degrees offset from cyan).

Spot shape. The last attribute of halftones is the shape of each spot. The spot may be circular, square, a straight line, or even little pinwheels (see Figure 13-18). The standard PostScript spot shape is a round black spot in the highlights, square at 50 percent, and an inverted circle (white on black) in the shadows. Changing the shape of the spot is rarely necessary. However, if you're producing cosmetics catalogs, or need to solve tonal shift problems printing on newsprint at coarse screen frequencies (to use two examples), controlling the halftone spot shape can definitely improve the quality of your job.

Contone Output

With binary devices such as platesetters and printers, you need to use a halftone to fool the eye into seeing shades of gray because you can't create color or gray pixels. With a contone device, you *can* vary the color or gray shade of each pixel. Continuous-tone imaging, usually called *contone*, is different from halftone imaging in two other ways.

▶   The pixels touch each other so that without very close inspection no paper or clear film shows through between marks.

▶   Each pixel is a specific color, made by building up varying densities of primary colors in the same spot.

The most common contone imaging device is your computer monitor. The color of each pixel you see (or don't see, if the screen's resolution is high enough) is made by mixing together varying amounts of red, green, and blue. For example, to make a pixel more red, the monitor must increase the number of electrons that are bombarding the red element of the pixel.

There's no threat of moiré patterns, because there are no grids involved. But then again, there's no chance of mass-reproducing the image, as no printing press can handle continuous-tone images (see "Hybrid Color Screening," on the next page). Aside from the monitor, there are two other types of contone devices that we should mention: film recorders and dye-sub printers.

Film recorders. A film recorder such as a Solitaire or a Fire1000 creates continuous-tone images in one of two ways. Some film recorders place a very high-resolution grayscale monitor in front of a piece of film, and then image the same piece of film three times—the first time with a red filter in front of the monitor, and then with a blue, and finally with a green filter. The same areas of the film are imaged each time, but with varying densities of each color.

Other film recorders color pixels in film by adjusting the amount of three bright light beams—each colored by a red, green, or blue filter—while they focus on a point on the film. Again, unlike halftones, each "pixel" on the film abuts the next, and is set to a specific color.

Film recorders are typically very high resolution devices, ranging from 1,024 (1 K) to 16,384 (16 K) pixels across. High resolutions are necessary because they're often imaging small pieces of film such as 35 mm slides or 4-by-5-inch film, though 16 K film recorders are usually reserved for writing 8-by-10 film.

Dye-sub printers. A second type of contone device is a dye-sub printer, which overlays varying amounts of ink to build a color. Dye-subs are typically 300-dpi devices, but the lack of halftoning or white space between each pixel makes images look surprisingly photorealistic at this seemingly low resolution.

Because of the lack of resolution, hard-edged objects such as type or line art may appear jaggy, but the soft edges and blends found in natural images usually appear nearly indistinguishable from photographs.

Hybrid Color Screening

There is one more method of simulating a "real-world" continuous-tone image: using tiny spots to simulate tints and colors, but making those spots so small and so diffuse that the image appears contone. The three primary examples of this sort of imaging are: high-resolution inkjet; color laser; and stochastic screening, either on a conventional press or on a direct-digital press such as the Indigo E-Print or the Agfa Chromapress.

Inkjet. In inkjet technology, the printer sprays a fine mist of colored inks onto paper. The amount of each ink is varied, much like a contone printer, but it results in tiny spots on paper, often with paper white showing through, more like halftones. While older low-resolution inkjets couldn't be mistaken for contone imaging devices, prints from current high-resolution inkjets are so smooth that for all practical purposes they can be considered contone devices. This holds true for both large-format inkjets like the Epson 9800 and their desktop-size siblings. They use tiny droplet sizes of four, six, or more inks, deployed with very sophisticated error-diffusion screening, to produce results that are indistinguishable to the naked eye from a true continuous-tone print.

Several vendors now supply inkjet cartridges with custom inks for effects such as quadtones built with four gray inks, while others supply third-party color inks either in cartridges or in bulk. But whether you use OEM or third-party inks, a major problem with most inkjet printers is that it's almost impossible to control the ink percentages exactly, so that if (for example) you ask for 50-percent cyan, you get exactly 50-percent cyan. If you send CMYK data to the printer, it typically converts the data to RGB and then back to CMYK at some point in the print stream. Even if you attach a PostScript RIP to the printer, there's little chance you'll get exactly the values you asked for. (Or, if you do, it's at the cost of the high-quality screening, and your image has dots like golf balls.)

Ultimately, CMYK RIPs are sometimes useful for inkjets used as proofing devices; but in our experience, if your goal is to produce final photorealistic output, you're better off using the Quartz (Mac) or GDI (Windows) drivers and feeding RGB data to the printer. That said, we have obtained stunning results with some of the RGB RIPs designed for photographic output on inkjets, such as Colorbyte Software's ImagePrint. But we use them as much for workflow reasons—it's easy to gang several images onto the sheet, for example—as for the real but fairly subtle improvement in image quality.

Tip: Printing PostScript to a Non-PostScript Printer. Few inkjets have PostScript RIPs built in to them, and we haven't been particularly happy with the software RIPs that you can buy along with the printers. So when we need to print from QuarkXPress or some other PostScript-dependent program, we create an Acrobat PDF file of our document. Then we print the file from Acrobat (which acts like a PostScript RIP) to the inkjet. However, Adobe InDesign CS prints beautifully through most inkjets' raster drivers, so we just print from InDesign's native application file rather than messing around with this PDF workaround.

Stochastic screening. Earlier in this chapter we discussed how halftones are formed by clumping together groups of printer dots into a regularly spaced grid of spots. However, we oversimplified; this is actually only one way to make a halftone. Remember, a halftone is just a way to simulate tints or colors with tiny spots. Another method of halftoning is a diffusion dither (see Figure 13-19).

Diffusion dithers can create near-contone quality, but they've been avoided until recently because they're often difficult to create and print, especially for full-color work. However, digital imaging has changed all this. Various vendors have created proprietary dithering techniques, usually called *stochastic screening*, that let you mass-reproduce contone-like images from a printing press. Note that proprietary stochastic screening is a type of "frequency modulated" (FM) screen, but it's certainly not the same as Photoshop's diffusion dither feature.

Figure 13-19
Diffusion dither
as halftone

*Grayscale image
screened by PostScript
at 133 lpi*

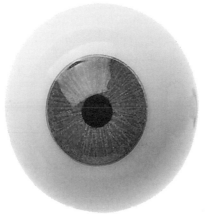

*250-dpi diffusion
dither from Photoshop*

*1000-dpi,
40-lpi halftone
from Photoshop*

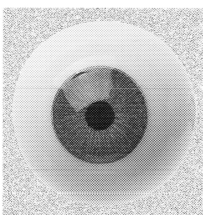

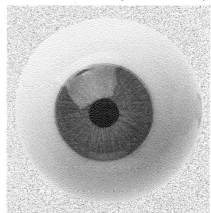

Stochastic screening is very cool for a number of reasons, including:

► Image content that has been difficult to reproduce using traditional
halftoning methods—such as fabric or other fine-detail objects—is
much more easily reproduced with stochastic screening because it
eliminates *subject moiré*, where the pattern in the subject creates a
moiré by interfering with the regular pattern of the halftone screen.

► You can print with more than four colored inks without worrying about
moiré patterns due to conflicting halftone angles (there are no angles
in a diffusion dither).

► It's much easier to reproduce near-contone images. Some printers
are even getting good results with low-resolution stochastic screens
printed on low-quality paper.

► You can print more detail at a given image resolution. While the ideal image resolution is around 300 ppi, if all you have is a low-resolution Web graphic, stochastic gives better quality than regular halftones.

On the other hand, stochastic screening, like any new technology, can bring with it a host of new troubles ("challenges," says the ever-optimistic David). For instance, stochastic screening raises the concept of dot gain to new heights, causing many to retreat from printing with it soon after seeing their first printed images appear as big ink blobs. The size of the stochastic dot also limits the amount of highlight detail you can reproduce, which is why many inkjet printers add Light Cyan and Light Magenta inks—the dots aren't any smaller, but they appear smaller because they're printed with the lighter inks.

You can create stochastic screens for your images with several pieces of software, including Isis Imaging's IceFields utility. Or you can use any

Making Halftones in Photoshop

When you print an image from Photoshop or from a page-layout program, the PostScript printer converts your grayscale or color data into halftones. That doesn't mean, though, that you couldn't do it yourself in Photoshop if you really wanted to. In fact, there are a few times when it's advantageous to convert images into halftones in Photoshop.

► You are printing to a non-Post-Script printer and you want controllable halftones and smaller image files.

► You want a diffusion dither—a stippled screen very similar to the stochastic screening available on many imagesetters,
but useful for lower-resolution output as well (see Figure 13-19, on the previous page, for an example).

► You want to create special half-tone-like effects.

► You want to learn about how halftones work. Creating half-tones in Photoshop is a great way to learn what halftoning is all about. (When we do sem-inars, it's only when we show people how to do halftoning in Photoshop that they really understand what we've been talking about.)

Here's how to convert a gray-scale image into a halftone in Pho-
toshop (yes, this only works with grayscale images; if you're working on a color image, select Grayscale, or duplicate a color channel into a new grayscale document).

1. Select Bitmap from the Mode submenu under the Image menu (see Figure 13-20).

2. In the Bitmap dialog box, choose an output resolution appropriate for your output. All the same rules for line art images that we talked about back in Chapter 10, *Spot Colors and Duotones*, apply here.

   So if your final output is on a 600-dpi laser printer, you don't need more than 600-ppi image resolution. If your final output of a number of vendors' built-in platesetter screening algorithms such as Agfa's CrystalRaster or Linotype-Hell's Diamond Screens.

Color laser printer. Most color laser printers use some kind of diffusion dither to simulate a very high screen frequency. We've found that it's almost always best to let the laser printer take care of the screening using its own proprietary algorithms, rather than doing it ourselves.

Controlling color on these devices isn't easy—where possible, we prefer to send a calibrated RGB image through a color management system (see Chapter 5, *Color Settings*). If you do want to create your own CMYK separations from Photoshop for a color laser device, the biggest potential pitfalls are specifying too high an ink density and underestimating dot gain. Color laser printers don't have dot gain in the usual sense, and they use dry toner or solid ink technology, so you might think that you could go all the way to a 400-percent total ink limit and 100-percent black ink

is on an imagesetter, you may need to raise this to 1000 or even 2000 ppi.

3. Select Halftone Screen from the Method menu in the Bitmap dialog box, and click OK. (While you're here, you should also check out the Diffusion option; it's a very different look.)

4. In the Halftone Screen dialog box, set the frequency, angle, and spot shape, then click OK.

If you don't like the halftone effect that results, you can undo the mode change and start over with different settings.

Note that once you halftone a grayscale image, you can no longer make many edits to it—no tonal adjustments, filters, or the like (there's nothing there for the tools

to work with). Also, you shouldn't scale the image, even a little, or you can expect to get very strange patterning when you print.

We generally let the RIP in the platesetter or imagesetter take

care of the screening for us. We never do this kind of Photoshop halftoning on color images (unless we're trying to create a special effect). But for drop shadows and the like, this is a great technique.

Figure 13-20 Bitmap dialog box

When you choose Halftone Screen in the Bitmap dialog box, the Halftone Screen dialog box provides screening options.

limit. If you do, you'll get very dense shadows and saturated colors that look as though they belong in some other image. As a starting point, try 260-percent total ink with an 85-percent black limit in the CMYK Setup dialog box.

Image Differences

Now that we've explored the various imaging methods, we should recap and highlight some of the different techniques you can use in building images suitable for output on halftone and contone devices. We say "recap," because we've mentioned most (if not all) of these in previous chapters, though never in one place.

Resolution. The first and foremost difference between contone and halftone imaging is the required image resolution. It's quite a bit harder to work out the resolution needed for halftone output than it is for contone, so we'll deal with halftone output first.

▶ **Resolution requirements for halftone output.** The resolution of the output device isn't directly relevant in determining the resolution you need for the image. It's the halftone screen frequency that matters. You never need an image resolution above two times (2×) the halftone screen frequency (and often you can get almost-equivalent results with as little as 1.2× or 1.4×). That means that even if you're printing on a 2400-dpi imagesetter, your image resolution can (and should) be much lower. For instance, printing at 150 lpi, you never need more than a 300-ppi image, and usually no higher than 225 ppi (we generally use the 1.5 multiplier; see Chapter 3, *Image Essentials*.)

▶ **Resolution requirements for contone output.** The resolution needed for a contone output device is easy to figure, but it can sometimes be hard to deliver. Your output resolution should simply match the resolution of the output device. If you're printing to a 300-dpi dye-sub printer, your image resolution should be 300 ppi. When printing to a 4 K film recorder, your image should have a horizontal measure of 4096 pixels, or about 60 MB for a 4-by-5 print. An 8 K film recorder really wants 240 MB—an 8192-by-10240-pixel image.

In truth, many high-resolution film recorders are more forgiving, and you can halve the resolution. For instance, we know of few people who actually send a 960 MB image to a 16 K film recorder, and we know quite a few who get good results sending a 60 MB file to an 8 K film recorder (about half the amount of data it "requires"). Sending less than a full 60 MB to a 4 K film recorder, however, is a much more marginal proposition. Make sure, though, that you send an integral multiple of the device's resolution. If you send 4095 pixels to a device that wants 4096, it'll either barf when it gets the file, or you'll get some very strange interpolation artifacts.

The appropriate resolution for stochastic screening is less clear, but in general you rarely need over 300-ppi images.

▶ **Resolution requirements for inkjet output.** The necessary resolution for today's photorealistic inkjets is to some extent a guessing game. In part, it depends on the paper stock—matte papers generally require less resolution than glossy ones. Anecdotal evidence suggests that a resolution around 240 ppi is sufficient for most images, but if you're really picky, you may want to determine the ideal resolution for a particular paper stock yourself using good old trial and error. It's certainly possible to send too much data to an inkjet printer, not only increasing print times unconscionably but also degrading the image: you do *not* want to send a 1440-ppi image to a 1440-dpi inkjet!

Synthetic targets composed of black and white line pairs show an improvement when they're printed at an integral divisor of the printer resolution, such as 360 ppi on a 1440-dpi inkjet, but it's uncertain how applicable this is to images with more natural content. Bruce usually prints to 1440-dpi inkjets at 360 ppi if the image contains enough real pixel data to start with. On small prints (8-by-10-inches or less) he may even send 480 ppi and print at the much slower 2880-dpi setting. However, although Bruce insists the benefit is real, it takes careful sharpening to see it. If the image doesn't contain enough pixels to print at these fairly high resolutions, we'll simply send what we have rather than interpolating.

Tonal and color correction. We talk a great deal about compressing tonal range ("targeting") for halftone output in Chapter 6, *Image Adjustment Fundamentals*, so we won't go into it here. Contone output needs less in the way of tonal and gamut compression than halftone output, because contone devices generally have a greater dynamic range and a wider gamut than do halftone devices. However, this can bring its own problems, particularly when you have a scanner with a tendency to oversaturate some colors, as do many inexpensive scanners (and even some expensive ones). Keep a watchful eye on saturated colors. Some dye-sublimation printers feature a magenta that's almost fluorescent!

Sharpening. As we noted back in Chapter 9, *Sharpeness, Detail, and Noise Reduction*, contone images need less sharpening than halftone images. But that doesn't mean they don't need any at all. Halftones, again because of their coarse screens and significant dot gain, mask details and edges in an image; sharpening can help compensate for both the blurriness of the scan and the blurriness of the halftone. And, halftones being what they are, you have a lot of room to play with sharpening before the picture becomes oversharpened (most people end up undersharpening).

In contone images, however, there's a real risk of oversharpening. Not only should you use a lower Amount setting for unsharp masking, but also a smaller Radius. Where a Radius less than one is often lost in a halftone image, it's usually appropriate in contone images. In this context, inkjet printers tend to behave more like contone devices than halftone devices.

Image mode. This last item, image mode, isn't really dependent on what output method you're using. However, because we still see people confused about image mode, we thought we'd throw in a recap here, too.

Again: if you're printing to a color contone device that outputs to film (or if the image is only seen on a color screen), you should leave your image in RGB mode. Contone and hybrid devices that print on paper use CMYK inks or toners, but in most cases you'll get better results sending RGB and letting Photoshop or the printer handle the conversion. If you have a good profile for the output device, you can preview the output using Proof Setup, and convert the image from your RGB editing space to the device's space at print time (we discuss this in the next section). If you're printing separations, though, you need to send a CMYK file.

We've tried many times to build Photoshop Classic CMYK setups for CMYK dye-sublimation printers, but it simply doesn't work. Photoshop's separation engine is geared toward halftone output, where the ink density remains constant and the dot size varies. It simply can't handle the variable density on dye-sublimation printers. It would work for inkjets if we could control the inks directly, but since we can't, it doesn't.

Imaging from Photoshop

When we started writing the *Real World Photoshop* series back in the days of version 3, it was almost a given that most people who used Photoshop didn't print directly from it; instead, they saved their images in some other format and then imported them into some other program to print later. But the revolution in inkjet printing has changed all that, as legions of photographers discover that the digital darkroom is infinitely more controllable and predictable than the wet one. So we're going to tackle the topic of imaging directly from Photoshop before we move out of Photoshop and into QuarkXPress, InDesign, or other programs.

As in almost every other Macintosh or Windows program, there are two menu items (and accompanying dialog boxes) tied to imaging: Page Setup and Print, both found under the File menu. But Photoshop also offers a third item, Print with Preview, that serves as command central for the two more common ones and adds Photoshop-specific options.

Because Mac OS X and Windows XP currently don't allow applications to add features to the Print and Page Setup dialog boxes, Adobe added the Print with Preview command. Most of the options you need to change when you're printing from Photoshop can be accessed easily in Print with Preview, so when we print from Photoshop, this dialog box is always our first stop (see Figure 13-21).

Print with Preview

In its basic form—what you get when you click the Fewer Options button in the dialog box—the Print with Preview dialog box (which is confusingly labeled "Print") lets you control the position and scaling of your image on the page. You can do so either visually, by dragging the image proxy to position it and dragging the bounding box handles to scale it, or numerically, by entering values in the appropriate fields. To scale or position the image by dragging, you must turn on "Show Bounding Box," and if "Center Image" is turned on, you can only scale the image, not position it.

Figure 13-21
Print with Preview
dialog box

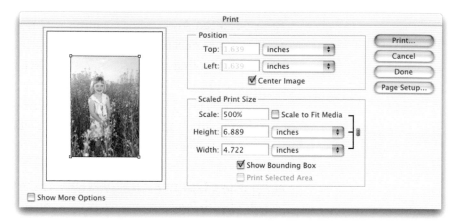

Note that the proxy image is For Position Only—specifically, it isn't color-managed, so don't try to draw any conclusions from its appearance!

Position. The Position fields let you enter the position of the image's top-left corner on the page, in inches, centimeters, points, or picas. If the Center Image checkbox is turned on, the position fields are dimmed.

Scaled Print Size. The Scaled Print Size fields let you enter a scaling percentage, or a height or width in inches, centimeters, points, or picas. The Scale to Fit Media checkbox, when turned on, scales the image to cover as much of the printer's printable area as the image's aspect ratio allows. All three fields are locked together—you can't change the aspect ratio of the image.

The base size that's first reported when you open Print with Preview is based on the settings in the Image Size dialog box. When you change the scaling, be aware that you aren't creating any new pixels—the scaling options are just like changing the size or resolution in Image Size with the Resample Image checkbox turned off.

Tip: Don't Scale in Page Setup. Photoshop lets you apply scaling to the printed image in Print with Preview *or* in Page Setup, but Print with Preview doesn't "know" about scaling applied in Page Setup; so if you apply scaling there, the preview and dimensions in Print with Preview will be incorrect. We recommend you always apply scaling in Print with Preview, and leave the scaling in Page Setup at 100 percent.

Print Selected Area. You'd be surprised how many people wonder how to print just a small portion of their enormous image. They go through all sorts of duplicating and cropping convolutions instead of simply drawing a marquee around the area they want printed, then turning on the Print Selected Area checkbox in the Print with Preview dialog box. If no pixels are selected, or if the selected area isn't a rectangle (like if it's feathered), this checkbox is grayed out.

Show More Options. When you click on the Show More Options check-box, Print with Preview gives access to even more controls (we never turn this off). The Photoshop-specific items appear when you choose Output from the popup menu, and (surprise!) the various color management output options appear when you choose Color Management from the popup menu. Let's cover the Output options first (see Figure 13-22).

Figure 13-22
Show More Options

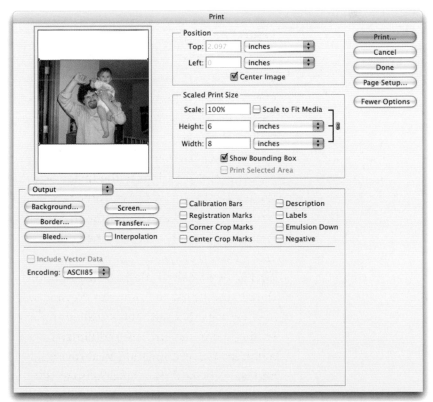

Output Options

The Output Options tell Photoshop how to print the document. A couple of these items (screens and transfer curves) also apply when you save files in various file formats. Some features in the dialog box are determined by which printer driver you currently have selected. Because these are standard system-level features, we're going to skip them and get right to the good stuff: the Photoshop-specific items. Note that some of these options apply only to PostScript printing. If you're printing to a non-PostScript printer, they have no effect, and Photoshop will alert you to the fact by popping up the dialog box shown in Figure 13-23.

Figure 13-23
The non-PostScript
printer alert

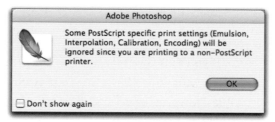

Screen. This is a PostScript-only option. When you click the Screen button, Photoshop brings up the Halftone Screens dialog box, where you can specify the halftone screen angle, frequency, and spot shape for your image (see Figure 13-24). When the Use Printer's Default Screens checkbox is turned on (it is unless you go and change it), Photoshop won't tell the printer anything about how the image should be screened.

Figure 13-24
Halftone Screens
dialog box

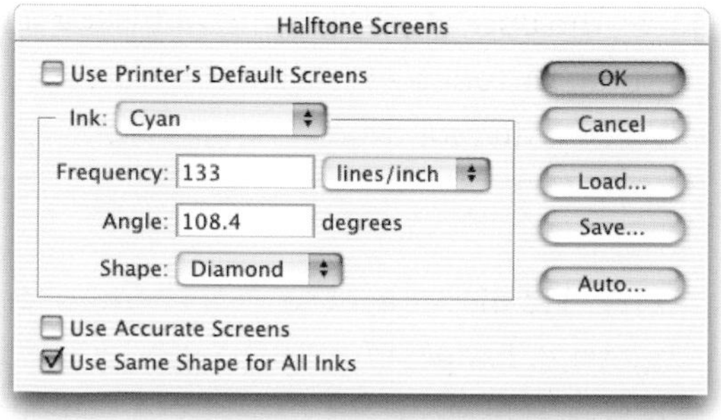

Leave this checkbox on unless you want to take responsibility for setting your own halftone screens. Photoshop gives you a wide array of possibilities for setting the halftone screen. However, most platesetters and imagesetters override the screen values (see "Overriding Screen Settings," earlier in this chapter).

▶ **Frequency and Angle.** The frequency and angle are self-explanatory.

▶ **Shape.** When the Use Same Shape for All Inks checkbox is on, the Shape popup menu applies to each process color. We'd only change this for special low-frequency effects.

▶ **Use Accurate Screens.** When you turn on the Use Accurate Screens checkbox, Photoshop includes the PostScript code to activate Accurate Screens in your PostScript RIP. However, if your RIP doesn't have Accurate Screens technology, or if it uses some other screening technology—such as Balanced Screens or HQS—you should just leave this off.

▶ **Auto.** If you don't know what frequency/angle combinations to type in, check with your RIP vendor. If they don't know, you're probably in trouble. However, as a last resort, you could try clicking the Auto button and telling Photoshop approximately what screen frequency you want and what resolution printer you're using.

Note that you can include these screen settings in EPS files (see "Encapsulated PostScript (EPS)" earlier in this chapter).

Tip: Use Diamond Spot. Peter Fink's PostScript prowess perfected the diamond spot (say that ten times fast). The diamond spot is better in almost every instance than the standard round spot because it greatly reduces the optical tonal jump that is sometimes visible in the mid-to-three-quarter tones—the 50-to-75-percent gray areas. We've also been told that the diamond spot is much better for silkscreening.

Transfer. We discussed the idea of input/output contrast curves back in Chapter 6, *Image Adjustment Fundamentals*, and in Chapter 10, *Spot Colors and Duotones*. Well, here they are once again, in Print with Preview. A transfer curve is like taking a curve that you made in the Curves dialog box and downloading it to your printer. It won't change the image data on your hard drive, but when you print with the transfer curve, it modifies the printed gray levels. This option works on non-PostScript printers.

It's a rare occasion that you'd need to use a transfer curve these days. But if you do, click the Transfer button (see Figure 13-25). Note that while you can save a transfer curve with an image in any format that Photoshop supports, the curve is only recognized when you print directly from Photoshop. To print images with transfer curves from a page-layout application, you need to use EPS files. But there's a danger in using transfer curves with EPS images, because there's no obvious signal to tell anyone working with the image that it contains a transfer curve, except that the values in the file aren't the same as those that print. The only way to tell is to open the image in Photoshop and check to see if there's a transfer curve specified. If you do use a transfer curve, make sure that whoever is responsible for printing the file knows it's lurking there!

Figure 13-25
Transfer Functions
dialog box

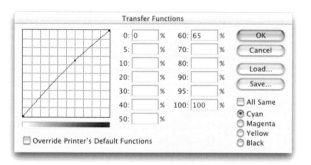

Tip: Interchangeable Curves. While Bruce can think about transfer curves in terms of numbers, David needs a more touchy-feely approach. So he tries out his transfer curves in the Curves dialog box first. When he gets a curve just the way he wants it, he saves the curve to disk (using the Save button in the Curves dialog box), then he goes to the Transfer Functions dialog box and loads it in.

Note that Photoshop provides you with a checkbox at the bottom of the Transfer Functions dialog box: Override Printer's Default Functions. Don't turn this on unless you really know what you're doing with transfer functions. If you're printing through a linearized RIP, turning this checkbox on will override the linearization, and could give you nasty results. While it's nice that Adobe gives us this control, it's one we tend to ignore.

Background. Background—and the next 11 features—are only relevant when you're printing from Photoshop; you cannot save them in an EPS format (or any other, for that matter) and expect them to carry over to other programs, like you can with Screen and Transfer.

When you print your image from Photoshop to a color printer, the area surrounding the image is typically left white (or clear if you're printing on film). The Background feature lets you change the color that surrounds the image, using the standard Photoshop Color Picker. The background color that you pick acts like a matte frame around the image to the edges of the printable area.

Tip: Make Your Highlights Pop. If you typically make prints with a white border, you can make your highlights appear much snappier if you lay down a *small* amount of ink in the border. Our eyes adapt to the paper-white border: when you print a very light gray or yellow tone in the border, the eye still accepts this as paper white; so, any specular highlights that use the actual paper white appear brighter than they really are, because the viewer's eye is adapted to the white of the surround.

Border. If you specify a border around an image (the border can be up to 0.15 inches, 10 points, or 3.5 millimeters), Photoshop centers the frame on the edge of the image when you print; that is, half the frame overlaps the image, and half the frame overlaps the background. You cannot, unfortunately, change the color of the frame; it's always black.

Unless we're printing directly from Photoshop *and* we want a print with a black border, we can't think of any reason to use this feature, except perhaps to print an image with a pretrapped frame directly from Photoshop, then strip it in with the rest of the film manually. Yuck. We'd rather import the file into QuarkXPress or InDesign and keyline it there.

Bleed. Setting a Bleed value adjusts where Photoshop places the corner crop marks. You can choose a bleed up to 9.01 points, 3.18 millimeters, or 0.125 inches (who knows who came up with these values). Again, this is most useful if you're planning on doing manual stripping later. Note that if you specify a 0.125-inch bleed, Photoshop sets the crop marks in by that amount from the image boundary, not out: it effectively says, "cut off the edges of this image."

Interpolation. This PostScript-only item usually does absolutely nothing. In theory, this feature tells your printer to upsample low-resolution images at print time. We've heard various claims that some PostScript Level 2 or greater printers are actually capable of doing this, but we've yet to see evidence of it. But thanks, Adobe, for giving us the choice!

Description. David loves Photoshop's ability to save a description with a file because of the File Info metadata tie-in to InDesign, but it's also helpful when printing a whole mess of images that you need to peruse, file, or send to someone. When you turn on the Description checkbox in Print with Preview, the program prints whatever caption you have saved in File Info (under the File menu) beneath the image. If you haven't saved a description, this feature doesn't do anything.

You might even include your name or copyright information in the Description field of the File Info dialog box, even though there are other fields for this. At least your name prints out with your images.

Newspapers and stock photo agencies can make much more elaborate use of the File Info feature, including credit lines, handling instructions, and keywords for database searches.

Calibration Bars. This is a PostScript-only option. When you turn on the Calibration Bars checkbox in Print with Preview, Photoshop prints one (for grayscale images) or several (for color images) series of rectangles around the image (see Figure 13-26). Beneath the image is a ten-step gray wedge; to the left is the same gray wedge, but on each color plate; to the right is a series of colors, listed below. Each color is 100 percent (solid).

- ▶ Yellow

- ▶ Yellow and magenta

- ▶ Magenta

- ▶ Magenta and cyan

- ▶ Cyan

- ▶ Cyan and yellow

- ▶ Cyan, magenta, and yellow

- ▶ Black

Figure 13-26
Printer marks

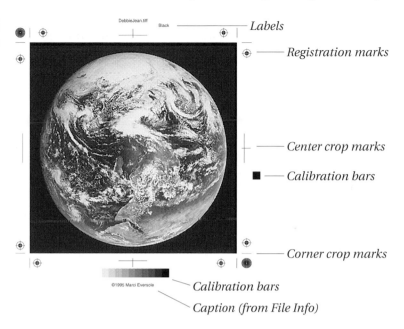

Labels

Registration marks

Center crop marks

Calibration bars

Corner crop marks

Calibration bars

Caption (from File Info)

Registration Marks. If you're outputting separations, you need to add registration marks so that the printer can align the four colors properly. Turning on the Registration Marks checkbox adds ten registration marks (eight bull's-eyes and two pinpoint types).

Corner Crop Marks. Even if your printer is going to strip your image into another layout, it's helpful to print with corner crop marks, which specify clearly where the edges of the image are. This can help the stripper align the image with a straight edge. In fact, it's essential if the image has a clear white background (like a silhouette); without crop marks, it's impossible to tell where the image boundaries are.

Center Crop Marks. If you need to specify the center point of your image, turn on the Center Crop Marks checkbox. We always turn this on along with Corner Crop Marks as an added bonus, although we aren't always sure why we do so. Note that when you turn this feature on, Photoshop adds two pinpoint registration marks, even on grayscale images, which in theory don't need them.

Labels. When you're printing color separations, turning on the Labels checkbox is a must. This feature adds the file name above the image on each separation, and also adds the color plate name (cyan, magenta, yellow, black, or whatever other channel you're printing). If you're printing a spot color in addition to process colors, it's even more vital that you label the spot separation.

Negative and Emulsion Down. When it comes to the Negative and Emulsion Down options, our best advice is to ignore them unless you're a service bureau printing to an imagesetter, and even then, these options are usually better set in the imagesetter RIP itself. For the record, Emulsion Down is a PostScript-only option, while Negative applies to non-PostScript printers too.

Encoding. As we mentioned earlier, image data can be stored and sent to a PostScript printer as ASCII or binary data. ASCII takes much more space to describe the data than does binary, but it's universally understandable no matter how your PostScript device is connected to the world; so it's often preferable on networks that are administered using DOS or UNIX machines. We recommend saving time and using binary; if it doesn't work, try ASCII85, which is somewhat more compact than ASCII and almost always works.

There's one more option: JPEG. While JPEG is much more compact than either binary or ASCII, and therefore is sent down the wires to the printer faster, the compression is lossy, so image quality degrades slightly. However, when printing with JPEG encoding, Photoshop only compresses the image slightly, so degradation is kept to a minimum. (We'd be surprised if you could see the difference on a scanned image of decent resolution.) JPEG encoding only works when printing to PostScript Level 2 or 3 printers, because they know how to decompress JPEG.

Color Management Options

The Color Management options inside the Print with Preview dialog box let you tell Photoshop to do one of three things: perform a color conversion on the data that gets sent to the printer, pass the image data and the profile that describes it to the printer driver for printer driver color management, or simply send the pixels to the printer (see Figure 13-27).

Whether we're making final prints from Photoshop or generating proofs, we find these options invaluable. However, if you make Photoshop convert the color, you *must* make sure that the printer driver doesn't also make a conversion, because then you'll get hideous results.

Figure 13-27
Color Management
options

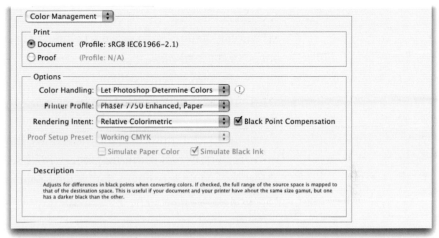

Document versus Proof. By default, the Print option is always set to Document, which is either the space represented by the profile embedded in the image or, in the case of untagged images, by the current working space you've set for the document's color mode in the Color Settings dialog box (see Chapter 5, *Color Settings*).

The other option, Proof, tells Photoshop to convert the image from the document space to the profile specified in Proof Setup, using the rendering intent set in Proof Setup, before handing off the data to the printer. We use this feature when we're trying to make a desktop printer simulate final printed output when we haven't yet converted the file to the final output space. If, for example, we have a ProPhoto RGB image destined for press output, and we want to simulate the press on an inkjet printer, we set Proof Setup to simulate the press by choosing the press profile there, then we click the Proof button in Print with Preview.

When we do so, the Proof Setup Preset menu and the Simulate Paper Color and Simulate Black Ink checkboxes become enabled, and the Rendering Intent menu becomes disabled. See "Proof Setup Preset," slightly later in this chapter.

Color Handling. The Color Handling popup menu allows you to specify whether or not Photoshop will apply a color conversion before sending the data to the printer. There are four options:

▶ **Let Printer Determine Colors.** This option tells Photoshop to send the data to the printer in its native document space, with that space's profile embedded. This option is designed for use with printers or printer drivers that perform their own color management.

We almost never use this option. We've yet to see PostScript color management work reliably, though we've heard of a handful of sites that have made it work. One situation when we do use this option is when we're debugging color management. In theory, choosing this option should produce identical results to the next option—Let Photoshop Determine Colors—when the same printer profile is used and the printer driver is correctly configured. If it doesn't, that fact can be a useful data point. The other is when we're printing to an inkjet through a RIP that has been configured to translate the color correctly.

▶ **Let Photoshop Determine Colors.** This does what it says—it tells Photoshop to send the data to the printer in the space specified by the Printer Profile in the next menu. This is our preferred method of printing from Photoshop. It lets Photoshop perform all the necessary color conversions, which in our experience is the most reliable workflow. When you use this method, though, you must make sure that any color management options in the non-Photoshop section of your printer's driver are turned off; otherwise you'll get a double conversion, with results that range from unacceptable to ghastly.

If you choose Let Photoshop Determine Colors in the Color Handling popup menu, you can pick any ICC profile from the Printer Profile menu to tell Photoshop to convert the image to that profile's space before handing it off to the printer. When you choose a profile, you also are given the opportunity to choose the rendering intent used for the conversion. This is usually the easiest, and sometimes the only way to use custom, rather than vendor-supplied profiles with inkjet printers.

▶ **No Color Management.** The only situations where we use No Color Management are when we're printing a calibration target and only care about the numbers in the file, not the colors they represent, or when we're printing an image that has already been converted to output space.

▶ **Separations.** Have you been trying to get Photoshop to print color separations of your CMYK and duotone images? The folks at Adobe hid the controls! To print each color on its own plate (rather than a composite color image), you must select Separations from the Color Handling popup menu. (This option only appears when you're printing an image that's already in CMYK or Duotone mode.)

Tip: Printing Single Colors in Separations. Photoshop doesn't give you an obvious way to print fewer than all four process colors when printing color separations; you only have the option to choose Separations, not "only the cyan and magenta, please." Nonetheless, you can do just this in one of two ways.

▶ Photoshop only prints the color plates that are displayed in the document window. For instance, if you only want to print magenta and black, click on the yellow and cyan eyeballs in the Channels palette to hide them. Now when you print, Photoshop automatically prints separations of the remaining two colors. (The Space popup menu only displays one option, Grayscale, when you do this.)

▶ You can also use the Pages field in the Print dialog box to print fewer than four color separations. For example, when Print Separations is turned on, you can tell Photoshop to print from page two to page two; page two in a CMYK image is the magenta plate. If all the colors are not visible (because you've hidden them, as in the last bullet item), then page two is whatever the second *visible* color is. Note that this doesn't work when Print Selection is turned on in Windows.

Be aware that printing different plates for a separation at different times or from different devices can cause problems with registration and tint (hence color) consistency. If you have to rerun a single plate, it's typically better to rerun all four.

Tip: Don't Downsample High-Bit Files for Printing. If you're printing a high-bit file directly from Photoshop, it's both unnecessary and unwise to downsample it to 8 bits per channel prior to printing. It's unnecessary because Photoshop is smart enough to downsample the data before handing it off to the printer. It's unwise because if you request color space conversions, you'll get better results allowing Photoshop to do the conversion on the high-bit data before it does its automatic downsampling than you will forcing Photoshop to make the conversion on an image that's already been downsampled to 8 bits per channel.

Proof Setup Preset. When you choose Proof as the source space, the Proof Setup Preset menu becomes enabled, and the Rendering Intent menu becomes disabled. You can choose any saved Proof Setup preset from this menu—if you've applied a Proof Setup to the document, it defaults to that setup. When you print, Photoshop first converts the documents colors from the source space to the Proof Setup space, using the rendering intent specified in Proof Setup. It then converts the Proof Setup colors to the printer space specified by Printer Profile. The rendering intent is controlled by the two Simulate checkboxes—Simulate Paper Color and Simulate Black Ink—as follows:

▶ When both checkboxes are turned off, Photoshop converts the Proof Setup colors to the printer space using Relative Colorimetric rendering with Black Point Compensation, so the Proof Setup paper white is translated to the printer's paper white, and the Proof Setup black is rendered as the blackest black the printer can reproduce.

▶ When Simulate Black Ink is turned on, Photoshop converts the Proof Setup colors to the printer space using Relative Colorimetric rendering *without* Black Point Compensation: The Proof Setup paper white is still translated to the printer's paper white, but the Proof Setup black is rendered as the actual shade of black that the final output being simulated will produce.

▶ When Simulate Paper Color is turned on, Simulate Ink Black is turned on and dimmed. Photoshop converts the Proof Setup colors to the printer space using Absolute Colorimetric rendering: The Proof Setup paper white and ink black are reproduced exactly. If you're simulating newsprint, for example, the paper white areas will print with some black and yellow to simulate the yellow-gray newsprint stock, and the blacks will print as relatively washed-out newsprint blacks.

If you're used to earlier versions of Photoshop, you'll have noticed that all the color management options in Print with Preview have been changed. But no functionality has been added or taken away, and if the new options aren't any more intuitive than the old ones, they aren't any less so, either. It may take you a little while to translate the old settings to the new ones, but the functionality remains the same.

Using an Online Service

Don't own a printer? Prefer photographic prints to inkjet output? Want a poster-sized print? No problem! You can use an online service to print your photographs. When you choose Print Online from the File menu, Photoshop launches Adobe Bridge, selects current image, and automatically chooses Photo Prints from the Photoshop Services submenu (under the Tools menu). The Photo Print service lets you upload one or more images to Kodak EasyShare Gallery. (This service is also known as Ofoto.com; back in Photoshop CS, Adobe worked with Shutterfly.com.)

Of course, if you don't already have a free Kodak EasyShare Gallery account, you can create one here. Then Bridge will send the file(s) to the service—just as you might do manually via the Ofoto.com Web site—and (Kodak hopes) buy lots of prints.

Note that Kodak automatically applies brightness and contrast adjustments to your images unless you turn off the proprietary Kodak Perfect Touch feature. If you have carefully tweaked your image in Photoshop, the last thing you want is for those settings to be overridden by a computer that thinks it knows better. Ofoto's system assumes that your JPEG images (it only works with JPEG images) are in the sRGB color space. We don't believe for a moment that its system is truly sRGB, but using that is better than shooting blind.

Imaging from a Page-Layout Program

In the prepress world, most people don't print directly from Photoshop—at least for their final output. Instead, they print from separation programs, presentation programs, or page-layout programs. In this section, we're going to focus on the latter item: page-layout programs such as Adobe InDesign, Adobe PageMaker, and QuarkXPress.

Our assumption here is that if you're printing from a page-layout program, you're probably printing to a PostScript imagesetter or platesetter, resulting in paper, film, or plates with black-and-white halftoned images.

QuarkXPress, InDesign, and PageMaker

In the last gasp of the twentieth century, QuarkXPress became the imaging tool of choice for graphic designers, service bureaus, ad agencies, and other heavy color users. Whether or not it deserved this title should be (and is) argued anywhere but here (otherwise Bruce and David would debate themselves into a tizzy). Currently, it appears that Adobe PageMaker is a dead product, and that Adobe InDesign is poised to take the crown from XPress sooner rather than later.

No matter which page-layout tool you use, it's crucial that you consider how your images will transport from Photoshop to the printed page. There are some basic rules you should follow.

File formats. Earlier in this chapter, we covered file formats in some detail, including which ones to use for page layout. To recap quickly: when it comes to printing from page-layout programs, always use TIFF, PDF, DCS, or EPS. With InDesign or QuarkXPress 6.5, you can also use the native Photoshop (PSD) format. We tend toward the TIFF format for almost all our files, though we'll occasionally use EPS or DCS for specialized effects—such as duotones or custom screening. If your image has vector artwork (like text layers) in it, you should use EPS or (preferably) PDF.

CMYK vs. RGB. The choice between importing RGB or CMYK images involves two decisions—when do you want to do your separations, and what program do you want to do them in? You can preseparate all your images with Photoshop (or another program), or you can place RGB images in QuarkXPress, InDesign, or PageMaker, and rely on their color management systems to do the separations for you.

Preseparating has a lot going for it. Images land on pages ready to print; the page-layout program just sends the channels down, with no processing at print time. Note that CMYK EPS files are not color managed in the page-layout program, though CMYK TIFF files may be. That is, if the page-layout program's CMS is turned on, your CMYK values may be altered at print time. To ensure the image data stays the same, choose an output (target) profile that matches the image (source) profile.

Placing unseparated RGB files has advantages as well, though. You can use the page-layout program's color management system to produce better proofs off color printers, and you don't have to target the images until the last minute, when you know all your press conditions and are ready to pull final seps. However, when it comes right down to it, we separate almost all our images in Photoshop first. (But we archive the RGB files, just in case we need to reseparate to some other target.)

Rotating. Rotating large pixel-based images is a major pain on anything but the fastest machines. When you import an image into a page layout application and rotate it on the page, it seems to rotate very quickly. But the real math work is done at print time inside your PostScript printer. That means that every time you print (either a proof on a PostScript device or your final piece), your printer has to do the same time-consuming calculations that you could have done once in Photoshop. If you know you're going to rotate an image 15 degrees, do it in Photoshop first, then import it onto your page.

Cropping and clipping. Let's say you've imported a 24 MB photograph of your class of '74 onto your page, but out of 1,400 people, you only want to print the 31 people who were on the lacrosse team. You use the cropping tool (in PageMaker) or the picture box handles (in XPress and InDesign) to crop out everyone else, duplicate the image, recrop, and so on, for 31 people. And then you print the page....

If you saved the image from Photoshop as an EPS, prepare to wait a while for the page to print. In fact, you might want to consider a quick jaunt to the Caribbean. The entire image, no matter how much is showing, has to be sent to the printer for every iteration. Don't laugh. We've seen this plenty of times (usually in the same publications that are littered with gratuitous tabs and space characters).

On the other hand, if you saved the image as a TIFF, PSD, or a JPEG, the file shouldn't take too long because the layout apps can pull out just the data they need to image your page. However, it does take the program a little extra time at print time to throw away the data it doesn't need.

In either case, the page-layout program has to import and save a low-resolution preview of the *entire* image. That means unnecessary time and file size. The best solution: crop your images in Photoshop before importing them.

Image editing. Both PageMaker and QuarkXPress let you perform some basic tonal manipulation on TIFF files. (InDesign does not.) In PageMaker (with grayscale images only), select Image Control from the Element menu. In XPress, select Other Contrast from the Style menu or use the QuarkVista palette to apply filters. However, this is like saying that your kitchen knife lets you perform heart surgery. Sure you can do it, but it's gonna get ugly. Except for special effects (and controlling screen settings on an image-by-image basis), we recommend that people simply not use these features; instead, use Photoshop.

Getting It Out

Photoshop is the best all-around tool we've encountered for working with images, massaging images, and targeting images for specific output devices. However, page-layout programs such as InDesign and Quark-XPress excel at integrating text and graphics into complete pages.

If you keep that distinction clear, you'll use Photoshop to do everything that needs to be done to your images, and give the page-layout program an image file that it can simply pass on to the output device. Your work will proceed more smoothly, and you (or your service bureau) will encounter fewer unpleasant surprises. Sometimes it's nice when life is boring....

14 Multimedia and the Web

Purposing Pixels for the Screen

It's pretty clear that we've spent most of our professional lives focused on preparing images that are destined for a printing press. But the times they are a-changing, and one of the most common uses for Photoshop today is preparing images for screen display, whether in an interactive multimedia presentation or a Web site. And just as there are techniques for optimizing an image for paper, there are methods you can use to ensure good quality on screen (as well as tips for preparing your on-screen image efficiently).

In this chapter, we take a look at several important issues you need to consider when preparing images for multimedia or the Web, including deciding on a graphic file format and dealing with indexed-color images. Note that we don't discuss all the cool ways you can make funky buttons, rules, bullets, and other page elements; there are other great books on the market that include those techniques.

ImageReady. Once upon a time, Adobe had an idea that people creating images for print would use Photoshop and those that wanted Web graphics would use Adobe ImageReady. They even bundled the two programs together (and still do), and made it easy for people to switch between the two programs via the Jump button at the bottom of the Tool palette (or from the File menu). If your image is open when you click this button, the image automatically opens (or updates) in the other program. Plus, ImageReady and Photoshop can read the same native file format, with layers and so on.

However, it appears that most people want the flexibility of creating either print or Web graphics in Photoshop. The result: Adobe is slowly but inexorably moving features from ImageReady into Photoshop. The newest transfers are Variables (see Chapter 12, *Essential Image Techniques*) and the Animation palette, which lets you create little flip-book movies that you can save as animated GIF files (see "The Animation Palette," later in this chapter).

The upshot is that Photoshop provides most of the tools you need for Web graphics, and the majority of Web graphics never require ImageReady. Therefore, we won't be discussing ImageReady in this chapter. There are several other programs currently on the market that are expressly designed to build Web graphics, such as Macromedia's Fireworks. However, this is a book on what you can do with Photoshop, so we won't be covering those programs, either.

Preparing Images

No matter whether an image is destined for print or for screen, we always recommend that you do the tonal correction, color correction, and sharpening in Photoshop. But the kind of correction and sharpening you need for on-screen images is almost always different than for printed images.

Ultimately, the one rule that almost always applies to images for the screen is that no matter what the image looks like on your screen, it will look different on everyone else's. Preparing images for multimedia and the Internet is an exercise in frustration for anyone who is used to print production; even the whims of a web press seem trivial compared to the variations from one person's screen to another on the Web.

Tone

Electronic commerce demands that Web color get more consistent; the number one reason for merchandise returns is, "it wasn't the color I saw in the catalog." Without an easy way for people to characterize their monitor and for images to be compensated on the fly, customers will never be able to tell whether the shirt they're looking at is a dark burgundy or a light red, and e-commerce will flounder. With so much money riding on this, you'd think that there would already be good commercial solutions to ensure accurate color. Unfortunately, the tough part is getting the person-on-the-street to create custom monitor profiles on their machines.

While the display on some computer monitors is darker than on others, monitors connected to a Macintosh tend to display images lighter than those on a PC (see Figure 14-1). You can compensate for this to some extent by choosing an appropriate RGB space for your images (see Chapter 5, *Color Settings*); but it's unlikely that the people who view your images will have calibrated monitors, so the above gamma numbers are no more than a general guideline.

There are several strategies for dealing with this mismatch. All involve some compromises. Since the destination monitor is essentially an unknown, you can be fairly certain that until self-calibrating monitors are ubiquitous and all browsers support system-level color management, your images are going to look much better (or worse) on some systems than on others. Ultimately, it's simply impossible to produce images that will look good to every Web user.

Figure 14-1
Monitor gamma
and image tone

Macintosh screen,
(around gamma 1.8)

Windows screen,
(around gamma 2.2)

Given the current state of the art, the best you can do is to choose an aim point appropriate for the audience you're trying to reach. We suggest you choose one of the following alternatives.

▶ **Convert to sRGB.** Back in Chapter 5, *Color Settings*, we discussed the sRGB color space, developed by several industry giants to describe the general characteristics of the "typical" Windows monitor. Of course, the sRGB color gamut excludes many of the intense colors that you may want to display. (Ironically, the logo color of one of sRGB's main proponents, Hewlett-Packard, lies outside the sRGB gamut.) Also, we doubt that the majority of monitors on the market actually display sRGB. Still, you can convert your edited images into the sRGB space before saving them, accepting its inherent limitations.

Given the marketing muscle behind sRGB, it's probably the most sensible choice unless you're trying to sell color-critical merchandise or show fine art on the Web. However, there are many good reasons to work in a better RGB workspace and only convert to sRGB just before saving the file (see "Tip: Work in a Big Space," on the next page).

▶ **Prepare two sets of images.** We know some photographers who care so much about color that they've prepared two sets of their images, one at gamma 1.8 and one at gamma 2.2. Then they set up their sites so that Mac users see the gamma 1.8 version while Windows users see the gamma 2.2 version. It's a good theory, except that it still doesn't take into account that out in the real world some Mac monitors actually display more darkly than Windows monitors, and *vice versa*. It is also a lot more work to do this, of course.

▶ **Embed the profile.** The best solution to the color mismatch problem is to embed an ICC profile in each image. Unfortunately, this approach relies on two things: that every person looking at your images has created their own custom monitor profile, and that their browser supports (and corrects for) embedded profiles. But let's get real: Neither of these is likely in the real world, at least not anytime soon. For instance, as far as we know, only Safari and Internet Explorer 4.x and 5.x for the Mac support embedded profiles (and in the latter, only when you turn on the ColorSync checkbox in the Preferences dialog box).

Note that Photoshop does not embed profiles in GIF files because they're always in Indexed Color mode rather than RGB. However, there are ways that you can specify a profile for a GIF file (see the Web site *www.colorsync.com* for more information on specifying an associated profile within your HTML code). Embedding an RGB working space profile usually only adds about 0.5 K to a JPEG image, so file size shouldn't be a consideration.

All three approaches have their strengths and weaknesses, and each of these three strategies optimizes the image for a different set of users.

Tip: Work in a Big Space. Even if every image you create is for the Web, we still suggest setting the RGB popup menu in your Color Settings dialog box to a reasonable color space, like Adobe RGB (if you don't know what we're talking about here, check out Chapter 5, *Color Settings*). Then, if you want to convert your images to the sRGB space before saving them, you can use Convert to Profile (from the Edit menu) to convert from your RGB space to sRGB. If you use the smaller sRGB space as your RGB working space, you're limiting your color options unnecessarily when editing your images.

Color

Not only can you rarely predict tonal shifts in images for the screen, you can't assume anything about color. Most graphic arts professionals have 24-bit color ("true color") monitors, but just because you have one doesn't mean that your audience will. In fact, some users of older computers can only view 256 colors at a time, due to the constraints of their video hardware (or the games they like to play on their computer). The occasional computer user only has a grayscale screen, so they won't see color at all.

What's worse, even two people with the same kind of screen and computer system will probably see the same image differently on each of their monitors. Again, monitor calibration can help considerably, but it's too rare to depend upon. (And a thoughtless quick twist of the brightness or contrast knobs means that the color is even further off.)

However, there are a few rules you can generally trust.

▶ It's usually more important to retain the contrast between colors than the particular colors themselves. Image details that result from subtle changes in color (like the gentle folds in a red silk scarf) are often lost in translation.

- ▶ Solid areas of color, including text, should be set to one of the 216 "Web-safe" colors (see "Tip: Web-Safe Colors," below) so that they won't dither on old 8-bit screens.

- ▶ If you built your image on a 24-bit color monitor (which is a good idea, even when making Web graphics), switch your monitor to 8-bit color (256 colors) to test how less-well-equipped folks will see your image. (Or, use the Browser Dither feature in the Save For Web dialog box, which we talk about later in this chapter.)

- ▶ While you're testing, also try looking at your image on both Macintosh and Windows systems. You can also select Windows RGB or Macintosh RGB from the Proof Setup submenu (under the View menu), and then turn on Proof Colors (press Command-Y) to see how they change. This isn't perfect, but it should give you a general idea of how the image may look on a different system.

- ▶ Images for multimedia and the Web should always be in RGB or Indexed Color mode.

Tip: Web-Safe Colors. There is a myth that people making GIF images should always save them using Web-safe colors. The problem is that "Web-safe" really should be called "Save for 8-bit monitors" because this is only relevant when viewing images on a monitor set to 8-bit color (256 colors). The vast majority of computers on the planet now display 16-bit ("thousands of colors") or 24-bit ("millions of colors" or "true color") color, so Web-safe just isn't that important anymore.

However, if you do use a non-Web-safe color in your image, it—by necessity—gets dithered using the system palette's colors when viewed on an 8-bit color monitor (see Figure 14-2). The dithering is distracting in many images (especially images with text), but is usually unavoidable in pictures that contain anti-aliasing, gradients, or photographic images.

There are various ways to choose Web-safe colors for a Photoshop image, but the easiest is simply to turn on the Only Web Colors checkbox in Photoshop's Color Picker dialog box. Or, you could open the Swatches palette and choose any of the Web-safe palettes from the palette's popout menu (any palette that begins with the word "Web" or "Visibone").

By the way, if you do the math, you'll find that all the Web-safe colors are in 20-percent steps within the 256-level scale. That is, a typical Web-

Figure 14-2
Web-safe colors

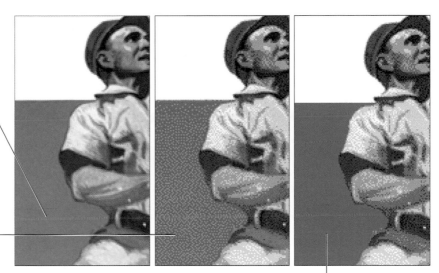

On a 24-bit color monitor, these colors wouldn't dither.

On an 8-bit color monitor, however, these colors simply aren't available.

If the color is Web-safe, it won't dither on 8-bit color screens.

safe color might be 20-percent red and 60-percent green. You might be tempted with this knowledge to change your Color Picker (in the Preferences dialog box) in order to specify colors by percentage. Don't do it! Photoshop translates these values based on the RGB profile in the Color Settings dialog box, so you won't get the proper values at all. Instead, if you want to type specific numbers into the Color Picker dialog box, use 0, 51, 102, 153, 204, or 255 (these correlate directly with 0, 20, 40, 60, 80, and 100 percent).

Resolution

One of the wonderful advantages to working on images for screen display is that resolution is almost always 72 ppi, making for very small images (relative to prepress sizes, at least). A 4-by-5-inch image at 72 ppi takes up 300 K, where the equivalent prepress image might consume over 4.5 MB of disk space and RAM. With smaller file size come faster processing times and lower RAM requirements. You can actually use any resolution you want, but when it comes time to put the image on screen, each image pixel is mapped to a screen pixel. A 300-ppi image will become enormous on screen!

Of course, similar to the vagaries of color and tone on the Internet, you rarely know what resolution screen your images will be viewed on—your 72-ppi illustration quickly becomes much smaller if someone views it on a high-resolution monitor. Because you cannot assume monitor resolution, it's often a good idea to design your 72-ppi images slightly larger in size so they'll look okay on a higher-resolution screen. The "standard" resolution of most Windows and Macintosh monitors is around 96 ppi. Bruce runs a 22-inch monitor at 1920-by-1440-pixel resolution, which is close to 125 ppi! (This makes all Web images on his screen appear about half the size they were intended.)

Note that when scanning images destined for the screen, we still almost always scan them at a higher resolution (often the full optical resolution of the scanner) and then downsample them in Photoshop.

Tip: Pages to Graphics. People spend a lot of time trying to figure out how to get their InDesign or QuarkXPress pages up on the Internet. Converting to HTML is one option, though the page almost never looks the same as it did originally. Saving in the PDF format is another option, but then people need Acrobat Reader to view the page, which is a hassle.

Our favorite method of getting pages from XPress or InDesign (or any other program) up on the 'Net is to make a picture out of each one. Adobe InDesign CS lets you export a document page as a JPEG file (select Export from the File menu). If you're using XPress, an earlier version of InDesign, or some other program, here's what to do:

1. Save a page from the program as an EPS or PDF. InDesign and Quark-XPress have specific features to do this; if your program doesn't, you can print to disk as an EPS file using the LaserWriter PostScript driver.

2. Open this file in Photoshop. When Photoshop opens the Generic EPS or Rasterize PDF dialog box, choose to open the image as an RGB file at 72 dpi. Small type doesn't convert well to bitmap, but you might get a better result by turning on Anti-alias in the Open EPS dialog box.

3. Select Flatten from the Layer menu.

4. Save the file as either a GIF or a JPEG, depending on the content of the page and how much compression you're likely to achieve (see the next section for more on these file formats).

By turning the page into a picture, anyone with a Web browser can see it on the Internet. And surprisingly, even a full-page "page image" can be made very small if it's mostly text.

Saving Your Images

It's likely that the majority of images displayed on Web pages today were produced or edited with Photoshop. However, making images for the Web is a study in compromise: You can have either great-looking images or pictures that download quickly. You choose. The problem is that you need to see all the options to make an informed decision about how much to degrade your image in the name of small file sizes. The solution is the Save For Web feature.

Save For Web (select it from the File menu or press Command-Option-Shift-S) lets you see exactly what will happen to your images when you convert them to GIF or JPEG. Better yet, it can display two or four versions at a time and let you tweak each of them until you get just the effect you want (see Figure 14-3).

On-Screen File Formats

We discussed graphic file formats back in Chapter 13, *Image Storage and Output*, but we need to explore two formats—GIF and JPEG—in more depth here, because they're key to the way images appear on the Internet.

Figure 14-3
Save For Web

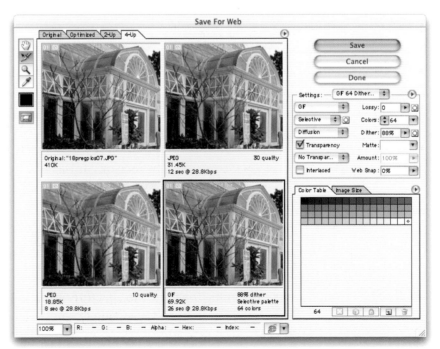

If your images are destined for a multimedia program such as Microsoft PowerPoint or Macromedia Director, you can probably save them in the PICT or TIFF file format. But for Web use, you almost certainly need to save your images in either GIF or JPEG format.

Tip: Checking File Size. The file size that Photoshop provides in the lower-left corner of the document window is far from accurate, mostly because it doesn't take into account any form of compression you will achieve with either JPEG or GIF images. The file size you see in the Save For Web dialog box is more accurate, but it's still not perfect. The only way to find an image's true (post-compression) file size is to save it to disk and switch out of Photoshop. If you have a Macintosh, use Get Info in the Finder (select the file and choose Get Info from the File menu); if you're working on a Windows machine, use Properties on the Desktop (click on the file with the right mouse button and choose Properties from the list of options; see Figure 14-4).

Figure 14-4
Finding file size

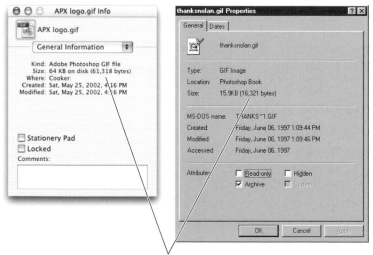

Pay attention to this value.

If the file size is displayed as "27 K on disk (22,045 bytes used)," only pay attention to the second number. The first value is the amount of space the image takes up on your hard disk: this depends on the block size your hard disk uses. If your disk uses 32 K blocks, a 2 K file will occupy 32 K on disk, and a 33 K file will use 64 K of disk space. The second number shows the actual amount of data someone would have to download to see the image, and it's usually smaller than the disk space number.

Save For Web

The trick to the Save For Web feature is to be methodical. Here are the basic steps you should follow once you have the dialog box open.

1. Switch to the 2-Up or 4-Up tab of the window. We like 4-Up except on those rare occasions where we're almost sure what settings we're going to use.

2. Leave the first panel set to Original (so you have something with which to compare your tests). Click on each of the other images and choose for it a preset configuration from the Settings popup menu. For a good spectrum of results, David usually starts with these three: JPEG Medium, GIF 64 Dither, and GIF 32 No Dither.

3. Check each image's quality (visually) and size, and approximate download time (shown under each image).

4. Pick the one that is closest to what you're trying to achieve, and tweak the settings to minimize the size while maintaining quality. We cover each of the settings and how they work below.

5. When you're ready, click OK (make sure the proper image is highlighted; whichever one is highlighted is the one that gets saved to disk).

The problem is that there are so many settings in the dialog box to tweak, many of them obscure. The Settings and Format popup menus are relevant for any file format you use, so we'll cover them first. Then we'll get into the settings that are specific to GIF, JPEG, WBMP, and PNG.

Settings. The Settings popup menu lets you recall saved sets of settings. There's nothing magic about the settings that are already built-in; they're only there to get you started. If you don't like Adobe's settings, you can delete them by choosing Delete Settings from the popout menu to the right of the Settings popup menu. If you want to add your own group of settings to the list, choose Save Settings instead; make sure the settings are saved in the Optimized Settings folder (inside your Photoshop Presets folder), with an .irs file name extension.

Format. If you prefer to arrange the settings manually, you should start by choosing GIF, JPEG, PNG, or WBMP from the Format popup menu. We discuss these formats in some detail in the last chapter and below.

JPEG

For best reproduction on the Web, scanned photographic images should almost always be saved in the JPEG file format. This way, people viewing the image on a 24-bit color monitor will see all the colors in the image, and those on 8-bit monitors will see a dithered version. Fortunately, the dithered version is usually pretty good—almost as good as if you had converted the image to 8-bit in Photoshop yourself.

JPEG compresses RGB natural images really well, even if the image does suffer some degradation in the process. On the other hand, JPEG is not suitable for images that have a lot of solid colors, especially computer-generated images, type, and line art. It's also not appropriate for images in which you've used Web-safe colors—because colors often shift in JPEG images—or images that require transparency.

You can save images in the JPEG format from the Save As dialog box (see Chapter 13, *Image Storage and Output*), but you get much more control in the Save For Web dialog box (see Figure 14-5).

Optimized. The only time you want to turn off the Optimized checkbox is if you're sure your image will be displayed on a very old Web browser that may not support the Optimized JPEG format. Almost every browser in use these days supports this format, however.

Compression quality. The more compression you apply in Photoshop, the worse the resulting image quality. Where you only have 12 levels of JPEG compression in the Save as JPEG dialog box, the Save For Web dialog box offers you 100 levels. The four settings in the Quality popup menu (Low, Medium, High, and Maximum) are simply presets for values in the Quality field to the right. (The four settings correspond to numerical values of 10, 30, 60, and 80, in case you care.) You can change the value to any number between 1 and 100 (100 being the highest quality and least amount of compression).

If you're a prima donna about your images, and you don't want *any* degradation, you're probably in the wrong business here. Remember that you can usually get away with a lot of degradation. David rarely uses a Quality value over 50 for Web images, though he probably wouldn't use less than 90 (a 9 or 10 setting in the Save As dialog box) for prepress images. Ultimately, it's all trial and error.

Figure 14-5
Save For Web:
JPEG images

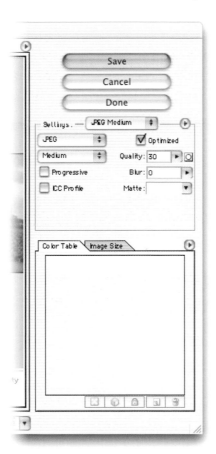

Note that if there are particular areas in your image that you don't want as degraded as others by the JPEG compression, you can select those areas, and save the selection as a channel. Then, click the little button next to the Quality field (the one that has a little dotted circle in it), and choose your channel from the Channel popup menu. Here, Photoshop lets you choose compression values for the black and white areas of the channel. Similarly, you can just specify a text or vector layer rather than building a channel. However, watch out: files that have this sort of compression-prioritizing area may look slightly better, but are almost always larger than those in which you have a single compression value throughout.

Progressive. Like Optimized, we almost always leave the Progressive feature turned on. When it's on, Web browsers will display a low-resolution version of the image first, then replace it with a high-resolution version. Strangely, progressive JPEG images are even slightly smaller than nonprogressive JPEGs, so the only reason not to leave this turned on is for displaying on very old browsers.

Blur. The problem with JPEG images is that the more you compress them, the more blocky they appear. These blocky artifacts are distracting to the eye, and primarily appear around high-contrast edges in your image. One option to combat these artifacts is to blur your image slightly so the edges aren't so pronounced. You can either apply the Gaussian Blur filter to your image before opening the Save For Web dialog box, or you can type a blur value into the Blur field here. Both do exactly the same thing, so if you're going to use it (we rarely do—perhaps only for thumbnails) we recommend just applying it in the dialog box.

ICC Profile. The ICC Profile checkbox lets you tell Photoshop whether to embed your RGB workspace profile in your JPEG image. Currently, the only Web browsers that care about color management assume that images are in sRGB unless an embedded profile tells them otherwise. We generally recommend converting Web images to sRGB before opening Save For Web, which makes profile embedding moot. But if for one reason or another you don't want to convert the image to sRGB, and you think your target audience will have color management configured correctly, by all means embed your working space profile—it usually adds less than 1 K of data to the file. For more information about ICC profiles and color management, check out Chapter 5, *Color Settings*.

Matte. JPEG images are always opaque and they're always rectangular. That's just the way it is; if you want real transparency, use the GIF or PNG format. So what happens if your image is on a layer that includes transparency? Photoshop fills in all your transparent pixels with whatever color you've chosen in the Matte field. In general, you want the Matte color to be the same color as either the background of the image or the background of your Web page. Note that the color you choose may shift slightly in the conversion to JPEG, especially if you're applying a lot of compression; check the RGB and Hex settings at the bottom of the Save For Web dialog box.

Tip: Keep Your Originals. Remember that if you open a JPEG image in Photoshop and then save it out again as a JPEG, the compression damages the image even more. So remember to always keep the original non-JPEG version of your image. That way, you can go back and make edits on the original and save out the JPEG version fresh again.

GIF

While JPEG is the preferred format for natural ("photographic") scanned images, GIF (don't even get us started on the "how should this be pronounced" argument) is currently *the* format for everything else.

▶ Images that contain areas of solid colors (including most blocks of text and computer-generated pictures)

▶ Animations

▶ Images containing transparency

▶ Images that rely on Web-safe colors

Theoretically, the GIF specification allows for a full 24-bit color image; however, nobody really supports this, so GIF images are always saved in 8-bit indexed color. (For more on this mode, see "Indexed Color" in Chapter 3, *Image Essentials*, and "Indexed Colors," later in this chapter.) That means you can't have more than 256 colors in your image. Fortunately, you can usually specify which 256 colors you want to use.

Tip: Stay in RGB. Some folks convert their RGB images to Indexed Color mode (on the Mode submenu) before saving them as a GIF. There's nothing wrong with doing this, but the Save For Web dialog box makes this workflow obsolete. Just leave the image in RGB and let Photoshop convert to Indexed Color mode on the fly when you save the file. The RGB mode is much more efficient in the long run because it affords the most flexibility in editing the image.

Here are the various options you have when saving a GIF image in the Save For Web dialog box (see Figure 14-6).

Lossy. No, Adobe isn't breaking the rules of GIF images: the GIF file format is still a lossless format (it doesn't degrade your image like JPEG does). Instead, the Lossy feature in the Save For Web dialog box lets you degrade

Figure 14-6
Save For Web:
GIF images

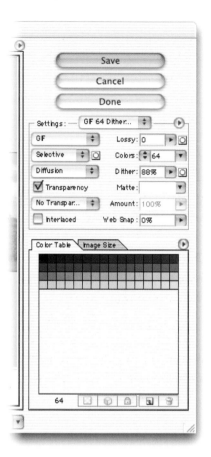

the image before it's saved as a GIF. Photoshop is taking advantage of several characteristics of the compression algorithm that GIF uses; by degrading the image in certain intelligent ways, it can compress the file further. This is most helpful when you have to save a scanned photographic image as a GIF instead of a JPEG (for instance, if you want portions of the image to be transparent). You can often get a significant increase in compression with hardly any visual noise by increasing the Lossy value to 10 or 20.

Color reduction method. GIF images are saved in the Indexed Color mode, which means a maximum of 256 colors. If you're converting an RGB image, or reducing the number of colors in an indexed color image, you need to tell Photoshop what method of color reduction to use (these are the same as the reduction methods listed in the Indexed Color dialog box): Adaptive, Selective, or Perceptual. Where Adaptive picks colors from your image based on how often they appear in the image, Perceptual picks a color palette based on how the colors look to the eye; in particular, Perceptual creates much nicer transitions between colors, so it's best for scanned photographic images. The Selective method is slightly better for images that have sharp high-contrast edges, such as synthetic images (like those from Illustrator or FreeHand). We hardly ever use Adaptive anymore.

If you insist on using a Web-safe palette, go ahead and select "Restrictive (Web)" from the popup menu. Or, if you've already built a custom color palette, you can choose it by selecting Load Color Palette from the popout menu next to the Color Table and Image Size tabs (if they labeled these popout menus, it would sure make it easier to describe this stuff to you).

Tip: Giving Preferential Treatment. Do you care about the color in one part of your image more than in other areas? No problem. Make a rough selection of the pixels you care about using the Marquee or Lasso tool, and save the selection in the Channels palette (see Chapter 8, *Making Selections*). Then, in the Save For Web dialog box, click the little button next to the Color popup menu (the one where you select Adaptive, Perceptive, and so on). Photoshop lets you pick the saved channel, and re-creates the color palette, giving a weighted preference for colors in that area.

Colors. The fewer colors in an image, the more solid or patterned areas in the image, so the better compression you can get. Very few GIF images need a full 256 colors; in fact, it's rare to find an image that won't look reasonable on screen with only 64. Note that the colors are shown in the Color Table at the bottom right of the dialog box (see "Color Table," later in this chapter).

Dither. Reducing the number of colors in an image is an imperfect science, and the results are often better if you dither the final colors a little bit. Photoshop has always included the Diffusion and Pattern dithers in the Indexed Color dialog boxes (the first is good, the second is bad). New to the lineup is the Noise option. The results are similar to—though a little "noisier" than—the Diffusion dither; however, you should use the Noise option if you're also slicing the image into smaller pieces (see "Slices," later in this chapter). The reason has to do with the way that diffusion dithers are created (Photoshop looks at each pixel and the pixels around it; if you later slice an image, the pixel values might change and the dither would no longer look right).

If you choose the Diffusion method, you can also pick a Dither amount in the Dither field. Personally, we feel that if you're going to be dithering an image at all, you might as well pick a value in the 70 or 80 percent area. However, the choice is up to you and really is image-specific.

Transparency. If your image contains transparent pixels (that is, it has no opaque Background layer), you can choose whether or not those pixels should be transparent in the final image by turning on or off the Transparency checkbox. When the checkbox is turned off, all transparent pixels are set to the color in the Matte field. If Matte is set to None, then Photoshop sets the colors to white.

On the other hand, if you turn on the Transparency checkbox, Photoshop leaves fully transparent pixels transparent, and blends partially transparent pixels with the color in the Matte setting. This is very useful when you're trying to blend your GIF image into your Web page's background color (see Figure 14-7). If Matte is set to None, then Photoshop simply clips off all partially transparent pixels, and you get a hard, aliased-edged image.

If your image doesn't contain any transparent pixels, you can force particular colors to be transparent in the Save For Web dialog box by selecting them in the Color Table (you can choose more than one by Command-clicking on each color) and clicking the Transparency button. But unless you have very few colors in your image, it's usually just much faster to exit the Save For Web dialog box and create transparency in the image itself.

You can also create "dithered transparency" by selecting from the popup menu directly beneath the Transparency checkbox. This only has an effect when there are pixels that are partially transparent in your image (like a drop shadow might be). Unfortunately, the result is typically so extraordinarily ugly that we find it hardly worth the time.

Tip: Finding a Good Matte Color. When choosing a matte color to which Photoshop can blend your semitransparent pixels, you generally want to pick a color dominant in whatever background you're placing the image over. If you can't remember what that color is, but it appears somewhere on screen (the Photoshop Color Picker, the Swatches palette, or in some image window), you can choose it by clicking once on the Matte color

Figure 14-7
Transparency in
GIF images

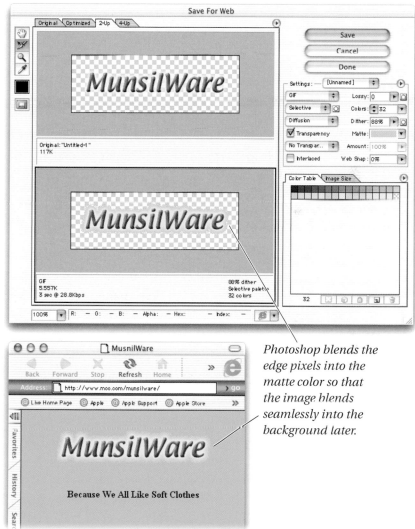

*Photoshop blends the
edge pixels into the
matte color so that
the image blends
seamlessly into the
background later.*

swatch, then clicking on the desired color with the automatically provided eyedropper tool. If the Swatches palette isn't visible (and you want it to be), choose Show Swatches from the Window menu first.

Interlaced. Whereas turning on the Progressive checkbox for JPEGs generally makes the image slightly smaller (a fact which truly confounds us, as the image doesn't appear to change any), turning on the Interlaced checkbox for GIF images actually makes the image very slightly larger. Because of this, we only turn this on when having an image appear slowly (like a venetian blind opening) actually benefits the viewer. For instance, we rarely use this for buttons, but we typically do use it for image maps, because the audience might be able to click on an area of the image map before the final image is complete.

Web Snap. Maybe we just don't get it, but the Web Snap feature seems really useless to us. The concept is that as you increase the Web Snap percentage, some number of colors in your image will snap to a Web-safe color palette. Unfortunately, you have no control over what colors are changed. We never use this; if we want to snap colors to a Web-safe palette, we do it manually in the Color Table area.

Color Table. The Color Table not only displays which colors appear in your final image, but also lets you change them or keep them from being changed. While it's rare that you'd need to do so, if you double-click on any color swatch, Photoshop lets you change its color (using the standard Color Picker). More common is tweaking the color to match the nearest Web-safe color. Fortunately, Photoshop makes this really easy: just select the color (or more than one color by holding down the Command key when you click) and click the Snap to Web-safe Color button (that's the one that looks like a little cube). Web-safe swatches appear with a white dot in their centers. The popout menu next to the Color Table lets you add and delete colors, select specific colors, and—best of all—control how Photoshop displays the color swatches. We generally choose to display the swatches by Hue or Luminance, as we find these easiest to comprehend.

Tip: Save That Color! Let's say you've got an image of a banana with a small bit of red text over it. Because the image is composed of mostly yellow colors, the red text might change to a dark yellow color if you lower the number of colors in the image. To save the red pixels, increase the number of colors in the Save For Web dialog box to 128 or so (enough so that the red pixels appear in the Color Table), then select the red swatch and click the Lock button (the one that looks like a little padlock). Now, as you lower the number of colors in the image, that swatch will always remain red. You can unlock it again by selecting it and clicking the button again. Note that locked colors always show a small white square in the bottom-right corner.

Tip: Optimize to File Size. Computers are supposed to figure stuff out for us, right? So if you know that you need an image to be smaller than 10 K, why not let Photoshop figure out the proper settings for you? Click on one of the images in the Save For Web dialog box and select Optimize to File Size from the unlabeled popout menu next to the Settings popup menu. The Optimize To File Size dialog box lets you choose a file format (JPEG or GIF), but we tend simply to choose the Automatic feature and let Photoshop figure out the best solution for us (see Figure 14-8). Whatever you do, though, don't just accept whatever Photoshop gives you: the best images still require some tweaking.

Figure 14-8
Optimize To File Size

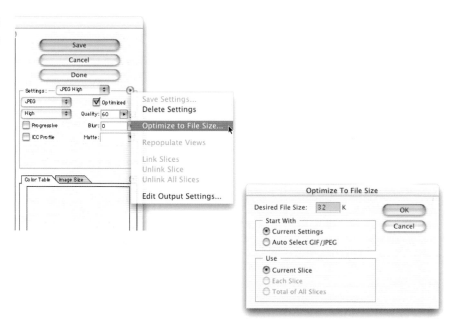

Tip: Eking Out the Bytes. A great many images on the Internet (or "information superhighway," or "Infobahn," or whatever you want to call it) are saved in GIF format, especially those that appear on World Wide Web sites. The reason is simple: they're very compact. But sometimes they're just not compact enough. For instance, on slower modem lines, there's a big difference between watching a 30 K image slowly appear on your screen and a 15 K image appear without trouble.

If you're trying to eke out every little bit of compression in a GIF file, keep in mind how LZW compression works: it looks for repeating patterns of colors. For instance, it can tokenize "red, blue, red, blue, red, blue" into one piece of information. Therefore, the images that get compressed the most contain lots of these repeating patterns.

Here are several ways you can make Photoshop use more repeating patterns when you're converting images from RGB to Indexed Color.

▶ Use solid areas rather than gradations or textures.

▶ If you do use gradations (blends), consider unchecking the Dither option in the Gradient tool's Options palette and making the blend vertical (top to bottom) rather than horizontal (side to side). (This ensures that more pixels of the same color will sit next to each other.)

▶ Using specific color schemes is better than using lots of different colors. The fewer colors you use, the more compression you'll achieve.

▶ Use a smaller bit depth (use 16 or 32 colors instead of 128 or 255). Of course, many images degrade significantly with fewer colors, so you should play around with this.

▶ If you're converting to Indexed Color mode before you export the GIF, choose Pattern dither instead of Diffusion dither (in the Indexed Color dialog box).

▶ Using System palette (or Uniform, if you're using fewer than 8 bits per pixel) instead of Adaptive can save 1 or 2 KB, which is important in some cases. If this doesn't matter as much to you, Adaptive is probably better.

With any of these techniques, the image's dither is almost always slightly more obvious, but you can make the image transfer over phone lines faster.

PNG Images

There are very few settings you can change when saving files in the PNG-24 format (the primary choice is whether or not they should include transparent areas), and the settings for the PNG-8 file format are almost identical to those of the GIF format (see Figure 14-9). As we explained back in Chapter 13, *Image Storage and Output*, we think the PNG format is cool, but it is still isn't widely used or supported fully by Web browsers. Also, note that PNG images are generally larger than their GIF or JPEG

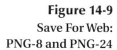

Figure 14-9
Save For Web:
PNG-8 and PNG-24

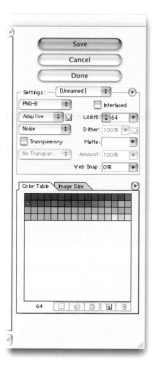

counterparts, so there has to be a really good reason to use them (which there isn't yet).

WBMP Images

Web pages are beginning to appear on every sort of device, from cell phones to PDAs to kitchen blenders (well, not yet, but probably soon). However, most of these devices only display black and white pixels—it's like a return to 1984! Standards are shifting, but one file format for displaying these Bitmap images has gained popularity: WBMP (which isn't the same thing as Windows BMP). Photoshop lets you save WBMP files in two ways. If your file is already converted to Bitmap mode from the Mode submenu (in the Image menu), you can simply save as WBMP from the Save As dialog box. Otherwise, the Save For Web dialog box lets you save any kind of image in the WBMP format.

The only control you have for WBMP files is the type of dither: None, Diffusion, Pattern, or Noise. Note that Diffusion and None look the same until you increase the dither percentage for the Dither setting. Curiously, the WBMP format doesn't appear to include any compression algorithms, so whatever dither you use creates the same-sized file.

Other Save For Web Controls

Before we move on to other aspects of Photoshop's Web capabilities, we should note just a few other nifty features in the Save For Web dialog box.

Navigating. You can navigate around your graphic to check for image degradation in different areas. First, you can use the Grabber Hand tool (press H) by clicking-and-dragging on any one of the images. As you drag one image, all the other images move, too. Next, you can zoom in and out on the image by changing the view percentage in the lower-left corner of the Save For Web dialog box (though it's usually faster to Control-click or right-mouse-click on an image and change the scale from the context-sensitive menu). Zooming out rarely helps, but we sometimes zoom in to see the effects of the JPEG or GIF conversion more clearly. Note that you can also resize the Save For Web dialog box by dragging in the lower-right corner of the window.

Image Size. Need your final Web graphic to be smaller than the high-resolution version you've got? You can use the Image Size dialog box to downsample the image before using Save For Web, or you can use the Image Size tab in the Save For Web dialog box. Both do exactly the same thing. The one difference is that the Save For Web dialog box only offers you pixel dimensions, and the result will always be at 72 ppi. This is okay because inches, millimeters, and picas don't mean anything in a Web world where everyone's monitors display at different resolutions.

Browser Dither. Sure, you have a 24-bit color monitor, but your audience might not. A few people still have old 8-bit color monitors, and your glorious color images will get dithered using the 256 colors in their Web browser's color palette. If you care about what those people see, you can turn on the Browser Dither option in the unlabeled popout menu at the top right of the Save For Web dialog box's image area (or, better yet, just select it from the context-sensitive menu).

Download speed. Each image in the Save For Web dialog box lists the approximate time it would take to download this image at 28.8 Kbps. However, if you're pretty sure that most of your audience will be connected with a 256 Kbps cable modem, you can change the setting in the popout menu at the top of the dialog box (or in the context-sensitive menu). To be honest, though, we rarely pay attention to this readout, as there are many variables that affect download times (server load, processor speed, cosmic rays…).

Gamma. As we pointed out earlier, Windows boxes typically display images darker than Macintosh boxes. You can simulate this by turning on Standard Windows Color, which simulates a display gamma of 2.2; or Standard Macintosh Color, which simulates a display gamma of 1.8 (either from the popout menu at the top of the dialog box or from the context-sensitive menu). But ultimately, when it comes to color and tone correction for the Web, it's still really hit or miss.

Let Photoshop Write Your HTML

Who wants to write HTML code anymore? Certainly not us. We paid our dues already, and now we just want to let the computer do what it's good at. Fortunately, the Save For Web dialog box will write HTML code that describes our images.

There's two ways to get HTML out of this dialog box. First, you can click on the preview button to open the currently selected image in your Web browser. Not only does the image appear, but so does information about the image and the source code that the Web browser can read. You can then copy the pieces of the HTML that you require (generally the IMG tag).

There's a better way, though: After you select which image you want to save and click OK, Photoshop displays the Save Optimized As dialog box, where you can actually name your file and tell Photoshop where to save it (see Figure 14-10). What's more, you can choose HTML and Images from the Format popup menu. (If you're saving Slices, this is really important;

Figure 14-10
Save Optimized As

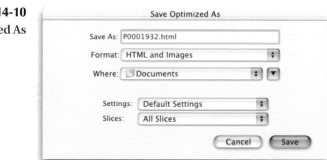

see "Slices," in the next section.) You can then open the HTML file in a text editor and copy and paste the relevant information.

More Web Tools

Adobe Photoshop offers many more tools for getting great-looking Web images. In fact, with each new version, we see that the line between Image-Ready and Photoshop becomes less distinct. Where will it ever end?

In this section, we'll explore image slicing, converting images to indexed color, making Web page galleries for browsing your photographs, and building animated GIFs. This certainly doesn't cover every Web feature in Photoshop, but we think it covers the most important ones.

Slices

Not every part of an image is equal, and not all parts deserve equal treatment. Often, some parts of an image can be compressed significantly more (with greater image degradation) than others. Or some parts are destined to be rollovers (areas that change when the cursor rolls over them in the Web browser), animations, or Web links. In any of these instances, you might consider slicing your graphic into smaller pieces with Photoshop's Slice tool. When you do this, and then save the image with the Save For Web feature, Photoshop saves each slice as a separate file to disk with its own compression settings. Or, if you open the sliced image in ImageReady, you can set each slice to be a rollover or other type of dynamic media.

Tip: Slices vs. Image Maps. If your entire image will be optimized the same way, you're not creating rollovers or other dynamic areas in the graphic, but you do want certain areas to be "buttons" or "hot links" (areas that, when clicked, take you to a different URL), then you might want to make the image an "image map" instead of slicing it up. It's easy to make image maps in ImageReady (there's even a special tool for it), and this way you only export a single image rather than one file for each slice. Plus, the "hot" areas in an image map can be rectangular, oval, or even a polygon—whereas slices are always rectangular.

Making (and breaking) slices. Photoshop offers two tools for creating slices: the Slice tool (it looks like a little blade in the Tool palette; press K to select it quickly), and the New Layer Based Slice feature (in the Layer menu).

▶ **Slice tool.** The Slice tool acts much like the Marquee selection tool: just drag it over the area you want to define as a slice. You can constrain the shape or size of the slice by choosing Constrained Aspect Ratio or Fixed Size from the Style popup menu in the Options bar (see Chapter 8, *Making Selections*, for more on how to use these options).

▶ **New Layer Based Slice.** Let's say you've got five buttons in your image and you want each one to be a separate slice. If each one is on its own layer, then you can avoid the Slice tool entirely by selecting a layer and choosing New Layer Based Slice from the Layer menu (then repeating this for each layer with a button on it). Photoshop creates slices based on the boundaries of whatever is on each layer. Better yet, if you change a layer, the slices update automatically.

You can't have a single slice of an image; however you make the slice, Photoshop automatically slices the rest of the image up. For example, if you make a square slice in the middle of the picture, Photoshop adds four other "auto-slices" to fill in the area around the square (see Figure 14-11). The slice you make is called a "user slice," and it looks slightly different on screen: user slices have solid boundaries, auto-slices have dotted bound-

Figure 14-11
Slicing an image

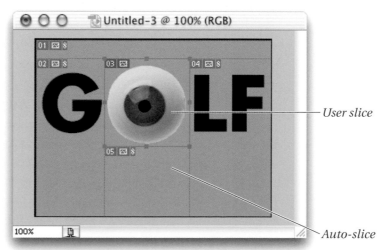

— User slice

— Auto-slice

aries. Each time you change or add a user slice, Photoshop reconfigures the auto-slices automatically.

How do you change a slice once you've made it? Use the Slice Selection tool. This tool is hiding behind the Slice tool in the Tool palette; you can get it by pressing Shift-K, or, temporarily, by holding down the Command key while the Slice tool is selected. The Slice Selection tool lets you move the slice (click inside the slice and drag) or change the slice boundaries (drag the slice's corner or edge handles). You can only edit or move user slices, though. If you want to change an auto-slice into a user slice, click on it with the Slice Selection tool (you can't use the Command key trick here) and then click the Promote to User Slice button in the Options bar.

Tip: Minimize Your Slices. The main problem with automatic layer-based slices is that you often get many more slices using this feature than if you use the Slice tool with care. The more slices, the more files you have to keep track of on disk, and the longer it takes to transfer the image to the Web browser. We'll often start our sliced images with layer-based slicing, but then edit the slice boundaries once we're pretty sure the graphic won't change again. To edit the slice boundaries, you have to click on the slice with the Slice Selection tool and then click the Promote to User Slice button in the Options bar. Of course, after you do this, the slices are no longer tied to the layers (see Figure 14-12).

Tip: Overlapping Slices. Slices often overlap each other, especially when you use the New Layer Based Slice feature. In these cases, Photoshop adds "sub-slices" in the overlapping areas, which act just like regular slices, but cannot be selected with the Slice Selection tool. If you don't like the order in which the overlapping slices are arranged, you can change them by selecting the slice and clicking on the Bring to Front or Send to Back button in the Options bar (these buttons appear when you have the Slice Selection tool chosen in the Tool palette). In general, you should try to avoid overlapping slices unless you're going to apply the same optimization/compression techniques to each of them.

By the way, once you make your slices, you can lock them in place by selecting Lock Slices from the View menu. That way, you (or some careless colleague) won't accidentally move or resize the slice boundaries.

Figure 14-12
Reducing the
number of slices

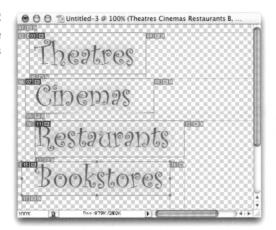

*Sloppy slicing
creates 17 slices.*

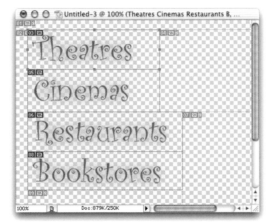

*By aligning the
slice borders, we
get only nine
slices.*

If you want to delete a single slice, click on it with the Slice Selection tool and press the Delete or Backspace key. If you want to delete all the slices, choose Clear Slices from the View menu. (No, we have no idea why these features are in the View menu; we figure they just couldn't decide where else to put them.)

Slice Options. While you need ImageReady to create dynamic media such as rollovers, you can control each slice and add some basic actions right in Photoshop by selecting the slice with the Slice Selection tool and clicking the Slice Options button in the Options bar. (Even faster, just Command-double-click on the slice with the Slice tool.) This opens the Slice Options dialog box (see Figure 14-13). Here's a quick rundown of the options.

Figure 14-13
Slice Options
dialog box

▶ **Name.** Photoshop automatically gives your slice a name based on the name of the file itself. When you save the slices to disk, it'll have this name (plus .gif or .jpg, depending on the file type). You can override the name here, if you like. Note that if you're using Cascading Style Sheets (CSS), this is also the object name (see "Saving Slices," below).

▶ **URL.** You can make this slice "hot" (so that you can click on it to jump to a different Web page) by typing a URL into the URL field. If the Web page you're linking to will be in the same folder as the current page's folder, then you can just type the file's name (like "mypage.html"). However, if you're linking to a different site's page, you need the full URL (like "http://www.moo.com").

▶ **Target.** The Target field tells your Web browser where to open the new Web page that you linked to in the URL field. If you leave this blank, the Web page replaces the current Web page (if you're using frames, then it replaces the current frame). On the other hand, you can type "_top" in the Target field to force the linked page to replace the entire window (even if there's a frame there), or "_blank" to open the link in a new window. If you're using frames in your HTML, you can also type the target frame name.

▶ **Message Text.** By default, when you move your cursor over a link in a Web browser, the link URL shows up at the bottom of the browser window. You can replace that URL with a specific message by typing in the Message Text field. We usually leave this blank.

▶ **Alt Tag.** If the person viewing your Web page has a slow Internet connection, it might take a while to download an image. While they're waiting, it's often helpful to show them an alt tag—some text that describes what the image will be. This is even more important if they've set their browser's preferences so that no images are downloaded at all. The alt tag (if you type one in this field) appears in place of the image. For instance, this isn't important in a slice that has no relevant information in it, but it's crucial that you label slices that are buttons with their action. Otherwise, some of your viewers may not be able to navigate your Web site.

▶ **Dimensions.** The Dimensions fields let you specify where the slice is in your image and how wide and tall it is (in pixels). This is most useful when you're trying to align slices along their edges.

▶ **No Image.** If you choose No Image from the Slice Type popup menu, Photoshop won't save this slice to disk. Instead, it includes some custom HTML in its place (whatever you type in the HTML field of the Slice Options dialog box). For example, if you type text here, you'll see that text in place of the slice in the Web browser. If you leave the field blank, it'll leave a hole in the image (the Web page's background will show through, unless you change the Background setting in Output Options, which we'll talk about in a moment). You can type any HTML you want here (up to 255 characters). But make sure whatever you put in the HTML field is no bigger than the slice itself. If it is, and you use the default Table method of writing HTML, then all hell will break loose and your image will fall apart.

The values you set in the Slice Options dialog box are saved with your Photoshop image, and are also transferred to ImageReady if you open the graphic in that program. But you still have to export the picture along with HTML in order for the values to actually be functional.

Saving slices. In the good old days, we used to have to slice up images manually, using the Crop tool, then write down the pixel dimensions for each slice, and then piece them together into a table using hand-coded HTML. And we liked it! (Well, not really, but what choice did we have?) Fortunately, Photoshop can write our HTML for us now, making the whole process pain-free and very quick. The trick is to save the sliced image using Save For Web, as described earlier in the chapter, and make sure that you choose Images and HTML from the Format popup menu in the Save Optimized As dialog box.

When you open the Save For Web dialog box, choose the Slice Selection tool (press K), click on each user slice, and specify how you want it to be optimized (GIF versus JPEG, number of colors, and so on). You can also click on one of the auto-slices and choose its optimization settings (all the auto-slices get the same optimization settings).

After you click the Save button, you'll see the Save Optimized As dialog box; choose Other from the Settings popup menu here. The Output Settings dialog box (see Figure 14-14) lets you control how Photoshop writes

Figure 14-14
Output Settings

This is actually four dialog boxes rolled into one.

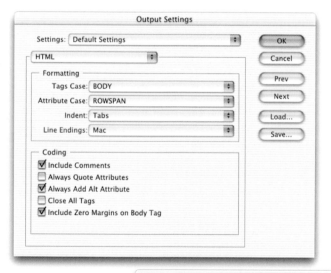

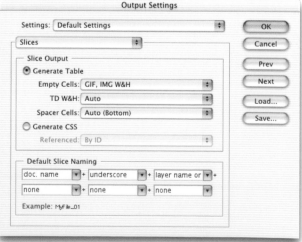

the HTML to disk, including how it names each slice that you haven't already named in Slice Options, whether the slices are arranged in an HTML table or with CSS tags, and a host of other options. Most of the settings aren't that exciting, or they're self-explanatory. Here are a few that we should mention, though.

► **Formatting.** There's a certain breed of person who deeply cares about exactly how the HTML is typed—for instance, whether certain words are in all capital letters, in lowercase, or in initial caps. You can specify this sort of thing in the Formatting section of Output Settings. We tend to be more mellow about these things, so we just ignore this section.

Figure 14-14
More Output Settings,
continued

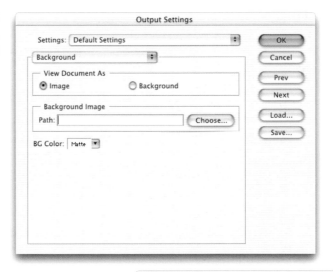

▶ **Slice Output.** Photoshop can piece together your slices in one of two ways: as an HTML table or using CSS. The default setting is Table, which is probably the way you should go in most instances. The only time we can think of when CSS would make more sense is if you were doing something like animating the pieces of the slice so that they fly around the screen. Otherwise, Table offers easier and smaller HTML. (And you can always position the table on your Web page with CSS later, using something like GoLive or Dreamweaver, if you really want to.) Whichever you choose, we recommend leaving the other settings in this section at their defaults, unless you have a very good reason to change them.

▶ **View As.** If your image is destined to be a background image (a picture that gets tiled so that it covers the whole Web browser window), you should choose View As from the Background tab of the Output Settings dialog box (press Command-2 to jump there quickly). However, you can't make a sliced image a background image, so this is grayed out if you have any slices. Of course, this is only relevant if you're asking Photoshop to write your HTML, which you often don't need if you're just making a background image.

▶ **Background.** The field labeled Background (inside the Background tab of the dialog box) lets you tell Photoshop what to use as a background image in the HTML it writes. For example, if you choose a color from the Color popup menu, Photoshop places your image (even if it's sliced) on top of that color. This isn't really relevant if you're planning on placing the sliced image onto some other Web page using GoLive or Dreamweaver.

▶ **Saving Files.** The Saving Files tab of the Output Settings dialog box (press Command-3 to get there quickly) gives you lots of control over exactly how Photoshop names each file, and where it puts these files. But the file names in this section relate more to dynamic images, such as rollovers created in ImageReady. If we change anything here, it's the name of the folder where the files are saved (the default "images" is fine, but we often use different names, depending on what we're doing; or, if you turn off the Save Images In checkbox, then Photoshop just saves the images and HTML in the same folder).

▶ **Slices.** The place to specify how Photoshop names slices when it saves them to disk is the Slices tab of the Output Settings dialog box (press Command-4 to jump to this tab). Again, we usually just leave this set to the defaults, but you can tweak it if you've got a favorite naming algorithm. Note that we were confused by this setting until we realized that the second line of popup menus is connected to the first line by the little plus symbol.

You can get to the Output Settings dialog box from either the Save For Web dialog box or the Save Optimized As dialog box (the dialog box that you get once you click OK from Save For Web). Both take you to exactly the same place.

Tip: Saving Output Settings. If you think you'll use a particular configuration of options in the Output Settings dialog box more than once or twice, you might as well save your settings to disk by clicking the Save button in the Output Settings dialog box. (Photoshop saves it in the proper place by default: the Optimized Output Settings folder, inside the Presets folder, inside the Photoshop folder.) Then, next time you want to use the same configuration, you can simply choose your saved file from the Settings popup menu (or click the Load button). Note, however, that the Save button only appears in the Output Options dialog box when you open it from the Save As Web dialog box; it's missing in action when you open Output Options from the Save Optimized As dialog box.

Indexed Colors

As we said in Chapter 3, *Image Essentials*, and earlier in this chapter, GIF images and many other graphics designed for games and multimedia are stored in Indexed Color mode. Indexed color images are small (about the same size as grayscale images), they often compress in file size really well, and they're perfect for those old and obsolete 8-bit color monitors that some folks still have.

Earlier, we said that converting images to Indexed Color mode before saving them as GIF files was obsolete, because it's more convenient to leave the image in RGB mode and use Save For Web to convert it on the fly. However, many people still need to work with indexed color images in Photoshop, and the program offers two features to help manage this process: the Indexed Color dialog box and the Color Table dialog box. There are also several ways to pick and manage Web-safe colors, which we'll discuss in the next section.

Indexed Color dialog box. You can convert an RGB or grayscale image to indexed color by selecting Indexed Color from the Mode submenu (under the Image menu). This brings up the Indexed Color dialog box (see Figure 14-15). Many of the controls here work in exactly the same manner as those we talked about in the Save For Web dialog box (see "GIF," earlier in this chapter). However, there are a few special things to think about.

▶ **Preview.** The Preview checkbox lets you see exactly how you're messing up your image. There are few (if any) reasons to turn this off.

▶ **Palettes.** The Palette popup menu offers a number of different options, including Perceptual, Selective, and Adaptive color reduction methods in both "Local" and "Master" flavors. As far as we can tell, there's no reason to use the Master versions in Photoshop; they're errant holdovers from ImageReady. If you want to use master palettes (palettes that are consistent across multiple images), ImageReady is probably a better bet. Again, we generally use Perceptual for scanned photographic images, and Selective for synthetic images with sharp edges.

▶ **Transparency.** Any pixels that are transparent in your image can be transparent in the final indexed color image, too. However, if you don't have any transparent pixels, then turn off the Transparency checkbox in the Indexed Color dialog box; otherwise, Photoshop adds a color swatch to your color table and specifies that swatch as a transparent color (taking up a swatch that could better be used for a color).

   Of course, indexed color documents cannot contain partially transparent pixels, so the Matte feature lets you anti-alias these pixels into some other color (whatever color the image will later sit on). If you set the Matte popup menu to None, Photoshop gives you a hard-edged boundary. This sounds bad, and images that have no anti-aliasing around them often look really jaggy in Photoshop; but when they're placed over a colored or patterned background, you often don't notice the jaggies at all (or if you do, they're still better than a halo around the image; see Figure 14-16).

▶ **Forced.** The Forced popup menu lets you force particular colors into the image's color palette. For instance, if you choose Black and White (which is on by default), Photoshop ensures that those two colors are in the palette. This is especially important when you're using very few colors or when you need to make sure that a specific color is locked in and won't change. Besides Black and White, the Forced popup menu

Figure 14-15
Indexed Color
dialog box

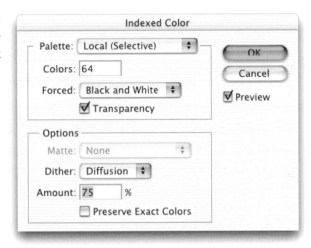

Figure 14-16
Anti-aliasing images

Anti-aliased to white background

Aliased (jaggy edges)

The anti-aliased version looks terrible on a colored background.

The aliased version looks good.

offers you Primaries (which forces red, green, blue, cyan, magenta, yellow, black, and white into the palette), Web (which ensures that all 216 Web-safe colors are in your palette), and Custom (which lets you specify your own colors that should be in the final palette).

Tip: Prioritizing Colors. Occasionally you and Photoshop might disagree as to what colors in the image are the most important. For instance, if you convert a photographic portrait of someone against a bright blue background, the color palette will include a lot of blues that you might not necessarily care about—you probably want Photoshop to include more skin tones instead. You can force Photoshop to prioritize colors by selecting the area containing the colors you want, then converting to Indexed Color mode. Note that Photoshop may still change the colors slightly.

Tip: Saving Palettes. After converting an image to indexed color, you can view the palette by selecting Color Table from the Mode submenu (under the Image menu). More important, from there you can save this palette to disk in order to use it for other conversions (click the Save button). In this way, you can standardize a number of images on the same palette. Plus, custom color palettes that you've saved to disk from Photoshop can also be used in some multimedia programs. Note that you need to save the palette with an ".aco" extension if you want it to work on Windows or cross-platform machines.

Editing the color table. In an indexed-color image, each pixel is assigned a number from 0 to 255. The pixel's color comes only by comparing the number with a color lookup table (CLUT). Fortunately, this is all done behind the scenes, so you don't have to think about it much. One reason to convert an image to Indexed Color is so you can edit the particular colors in an image by editing the CLUT. If you choose Color Table from the Mode submenu, you can click on any color in the table to edit it. In color tables that have more than eight or 16 colors, this kind of editing is cumbersome; but in some instances, editing an image's color table can be a very powerful tool.

Tip: Swapping Indexed Colors. Let's say you have a logo on your Web page, which you want to be a different color every week. One way to make this color change would be to edit the GIF image's color lookup table (see Figure 14-17).

1. Open the GIF image and select Color Table from the Mode submenu (under the Image menu).

2. Click on the color you want to change, and when Photoshop asks you to, select a new color from the Color Picker (or type in RGB values). You probably want to make sure that the color you select is Web safe.

Figure 14-17
Swapping indexed colors

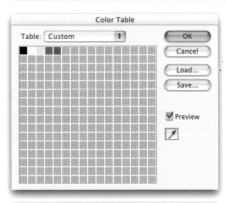

Click on a swatch to change its color. This alters the color throughout the image.

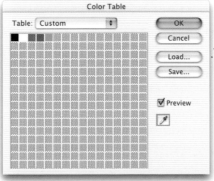

If the image is anti-aliased and all the intermediary colors are clumped together in the palette (as they often are), you can change them all at once. For example, if you have five different red swatches—from light pink to bright red—you can drag the mouse from the first swatch to the last. When you let go of the mouse button, Photoshop asks you for the new first color (to replace the light pink), and then for the new last color (to replace the bright red). It will then build all the intermediary colors for you, based on the two you choose.

3. Click OK and save the image.

Of course, this tip works best when the image has only a few colors.

Tip: Which Swatch to What Color? Trying to figure out exactly which swatch in the color lookup table represents each color in your indexed color image is almost impossible until you notice that the Info palette gives you this information automatically as you move the cursor over each pixel.

Web Colors

What's a Web color? In Photoshop, this term means two different things, depending on where you find it. Photoshop can display "Web Color" in the Info palette (select Palette Options from the palette's popout menu, or click on one of the little triangles in the Info palette to change the display). In this mode, the Info palette shows you the hexadecimal equivalents of your RGB colors (see Figure 14-18).

(For those of you who care but don't already know: Hexadecimal is simply base-16, which means that after the number 9 comes A, then B, then C, and so on to F, which represents the number 15. So the digits 00 signify zero and FF signifies 255.)

The second use of the term "Web Color" is in Photoshop's Color Picker dialog box, where you can turn on the Only Web Colors checkbox. What this *should* read is Only Web-safe Colors. Or, even more specifically, "Only let me pick colors that won't dither when displayed in a Web browser on archaic 8-bit color monitors."

Tip: Copying Web Colors. The only time you would really need to know the hexadecimal equivalent of a color in your document is if you

Figure 14-18
Hexadecimal
equivalents of colors

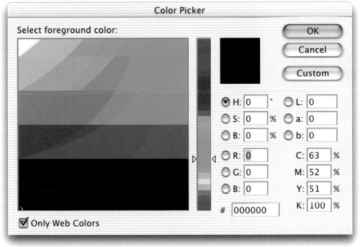

needed to duplicate it in another program, like GoLive or Dreamweaver. Fortunately, if you select the Eyedropper tool (press I), then hold down the Control key (on the Mac) or the right mouse button (in Windows) while you click, the context-sensitive menu offers to "Copy Color as HTML." The result: the HTML tag for the color you clicked on. For instance, it might copy COLOR="#E7ECF6" on to the Clipboard. You can then paste this into some other program.

If you want the hexadecimal equivalent without the HTML tag, you can simply click once with the Eyedropper tool, then click on the foreground color swatch in the Tool palette. The Color Picker dialog box now displays the hexadecimal values, as well as RGB, CMYK, Lab, and HSB.

Tip: Changing Your Jump To Application. If you use Photoshop and ImageReady together, it's worth noting that Adobe has a Jump To feature in the File menu and at the bottom of the Tool palette (or you can press Command-Shift-M). The Jump To feature does just one thing: it switches to ImageReady. If you have an image open when you invoke this command, Photoshop prompts you to save it (if it's not already saved), and then it opens the same picture in ImageReady.

However, the Jump To feature doesn't have to switch to ImageReady. If there's some other image-editing program that you'd rather use, you can easily change Photoshop's default behavior. Inside the Photoshop Settings folder there's a folder called Helpers. Inside the Helpers folder there's another folder called Jump To Graphics Editor. Inside this folder are aliases (or shortcuts on Windows). The alias with the curly braces around its name is the application that Photoshop switches to when you click the Jump To button on the Tool palette. We'll leave the rest to your imagination. Of course, whatever application you use must be able to open the file format of the images you're working on.

Web Photo Gallery

The Web Photo Gallery, found in the Automate submenu (under the File menu), is like the other automated features: it performs a task that you could do by hand, but it would be so painful and boring that you might fall out of your chair from the sheer monotony of the chore. In a nutshell, the Web Photo Gallery creates a Web page full of image thumbnails (see Figure 14-19). If you click on one of the thumbnails, it automatically links to a larger-size version of the picture. That's about it.

Fortunately, Adobe has come up with some nicer layout templates than earlier versions of Photoshop offered. Some layouts are pretty basic, but any of the layouts are more than adequate when it comes to a quick 'n' dirty display of images from a digital camera that need to be shared among several people on the Web. Some layouts even offer a clever mechanism for your audience to send you e-mail feedback on each image. And if you want to design your own layout, Photoshop lets you (see "Tip: Customize Your Galleries," later in this section).

Using one of these built-in Web photo galleries is pretty easy.

1. After choosing Web Photo Gallery from the Automate submenu, choose a gallery style from the Styles menu, such as Horizontal Blue & Gray, Horizontal Gray, Centered Frame, or Dotted Border. Some of these are built (behind the scenes) using HTML tables; others are based on frames or Flash.

2. Look at the settings in each tab of the Options popup menu (Banner, Gallery Images, Gallery Thumbnails, Custom Colors, and Security). These choices determine what your final Web gallery will look like

(see Figure 14-20). For example, in the Banner tab, you should type the name of the photographer and the date the pictures were taken (or today's date). The Site Name field determines the title of the gallery (it's the Web site name, not usually the site where the photos were taken). Similarly, the two Images tabs let you choose how large and how compressed the final images should be.

When it comes to image and thumbnail size, the pixel dimension you specify (for instance "Small" means 250 pixels) determines the width or height of the image, whichever side is larger. The only way to find out the actual file size (on disk) is by trial and error, though Large images tend to be around 40–60 K each, while Medium thumbnails tend to be around 25 K each.

You can assign captions for the thumbnails and/or for the larger images. The captions can just be the file name. Or, if you have filled out the fields in the File Info dialog box (under the File menu), Photoshop can use this data—just turn on the Title, Copyright, Caption, and Credits checkboxes.

The Security features let you tell Photoshop to add text to each image. For example, if you want your company name to be added in the lower-

Figure 14-19
Web Photo Gallery

Figure 14-20
The five tabs of the
Web Photo Gallery
dialog box

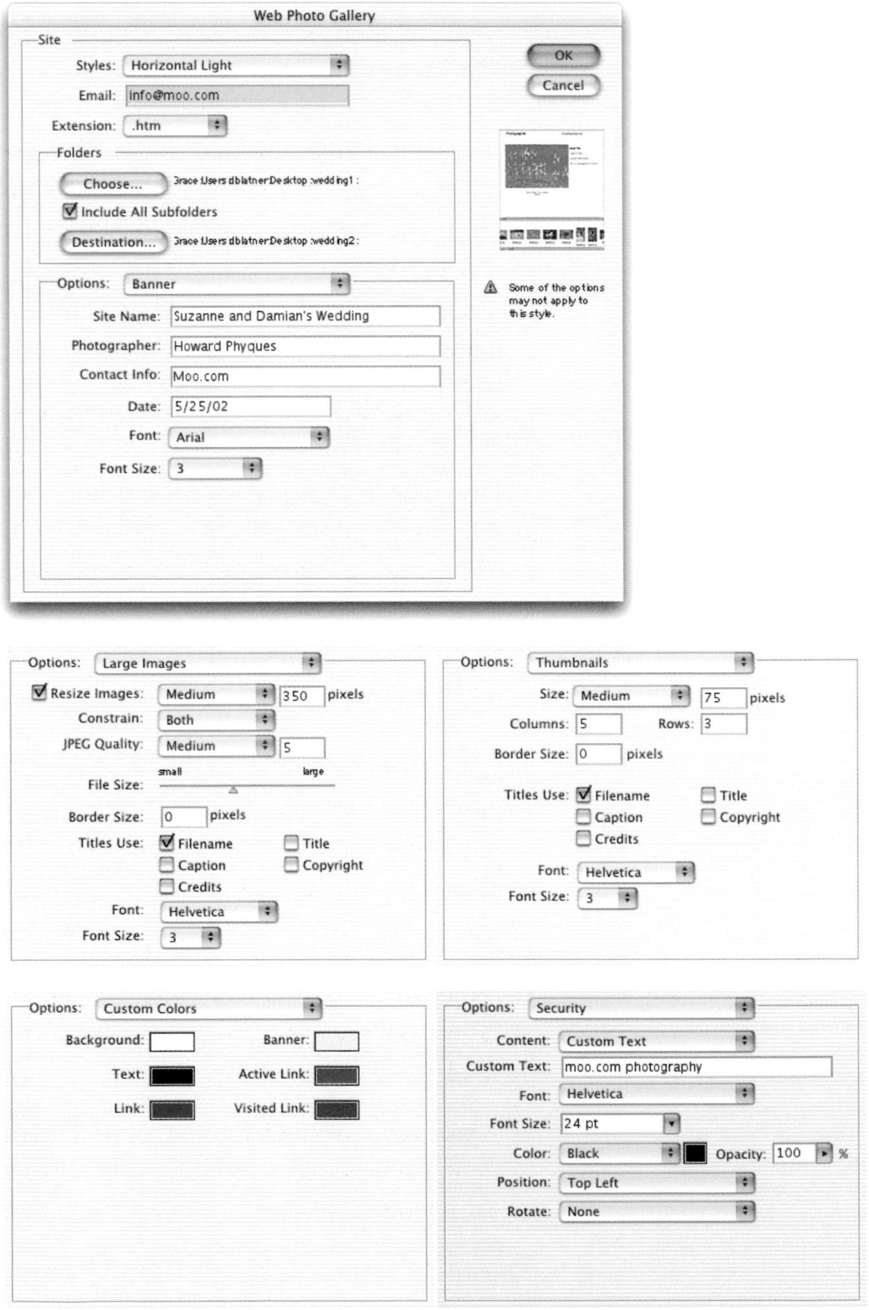

left corner of each image, you can select Custom Text from the Content
popup menu. (You can also specify where you want Photoshop to place
the text and in what font, size, and so on.) Of course, Adobe is using
the word "Security" pretty loosely—there's no reason someone can't

copy the image and just crop out your name. But something is certainly better than nothing in this game.

3. Click the Source and Destination buttons to specify a folder that contains all the pictures as well as a folder in which to put all the final files. If you want Photoshop to look inside subfolders, turn on the Include All Subdirectories checkbox. (Note that if you include an alias or a shortcut to another folder, Photoshop is smart enough to look inside those folders, too.)

After you click OK, Photoshop processes each of the images in your folder(s) and saves them as JPEGs (this is a good time to go grab a cup of coffee). The final result is three folders—one for the thumbnail images, one for the larger-size images, and one for the HTML pages that display the larger-sized images—plus two other text files. You can throw away the file called "UserSelections.txt." This is just a record of the settings you used in the Web Photo Gallery dialog box (we're not sure why Photoshop saves this, but there's probably a *really* good reason).

Tip: Customize Your Galleries. You don't like the galleries that Photoshop creates? Not jazzy enough for you? No problem, you can always edit the HTML files in GoLive, Dreamweaver, or some other editor later. However, if you're going to be making a lot of galleries, it would be more efficient to edit Photoshop's built-in templates instead.

1. Find the folder that contains the gallery templates (it's called Web Photo Gallery, and it's inside the Presets folder, in the main Photoshop folder).

2. Make a copy of one of the template folders here, and name the duplicate folder as whatever you want your template to be called in Photoshop's Web Photo Gallery dialog box.

3. Edit the files inside this folder using a text editor. You can edit them to some degree with Adobe GoLive or Macromedia Dreamweaver, but because these files are templates (rather than real Web pages), it's safer to make your changes in the actual HTML code.

    Note that the template works by replacing certain codes with the settings you make in Photoshop. For instance, the %%BGCOLOR%% code in the template automatically gets stripped out and replaced with the background color you chose in the Web Photo Gallery dialog box. If you always want the same background color, though, you can remove this code from the template and type in your own color.

Now, when you open the Web Photo Gallery dialog box, your new template should appear in the Styles popup menu. Obviously, making templates requires some knowledge of HTML, but it's surprisingly easy once you get the hang of it.

The Animation Palette

As we mentioned earlier, the Animation palette is a recent arrival, having earlier been seen only in ImageReady. The ability to create animated GIFs in Photoshop will either strike you as ridiculous (Bruce's eyebrows almost raised off his forehead upon finding this feature) or appropriate (David is just plain tired of launching ImageReady). But whatever the case, it's here, so we'd better at least touch on it.

Tip: Opening Animated GIFs. Oddly, when you open an animated GIF file in Photoshop, the program sees only its first frame. In order to get all the GIF's frames, you must open it in ImageReady, then use that program's Jump to Photoshop feature. If we're lucky, then this is just a bug that will be fixed before too long.

To create an animation, open the Animation palette from the Window menu (see Figure 14-21). At first, every document has a single animation frame. You can think of each frame in an animation as a state in the Layer Comp palette—that is, each frame remembers a given state in the Layer palette. If you click the New Frame button in the palette (technically it's called the Duplicates Selected Frames button, but we prefer our naming) you get a second frame. Now you can change which layers are visible in the Layer palette, where the pixels are on each layer (with the Move tool), or what layer styles are applied to each visible layer. The changes you make apply only to this second frame, so you can click on the first frame to return to the original settings.

The fact that each frame remembers all those things (layer visibility, layer position, and layer styles) makes Photoshop's animation feature very flexible. For example, here's how to make some text move across the page while changing color:

Figure 14-21
Animation palette and
palette menu

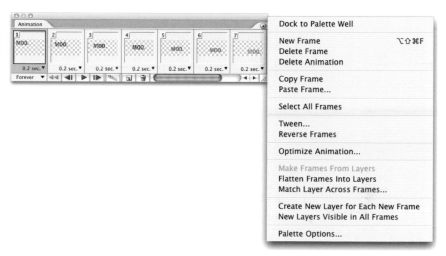

1. Place some black text where to want it to start.

2. Give the text layer a Color Overlay layer style using the start color.

3. Create a second animation frame in the Animation palette.

4. Use the Move tool to move the text to where you want it to end up.

5. Double click the layer style icon in the Layers palette to change the Color Overlay style to the end color.

6. Choose Tween from the Animation palette flyout menu (it's hiding far off in the upper-right corner) and enter the number of in-between steps you want to create (use at least 5 or 10 to see the effect clearly). When you click OK, Photoshop adds the frames between the beginning and ending frames you had created.

To preview the animation you just created, click the Play Animation button in the palette. (Click the same button to stop playing.) You'll often find that the animation plays too quickly. You can slow down each frame by choosing a delay time from the popup menu at the bottom of each frame. To apply the same delay time to all the frames, click on the first one, then Shift-click on the last frame (to select it and all frames between), then change the delay for any one of them.

There are many other cool features hiding in the Animation palette menu, including the Make Frames from Layers feature, which—as you'd guess—makes one frame for each layer in your document.

Note that several features appear in the Layers palette whenever the Animation palette is visible. These animation-specific features don't make a lot of sense when you're not animating, but you can still make them stick around when the Animation palette is closed (or stay closed when that palette is open) by choosing from the Animation Options submenu in the Layers palette menu.

To save your animated GIF to disk, use the Save For Web feature and choose a GIF format, as described earlier in this chapter.

The Future of Publishing

While much of the wild rush to the Web has been driven by vague fears of being left behind by the competition, people are beginning to invent Web business models that actually make sense and occasionally even make money as well. Whatever your reason for being on the Web, one of the keys to success is to produce images that are small and compress well, yet still have impact. Photoshop gives you the tools to accomplish this. As for making money at it: if we knew how, would we have written this book?

Production Notes

How We Made This Book

In many ways, producing this book was as interesting as writing it. So we thought that something a bit more complete than a normal colophon was in order. What follows is an overview of the systems and procedures that we used to produce this book.

Our Systems

We're often asked about our personal system setups. Here's a quick rundown of what equipment we used while making this book. This isn't everything we use, of course . . . there's always some new toy.

Bruce. System 1: Power Macintosh G4/800MHz x2, 1.5 GB RAM, 570 GB hard drive space, LaCie electron22blue III and LaCie PhotonII 18 monitors, GretagMacbeth EyeOne spectrophotometer, LaCie BlueEye colorimeter, LaCie BlueEye and GretagMacbeth ProfileMaker Pro monitor calibration. **System 2:** Power Macintosh G5 2GHz x2, 3.5 GB RAM, 1.5 TB hard drive space, Sony Artisan and EIZO ColorEdge 21 monitors, GretagMacbeth ICColor 210 Spectrophotometer, Imacon Flextight 848 scanner. **System 3:** Apple PowerBook G4/1GHz 12-inch, 768MB RAM, 120 GB hard drive space. **System 4:** Power Macintosh G4/450, 1.5 GB RAM. 320 GB total hard disk space, Epson Stylus Photo 2200 printer, Apple LaserWriter Pro 630 laser printer, GretagMacbeth SpectroScan spectrophotometer.

David. Macintosh 17-inch PowerBook G4 with 1 GB RAM and Mac OS X 10.2, IBM ThinkPad T41 with 1.5 GB RAM and Windows XP Professional, Gretag Macbeth EyeOne monitor calibrator, Epson Stylus inkjet printer, Xerox Phaser 8850 solid-ink color printer.

Writing, Editing, and Page Layout

Originally, we wrote this book in Microsoft Word on the Mac. Early editions were laid out with Adobe PageMaker; but for the last edition, we reflowed the book using Adobe InDesign CS. This edition was laid out in InDesign CS2. Then, some chapters were exported to Microsoft Word for editing, some were edited using Adobe InCopy, and some were edited directly within InDesign (using the Story Editor).

Design and Type. The body text typeface is Adobe Utopia (various weights)—9.8 on 15 for the main text, 8.8 on 12.5 for sidebars. Heads are set in ITC Optima Black. Figure callouts use Utopia Italic 9 on 12.

Images

Many of the images were scanned from film on a LeafScan 35, and more recently, on an Imacon Flextight Precision III. Prints were scanned on a variety of flatbed scanners, including an Agfa Arcus Plus, a Linotype-Hell Saphir Ultra, a Heidelberg CPS Opal Ultra, a UMAX PowerLook 3000, and a low-end UMAX Astra1220. We also used direct digital captures from Canon 300D, Canon 1Ds, Kodak DCS 420, Kodak DCS 460, Olympus DC265, Polaroid PDC-2000, Nikon/Fuji E2S and Nikon CoolPix 5000 digital cameras. The remaining images came from various CD collections (see "Image Credits"). We captured all the screen shots using the indispensable SnapzPro X from Ambrosia Software. All the images in this book started out in RGB form; we used no drum scans.

We placed all the color images as preseparated CMYK TIFFs (with the exception of duotones and graphics from Illustrator and FreeHand, all of which required that we use EPS).

Separations. All the color images in this book were separated in Photoshop using a variety of RGB Working spaces and one of two CMYK output profiles:

▶ **RGB Working Space.** Most of the images in this book were edited in Adobe RGB (1998), or Kodak ProPhoto RGB. A few legacy images were edited in ColorMatch RGB or Bruce RGB. For monitor calibration, Bruce used Sony's Artisan colorimeter and software, EIZO's Color Navigator software with a GretagMacbeth Eye-One Pro, LaCie BlueEye software with a Sequel BlueEye colorimeter, and GretagMacbeth ProfileMaker Pro 4.1.5 with an Eye-One Display colorimeter.

▶ **CMYK Setup.** Since the book was printed direct-to-plate, we printed GretagMacbeth's TC 6.05 profiling target on press. We built a set of ICC profiles with GretagMacbeth ProfileMaker Pro profiling software, using the average of five readings each from ten different press sheets for a total of 50 sets of measurements. We used a GretagMacbeth Spectrolino mounted on a GretagMacbeth Spectroscan xy table to automate the data collection. We built two profiles from this data set, one with light GCR for images, the other with heavy GCR for screen shots.

Preproofing

When we compared the test images on the print test with the digital files viewed on our reference monitor, we found that our custom ICC profile, in combination with solid monitor characterization, gave us a very accurate on-screen view of the CMYK data in Photoshop.

We also used our ICC profiles to provide accurate viewing of the color within InDesign CS. This proved surprisingly useful: in several cases we went back and edited the images after we had seen them in context on the page.

For hard-copy preproofing, we used the press ICC profile as our source profile and a custom profile for the Epson Stylus Photo 2200 printer with Epson Enhanced Matte paper that we built using GretagMacbeth's ProfileMaker Pro 4.1.5 software as our output profile.

For non-color proofing, we built PDF files for each chapter and emailed them to our editors. Our editors exported their comments as small Acrobat FDF files and e-mailed them to us; we reimported these comment files into the original PDF files before making final edits in pages. We killed as few trees as possible during the production of this book.

Author! Author!

Where to Reach Us

Bruce Fraser spent 25 years in Edinburgh, Scotland, before moving to the equally gray fog belt of San Francisco, which may explain his fascination with color. Bruce is currently a contributing editor for both *Macworld* and *Creativepro.com*, and is the author of *Real World Camera Raw* and coauthor of *Real World Color Management*. He has lectured on color reproduction in North America, Europe, and Australia, and is a founder and principal of Pixel Genius LLC. Bruce has been a Photoshop user since the program made its first appearance as BarneyScan XP, and was an alpha tester for Photoshop CS2. You can reach him via email at *bruce@pixelboyz.com*.

David Blatner is a Seattle-based consultant specializing in electronic publishing. He has authored or coauthored 15 books, including *Adobe Photoshop CS/CS2 Breakthroughs,* the award-winning *Real World Quark-XPress* (formerly titled *The QuarkXPress Book), Real World InDesign CS2, The Flying Book, Judaism For Dummies,* and *The Joy of Pi*. Over a half a million copies of his books are in print in 13 languages. David is a contributing editor for *Creativepro.com*, and has presented at conferences around North America, Europe, South Africa, and Japan. His email address is *david@moo.com*.

Image Credits

And Permissions

Earth image used on chapter opening pages, courtesy National Aeronautics and Space Administration.

Page 17. Impossible Shot ©2004 Bruce Fraser.

Page 20. Taj Mahal ©1995 Bruce Fraser, Imacon Flextight Precision II, Kodak Ektar 25.

Page 32. From "Animals and Wildlife," courtesy Digital Stock.

Page 47. Courtesy, Pomona College Mystery Number.

Page 53. From "Visual Symbols Sampler 2," courtesy PhotoDisc

Page 55. Mosaic, Madaba, Jordan ©2000 David Blatner, Olympus DC265 camera

Page 59. From "Sharks and Whales," courtesy Digital Stock.

Page 98. Cat ©2005 Bruce Fraser.

Page 99. From "Faces and Hands," courtesy PhotoDisc.

Page 100. From "PhotoDisc Sampler" courtesy PhotoDisc.

Page 103. From "Fine Art and Historical Photos," courtesy PhotoDisc.

Page 106. Michael Kelly Guitar ©2005 Bruce Fraser.

Page 107. From "Fine Art and Historical Photos," courtesy PhotoDisc.

Page 108. Bike Parts ©1991 MacUser Magazine, by Peter Allen Gould. Leafscan45, Kodak Ektachrome 4x5.

Page 109. From "Classic Sampler," courtesy Classic PIO Partners.

Page 134. Koi © 2005 Bruce Fraser.

Page 173. Golden Gate Park windmill, ©2003 Bruce Fraser, Canon EOS 1Ds camera.

Page 191. Boothbay Harbor, Maine ©1993 Bruce Fraser. Leafscan 35, Kodak Lumiere 100.

Page 229-230. Valparaiso Moa, ©1994 Bruce Fraser, Imacon Flextight 848, Kodak EPP 100.

Page 233. Owl ©2005 Bruce Fraser.

Page 236. Lillies ©2005 Bruce Fraser.

Page 236-237. Trees ©2005 Bruce Fraser.

Page 243. Train by Eric Wunrow, from "ColorBytes Sampler One," courtesy ColorBytes, Inc.

Page 248. Bridge ©2005 Bruce Fraser.

Page 253. Ocean ©2005 Bruce Fraser.

Page 254. Garden ©2005 Bruce Fraser.

Page 261. Building from "ColorBytes Sampler One," courtesy ColorBytes, Inc.

Page 266. Alcatraz ©1995 Bruce Fraser. Kodak DCS 420 camera.

Page 272. Wheel ©2005 Bruce Fraser.

Page 272. Strorm ©2005 Bruce Fraser.

Page 284. Ocean 2 ©2005 Bruce Fraser.

Page 287. Flower ©2005 Bruce Fraser.

Page 289. Swan ©2005 Bruce Fraser.

Page 292. Telephone Man ©2005 Bruce Fraser.

Page 297. The Last Place on Earth ©2005 Bruce Fraser.

Page 298. Llamas ©2005 Bruce Fraser.

Page 301. Na Pali Coast ©2000 Bruce Fraser. Imacon Flextight Precision III, Kodak Ektar 25.

Page 303. "Bruce." ©2004 Jeff Schewe.

Page 307. Masked Dancer ©1994 Bruce Fraser. Leafscan 35 Kodak PJA 100.

Page 315. Woman in Red Hat ©1990 Eastman Kodak Co.,

photographer Bob Clemens, Kodak Photo CD Sampler.

Page 317. Boats ©2004 Bruce Fraser.

Page 320. Trees 2 ©2004 Bruce Fraser.

Page 321. After ©2004 Bruce Fraser.

Page 335. Stack o' Shine ©2004 Bruce Fraser.

Page 346. Chichen Itza Pyramid 2 © 2000 Bruce Fraser. Imacon Flextight Precision, Kodak PJA-100.

Page 348. Double Peaks ©2004 Bruce Fraser.

Page 359. Dawn at Varanasi ©1995 Bruce Fraser. Leafscan 35, Kodak PJA 100.

Page 362. From My Deck ©2005 Bruce Fraser.

Page 449. Men in Kilts ©1995 Pamela Pfiffner. Leafscan 35, Kodak PJA 100.

Page 372. Zabriskie Point, ©2001 Bruce Fraser, Flextight Precision 848, Kodak Portra NC.

Page 378. Lexxi ©2000 Alan Womack, used by permission.

Page 392. Sagebrush at Mono Lake, ©2003 Bruce Fraser, Flextight Precision 848, Kodak Portra 160 NC.

Page 397. Chichen Itza Pyramid 1 © 2000 Bruce Fraser. Imacon Flextight Precision III, Kodak PJA 100.

Page 397. Kremlin Domes © 1997 Bruce Fraser. Imacon Flextight Precision, Kodak PJA 100.

Page 407. Blue Bottle, ©2002 David Blatner, Nikon CoolPix 5000 camera.

Page 412. From "Visual Symbols Sampler 2," courtesy PhotoDisc.

Page 414. Bahai Temple, Haifa. ©2000 David Blatner, David Blatner, Olympus DC265 camera

Page 416. From "Sports and Recreation," courtesy PhotoDisc

Page 420. From "Fine Art and Historical Photos," courtesy PhotoDisc.

Page 424. From "Object Series 1: Fruits and Vegetables," courtesy PhotoDisc.

Page 426. From "Signature Series 8: Study of Form and Color," courtesy PhotoDisc.

Page 429. From "Children of the World," courtesy PhotoDisc.

Page 431. Apples image from "The Painted Table," courtesy PhotoDisc.

Page 432. Fishing lure from "Object Series 4: Retro Relics," courtesy PhotoDisc.

Page 433. From "Object Series 1: Fruits and Vegetables," courtesy PhotoDisc.

Page 442. From "Visual Symbols Sampler 2," courtesy PhotoDisc

Page 443. From "Signature Series 8: Study of Form and Color," courtesy PhotoDisc.

Page 447. From "Visual Symbols Sampler 2," courtesy PhotoDisc, and "Streets of London," courtesy ImageFarm

Page 449. From "Object Series 4: Retro Relics," courtesy PhotoDisc.

Page 450. From "Signature Series 8: Study of Form and Color," courtesy PhotoDisc.

Page 451. Trees image from "Signature Series 8: Study of Form and Color," courtesy PhotoDisc.

Page 453. Waterfall image from "Signature Series 8: Study of Form and Color," courtesy PhotoDisc.

Page 460. Duck ©2004 Bruce Fraser.

Page 460. Clown Parrots, ©2003 Bruce Fraser, Canon EOS 300D camera.

Page 461. Clown Parrots, ©2003 Bruce Fraser, Canon EOS 300D camera.

Page 467. Trees image from "Signature Series 8: Study of Form and Color," courtesy PhotoDisc.

Page 467. Pumpkin image from "Object Series 1: Fruits and Vegetables," courtesy PhotoDisc.

Page 477. Golden Gate Park Windmill (detail), © 2003 Bruce Fraser, Canon EOS 1Ds camera.

Page 479. Alice-Anne, ©2000 Bruce Fraser, Nikon LS 4000, Kodak Portra 160 NC.

Page 483. Niña con Conejo ©2000 Bruce Fraser. Imacon Flextight Precision, Kodak Lumiere.

Page 486. Golden Gate Bridge ©2000 Bruce Fraser. Kodak DCS 460 camera.

Page 488. Stone Forest ©2003 Bruce Fraser.

Page 493. Shell Gasoline ©2004 Bruce Fraser.

Page 505. Crooked Street ©2004 Bruce Fraser.

Page 524. Barn image from "Signature Series 8: Study of Form and Color," courtesy PhotoDisc.

Page 525. Leaf image from "Signature Series 8: Study of Form and Color," courtesy PhotoDisc.

Page 531. From "Signature Series 8: Study of Form and Color," courtesy PhotoDisc.

Page 534. Zabriskie Point, ©2001 Bruce Fraser, Flextight Precision 848, Kodak Portra NC.

Page 536. From "Signature Series 8: Study of Form and Color," courtesy PhotoDisc.

Page 540. Hearst pool image from "Color Digital Photos: Paramount," courtesy Seattle Support Group.

Page 540. From "Animals," Dover Publications.

Page 554. Log ©2005 Bruce Fraser.

Page 557. Girl ©2005 Bruce Fraser.

Page 557. Ox ©2005 Bruce Fraser.

Page 563. Flowers ©2005 Bruce Fraser.

Page 579. Big Hill ©2005 Bruce Fraser.

Page 582. Water ©2005 Bruce Fraser.

Page 585. Heather ©2005 Bruce Fraser.

Page 589. Boats ©2005 Bruce Fraser.

Page 590. Fireworks ©2005 Bruce Fraser.

Page 596. Odd House ©2005 Bruce Fraser.

Page 602. Rainbow ©2005 Bruce Fraser.

Page 677. Amusements ©2005 Bruce Fraser.

Page 679. From "William Morris: Ornamentation & Illustrations from The Kelmscott Chaucer," Dover Publications.

Page 682. From "Animals," Dover Publications.

Page 683. From "Animals," Dover Publications.

Page 684. Special collections division, University Washington Libraries. UW negative #10542.

Page 691. San Francisco ©2005 Bruce Fraser.

Page 698. Gabriel, ©2002 David Blatner, Nikon CoolPix 5000.

Page 699. Church ©2004 Bruce Fraser.

Page 702. "Author at Work" by Howard Blatner, from Blatner family collection.

Page 704. "Seattle Lamppost" ©1995 David Blatner.

Page 705. "Debbie" by Donald Carlson, part of a collection by David Blatner.

Page 708. Seattle Sunrise ©2001 Debra Carlson, Olympus DC265 camera.

Page 711. Wall. ©2004 David Blatner.

Page 713. Edinburgh ©2005 Bruce Fraser.

Page 714. Giant Snow Morels ©2001 David Blatner, Olympus DC265 camera.

Page 715. From "Fine Art and Historical Photos," courtesy PhotoDisc.

Page 719. From "Fruits and Vegetables," courtesy PhotoDisc

Page 725. From "Fruits and Vegetables," courtesy PhotoDisc

Page 738. "Edna Hassinger" courtesy Allee Blatner. Photographer unknown.

Page 742. Mount Rushmore from Volume 5: Mountainscapes, 1993 courtesy ImageClub.

Page 747. Jerash Ruins, Jordan ©2000 David Blatner, Olympus DC265 camera

Page 760. "Mr. Schewe," ©1999 David Blatner.

Page 761. Birthday Tulips ©2000 Debra Carlson

Page 833. Taj Mahal image ©1993 by Carol Thuman.

Page 853. Earth image courtesy National Aeronautics and Space Administration.

Page 869. From "PhotoDisc Fine Art Sampler," courtesy PhotoDisc.

Page 905. Day at the Ballpark ©2002 David Blatner, Nikon CoolPix 5000 camera.

Index

L

Lab color model, 135, 166
Lab mode
  converting to Grayscale, 673, 677
  overview, 120–121
  TIFF images, 796
Label feature, 623, 853–854
Label menu, 628–630
labels
  applying, 628–630
  described, 630
  preferences, 617–618
  as preproduction tool, 649–651
  searching by, 629–630
  strategies for, 640
  uses for, 637
  vs. keyboard shortcuts, 628–629
  vs. ratings, 651
  working with, 628–630
languages, scripting, 778
Large Document Format files (PSB), 818
large-gamut spaces, 166–167, 209–210
laser printers, 105–106, 841–842
Lasso tool, 406–409, 430
Lasso Width, 408–409
Late Night Software, 781
layer blending, 351–377. *See also* blending modes
  advanced techniques, 364–371
  color casts correction, 364–365
  Curves layers vs. pixel layers, 351
  tip for, 714–715
layer blending modes, 351–357
layer clipping paths, 741–747
layer comps
  blending modes, 67–71
  creating, 67–68
  displaying, 69–70
  exporting, 780
  layer effects, 69
  layer visibility, 67–69
  pixel positions, 69
  saving, 780
  saving as presentations, 70
  updating, 70
  warnings, 70–71
Layer Comps palette, 67–71
layer data, 55–56
layer groups, 65–66
layer masks, 442–446
  adjustment layer creation and, 338, 343
  calculating file size, 123–124
  copying, 29, 346–347
  copying channels to, 342–343
  creating, 28–29, 363, 443–445
  deleting, 445
  editing, 444–446
  effects, painting in, 445
  enabling/disabling, 345
  filtering, 761
  gradients, 344, 348, 445
  hiding/showing, 345

loading luminosity, 383–385
loading selections as, 341–343
matching adjustment layers between images, 333
moving layers, 446
for noise reduction, 474–475
painting on, 332, 343–345, 703
reversing, 341–342
selecting and displaying, 337, 443–444, 446
turning on and off, 445
using edge masks, 474
layer sets, 394
layered files
  converting images between profiles, 215
  saving as PDFs, 333–334
  saving as TIFFs, 333–334
  saving in Photoshop format, 333
layers
  acting as masks, 446–447
  applying filters, 759–761
  applying selections to, 337
  calculating file size, 123–124
  changing layer types, 746
  clipping groups, 446
  cloning to, 710
  Color Fill, 372–377
  compression and, 798
  converting to spot color channels, 516
  creating, 64–65
  displaying, 64
  distributing, 31–32
  dragging/dropping, 28
  duplicating, 27
  filters on neutral layers, 760–761
  floating selections, 412–413
  future layer-blending algorithms, 793
  gradients on, 49–50
  grouping, 65–66, 446–447
  hiding, 64
  in JPEG files, 875
  layer comps, 67–71, 780
  layer groups, 65–66
  layer masks, 442–446
  layered TIFFs, 82–83
  linked, 14, 27, 31
  locking, 31
  manipulating in actions, 763–765
  merging, 27
  moving, 26–28
  moving between, 23–25
  names, 328, 370–371
  in PDF files, 809–811
  in PICT files, 813
  pixel, 380
  in PSD files, 791–793
  renaming, 64
  retouching images, 697
  saving to separate files, 780
  saving with files, 787
  selecting, 14, 24–25, 27
  sharpening layers, 471–472
  in TIFF files, 792, 796–797
  transparency masks, 441–442